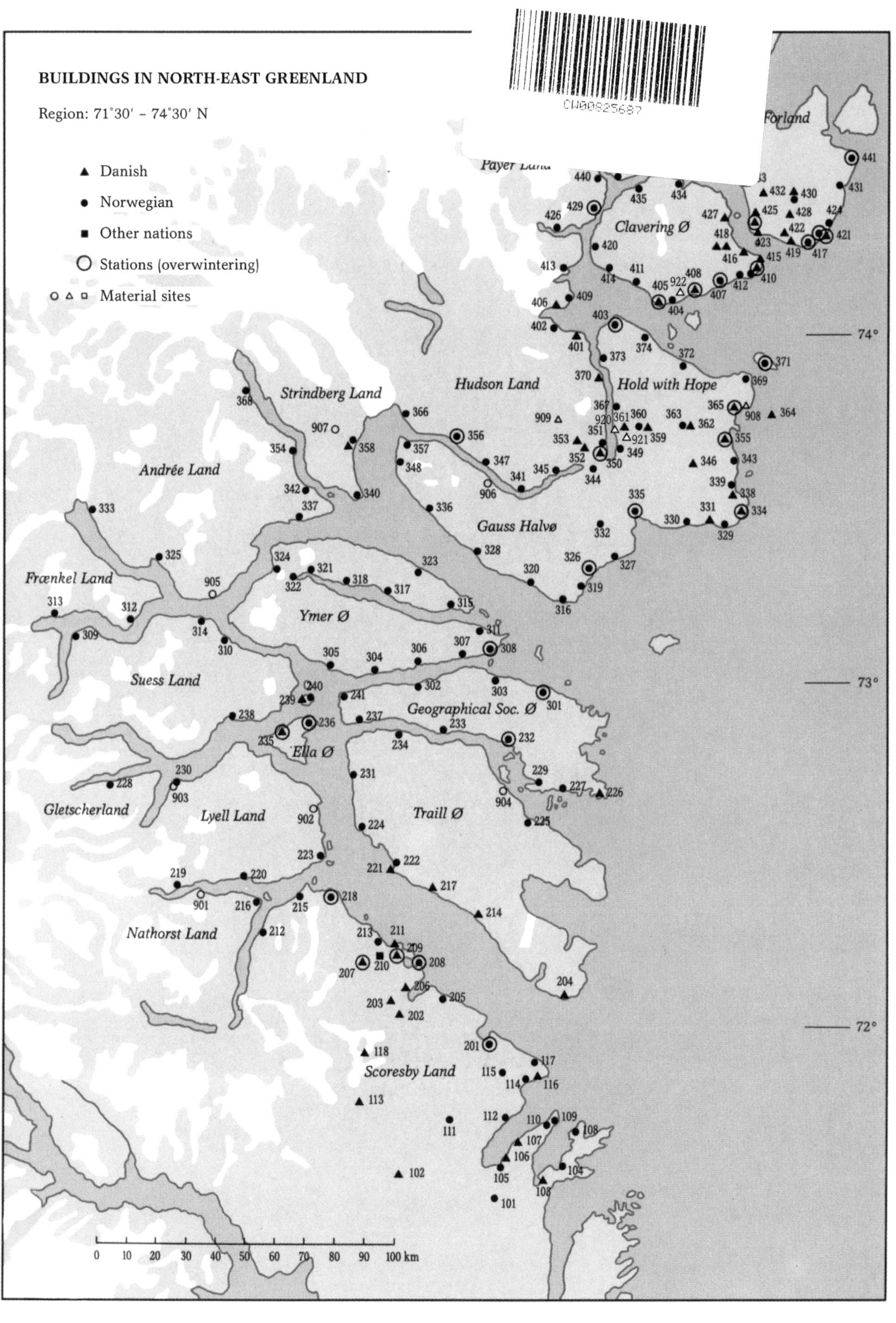

BUILDINGS IN NORTH-EAST GREENLAND
Region: 71°30′ – 74°30′ N
Danish
Norwegian
Other nations
Stations (overwintering)
Material sites
Forland
Payer Land
Clavering Ø
Hudson Land
Hold with Hope
Strindberg Land
Andrée Land
Gauss Halvø
Frænkel Land
Ymer Ø
Suess Land
Geographical Soc. Ø
Ella Ø
Gletscherland
Lyell Land
Traill Ø
Nathorst Land
Scoresby Land
74°
73°
72°
0 10 20 30 40 50 60 70 80 90 100 km

NORTH-EAST GREENLAND 1908-60

The Trapper Era

NORTH-EAST GREENLAND 1908-60

THE TRAPPER ERA

PETER SCHMIDT MIKKELSEN

SCOTT POLAR RESEARCH INSTITUTE
University of Cambridge

North-East Greenland 1908-60. The Trapper Era

Rosenhøjvej 10, DK-8410 Rønde, Denmark
www.xsirius.dk
ISBN: 978-0-901021-06-9

Publication of this book was supported by

Front cover: Danish trappers in front of Villaen, the old house of the Danmark Expedition, at Danmark Havn in the autumn of 1919. From left: Hans Ludvig Jensen, Robert Frørup, Niels Peter Andersen and Christian Ahlstrand. ©Jonna Jensen

Back cover:
Evening sun in Kong Oscar Fjord, August 1989. ©Peter Schmidt Mikkelsen

Published by Polarworld on behalf of the Scott Polar Research Institute, University of Cambridge.
www.polarworld.co.uk

Printed in Malaysia for Imago Publishing Ltd

To Lisa Maria and Niels

Publisher's Note:

We are delighted to have had the opportunity to work with Peter Schmidt Mikkelsen, the Scott Polar Research Institute and the Aage Jensen Foundation on this English edition of North-East Greenland 1908-60: The Trapper Era. In order to preserve the character of the original Danish edition of this book, the author has been given full control over the content, style of editing and design, proof-reading, and quality of the images.

TABLE OF CONTENTS

FOREWORD

Dear Reader,

At last we have an English edition of Peter Schmidt Mikkelsen's book *"North-East Greenland 1908-60. The Trapper Era"*. This is an updated and enlarged translation of the Danish edition published in 1994 and reprinted in 2001. An English edition has long been desired by the many British and foreign scientific and sporting expeditions, and many other people, who visit North-East Greenland in increasing numbers.

This book is the story of the pioneers who worked in one of Europe's largest and last wildernesses, now a major part of the World's largest national park. It is also the story of a little known and almost forgotten high-arctic region that was the centre of a historic and dramatic trapping enterprise. This book is based on trappers' published and unpublished diaries, and personal interviews with surviving trappers and other pioneers in the 1980s and early 1990. The descriptions are detailed and historically correct, and illustrated with many old and new photographs. There are fascinating accounts of the lives of individual trappers, often special characters who endured a lonely and risky existence far from the comforts of civilization. In this vast and great high-arctic region they built hundreds of small and primitive huts which provided shelter against the storms and cold of the Arctic winters, and they taught themselves to live off the land and its rich fauna in a harmonious way.

The book is much more than just a good history book. It also functions as a useful and necessary traveller's guide for all visitors to North-East Greenland - scientific and sporting expeditions, and tourists. It provides the background to the building of all the more than 300 stations and huts, their varied occupants, and their present condition and location (GPS), important information for present-day expeditions and visitors. The book also contains important indexes, references to sources and to published literature useful to the reader.

The book also illustrates the dramatic effects of the Arctic climate and environmental changes that have led to some of the old buildings vanishing or falling apart. It also says something about the "North-East Greenland Company Nanok" (that takes its name from the former Danish trapping company "Nanok"), and is a private, non-profit organization that since 1991 has undertaken voluntary surveys, restoration and maintenance of the hunting stations and huts, in co-operation with the Greenland National Museum & Archive and the Department of Environment & Nature in Nuuk. This important work is sponsored by the Aage V. Jensens Fonde, a large Danish charitable foundation that exists to protect and conserve Danish nature and wildlife. The restoration work in Greenland is supported by many individuals, and carried out in close co-operation with the Sirius Dog Sledge Patrol and other Greenlandic and Danish authorities.

The author, Peter Schmidt Mikkelsen, has produced an excellent, authoritative and superbly illustrated book, that like his other books about North-East Greenland draws on his service in the military Sirius Dog Sledge Patrol, his participation in numerous expeditions as well as his long-time leadership of the new Nanok organization. Very few people have such a thorough knowledge of North-East Greenland and its history as he does.

This year, 2008, is exactly 100 years since the Danmark Expedition of 1906-08 returned after mapping the last unknown stretch of the coastline of Greenland; it is also 100 years since the first trapping expedition wintered in North-East Greenland; and it will soon be 50 years since the end of the "Trapper Era". Finally, it can be noted that this is the second season of the International Polar Year 2007-2008.

I am myself a Norwegian, and one of the few remaining trappers. In recent years I have enjoyed the opportunity to participate in Nanok's restoration expeditions and thus had the privilege of experiencing North-East Greenland over a span of sixty years (1946-2006).

With kind regards,

Ivar Ytreland
Aamaalvegen 54
N-1440 Drøbak
Norway

ABOUT THIS BOOK ...

The collection of information presented in this volume really began in 1987, when planning an expedition to North-East Greenland. The journey was to take place during the summer of 1989, and we were four friends sharing the idea - a kayak trip from Daneborg to Mestersvig. The region we were going to visit was already well-known to me from my military service with the Sirius Dog Sledge Patrol from 1977-1979. I looked forward to revisiting the region, and as a holiday in North-East Greenland is no everyday occurrence, I tried my best to prepare for the adventure.

The scenery of North-East Greenland is desolate and magnificent, but somewhat unpredictable with respect to the weather. The Arctic animals, birds and sea life are at home here. North-East Greenland had captivated me since I first set eyes on it while with the Sledge Patrol, where I had learnt to take just one day at a time! What else would we encounter along the way? Nothing, apart from some small huts found at intervals along the coasts of the fjords. The huts were very familiar to me, and had often provided me and my companions with shelter during snow storms or bad weather. Except for groups of stone circles and house ruins built by the Inuit centuries ago, the only evidence of other human activities we would come across were these huts. But who had built them? When and why? I knew a little of their history, but wanted to learn more.

The research started on my own bookshelves, in the miscellaneous collection of books about North-East Greenland I had assembled over the years. Here I found a part of their history. Most of the huts had been built by Norwegian and Danish fox-trappers, a few had been established for scientific purposes, some dated back to the Second World War, and others were shelters built by people working at the weather and military stations on the coast. Almost everyone knew something about the huts. For travellers in the region the huts were often an obvious destination after a good day's journey and a rustic but safe shelter for the night. This preliminary search was compiled into a simple leaflet, which proved very useful on our 1989 kayak journey.

The expedition in 1989 inspired me to continue research into the history of the huts and buildings, and the idea of gathering the results into a book also began to evolve. The published sources had only answered some of my questions, and the answers were often vague. The trail now led me to archives in Norway and Denmark. These proved to contain a vast and varied material, including trappers' diaries, travellers' log books, etc. Now the names of some of the people involved began to emerge from their anonymity. The huts, after all, consisted of only rough timbers and roofing felt. It was the people who had built and used them that provided the huts with identity. Where were they now? How many were still alive, and would it be possible to find them?

A couple of names and addresses formed the starting point, and soon - through a letter or a phone call - names became living persons, who could tell me things which the books and the archives could never answer. With every new contact I was met by an overwhelming kindness and willingness to help me in my quest. The network spread like rings in water, new names turned up, sometimes only the name of a city or a county, but a lead nonetheless. That the region 'up there' is something quite special was confirmed by the almost identical reply: *"North-East Greenland? – Yes, that's where I spent the best years of my life...."*

Journeys in Norway and Denmark now followed and led to many a friendly talk of days gone by in North-East Greenland. The continued search turned out to be very time-consuming, but at the same time very interesting and satisfying as I made contact with more and more of the former fox-trappers and other Greenland old-timers, and learnt more of their lives and adventures. This volume is the story of these people, and of the huts and houses they built in North-East Greenland!

In 1990 the idea of publishing the material took a definite structure, and in 1992 the work with the manuscript began. The source material continued to grow, and it became evident that measures had to be taken to limit the scope. As the majority of the huts had been built in connection with the Norwegian and Danish trappers, the trapper era became the main theme of the book; but as the trapping was very much connected with exploration, as well as Norwegian and Danish administration and politics, these are mentioned too.

In 1994, the first edition of *"Nordøstgrønland 1908-60, Fangstmandsperioden"* was published by the Danish Polar Center. The book was well received by the public and press, and when the 1st edition was out of print, an updated 2nd edition was published in 2001.

In 2003, the Greenland National Museum & Archives in Nuuk (the capital city of Greenland) asked Nanok to carry out a major project to establish a new, up-to-date register of all the old trappers' huts in North-East Greenland, including photographs and GPS-data. As a member of the Nanok leadership, I was fortunate enough to take part in both the planning and the fieldwork for this project, which lasted for five years and included more that 20 individual expedition members.

From the start, many people had asked when there would be an English version of my book, and in 2006 I began the translation. However, as many new sources and much new information had come to light since 1994, this English edition has been thoroughly updated and enlarged. In particular, opportunity has been taken to reproduce many of the new photographs in colour.

ACKNOWLEDGEMENTS

The author wishes to express his sincere gratitude to:

Ulla Gyldenlund Kristensen, my wife, who with great patience and during many months of inspiring teamwork has produced the excellent translation from the Danish edition.

Lisa Maria Gyldenlund Mikkelsen and Niels Gyldenlund Mikkelsen, our children, for their constant and loving support. I dedicate this book to them.

Tony Higgins, whose improvements to the text went beyond the task of English correction and raised the quality of the entire manuscript, thanks to his knowledge of the region and insights into the history of its place names gained during fifteen summers of geological mapping.

Erik Jochumsen, photographer and a former member of Sirius, whose professional adaptation of the extensive photographic material has given the volume a balanced and integrated appearance.

Ove Hermansen, air traffic controller at Kastrup, who with never failing enthusiasm raised many critical questions and gave the manuscript another thorough and constructive read through.

Derek Fordham, Honorary Secretary of the Arctic Club, who without hesitation volunteered to make contact with potential publishers in England.

Julian Dowdeswell, Director of the Scott Polar Research Institute, and Heather Lane, Librarian of the Scott Polar Research Institute, who by their encouraging co-operation have provided the best possible framework for publication of the book.

Kari Herbert, Director of the publishing company Polarworld, and the graphics designer team at Bumblebee Design, for production of an attractive and durable volume, and for their excellent collaboration during the publishing process.

Ivar Ytreland, former trapper, for the complimentary Foreword to this book, and his continuous and visionary encouragement during our long friendship.

Leif Skov, Chairman of the Aage V. Jensens Fonde, for his constant support, both personally and through financial grants from the Aage V. Jensens Fonde.

In addition, I would like to express my appreciation to all of the following who have made special contributions to this edition: Claus Andreasen, Knud Bavngaard, Nils-Martin Hanken, Anne Lise Jensen, Will C. Knutsen, Ruth Kragh, Hans Lapstun, Otto Lapstun, Birger Larsen, Norma Larsen, Sonja Madsen, Jens Mathiesen, Jørgen Nielsen, Anne Marit Myrvold, Bent Philbert, Jørgen Rasmussen and Svein Torske.

My warm appreciation also goes to Claus Andreasen, Kirsten Caning, and Karsten Secher, for their dedicated participation in the publication of the original Danish edition.

Thanks are also due to the staff of the Arctic Institute and Danish Polar Centre in Copenhagen, the Norwegian Polar Institute in Tromsø, the Scott Polar Research Institute in Cambridge, England, the Greenland National Museum & Archives in Nuuk, and the Department of Environment & Nature in Nuuk.

Finally my thanks go to the numerous Nanok and Sirius colleagues, scientists, Greenland enthusiasts and different organisations that for two decades have contributed their knowledge and material to help making the final shape and form of this book.

Peter Schmidt Mikkelsen
Rønde, 9th March 2008

PRACTICAL INFORMATION

Scope
This book deals with the activities of Norwegian and Danish trappers, and in particular the hunting stations and huts used while engaged in trapping and over-wintering on the east coast of Greenland between latitudes 71°30′ and 77°30′N. Fox-trapping is a winter activity, as only the thick winter fox furs have commercial value. In addition, information on individual trappers as well as brief details of scientific, commercial and administrative activities up to 1960, are included. The book does not deal with sites of Inuit origin, nor the huts erected after 1970 by the Sirius Dog Sledge Patrol (Slædepatruljen Sirius). Buildings, houses and huts associated with the town of Ittoqqortoormiit (Scoresbysund) and surrounding settlements are beyond the scope of this volume.

Quotations, sources and language
Quotations from published literature and unpublished sources are given in *italics*, followed by the source (reference). Further literature is noted at the end of each section. Where the sources quoted are in Danish or Norwegian, they have been translated for this English edition.

Huts, houses and stations
Traditionally buildings and settlements in North-East Greenland related to hunting activities are known as huts or cabins (hytter), houses (huse) or stations (stationer). These designations have not been used according to any rigid definition. In general a "hut" is a small building, typically 5-7 m² in area, used for shelter and for overnight stays during hunting travels. A "house" is a larger, or more important hut, or a small station. A "station" is a large building, or group of buildings, often centrally placed in a hunting terrain, that acts as a main base for summer or winter activities.

Categories
In this volume, stations and buildings are grouped according to how they have been utilised.

Category I: Stations, which have been used for wintering for at least one winter, divided into category IA and IB:

Category IA: Trappers' stations, principal bases used for trapping activities.

Category IB: Other stations, such as weather stations and scientific stations, not used by fox trappers for wintering.

Category II A-C: Locations (huts) used for overnight stays on hunting tours, but not used for wintering.

The history of the trappers' stations is the main focus of this volume, whereas the other stations and the numerous primitive hunting huts are described only briefly.

Name and location number
Each building, hut, house or station, has been assigned a primary name and a three-digit location number, e.g. Myggbukta [335]. The first digit in the location number indicates the latitude of the building: Myggbukta is located between latitudes 73° and 74°N. The second and third digits (35 for Myggbukta) are locations of consecutive buildings generally in a northern direction between latitudes. Location numbers in the interval 901 to 923 do not relate to latitude, but are indicative of depots, planned huts that were never built, and other special circumstances.

Place names and Danish letters
Place names in Greenland are spelled in accordance with the official Greenland place name registry, e.g. Kap Morris Jesup (Cape Morris Jesup). In other literature and notably in quotations, place names may be spelt otherwise.

Some place names in North-East Greenland are found in both two-word and one-word variants. Thus Scoresbysund is the Greenlandic town on the north side of the fjord Scoresby Sund. Similarly, Mestersvig is the airport west of the inlet Mesters Vig, Germaniahavn is the hunting station at the harbour Germania Havn and Danmarkshavn the meteorological station at the harbour Danmark Havn. In most cases both the one-word and two-word variants have official approved status.

Note that the Danish letters Æ (= AE), Ø (= OE) and Å (= AA) come at the end of the Danish alphabet. Thus the station Mønstedhus is described after Myggbukta, and the Aalborghus station is last in the descriptions of stations.

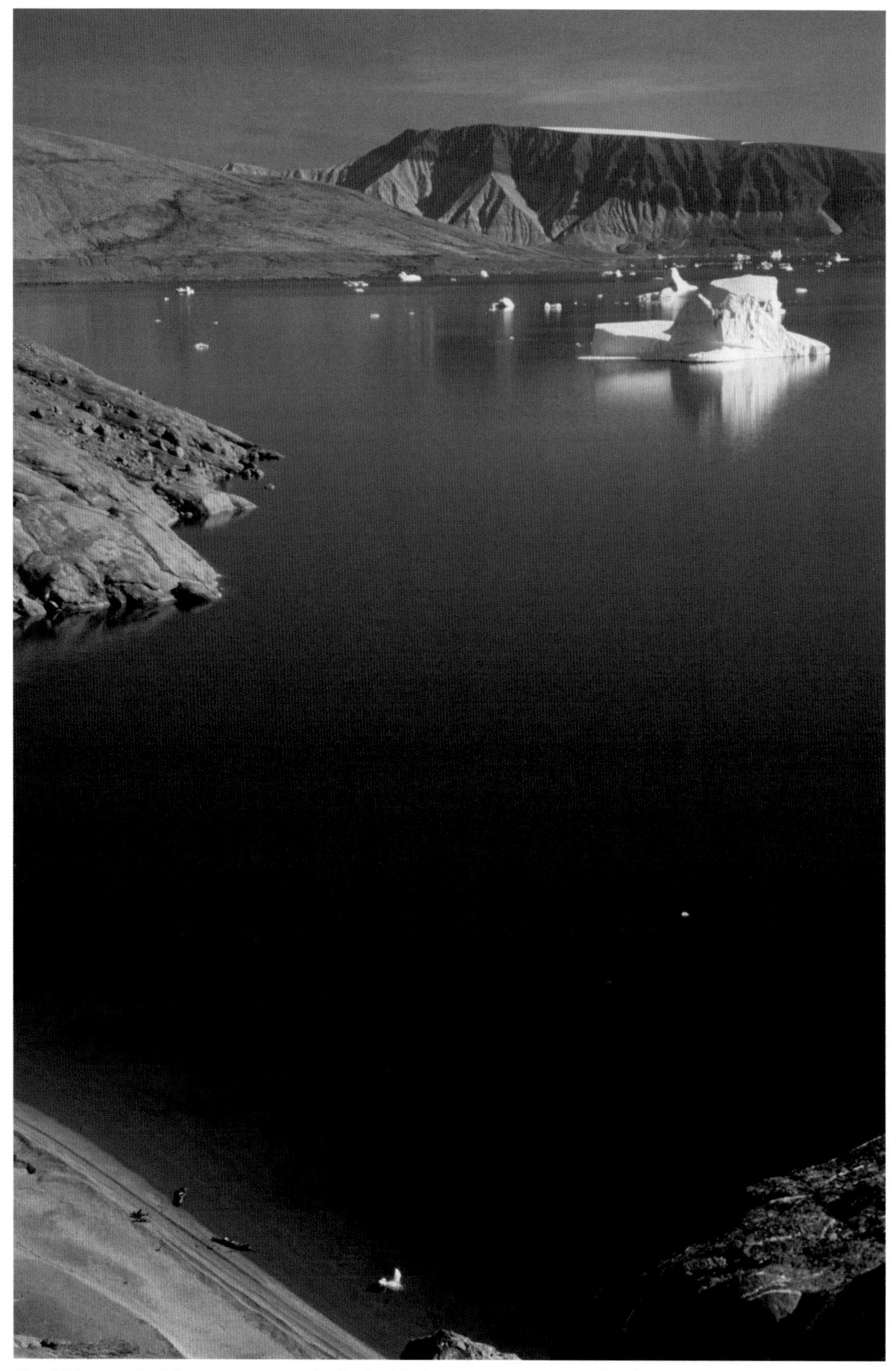

Kap Weber south of the entrance to Geologfjord, 10th August 1989. © Peter Schmidt Mikkelsen

INTRODUCTION

GREENLAND

Geographically, Greenland is the largest island in the world, and belongs to the North American continent. It has an area of 2,166,086 km^2, of which 410,449 km^2 is ice-free. The northernmost point of Greenland, Kap Morris Jesup, is only 740 km from the North Pole. The central part of Greenland is covered by an extensive ice cap, the so-called "Inland Ice" (Indlandsisen), which has a maximum thickness of 3200 m.[1]

The population of Greenland was 56,648 in 2007,[2] of whom 88% were born in Greenland and 12% outside Greenland. The majority live in South-West and West Greenland, where fishing, hunting and sheep-breeding are the main industries.

A Danish colony since 1721, Greenland became an equal part of Denmark in 1953, and in 1979 obtained Home Rule status as a distinct community within the Realm of Denmark and the Faeroe Islands. The *Landsting* is the parliament of Greenland, and the *Landsstyret* the Cabinet. Nuuk, the largest town in Greenland with 15,047 inhabitants in 2007, is the capital and seat of government.

NORTH-EAST GREENLAND

The geographical designation North-East Greenland, is usually taken to denote the ice-free coastal region between Ittoqqortoormiit (Scoresbysund; 70°29'N) and Nordostrundingen (81°21'N). The activities of Norwegian and Danish trappers, the main subject of this book, were essentially restricted to that part of North-East Greenland between Liverpool Land (71°30'N) and Skærfjorden (77°30'N). In this volume, the designation North-East Greenland can therefore be assumed to refer to the latter region.

The wide belt of drifting pack ice off the coast of North-East Greenland acts like snow-covered land and effectively gives the region a high arctic continental climate. Entirely located north of the Arctic Circle, the long polar night lasts for about three months, with a corresponding period with 24 hours daylight (midnight sun) in the summer. The annual precipitation in Danmarkshavn (76°46'N) is 100-200 mm, and the average temperature minus 12°C.

Geologically North-East Greenland is part of the circum-Atlantic Caledonian realm, formed about 420 million years ago. Due to the sparse arctic vegetation, the core zone of the Caledonian mountain belt is magnificently exposed in steep mountain walls in the inner parts of the fjords. In the outer fjord zone, thick successions of brightly coloured, gently folded, shales, limestones and dolomites are conspicuous. Younger, post-Caledonian sediments make up large parts of the lower terrain of the outer coastal islands.

The network of broad valleys cutting through the mountainous interior, and the large coastal islands are home to large numbers of muskoxen; the population varies drastically, but is probably between 8,000 and 20,000 animals. Other terrestrial mammals include the polar bear, arctic wolf, arctic fox, ermine, alpine hare and collared lemming. Marine mammals such as walrus and various species of whale and seal are found in the fjords. Throughout the summer many of the rivers support large numbers of arctic char. Many species of migratory birds breed in North-East Greenland, notably the barnacle and pink-footed goose, but only the snowy owl, gyrfalcon, raven and ptarmigan winter here.

The most northern permanent town in East Greenland is Ittoqqortoormiit (Scoresbysund; 70°29'N), that with outlying settlements had a population of 529 in 2007. The present-day inhabitants of the town are mainly descendents of the 85 Greenlanders (70 from Ammassalik and 15 from West Greenland) who arrived with "Gustav Holm" on September 1st 1925. Further north, the airfields at Constable Pynt (70°44'N) and Mestersvig (72°13'N), the military base of Sirius Daneborg (74°18'N), the Danmarkshavn Weather Station (76°46'N), and Station Nord (81°36'N) are mainly manned by Danish personnel.

Böcher 2000; Génsbøl & Tofte 1998; Henriksen 2005; Koch 1945; Muus et al. 1990; Topografisk ... 2000.

DISCOVERY AND EXPLORATION

Inuit cultures first reached North-East Greenland about 4400 years ago. They followed the migration routes of the animals they depended upon for their existence across North Greenland, and then southwards along the coast of North-East Greenland. Their house ruins are widely distributed throughout the region, but the conditions of existence were marginal, and in response to changes in climate and wildlife fluctuations the successive Inuit cultures (Independence I, Independence II, Thule, North Greenland mixed culture) flourished and died out. The last remnants of the North Greenland mixed culture in North-East Greenland were probably the group of 12 encountered by Douglas C. Clavering at Clavering Ø in 1823.[3]

The Norse seafarers sailing from Iceland to southern Greenland in the period c. 1000-1250 are known to have used prominent East Greenland mountains as landmarks in their sailing directions, but it is unknown how far north along the coast of East Greenland they may have reached. Finds of silver beads and buttons in Inuit graves near Ittoqqortoormiit have been considered by some as evidence of some contact between the Norse and the former Inuit population.

It was not until the early 1600s that European explorers gained actual knowledge of North-East Greenland, the land behind the drifting pack-ice barrier.

Grønlands forhistorie 2004; Traces 2004.

THE EARLIEST ACCOUNTS

HENRY HUDSON 1607

In the middle of the 1400s the Ottoman empire blocked the normal trade routes to the Far East, and the need arose for other safer passages to the Orient and the fabled Spice Islands. Throughout the centuries, spices, and pepper in particular, were highly valued and in constant demand amongst Europeans. Portuguese mariners were the first to discover a sea route to the Far East, south of Africa, but it was the possibility of reaching the Orient via shorter routes that prompted the search for a North-West or a North-East passage, that brought with it exploration of the Arctic including Greenland.

In April 1607 the British Muscovy Company sent out the mariner Henry Hudson (c. 1550-1611) aboard the "Hopewell", whose mission was to discover a passage via the North Pole to China and India. Hudson headed north-west, reached the largely unknown east coast of Greenland and followed it northwards at a distance. On the 21st June 1607, the coast was so close that Hudson records: *"And considering wee knew no name given to this land, wee thought good to name it Hold-with-Hope, lying in 73 degrees of latitude"*.[4] Hold with Hope is the oldest place name in North-East Greenland still in use. The floating ice belt hindered further advance along the coast north of Hold with Hope, and Hudson followed the outer border of the pack ice as far as Svalbard, the archipelago discovered in 1596 by two Dutchmen,

Walfang im nördlichen Eismeer 1776. (Whale fishery in the northern sea 1776). The painting shows a fleet of Dutch, British and Danish whaling ships. The latin inscription "VIS VINCITUR ARTE" translates roughly to "Force is defeated through cleverness". © Altonaer Museum in Hamburg, Germany

Willem Barendzoon (or Barents) and Jacob van Heemskercke Hendrickszoon, who had also sought in vain for a new route to the Orient.

THE WHALERS

Although Hudson did not discover the North-East Passage, and his observations had no direct significance for trading with the Far East, his reports of the abundant whales in Svalbard waters led to the development of the northern whale fishery. Europeans needed a constant supply of oil for their train-oil lamps, and a giant whaling industry soon developed along the coasts of the North Atlantic Ocean. The whalers came from many European countries, notably from the Netherlands but also from the Danish-Norwegian kingdom; the Danish whalers came in particular from Rømø.

Svalbard and Jan Mayen were situated in open waters and became the centre of the new whaling industry at the beginning of the 16th century. However, whales became scarce in Svalbard waters after c. 1630, and whalers moved their hunting grounds to the floating ice barrier that blocked access to North-East Greenland. The whalers approached the floating ice with great reluctance, knowing through bitter experience the crushing forces exerted by the ice. The ice limit varies from year to year, and a few whaling captains came sufficiently close to the coast to mark their names on their charts. A Dutch sea chart dated 1710 records:

At about 74°N: *"t. Baey van Gael Hamkes opgedaen Anno 1654"*.

At about 73°N: *"t. Land van Broer Ruys opgedaen Anno 1655"*.

At about 78°N: *"t. Land van Lambert opgedaen Anno 1670"*.

Whaling was a tough job for tough men. Arctic sailors were as a class: *"rough, hard-bitten men, whose only motive for enduring the dangers and hardships of their voyages was to make enough money for an orgy of drinking and whoring when they came back to port. They were usually brilliant seamen – they had to be in order to survive – but they did not possess sensitive feelings, cultural intellects, polite manners or scientific curiosity"*.[5] Captain William Scoresby Junior was a rare exception.

Amdrup et al. 1913; Keulen 1710; Mulvad 2002; Münzing 1978; Zorgdrager 1723.

William Scoresby Junior (1789-1857) is considered one of the founders of modern arctic exploration. © Stamp 1975

MAPPING 1822-1908

WILLIAM SCORESBY 1822

William Scoresby Junior and his father William Scoresby Senior were important and successful figures in British arctic whaling. Even while engaged in the search for whales they concerned themselves with scientific observations and experiments of all kinds.[6] Although he was only about thirty years old: *"Scoresby Junior was already distinguished for his work on navigation and the earth's magnetism. ... He was a gentleman and a scientist, soft-spoken, highly moral and deeply religious"*.[7] One major result of Scoresby Junior's whaling career was his celebrated *"An account of the Arctic regions with a history and description of the Northern Whale-Fishery"*, published in 1820, and another the *"Journal of a Voyage to the Northern Whale-fishery; including the researches and discoveries on the eastern coast of West Greenland, made in the summer of 1822, in the ship Baffin of Liverpool"*. Published in 1823, the journal of his 1822 voyage brought back for the first time anything approaching accurate information on the fjord region of North-East Greenland, and his charts corrected serious errors in longitude.

Between June and August 1822 Scoresby in the "Baffin" was on numerous occasions close to land, sometimes in company with his father in the "Fame", sometimes with other whalers - up to 20 or 30 whalers were at times reported in sight. Scoresby succeeded in laying down a chart of the North-East Greenland coast between latitudes 69°-75°N, made landings at several places, and more than 80 localities were given names. He named Scoresby Sund after his father, who was the first to explore the mouth of the fjord. William Scoresby Junior (1789-1857) is considered one of the founders of modern arctic exploration.

Jackson 2003; Stamp 1975, 1976

DOUGLAS C. CLAVERING & EDWARD SABINE 1823

In 1823 the British Board of Longitude sent out an expedition led by Captain Edward Sabine (1788-1883) in order to determine the figure of the Earth, by swinging the pendulum at the northernmost latitudes possible. In 1822 Sabine had made similar observations in the southern and central parts of the Atlantic Ocean. In 1823 the Royal Navy placed the "Griper", captained by Douglas Charles Clavering (1794-1827), at his disposal. The "Griper" was one of the vessels used by Captain William Parry on his first expedition to the Arctic in 1819-20. After completion of observations in Svalbard, course was set for Greenland. An attempt to penetrate the ice belt at 77°N failed, and the coast was eventually reached near Wollaston Forland at about 74°N on the 8th August 1823. The area was explored for a week or so, and Shannon was visited, but the pendulum observations were carried out at the sheltered harbour of the present Germania Havn.

While Sabine was occupied with his observations, Clavering and his crew sailed south to explore Gael Hamke Bugt, and it was here at Dødemandsbugten on the coast of Clavering Ø, that on the 18th August 1823 they discovered an Inuit camp of 12 individuals - men, women and children. Clavering and his men stayed with the natives for a few days, and this is the only recorded encounter between Europeans and the original Inuit of North-East Greenland.[8] The encounter ended dramatically when the sailors demonstrated the power of their guns, and shot a seal with a musket. An Inuit was persuaded to try and fire a pistol, but the experience paralysed the group with fear; the next morning they had disappeared and were never seen again.

Edinburgh New Philosophical Journal 1830; Sabine 1825.

GERMAN ARCTIC EXPEDITION 1869-70

The noted German geographer August Petermann (1822-78) had suggested that an attempt be made to reach the North Pole along the coast of Greenland or Svalbard, and in 1868 a reconnaissance expedition led by Captain Karl Koldewey in the "Grönland" was sent out. Failing to penetrate the pack ice off North-East Greenland, the "Grönland" eventually reached Svalbard. Based on this experience, a larger scale expedition was organised in 1869.

The German Arctic Expedition of 1869-70 (Die zweite deutsche Nordpolarfahrt), is often referred to as the Koldewey Expedition after its leader, Karl Koldewey (1837-1908).[9] It was the first major expedition to overwinter in North-East Greenland, and the first to undertake systematic scientific observations. The plan was to explore the unknown east coast of Greenland north of 74°N, and if possible reach the North Pole, and their two vessels were equipped for two years.

The expedition left Bremerhaven on the 15th June 1869. On board the steamer "Germania" were Captain Koldewey, four scientists and a crew

"Germania" in her winter harbour at Sabine Ø 1869-70. © Koldewey 1873

of twelve. The schooner "Hansa" was commanded by Captain Hegemann and carried two scientists and a crew of eleven. When passing through the ice belt, close to the coast of Greenland, the ships lost contact with each other due to a misinterpreted signal. The "Hansa" was subsequently trapped in the drift ice, carried southwards, and was wrecked in October off the coast of Liverpool Land. The crew made camp on an ice floe, and miraculously survived a 200-day drift down the east coast, around Nunap Isua (Kap Farvel), and as far as Narsaq Kujalleq (Frederiksdal) in South-West Greenland.

Meanwhile the "Germania" safely reached the coast of North-East Greenland on 3rd August 1869. Attempts to sail northwards along the outer coast of Shannon were frustrated by ice, and after a month of difficult navigation Koldewey decided to overwinter in a natural harbour at the south point of Sabine Ø, subsequently known as Germania Havn. Two stone shelters [447-1] were built on the west coast of the harbour, one used as an observatory and the other a depot house.

During the winter and following spring the expedition members made a series of journeys with man-hauled sledges to Kuhn Ø, Tyrolerfjord and Germania Land. In 1870, after the ice had broken up, Koldewey took the "Germania" into Kejser Franz Joseph Fjord, where after climbing to a vantage point near the present Payer Tinde, the highest mountain in North-East Greenland was seen at the margin of the Inland Ice, and named Petermann Bjerg (2940 m). The Koldewey Expedition brought back abundant scientific observations, and extended the basic mapping of the coastal region from 73°to 77°N. Without any loss of life the "Germania" crew arrived back in Germany on 11th September 1870.

The tables later in this volume (p. 52-56) list details for this and subsequent expeditions with respect to numbers of participants overwintering, huts and houses built, foxes killed, etc.

125 Jahre ... 1993; Koldewey 1873, 1874; Payer 1877.

DANISH EAST GREENLAND EXPEDITION 1891-92

In 1891 the Danish Admiralty sent out the East Greenland Expedition 1891-92 under the leadership of First Lieutenant Carl Ryder. Their task was to continue the exploration of Kejser Franz Joseph Fjord and Scoresby Sund. The expedition, often referred to as the Ryder Expedition, numbered 30 participants, including the Norwegian crew on the expedition vessel "Hekla", that was commanded by Captain Ragnvald Knudsen.

On the 23rd July 1891 the expedition reached the entrance of Kejser Franz Joseph Fjord, but finding the fjord was blocked by ice sailed south and entered Scoresby Sund. Sailing westwards into the unknown reaches of inner Scoresby Sund, a sheltered harbour (Hekla Havn) was discovered on Danmark Ø and became their winter quarters.

During the autumn journeys were made by motor boat into the unknown fjord system to the west. After an undramatic wintering, exploration was continued in a series of spring sledge journeys.

The Ryder Expedition left Scoresby Sund in the middle of August 1892, returning with valuable botanical, zoological and geological observations and a map of the fjord system, later published in the Danish scientific series "Meddelelser om Grønland".

Gulløv 1991; Ryder 1895.

ALFRED NATHORST 1899 & GUSTAF KOLTHOFF 1900

Alfred Gabriel Nathorst, a Swedish geologist, led two expeditions in search of traces of Salomon August Andrée and his companions, who in 1897 had disappeared during a balloon voyage to the North Pole. The first in 1898 was to Svalbard, and the second in 1899 to North-East Greenland.

"Antarctic" made an unusually rapid passage through the drift-ice belt, and was close to Lille Pendulum on 2nd July 1899, the earliest date on record. They reached Sabine Ø on the 6th July 1899. However, the fjord ice was still intact, and after placing a depot on Hvalrosø, they continued southwards to Scoresby Sund where the head of Hurry Inlet was visited. When ice conditions in the fjords improved, they sailed north again and into

"Antarctic" leaves Copenhagen. Summer 1900.
© Arctic Institute

Kejser Franz Joseph Fjord on the 9th August; the innermost part of the fjord was reached by Europeans for the first time. Discoveries now occurred one after the other, and during three hectic weeks the expedition managed to map the entire widely branched fjord complex between latitudes 72° and 74°N. Nathorst gave priority to geographical discovery rather than scientific observation, as each day unknown fjords and new mountains were discovered. The mapping work of Per Dusén, the cartographer of the expedition who also undertook the botanical and photographical work, is regarded as his life's greatest achievement. His map has only one significant distortion, namely Dusén Fjord, which was drawn much too short. It has to be said in the defence of Dusén that the fjord bearing his name was discovered only the day before the home voyage. Nathorst probably expressed the thoughts of Dusén at this incident, when he wrote: *"At first, I admit, I wished that this fjord had not existed".*[10]

In 1900 another Swedish expedition visited North-East Greenland, a zoological expedition led by the zoologist Gustaf Kolthoff. The Norwegian sealer "Frithjof" had been chartered for the expedition that reached Mackenzie Bugt (73°25'N) on the 31st July 1900.[11] After visiting Nathorst's depot on Hvalrosø, where post was deposited, the expedition continued into Kejser Franz Joseph Fjord and Moskusoksefjord, where they stayed until the 23rd August. A large collection of birds and animals was taken home including two wolves, and two captured muskox calves.

Andrée et al. 1930; 1925; Kolthoff 1901.

CARLSBERG FOUNDATION EXPEDITION TO EAST GREENLAND 1900

In 1900 First Lieutenant Georg Carl Amdrup (1866-1947) led the Carlsberg Foundation Expedition to East Greenland (Carlsbergfondets Ekspedition til Østgrønland). The plan was to undertake a journey by an 18 foot open boat along the unknown coast between Scoresby Sund (70°N) and Agga Ø (67°22'N) near Ammassalik. On the 21st July, when Amdrup and his three companions started their journey, the command of the "Antarctic" was delegated to Dr. Nicolaj Hartz, and under his leadership the coast between Scoresby Sund and Fleming Fjord was mapped. On the 2nd September 1900 Amdrup and his crew reached Ammassalik, where they later in September were picked up by the "Antarctic".

Amdrup et al. 1913; Hartz 1902; Koch 1902.

DUKE OF ORLÉANS 1905 & 1909

In the summer of 1905, the Frenchman Louis Philippe Robert Duc d'Orléans hired the "Belgica", the former Norwegian sealer "Patria", for a cruise to Svalbard and North-East Greenland. "Belgica", under the command of Adrian de Gerlache, first visited the west coast of Spitsbergen before sailing for North-East Greenland. Near Kap Bismarck (76°42'N) they met the Norwegian sealer "Søstrene", whose skipper reported ice conditions to be the best he had known in 30 years. Thus encouraged "Belgica" pressed northwards, landing at Kap Philippe on Île de France (77°35'N), and reaching 78°16'N before the ship was stopped by unbroken winter ice. Panoramic sketches of the coast were made up to about 79°N. After the return, the Duc Orléans purchased "Belgica", and in the summer of 1909 visited the area between Kejser Franz Joseph Fjord and Shannon.[12]

Isachsen 1925; Kjær 2005; Orléans 1905.

DANMARK EXPEDITION 1906-08

In the summer of 1906 the "Committee for the Danmark Expedition to the North-East Coast of Greenland" sent out an expedition under the leadership of the journalist and writer Ludvig Mylius-Erichsen (1872-1907). The expedition numbered 28 participants. The main objective was to explore and map the entirely unknown regions north of latitude 78°16°N, between the northernmost point reached by the French Duc D'Orléans in 1905, and Kap Clarence Wyckoff (82°57'N) on the east coast of Peary Land, the easternmost point reached by the American Robert Edwin Peary on the 22nd May 1900 after travelling along the north coast of Greenland from the Thule area.

The Danmark Expedition left Copenhagen on the 24th June 1906, and reached the coast near Store Koldewey on 12th August. On the 16th August the expedition ship "Danmark" - formerly "Magdalena" of Tønsberg, Norway, anchored for the winter in a small south-facing bay close to Kap Bismarck. The harbour, named Danmark Havn (76°46'N), became the headquarters of the expedition for the next two years. Ashore and close to the ship, a house for four persons was built, known as "Villaen" [628-1]. About 60 km to the west, at a bay in Mørkefjord, an advanced meteorological station was established, and was known as "Pustervig" [640].

At the end of March 1907 four sledge teams set out to map the last unknown stretch of North-East Greenland north of Danmark Havn. On the 12th May 1907 a sledge team led by First Lieutenant Johan Peter Koch (1870-1928) reached Peary's cairn at Kap Clarence

"Danmark" and "Villaen" in Danmark Havn, 1908.
© Arctic Institute

Wyckoff and three days later Kap Bridgman (83°29'N). The coast of Greenland had finally been travelled in its entirety.

During the spring three out of the four sledge teams returned safely to Danmark Havn, but the fourth, consisting of Mylius-Erichsen, First Lieutenant Niels Peter Høeg-Hagen and the Greenlander Jørgen Brønlund did not return. It was not until March 1908 that the fate of the three men was revealed. The spring thaw of 1907 had stranded them on the inhospitable west side of Danmark Fjord throughout the summer. Weakened by the scarcity of game, they all perished during the attempt to return to Danmark Havn in November-December 1907, presumably via the Inland Ice. The body of Brønlund was found near the east point of Lambert Land (79°15'N). With this sad message the expedition returned to Copenhagen on the 23rd August 1908.

The Danmark Expedition brought back extensive, scientific observations of all kinds, that were published in six large volumes in the series "Meddelelser om Grønland".

Amdrup et al. 1913; Freuchen 1936; Friis 1909; Kjær and Foxworthy 2004: Lundbye 1984; Manniche 1909; Poulsen 1991; Ventegodt 1997.

SCIENTIFIC EXPLORATION 1909-60

The Danmark Expedition 1906-08 completed the final gap in the outline map of North-East Greenland, and as such the entire coast of Greenland. However, many inland areas of North-East Greenland were essentially unknown prior to the pioneer exploration undertaken from the land and from the air during the Three-year Expedition 1931-34 led by Lauge Koch. The products of this expedition included a 1:1 million topographic map of North-East Greenland, and the first of a series of 1:250,000 map sheets prepared by the Danish Geodetic Institute (Geodætisk Institut). One of the many new discoveries was the 70 km long Grandjean Fjord, first explored in 1932. A number of stations and huts described in this volume were erected by this and other scientific expeditions.

ALABAMA EXPEDITION 1909-12

After the return of the Danmark Expedition, a desire to establish for certain what had happened to Ludvig Mylius-Erichsen, Niels Peter Høeg-Hagen and their diaries arose. In 1909 Captain Ejnar Mikkelsen (1880-1971) obtained the support of the Committee of the Danmark Expedition and, with the help of private funds, embarked on an expedition - the Alabama Expedition 1909-12 - to unravel the circumstances of the disaster, and if possible find the missing diaries. The expedition ship "Alabama" of Stavanger was purchased, and Ejnar Mikkelsen with six companions and provisions for 18 months set sail on 20th June 1909.

After a difficult passage through the pack ice the "Alabama" was forced to winter on the east coast of Shannon, south of Kap Sussi. In the autumn of 1909 a sledge journey was made to Lambert Land, where the body of Jørgen Brønlund was found once again, together with some possessions.

In March 1910 Ejnar Mikkelsen and Iver P. Iversen set out on a sledge journey across the Inland Ice to Danmark Fjord. In Danmark Fjord two cairn records

The discovery of North and North-East Greenland has followed two different routes, a route from the west through Smith Sound and the Nares Strait, and a route from the south-east along the east coast of Greenland. © Peter Schmidt Mikkelsen

left by Mylius-Erichsen were recovered, reporting the sensational news that "Peary Channel" did not exist, and that Peary Land was not an island. However, the cairn records did not solve the mystery of the route the party had taken in an attempt to reach Danmark Havn. Mikkelsen and Iversen followed the outer coast, with great difficulty and much hardship as Mikkelsen was ill much of the time. They eventually reached Shannon in November 1910, only to discover, that "Alabama" had been wrecked. The other expedition members had been rescued by the Norwegian "7de juni" Expedition, after having built a hut "Alabamahuset" [518], from the wreckage of the ship, and leaving a depot of provisions. Mikkelsen and Iversen were

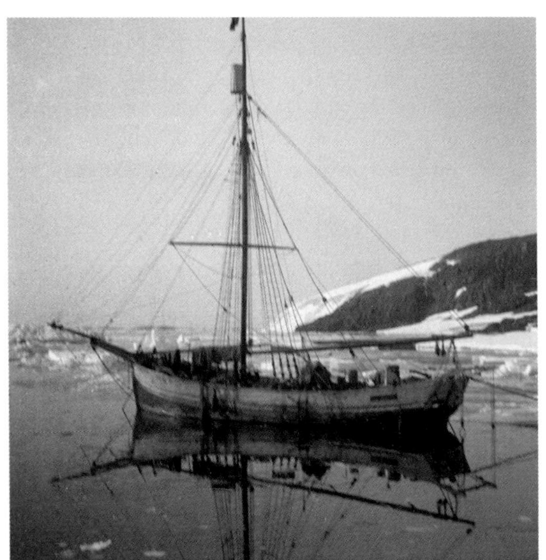

"Alabama" at Kap Sussi, 6th September 1909. © Arctic Institute

stranded, and spent two further winters at Alabamahuset and the houses at Bass Rock [461] until they were rescued in July 1912 by the Norwegian sealer "Sjøblomsten".

Mikkelsen 1914, 1922.

DANISH EXPEDITION TO DRONNING LOUISE LAND AND ACROSS THE INLAND ICE 1912-13

This four-man expedition, that included Alfred Wegener (1880-1930) the German scientist who first proposed the theory of "continental drift", was led by Johan Peter Koch (1870-1928). The plan was to explore the atmospherical and glaciological conditions along the marginal zone of the Inland Ice. In July 1912 the expedition was landed by the "Godthaab" in Dove Bugt, together with 16 Icelandic ponies and a motor boat. The expedition spent the winter of 1912-13 in a wintering house, "Borg" [919], which they built on Brede Bræ. In April 1913 the expedition continued westwards to Dronning Louise Land using pony-drawn sledges, and then further west across the Inland Ice to the west coast of Greenland.

Koch 1913; Tusaat 1994.

JOHAN A. OLSEN EXPEDITION 1922-23

In 1922 the Geofysisk Institutt in Tromsø sent up the Johan A. Olsen Expedition with the "Anni I" to establish the radio- and weather station "Myggbukta" [335] in Mackenzie Bugt. They provided the first wireless connection between Greenland and Europe, and the first regular weather service from

"Godthaab", 1928 © Arctic Institute

East Greenland. In 1923 the expedition left Greenland for Norway, but "Anni I" disappeared without trace, presumably crushed in the pack ice. Radio communications and weather reports were restored in 1926, and Myggbukta was the centre of Norwegian activity in North-East Greenland until 1959.
Isachsen 1925.

CAMBRIDGE EAST GREENLAND EXPEDITIONS 1926 & 1929

James Mann Wordie, a British geologist and mountaineer, attempted to reach North-East Greenland in 1923 on the "Heimen" but failed to reach the coast due to the very bad ice conditions that sank "Anni I". The 1926 and 1929 voyages with the larger "Heimland" were more successful, and explored the area between the Pendulum Øer and Kong Oscar Fjord.

At Germania Havn in 1926 the expedition repeated Edward Sabine's pendulum observations of 1823, and continued the surveying and exploration initiated by William Scoresby, Douglas C. Clavering and Alfred Nathorst.

In 1929, on the 15th of August, Wordie and two companions were the first to climb Petermann Bjerg (2940 m), the highest mountain in North-East Greenland.
Wordie 1927, 1930.

NORWEGIAN SVALBARD- & ARCTIC OCEAN SURVEY (NSIU) 1929-33

In the years 1929-33 five summer expeditions to North-East Greenland were sent out by the Norwegian Svalbard- & Arctic Ocean Survey (Norges Svalbard- og Ishavs-undersøkelser; NSIU). Adolf Hoel (1879-1964), a Norwegian geologist, was the originator of the expeditions which took place when the Danish-Norwegian conflict over sovereignty of East Greenland was entering its final phase. Hoel led the expeditions in 1930, 1931 and 1933, and geologist Anders Kristian Orvin the remaining years.

The NSIU expeditions operated primarily in the area between Kong Oscar Fjord and Clavering Ø. They were carried out as a close co-operation between NSIU and the Norwegian trapping company Arctic Commercial Enterprise (Arktisk Næringsdrift).
The vessels "Veslekari" (M-20-VD) and "Polarbjørn" (M-12-HD) were chartered for transport to and from Greenland.
NSIU 1937; Erskine and Kjaer 1998; Kjær and Sefland 2006; Orvin 1930, 1931, 1934; Richter 1934.

LAUGE KOCH EXPEDITIONS 1926-58

In the years 1926-39 and 1947-58 the Danish geologist Lauge Koch (1892-1964) led a long series of largely geological expeditions to North-East Greenland, with government support and using the ships "Gustav Holm" and "Godthaab" loaned by the Royal Greenland Trading Company (KGH).

In 1926-27 Koch wintered in Scoresbysund, from where in the spring of 1927 he made a sledge journey to Danmark Havn. Summer expeditions followed in 1929 and 1930. The Three-Year Expedition 1931-34 was the largest and most comprehensive expedition hitherto sent to Greenland by Denmark, and received the support of the Carlsberg Foundation and private funds, as well as the Government. Topographic

Lauge Koch, an outstanding expedition leader and a controversial personality, 1958. © Oliver Wackernagel

surveying was entrusted to the Geodetic Institute. The expedition was to extend over four summers and three winters, with the scientists wintering in specially built stations. Another Two-Year Expedition followed in 1936-38. After the war Koch resumed his expeditions in 1947, but following the building of the airfield at Mestersvig, wintering expeditions were given up in 1954. Summer expeditions continued until 1958, when Government funding was suspended.

In connection with Lauge Koch's expeditions, wintering stations were built at "Eskimonæs" [405] and "Ella Ø" [235] in 1931, and the smaller travel houses "Nordfjordhuset" [358-2] and "Kap Brown huset" [107] were also erected. In 1932 the station "Kulhus" [511] was built farther north, in 1949 "Ekspeditionshuset" [206-1] was built near Mesters Vig, and in 1950 the summer base "Maria Ø station" [239-2] was established.

Galena-bearing quartz veins were discovered near Mesters Vig in 1948, which led to the founding of Nordisk Mineselskab A/S (The Northern Mining Company Ltd., or "Nordmine"). The airfield, "Mestersvig Airfield" [209-1] was constructed in 1952, to serve the mining village "Minebyen" [207], which operated from 1952-61.

Lauge Koch was a controversial personality, but an outstanding expedition leader.

Koch 1934, 1938, 1939, 1940; 1955; Lassen 2005; Odsbjerg 1992; Ries 2003; Schwarzenbach 1993; Seidenfaden 1936, 1938; Thorson 1937; Tusaat 1992.

ROBERT BARTLETT 1930-31 & JOHN HOWARD 1933

In the summers of 1930 and 1931 the American Robert A. Bartlett visited North-East Greenland in the "Effie M. Morrissey". The purpose of these summer expeditions was to collect archaeological and anthropological material for American museums. In 1931 the ship was trapped in the drift ice for 37 days before reaching land.

The "Norkap II" Expedition in 1933 was led by the American John K. Howard. The main purpose was hunting, although some geological work was carried out on Ymer Ø.

Bartlett & Bird 1931; Bartlett 1934; Talcott 1937.

LOUISE BOYD EXPEDITIONS 1931-38

The American Louise Arner Boyd undertook a number of voyages to North-East Greenland, in the summers of 1931, 1933, 1937 and 1938. Louise Boyd had inherited a fortune from her father, a pioneer in the U.S. mining industry who made his money in the California gold rush, and she planned and financed all her Arctic expeditions herself. For her expeditions Louise Boyd chartered the Norwegian sealer "Veslekari", and brought back extensive photographic and topographical material, later published in two publications of the American Geographical Society.

Boyd 1935, 1948; Kjær and Sefland 2004.

CHARLES BIRD & EDWARD BIRD 1936-38

In 1936-37 Charles Bird and Edward Bird, two English ornithologists from Cambridge University, spent the winter with the Norwegians in Myggbukta. Edward Bird went home in 1937, but his brother Charles stayed for another year.

Orvin 1937; Report on the activities ... 1937.

MØRKEFJORD EXPEDITION 1938-41

In the summer of 1938 the "Danish North-East Greenland Expedition 1938-39, sent out by Alf Trolle, Ebbe Munck and Eigil Knuth in memory of the Danmark Expedition", established the station

Reunion of former Swiss members of the Lauge Koch Expeditions meeting in Tennwil, Switzerland, 7th September 1995. From left: Oliver Wackernagel, Kurt Bürgi, Gerold Stryger, Klaus Stucky, Rudolf Frei, Emil Witzig, Peter Braun, Hans-Peter Thöni, Rudolf Trümpy, Theo Bearth, Armin Wyttenbach, Hansruedi von Gunten, Hans Röthlisberger, Fritz Hans Schwarzenbach (host), Hanspeter Hartmann-Frick, Peter Schmidt Mikkelsen (guest), Wolf Maync, Markus Aellen, Bernardo Moser, Urs Hoessly, Walter Bisig, Eduard Wenk, Erdhart Fränkl (host), Stefan Götz, Urs Grunder, Hanspeter Buess, Emil Graven, Paul Graeter. © Atelier Meyer 5610 Wohlen

The (old) "Polarbjørn" (M-12-HD), 20th July 1932. © Thor Askheim / Norwegian Polar Institute

"Mørkefjord" [641] in the north-western part of Dove Bugt. Usually known as the "Mørkefjord Expedition", it was led by the archaeologist and artist Eigil Knuth. In the spring of 1939, Knuth undertook a sledge journey northwards along the coast that reached 81°50'N. The zoologist Alwin Pedersen was an independent member of the expedition and had his own house, "Alwin Pedersens hus" [639-2], built at Hvalrosodden. The expedition ended officially in 1939, but due to WWII, the Mørkefjord station remained manned until 1941.

Andreassen 2003 pp. 143-180; Knuth 1940, 1942.

NORWEGIAN-FRENCH POLAR EXPEDITION 1938-39

In 1938 the Norwegian-French Polar Expedition, led by the Norwegian-American Willie Knutsen and financed by the French count Gaston Micard, established the station "Micardbu" [704] on the east coast of Germania Land. The purposes of the expedition were trapping as well as scientific research. The expedition vessel "En Avant" - the former "Ringsel" (T-30-T), was anchored during the winter in a natural harbour at the north point of Store Koldewey. This expedition is also mentioned in the chapter "Trapping - winter expeditions".

Knutsen 1992, 2005.

DANISH DOG SLEDGE EXPEDITION 1938-39

In 1938-39 the writer and trapper Elmar Drastrup led a two-man dog sledge expedition whose objectives were to find a better sledge route to Peary Land and, - if possible - across North Greenland to West Greenland. The expedition was financed by the Scoresbysund Committee. However, after reaching Romer Sø at 81°N they were frustrated by open water and heavier than usual snow conditions, and forced to retreat back along the East Greenland coast. After a journey of 2350 km in 105 travelling days they reached their starting point, Sandodden in Young Sund.

Drastrup 1945.

HANS AHLMANN & KÅRE RODAHL 1939-40

During the summer of 1939, the Swedish professor Hans W:son Ahlmann carried out glaciological investigations on a glacier in northern Clavering Ø assisted by the meteorologist Backa Eriksson and the Norwegian medical student Kåre Rodahl. Rodahl continued his own biological investigations in the winter of 1939-40 at Moskusheimen [429] trappers' station, and amongst other things discovered that poisoning from eating polar bear liver is due to the high vitamin A content.

Rodahl 1946 (1), 1946 (2), 1949 (1), 1949 (2), 1992.

DANISH PEARY LAND EXPEDITION 1947-50

After World War II, Eigil Knuth and Ebbe Munck resumed the interrupted work of the Mørkefjord Expedition. In the summer of 1947 the Danish Peary Land Expedition established "Zackenberg-basen" [438-3] at Young Sund, from where building materials and provisions were air-lifted to Peary Land, and a station was established beside Jørgen Brønlund Fjord.

Under Knuth's leadership the expedition wintered here in 1948-50. Eigil Knuth subsequently led numerous summer expeditions to Peary Land, and later Île de France up to 1995, mainly summer expeditions with archaeological objectives.
Andreassen 2003; Høy 2003; Johnsen 1967; Knuth 1947, 1948, 1952, 1973; Laursen 1972; Martens et al. 2003: Rodahl 1948; Tusaat 1994.

BRITISH NORTH GREENLAND EXPEDITION 1952-54

After a reconnaissance in the summer of 1951 Commander C.J.W. Simpson of the Royal Navy led the British North Greenland Expedition 1952-54 to Dronning Louise Land. From Zackenberg-basen [438-3] at Young Sund materials and equipment were air-lifted to Britannia Sø in Dronning Louise Land. The base station "Britannia Sø" [706] was established on the east side of the lake, and the expedition wintered here in 1952-54.
Banks 1957; Simpson 1957; Hamilton 1958; Lister 2005.

MESTERS VIG GEOMORPHIC RESEARCH PROGRAM 1955-64

In 1955, Albert Lincoln Washburn embarked on a long-running programme of geomorphological studies from a base near the airfield at Mestersvig. Reconnaissance studies in 1955 and 1956 were followed by the main phase of the study which lasted from 1957-61, with follow-up studies in 1964. The headquarters of the expedition were at "Washburns hus" [210], but the house was not used for over-wintering.
Washburn 1965.

OTHER SCIENTIFIC EXPEDITIONS 1948-60

In addition to the scientific expeditions mentioned above, a number of other research groups visited North-East Greenland from 1948-60.

Danish expeditions included: Geodetic Institute 1949-54 and 1959-64 (aerial photography, surveying), Christian Vibe 1953, 1954, 1956, 1958 (zoology), The Carlsberg Foundation Scoresbysund Expedition 1958 (botany and biology), Geological Survey of Greenland (GGU) 1958, 1959 (geology).

Work sponsored by other nations included: Leeds University Greenland Expedition 1948 (glaciology and geology), W.R.B. Battle Expedition 1949 (glaciology), Expéditions Polaires Francaises 1950-51 (geophysics), Cambridge Expedition to East Greenland 1955 (zoology), British North-East Greenland Expedition 1956 (zoology), U.S. Air Force Cambridge Research Center 1956 and 1959 (aircraft landing sites), American Glaciological Expeditions 1959 and 1961.
A.K. Higgins, pers. comm.

THE RESEARCH CONTINUES ...

From 1960 to 2008 about 250 scientific expeditions have continued all kinds of scientific research in North-East Greenland.[13] These have included large, state financed expeditions as well as smaller, university or privately sponsored groups. Danish, British, French, Swedish and Norwegian expeditions have been particularly active.
In 1995 a permanent research station was established at Zackenberg, 25 km north-west of Daneborg. The "Zackenberg Ecological Research Station" (ZERO) - or "Zackenberg ZERO" - [438-5] was officially opened in August 1997. A branch facility is located at Daneborg in the former Daneborg Vejrstation [425-2], which in 1998 was reopened and repaired to be used for marine research. ZERO is sponsored by the Greenland Home Rule authority and operated by the Danish Polar Center. The work at Zackenberg is coordinated through the programme "Zackenberg Ecological Research Operations" with the following institutions as partners: Danish Polar Center, Danish National Environmental Research Institute, Greenland Institute of Natural Resources, University of Copenhagen and Asiaq. The work at Zackenberg is financially supported by the Danish Environmental Protection Agency, The Ministry of Science, Technology and Innovation, the Greenland Home Rule authority and the Aage V. Jensens Fonde.[14]
A.K. Higgins, pers. comm.

COMMERCIAL EXPLORATION – SUMMER EXPEDITIONS

North-East Greenland hosts vast resources, both onshore and offshore. A wide range of minerals are known, but few occurrences have been exploited due to the location of North-East Greenland - bordered to the west by the continental ice cap (Inland Ice) and to the east by the wide belt of drift ice. Until the introduction of aircraft, the coast was only accessible by ship for at few weeks each summer. In the days of sailing ships this was a highly risky affair, and for centuries the dangers of navigating in the drift ice prevented mariners from approaching the shore. Even in recent years, modern ice-strengthened ships have been unable to reach land in bad ice-years, returning home without success. Until the 19th century the navigation difficulties hindered any thought of commercial exploitation of North-East Greenland's resources.

THE NAVIGATION

The commercial and scientific exploration of North-East Greenland started more or less simultaneously. It was the search for whales and new hunting grounds that led William Scoresby Junior and his father to penetrate the ice belt in 1822, and try their luck in coastal waters. Thanks to their wide-ranging scientific interests, their short visit brought back the first reliable information on the land behind the drift ice. The invention of the steam machine and ship's propeller were two other important factors that finally made navigation independent of the wind. Although many ships still carried sail, this new means of manoeuvring through the drift ice improved accessibility to the coast of North-East Greenland and opened up the possibility of commercial activities.

At first it was the sea mammals that attracted attention. Whaling and sealing had taken place along the edge of the drift ice since the early 17th century, but visits to the coastal waters such as that by William Scoresby were rarely possible until the introduction of steam-powered trapping ships. These allowed easier passage of the drift ice and the hunting of walrus, seal and other mammals in coastal waters. Helge Vedel, who participated in the Danish East Greenland Expedition 1891-92, recorded a meeting with Scottish whalers on the 6th July 1892 *en route* to the coast. The Danish expedition met up with the "Hope" and the "Eclipse" of Peterhead, and their well-known skippers, the brothers David Gray and John Gray. Vedel writes: *""Eclipse" was constructed in 1871 for whaling, a 450 ton vessel with full-rigged patent topsail. The engine 450 HP (nominal) runs 8 1/2 knots on steam, usually 5-6." ..."The crew, 50 men from Peterhead and the Shetland Islands, could man the eight whaling boats" ... "In 1868 Captain David Gray went ashore on Clavering island, and has on numerous occasions been in coastal waters on the east coast of Greenland north of 70°N.*[15] The 63-year-old David Gray had then been sailing and whaling in the Arctic for 46 summers in a row, while John Gray had "only" been navigating the Arctic Ocean since 1848.

Isachsen 1922.

NORTH-EAST GREENLAND, A NEW HUNTING GROUND

Norwegians have always had close relations with the Arctic Ocean, an association that goes back to long before the trans-Atlantic voyages of the Viking era. Living beside the north Atlantic Ocean, they have continued trapping and fishing along the northern ice border until the present-day.

In the beginning of July 1889, part of the Norwegian sealer fleet was in the waters west of Svalbard, where for a month the sealers had cruised back and forth along the "West Ice" (Vestisen) in the Greenland Sea between Jan Mayen and Svalbard, looking for hooded seal. The catch had been poor, so some sealers started looking for better hunting grounds. Amongst the sealers was "Hekla" of Tønsberg, skippered by Ragnvald Knudsen (1858-1930). Knudsen had had a comet-like career. At age 19 he was second mate on Norway's second largest ship, and after completing his master's certificate, spent several years with the navy and merchant fleet, until becoming master of the sealer steam ship "Hekla" in 1888. Knudsen had then no experience with sealing, and the owners were blamed for having hired such a young and inexperienced man as skipper; however, Knudsen was an able sailor and a lucky one.

Leaving the other sealers, Ragnvald Knudsen took the "Hekla" and its crew of 48 westward. In his diary he writes: *"As I had previously read some accounts of expeditions to the east coast of Greenland, giving information about walrus and seal there, it occurred to me that there might be some business to be done there".*[16]

Walrus on an ice floe near Kap Berghaus. June 1979.
© Peter Schmidt Mikkelsen

This was a big risk to take, and Knudsen had his worries about the reactions of the ship owners and the crew. But they advanced quickly, and on the 16th July 1888 "Hekla" reached the East Greenland coast near Kap Broer Ruys. The ice was packed to the south so Knudsen went northwards to the more open waters of Young Sund. *"There were plenty of animals there, reindeer and muskoxen. A polar bear walked cautiously around further away. The mood on board became more spirited. The crew, who during the passage through the ice had been somewhat down-hearted, began to enjoy themselves and would have liked to hunt the bear as well as the reindeer and muskoxen. But we had no time for such things. The walrus was now our target and away we went".* [17] Only a few hours later Knudsen found what he was looking for. On the beach by Kap Berghaus a huge herd of walruses was observed and for the sleeping animals the discovery was fatal - within the next half hour 100 walrus lay slaughtered on the beach. Since that day Kap Berghaus is often referred to as "Heklas Hvalrosnæs".

The hunt proceeded to the fjord area between Gael Hamke Bugt and Shannon, but the autumn was now rapidly approaching, and in August the crew became uneasy. They feared "Hekla" could become icebound. Knudsen could not resist the wishes of the crew and course was set for home. On the 14th August "Hekla" was back in open waters again and arrived in Hammerfest on the 28th August. The catch from their three months in the "West Ice" and North-East Greenland amounted to 1000 barrels of blubber, 2730 seals, 44 baby seals, 807 hooded seals, 21 bearded seals, 267 walruses (about 27 tons), 220 kg walrus teeth, nine polar bears and 24 muskoxen.

In 1891-92 Ragnvald Knudsen and "Hekla" wintered in North-East Greenland with The Danish East Greenland Expedition 1891-92.

Isachsen 1925.

NORWEGIAN SEALERS AND FISHERMEN

The success of Ragnvald Knudsen's voyage in 1889 encouraged other Norwegians to try their luck in the Greenland Sea and in East Greenland coastal waters. From 1897 Norwegian vessels regularly visited the east coast in order to supplement their catch with walrus, polar bear and muskox, or to fish arctic char in the rivers. It was not without risk, and over the years many Norwegian sealers and their crews disappeared in the dangerous ice belt off the Greenland east coast.

Between 1889 and 1931 a total of 124 visits to North-East Greenland by Norwegian sealers were recorded.[18] After a pause during World War I (WWI), Norwegian activity increased considerably from 1919, only to cease around 1930. Sealers had now begun to supplement their catch with Greenland shark, but another reason for the change was that Norwegians had been shut out of the Scoresby Sund region after the founding of the Scoresbysund colony in 1924. However, Norwegian vessels continued to visit North-East Greenland annually until 1959, providing support and supplies as well as transport to and from Greenland for the wintering trappers.

TOURISM AND TRANSPORTATION

For many years, Norwegians played a dominant role in the navigation of the East Greenland coast, and not solely for trapping. Their great experience made them and their ships the obvious choice for transportation of scientific expeditions. Celebrated ships such as the "Antarctic", "Belgica" and "Danmark" had previously all sailed under the Norwegian flag, and the East Greenland expeditions often employed a Norwegian crew or a Norwegian ice pilot.

Norwegian ship owners also saw other opportunities for commercial enterprise in North-East Greenland. As early as 1902, Magnus K. Giæver of Tromsø developed the idea of arranging hunting safaris for rich tourists. In his memoirs he writes: *"My idea was that these expeditions should be of a very intimate character – only three to four hunters – and not mass killings of any kind of animals. For this reason participation in the expedition had to be a quite expensive affair; however, I confidently went ahead with realizing my plan".*[19] Giæver equipped the "Laura" with comfortable cabins, provided the services of chef and waiter, and carried on board abundant supplies of champagne - even clay pigeon machines were provided in case the hunt should fail.

After fruitless efforts in 1904 and 1906, Giæver succeeded in reaching the East Greenland coast in

1907 with four wealthy tourists on board. "Laura" visited Hvalrosø, Bass Rock, Shannon and later Dusén Fjord. The hunting result of the trip included 30 polar bears, 14 muskoxen, 9 hooded seals, 11 seals and one narwhale. The tourists were more than pleased, but the expedition ended tragically. On the home voyage "Laura" was trapped by the ice, drifted southwards and did not break free until the end of September. Meanwhile, the company's other ship "Frithjof" had been sent out to search for "Laura". Unfortunately, "Laura" reached Jan Mayen just one day after "Frithjof" had left the island to enter the pack ice. While "Laura" returned safely to Norway, "Frithjof", was damaged during a storm and headed for Iceland where the ship was wrecked. Only one of the 18 crew members was rescued.

In 1900 "Frithjof" had been chartered by the Gustav Kolthoff expedition for a voyage to Greenland, and in 1901 the ship was chartered by the Baldwin-Ziegler Expedition. The American Evelyn Baldwin planned to reach the North Pole via Franz Joseph Land, and to support a possible return via the east coast of Greenland depots were established in 1901 at Kap Philip Broke and at Bass Rock. However, the expedition suffered from poor leadership, and the attempt on the North Pole was abandoned. Although Baldwin never utilized his own depots, the depot houses and provisions at "Kap Philip Broke" [470] and "Bass Rock" [461] were of vital importance for others, notably the stranded members of the Alabama Expedition in 1909-12.

Giæver's ships again carried wealthy tourists to North-East Greenland in 1910 and 1911; but others were trying to break into the same business. Jens Øien, formerly one of Giæver's skippers, bought himself a ship and started his own arctic safaris.

This pioneer tourism venture came to an end in 1914 with the outbreak of WWI. When the war ended much had changed in Europe, and tourism did not resume until the 1930s, when tourists, hunters and journalists once again joined expeditions to North-East Greenland; however, these were now rather more modest affairs.

Giæver 1939; Isachsen 1932; Kjær 2006; Kmunke 1910; Kolthoff 1901; Leverkus 1909; Norsk Polarklubb 1980; Vollan 1951.

SPORT EXPEDITIONS

At the present-day expeditions to North-East Greenland are divided into two categories, "scientific expeditions" and "sport expeditions". The latter group includes climbing expeditions, tourist visits and other expedition activities not primarily with scientific aims.

One of the earliest sport expeditions was that of the Norwegians Arne Høygaard and Martin Mehren, who in August 1931 reached Nordfjord via Waltershausen Gletscher, after a crossing of the Inland Ice. However, it was not until the beginning of the 1950s, that the vast recreative possibilities of North-East Greenland were seriously recognized and exploited by enthusiastic outdoor people. To begin with it was the high unconquered mountain peaks of the Stauning Alper that attracted attention, not least because of their location a few tens of kilometres west of the airfield at Mestersvig.

Up to 1960 the following climbing expeditions visited the region: a Norwegian mountaineering expedition (Arne Randers Heen, Øistein Røed and Kjeld Fris Baasted) in 1951, the Norwegian-Danish Expedition to the Stauning Alper in 1954, a mountaineering expedition led by W.D. Brooker in 1956, the Austrian Greenland Expedition 1957, the Scottish East Greenland Expedition 1958 and the British East Greenland Expedition 1960.

Between 1960 and 2007 about 170 sport expeditions have visited North-East Greenland,[20] and have increasingly taken advantage of chartered aircraft such as helicopters and Twin Otter aircraft to reach more distant areas of interest.

Elander 1992; Hoff 1992; Høygaard & Mehren 1931; Mikkelsen 1990, 2006; Pedersen 1979; A.K. Higgins pers. comm.

For summer travels in North-East Greenland the kayak is still an unsurpassed means of transportation. The ratio between payload and energy consumption is large, and in addition it is pollution-free. Peter Schmidt Mikkelsen (left) and Magnus Elander of the "Danish-Swedish Kayak Expedition 1989" in front of the old expedition house "Ørnereden" (The Eagle's Nest) at Ella Ø, 16th August 1989. © Peter Schmidt Mikkelsen

TRAPPING – WINTER EXPEDITIONS

The commercial enterprise that has left the most visible traces in North-East Greenland is the trapping of foxes by Norwegian and Danish hunters, specifically the winter trapping. The objectives were simply to trap arctic fox and to sell their skins. In the cold climate of North-East Greenland, the arctic fox develops a thick winter fur of high quality as protection against the cold. There are two colour variations: white fox and 'blue fox', of which the white is dominant. In the summers foxes shed their fur, and the thin brown summer coats have no value. Only the thick winter skins, from foxes trapped in the period from November to April, have commercial value, and since North-East Greenland can only be reached by ship in the short summer months, the trappers - or hunters - had to over-winter in Greenland.

The trapping was undertaken by hunting companies based in Norway and Denmark, with the principal activities essentially restricted to the period 1908-60. In reality, fox-trapping was only profitable for a few years, and was only continued due to government subsidies and the support of private sponsors, that was linked mainly to political circumstances.

Both Danes and Norwegians generally used the same trapping methods. In the years 1908-24, usually three to four trappers lived at a so-called trappers' station. From the station regular trips were made to check their traps, which were placed within a radius of a day's walk. This method was known from Svalbard, but was not optimal in North-East Greenland, where the fox roam more widely. From the end of the 1920s a different system was introduced that greatly expanded the region covered from each trappers' station. For each trapping territory a network of small trappers' huts or cabins were built, so that one or two trappers from each station could undertake long trapping journeys using dog sledges, visiting large numbers of traps and staying overnight in the often very primitive trappers' huts, returning to the station with their catch after an absence of a week or more.

The type of traps used developed and changed through the years. At first foot-traps and poisoned bait were used along with box traps for catching foxes

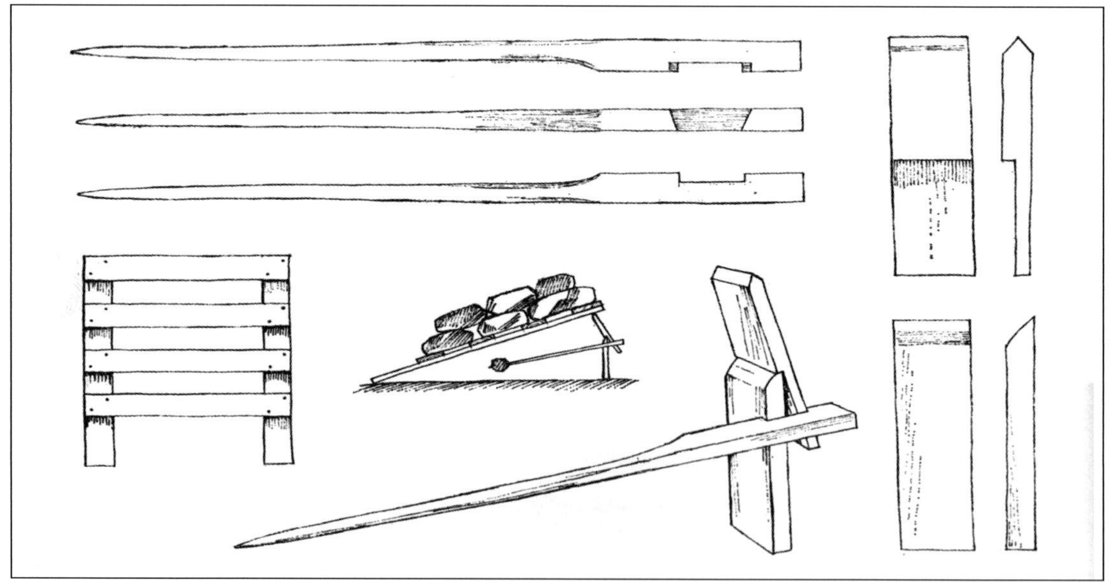

"As far as I know, the most used wooden fall-trap originates from Arctic Canada. After 1930 Danish and Norwegian trappers almost exclusively used this trap. The fall-trap has the advantage that it kills the fox instantly, and when the trap is checked the prey is found dead and frozen stiff. The trap consists of two wooden boards, to which four cross-boards of untreated wood or drift wood are nailed. This wood framework is loaded with heavy stones and suspended at one end, at an angle of about 30° from the ground, by two short, shaped wood planks and a locking stick, that also holds the bait. The pressure from the weight of the stones on the trap holds the two shaped planks in the notch of the locking stick. When the fox grabs the bait on the locking stick, the trap collapses". © Kristoffersen 1969

White arctic fox in its summer fur. The Greenlandic fox population consists of two colour variants, the white fox and the blue fox. In North-East Greenland the white fox makes up 90% of the fox population. The blue fox keeps its dark fur throughout the year, whereas the winter fur of the white fox is completely white. The fur of the blue fox is finer and more delicate than the white fox, and during the trapping era it would bring three times the price of the white fox fur. Since 1974, the fox has been completely protected within the area of the National Park. Ella Ø, 1979. © Peter Schmidt Mikkelsen

The polar bear is the largest known furred carnivore. Since 1974, only registered hunters living in the Greenlandic settlements are permitted to hunt polar bear in the National Park. To the Danish and Norwegian trappers of the trapping era the skins of the polar bear had only secondary value in comparison to those of the arctic fox. Kap Franklin, May 1979. © Peter Schmidt Mikkelsen

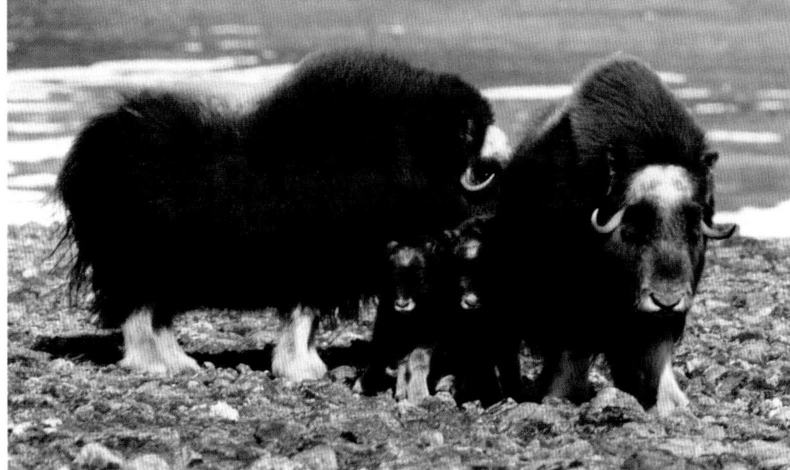

Muskox cows with calves. The muskox population in North-East Greenland varies greatly, and estimates range from about 8,000 to 20,000 animals. The muskox was the most important source of fresh meat during the trapping era, for both the hunters and their sledge dogs. Since 1974, the muskox has been protected within the area of the National Park. Daneborg, June 1979. © Peter Schmidt Mikkelsen

Bearded seal sun-bathing on an ice floe. Various species of seal are found in North-East Greenland, the most common being the ringed seal. Seal meat was also good dog food, and part of the trappers' traditional summer duties was to hunt seal. At the present-day the Sirius Dog Sledge Patrol is permitted to hunt a certain number of seal for dog food. Kong Oscar Fjord, August 1979. © Peter Schmidt Mikkelsen

alive. From about the 1930s common wooden fall-traps and box traps were mainly used.

Due to the seasonal accessibility, the year in North-East Greenland traditionally extends from summer to summer. You arrive on the coast in the summer, and leave again after one or more winterings. To the trappers the hunting year would typically pass as follows - Arrival in North-East Greenland in July-August. Preparation of the trapping territory, with building, provisioning and equipping of trappers' huts in August-September. Construction of the required number of traps and other equipment in September-October. Trapping journeys in the territory from about 20th October until 1st May. Cleaning and curing of the fox-skins, maintenance of the trappers' station, repair of boats and other equipment, and "vacation" in May-June. Apart from all these activities, the trappers also had to hunt to obtain food for themselves and their dogs, with the main prey being muskoxen, which could be hunted throughout the year. In the summer time it was also possible to hunt seal, walrus and birds. The polar bear was also hunted throughout the year, but the bear skins had only secondary value compared to that of the arctic fox skins.

Despite the similar trapping methods, the Norwegian and Danish trappers had widely different backgrounds. In Norway fox-trapping was a commercial versatile business, rich in tradition. However, to the common man in Denmark fox-trapping in Greenland was viewed as adventure - only well-informed circles knew what the Arctic and the trapping was really about.

With respect to the number of trappers taking part in expeditions, over-winterings, buildings and huts erected, and foxes trapped, see the tables later in this book (p.32-56).

TRAPPING 1908-24

The years 1908-1924 were a pioneer period for fox-trapping in North-East Greenland, a region then with no recognised owner, and open to anyone to try their luck. It was not until the end of this period that sovereignty was seriously considered. Although fox-trapping was not continuous, various attempts were made by both Norwegians and Danes.

THE INITIATIVE FROM SUNNMØRE

Sunnmøre is located about a quarter of the way up the coast of Norway. At the beginning of the 20th century the region was a power centre for Norwegian activity in the Arctic Ocean. The ports of Ålesund, Brandal and Hareid were home to a huge fleet of ships, as well as crews prepared to venture anywhere where pack ice was to be found. About 1900 the sealers from Sunnmøre began to undertake regular summer journeys to the waters off North-East Greenland, and the participants in these voyages would often discuss whether a wintering in North-East Greenland would be worthwhile. The main possibilities were in the arctic fox, as the price for good fox skins was high. Norwegian trappers had wintered in Svalbard since 1893, and made good profits from fox-trapping, and North-East Greenland was in many respects very similar terrain. In North-East Greenland, as in Svalbard, fox-trapping could be combined with hunting of polar bear. Although reindeer in North-East Greenland became extinct about 1900, alternative sources for fresh meat were to be found in the abundant herds of muskoxen.

To the sealers from Sunnmøre the idea of wintering in North-East Greenland was not a big step, but rather a natural expansion of an old trade.
Torkildsen 1991; Vollan 1951.

FLOREN EXPEDITION 1908-09

The first initiative came from Severin Gåsnes Liavåg. Born in 1879 in Hjørungavåg, he had sailed the Arctic Ocean from his youth. He was: *"one of those born to be an arctic sailor. He was calm and reliable, most calm when it came to the crunch",*[21] - and had a steady trigger finger which made him a marksman on the "Minna" (M-47-HD), which in 1900 was the first Sunnmøre sealer to operate in North-East Greenland waters. In 1904 Liavåg was the master on the "Avanse", which he co-owned with Hans Koppernes, a merchant in Ålesund. Through his loans for equipment, Koppernes made it possible for the people from Sunnmøre to start their trapping business. When "Avanse" was shipwrecked while herring fishing near Iceland, Liavåg and Koppernes ordered a new ship for the purpose of winter trapping in North-East Greenland. This vessel, a 37 ton sailing ship, was named "Floren".

In May 1908 they started to prepare for the expedition. All supplies were calculated for an absence of two years, as the risk of an extra involuntary wintering was not unrealistic. Materials for a winter house were also loaded. The "Floren" and her crew of seven left Ålesund on 18th June 1908 and set course towards: *"the large bay which from time to time forms north to north-east of Jan Mayen".*[22] On the 3rd July they arrived at the Pendulum Øer. Liavåg chose to erect their winter house "Koppernesshuset" [441-1] at Kap Wynn, the easternmost point of

Wollaston Forland. Here four men wintered, while the remaining three lived at "Borganes" [421-1], a primitive hut constructed on the ruins of an old Inuit house at Kap Borlase Warren.

It was a quiet winter. While the men had no personal experience of fox-trapping, they did as the trappers in Svalbard used to do with good results. A number of box traps were placed in the vicinity of the station house, and checked on a regular basis. The outcome was 32 arctic foxes, and no less than 28 polar bears. Probably without knowing it, they had settled in an area with one of the largest bear populations in Greenland.

On the 12th May 1909 tragedy struck the expedition, when Severin Liavåg and Johan A. Hareide drowned during a bear hunt close to Kap Wynn. The remaining crew returned safely to Ålesund on the 27th August 1909; one of them, Adolf Brandal, concluded his diary of the expedition with the words: *"Must say, it was good to see the green grass of home again".*[23]

Brandal 1930; Giæver 1957; Vollan 1951; N087.

7DE JUNI EXPEDITION 1909-10

The tragic news of the drowning of Liavåg and Hareide had not reached Ålesund when the motor galeas "7de juni" (7th June) set out on the 900 nautical mile journey to North-East Greenland. Local people shook their heads and predicted death and misery would accompany this act of madness. Unfortunately the pessimists were to be proved right.

S.Th. Sverre of Oslo sponsored this expedition, which numbered six members led by Vebjørn Landmark from Brandal. On the 30th July 1909 the expedition arrived near Shannon, and at the beginning of August they built their winter house, "Kap Mary huset" [410-1], on Clavering Ø. Afterwards they looked for a safe harbour for the ship, and chose Germania Havn on Sabine Ø, where they built a turf-house strengthened with stone walls, "Germania-hamn" [447-2].

During the autumn about half of the men lived at Kap Mary huset, but at the end of November they all moved to Germania Havn, as they hoped to stay on the ship during the polar night. Shortly after New Year the area was ravaged by a blizzard. The sea ice broke up on all sides of Sabine Ø, and there was open water only 40 paces from "7de juni". The situation was critical, and some of the men moved into the Germania-hamn house onshore. In January and February three of the men fell ill with scurvy and a fourth was suffering from severe frostbite. With the fifth man nursing the others, only Landmark was able to tend to the trapping. On May 14th one of the sick men, Henning Idrevik, died and his grave is to be found at Germania Havn.

On their way home, the surviving members of the "7de juni Expedition" rescued five stranded Danes from the Alabama Expedition, and reached Norway on the 19th August 1910.

Giæver 1939; Hareid Historielag 1984; N086.

EAST GREENLAND COMPANY LTD. 1919-24

Members of the Danmark Expedition had discussed the possibilities of commercial exploitation of North-East Greenland during their winterings from 1906 to 1908. Fox trapping was an obvious possibility, but little came of it at first; supporting risky activities in North-East Greenland was not the most obvious area of investment for Danish capital.

However, some of the expedition members, notably Hans Ludvig Jensen, kept the idea alive, and on the 12th February 1919 the East Greenland Company Ltd. (A/S Østgrønlandsk Kompagni) was founded in Copenhagen. The board of directors included two of the participants from the Danmark Expedition, A.L.V. Manniche (a taxidermist) and Captain Alf Trolle. Other members of the board were N.C.Th. Møller (a businessman), C. Thielst (a company director) and M. Wiehe (a businessman). According to the regulations of the company, their mission was: *"to engage in rational exploitation of business possibilities in and around East Greenland in connection with trade and shipping".*[24] In reality the plan was to run a fox-trapping enterprise in the region between the Pendulum Øer and Germania Land. To carry out this plan the company needed to acquire a suitable vessel for transportation of trappers and supplies to North-East Greenland each summer, and to carry back the catch and the trappers returning home. With a substantial share capital of no less than 300,000 kroner they started to realize their plan.

On the 26th April 1919 the company purchased the motor schooner "Dagny" at a price of 90,000 kroner. As master the company hired Gustav Thostrup, the best arctic skipper in Denmark, and another former participant in the Danmark Expedition. As trappers, men with practical experience were preferred, and these included professional hunters or fishermen. Nine men were hired, together with Hans Ludvig Jensen who was to be in charge of the party.

The choice of trapping territory had naturally fallen on that part of the coast, which the participants from the Danmark Expedition already knew so well;

it was here they had initially dreamt of the possibilities of trapping. However, it is interesting to observe in hindsight that this choice had a fatal impact on the success of Danish trapping. Ice conditions so far north are far more difficult than in the area to the south around the Pendulum Øer where the Norwegian trapping business had started, and later became established. If the Danes in 1919 had known more about overall ice and navigation conditions, their enterprise might have developed more favourably. It was their problems with the East Greenland pack ice that, from the beginning to the end, caused the most severe setbacks for the Danish fox-trapping companies.

"Dagny" departed from Copenhagen on the 5th June 1919 and arrived at the south point of Sabine Ø on June 29th. Here they erected the trappers' station "Germaniahavn" [447-3]. Three trappers were left here, and "Dagny" then continued northwards into Dove Bugt. Next stop was Danmark Havn, where they took over Villaen, the old winter house of the Danmark Expedition. According to plan, "Dagny" should then have established a new station within Dove Bugt. However, the winter ice to the west had not yet broken up, and it was left to the seven trappers left at Danmark Havn to transport building materials to the destination themselves. Later in the summer they succeeded in moving the materials by motor boat 25 km westwards, where the planned station was established, "Hvalrosodden" [639-1].

"Dagny" returned safely to Denmark, arriving in Copenhagen on the 29th August 1919, and the future for the new company looked promising. However, the summer of 1920 saw the first of several serious setbacks. "Dagny" arrived safely in Greenland with a relief expedition, carrying supplies and new trappers. Two new stations were established, "Carlshavn" [365] and "Kap Broer Ruys" [334], but while travelling northwards towards Danmark Havn "Dagny" was wrecked in the ice off Shannon on the 8th August. Captain Ferdinand Hansen and the crew managed to get ashore, but were forced to over-winter.

In Denmark the return of "Dagny" had been anticipated with some excitement, and it naturally caused concern when the ship was overdue. To the company the situation was critical, as the absence of the expected catch and the consequent loss of income led to financial problems. It became obvious that a new ship would have to be acquired, and the crisis was temporarily overcome by increasing the share capital to 400,000 kroner. The company also obtained an interest-free government loan amounting to 250,000 kroner, since leading figures in Danish government circles had finally come to realise that Denmark must become more actively involved in East Greenland. While the Danes had made major efforts to explore the coast, the Norwegians had shown more enterprise in commercial exploitation of the land areas. Through their regular sealing and navigation of the pack-ice, and pioneer fox-trapping ventures, Norway was little by little gaining prescriptive rights to the region, a tendency of particular concern to J.C. Christensen, a leading Danish politician. His influence led to arrangement of the government loan, and allowed the East Greenland Company to buy a new ship, "Teddy". For the 1921 relief voyage, Gustav Thostrup was once again hired as master.

When Thostrup returned to Copenhagen on the 22nd September 1921 with "Teddy", after a successful voyage, he was welcomed as a hero. However, while he had carried out the rescue mission in the best possible way, he also brought back with him sad news. Three men had lost their lives during the winter of 1920-21, two of whom had died of scurvy and one killed by a polar bear. The trappers' station "Christianshavn" [410-2] had been established, but ice conditions made it impossible to call at the northern stations where a part of the catch had been left. Once again, the company was in need of money, and again it succeeded in gaining a government loan of 250,000 kroner, based on the assumption that if Denmark was to make its presence felt, the cheapest way of doing so was to support the continuing operation of the East Greenland Company.

In the summer of 1922 Thostrup once again sailed to North-East Greenland as master of "Teddy", but due to difficult ice conditions did not reach the coast until the 28th July. The "Teddy" then suffered a broken crank-shaft, the repair of which took almost a month, by which time it was too late to relieve the northern trappers' stations. However, they did manage to build the station "Valdemarshaab" [421-2].

By the end of 1922 the East Greenland Company still had enough assets to continue its business, but in the summer of 1923 things went wrong again. "Teddy", in 1923 mastered by Henning Bistrup, another participant of the Danmark Expedition, did not return as scheduled. It was not until the summer of 1924 that the fate of the ship and its crew became known. On its voyage back to Denmark, "Teddy" had been caught in the pack-ice and wrecked. The crew had drifted southwards on an ice floe, and in November 1924 miraculously managed to bring themselves safely ashore near Ammassalik.

The wreck of "Teddy" sealed the fate of the East Greenland Company. The company asked for yet another grant from the Danish state. The result was that the Greenland Administration's ship "Godthaab"

"Teddy". © Jonna Jensen

and its Captain, Julius Hansen, were put at their disposal for the voyage in 1924. It was left in the hands of Captain Hansen to decide, on the basis of the last year's catch, whether to continue trapping or abandon the trappers' stations. The catch was not satisfactory, and the situation was not improved by the fact that a trapper at the new station "Sandodden" [425-1] had accidentally shot and killed himself in August 1923. The decision was made on the 14th July 1924: the trappers were to return home, and the dogs killed.

The company's management was not in favour of an immediate liquidation, and in the event the state took over the stations against a receipt in settlement of all claims. The aggravated political situation that had gradually been building up concerning the sovereignty of East Greenland made it desirable to maintain all Danish assets in the area for as long as possible. However, on 15th July 1926 it was all over. The company was dissolved, and an era in Danish trapping was concluded.

During the period 1919-24 the East Greenland Company had built seven trappers' stations and three smaller trappers' huts; 38 trappers - including the four who had died - had altogether undertaken 61 over-winterings.

Bistrup 1924; Dahl 1924, 1925, 1926; Lauritsen 1984; Lund 1926; Madsen 1963, 1989; Møller 1939; Rostock-Jensen 2004; Tutein 1945, 1951; Ø002.

JOHAN A. OLSEN EXPEDITION 1922-23

In the summer of 1922 a seven-man Norwegian expedition arrived in North-East Greenland on board "Anni I". The expedition was led by Captain Johan A. Olsen from Skulsfjord, and had two main objectives. One was to trap foxes, and the second was to establish and operate a radio weather station for the Geofysisk Institutt in Tromsø. The expedition settled on the coast north of Foster Bugt. Here they built two stations, "Myggbukta" [335] which was to operate as the radio station, and "Franklin-huset" [326]. On 14th October 1922 the first weather report was sent from Myggbukta to Tromsø. Weather reports were then transmitted three times a day, almost without any interruptions, until the 15th August 1923 when the expedition began its homeward voyage. The "Anni I" never reached Norway. Ice conditions were extremely difficult in 1923, and ship and crew disappeared without trace.

It had been planned that the weather station at Myggbukta would be taken over in 1923 by Mikal Olsen and B.H. Tolløfsen, but their ship "Conrad Holmboe" was unable to penetrate the pack-ice and the expedition had to return to Norway.

An attempt to solve the mystery of the disappearance of "Anni I" was made by the Norwegian polar explorer Gunnar Isachsen, who visited East Greenland with the "Quest" (494-BN) in the summer of 1924. The party also visited Myggbukta, and the possibility of manning the station was discussed. However, the station's radio equipment was in too bad a condition, and the idea was abandoned.

Devold 1940; Erskine and Kjaer 1998; Giæver 1939; Isachsen 1925.

TRAPPING 1926-42

No fox trapping was undertaken in North-East Greenland between 1924 and 1926, but 1926 saw the beginning of a new and more successful era that lasted until 1942. Fox trapping became more organised and efficient, and in some years produced a good economic return. The beginning of the period was marked by the culmination of the Danish-Norwegian dispute over the sovereignty over East Greenland. The results of the fox-trapping expeditions were part of the evidence laid before the Permanent Court of International Justice at The Hague. Trapping continued throughout the period, and was only brought to an end after the outbreak of WWII in Europe, when both Norwegian and Danish fox trappers became involved in the defence of East Greenland in 1942.

FOLDVIK EXPEDITION 1926-28

It was Ole Andreas Krogness, the director of the Geofysisk Institutt in Tromsø, who took the initiative to establish the weather station in Myggbukta in 1922. When "Conrad Holmboe" failed to reach Myggbukta in 1923, North-East Greenland once again became a blank spot on the weather chart. Yet, one day in 1925, Nils Foldvik and Hallvard Devold, both wireless operators working for Krogness, told him of their plans to equip a two-year expedition to North-East Greenland to trap foxes and resume the weather service in Myggbukta. Krogness promised them his full support, and on 17th July 1926 the Foldvik Expedition left Norway aboard the "Ringsel" of Tromsø. The six participants, under the leadership of Nils Foldvik, called first at Kap Stosch, where a new trappers' station "Krogness" [403] was established. The Foldvik Expedition experimented with new principals for fox trapping in North-East Greenland. They had at their disposal the stations at Myggbukta, Krogness, as well as the unused Danish stations on the east coast of Hold with Hope. Between the stations they now erected a number of small huts at a distance of a day's journey between each other, forming a network across an extensive terrain that made trapping significantly more efficient. Initially the trappers walked from hut to hut, as the Foldvik Expedition had only brought along a few dogs with them. However, the potential of using dog sledges was realised, and by the 1930s, when the stock of sledge dogs had increased sufficiently, later expeditions provided each trapper with his own sledge and a team of four to eight dogs, enabling much larger areas to be reached. The three wireless operators of the Foldvik Expedition took turns at trapping fox and tending the weather station at Myggbukta.

In the summer of 1927 the Foldvik Expedition expanded their trapping territory further, building at Revet, west of Clavering Ø, a new station they called "Tyrolerheimen" [429], replaced in 1928 by a larger station "Moskusheimen". They also built a number of trappers' huts along the east coast of Clavering Ø, and moved some of the huts built in 1926 to better locations.

After two successful winterings the expedition returned to Norway in the summer of 1928 with the "Terningen" of Tromsø. In addition to the two new stations, the expedition had built a total of sixteen new trappers' huts.

Devold 1940; Giæver 1939; N085; Thomsen et al. 1998.

HIRD EXPEDITION 1927-29

On the 14th July 1927 the small motor cutter "Hird" left Ålesund with six men led by Jonas Karlsbak. They reached North-East Greenland at Kap Mary on the 25th July. Seventeen years had passed since another Sunnmøre expedition, Vebjørn Landmark's "7de juni" Expedition, had wintered at Germania Havn, where "7de juni" had been anchored during the winter. The "Hird Expedition" also had to find a safe harbour for the winter, and the expedition therefore sailed from Kap Mary northwards to Germania Havn, where they found the station Germaniahavn built in 1919 by the East Greenland Company. The Danes had not visited their Germaniahavn station since 1924, and in the absence of any prohibition notice, the Hird Expedition decided to take possession of the station. The following day they suddenly observed smoke from an approaching steamer, which proved to be the "Fangstmand" of Ålesund with Vebjørn Landmark as master. Landmark dissuaded them from using the Danish station, as the Danes might return, so following his advice the Hird expedition loaded their equipment and headed southwards again. They now needed to find another winter harbour, as well as suitable locations for two station houses.

On the south coast of Wollaston Forland they found a suitable location where they built "Kap Herschell" [417]. The other station, "Elvsborg" [407] was placed on the south coast of Clavering Ø.

From old shipmasters reports they were aware of a recommended good harbour on the north-west side of Store Finsch, and it was here they anchored "Hird" for the winter. However, only a few weeks later, at the end of August 1927, a violent hurricane hit the area, destroying the moorings and the "Hird" was wrecked.

The first winter three men stayed at each of the two stations, but during the summer of 1928 they adopted the techniques of the Foldvik Expedition and provided their territory with additional small huts. They also established another new station, "Jackson-stua" [371], built on Jackson Ø.

In 1928 one man left for home, while the remaining five stayed for another winter, hunting from the Danish station in Germania Havn, as well as from Kap Herschell and Jackson-stua.

The five men of the Hird Expedition went home aboard "Veslekari" in 1929. The catch had been excellent, and four of the participants later returned with other expeditions. The Hird Expedition was particularly significant for expanding Norwegian trapping in North-East Greenland to the northern Sunnmøre terrain, the so-called Kap Herschell territory. In addition to the three stations, the expedition also built six trappers' huts.

Giæver 1939; N032; N142; N143; P134; P135.

FINN DEVOLD EXPEDITION 1928-30

In the spring of 1928, the Foldvik Expedition at Myggbukta received a telegram from Hallvard Devold in Tromsø that Finn Devold, Hallvard's younger brother, was busy equipping an expedition to take over the weather station in Myggbukta and the adjacent trapping territory. *"Finn had been the manager on Jan Mayen during our first year in Myggbukta and through the radio he had heard reports of the hunting of wolf, bear and muskoxen around Myggbukta. He naturally longed for a journey to East Greenland to see for himself. The direct initiative for starting his project was that Lauge Koch had been in Oslo, giving a lecture to the Norsk Geografisk Selskap. In his lecture Koch presented some statements not immediately digestible for a part of the audience. Among these were professor Adolf Hoel and my brother Finn. The outcome was that Finn received a grant from the state to enable him to relieve the Foldvik Expedition"*.[25] Hallvard Devold does not directly say which of Koch's statements the Norwegians had found provocative. However, in 1928 the Norwegian Greenland Expedition 1928-30, better known as the Finn Devold Expedition, arrived in North-East Greenland aboard the "Terningen". The expedition numbered six members, all but one experienced winterers from Svalbard and Jan Mayen. During the first summer they built a new station house at Revet to replace that built by the Foldvik Expedition in 1927; this station was named "Moskusheimen" [429]. The expedition had not brought enough wood with them to expand the Norwegian trapping territories as they had planned, and only managed to build four huts, including two in Moskusoksefjord which were annexed to the Norwegian domain.

After two winterings the Finn Devold Expedition returned to Norway in 1930.

Giæver 1939.

NANOK LTD. 1929-41

The East Greenland Trapping Company Nanok Ltd. (Østgrønlandsk Fangstkompagni Nanok A/S), usually referred to simply as "Nanok", was founded on the 20th May 1929. The founders were Leander E. Emskær Larsen (a fisherman), Svend Engelhardt (a barrister) and Johannes Gerhardt Jennov (a lawyer). The first board of directors comprised Henry Tuxen (an engineer), Commander Godfred Hansen and Svend Engelhardt. The object of the company was: *"to the extent allowed by the circumstances to make a scientific as well as practical survey of the available commercial possibilities in and around East Greenland, and to exploit these as well as run trading and shipping"*.[26] The share capital of 90,000 kroner was provided by Nordisk Trust Kompagni, Øresunds Chemiske Fabriker (the Cryolite Company) and private shareholders.

The idea of a new Danish trapping company had been kept alive by veterans from the old East Greenland Company. For years Hans Ludvig Jensen had worked for the cause, as usual mainly behind the scenes. Leander E. Emskær Larsen was also a veteran trapper from the old company. However, it was Johannes Gerhardt Jennov (1886-1980) who became the managing director and the unchallenged leader of Nanok, a position he retained for many years, even after Nanok ceased trapping in 1952.

On the 2nd August 1929 Nanok sent out its first expedition from Copenhagen. Nanok had chartered the Norwegian ship "Birkild" (M8M) as no suitable Danish vessel was available. At the last moment it was confirmed that Nanok could re-possess the trappers' stations which the government had taken over from the old company. The wintering party numbered twelve men, and a miscellaneous collection of twelve dogs representing even more dog breeds. The ten trappers included four veterans from the old company. Richard Bøgvad from Øresunds Chemiske Fabriker accompanied the group in order to survey some supposed cryolite deposits. The wintering party was completed by J.G. Jennov, who personally wanted to familiarize himself with the conditions in North-East Greenland.

On the 19th August 1929 "Birkild" reached the Germaniahavn station, where they were met by three men from the new Norwegian trapping company Arctic Commercial Enterprise (Arktisk Næringsdrift). Their leader, Arnulf Gisvold, explained that their company planned to organise trapping in the region from Wollaston Forland northwards, and would also erect huts along the coast. However, they had been stopped by unbroken winter ice, and their materials were now placed in a depot at a valley (Landingsdalen) south of Kap Wynn. Gisvold also reported that Hallvard Devold had accidentally set fire to, and burnt down, the Danish Carlshavn station in 1927. This was surprising and disturbing news, but Jennov and Gisvold were prepared to make the best of the situation and agreed a friendly compromise. They negotiated a partition of the territory, and Gisvold promised that the Norwegians would rebuild Carlshavn the following year and place it at the disposal of the Danes. However, this promise was never fulfilled.

On the 20th August 1929 "Birkild" reached the south coast of Hochstetter Forland, and here the Nanok party started to build "Hochstetter" [510], which became the most important station to the company.

Since the Carlshavn station was not available, the ten trappers in 1929-30 spread themselves out between the stations Sandodden, Germaniahavn and Hochstetter. In November 1929 Hans Ludvig Jensen fell into a tidal crack, and suffered bad frostbite. Although he had not entirely recovered, he participated in a sledge journey to Danmark Havn in May 1930 in an attempt to locate the supposed cryolite deposit. Unfortunately, Bøgvad's investigations proved the reported find to be incorrect.

While the Nanok party in North-East Greenland had encountered unexpected difficulties, the situation for the board of the company in Denmark was no better. In October 1929 the Harald Plum Koncern collapsed, taking with it the Nordisk Trust Kompagni. Nanok suffered a loss of 34,000 kroner, but the board was able to save the company and rebuild a share capital of 100,000 kroner.

1930-31

In the summer of 1929 J.G. Jennov had kindly helped Arnulf Gisvold and his party to transport their building materials to Kap Wynn. In 1930 Jennov realized that he had been far too trusting, and had simply underestimated the political situation. While individual Danish and Norwegian trappers were on good terms in North-East Greenland, there were other powers at home to whom trapping territories and trappers' huts were not just local matters, but were important factors in the dispute over the sovereignty of East Greenland.

Jennov discovered that the Arctic Commercial Enterprise company did not intend to rebuild Carlshavn as they had promised; there was also the incident of a telegram which never reached the board of Nanok. The Danes needed to order more building materials from Denmark, but as there was no Danish transmitter nearer than Scoresbysund, Jennov somewhat naively sent the order via the Norwegian radio station at Myggbukta. Hallvard Devold had deliberately blocked the telegram, for which reason the materials required did not arrive with "Godthaab" in the summer of 1930.

A third incident also left Jennov with bitterness. In 1923 the first Danish trapping company had deposited a large quantity of building material at Kap Mary, but this had now disappeared. It turned out that the Foldvik Expedition had used it in 1927 to build a number of Norwegian huts. Indeed the Norwegians claimed this had been undertaken with Lauge Koch's permission, which Koch of course denied. In this case it was one person's word against another's, and Jennov and Nanok were the losers. As a result, by 1930 Jennov had lost his trust not only in the Norwegian leaders, but also in Lauge Koch. Despite the lack of material, Nanok was able to put up a few buildings in 1930, including a replacement for Carlshavn station, the "Knudshoved" [335] station on Hold with Hope. The Norwegian trapping system was adopted, meaning the Danes also erected small huts to be used for staying the night when travelling. Nanok built a total of nine trappers' huts in the area between Young Sund and Hochstetter Forland. Late in the autumn of 1931, another three huts were built in the area between Hochstetter and Bessel Fjord. These three huts were actually "dummy" huts, put up in haste in order to annex the area, and were therefore later replaced.

In 1930-31 Jennov and his ten trappers wintered at the stations Sandodden/Knudshoved, Germaniahavn and Hochstetter. In the spring of 1931, Jennov - having learnt by bitter experience - sent two of his men the long way south to the Danish radio station at Scoresbysund. This time he wanted to be certain that his order for supplies was sent.

1931-32

During the winter of 1931 North-East Greenland became the focus of newspaper articles in both Norway and Denmark. Lauge Koch's plans for a large-scale three-year scientific expedition to North-East Greenland were unwelcome in Norway. When the matter of the blocked telegram became known in Denmark, patriotic fervour rose to fever-pitch, and created sympathy for Nanok. The newspaper "Ekstrabladet" took the lead and established a fund towards the purchase of radio equipment and other supplies for Nanok that soon collected 10,500 kroner. At the annual general meeting of the company held on the 14th April 1931, the board of Nanok expressed its delight at the increasing interest in the company, and tried to take advantage of the sudden patriotic atmosphere. The crisis was reached when on 29th June 1931 Hallvard Devold raised the Norwegian flag at Myggbukta and took possession of *Eirik Raudes Land*, the name they gave to the coastal region between 71°30' and 75°40'N where Norwegian hunters had been most active. A few days later, on 10th July 1931, the Norwegian government proclaimed annexation. The claim was contested by Denmark, who appealed to the Permanent Court of International Justice at The Hague. Until the case was settled, it was easy for Nanok to gain a hearing as well as financial support.

In the summer of 1931 Nanok's trappers had free transportation to North-East Greenland with the "Godthaab", one of the ships used by Lauge Koch's Three-Year Expedition. Nanok used some of its funds to purchase a small radio station, which was installed at the Hochstetter station, but it never came into operation. Firstly, the battery was defective, and secondly, the wireless operator and one of the trappers suffered severe frostbite during a sledge journey southwards in December 1931; they were forced to stay at Eskimonæs for the rest of the winter. Apart from these two men, Nanok had three trappers staying at the stations Sandodden and Hochstetter in 1931-32.

1932-33

In 1932 Nanok had free transport with another of Lauge Koch's ships, "Gustav Holm". During this summer the company was able to build the trapping station "Bessel Fjord" [601-2]. In addition, J.G. Jennov led a separate expedition with the ship "Gefion" to the Dove Bugt area.[27] A radio station was installed at Hvalrosodden and trappers' huts were built in the surrounding territory. During 1932-33 Nanok had nine men, including two radio operators, wintering at the stations Hochstetter, Bessel Fjord and Hvalrosodden. One of the radio operators died during a blizzard on the 8th April 1933.

1933-34

On the 5th April 1933 the Permanent Court of International Justice at The Hague announced its verdict on the Danish-Norwegian dispute over the sovereignty of East Greenland. The board of Nanok could pride itself on the fact that Danish trapping activities, including those of Nanok, were given as one of the factors that settled the dispute in Danmark's favour. Nanok had taken part in the fight for East Greenland, but now came the morning-after.

"Gustav Holm" in the pack-ice, July 1932. © Arne Philbert

The Danish public was looking for new and more interesting subjects, and the government initially refused to support Nanok in any other way than free transport, in the government ships that were in any case visiting North-East Greenland. All at once it had become much more difficult to find reasons to support a trapping enterprise whose economic expectations were somewhat dubious.

In the summer of 1933 Nanok once again had transport with the vessels of the Three-Year Expedition, "Gustav Holm" and "Godthaab". The following winter only the stations Hochstetter and Hvalrosodden were manned, by six trappers, of whom one also acted as radio operator.

1934-35

In the spring of 1934 Nanok was granted a government grant in cash of 5000 kroner. This was much less than required, but still a symbolic gesture. In the summer the trappers were transported to Greenland with "Gustav Holm", free of charge. However, this turned out to be a qualified truth. After his personal airborne reconnaissance on the 10th August 1934, Lauge Koch, the leader of the Three-Year Expedition, refused to allow "Gustav Holm" to call at the Nanok stations north of Sandodden because, he claimed, the passage was blocked by ice. J.G. Jennov was furious. From several other sources, including Norwegian, it was confirmed that the ice conditions would not have been any hindrance to "Gustav Holm", and J.G. Jennov wrote that: *"Dr. Lauge Koch's unwillingness to navigate our stations had the consequence that three trappers from Hvalrosodden were forced to stay for yet another winter".*[28] The experts agreed with Jennov, but his continuous criticism of Koch's dispositions and the resulting press coverage only caused: *"bad feelings in the government".*[29] Danish authorities had begun to regard J.G. Jennov as a quarrelsome individual.

The Danish cine-photographer, Leo Hansen, and eleven trappers over-wintered, distributed at Sandodden, Hochstetter and Kulhus.

1935-36

In 1935 the government once more refused to support Nanok financially, but again granted free transport. Unfortunately ice conditions were the most difficult for many years and "Godthaab" did not succeed in reaching the coast. As a consequence Nanok could not resupply their trappers or place new people ashore. However, it was possible - using an aeroplane and with Norwegian assistance - to rescue Leo Hansen and four trappers, including Christian Jensen, who had become ill with scurvy. The missing supplies led to a difficult winter for Nanok's seven trappers, who stayed at Sandodden and Hochstetter.

1936-37

Even after a contribution from the major newspaper "Berlingske Tidende", Nanok's tight economy in 1936 made it necessary to sign a special contract with three trappers - they were to travel to Greenland on board the "Gustav Holm" to hunt in Dove Bugt; they were willing to equip themselves at their own expense, but in return would receive a larger share of the catch than usual. Once again, an absent supply call had a major impact on Nanok's unsatisfactory economy. Due to the difficult ice conditions in 1935, the Captain of "Gustav Holm" had been instructed not to call at places north of Hochstetter Forland. It was deemed irrelevant that the waters of North-East Greenland in the summer of 1936 were almost totally free of ice - an order was an order. The three trappers and the supplies for Hvalrosodden were therefore unloaded at Hochstetter. As an additional slap in the face, the Maritime and Commercial Court (Sø- og Handelsretten) in Copenhagen passed judgment on Nanok on the 9th November 1936, to pay compensation of 6000 kroner to the three trappers who could not be fetched from Hvalrosodden in 1934. Amongst the six trappers who over-wintered at Sandodden, Hochstetter and the unused Norwegian station Ottostrand in 1936-37, was the then 62-year-old veteran, Hans Ludvig Jensen.

1937-38

In 1937 the annual supply voyage for Nanok once again failed. "Gustav Holm" was trapped by the ice in Scoresby Sund, and the relief party of new trappers had to return with the ship to Denmark. Fresh fruit, vitamins and other supplies did not arrive in time, and of the five trappers who wintered at Sandodden and Hochstetter, one was ill with scurvy most of the time.

1938-39

In 1938 Nanok succeeded in raising capital from a variety of sources. In addition to a promise of a fixed annual government grant of 5000 kroner, Nanok also received 40,000 kroner from the "Otto Mønsteds Fond". Furthermore private fund-raising, especially in the cities of Aalborg and Nørresundby, resulted in sufficient funds to buy material for a completely new trappers' station. The best news of the year was the almost unrestricted use of "Gustav Holm". During the summer of 1938 Nanok established two new trappers' stations, "Mønstedhus" [532-2] and "Aalborghus" [613-2]. The thirteen trappers wintered at Sandodden, Hochstetter, Mønstedhus, Aalborghus and Hvalrosodden.

In February 1939 two of the trappers, Svend Aage

Jespersen and Anders Kristian Østerlund Johannesen, vanished during a sledge journey. Their bodies were never found and the nature of the accident that overcame them remains a mystery.

1939-40
The relief voyage in 1939 took place with "Gustav Holm". Due to difficult ice conditions neither Hochstetter nor Mønstedhus could be reached. The twelve Nanok trappers wintered at the stations Sandodden, Hochstetter, Mønstedhus, Aalborghus and Hvalrosodden.

1940-41
The German occupation of Denmark caused various complications with respect to navigation of North-East Greenland. When it became known at the beginning of June 1940 that NSIU was to send out a relief expedition with "Veslekari" for the Norwegian trappers, Nanok proposed to the Greenland Administration that the Danish relief expedition - for political reasons - should be sent out under Nanok's name. The proposition was well received, and discussions took place between the Greenland Administration, Rigsdagens Grønlandsudvalg and Nanok with respect to using "Gamma", the ship of the Mørkefjord Expedition. The plan, however, was not implemented, as the Prime Minister eventually declared that in his belief, the necessary funding could not be raised.

About the same time as this plan was abandoned, a person presenting himself as "Charles Hansen", contacted Nanok with an offer to promote a Danish expedition to North-East Greenland using a Norwegian vessel - for patriotic reasons. From Nanok's minutes of proceedings it appears that a meeting was held on the 23rd July 1940, but: *"Bøgvad, with whom Charles Hansen negotiated, realized during the discussions that Mr. Charles Hansen was identical with the notorious Nazi, Curt Carlis Hansen, who is probably employed by the Gestapo. It could be assumed that his main interest was to operate a radio station on the east coast of Greenland which would work for the German Wehrmacht. After discussions with the board members at home, and having presented his views to the Greenland Administration, it was decided not to allow the expedition to leave under the name of Nanok".*[30] However, Curt Carlis Hansen managed to send out another expedition with a Danish crew with the "Furenak" of Ålesund.

In the summer of 1940 all trappers in North-East Greenland were confronted with the choice of either remaining, or leaving for Iceland with the patrol boat "Fridtjof Nansen". Berndt Jensen, Christian Petersen and Carl Henrik Schultz left with the ship, and the remaining nine Danish trappers stayed the winter of 1940-41 at the stations Sandodden, Hochstetter, Mønstedhus, Aalborghus and Hvalrosodden. The catch of 459 arctic fox furs was the largest in the history of Nanok.

1941
In the summer of 1941, Danish trapping in North-East Greenland was ordered to cease. The US Coast Guard (USCG) cutter "Northland" commanded by Edward Hanson Smith undertook the evacuation. Four trappers left with the ship, while Eli Knudsen, Mads Christensen, Niels Hansen and Peter Nielsen joined the North-East Greenland Sledge Patrol.

During 1941-45, a total of nine former Nanok trappers served in the North-East Greenland Sledge Patrol. However, due to the complete separation of Greenland and Denmark the board of Nanok did not learn about these men's service until the end of the war.
Drastrup 1932; Hansen 1939; Hvidberg 1932; Jennov 1937, 1938, 1940; Kristoffersen 1969; Lauritsen 1984; Nyholm-Poulsen 1985; G127-G130; A127-A134.

ARCTIC COMMERCIAL ENTERPRISE LTD. 1929-42

When Hallvard Devold returned from the Foldvik Expedition in 1928, he was firmly convinced that the Danish authorities had adopted a strategy to force Norwegian interests out of East Greenland. He wanted to prevent this, and therefore decided to contact prominent figures in Norway with the same opinion. He soon made contact with the geologist Adolf Hoel, who was the leader of Norges Svalbard- og Ishavs-undersøkelser (NSIU). NSIU had been founded in March 1928 with the objective of gathering the Norwegian administration of arctic matters into one institution. Gustav Smedal, a lawyer and the leader of Norges Grønlandslag, was one of the founders of NSIU, and the strategist behind the Norwegian struggle to acquire the sovereignty of East Greenland.

Until 1928 Norwegian expeditions to Greenland had lacked any scientific focus or central coordination, and previous attempts to send out scientific expeditions to North-East Greenland had largely failed. However, by the end of 1928, a close co-operation had been established between Norges Grønlandslag (Gustav Smedal), NSIU (Adolf Hoel) and fox-trapping interests (Hallvard Devold), a partnership capable of planning and undertaking major decisions. Devold had discussed his plans to expand the fox-trapping enterprise with Hoel, who for his part was intensely interested in launching scientific investigations, which could prove decisive in determining the question of sovereignty of East Greenland. It was obvious to combine these activities in an effective manner. Thus trappers and scientists could use the same ships for transport, and use the same stations and huts. This co-operation soon led to the founding of Arctic Commercial Enterprise Ltd. (Arktisk Næringsdrift A/S) on the 24th June 1929, with the purpose of carrying out: *"trapping and mining in arctic areas"*.[31]

The share capital of the new company amounted to 37,750 kroner, distributed amongst 151 shares. With the common goal of strengthening Norway's position in the struggle for East Greenland, the stock holders included representatives from almost every Norwegian interest group, commercial as well as political. Support came from the wintering fox-trapping expeditions (Hallvard Devold and Arnulf Gisvold), the traditional sealers (A/S Søndmøre, Peter S. Brandal, Martin Karlsen and G.C. Rieber), scientific expeditions (Adolf Hoel) and political groupings (Norges Grønlandslag, Kristiansand Grønlandsnevnd). Furthermore, the Norwegian press "Tidens Tegn", "Aftenposten" and many private individuals and groups were in favour.

Until the Permanent Court of International Justice at The Hague settled the sovereignty of East Greenland, Arctic Commercial Enterprise and NSIU enjoyed a close partnership. From 1929 to 1933 five joint research and trapping expeditions were sent out. During this period the strategy was clear. Scientific exploration of all kinds was to focus on appropriating the area annexed by Norwegian fox-trappers. At the same time the trappers embarked on an extensive and systematic extension of their trapping terrain, with the erection of numerous Norwegian trappers' huts. The huts were to serve not only the practical purposes of shelter for trappers and scientists, but also to mark out the annexed areas.

1929-30

On the 14th July 1929 the first joint NSIU and Arctic Commercial Enterprise expedition left Ålesund, with Hallvard Devold as the leader of the ten trappers.

The expedition had chartered "Veslekari", one of Norway's most famous polar vessels. "Veslekari" was a 296 ton sealer, built in 1918 and equipped with a 300 hp steam engine.[32] Hans Rekdal was master, and Vebjørn Landmark - the leader of the "7de juni Expedition" - had been hired as first mate for the summer. The shipping company had obtained dispensation as regards load marks, which was needed, as the ship lay deep in the water due to the heavy cargo. The major part belonged to Arctic Commercial Enterprise, and included three motor boats, two rowing boats, wood and timber for three trappers' stations and 37 huts, together with coal, petrol, tools and trapping equipment and a three year supply of provisions for 10 men. In addition, there were eight dogs and five puppies.

During the summer of 1929, Arctic Commercial Enterprise succeeded in developing the trapping territory between Kong Oscar Fjord and Myggbukta. The trappers' station "Kap Humboldt" [308] was built on Ymer Ø, "Sverresborg" [232] in Vega Sund, and 14 trappers' huts were erected.

A planned expansion of the territory north of Wollaston Forland had to be abandoned due to the difficult ice conditions, and they only managed to build the station "Liavåg" [441-3] at Kap Wynn. The trappers wintered at the stations Sverresborg, Kap Humboldt, Kap Herschell and Liavåg.

1930-31

In 1930 Arctic Commercial Enterprise built the trappers' station "Hoelsbu" [356] in Moskusoksefjord, and a series of huts in the fjord and along the south coast of Gauss Halvø. The Sverresborg station was abandoned, and replaced by the "Maristua" [256] station on Ella Ø. "Veslekari" was again used as supply ship.

"Veslekari" in the East Greenland pack-ice, 26th July 1929. © Bernhard Luncke / Norwegian Polar Institute

In the summer of 1930 Arctic Commercial Enterprise took over the operation of Myggbukta Radio and the territories and huts used by the Foldvik Expedition. Myggbukta now became a natural centre of Norwegian activities in North-East Greenland. Here a new station house was erected and a new radio transmitter installed.

Trappers with a wireless operator's licence undertook the weather service during the first years, but from 1932 the company employed a professional radio operator, whose only task was to carry out the weather observations up to five times a day, and transmit these to Norway. This was a demanding job for one man, and from 1947 a second wireless operator was employed.

Myggbukta Radio operated from 1930 to 1940, and again from 1946 to 1959. Arctic Commercial Enterprise received an annual government grant to support the weather service, but covered other expenses themselves.

It was here, in Myggbukta, that Hallvard Devold on the 27th June 1931 declared the occupation of *Eirik Raudes Land* which led to the international trial at The Hague. While this action was intended to appear as a spontaneous reaction by Norwegian trappers, who saw their interests threatened by Danish government policies concerning East Greenland, in reality this provocative act of occupation had been organised by leading figures in Norway, notably Gustav Smedal and Adolf Hoel.

In 1930-31 Arctic Commercial Enterprise had nine trappers and one wireless operator wintering at the stations Maristua, Kap Humboldt, Myggbukta and Hoelsbu.

1931-34

In the summers of 1930 to 1934 the Norwegian expeditions used "Polarbjørn" as their supply vessel. The joint expedition in the summer of 1933 was the fifth and last sent out by Arctic Commercial Enterprise and NSIU.

In 1931-32 Hallvard Devold was leader of the five wintering trappers at Myggbukta and Moskusheimen. Sverre J. Sørensen and later Eilif Herdal were in charge of the parties in 1932-34; the first year there were seven trappers and one wireless operator, and the second year five trappers and one wireless operator. During these years Arctic Commercial Enterprise only used the stations at Kap Humboldt, Myggbukta and Hoelsbu, as Moskusheimen was lent out to the Sigurd Tolløfsen Expedition.

In the autumn of 1933, Knut O. Brandal, one of the trappers at Hoelsbu, died from an acute stomach disorder and was buried near Hoelsbu.

1934-35

From 1934, Arctic Commercial Enterprise was, in theory, obliged to charter their own vessel for the annual relief expeditions. In practice, NSIU continued to arrange transportation on behalf of Arctic Commercial Enterprise, just as they had when supporting the government-financed radio service at Myggbukta. The summer expedition in 1934 used the "Selbarden" (M140-A) of Ålesund. During the 1934-35 winter Eilif Herdal was leader of the six trappers and one radio operator, who resided at Kap Humboldt, Myggbukta, Hoelsbu and Moskusheimen.

1935-36

In the summer of 1935, pack-ice conditions along the coast of North-East Greenland were extraordinarily difficult. The ice was tightly packed along the entire coast, and the relief ship "Buskø" (M17-VD) was unable to reach land at the first attempt. NSIU sent "Veslekari" to provide assistance on the 18th August. However, on the 22nd August an opening appeared in the ice enabling "Buskø" to slip through to the Clavering Ø area and to commence unloading its cargo. "Veslekari" was then ordered to proceed directly to Myggbukta, but was trapped in the pack-ice and almost wrecked. On the 24th August 1935 the Norwegians were requested by the Danish government to try and rescue four Danish trappers, who were stuck in the ice north of Wollaston Forland together with their motor boat. Due to the ice conditions "Buskø" was unable to force her way further north, but fortunately four Norwegians succeeded in rescuing the Danes by motor boat. While this was going on, hurricane-force winds pushed the ice against the coast, and "Buskø" had to abandon the supply of the Norwegian southern stations. Supplies for Myggbukta were instead unloaded at the head of Loch Fyne. On the 6th September "Buskø" and "Veslekari" left East Greenland together, and reached Ålesund a week later. The Danish government paid compensation of a total of 28,860 kroner to the Norwegian trappers and Arctic Commercial Enterprise to cover their losses and inconvenience due to "Buskø" having been forced to change her original schedule.

Due to the absence of supplies, Kap Humboldt was not manned the following winter, and the six trappers and one radio operator, led by Finn Framnes-Hansen, wintered at the stations Myggbukta, Hoelsbu, Krogness and Moskusheimen. A young student, Øivind Holm Johnsen, also stayed at Myggbukta. He had been hired by Arctic Commercial Enterprise to transport supplies from Loch Fyne to Myggbukta by dog sledge.

"Selbarden" in 1934.
© Nils-Martin Hanken

"Buskø" in 1935.
© Arctic Institute

1936-39

As a consequence of the problematical ice conditions in 1935, NSIU decided that in future they would only use the strongest ice-strengthened ships available in Norway for the annual relief service. In 1936 "Isbjørn" was therefore hired, and in the following two summers "Polarbjørn". In order to cover a part of the additional expenses, Arctic Commercial Enterprise began from 1936 to take along a limited number of tourists.

In the period 1936-39, Arctic Commercial Enterprise had each year six trappers and one wireless operator staying at the stations Kap Humboldt, Myggbukta, Hoelsbu and Moskusheimen. During the two first winters Finn Framnes-Hansen was leader of the party, while Eilif Herdal was leader in 1938-39.

During the 1936-37 winter two British ornithologists, Edward Bird and Charles Bird, stayed at Myggbukta. Charles Bird also wintered in 1937-38, the noted winter when the total fox catch numbered 1400 - the largest in the history of Arctic Commercial Enterprise.

During the winter of 1938-39 Gerhard Antonsen, the trapper at Moskusheimen accidentally stabbed himself in the eye. In the summer of 1939 he was evacuated to Norway, after having spent seven consecutive winters in North-East Greenland.

"Isbjørn", July 1932. *© Norwegian Polar Institute*

1939-40

The relief ship in 1939-40 was again "Polarbjørn". Levin Winther, the trapper at Hoelsbu, was accompanied by his wife Petra Winther, who became the first Caucasian woman to over-winter in North-East Greenland. They stayed at Hoelsbu until the summer of 1942. In 1939-40 seven trappers and one wireless operator wintered at the stations Kap Humboldt, Myggbukta, Hoelsbu and Moskusheimen. The medical student Kåre Rodahl, who was to carry out nutritional research, also stayed at Moskusheimen.

1940-41

John Giæver led the relief expedition that took place with "Veslekari". All the Norwegian stations were visited and re-supplied. However, in Narhvalsund "Veslekari" was arrested by "Fridtjof Nansen", a Norwegian naval vessel in allied service. None of the newly arrived trappers were allowed to remain, and all on board the "Veslekari" - except three Danes - were ordered to leave North-East Greenland with "Fridtjof Nansen", as they were suspected of being in collusion with the German Wehrmacht. Giæver spent about two months in a British prison before he was acquitted, and allowed to join the allied forces.

The trappers who were already in North-East Greenland before the outbreak of war were given the choice of remaining in Greenland or being evacuated to Iceland. Some left the coast and later joined the Norwegian allied forces, but six trappers, including Levin Winther and Petra Winther at Hoelsbu, chose to stay. The Norwegian stations Myggbukta, Kap Humboldt and Moskusheimen were manned in 1940-41.

While "Fridtjof Nansen" and "Veslekari" were still in Greenland, "Polarbjørn" arrived from Canada with supplies. It had been dispatched by the Norwegian government in exile in England. When it was realized that the stations had already been visited, "Polarbjørn" returned with its cargo.

1941-42

In the summer of 1941 a relief expedition led by Hallvard Devold was sent out with "Buskø". The expedition was financed by the Norwegian state but sent out by Arctic Commercial Enterprise. The expedition numbered seven trappers, including a woman. On board was a wireless operator, as well as a new radio station that the Germans had demanded be unloaded at Jonsbu in Peters Bugt.

"Buskø" called at several of the Norwegian stations, but was finally seized by the USCG cutter "Northland". The Americans picked up the trappers and equipment - which "Buskø" had just unloaded - and continued to Myggbukta. Here, another American ship, the "Bear", took over the "Buskø" that with its crew and cargo was sailed to Boston. The trappers, who had been forced to accompany the ship to the USA, were acquitted by the American authorities and later joined the allied forces. A demand from the allied forces that all trappers must be evacuated from North-East Greenland was not executed, which allowed Henry Rudi at Moskusheimen, Johan Johansen at Myggbukta and the Winthers at Hoelsbu to remain at their stations. The Norwegian trapper Hans K. Siewers joined the North-East Greenland Sledge Patrol (Nordøstgrønlands Slædepatrulje).

1942

In the summer of 1942 the order that trapping should cease and all trappers be evacuated was put into force. Levin Winther and Petra Winther were taken to West Greenland, Johan Johansen joined the American forces, and Henry Rudi joined the North-East Greenland Sledge Patrol. During 1941-45 a total of four former Norwegian trappers served in the sledge patrol. Arctic Commercial Enterprise resumed trapping in 1946.

Arnesen 1932; Blom 1973; Devold 1940; Giæver 1930, 1931, 1937a, 1939, 1957; Hydle 1931; Jennov 1939; Münsterhjelm 1937; Norsk Polarklubb 1964; Orvin 1930, 1931, 1934, 1935, 1937; Pantenburg 1944.

MØRE EXPEDITION 1930-32

In the summer of 1930 a new trapping expedition was sent out from Sunnmøre led by Jonas Karlsbak. The Møre Greenland Expedition, or the Møre Expedition, comprised six members who were given free transport to North-East Greenland on board the "Veslekari", which had been chartered by NSIU's scientific expedition. The participants had outfitted the expedition at their own cost, but received a government grant of 10,000 kroner in return for handing over to the Norwegian state the rights to use all old and new trappers' stations and huts.

Four of the Møre Expedition members were veterans from the Hird Expedition 1927-29. Two members resumed trapping along the coasts of Wollaston Forland and Gael Hamke Bugt using Kap Herschell as a base station. Three new huts were built and another moved to a different location. The remaining four members continued to Kong Oscar Fjord in order to establish a new trapping territory, the so-called southern Sunnmøre territory. Here they split into two groups, and built the stations "Kap Peterséns" [218] and "Antarctichavn" [201] as well as eleven new huts.

In the summer of 1931 two of the participants returned to Norway because of illness. Experience during the first winter showed that one trapper at each station in Kong Oscar Fjord was sufficient. In December 1931 Knut Røbek fell through thin ice in Gael Hamke Bugt and drowned. The other expedition members returned to Norway in 1932 with the NSIU vessel "Polarbjørn".

Giæver 1939.

HELGE INGSTAD EXPEDITION 1932-34

After the Norwegian government had ratified the occupation of so-called "Eirik Raudes Land" in 1931, the barrister Helge Ingstad was appointed 'sysselmand' (governor) and ordered to remain in North-East Greenland until further notice. Ingstad equipped a trapping expedition with five members and in 1932-34 took over the Møre Expedition's territory in Kong Oscar Fjord. The Helge Ingstad Expedition travelled up with NSIU's expedition ship "Polarbjørn". Ingstad together with a wireless operator and a trapper settled at Antarctichavn, while the other two trappers took over Kap Peterséns. The expedition built 10 new trappers' huts in the territory, most of them in the area south and east of Kap Biot.

When Norway lost the court case at The Hague, Ingstad was appointed sysselmand on Svalbard. He left Greenland in 1933, while the remainder of the expedition continued trapping until 1934.

Giæver 1939; Ingstad 1935, 1937, 1996.

SIGURD TOLLØFSEN EXPEDITIONS 1932-34 & 1937-40

In the summer of 1932 Sigurd Tolløfsen from Måsøy in Finnmark equipped an expedition of six participants. He had been given the right for a two-year period to utilize the territories of Arctic Commercial Enterprise at Moskusheimen and the Sunnmøre territory at Kap Herschell. Furthermore, he was to establish a new territory around Kuhn Ø.

Tolløfsen, together with the John Giæver Expedition and a third group of char fishermen from W. Holmboe in Tromsø, chartered the "Isbjørn" of Tromsø for transport. Tolløfsen built the trappers' station "Sigurdsheim" [468] on the east coast of Kuhn Ø, and six huts in the surrounding terrain. An additional hut was built in the Moskusheimen territory.

At the end of May 1933, Tolløfsen's son, Arnljot, disappeared during a sledge journey between Eskimonæs and Kap Herschell. His body was never found, but he is believed to have gone through the ice somewhere between Kap Breusing and Kap Herschell. Sigurd Tolløfsen and three other members of the expedition returned to Norway in 1934. The sixth participant, Gerhard Antonsen, stayed on for another five years in a row as a trapper for Arctic Commercial Enterprise.

The Sigurdsheim territory was only used for a few years, as it was cramped between other Danish and Norwegian territories in Wollaston Forland and Hochstetter Forland. In time it was split up and distributed between these other terrains.

In 1937 Tolløfsen equipped another six-man expedition to trap in his own and John Giæver's territories between Kuhn Ø and Dove Bugt. The expedition travelled up with "Polarbjørn", but unbroken winter ice prevented the ship sailing north of Bass Rock. The expedition fished for arctic char at Zackenberg, but Tolløfsen returned to Norway with great financial losses. In 1938 he again managed to equip a new four-

man expedition, and this time "Polarbjørn" succeeded in calling at the stations Jonsbu and Ottostrand. Tolløfsen and two trappers went home in 1939, while his son Eivind Tolløfsen stayed until 1940.
Giæver 1939.

JOHN GIÆVER EXPEDITION 1932-34

In the years 1929-31, the journalist and writer John Giæver had been a trapper for Arctic Commercial Enterprise. In the summer of 1932 he led his own six-man expedition. Just like Helge Ingstad and Sigurd Tolløfsen, he had planned the expedition in co-operation with NSIU. The three expeditions were intended to strengthen the Norwegian position in the struggle for East Greenland. Giæver had been appointed to establish a radio station in the area north of Wollaston Forland for the Norwegian state, in order to transmit daily weather reports.

The radio- and trappers' station "Jonsbu" [521] was established on the west side of Peters Bugt. and Giæver wintered here together with the wireless operator. Further north the expedition built two other trappers' stations, "Ottostrand" [531] south of Haystack on the east side of Hochstetter Forland, and "Olestua" [603] at Kap Carl Ritter on the east side of Ad. S. Jensen Land. Furthermore, a total of 18 huts were erected in the surrounding terrain.

After Norway lost the court case in The Hague, the weather service at Jonsbu was discontinued, and the wireless operator transferred to Myggbukta to undertake the radio- and weather service for Arctic Commercial Enterprise. John Giæver's expedition returned to Norway in 1934 with "Selbarden".
Giæver 1939; N082.

SULØYA GREENLAND EXPEDITION 1934-37

Hermann Andresen and Peder Sulebak, two veterans from the Hird- and Møre expeditions, returned in 1934 to Greenland with a new four-man expedition after two years in Norway. The expedition, called the Suløya Greenland Expedition or the Suløya Expedition, arrived with the "Selbarden" and resumed trapping in the Kap Herschell and Kong Oscar Fjord territories.

In January 1935 Nils Hanken, who was working with Andresen from Kap Herschell, unfortunately broke his leg during a trapping journey. He succeeded in reaching the Eskimonæs station, where the Danes helped him and allowed him to stay until his leg healed.

Hermann Andresen and Peder Sulebak returned to Norway in 1936, while Nils Hanken and Karsten Sulebak took over the territory in Kong Oscar Fjord, trapping there at their own expense. They returned in 1937 to Norway with the "Polarbjørn". The Suløya Expedition only built one hut.
Giæver 1939; P101.

QUEST EXPEDITION 1936-37

Gaston Micard, a French count and polar enthusiast, hired the sealer "Quest" of Bodø in 1936 for a wintering in North-East Greenland. Ludolf Schjelderup, the owner and master of the ship, was allowed under the terms of the contract to trap fox on his own account, and arranged with Arctic Commercial Enterprise to use a trapping territory in Loch Fyne. The expedition numbered 13 participants, of whom only a few took part in the trapping. Two trappers wintered at Krogness, while the others lived aboard "Quest" while it was icebound near the head of Loch Fyne. The Quest Expedition built four trappers' huts, as well as a provisions house near the ship which was dismantled when the expedition went home in the summer of 1937.
Erskine and Kjaer 1998; Giæver 1939; Knutsen 1992, 2005.

HERMANN ANDRESEN EXPEDITION 1937-39

In the summer of 1937 Hermann Andresen returned to Greenland for his fourth wintering. This time he had equipped his own expedition, which consisted of himself and a novice. As in his previous winterings, the Kap Herschell station was the base for his trapping activities. His partner went home in 1938, leaving Andresen to tend the entire territory himself. While 1938-39 was a poor winter for trapping in other Norwegian stations with an average catch of 38 foxes,

"Quest" at Sandodden, July 1932. © Arne Philbert

Andresen set a record with 642 foxes, the largest number ever for a single trapper in the history of trapping in North-East Greenland. The huge catch was partly due to local maxima in the population of lemming, the most important food for the arctic fox. Andresen returned home in 1939, this time for good. He had wintered for eight years altogether.

Giæver 1939; Norsk Polarklubb 1964.

SØREN RICHTER EXPEDITIONS 1937-38 & 1939-40

Søren Richter was both an archaeologist and a trapper. During 1929-31 he was a member of the first wintering party of Arctic Commercial Enterprise. In 1932 and 1933 he participated as archaeologist in the NSIU summer expeditions. Again in 1935-36 he wintered as a trapper for Arctic Commercial Enterprise.

As Richter wanted to carry out further archaeological excavations in Kong Oscar Fjord, he teamed up with Peder Sulebak for a wintering expedition to this area in 1937. They planned to catch foxes alive, and had brought along with them a young man as fox tender. The expedition travelled to Greenland with "Polarbjørn", and occupied the stations Antarctichavn and Kap Peterséns. Richter and the fox tender went home with the same ship in 1938, while Peder Sulebak continued on his own. The expedition may have built a single trappers' hut.

In the summer of 1939 Søren Richter returned to Kong Oscar Fjord with two companions on his own private expedition. One of the men was an experienced fox tender, and their plan was mainly to catch live foxes. The expedition built a new trappers' station, "Hamna" [208-2] at Noret in Kong Oscar Fjord. Despite a poor fox year, they succeeded in catching 34 live foxes that were to be shipped back to Norway for breeding. However, the war hindered these plans and prevented them staying on for a planned second year. In the summer of 1940 they were evacuated to Iceland by "Fridtjof Nansen", where they joined a Norwegian military force that was based there. No new trappers' huts were built.

Aune 1991; Giæver 1939; Norsk Polarklubb 1964; Nyquist 1945; Richter 1946.

PEDER SULEBAK EXPEDITION 1938-39

When Søren Richter went home in 1938, Peder Sulebak took over the entire Kong Oscar Fjord territory and trapped there on his own. This was to be Sulebak's eighth and last wintering in North-East Greenland. He did not erect any new trappers' huts in 1938-39.

Giæver 1939; Norsk Polarklubb 1964.

NORWEGIAN-FRENCH POLAR EXPEDITION 1938-39

In 1938-39 the Norwegian-American Willie Knutsen led a combined research- and trapping expedition financed by the French count Gaston Micard. The Norwegian-French Polar Expedition built the station "Micardbu" [704] on the east coast of Germania Land and also four trappers' huts. Two of the huts were on Store Koldewey, where the expedition vessel "En Avant" (formerly "Ringsel") had anchored for the winter. Some of the 13 expedition members lived on the ship, and four of them took part in trapping.

During the winter Micard became seriously ill, and it became necessary to call for help from Norway. The "Veslekari" was sent to rescue Micard, bringing along a float-equipped aircraft by which Micard was successfully evacuated. Knutsen accompanied Micard to Norway, with the result that the original plans to continue for another year were abandoned. The remaining participants returned home in the summer of 1939.

Knutsen 1992, 2005; Norsk Polarklubb 1964.

OLE KLOKSET EXPEDITION 1938-39

In 1933-35 Ole Klokset, from Tennfjord near Sunnmøre, had trapped foxes in North-East Greenland for Arctic Commercial Enterprise. In 1938 he equipped his own wintering expedition, and had planned to build a trappers' station as far north as possible. However, ice conditions forced the expedition ship "Grande" of Sandshamn to turn back at Bass Rock, and Klokset instead build his station on the north coast of Geographical Society Ø. The station, which was called "Laplace" [301], was placed close to the Kap Humboldt territory of Arctic Commercial Enterprise. Klokset's trapping area was thus restricted to the unused area east of the station and southwards along the outer coast; he also trapped in the inner part of Hudson Land. His trapping area thus extended over 100 km from Laplace, which was a long journey, so he built two travellers' huts; one on the north coast of Ymer Ø and one in Nordfjord.

Norsk Polarklubb 1964; Pedersen 1969.

TRAPPING 1945-60

The war had interrupted fox-trapping in North-East Greenland. The Danish trappers had been evacuated in 1941, and Norwegian trapping activity was brought to a close in 1942. American forces had taken over the protection of Greenland by an agreement signed on the 9th April 1941, but Greenland waters were still a war zone in the summer of 1945. However, while Nanok was able to resume trapping in 1945, the aftermath of the war and other circumstances delayed the resumption of Norwegian trapping activity until 1946.

The years from 1945 to 1960 were marked by a gradual decline in fox-trapping, and the effective end of the trapping era. Declining fur prices and increasing costs meant that trapping became unprofitable, and without government grants or other support the trapping finally came to a close.

Norwegian trapping ceased in the summer of 1959. On 19th October 1965 the Danish government officially terminated the East Greenland agreement between Denmark and Norway of 9th July 1924. As a consequence the commercial Norwegian rights in North-East Greenland were terminated on 9th July 1967. Negotiations with the Norwegian government in 1968 led to the Danish state taking formal possession of all Norwegian hunting stations and hunting huts in North-East Greenland in 1969, in return for 50,000 kroner in compensation to the owners.

NANOK LTD. 1945-52

When the German Wehrmacht in Denmark surrendered in May 1945, J.G. Jennov and the board of Nanok began planning the resumption of fox-trapping. At the board meeting held on the 31st May it was still uncertain whether it would be possible to obtain transportation. However, in the summer of 1945, when the ministry of naval affairs decided to dispatch the "Godthaab" to North-East Greenland, J.G. Jennov and seven Nanok trappers were on board.

As expected the war had left its traces. The supplies deposited at the various trappers' stations had been used, removed or destroyed. And the same applied to motor boats and other material. No attempts were made to call at the northernmost territories, but two new stations "Zackenberg" [438-2] and "Loch Fyne" [350] were built. The latter was placed at the head of Loch Fyne in an area regarded as part of Norwegian trapping territory, even by most Danes. At the board meeting on the 12th October, several board members expressed their reservations about this disposition, which was not exactly in the spirit of Danish-Norwegian co-operation. It could even damage Nanok's limited goodwill in Denmark, where neither the authorities nor the Danish people wanted any new confrontation with Norwegian interests. As expected, the location of the Loch Fyne station did result in complaints from the Norwegian leaders, but the incident quickly died away without any consequences worth mentioning.

During the years 1946-52, J.G. Jennov continued to lead the Nanok relief expeditions. The company still had the benefit of free transport with government ships, but as in the years before the war, the ships were refused permission to call at the Nanok stations north of Wollaston Forland. The Hochstetter and Mønstedhus stations received no visits until 1948, when the "Søndmøringen" (M-349-HØ), chartered in Norway was used. The poorest trapping season in the history of Nanok was the year 1948-49 with a total catch of only 33 fox skins.

Nanok and J.G. Jennov experienced their greatest problems with the authorities at home. Claims for compensation for lost property and income during the war years were not settled until August 1947, when respectively 21,314 kroner and 35,000 kroner were awarded. Nanok continued to receive free transport for its hunters and cargo, and in 1949 the annual government grant was raised to 40,000 kroner. For the years 1950 and 1951 the government grants amounted to 75,000 kroner and 37,000 kroner respectively, with various smaller amounts derived from foundations, companies and private sponsors.

Nanok's overstretched economy led to discussion of alternative solutions. Since financial conditions were also difficult for the Norwegian trapping companies, despite their considerably larger grants from the Norwegian government, a possible merger of Danish and Norwegian trapping interests was discussed as early as 1949. However, negotiations at the Norwegian Polar Institute in Oslo closed without result; the Norwegians were in favour of a more convenient division of trapping territories, but were not interested in any kind of merger. The possibility of transferring Nanok's interests to a foundation were also discussed, but could not be put into practice. For Nanok, the post-war period was a continuous fight for survival.

The verdict at The Hague meant that the Danish state had been able to profit from Nanok's presence in North-East Greenland up until WW2. The presence of Nanok's trappers, and with the police force represented by Lauge Koch, was enough to maintain Danish sovereignty. However, the war years had brought the attention of the authorities to the need for a military presence to monitor and prevent unwanted foreign intrusion in the uninhabited areas north of Scoresbysund, across all of North Greenland and south-westwards to Thule. The increasing east-west confrontations of the post-war years made the possibility of territorial violation more likely. As a consequence a military sledge patrol was founded in 1950, which from 1953 became "Sirius". This patrol was given responsibility for military surveillance and also became the police authority, such that from a political point of view the presence of Danish trappers was no longer essential.

In 1952 the government grant to Nanok was suspended, a move that sealed the fate of Nanok. An intense and emotional debate continued until the last moment, with individuals as well as part of the press supporting Nanok and complaining that private initiative had once again been handed over to the Norwegians. The decision of the government was final. However, since Sirius also had a need for shelter when patrolling North-East Greenland, an agreement was signed with Nanok for an annual state payment of 12,000 kroner to allow members of Sirius the use of Nanok's stations and huts. Records show that in the years 1957 and 1967 Sirius made use of respectively 60 and 35 Nanok stations and huts. However, the state would neither buy the huts nor index-link the rent, and in 1980 Nanok gave notice that the contract would be terminated. In fact the Sirius patrol has continued to use a number of Nanok's buildings up to the present day.

Although Nanok ceased fox-trapping in 1952, the company continued to exist. Since 1952 Nanok has in reality provided a meeting place for a group of people who felt that there ought to be an opportunity for private Danish initiatives in North-East Greenland. Many different ideas have over the years been discussed during board meetings, but all have failed for the same reason: lack of finance.

J.G. Jennov continued as director of the company until 1976 when he was succeeded by Mogens Graae, who had been a member of the board since 1953. In 1970 Graae obtained permission to use the name Nanok for his textile factory. Graae never gave up the idea of a fresh start for Nanok, but in November 1990 the Østgrønlandsk Fangstkompagni Nanok Ltd. was finally liquidated and the assets from the old company were passed over to Graae. As late as the summer of 1991 Graae visited North-East Greenland to inspect his properties.

In respect of the post-war period mention should be made of the death of the trapper Aksel Nielsen in February 1946, when he fell through the ice near Kap Breusing; another trapper, Jack E. Christensen, suffered severe frostbite in his feet in the winter of 1949-50; and finally it deserves comment that J.G. Jennov and three trappers in 1954 made a summer expedition to move Mønstedhus 20 metres further inland, to stop it from falling into the sea. This action actually saved Mønstedhus for half a century, until 2002 when it finally was taken by the sea.

Lauritsen 1984; A135-A143; G130; G131.

NANOK 1991–

On 29th July 1991 a group of six North-East Greenland enthusiasts gathered at Mogens Graae's cottage in Tuen in northern Jutland, Denmark. As well as Mogens Graae, the group consisted of Aage Hjorth Hansen, Erik Jensen, Peter Schmidt Mikkelsen, Henning Schwegler Poulsen and Jens Erik Schultz. This initial meeting led to a two-man Nanok expedition travelling to North-East Greenland in August-September 1991, and a few months later the rebirth of Nanok.

On 12th January 1992 the group again met at Mogens Graae's cottage, and the official name of Nanok was changed to "Nordøstgrønlandsk Kompagni Nanok" (The North-East Greenland Company Nanok).

"Søndmøringen" c. 1948. © Mogens Graae

With director Mogens Graae as the central figure, the founding six-man group initiated an attempt to breathe new life into the dying embers of Nanok. With fox-trapping long abandoned, the vision was now on a non-profit basis to: *"disseminate knowledge of North-East Greenland and its cultural history, and to contribute to maintenance of the cultural relics and buildings of the area ..."*. With this new initiative as a basis, the new Nanok has drawn public attention to the need for an effort to maintain some of the old, historic Norwegian and Danish buildings in North-East Greenland, since many would otherwise disappear within the foreseeable future. The initiative has proved successful, and since 1991 Nanok has been able to send out an expedition to Greenland every summer. On 28th February 1999, Mogens Graae, director of Nanok since 1976, died at the age of 82 - the end of an era.

Peter Schmidt Mikkelsen was appointed managing director of Nanok on 6th March 1999. The remaining board of management today (2008) comprises Søren Andersen, Palle Vagn Norit, Tommy Pedersen, Martin Reenberg, Søren Rysgaard and Jens Erik Schultz. In addition, the management receives the enthusiastic support of a number of individuals - "Nanok'ers" - who participate actively in Nanok's projects. All work in Nanok is voluntary and unpaid. In the autumn of 1999, the Aage V. Jensens Fonde offered to finance Nanok's activities, and since 2000 the Aage V. Jensens Fonde has been Nanok's primary sponsor. Nanok is also supported by a number of private contributors. Each summer Nanok sends an expedition consisting of 5-10 persons, divided into 2-3 teams, to work in North-East Greenland for 2-5 weeks. The expedition participants are hand-picked by the Nanok management. In the years 1991-2007, Nanok has sent about 100 Nanok'ers to North-East Greenland.

Since 1991 Nanok has restored about 20 historic buildings in North-East Greenland related to the trapping era, and gained considerable recognition and support from, amongst others, the Greenland Home Rule authority and the Greenland National Museum & Archives. It is today acknowledged by the authorities that the old buildings have not only historical value, but also a practical value for people working or visiting the area, such as scientists and tourists.

Nanok does not own any buildings or possessions in North-East Greenland, as most of the old buildings from the trapper era officially belong to the Danish state. A draft law to transfer ownership to the Greenland Home Rule authority was prepared in 2002, but at the time of writing has still not been implemented.[33]

In 2003-2007 Nanok, with the encouragement and support of the Greenland Home Rule authority, carried out a major survey of all building locations in North-East Greenland dating from the trapper era. More than 300 sites were visited and surveyed. The data collected has been handed over free of charge to the Greenland National Museum & Archives in Nuuk. Nanok publishes an annual report of its activities in Danish and English.

NANOK EXPEDITIONS 1991 -

Nanok expeditions have included the following participants and locations:

1991: Mogens Graae, Henning Schwegler Poulsen, Zackenberg [438-2].

1992: Erik Jensen, Jens Erik Schultz: Zackenberg [438-2].

1993: Allan Nielsen, Henning Schwegler Poulsen, Martin Reenberg: Loch Fyne [350].

1994: Erik Jensen, Martin Reenberg: Moskusheimen [429], Sandodden [425-1].

1995: Martin Reenberg, Jens Erik Schultz, Bent Zwergius: Ny Jonsbu [514-2].

1996: Søren Andersen, Erik Jensen, Henning Schwegler Poulsen, Jens Erik Schultz: Hochstetter [510].

1997: Dennis Carter, Martin Reenberg, Ivar Ytreland: Kap Humboldt [308].

1998: Henning Schwegler Poulsen, Jens Erik Schultz: Eskimonæs [405].
Søren Andersen, Aksel Mikkelsen, Carsten Thordal: Hochstetter [510].
Jannik Berntsen, Wagn Kromann, Niels Lindegaard, Bent Zwergius: Kap Peterséns [218].

1999: Claus Birkbøll, Magnus Elander, Peter Schmidt Mikkelsen, Hasse Nielsen Staunstrup: Germaniahavn [447-3].
Jannik Berntsen, Wagn Kromann, Niels Lindegaard: Hoelsbu [356].
Øystein Killie, Thor Melhuus, Ivar Ytreland: Myggbukta [335].

2000: Søren Andersen, Jannik Berntsen, Lars Nielsen, Carsten Thordal: Hoelsbu [356], Kap Ovibos hytten [340].
Claus Vahlkvist, Bent Zwergius: Hotel Karina [part of Sandodden 425-1].

2001: Lars Kock Andersen, Jannik Berntsen, Jens Chr. Gotfredsen, Jesper Graae, Wagn Kromann, Niels Lindegaard, Martin Reenberg: Antarctichavn [201], Holm Bugt hytten [222], Kongeborgen [224-2].
Søren Andersen, Jette Bøgsted, Erik Jensen,

In 1992 the North-East Greenland Company Nanok (Nordøstgrønlandsk Kompagni Nanok) was founded by a group of Greenland enthusiasts. The photograph was taken at the actual occasion at Mogens Graae's cottage. The founding group from left: Peter Schmidt Mikkelsen, Jens Erik Schultz, Erik Jensen, Mogens Graae and Henning Schwegler Poulsen. Aage Hjorth Hansen is absent from the photograph. Tuen, 12th January 1992. © Peter Schmidt Mikkelsen

Today (2008), the board of North-East Greenland Company Nanok (from left): Peter Schmidt Mikkelsen, Jens Erik Schultz, Palle Vagn Norit, Tommy Pedersen, Martin Reenberg, Søren Andersen. Board member Søren Rysgaard is absent from picture. Hølkerup, 12th November 2005, © Peter Schmidt Mikkelsen

Helle Mogensen, Tommy Pedersen, Jens Erik Schultz: Kap Harald Moltke: Brønlundhus, both located in Peary Land.

2002: Anders Bjerregaard, Otto M. Martens, Peter Schmidt Mikkelsen, Ivar Ytreland, Knut Ytreland: Kap Herschell [417], Myggbukta [335]. Jannik Berntsen, Niels Lindegaard, Fritz Ploug Nielsen, Palle Vagn Norit: Varghytten [324].

2003: Søren Andersen, Erik Jochumsen, Klaus Myntzberg Jensen: Clavering Ø area. Morten Lindhard, Ole Schirmer Nielsen, Jens Erik Schultz, Jesper Mølbæk Stentoft, Niels Fæster Sørensen: Ella Ø area.

2004: Erik Jochumsen, Søren Kristensen, Peter Schmidt Mikkelsen: Hochstetter area.
Lars Bønding, Ole Schirmer Nielsen, Jesper Mølbæk Stentoft: Ella Ø area.

2005: Hans Henrik Carlsen, Erik Jochumsen, Anders Ibsen: Dove Bugt area.
Christian Holm Andersen, Rasmus Gregersen, Kunuk Olsen Lennert: Clavering Ø area.

2006: Jannik Berntsen, Hans Henrik Carlsen, Erik Jochumsen, Jens Erik Schultz: Germania Land area, Villaen [628-1].
Torben Jeppesen, Ole Schirmer Nielsen, Jesper Mølbæk Stentoft: Ella Ø area.

2007: Niels Gyldenlund Mikkelsen, Peter Schmidt Mikkelsen: Miscellaneous areas. Hans Henrik Carlsen, Allan Broholm Pedersen, Justin Mark Smallbone: Clavering Ø area.
Steffen Holberg, Henrik Nevers, Kristian Nevers: Ella Ø area.

ARCTIC COMMERCIAL ENTERPRISE LTD. 1946-59

In 1946 Arctic Commercial Enterprise Ltd. (Arktisk Næringsdrift A/S) resumed its fox-trapping activities and Myggbukta Radio was reopened. The Norwegian state provided a grant of 93,000 kroner for chartering an expedition vessel, and in addition a loan of 75,000 kroner towards the costs of repairs and provisions to allow a restart of trapping. Transport to Greenland took place with "Polarbjørn" with John Giæver as leader of the expedition.

On arrival the main Norwegian hunting stations of the company were found to be in poor condition after the war, and much equipment was either missing or broken. The radio masts at Myggbukta had been cut down and all the radio- and meteorological equipment had been removed. The trappers' huts were in a somewhat better state. However, these problems had been anticipated, and the expedition had brought along the necessary replacements. The Myggbukta weather service was resumed on the 18th August 1946. While "Polarbjørn" was at Myggbukta, one of the trappers, Bjarne Myrvold, injured his hand when a shotgun barrel split. "Polarbjørn" headed immediately for Iceland where Myrvold received medical attention, and he later returned to Norway. As a consequence only five trappers and one wireless operator wintered at the stations Myggbukta, Hoelsbu and Moskusheimen in 1946-47.

In the post-war years John Giæver usually led the Arctic Commercial Enterprise relief expeditions. For a few years - while Giæver participated in an expedition to Antarctica - the expeditions were instead led by Søren Richter. In the post-war period Arctic Commercial Enterprise received on average an annual grant of 156,420 kroner from the Norwegian state.

In 1947 the manning at Myggbukta was reorganised, with one trapper and two radio operators. This allowed the radio operators to share duties, giving them every second week free.

Gudrun Andersen accompanied her husband, the trapper Normann Andersen, to Greenland in 1947. In total the couple spent four years at Moskusheimen, namely 1947-49 and 1952-54.

In 1948, Arctic Commercial Enterprise received 85,000 kroner from the Norwegian government to help rebuild the Norwegian territories formerly used by John Giæver and Sigurd Tolløfsen. The Jonsbu station had been burnt down during the war, and was replaced by "Ny Jonsbu" [514-2], erected in Ardencaple Fjord, about 15 km south of the old Jonsbu station.

Due to the fire and wreck of the (old) "Polarbjørn" in the East Greenland pack-ice in 1948, "Quest" was used for the relief expedition in 1949. However, ice conditions were very difficult and it was not possible to reach the northern stations of Ny Jonsbu and Ottostrand. Instead the supplies were unloaded at Kap Stosch and Revet. The four trappers at the northern stations had fished for arctic char in Langelv during the summer of 1949, and had a total of 28 barrels ready to take home. As the ship failed to reach them their efforts were in vain; the fish were useless the following year.

In the years 1950-57, the (new) "Polarbjørn" was used for the relief expeditions. In the summer of 1951 the ice was closely packed from Myggbukta northwards, so visits to the northernmost stations had to be abandoned. The Hoelsbu station could not be reached either, and its provisions were sent via Loch Fyne.

In the summer of 1952 the winter-ice between Shannon and Bass Rock remained unbroken, so the trappers for Ottostrand had to be landed at Kap David Gray on Shannon. From here they travelled to the station in the autumn.

Arctic Commercial Enterprise decided to close down the trapping in their northern territories from 1953, as the ice conditions were generally very difficult. The stations Ottostrand and Ny Jonsbu were subsequently not used. Kap Humboldt was not used for wintering after 1952.

In 1953 Solveig Sæterdal came to stay with her husband, Fredrik Sæterdal. The Sæterdals spent the years 1953-56 at Hoelsbu.

In 1954, Arctic Commercial Enterprise made an agreement with the Sirius Dog Sledge Patrol with

The (new) "Polarbjørn" in 1950. © Søren Richter / Norwegian Polar Institute

respect to mutual use of their stations and huts. Arctic Commercial Enterprise experienced its poorest catch ever in the winter of 1956-57. The three trappers at Myggbukta, Hoelsbu and Moskusheimen caught only 36 foxes altogether.

Ice conditions in North-East Greenland were again difficult in the summer of 1957. "Polarbjørn" left Young Sund on the 17th August on its way home, but in an easterly gale was trapped in the ice about 20 sea-miles east of Jackson Ø, and drifted helplessly towards land. Although the ship managed to get free, the following week was a continuous struggle against the ice masses off the coast. On the 24th August the ice pressure was so strong that the deck bulged amidships, and the ship sprang a leak and began to take in water. Myggbukta and Mestersvig were alerted by the sinking ship. The American forces at Thule Air Base were requested to help, and immediately sent a cargo plane carrying a rescue helicopter. On August 26th the ice loosened its grip, but because of the severe damage "Polarbjørn" was doomed. The helicopter evacuation of the 13 crew members and 10 passengers took place on the 28th and 29th August 1957. "Polarbjørn" was never seen again, and probably sank soon afterwards. In 1958 and 1959 "Polarsel" was used for the relief expeditions.

In the summer of 1959 Myggbukta Radio and all the Norwegian trappers' stations in North-East Greenland were closed down. The Norwegian Meteorological Institute considered Myggbukta Radio to be no longer necessary as the Danes had established a series of large weather stations along the East Greenland coast, from which any required weather information could be obtained at no cost. Another contributory factor was that the profits of fox-trapping had diminished year by year due to falling fur prices and increased transport expenses. As the Norwegian state was not prepared to support trapping on its own merits, the economic basis for Arctic Commercial Enterprise vanished, and trapping ceased. Officially the closure was only temporary, but in practice trapping was never resumed.

Norsk Polarklubb 1964.

HERMANN ANDRESEN EXPEDITIONS 1946-59

After the war Hermann Andresen was able to send trappers to both of the Sunnmøre territories, the Kap Herschell territory in the north and in the south the area around the Antarctichavn, Kap Peterséns and Hamna stations. Andresen did not winter himself after the war, but travelled up every summer with his hired trappers and fishermen. He was one of the legendary characters of the Norwegian trapping industry.

In the summer of 1946 his first post-war expedition numbered four trappers. As the stations and huts, especially in the Kap Herschell territory, were expected to be in poor condition following the war, Andresen received a government grant of 50,000 kroner to re-establish the trapping territories. Except for 1947-48, Hermann Andresen received an average annual grant of 28,490 kroner from the Norwegian government.

From 1947 onwards Andresen employed two to five extra men to fish char, mainly led by Kristian Ytreland and Ivar Ytreland. Fishing took place at different locations, but mainly at the mouth of the river that flows east of Zackenberg into Zackenberg Bugt.

Until 1953 Andresen usually hired four trappers for wintering: two at Kap Herschell and two in the southern territory. However, after the Danish lead mine at Mestersvig was established trappers working in the southern territory broke their contracts on several occasions to work in the mine, as working conditions and pay were both better.

The Kap Peterséns station was last used for wintering in 1955-56. In the summer of 1958 difficult ice conditions hindered "Polarsel" from reaching the Kap Herschell station, and the two new trappers, Sverre Storholt and Oskar Tørmoe, returned home with the ship. The Kap Herschell station has not been used for wintering since 1957-58.

Since Andresen was totally dependent on the ships hired by Arctic Commercial Enterprise for transport, his trapping activities were also given up in 1959. His trappers had by then undertaken a total of 42 winterings.
Norsk Polarklubb 1964; Norsk Polarklubb 1966.

HANS FREDERIKSEN & ERIK B. LARSEN EXPEDITION 1954-55

Although Nanok gave up trapping in 1952 and sent their trappers home, one of the men, Hans Frederiksen, was exceptionally permitted to stay on for another year. He wintered at Zackenberg in 1952-53.

In 1954 Frederiksen once again wanted to try his luck as a trapper, this time at his own expense, and he teamed up with a colleague from Daneborg Weather Station, the wireless operator Erik B. Larsen. They obtained permission from Nanok to use the properties of the company in exchange for a 15% share of the catch.
G131.

MADSEN, BLOCK & REINDEL 1959-60 ... THE LAST TRAPPERS

While the last wintering Norwegian trappers prepared for their journey home in the spring of 1959, three Danes - Ib Palle Madsen, Viggo Block and Klaus Reindel - decided to give up their jobs at Station Nord and Danmarkshavn Weather Station and try their luck as trappers. With the permission of the authorities and Nanok, they trapped during the winter of 1959-60 from the stations at Zackenberg, Moskusheimen and Hvalrosodden.[34]

MISCELLANEOUS TRAPPING

To complete the list of trapping activities it should be mentioned that a limited amount of trapping also took place outside the established trapping companies. As early as the 1930s, personnel at the government stations of Ella Ø and Eskimonæs had trapped fox in their spare time. This tradition was continued post-war at Danmarkshavn as well as at Daneborg. At Daneborg unorganized trapping grew to such proportions that Nanok felt their own activities in the area were under threat. Despite vigorous objections, they did not succeed in stopping such "spare time trapping".

Table 1. Trapping expeditions

Expeditions			Vessels	Buildings			Wintering participants			Trapping results					
Period	Nation	Name	Vessel (arrival)	Category I	Category II	Material sites	Trappers	Other	Deaths	White fox	Blue fox	Arctic fox, total	Polar bear	Arctic wolf	Value of catch, kroner
1908-09	N	Floren Expedition	Floren	2	0	0	7	0	2	20	12	32	28	3	4000
1909-10	N	7de juni Expedition	7de juni	1	1	0	6	0	1	70	29	99	6	-	5000
1919-20	D	East Greenland Company	Dagny	2	0	0	10	0	0	105	22	127	19	see below	-
1920-21	D	East Greenland Company	Dagny	2	0	0	18	4	3	139	38	177	23	see below	-
1921-22	D	East Greenland Company	Teddy	1	2	0	8	0	0	125	26	151	26	see below	-
1922-23	D	East Greenland Company	Teddy	1	0	0	13	1	0	57	12	69	18	see below	-
1922-23	N	Johan A. Olsen Expedition	Anni I	2	0	0	6	1	7	70	16	86	11	6	30000
1923-24	D	East Greenland Company	Teddy	1	1	0	12	0	1	131	24	155	31	10	-
1926-27	N	Foldvik Expedition	Ringsel	1	5	0	6	0	0	total 1926-28, see below					
1927-28	N	Foldvik Expedition		1	11	0	6	0	0	243	44	287	18	7	55000
1927-28	N	Hird Expedition	Hird	2	0	0	6	0	0	total 1927-29, see below					
1928-29	N	Finn Devold Expedition	Ringsel	0	3	0	6	0	0	total 1928-30, see below					
1928-29	N	Hird Expedition		1	6	0	5	0	0	311	41	352	42	-	60000
1929-30	D	Nanok	Birkild	1	0	0	11	1	0	56	6	62	14	0	-
1929-30	N	Arctic Commercial Enterprise	Veslekari	3	15	1	10	0	0	total 1929-31, see below					
1929-30	N	Finn Devolds ekspedition		0	2	0	6	0	0	302	44	346	11	8	40000
1930-31	D	Nanok	Godthaab	1	12	0	11	0	0	100	11	111	10	0	-
1930-31	N	Arctic Commercial Enterprise	Veslekari	2	10	0	9	1	0	170	35	225	16	1	17000
1930-31	N	Møre Expedition	Veslekari	2	11	0	6	0	0	158	28	186	19	1	13000
1931-32	D	Nanok	Godthaab	0	5	0	5	1	0	153	16	169	4	1	-
1931-32	N	Arctic Commercial Enterprise	Polarbjørn	0	2	0	5	0	0	204	25	229	-	-	30000
1931-32	N	Møre Expedition		0	4	0	4	0	1	261	33	294	10	-	35000
1932-32	N	Holmboe's fishing expedition	Isbjørn	0	2	0	0	0	0	0	0	0	0	0	-
1932-33	D	Nanok	Gustav Holm	1	2	0	8	1	1	187	20	207	11	0	-
1932-33	N	Arctic Commercial Enterprise	Polarbjørn	0	0	2	7	1	0	196	31	227	-	-	28000
1932-33	N	Helge Ingstad Expedition	Polarbjørn	0	11	0	4	1	0	total 1932-34, see below					
1932-33	N	John Giæver Expedition	Isbjørn	3	11	2	5	1	0	total 1932-34, see below					
1932-33	N	Sigurd Tolløfsen Expedition	Isbjørn	1	7	0	6	0	1	total 1932-34, see below					
1933-34	D	Nanok	Gustav Holm	0	13	0	6	0	0	118	10	128	14	0	-
1933-34	N	Arctic Commercial Enterprise	Polarbjørn	0	2	0	5	1	1	277	30	307	5	-	25000
1933-34	N	Helge Ingstad Expedition		0	0	0	3	1	0	315	65	380	5	-	45000
1933-34	N	John Giæver Expedition		0	7	0	5	0	0	198	25	223	15	-	20000
1933-34	N	Sigurd Tolløfsen Expedition		0	0	0	5	0	0	358	34	392	11	-	48000
1934-35	D	Nanok	Gustav Holm	0	2	0	11	1	0	140	15	155	5	0	-
1934-35	N	Arctic Commercial Enterprise	Selbarden	0	6	1	6	1	0	381	41	422	-	-	35000
1934-35	N	Suløya Expedition	Selbarden	0	0	0	4	0	0	total 1934-36, see below					
1935-36	D	Nanok	Godthaab	0	1	0	7	0	0	30	5	35	1	0	-
1935-36	N	Arctic Commercial Enterprise	Buskø	0	1	0	6	2	0	188	16	304	-	-	15000
1935-36	N	Suløya Expedition	Buskø	0	1	0	4	0	0	153	29	182	21	-	16500
1936-37	D	Nanok	Gustav Holm	0	0	0	6	0	0	52	1	53	2	0	-
1936-37	N	Arctic Commercial Enterprise	Isbjørn	0	2	0	6	3	0	400	24	424	6	-	40000
1936-37	N	Quest Expedition	Quest	0	5	0	4	9	0	160	2	162	-	-	15000
1936-37	N	Suløya Expedition		0	0	0	2	0	0	60	16	76	-	-	9000
1937-38	D	Nanok	Gustav Holm	0	1	0	5	0	0	303	9	312	1	0	-
1937-38	N	Arctic Commercial Enterprise	Polarbjørn	0	3	0	6	2	0	1325	75	1400	-	-	110000
1937-38	N	Hermann Andresen Expedition	Polarbjørn	0	0	0	2	0	0	-	-	340	17	-	-
1937-38	N	Søren Richter Expedition	Polarbjørn	0	1	0	2	1	0	230	35	265	-	-	30000
1938-39	D	Nanok	Gustav Holm	2	13	0	12	0	2	-	-	186	6	0	-
1938-39	N	Arctic Commercial Enterprise	Polarbjørn	0	5	0	6	1	0	339	38	377	0	-	-
1938-39	N	Hermann Andresen Expedition		0	0	0	1	0	0	-	-	642	21	-	-
1938-39	N	Norwegian-French Polar Expedition	En Avant	1	4	0	4	9	0	-	-	12	-	-	-

Table 1. Trapping expeditions

Expeditions			Vessels	Buildings			Wintering participants			Trapping results					
Period	Nation	Name	Vessel (arrival)	Category I	Category II	Material sites	Trappers	Other	Deaths	White fox	Blue fox	Arctic fox, total	Polar bear	Arctic wolf	Value of catch, kroner
1938-39	N	Ole Klokset Expedition	Grande	1	2	0	2	0	0	48	10	58	2	-	-
1938-39	N	Peder Sulebak Expedition		0	0	0	1	0	0	15	8	23	0	-	-
1938-39	N	Sigurd Tolløfsen Expedition	Polarbjørn	0	0	1	4	0	0	50	-	50	0	-	-
1939-40	D	Nanok	Gustav Holm	0	3	2	12	0	0	total, 1939-41, see below					
1939-40	N	Arctic Commercial Enterprise	Polarbjørn	0	3	0	7	3	0	158	13	171	3	-	12400
1939-40	N	Sigurd Tolløfsen Expedition		0	0	0	1	0	0	13	0	13	0	-	-
1939-40	N	Søren Richter Expedition	Polarbjørn	1	0	0	3	0	0	60	22	82	0	-	-
1940-41	D	Nanok		0	0	0	9	0	0	-	-	459	-	0	-
1940-41	N	Arctic Commercial Enterprise	Veslekari	0	0	0	6	1	0	185	13	198	2	0	19760
1941-42	N	Arctic Commercial Enterprise	Buskø	0	0	0	3	1	0	-	-	388	2	0	-
1945-46	D	Nanok	Godthaab	2	4	0	7	0	1	-	-	339	-	0	-
1946-47	D	Nanok	Heimdal/ Godthaab	0	6	0	6	0	0	-	-	317	-	0	-
1946-47	N	Arctic Commercial Enterprise	Polarbjørn	0	0	1	5	1	0	535	34	569	1	0	4500
1946-47	N	Hermann Andresen Expedition	Polarbjørn	0	0	0	4	0	0	108	11	119	11	0	-
1947-48	D	Nanok	Gustav Holm	0	0	0	5	0	0	-	-	90	-	0	-
1947-48	N	Arctic Commercial Enterprise	Polarbjørn	0	1	0	6	3	0	248	27	275	1	0	37400
1947-48	N	Hermann Andresen Expedition	Polarbjørn	0	1	0	4	0	0	102	12	114	4	0	-
1948-49	D	Nanok	Søndmøringen	0	5	0	6	0	0	-	-	33	9	0	-
1948-49	N	Arctic Commercial Enterprise	Polarbjørn	1	3	0	9	3	0	159	14	173	1	0	26930
1948-49	N	Hermann Andresen Expedition	Polarbjørn	0	1	0	4	0	0	63	8	71	3	0	-
1949-50	D	Nanok	Søndmøringen	0	1	0	6	0	0	-	-	44	-	0	-
1949-50	N	Arctic Commercial Enterprise	Quest	0	4	0	9	2	0	678	42	720	10	0	8670
1949-50	N	Hermann Andresen Expedition	Quest	0	1	0	3	0	0	154	18	172	4	0	-
1950-51	D	Nanok	Søndmøringen	0	3	1	7	0	0	-	-	332	3	0	-
1950-51	N	Arctic Commercial Enterprise	Polarbjørn	0	2	0	4	2	0	513	51	564	5	0	76750
1950-51	N	Hermann Andresen Expedition	Polarbjørn	0	1	0	4	0	0	-	-	250	5	0	-
1951-52	D	Nanok	Søndmøringen	0	5	4	7	0	0	-	-	237	5	0	-
1951-52	N	Arctic Commercial Enterprise	Polarbjørn	0	0	0	5	2	0	-	-	150	5	0	27940
1951-52	N	Hermann Andresen Expedition	Polarbjørn	0	0	0	4	0	0	-	-	150	5	0	-
1952-53	D	Hans Frederiksen		0	0	0	1	0	0	-	-	12	-	0	-
1952-53	N	Arctic Commercial Enterprise	Polarbjørn	0	2	0	9	3	0	-	-	127	5	0	24680
1952-53	N	Hermann Andresen Expedition	Polarbjørn	0	0	0	4	0	0	-	-	19	1	0	-
1953-54	N	Arctic Commercial Enterprise	Polarbjørn	0	2	0	3	4	0	378	28	406	1	0	-
1953-54	N	Hermann Andresen Expedition	Polarbjørn	0	0	0	4	0	0	-	-	226	9	0	-
1954-55	D	H. Frederiksen & E.B. Larsen		0	0	0	2	0	0	-	-	180	-	0	-
1954-55	N	Arctic Commercial Enterprise	Polarbjørn	0	2	0	3	3	0	420	59	479	3	0	33000
1954-55	N	Hermann Andresen Expedition	Polarbjørn	0	1	0	3	0	0	-	-	165	5	0	-
1955-56	N	Arctic Commercial Enterprise	Polarbjørn	0	0	0	3	3	0	124	11	135	1	0	19720
1955-56	N	Hermann Andresen Expedition	Polarbjørn	0	1	0	3	0	0	-	-	156	10	0	-
1956-57	N	Arctic Commercial Enterprise	Polarbjørn	0	0	0	3	2	0	36	-	36	1	0	17380
1956-57	N	Hermann Andresen Expedition	Polarbjørn	0	0	0	2	0	0	-	-	52	3	0	-
1957-58	N	Arctic Commercial Enterprise	Polarbjørn	0	0	0	2	2	0	-	-	105	0	0	0
1957-58	N	Hermann Andresen Expedition	Polarbjørn	0	0	0	1	0	0	-	-	14	0	0	-
1958-59	N	Arctic Commercial Enterprise	Polarsel	0	0	0	2	2	0	-	-	426	4	0	45030
1958-59	N	Hermann Andresen Expedition	Polarsel	0	0	0	2	0	0	0	0	0	0	0	-
1959-60	D	Madsen, Bloch, Reindel		0	0	0	3	0	0	-	-	220	-	0	-
			Total	**39**	**244**	**15**	**527**	**81**	**21**	**12132**	**1364**	**19287**	**571**	**37**	**1079660**

Sources: Møller 1939; Giæver 1939; Jennov 1939, 1945; Polarboken 1964; A283; G130; G131.

Table 1 includes trapping expeditions, which have established buildings or have had personnel wintering in North-East Greenland 1908-60. A dash (-) indicates data are unknown.

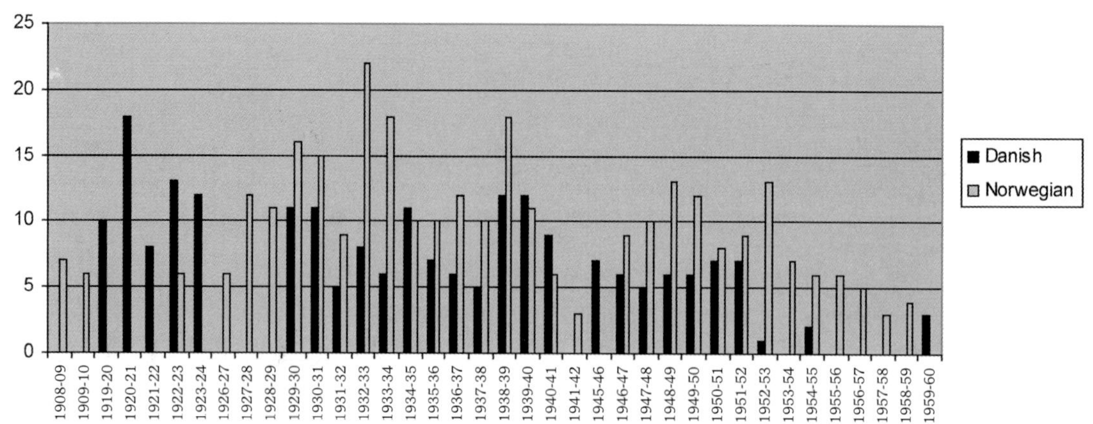

Fig. 1 shows the number of wintering Danish and Norwegian trappers over-wintering in North-East Greenland in the period 1908-60.

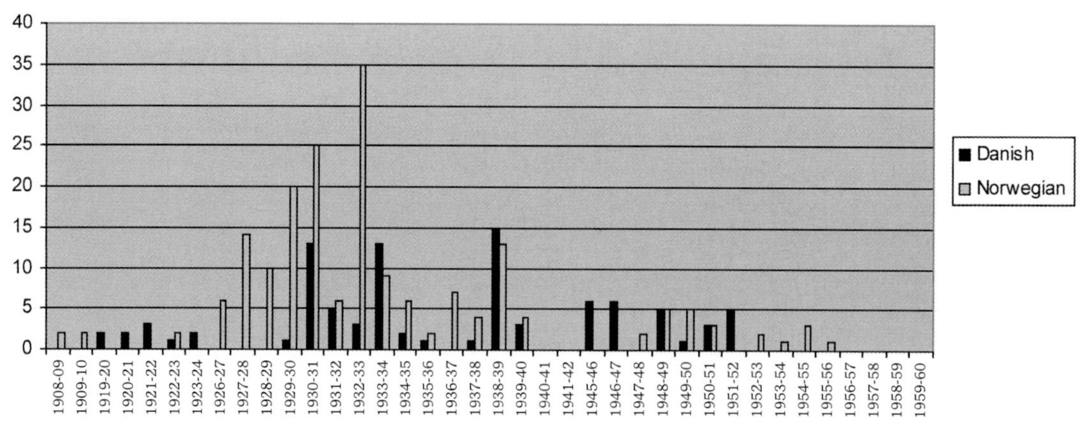

Fig. 2 shows the number of stations and huts built by Danish and Norwegian trappers during the Trapper Era 1908-60.

Fig. 3. Catch of fox pr. year

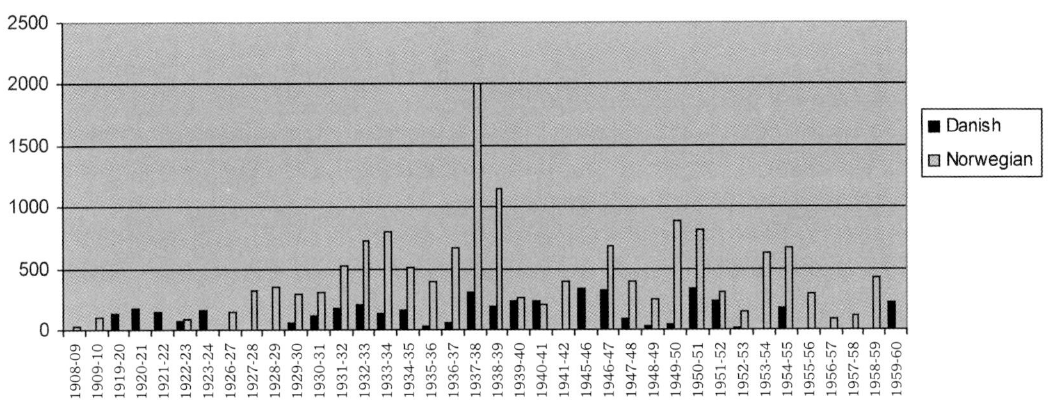

Fig. 3 shows the total of arctic fox trapped by Danes and Norwegian each year. Where totals are only known as a sum of several years (see Table 1), then the total is distributed equally amongst the years in question.

Fig. 4. Average catch of fox for each trapping season

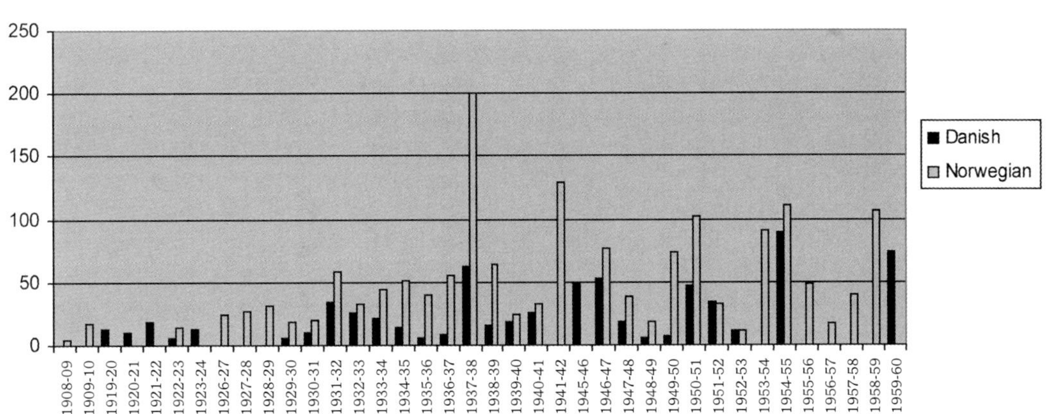

Fig. 4 shows the average Danish and Norwegian catch of arctic fox each year in the period 1908-60.

Table 2. Other expeditions / organisations

Expeditions			Vessels	Buildings			Wintering participants
Period	Nation	Name	Vessel (arrival)	Category I	Category II	Material sites	
1869-70	G	German Arctic Expedition 1869-70	Germania	0	1	0	17
1901-01	A	Baldwin-Ziegler Expedition	Belgica	2	0	0	0
1906-07	D	Danmark Expedition	Danmark	1	0	0	28
1907-08	D	Danmark Expedition		1	0	0	25
1909-10	D	Alabama Expedition	Alabama	1	0	0	7
1910-11	D	Alabama Expedition		0	0	0	2
1911-12	D	Alabama Expedition		0	0	0	2
1912-13	D	Danish Expedition to Dr. Louise Land	Godthaab	1	0	0	4
1931-32	D	Lauge Koch Expedition	Godthaab/Gustav Holm	2	2	0	16
1932-33	D	Lauge Koch Expedition	Godthaab/Gustav Holm	1	0	0	19
1933-34	D	Lauge Koch Expedition	Godthaab/Gustav Holm	0	0	1	13
1934-35	D	Lauge Koch Expedition / Police Service	Gustav Holm	0	1	0	4
1935-36	D	Lauge Koch Expedition / Police Service	Godthaab	0	0	0	4
1936-37	D	Lauge Koch Expedition / Police Service	Gustav Holm	0	0	0	15
1937-38	D	Lauge Koch Expedition / Police Service	Godthaab/Gustav Holm	0	0	0	15
1938-39	D	Lauge Koch Expedition / Police Service	Godthaab/Gustav Holm	0	1	0	9
1938-39	D	Mørkefjord Expedition	Gamma	2	0	0	10
1939-40	D	Lauge Koch Expedition / Police Service		0	0	0	5
1939-40	D	Mørkefjord Expedition		0	1	0	4
1940-40	D	Furenak Expedition	Furenak	0	1	0	0
1940-41	D	Lauge Koch Expedition / Police Service		0	0	0	5
1940-41	D	Mørkefjord Expedition	Veslekari	0	1	0	6
1941-42	*	North-East Greenland Sledge Patrol		0	1	0	12
1942-43	G	German Naval Weather Service	Sachsen	1	0	0	18
1942-43	*	North-East Greenland Sledge Patrol		0	0	0	12
1943-44	G	German Naval Weather Service	Coburg	1	0	0	26
1943-44	*	North-East Greenland Sledge Patrol		1	0	0	7
1944-44	G	German Naval Weather Service	Externsteine	0	0	1	0
1944-45	*	North-East Greenland Sledge Patrol		1	1	0	8
1945-75	D	Daneborg Weather Station		0	2	0	111
1947-50	D	Pearyland Expedition	Godthaab	0	1	0	
1947-58	D	Lauge Koch Expedition / Police Service		1	2	0	30
1948-	D	Danmarkshavn Weather Station		1	13	0	140
1950-	D	Sirius Dog Sledge Patrol		1	7	0	100
1952-91	D	Nordmine		0	5	0	
1952-	D	Mestersvig Airfield		1	6	0	
1952-54	B	British North Greenland Expedition	Tottan	1	0	0	46
1955-64	A	A.L. Washburn		0	1	0	
1997-	D	Danish Polar Center		1	0	0	
	D	Greenland Environmental Survey		0	1	0	
	D	Geological Surveys of Greenland		0	1	0	
			Total	21	49	2	720

D = Danish, G = German, A = American, B = British

* = The North-East Greenland Sledge Patrol was placed under the Greenland Administration. It had Danish, Norwegian and Greenlandic members, and was supplied by the US Coast Guard.

Table 2. Buildings erected by other expeditions/organisations in North-East Greenland 1960.

ADMINISTRATION

THE QUESTION OF SOVEREIGNTY

As long as North-East Greenland had no economic importance, no one was particularly concerned to whom it formally belonged. However, as fishing and sealing offshore increased, and exploitation of the land fauna together with fox-trapping began to expand, the question of sovereignty needed to be settled. Between 1921 and 1933 political arguments between Denmark and Norway concerning the historical affiliation of East Greenland escalated into a conflict.

HISTORICAL INTRODUCTION

In 986 the celebrated Viking, Eric "the Red" Thorvaldsson, led a Norse (Icelandic/Norwegian) expedition to western Greenland, a region he had spent three years exploring while banished from Iceland for murder. Eric the Red founded two Norse settlements, one "Østerbygden" in South-West Greenland, and the second "Vesterbygden", in West Greenland. In 1261 these settlements were annexed in the "Norgesvældet" by the Norwegian king. In 1380 Norway and Denmark were united, and their joint Kingdom included Iceland and the Greenland settlements. The Icelandic sagas record the history of settlement, and during the first three centuries of their existence the settlements flourished with the help of regular shipments of supplies from Europe. However, from about 1350 the supply ships from Europe declined in number, and contact was lost with the Norse settlements in the 15th century. The kingdom of Denmark/Norway sent out Hans Egede in 1721 to regain contact with the Norse settlements, but no survivors were found, and Hans Egede founded instead the colony of Godthaab. The disappearance of the Norse culture in Greenland remains a mystery. Deterioration in the climate with increased ice in the North Atlantic is sometimes blamed for the decline in shipping contacts. There has also been speculation that the Norsemen, left to fend for themselves, may have emigrated to North America at the end of the 15th century, a region they had navigated and explored since the days of Leif "the Lucky" Ericsson (Leifur Eiríksson Heppni). The Norse that remained in Greenland may have succumbed to the cold and illness, or according to some stories, were kidnapped and sold into slavery by pirates.

In 1776 all trading in Greenland became the monopoly of *Den kongelige grønlandske Handel* (KGH) (the Royal Greenland Trading Company) and was administered from Copenhagen. In 1814, as a consequence of the peace treaty of Kiel, the Danish-Norwegian kingdom was divided. In the 4th article of the treaty, it was stated that: *"The Kingdom of Norway... as well as the additional territories (Greenland, Faroe Islands and Iceland not included) will in the future belong to His Majesty the King of Sweden..."*.[35] The treaty of Kiel was never acknowledged in Norway, where the exclusions of article 4 (inserted in brackets) were a cause of much disapproval, argument and anger. However, the Norwegians were busy with other matters for the next century, and it was not until the end of WWI that Greenland entered the arena again.

By the end of the 19th century, fishing and trapping in both West and East Greenland had increased. Norwegian ships in particular considered access to Greenland an attractive objective, but the KGH monopoly on trade prevented all ships (even Danish) from calling at ports in Greenland without the formal permission of the Danish Home Secretary.

Various parties - including some Danes - were of the opinion that only the colonized areas of West Greenland and around Ammassalik in East Greenland, were to be considered included under Danish sovereignty. The Danish government wished to clear up any uncertainty, and began to seek approval from many different countries with interests in this region that all of Greenland was to be considered Danish territory.

Denmark brought up the issue with Norway in 1919 during the peace conference after WWI. Norway very much wanted sovereignty over Svalbard, and asked for and was given Danish approval. During the negotiations between the Danish minister Johan Christian Westergaard Kruse and the Norwegian minister and Foreign Secretary Nils Claus Ihlen, the Danes raised the question of sovereignty over Greenland. Niels Claus Ihlen promised that Norway would consider this matter, and although opinion within Norwegian government circles was divided, on the 22nd July 1919 Ihlen promised the Danish delegate that: *"the Norwegian government would not cause any difficulties during the sorting out of this matter"*. The Danes understood this statement to be a binding commitment and on the 28th July the Danish government declared that it would not oppose Norwegian sovereignty of Svalbard. It was

Idag, kl. 5 eftm. har vi heist det norske flagg og tatt landet fra Carlsbergfjorden i syd til Besselfjorden i nord i besiddelse i H. M. Kong Haakon den 7.s navn, og kaldt dette område Eirik Raudes Land.

Myggbukta den 27. juni 1931.

Hallvard Devold.

Ingvald Strøm Søren Richter

Eilif Herdal Thor Halle

The occupation document, which was written and signed in Myggbukta on 27th June 1931. The document translates to: "Today, at 5 p.m., we have hoisted the Norwegian flag and in the name of H.M. King Haakon VII annexed the land from Carlsberg Fjord in the south to Bessel Fjord in the north, and named this area Eirik Raudes Land. Myggbukta, 27th June 1931. Signed: Hallvard Devold, Ingvald Strøm, Søren Richter, Eilif Herdal, Thor Halle". © Norwegian Polar Institute

not until January 1921 that Denmark asked Norway for a written confirmation of Ihlen's oral statement. While Denmark obtained commitments from a number of other relevant nations during the period 1916-21 accepting that all of Greenland was Danish territory, Norway hesitated, and no acceptance was received.

Blom 1973.

THE EAST GREENLAND AGREEMENT

Between 1919 and 1921 the Norwegian government changed its mind over the Greenland issue. It had become clear that Norwegian sealers and fishermen had considerable economic interests in East Greenland, and these would be jeopardized by expanded Danish sovereignty. Following a number of diplomatic contacts between the two countries, Norway eventually claimed that Ihlen's oral statement had only been a preliminary and non-binding briefing. The Danes, on the other hand, considered Ihlen's statement to be a binding commitment, and it remained a central point of the Danish argument until the verdict at The Hague. Referring to Ihlen's statement, Denmark issued a decree on the 10th May 1921, announcing that Danish administration now covered the entire island of Greenland, including the uninhabited parts of East Greenland. Norway refused to accept this decree, and even though Denmark never in reality tried to restrict access to East Greenland, the decree created considerable anti-Danish feeling in Norway, awakening the old bitterness over the bracketed exclusions in the Kiel peace treaty of 1814.

From 1921 onwards a continuously growing opposition movement in Norway encouraged an occupation of East Greenland.

In the autumn of 1923 delegations from Norway and Denmark met to negotiate an agreement,[36] but it proved impossible to compromise on the issue of sovereignty. The Norwegians refused to recognize Danish sovereignty over East Greenland, but

The Norwegian flag is hoisted in Myggbukta at the occupation of "Eirik Raudes Land" on 27th June 1931. From left: Hallvard Devold, Eilif Herdal, Ingvald Strøm, Søren Richter and Thor Halle. © Hallvard Devold / Norwegian Polar Institute

reluctantly conceded that it could become *"no-man's land"*. The Danes for their part categorically rejected any discussion about the issue of sovereignty.
As a consequence, the agreement that the two parties signed on the 9th July 1924 solely concerned certain practical regulations of the situation in East Greenland. The agreement would stand for 20 years, but the sovereignty issue remained unsolved.

The East Greenland Agreement was criticized in Denmark as well as Norway. In Denmark it was claimed that Norway had been granted unnecessary rights, while in Norway those who had criticized the 6th article of the agreement allowing establishment of a native settlement in Scoresby Sund were soon proved right. As early as the summer of 1924, Ejnar Mikkelsen led an expedition to establish the Scoresbysund colony, and Norwegian companies found themselves excluded from yet another part of East Greenland; the Scoresbysund colony, like Ammassalik, was administered by the Greenland Administration directly from Denmark. Danes as well as Norwegians realized the inevitable approach of the hour at which the 8th article of the agreement, resolution of any disagreements at the Permanent Court of International Justice at The Hague, would need to be employed. During the period 1924-1930 both Denmark and Norway expanded their scientific activities and fox-trapping in North-East Greenland, a deliberate ploy designed to strengthen their position in any future court case.

In 1930 the conflict deepened. In Norway, the *Norges Svalbard- og Ishavs-råd*, also called *Ishavsrådet*, was founded. This committee included influential members such as Gustav Smedal and professor Adolf Hoel, who held the view that Norway should occupy those parts of East Greenland that were "no-man's land". The Norwegian government rejected this proposal from *Ishavsrådet*, but agreed to appoint three Norwegians (including Adolf Hoel) as the police authority over Norwegians in North-East Greenland, on the grounds that the country was "no-man's land". Denmark objected, and declared that Norway had no right to establish a police authority in Danish territory.

In December 1930, it became public knowledge that Denmark would launch a large-scale, three-year scientific expedition to North-East Greenland, under the leadership of Lauge Koch. The strategist behind the Norwegian Greenland movement, Gustav Smedal, had no doubts that this expedition would give Denmark a significant advantage in a future court case over sovereignty. Since the Norwegian government once again rejected the idea of a formal occupation of North-East Greenland, Smedal made a private one.
Blom 1973; Smedal 1928, 1934.

THE OCCUPATION

On the 29th June 1931 the press in Norway announced that Hallvard Devold and four other trappers from Arctic Commercial Enterprise had occupied the area between Carlsberg Fjord and Bessel Fjord in the name of the Norwegian king. On the 27th June they had hoisted the Norwegian flag in Myggbukta, and claimed "Eirik Raudes Land", the region between 71°30' and 75°40'N where Norwegian trapping activities were most widespread, as Norwegian territory. This news caused a hectic exchange of notes between the Danish and Norwegian governments. Denmark refused any compromise with respect to the sovereignty issue, while in Norway the government came under considerable pressure from the Norwegian public and press.

On the 10th July 1931, the Norwegian government yielded to public opinion, and confirmed by royal resolution that the area between 71°30' and 75°40'N on the east coast of Greenland was now under Norwegian sovereignty. On the 11th July the Danish government took the dispute to the Permanent Court of International Justice at The Hague, claiming that the Norwegian occupation was unlawful and invalid.
Blom 1973; Devold 1940; Smedal 1934.

THE HAGUE VERDICT

The Permanent Court of International Justice at The Hague declared the 14th October 1932 as the deadline for the countries involved to deliver their pleadings. From 21st November 1932 until the 7th February 1933 a number of public hearings were held, at which Norway maintained that Denmark had no right to "Eirik Raudes Land", whereas Denmark stated it had held uninterrupted sovereignty for centuries. On the 5th April 1933 the court announced its verdict, placing East Greenland under Danish sovereignty.
Blom 1973; Brøgger 1933; Lauritsen 1984; Udenrigsministeriet 1933.

THE POLICE SERVICE 1931-41

From 1930 and up until the verdict at The Hague, both Denmark and Norway had appointed public officials in North-East Greenland. Since 1931 the Danish government had assigned Lauge Koch, the leader of the Three-Year Expedition, as the Danish police authority, and when he left the coast, authority was delegated to the station managers of the wintering parties at Ella Ø and Eskimonæs. The Norwegians, on their part, had in 1931 assigned police authority to the leaders of the Norwegian trapping companies,

Hallvard Devold and Hermann Andresen. In 1932 Norway formally appointed the barrister Helge Ingstad as "sysselmand" over "Eirik Raudes Land"; Ingstad was obliged to move to the occupied territories "until further notice", and from 1931-32 he had his headquarters at the Antarctichavn trappers' station [201] in the southern Kong Oscar Fjord terrain. This altogether untenable authority situation was not resolved until the verdict at The Hague.

The Norwegian annexation of "Eirik Raudes Land" was annulled by the verdict at The Hague, but at the same time Denmark was criticized for not taking more active steps to assert its claimed sovereignty over North-East Greenland. One consequence was the appointment of Captain Ejnar Mikkelsen in 1934 as *Inspektør for Østkysten* (Inspector of East Greenland), under the Greenland Administration. North of the Scoresbysund colony, two police districts were established. The "North District" that extended from Nordostrundingen (81°21'N; the easternmost point of Greenland) down to an east-west line through the middle of Dusén Fjord (73°30'N); and the "South District" from Dusén Fjord to a line through Storefjord (71°06'N) on the coast of Liverpool Land and the watershed between Jameson Land and Scoresby Land. The scientific stations at Eskimonæs and Ella Ø became police headquarters for the two districts. Since Ejnar Mikkelsen never actually visited the police districts north of Scoresbysund, and Lauge Koch continued his expeditions in North-East Greenland until 1939 with wintering parties at Eskimonæs and Ella Ø, it was Lauge Koch who in reality exercised police authority. Ejnar Mikkelsen's interests were mainly focused upon the native populations in the Scoresbysund and Ammassalik settlements. During the years 1941-45 the duties of the police service were undertaken by the North-East Greenland Sledge Patrol.

THE SECOND WORLD WAR

From spring 1940 living conditions in North-East Greenland were increasingly affected by the war. Scientific explorations stopped, trapping was brought to an end more gradually, while administration and supply services were adjusted to the dictates of the war. Episodes from the war years have been described in several books. However, a number of incidents that took place during the war are still subject to reasonable doubt and discussion; an overall, thorough and objective account of the war years in Greenland has unfortunately not yet been produced.

THE AGREEMENT RELATING TO THE DEFENCE OF GREENLAND

On the 9th April 1940 Germany occupied Denmark, and it was not only the physical relations, such as supply services between Denmark and Greenland, that were interrupted. The invisible administration ties, which linked Greenland and Denmark were also broken.

Eske Brun (1904-1987), who was then Provincial Governor of North Greenland, interpreted the command from the Danish king for his people to surrender to the German Wehrmacht, as an announcement issued under threat. Brun chose instead to activate the emergency powers allowed for under the statutes of the Provincial Governor, that in: *"extraordinary circumstances"* he could: *"take such measures, as the need of the inhabitants might require".* Brun, and Axel Svane (1898-1991) the Provincial Governor of South Greenland, established a united administration, the Grønlands Administration, in Godthåb (Nuuk) and undertook to govern Greenland on their own responsibility. Eske Brun became the actual leader in Greenland, while Svane moved to the USA at the beginning of 1941 to become the Greenland representative to the US administration.

With respect to supplies, Greenland was now in a difficult situation, but in the event managed to replace the loss of supplies from Denmark with goods from the United States; the income from the cryolite mine at Ivigtut in West Greenland served as payment. Cryolite also had a significant role in the Greenland Defence Agreement, signed on the 9th April 1941 in Washington D.C. between the United States and the Danish ambassador, Henrik Kauffmann (1888-1963). Cryolite was then of vital importance as a flux used to produce aluminium for the aviation industry, and the mine at Ivigtut was the only source of natural cryolite. The mineral was so important, that Great Britain and Canada had discussed a Canadian occupation of Greenland to ensure that the cryolite mine remained in allied hands. This move proved unacceptable to the United States, and instead the United States and Canada agreed to jointly defend Greenland as long as it was cut off from Denmark, in return for supplies of cryolite. The USA was also allowed to establish air bases in Greenland, while US Coast Guard vessels would patrol the coastal waters. The squadron - Task Force 24.8 - was called *The Greenland Patrol* or *The Greenland Naval Patrol.*

THE WEATHER FRONT 1940-45

From 1941 onwards West Greenland could be regarded as well protected against any German aggression. The situation was, however, completely different with respect to North-East Greenland, where ice conditions limited ship patrols to the summer months. Furthermore, the military objectives in North-East Greenland were not about a specific place or anything tangible. This was *"a war about weather"*, as the noted Norwegian polar aviator, Colonel Bernt Balchen (1899-1973) expressed it: *"From this frozen island in the Arctic flow winds and currents that set up the storm fronts for all the North Atlantic, for England, for Norway, for the Continent itself. Greenland holds the key to tomorrow's weather in Europe"*. [37] And thus North-East Greenland became the focus of a series of attempts to establish German weather stations.

1940-41

As early as the summer of 1940, German interests tried via a Danish middleman to establish a weather service in North-East Greenland. The intermediary made contact with the *Igdloo* company, with a proposal for what he pretended was an ordinary trapping expedition. Jørgen Tvermose accepted the offer as leader, and hired three men for the job. The expedition left Ålesund on the 15th August 1940 with "Furenak", and arrived at Fleming Fjord on the 31st August. The four Danes went ashore at Kap Biot, where they started to build their winter house, "Kap Biot" [116]. The roof of the house was completed on the 7th September, but on the same day the naval vessel "Fridtjof Nansen" under allied command arrived. The Danes and their equipment were taken on board, the house was burnt down, and the four men were taken to England for interrogation. One became a prisoner of war, while Tvermose and the other two were found innocent and joined the allied forces.

"Fridtjof Nansen" was in British naval service and commanded by Captain Ernst Ullring, and in the summer of 1940 was sent to patrol East Greenland waters, and to prevent establishment of a German controlled weather service.[38] A group of British marines accompanied the ship. The Norwegian radio station at Myggbukta was destroyed, and the fuel supplies at the Danish stations of Ella Ø and Eskimonæs were removed. "Veslekari" was seized and everyone on board, except for the three Danes of the Mørkefjord Expedition, was forced to go with "Fridtjof Nansen". Those Danish and Norwegian trappers who had been in Greenland before the occupation of Denmark and Norway, were given the choice of remaining in Greenland or being taken to Iceland. Some went to Iceland, but 20 Danes and seven Norwegians remained in North-East Greenland.

1941-42

To the allied forces it was obvious that the Germans would make new attempts to establish a weather service in North-East Greenland, but how would it be possible to detect a German landing? Aerial surveillance and coast guard ship patrols might reveal a vessel on its way through the pack ice in the summer, but if the enemy had landed unseen there were numerous possibilities for hiding out on the deserted coast. The aerial and ship surveillance would need to be supplemented with something else, but what and by whom?

Eske Brun helped to solve this problem: *"In the summer of 1941 I made an agreement with the American authorities, that the Greenland administration would establish a sledge patrol service on this coast. The Americans were to provide support with transport of supplies and equipment in the summer, but the service was to operate under the jurisdiction of the Greenland administration. It was a police assignment, and the task was to patrol the entire coast from Kap Dalton south of Scoresbysund to Île de France, in a straight line approximately one thousand kilometres"*.[39] It was anticipated that dog sledge patrols by people familiar with the coast would reveal the presence of enemy activity, and prevent the operation of weather stations for any sustained period of time.

It was the chief of The Greenland Patrol, Commander Edward Hanson Smith (1889-1961), also called "Iceberg Smith", who was responsible for establishing the *North-East Greenland Sledge Patrol* (Nordøstgrønlands Slædepatrulje). In three identical letters, dated "Eskimonæs, 25th August, 1941" and signed by E.H. Smith, the three men Niels Ove Jensen, Aage de Lemos and Hendrik Høegh, the *kolonibestyrer* (Colony Manager) of Scoresbysund, were appointed as leaders of the patrols in the Eskimonæs, Ella Ø and Scoresbysund districts respectively. The letters of appointment described the purpose and objectives of the patrols, and the regions to be patrolled.

In the summer of 1941 Commander Smith had the three coast guard vessels, "Northland", "North Star" and "Bear" at his disposal. Yet another German attempt to establish a German-controlled weather station, this time at Jonsbu, was uncovered and hindered when "Northland" seized the "Buskø" that was carrying seven Norwegian trappers and a German oriented radio operator and his radio equipment.

In 1941-42 the sledge patrols north of Scoresbysund were made up of nine Danes and one Norwegian, supplemented by two Greenlander sledge drivers. The winter was undramatic, though a number of German aircraft were observed.

1942-43

In the summer of 1942 the American coast guard force returned with supplies and to patrol the coast

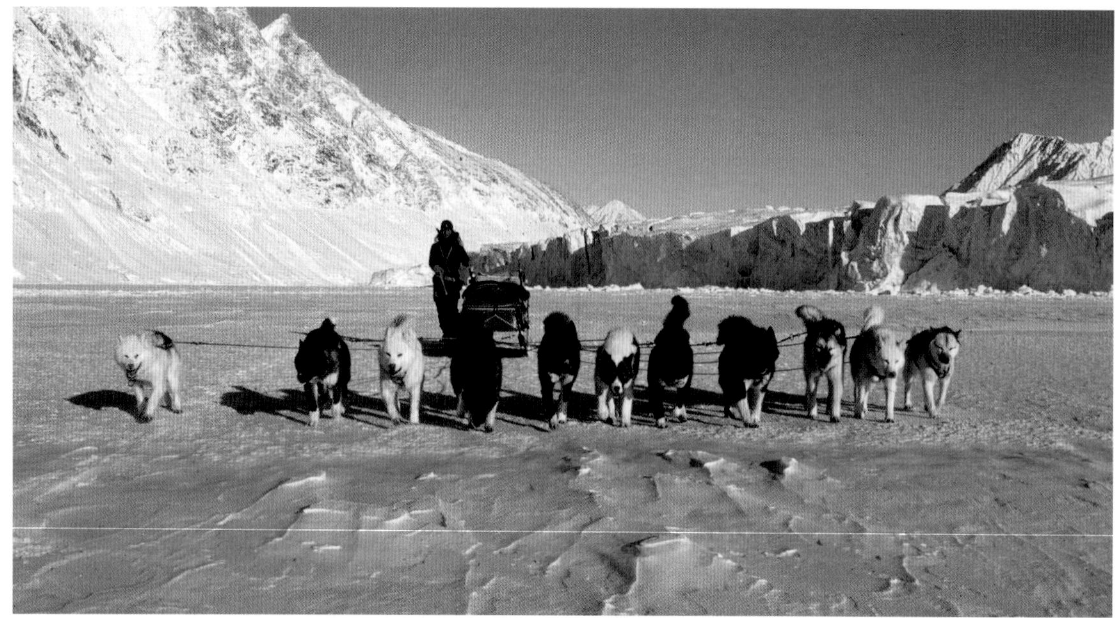

The Sirius dog sledge patrol maintains the sovereignty of the Danish Realm in North-East Greenland. Between 15,000 and 20,000 km are patrolled annually. Since 1950 almost 1 million kilometres has been travelled by dog-sledge patrols along the uninhabited coasts of North and North-East Greenland. Alpefjord, 16th March 1979. © Peter Schmidt Mikkelsen

with "Northland" and "North Star". The remaining Norwegian trappers were evacuated. Niels Ove Jensen left for West Greenland and was relieved by Ib Poulsen, who took charge of the five Danish and three Norwegian patrol men together with four Greenlandic sledge drivers stationed at Eskimonæs and Ella Ø.

At the end of August 1942 the German weather ship "Sachsen" succeeded in reaching Sabine Ø unnoticed. The expedition, named "Operation Holzauge" and numbering 18 members, was led by Hermann Ritter and Gottfried Weiss. Having established their winter quarters at "Hansa Bugt" [457] the expedition commenced a regular transmission of weather reports.

On the 11th March 1943 members of the sledge patrol discovered the presence of the German expedition. The Germans, realizing themselves unveiled, attacked Eskimonæs on the 23rd March 1943. The station was taken and partly destroyed. However the members of the sledge patrol managed to escape. On their way back to Hansa Bugt the Germans at Sandodden killed the Danish patrol member Eli Knudsen. On the same occasion they captured the patrol members Peter Nielsen and Marius Jensen. However, Peter Nielsen was soon released by the Germans and in May 1943 Hermann Ritter accompanied Marius Jensen to Scoresbysund, where all other patrol members had been ordered to go after the attack at Eskimonæs.

The Americans now tried to stop the German weather service. Bernt Balchen led two US Army Air Corps bombing raids. The first attack was on Eskimonæs on the 13th May 1943, the second was on Hansa Bugt on the 25th May.[40] However, these air raids did not stop the German weather service.

On the 21st July 1943 a commando force from "Northland" stormed the base on Sabine Ø, but found the place deserted. A month earlier the Germans had been evacuated by a seaplane. One German, Rudolf Sensse, was left behind. He had come too late for the rescue and like Hermann Ritter was taken into American captivity as a prisoner of war.

1943-44

In 1943 "Polarbjørn", now in American service, brought up materials for a new patrol headquarters, "Dødemandsbugten" [408], a replacement for the destroyed Eskimonæs station. The coastal patrols were again undertaken by "Northland" and "North Star". Niels Ove Jensen returned from West Greenland, and resumed his leadership of the sledge patrol north of Scoresbysund. His force now consisted of seven Danes.

After the attack on Eskimonæs, Eske Brun feared that the members of the patrol could be regarded as partisans with no rights of war. Thus, in April 1943, he changed the formal status of the patrol from police to military, so that the patrol members would be covered by the Geneva Convention.

In 1943-44 the sledge patrol revealed another German landing. On the 2nd October 1943 the German vessel "Coburg" (Wetterbeobachtungsschiff 2 or WBS 2) with 27 members had managed to reach

Shannon unnoticed. The German weather service was back in action.

In November 1943 members of the North-East Greenland Sledge Patrol had found the Germans' hide-out at "Kap Sussi" [520], which they attacked on the 22nd April 1944. The attacking force was observed by the German military leader, Lieutenant Gerhard Zacher, losing the element of surprise. In the ensuing fire fight Zacher was killed, and the Danes pulled out. The Germans continued their weather service unhindered until June 1944, when they were evacuated by aeroplane.

1944-45

In the summer of 1944 the sledge patrol moved from Dødemandsbugten to its new headquarters at "Daneborg" [425-2]. For the third season Niels Ove Jensen was in charge of the patrol north of Scoresbysund, which in 1944-45 numbered six Danes and two or three Greenlanders.

During the summer of 1944 the USCG patrol vessels on the East Greenland coast included "Northland", "Southwind", "Eastwind", "Evergreen" and "Storis". Captain Charles W. Thomas was in charge of the squadron.

On the 1st September 1944 "Northland" sank the German vessel "Kehdingen" (WBS 6) of the "Edelweiss I" operation at the south point of Store Koldewey. The crew of 28 was taken prisoner. On the 4th October a landing force from "Eastwind" captured 11 Germans from the operation "Edelweiss II" at "Tyskerdepotet" [917] on Lille Koldewey. The Germans had been set on shore a couple of days earlier from the "Externsteine" (WBS 11). "Externsteine" was later seized by the American naval force, which remained in North-East Greenland coastal waters until the end of October 1944.

Concerning the American naval task force, Niels Ove Jensen, the head of the North-East Greenland Sledge Patrol, wrote in his annual report for 1944-45: *"I will not here omit to mention that through all these difficult times, the Coast Guard vessels have been a true ray of light in our monotonous existence. Men such as Captain Carl Von Paulsen, Captain Charles Thomas and Lieutenant Commander Reginald F. Butcher, to mention only a few, will always be remembered with gratitude by the patrol for their great helpfulness and appreciation that they have shown with respect to the efforts of the patrol".*[41] The report by Niels Ove Jensen was dated: *"Daneborg, 26th July 1945"*. The war about the weather was over.

Akre 1983; Holzapfel 1950, 1951; Howarth 1957; Novak 2005; Nusser 1979; Odsbjerg 1990; Olsen 1965; Price 1995; Ruge 1954; Schatz 1951; Scheina 1982; Schwerdtfeger & Selinger 1982; Selinger 1991, 2001; Steen 1960; Stuhr 1974; Thomas 1951; Tilley 1992; Weiss 1949; Willoughby 1989.

THE POST-WAR PERIOD

After the war exploration and commercial activities in North-East Greenland were resumed.

Denmark had two important duties, partly to maintain continuous Danish sovereignty, and partly to collect regular weather observations. In order to carry out these tasks a chain of new, modern weather stations was established shortly after the war.

THE WEATHER SERVICE

Immediately after the war the *Greenland Radio and Weather Service* (Grønlands Radio- og Vejrtjeneste) started to reconstruct and reorganize the weather service in Greenland. The rapidly growing intercontinental air traffic made it necessary to expand the service. In co-operation with international meteorological and aviation organizations it was decided to build a network of new weather stations along the coast of Greenland, some of which would be financed by the International Civil Aviation Organisation (ICAO).

In the summer of 1945 the members of the North-East Greenland Sledge Patrol were able to return home to Denmark after several years of exile. The Daneborg station was manned by new personnel, whose tasks were to continue the weather service and maintain Danish sovereignty. For this purpose the station manager was assigned police authority.

In 1947 "Daneborg Weather Station" (Daneborg Vejrstation) [425-2] was extended with new houses and installations. Until it was closed in 1975 the station had an annual staff of about seven employees.

In 1948 a new weather station financed by ICAO was established at Danmark Havn. This station, "Danmarkshavn Weather Station" (Danmarkshavn Vejrstation) [628-2], has a staff of 10 to 12, and still functions as an important part of the international weather service.

THE SIRIUS DOG SLEDGE PATROL

In 1945, after the Germans capitulated and Denmark became a free nation once more, the North-East Greenland Sledge Patrol was disbanded. Police authority in the region north of Scoresbysund was handed over to the station managers at Daneborg and Danmarkshavn weather stations.

The escalation of the cold war soon led to a need for an improved, systematic surveillance of North- and North-East Greenland. The Danish Navy, which was responsible for military activities in Greenland, recommended the establishment of a military dog sledge patrol. This proposal was endorsed by the Danish government, and in 1950 - in the greatest secrecy - a sledge patrol was established by the Navy. The patrol was founded on the 18th August 1950 and named *Operation Resolut*. On this day the first team of five Danish servicemen gathered on Ella Ø, the headquarters of the patrol for the first year. Two Greenlander dog sledge drivers were attached to the patrol for the first year as instructors.

In the summer of 1951, the patrol moved to Daneborg, where a new headquarters, "Sirius Daneborg" [425-3] was established. The next team of five Danes soon arrived for their two-year service.

The name of the patrol was changed in 1951 to *Slædepatruljen Resolut* (Sledge Patrol Resolut). In 1953 the name was changed once again to prevent any confusion with the Canadian military station at "Resolute Bay" in northern Canada. The Danish sledge patrol took its new name from *Sirius* - the brightest star in the constellation of Canis Major (The Greater Dog). It was under the name *Sirius Dog Sledge Patrol* (Slædepatruljen Sirius) that the patrol first became known to the public.

The Sirius Dog Sledge Patrol has the main task of patrolling the uninhabited coastal regions of North-East and North Greenland, between Liverpool Land (71°N) in North-East Greenland and Nares Strait, the narrow channel between western North Greenland and Ellesmere Island in the Canadian Arctic. The patrolling of the 2100 km long stretch of coast is undertaken by dog sledge in the winter half-year, from about the 1st November until the 15th June. In the summer months the ice-free fjords of North-East Greenland are patrolled using small vessels. Apart from military surveillance and maintenance of sovereignty, the patrol since 1950 has also exercised police authority in the area. Within the borders of the North-East Greenland National Park, the patrol members also function as game keepers, and supervise the activities of scientific and sports expeditions during the summer.

From 1951 the Sirius Dog Sledge Patrol has numbered 10, later 12 members, selected from officers and sergeants of the Danish Navy, Army and Air Force who volunteer for two-years service in Greenland. Each sledge team, comprising two men and 11 dogs, is usually on continuous sledge patrol for a period of four to five months, during which they may only once or twice meet other people. Only one of the about 300 men who have served in the patrol between 1950 and 2008 has died on duty. Remembering the criticism accompanying the verdict in Denmark's favour at The Hague: *"that Denmark may have shown will but no results"* in asserting their claimed sovereignty, it is worthy of note that Sirius, since its foundation, has travelled almost one million kilometres by dog sledge patrols along the uninhabited coasts of North and North-East Greenland.

Bjerre 1980; Grønland under den kolde krig 1997; Inspektøren for Søværnet 1990; Mikkelsen 1986; Nielsen 1990; Sørensen 2002; Søværnskommandoen 1956; Thormann 1997.

THE NATIONAL PARK

Throughout the 1960s the vision of designating the uninhabited regions of North and North-East Greenland as a national park matured. The idea was to create a wildlife sanctuary and a biological "bank", which could ultimately accrue to the benefit of the native hunting communities of Ittoqqortoormiit (Scoresbysund) and Avanersuaq (Thule).[42]

On the 22nd May 1974 the Nature Conservation Act for Greenland was passed by the Danish Parliament, with the recommendation of the Greenland Provincial Council (the predecessor of the Landsting). The law came into force the same year on July 1st, and thus the world's largest national park became a fact. After an enlargement in 1988, the present-day *National Park North & East Greenland* covers 972,000 km^2, of which the largest part comprises a sector of the Inland Ice. The National Park has obtained the status of "Biosphere Reserve" under UNESCO's MAB-programme (Man and the Biosphere programme). The National Park is administered by the Home Rule Authorities.

According to the Home Rule Order and to the Ministry of Justice Executive Order on Access to and Conditions for Travelling in Certain Parts of Greenland of 7 December 2006, the public has access to the National Park: in principal that means everyone. With few exceptions, however, all visitors to the National Park must obtain prior permission from the Home Rule Authorities.[43] Anyone wishing to visit the National Park must fill out a special application form obtainable from the Danish Polar Center in Copenhagen; established on 1st January 1989, the Danish Polar Center functions as an information and service centre for polar research.

The National Park provides not only protection for the wildlife; archaeological sites, the landscape, arctic flora and relics of human activities are also protected, including trappers' huts and their contents of "antique" furniture and equipment.

Elander 1992; Grønlands Hjemmestyre 1990; Mikkelsen 1990; Roy 2004; Silis 1995; Statusrapport 2001.

REGISTER OF MANNED STATIONS 71° 30′ TO 77° 30′

1869-70:	"Germania"
1870-1906:	(none)
1906-07:	Villaen ("Danmark")
1907-08:	Pustervig
	Villaen ("Danmark")
1908-09:	Borganes
	Kopperneshuset
1909-10:	"Alabama"
	Germania-hamn
	("7de juni")
1910-11:	Alabamahuset
1911-12:	Bass Rock
1912-13:	Borg
1913-19:	(none)
1919-20:	Germaniahavn
	Hvalrosodden
	Villaen
1920-21:	Alabamahuset
	Bass Rock
	Carlshavn
	Hvalrosodden
	Kap Broer Ruys
	Kap Philip Broke
	Villaen
1921-22:	Carlshavn
	Christianshavn
	Germaniahavn
1922-23:	Bass Rock
	Carlshavn
	Christianshavn
	Franklin-huset
	Germaniahavn
	Myggbukta
	Valdemarshaab
1923-24:	Bass Rock
	Carlshavn
	Germaniahavn
	Kap Philip Broke
	Sandodden
1924-26:	(none)
1926-27:	Krogness
	Myggbukta
1927-28:	Elvsborg
	Kap Herschell
	Krogness
	Moskusheimen
	Myggbukta
1928-29:	Germaniahavn
	Jackson-stua
	Kap Herschell
	Krogness
	Moskusheimen
	Myggbukta
1929-30:	Germaniahavn
	Hochstetter
	Kap Herschell
	Kap Humboldt
	Krogness
	Liavåg
	Moskusheimen
	Myggbukta
	Sandodden
	Sverresborg
1930-31:	Antarctichavn
	Germaniahavn
	Hochstetter
	Hoelsbu
	Kap Herschell
	Kap Humboldt
	Kap Peterséns
	Maristua
	Myggbukta
	Sandodden
1931-32:	Antarctichavn
	Ella Ø
	Eskimonæs
	Hochstetter
	Kap Herschell
	Kap Peterséns
	Moskusheimen
	Myggbukta
	Sandodden
1932-33:	Antarctichavn
	Bessel Fjord
	Ella Ø
	Eskimonæs
	Hochstetter
	Hoelsbu
	Hvalrosodden
	Jonsbu
	Kap Herschell
	Kap Humboldt
	Kap Peterséns
	Kulhus
	Moskusheimen
	Myggbukta
	Olestua
	Ottostrand
	Sigurdsheim
1933-34:	Antarctichavn
	Ella Ø
	Eskimonæs
	Hochstetter
	Hoelsbu
	Hvalrosodden
	Jackson-stua
	Jonsbu
	Kap Herschell
	Kap Humboldt
	Kap Peterséns
	Moskusheimen
	Myggbukta
	Olestua
	Ottostrand
	Sigurdsheim
1934-35:	Antarctichavn
	Ella Ø
	Eskimonæs
	Hochstetter
	Hoelsbu
	Kap Herschell
	Kap Humboldt
	Kap Peterséns
	Kulhus
	Moskusheimen
	Myggbukta
	Sandodden
1935-36:	Antarctichavn
	Ella Ø
	Eskimonæs
	Hochstetter
	Hoelsbu
	Kap Herschell
	Kap Peterséns
	Krogness
	Moskusheimen
	Myggbukta
	Sandodden
1936-37:	Antarctichavn
	Ella Ø
	Eskimonæs
	Hochstetter
	Hoelsbu
	Kap Humboldt
	Kap Peterséns
	Krogness ("Quest")
	Moskusheimen
	Myggbukta
	Sandodden
1937-38:	Antarctichavn
	Ella Ø
	Eskimonæs
	Hochstetter
	Hoelsbu
	Kap Herschell
	Kap Humboldt
	Kap Peterséns
	Moskusheimen
	Myggbukta
	Sandodden
1938-39:	Alwin Pedersens hus
	Ella Ø
	Eskimonæs
	Hochstetter
	Hoelsbu
	Hvalrosodden
	Jonsbu
	Kap Herschell
	Kap Humboldt
	Kap Peterséns
	Laplace
	Micardbu ("En Avant")
	Moskusheimen
	Myggbukta
	Mønstedhus
	Mørkefjord
	Ottostrand
	Sandodden
	Aalborghus
1939-40:	Ella Ø
	Eskimonæs
	Hamna
	Hochstetter
	Hoelsbu
	Hvalrosodden
	Jonsbu
	Kap Humboldt
	Knudshoved
	Moskusheimen
	Myggbukta
	Mønstedhus
	Mørkefjord
	Sandodden
	Aalborghus
1940-41:	Ella Ø

Eskimonæs
Hochstetter
Hoelsbu
Hvalrosodden
Kap Herschell
Kap Humboldt
Moskusheimen
Myggbukta
Mønstedhus
Mørkefjord
Sandodden
Aalborghus

1941-42: Ella Ø
Eskimonæs
Hoelsbu
Moskusheimen
Myggbukta

1942-43 Ella Ø
Eskimonæs
Hansa Bugt

1943-44: Dødemandsbugten
Kap Sussi

1944-45: Daneborg

1945-46: Daneborg
Knudshoved
Loch Fyne
Sandodden
Zackenberg

1946-47: Antarctichavn
Daneborg
Hamna
Hochstetter
Hoelsbu
Kap Herschell
Loch Fyne
Moskusheimen
Myggbukta
Mønstedhus
Sandodden
Zackenberg

1947-48: Antarctichavn
Daneborg
Ella Ø
Hamna
Hochstetter
Hoelsbu
Kap Herschell
Kap Humboldt
Loch Fyne
Moskusheimen
Myggbukta
Sandodden
Zackenberg

1948-49: Antarctichavn
Daneborg
Danmarkshavn
Ella Ø
Hamna
Hochstetter
Hoelsbu
Kap Herschell
Kap Humboldt
Loch Fyne
Moskusheimen
Myggbukta
Ny Jonsbu
Ottostrand
Zackenberg

1949-50: Daneborg
Danmarkshavn
Ella Ø
Hamna
Hoelsbu
Kap Herschell
Kap Humboldt
Loch Fyne
Moskusheimen
Myggbukta
Ny Jonsbu
Ottostrand
Sandodden
Zackenberg

1950-51: Antarctichavn
Daneborg
Danmarkshavn
Ella Ø
Hamna
Hochstetter
Hoelsbu
Kap Herschell
Loch Fyne
Moskusheimen
Myggbukta
Ottostrand
Zackenberg
Aalborghus

1951-52: Antarctichavn
Daneborg
Danmarkshavn
Ella Ø
Hochstetter
Hoelsbu
Kap Herschell
Kap Humboldt
Kap Peterséns
Loch Fyne
Mestersvig
Moskusheimen
Myggbukta
Mønstedhus
Ottostrand
Zackenberg
Aalborghus

1952-53: Antarctichavn
Britannia Sø
Daneborg
Danmarkshavn
Ella Ø
Hoelsbu
Kap Herschell
Kap Humboldt
Kap Petersêns
Mestersvig
Moskusheimen
Myggbukta
Ottostrand
Zackenberg

1953-54: Antarctichavn
Britannia Sø
Daneborg
Danmarkshavn
Ella Ø
Hoelsbu
Kap Herschell
Kap Petersêns
Mestersvig
Moskusheimen
Myggbukta

1954-55: Antarctichavn
Daneborg
Danmarkshavn
Hochstetter
Hoelsbu
Kap Herschell
Mestersvig
Moskusheimen
Myggbukta

1955-56: Daneborg
Danmarkshavn
Hoelsbu
Kap Herschell
Kap Petersêns
Mestersvig
Moskusheimen
Myggbukta

1956-57: Antarctichavn
Daneborg
Danmarkshavn
Hoelsbu
Kap Herschell
Mestersvig
Moskusheimen
Myggbukta

1957-58: Antarctichavn
Daneborg
Danmarkshavn
Hoelsbu
Mestersvig
Moskusheimen
Myggbukta

1958-59: Antarctichavn
Daneborg
Danmarkshavn
Hoelsbu
Mestersvig
Moskusheimen
Myggbukta

1959-60: Daneborg
Danmarkshavn
Hvalrosodden
Mestersvig
Moskusheimen
Zackenberg

1960- Daneborg
Danmarkshavn
Mestersvig

Note: Daneborg includes: Daneborg Weather Station and Sirius Daneborg. Mestersvig includes: Mestersvig Airfield, Nyhavn and Minebyen. Daneborg Weather Station, Nyhavn and Mestersvig Airfield (partly) were closed down after 1960.

TRAPPERS' STATIONS

The following section deals in alphabetic order with Category IA buildings/building complexes in North-East Greenland, e.g. stations that have been used for overwintering in connection with trapping activities.

Note that the Danish letters Æ, Ø and Å (= AA) come at the end of the Danish alphabet. So the station Mønstedhus is described after Myggbukta, and the Aalborghus station is last in the descriptions of stations.

Getting fresh supplies of muskox meat. The muskox was vital for the trappers in North-East Greenland. It provided them as well as their sledge dogs with fresh food. © Arne Philbert, except upper right © Trygve Havold

ALABAMAHUSET
[518]

Wintering party
1910-11: Ejnar Mikkelsen and Iver P. Iversen
1920-21: Johan F. Petersen

When the Danmark Expedition returned to Denmark in the summer of 1908 it became known that Ludvig Mylius-Erichsen, Niels Peter Høeg Hagen and Jørgen Brønlund had lost their lives. However, only the body of Jørgen Brønlund had been found, and the diaries of Mylius-Erichsen and Høeg Hagen had not been recovered. On the initiative of Ejnar Mikkelsen, the Committee for the Danmark Expedition launched an expedition in the summer of 1909 to find the lost diaries, and if possible to discover the fate of the two missing men. For transport, the 50 ton "Alabama" - a so-called "Nordlandsjagt" - was purchased in Norway. The Alabama Expedition under the leadership of Ejnar Mikkelsen made winter harbour on the east coast of Shannon, a little south of Kap Sussi. The expedition members included Lieutenant Vilhelm Laub, Lieutenant Christian H. Jørgensen, the sailors Hans Olsen and Georg Paulsen, a carpenter Carl Unger and the engineer Iver P. Iversen.

In September-December 1909 Mikkelsen, Jørgensen and Iversen undertook a sledge journey to Lambert Land, where they re-discovered the body of Brønlund together with various belongings, including a notebook with sketches. A search in the vicinity for the bodies of Mylius-Erichsen and Høeg Hagen was not successful.

1910-11

In the beginning of March 1910, Mikkelsen and Iversen set forth on a sledge journey across the Inland Ice to Danmark Fjord. This journey did not solve the riddle of the missing bodies and diaries of the deceased, but two cairns containing messages from Mylius-Erichsen were located. The return journey of Mikkelsen and Iversen along the outer coast was very dangerous and full of incidents,

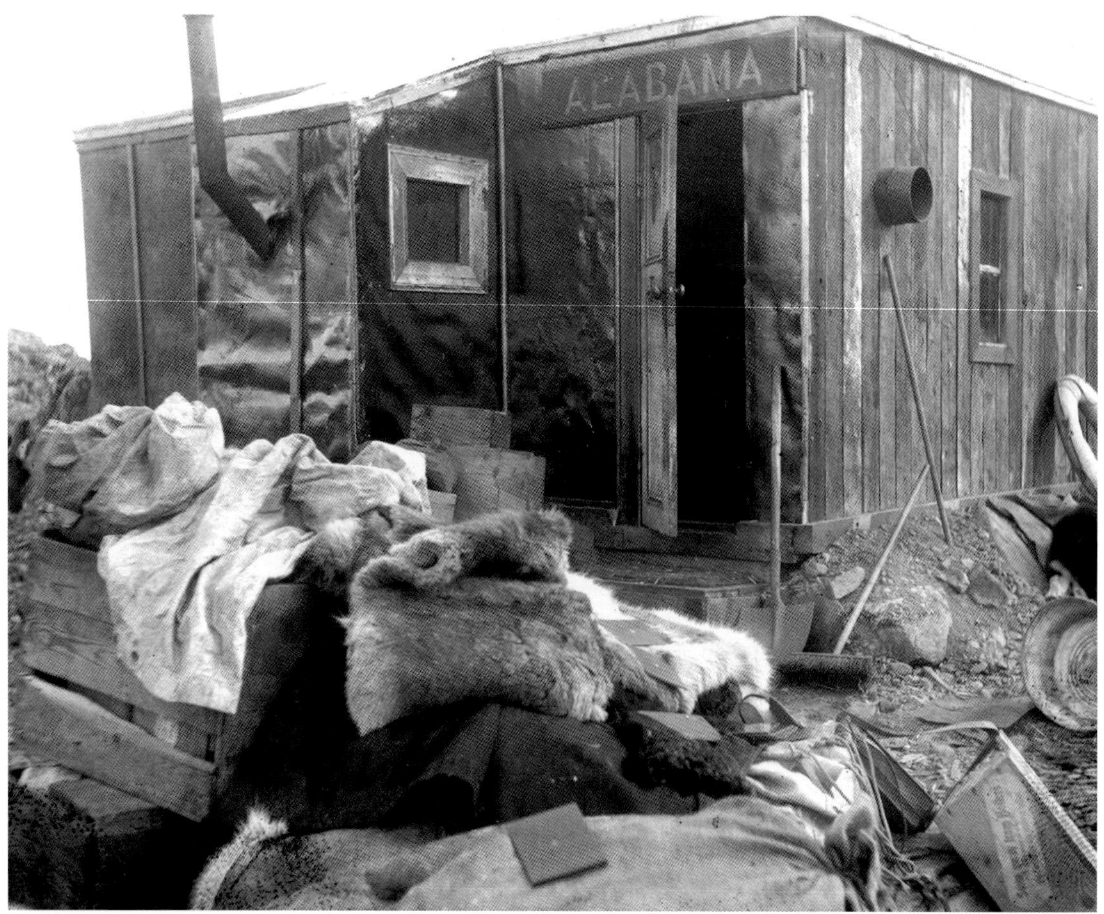

Alabamahuset, as it looked when Ejnar Mikkelsen and Iver Iversen used it a century ago. © Arctic Institute

and they did not reach Shannon until the 25th November 1910, only to discover that "Alabama" in the meantime had been wrecked and their companions had gone home.

During the winter of 1909-10 "Alabama" had sprung a leak and continuous attempts to stop the leak and save the ship proved in vain. The five stranded crew of "Alabama" now prepared themselves for a forced wintering and built a winter house from the wreckage of the ship - Alabamahuset. However, on the 27th July 1910 they were unexpectedly rescued by the Norwegian 7de juni Expedition. Vebjørn Landmark, the leader of the Norwegian expedition, had found a message at the Bass Rock depot left by Lieutenant Laub reporting the loss of "Alabama" and the location of the stranded crew members.

After spending the winter of 1910-11 at Alabamahuset, Mikkelsen and Iversen undertook a journey to Skærfjorden in the spring of 1911, to recover their own diaries and other equipment that they had been forced to abandon during their epic journey down the coast in autumn 1910. On their return to Shannon, they stayed at Alabamahuset until October 1911, then moved first to the Kap Philip Broke depot, and then to Bass Rock (see Bass Rock).

1920-21

While Alabamahuset is best known from its association with Ejnar Mikkelsen and Iver Iversen, the house has occasionally served as a winter base for trappers. After wintering in Germaniahavn during 1919-20, the trappers Hans Nielsen, Ejnar Falsøe and Johan F. Petersen decided to move to the house at Kap Philip Broke.

However, in the summer of 1920, the ship "Dagny" was wrecked in the ice off Shannon while carrying supplies to Danish trapping stations. The crew of "Dagny" all survived, and managed to reach Kap Philip Broke. Since the house was now becoming over-crowded, Johan F. Petersen moved to Alabamahuset where he lived by himself from August 17th 1920 until May 27th 1921. His friend, Marius Madsen, visited him in the spring of 1921, but finding the house too cold Petersen had decided to live in a snow cave nearby. In his cave Petersen had a snow couch covered with bear skins, which was reached by a crawl through an eight metre long passage.

After his return to Denmark in 1921, Johan F. Petersen wrote a report of his observations in North-East Greenland. It was a straight forward description of his fellow trappers and their trapping methods: *"When choosing the men it ought never to be forgotten that the future of the company depends on the abilities of these men. I admit that it is always difficult to hire a qualified Danish team, as Danes as a rule find it hard to adjust to new conditions and the arctic climate in particular. The Dane is generally over-particular, especially when it comes to food."* ... *"Employing sailors at the hunting stations is inadvisable, since as a rule they possess too many bad habits and Bolshevik tendencies that are not easy to remove."* ... *"The trapping methods ordained by Mr. Manniche ought to be abolished immediately, because they are impractical and old-fashioned, and furthermore inflict the most hideous cruelty to animals imaginable. I refer to fox trapping with foot traps. During my years as a trapper I myself have tried many different trapping methods. I have been horseback riding for fox in Argentina, I have seen the primitive fox traps of the Laplanders and the Patagonian Indians, hunted for fox with dogs in Finland and White Russia, and at home I have caught fox with strychnine and now in Greenland with foot traps. I prefer poison. If you only once have had the opportunity to watch a fox take poison, you would never use anything else. The foot trap is the cruellest of all trapping methods, a work of the devil, which it ought to be a crime to use."* ... *"A successful bear hunt can only be undertaken using good and strong dogs. Without a good team of dogs men cannot achieve anything at all".*[44] Johan F. Petersen later settled in Argentina.

Grønlandske Selskab 1983a; Madsen 1963, 1989; Mikkelsen 1914, 1922, 1955; P150.

Recent status

Since the 1920s Alabamahuset has only served as a travellers' hut, and probably only on very few occasions. For several decades it has been uninhabitable. However, the house and its surroundings is one of the most important historical sites in North-East Greenland.[45]

Alabamahuset [518], 2nd August 2004. Alabamahuset is a former Danish station, built in 1910 by the Alabama Expedition. It was used for over-wintering in 1910-11 and 1920-21. No maintenance has been carried out since the days of the Alabama Expedition, and Alabamahuset today is essentially a ruin and uninhabitable. However, the house was originally well built and its surroundings are protected by a thick layer of snow in the winter. Both the interior of the house and the surrounding area still contain many artefacts from the wreck of the "Alabama". © NCN

ANTARCTICHAVN [201]

Wintering party
1930-31: Odd Åmbak, Jonas Karlsbak
1931-32: Odd Åmbak
1932-33: Helge Ingstad, Normann Andersen, Bjørn Western
1933-34: Normann Andersen, Bjørn Western
1934-36: Peder Sulebak
1936-37: Nils Hanken
1937-38: Søren Richter, Ottar Årsvold
1938-46: None
1946-48: Andrew Kringstad
1948-49: Rolf Hauge
1949-50: None
1950-51: Alf Rustøen
1951-52: Mathias Aasen
1952-53: Stephan Meidell
1953-54: Johan Laine
1954-55: Otto Lapstun
1955-56: None
1956-57: Otto Lapstun
1957-58: Ingvar Haga
1958-59: Inge Sørlie and unnamed

In the evening of the 19th August 1899 the vessel "Antarctic" steered into a small bay on the south side of Kong Oscar Fjord. A.G. Nathorst wrote: *"this bay I have named Antarctic Harbour, and we anchored immediately after eight o'clock. One of my main reasons for steering hither was my concern that Per Dusén should not overstrain himself. He did not sleep all night, but has continued his cartography as eager as ever. To stay awake he drank a lot of coffee and smoked cigars almost incessantly"*.[46]

1930-31

On the 11th August 1930 another ship, the "Veslekari", arrived at Antarctichavn. Jonas Karlsbak, then 34 years old and leader of the Norwegian Møre Expedition, wrote: *"Today we came to Antarctichavn, where we went ashore to take a look at the terrain, and we found it suitable for a main station. There are muskoxen and tracks from all sorts of animals. We decided to stop and settle here." ... "We have now started to build a house at full speed, and before we went to bed we had raised the rafters"*.[47]

On the 15th August Jonas Karlsbak and Odd Åmbak were almost done: *"We have now covered the entire house with roofing felt, installed the stove and baked a cake. The stove is working perfectly and the house is fine and good. The main house is 8 x 10 ft and the porch is 10 x 10 ft and with a ridged roof, so this is our largest house in Greenland. Tonight we move into the house"*.[48] The station was officially named "Karlsbak", but is usually referred to as "Antarctichavn". When the station was complete, they went on to build the trappers' huts "Villa" [117], "Jostein" [205] and "Lavøira" [208-1].

The wintering of Karlsbak and Åmbak is well documented. They kept diaries, which was one of their obligations, as the Møre Expedition in 1930 had become an important part of Norwegian commercial activities in North-East Greenland. The expedition had been planned in co-operation with Ishavsrådet and NSIU. The leaders of the two institutions, Gustav Smedal and Adolf Hoel, had also secured a government grant of 10,000 kroner. In return the expedition members had to make commitments:

1. To establish trappers' huts and stations on behalf of the Norwegian government.
2. To formerly "take possession" of the territory needed for trapping surrounding their huts and stations.
3. To pass the rights to use the huts (not the ownership) to the Norwegian state if they were not using the huts themselves.
4. To keep diaries, and on behalf of NSIU make observations of wildlife and trapping conditions.
5. To prepare a written report to NSIU after the expedition.

These obligations later became mandatory for all expeditions supported by the Norwegian government. Neither Karlsbak nor Åmbak intimated in their diaries what they thought of the political aspect of their activities. To them their main purpose was to make a living. However, Karlsbak expressed much respect for Adolf Hoel: *"He is always supportive to us who live in the arctic wilderness, and if it were not for him things would not be so easy, everyone agrees on this"*.[49]

Odd Åmbak may have shared this opinion, but: *"Today Åmbak says that he looked upon politicking scientists and adventurers such as Ingstad, Giæver, Richter and others with scepticism. Even if he and his fellow trappers accepted the occupation then, today he believes that the Norwegians were too undiplomatic in provoking the trial in The Hague. Had the trappers who were up there simply kept their flags hidden and focused on the fox-trapping, the Norwegians would surely have eventually negotiated a solution with the Danes"*.[50]

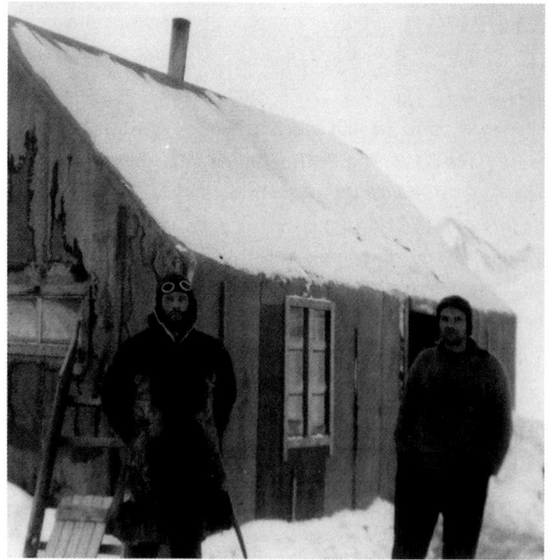

Jonas Karlsbak and Odd Åmbak at Antarctichavn. March 1931. © Jonas Karlsbak / Norwegian Polar Institute

Both Karlsbak and Åmbak were breadwinners and had young children back home in Norway. Karlsbak had been married, but his wife died giving birth to twins. In the summer of 1930 he became engaged to a girl, whom he later married. It was therefore not surprising that on Christmas Eve 1930 he wrote that: *"it is somehow the worst time during a wintering, this Christmas time when you yearn for old Norway – home to your loved ones. He who chooses to live this life ought not to have anyone back home, for thinking about them just makes living here miserable. If I had no one in Norway calling for me, I could live here like a fish in water all my life".* [51]

Åmbak, who at this time was 28 years old, was born on a farm in Åmdalen in Ørsta. His interest in Greenland was aroused as early as 1922 on a trip with the sealer "Kap Flora" to North-East Greenland waters. They came close to the coast, hunting for bear and muskox, and Åmbak was fascinated by the majestic nature and the clear atmosphere. The turning point came in the summer of 1929, when Åmbak was employed on "Veslekari", NSIU's supply ship to North-East Greenland. On the home voyage he listened with fascination to the accounts of the "Hird" trappers, and developed a burning desire to try a wintering. Moreover, he saw it as a possibility to earn enough money to buy his own farm in his native country.

Karlsbak and Åmbak started their trapping at the end of October, but not without drama: *"Åmbak took a trip to Nordnesset to see if the ice was safe. He went through the ice with the entire dog team, but managed to get himself back up onto solid ice. He had to shoot off the sledge trace in order to free the dogs, so that they could get out of the water, as he could not reach the sledge. The sledge was left floating where he went through".*[52] The next day the ice had become strong enough for Åmbak to fetch the sledge.

Their worst problems, however, came from the snow falling in large quantities and not packing properly. Loose snow was always a problem for sledging, and particularly in the Mesters Vig area.

At the end of the trapping season, Karlsbak and Åmbak had caught 50 foxes and four bears, and could hope for even more next year. However, for Karlsbak, the adventure ended here. In July he began to suffer from stomach pains, and when he was examined by the doctor on "Polarbjørn" the verdict was that he was suffering from appendicitis, and must go home.

1931-32

When "Polarbjørn" left Greenland in the summer of 1931, Odd Åmbak and Peder Sulebak were left behind to look after the Antarctichavn and Kap Peterséns territories respectively. During the autumn they helped each other make ready and extend their trapping territories, and in the Antarctichavn area they built two new trappers' huts: "Holstad" [110] and "Flatstranda" [114-1]. At the station they succeeded in growing rhubarb, a nutritious food supplement.

As winter approached they split up. Åmbak stayed at Antarctichavn, while Sulebak went to Kap Peterséns. Åmbak's territory now extended from Lavøira near Mesters Vig to Holstad on the east shore of Fleming Fjord. The catch of fox was even better than in 1930-31. Unfortunately, Åmbak lost a lot of fur, because ravens or foxes ate the catch while it was still in the traps.

From the middle of May until the end of July 1932, Åmbak stayed alone in Kong Oscar Fjord. At the end of the trapping season Sulebak had gone north to Kap Herschell, to participate in the search for the missing Knut Røbek (see Kap Herschell). While Sulebak was away Åmbak had to stay at Kap Peterséns, where they had gathered their entire catch. It was a long and lonely summer for Åmbak, and while he would have liked to visit the Danes at Ella Ø, the valuable fox furs had to be aired and tended, so he only made a single trip lasting a couple of days.

The total catch of the Møre Expedition brought in an income of 48,000 kroner. They had hoped for more, but fur prices had declined. Even so, his share was sufficient for Åmbak to buy the farm he had always wanted.

1932-33

When Helge Marcus Ingstad (1899-2001) arrived at Antarctichavn on 1st of August 1932, he was the right

Antarctichavn, 1st August 1932. © Anders K. Orvin / Norwegian Polar Institute

man in the right place at the right time. The outcome of the court case at The Hague was still unknown, and Norway needed a representative with the right qualifications; these the 32-year-old Ingstad certainly had. In 1922 he had graduated in law. The following two years he worked as a trainee lawyer, with the "sorenskriver" (assistant judge) in Stjør- and Værdal. He then worked as a barrister in Levanger. Having sold his property, he moved to France to study. From here he went to northern Canada, where he lived the life of a trapper among the Indians for four years. His last year was spent alone in a tent on the tundra. He returned to Norway in 1930.

In 1993, Helge Ingstad then aged 93, recalled: *"Shortly after my return from the wilderness of Canada, I became interested in the dispute about Greenland. I believed that the legal basis for the occupation was correct. At short notice, I received a request from the Norwegian government – handed over by Adolf Hoel, the director of Norges Svalbard- og Ishavs-undersøkelser – asking me if I was willing to go to East Greenland in the capacity of Sysselmand of "Eirik Raudes Land". I accepted, and the precondition was that I should lead my own trapping expedition. In 1932 we crossed the ocean, with men, sledge dogs and equipment on board the old polar ship "Polarbjørn"*.[53]

The term "sysselmand" originates from the old, Norse culture. A "syssel" was an administrative district, where the sysselmand was the king's official representative. In Denmark a division into syssels was also used in the Middle Ages, when Jutland was divided in 14 syssels, e.g. Vendsyssel. The Faroe Islands are still divided into seven syssels, and there is still a Norwegian sysselmand on Svalbard.

Ingstad's expedition consisted of himself, the wireless operator Bjørn Western and the trappers Normann Andersen, Arne Jacobsen and Sverre Røstad. Jacobsen and Røstad were to winter at Kap Peterséns.

In the evening of the 2nd August they had finished unloading the equipment at Antarctichavn, and since the fjords towards the south-east were free of ice, Ingstad asked to have material for trappers' huts transported into Fleming Fjord and Nathorst Fjord with the "Polarbjørn". Within 24 hours materials for the last hut were unloaded. It was time for parting, and: *"then we made a bonfire of driftwood, put over the coffee pot and drew on our pipes in silent reflection, our gaze following the "Polarbjørn" as she slowly melted out of sight against the white edge of the ice floes"*.[54]

Ingstad and Normann Andersen started to build their first hut, and: *"in the course of two days, there stood "Kåres-bu" – named after my brother, Kåre – and then we continued our way along the coast in the motor boat. One hut after another shot up behind us"*. [55]

It is still uncertain how many trappers' huts Ingstad's expedition really built during the years 1932-34, but the number is about 11, including the following eight huts in the Antarctichavn territory: "Kåres-bu" [109], "Ingstadheimen" [105], "Siste-huset" [104], "Snevigen" [108], "Ørsted Dal hytten" [111], "Syveren" [112], "Fleming Dal hytten" [101] and "Øyedalshytten" [115].

When the huts were completed, Ingstad and Andersen returned to Antarctichavn. Here the wireless operator Bjørn Western was waiting, and: *"one of the first tasks we had to do was to set up the wireless and put it in working order. The wireless room was built as an annex to the house, flush with the living room, the generator installed and cemented down, and the ninety-foot-high masts erected. While at work upon this, the operator was in a high fever of excitement, for this was his first job after receiving his official licence. And he came through with flying colours, not only then but later on that winter as well, when our aged wireless equipment presented us with some difficult problems; not the least of these being on those occasions when the generator would freeze or the masts were flattened by the wind"*.[56]

One day in the beginning of November Ingstad and Andersen set out with their two dog teams: *"For some months now we would support life in a tent and devote ourselves chiefly to trapping fox"*. [57] As indicated, Ingstad preferred to use a tent or igloo rather than trappers' huts. In this respect he differed from general practice.

The major part of the winter was spent examining the country; and then came the shock. One day Bjørn Western stepped out of his radio

The Helge Ingstad Expedition, en route to Greenland. in 1932. Standing (left): Sverre Røstad and Normann Andersen. Sitting (left): Arne Jakobsen, Helge Ingstad and Bjørn Western. © Anders K. Orvin / Norwegian Polar Institute

room and handed Ingstad a dispatch. It simply read: *"Norway by the decision of the Court at The Hague has lost the Greenland case on all points"*. [58] Plans and dreams fell apart; all at once the Norwegian syssel in "Eirik Raudes Land" was history.

During the summer Ingstad was offered the post of sysselmand of Svalbard. He therefore left Greenland in 1933, while the remaining participants of the expedition stayed on for another year.

In 1961 Ingstad and his wife Anne Stine, an archaeologist, found remnants of a Viking settlement in L'Anse aux Meadows on Newfoundland. They were the first to prove conclusively that the Greenlandic Norsemen had found their way across the Atlantic Ocean to North America, roughly 500 years before Christopher Columbus and John Cabot.

To Helge Ingstad, who became internationally known as a writer and scientist, his single year in North-East Greenland was probably merely an intermezzo. Even so, in 1990 he said to this author: *"I can easily understand your passion for North-East Greenland. Myself, I have never seen a more beautiful arctic country"*.[59] He still insisted that the verdict in The Hague was wrong.

Helge Ingstad died in March 2001 at the age of 101, a life-span involving three centuries!

1933-34

After Ingstad had left Greenland, Normann Andersen and Bjørn Western carried on at Antarctichavn for another winter. They both returned home to Norway in 1934, and later on Western worked at other Norwegian stations in the Arctic, but not in Greenland. Western did travel up to Greenland with "Veslekari" in 1940, but together with the rest of the crew was taken to Iceland with the "Fridtjof Nansen". Normann Andersen, on the other hand, returned to North-East Greenland after the war and stayed seven winters at Moskusheimen.

1934-35

In the middle of August 1934, Peder Sulebak and his nephew Karsten Sulebak arrived in Greenland with the "Selbarden". They settled at Peder Sulebak's old station at Kap Peterséns and spent the autumn there. In November they split up, Karsten remaining at Kap Peterséns, while Peder went south-eastwards to trap from Antarctichavn.

With his four years of experience, the winter was pure routine for Peder Sulebak. The winter passed without any significant events, and in his diary he usually only records the daily weather and that huge masses of snow fell in Kong Oscar Fjord.
The trapping received little mention. Together with

his nephew the total catch was only 35 foxes, a rather disappointing result.

Twice during the season Peder Sulebak sledged to Kap Peterséns to see how Karsten was doing. In May, when the season was over, he left Antarctichavn and spent the summer at Kap Peterséns with his nephew.

1935-36

At the beginning of November 1935 Peder Sulebak returned to Antarctichavn, after the summer at Kap Peterséns, reaching the station just as the last rays of the sun that year reached Antarctichavn: *"It's gone now"*, he wrote in his diary, *"I can only see where it's shining on other places, and that's a comfort too"*.[60]

The winter of 1935-36 as a whole, passed much like the previous winter, except that on the 15th December Peder Sulebak had the misfortune to suffer frostbite in his big toe. A couple of days later he wrote: *"Today I have been sewing myself some new footwear, as I cannot use the boot on my right foot, which has frostbite. I cannot risk freezing it again, so I need some larger and softer footwear, and I will have to finish it tomorrow if I am to reach Kap Peterséns for Christmas as planned"*.[61] In the event, the Christmas visit to Kap Peterséns never happened, for his toe healed slowly and he dared not risk the journey.

As in 1934-35, Peder Sulebak went to Kap Peterséns after the end of the trapping season, arriving on the 13th May 1936. The previous autumn Peder had been forced to leave their motor boat "Triks" in Noret, near Mesters Vig, and in order to salvage it, Peder and Karsten moved to the Lavøira hut at Noret, where they spent the summer.

1936-37

Peder Sulebak left Greenland in 1936, and was replaced by Nils Hanken, who had spent the years of 1934-36 at Kap Herschell. On the 27th August Hanken wrote in his diary: *"Karsten Sulebak arrived with the ship. Our main station will be here in Antarctichavn. Peder Sulebak has left for home. He went along with the "Selbarden". The "Isbjørn" left today immediately after noon. I have purchased Andresen's motor boat, but he was quite arrogant with his demands. I paid 760 kroner for the boat, which he himself had paid 700 kroner for two years ago. But we must have a motor boat. This is a nice place, but the house is a bit dilapidated"*.[62]

Nils Hanken was an energetic man, and with him as the driving force the entire territory was soon well provisioned. It was hard work, and they often got soaked, because the pack ice in 1936 was unusually scattered and provided the boat with little shelter from the heavy swells in the fjords.

Huge masses of snow fell in the area. On the 16th January 1937 Hanken wrote that: *"it is completely unbelievable that the dogs managed to keep up today. They sank in so deeply in the soft snow that only their noses were visible from time to time"*.[63] Day by day Hanken and the dogs had to struggle onward, and with the food beginning to run out he reached Øyedalshytten on the 21st January in the middle of a blizzard: *"I had to let Bamse be the pathfinder. And this time as so often before, he found both the traps and the house. It is good to be inside, but it would have been even better if I had a bit more to eat. Today I have eaten two slices of bread"* ... *"It is not a good hut. It is only 155 x 125 cm in size and made of a few pieces of wood and turf. But the hut has one advantage; it is both tight and warm"*.[64] After some days in the minute hut, held up by bad weather, Hanken finally succeeded in returning to Antarctichavn, and: *"here at the station the snow is flush with the chimney"*.[65]

It seemed as if the snowfall would never end that winter, and in Nathorst Fjord, Hanken wrote, there was: *"so much snow that I believe that the foxes would die from exhaustion trying to reach the traps"*.[66] In spite of the constant problems with the snow, Hanken's catch amounted to 98 foxes and nine polar bears.

Nils Hanken and Karsten Sulebak spent the summer at Antarctichavn, where Hanken ended his diary with the words: *"The 26th August I stood upon "Polarbjørn", watching the beloved places where I have spent these past years disappear from sight. Many memories come to mind and at this moment I understand how deep the roots are that bind me to this country, and the memories of this land in the west will live with me always"*.[67]

Nils Hanken was employed by the Norwegian customs authorities from 1939 until his retirement in 1978. He died in 1989.

1937-38

The archaeologist and trapper Søren Richter had wintered for Arctic Commercial Enterprise in 1929-31 and 1935-36. Furthermore, he had participated in two NSIU summer expeditions working as an archaeologist. Richter was interested in undertaking further excavations in the Kong Oscar Fjord region, and in 1937 Richter equipped a winter expedition together with Peder Sulebak. As they planned to trap live fox, Richter also took along his brother-in-law, Ottar Årsvold, as fox tender. The young man later wrote: *"I have never been so happy in my whole life as when I was told that my brother-in-law had decided to take me with him on a wintering to North-East Greenland. He had probably had some reservations, as I was only 16 years old, but I was big and strong for my age and willing to sacrifice anything to get away from my dreary everyday life and the hated school. We boys at home had read everything Ingstad and Giæver had written about the hard and rough life in the arctic wilderness and had joined them in our imagination".*[68]

When the winter came, Peder Sulebak went to Kap Peterséns, while Richter started trapping in the Antarctichavn territory. Årsvold already had 34 live foxes to take care of: *"They were a nightmare to look after, both day and night, for they were very wild. They never escaped, but they gnawed through the wire netting between the cages and fought so the air was thick with fur. They were also cannibals. In two of the cages the male had broken into the adjacent cage, and next morning had eaten the female, skin and bone. The only thing left was the lower jaw and some pieces of fur." ... "The solitude was terrible at first, and especially the evenings felt very long. But little by little I began to feel comfortable. The wilderness up north has its own atmosphere, which you have to experience to understand. I think I began to understand it bit by bit and the work slowly ran more smoothly. I shall never forget the nights, when the northern lights blazed over the sky in the most spectacular colours, and the full moon was shining like silver over the landscape as if it was in the middle of the day. On such an evening the skiing trip back home from the daily round in the trapping terrain was a celebration, filled with mysterious and beautiful visions".*[69]

In 1992 Ottar Årsvold recollected his wintering as an experience, which: *"has stayed with me all my life, mostly as a cosy and interesting outdoor life, but also tough in the winter darkness".*[70]

It was a year with many lemmings, and when Richter and Årsvold left for home in the summer of 1938, they took back with them an excellent catch of 265 foxes, including 17 live animals. With their departure an era in the history of Antarctichavn ended, as the station was not manned again until 1946.

1946-59

After WWII Hermann Andresen was allotted the Sunnmøre districts, which included Kap Herschell in the north and Antarctichavn, Kap Peterséns and Hamna in the south. Every year until 1959, Andresen's expeditions had trappers wintering; usually two men at Kap Herschell and two men at the stations in Kong Oscar Fjord.

During 1946-59 the stations Hamna, Kap Peterséns and Antarctichavn were alternately used as main and secondary stations. Depending on their trapping results and other factors, the trappers might one year choose to stay mainly at one station, the next year at another. This could change within a single season, so the wintering history of these three stations during 1946-59 is described as a whole in this section, since Antarctichavn was the most frequently used main station.

1946-47

In 1946-47 Hermann Andresen had two men, Andrew Kringstad and Hjalmar Hanson, wintering in Kong Oscar Fjord. Details of their wintering are not available, but on the 25th August 1946, J.G. Jennov on board the "Godthaab" noted: *"At Ella Ø we had two Norwegian trappers in tow. Due to a minor problem with the motor, their motor boat would not start. These two men, Hjalmar Hanson and Andrew Kringstad, had no experience in trapping; they had never even seen a fox trap. They were to stay at Havna".*[71] Kringstad, who was from Ålesund, used Antarctichavn as his station, whereas Hjalmar Hanson used the Hamna station. The latter returned to Norway in 1947 after one wintering.

1947-48

In 1947, Martin Larsen Lie, then 22-years old and from Svindal in Østfold, became Andrew Kringstad's new partner. In 1992, Lie told the author that he and a friend had wanted to go to Greenland in the summer of 1946.[72] They had been inspired by the polar books of Helge Ingstad. They went to see John Giæver,

Visitors to the Ella Ø station. Standing (left): trappers Martin Larsen Lie and Andrew Kringstad. Sitting in the kayaks: two Greenlander assistants of Lauge Koch's Expedition. © Martin Larsen Lie

who hired them at once and promised to write them a letter with further information; but time passed and strangely no letter came. They wondered about this for some time, and in the autumn the friend made a phone call to Giæver to enquire what had happened; Giæver was furious: *"Why the hell didn't you answer my letter?"*

Lie's friend did not understand at all, but then he suddenly realized that his wife must have got hold of Giæver's letter and burned it. It was therefore not until 1947 that Martin Larsen Lie managed to get to Greenland.

During the trapping season Lie and Kringstad stayed at the Hamna and Antarctichavn stations respectively. Of particular incidents, Lie recalled that Kringstad in the autumn had gone through the ice near Antarctichavn twice. The second time, on the 19th October, he wrote in his diary: *"Today I am sledging back to Havna. We had come some distance out on the ice, when Kringstad went straight through. His trousers were stiff, so when he got home, he had to thaw them to get them off. It is mere folly to walk on thin ice".* [73]

Martin Larsen Lie recollected in particular the pleasure of hunting muskox. On one occasion he shot 16; actually he ought not to have shot that many, but there was a large population of musk oxen in 1947-48. On one day they counted more than 400 animals, divided among several herds.

Economically his stay in Greenland was not a success. Back home, as a skilled carpenter, Martin Larsen Lie could earn up to 15,000 kroner in one season: *"They promised us the moon"*,[74] Lie said, but with a catch of 57 foxes he never came close to that amount of money, and therefore returned to Norway in 1948. Andrew Kringstad also returned that summer.

1948-49

In 1948 Rolf Hauge from Drammen and Per Myrvold from Myrvoll both signed a one-year contract with Hermann Andresen. They arrived in Kong Oscar Fjord on 9th August 1948 and stayed at Antarctichavn until 6th November, when Myrvold went to Hamna to trap. The following months were spent in solitude, apart from Christmas, which they spent together at Antarctichavn.

The trapping this year was very disappointing for the 28-year-old Myrvold. The autumn produced only one fox, and after another two weeks of unsuccessful travel he wrote in his diary on the 13th February 1949: *"It doesn't look good. I have been over the entire territory except for the last piece on Traill Ø, and seen tracks from only two foxes. I have replaced the bait on almost all the traps. Soon four months of the trapping season will have passed and so far I have managed to equal Hansen. The difference is however, that I have not myself caught the one I've got. It is time to catch fox if there ever was a fox in Greenland. If only the going would improve, I will climb the heights to look for tracks. I shan't travel the outer territory until March. It is just a waste of time".*[75]

It was a hope in vain. On the 30th April, Myrvold could count his catch as three foxes and one seal.

In the beginning of May 1949, Rolf Hauge moved to Kap Herschell, where he was to stay for the following year.

1949-50

Per Myrvold wintered alone in the Kong Oscar Fjord territory in 1949-50, for: *"the trapper who was supposed to stay at Antarctichavn alone, has gone to the Danish doctor in Mestersvig, and wants to go home because of anxiety and stress".*[76]

Apart from the visit of the "Quest" in August, and rare contacts with the Danes from Ella Ø, Per Myrvold spent the entire summer of 1949 in solitude. When the trapping season was finally about to begin, he developed stomach pains, and fearing it might be something serious he left his territory and went to Myggbukta. After New Year, he returned to Kong Oscar Fjord where he spent the following months trapping from Hamna and Antarctichavn in turn. The catch was about 20 foxes, a little more than the previous year. In general, trapping was considerably hindered by huge amounts of snow.

On the 13th February Myrvold unexpectedly had a visit from a Greenlander: *"Elias Arke arrived on skis from Havna. He had had a terrible trip from Ella Ø. As far as I could understand, Jon Brønlund has died. Elias was very poorly equipped and arrived wearing a couple of old boots and mittens which I had thrown away last year".*[77]

The following day Per Myrvold wrote down what Elias Arke had told him about his dreadful journey from Ella Ø: *"He had left Ella Ø on 27th January without sleeping bag or food and took four days to reach Kap Petersèns. The snow was deep all the way, and it was snowing and foggy. On the second day he left his rifle behind. Then he abandoned one of his ski poles because his hand was so frostbitten he couldn't use it. On the way he had dug himself into a snowdrift and rested for about half an hour. Then up and off again, to get a little warmth into his body. His trousers and sweater were frozen with ice. He had only some small ski boots on his feet, with the result that he developed bad frostbite. Jon Brønlund was together with Elias for three days, but couldn't manage any more, and remained on Kong Oscar Fjord for ever. He was only 18 years old, and of mixed Greenlandic-European origin.*

When the hunger and the thirst became too much, Elias had eaten snow. On the fourth day he knew that he was in the vicinity of Kap Peterséns, but had almost given up finding it because of the weather. Nevertheless, he found the station and remained there for nine days so his leg could improve a bit. He had to keep the fire going, so he probably did not get much sleep there either".[78]

Elias Arke stayed with Myrvold for about two weeks, until he was picked up by some relatives from Scoresbysund/Ittoqqortoormiit. A search was made for the body of Jon (or Jørgen) Brønlund, but he was never found. He is said to have been related to the Jørgen Brønlund who died during the Danmark Expedition 1906-08.

After a trip north in May to Myggbukta, Per Myrvold spent the 1950 summer alone again. "Polarbjørn" arrived on 9th August, and the following day the journey home began: *"having said goodbye to the dogs, six faithful, hard workers through two arctic winters".*[79]

1950-51

Halvor Bjørdal from Stranda and Alf Rustøen from Olden took over the Kong Oscar Fjord terrain after Per Myrvold. In the summer of 1950 they built "Kongeborgen" [224-2] as a replacement for the old Kongeborg hytte [224-1].

In the trapping season Bjørdal primarily used Hamna as his base, while the 21-year-old Rustøen used Antarctichavn. Their total catch numbered 63 foxes. In the summer of 1951 they changed employer, and worked for Arctic Commercial Enterprise. Bjørdal moved to the Kap Humboldt station, while Rustøen trapped from Myggbukta. Both went home in 1952.

1951-52

Mathias Aasen from Ålesund was 32-years old when he and another trapper, Bakke (first name unknown) took over the Kong Oscar Fjord territory. They mainly used Antarctichavn as their base, but Bakke also used Kap Peterséns in the trapping season. Both wintered for just one year. Aasen told the author in 1993 that it was a very disappointing season, as they had a lot of snow that winter and only caught seven or eight foxes. Fortunately the journey from and to Ålesund was free of charge, and: *"it was actually a nice trip with "Polarbjørn" and fortunately I was not seasick".*[80]

1952-53

In 1952 Stephan Meidell and Lars Myhrvold took over the Kong Oscar Fjord territory. Myhrvold, who came directly from UN service in Korea, had an artificial foot. It was not intended that he should over-winter, but he took the place of another trapper who changed his mind. In any case, Myhrvold was a: *"sporty and able man"*,[81] so that you hardly noticed his handicap.

He did not refrain from using his disability for a good joke. In 1992 Lauritz Storholt recalled: *"On the ship during our journey to Greenland there was a young lad of 15-16 years. His uncle was Captain Marø, and the boy had been allowed to come along as cabin boy. And we had a lot of fun with each other, you know. And, well, it was probably not very nice, but at one time when Lars Myhrvold was sitting on the deck, he asked the cabin boy: "Do you have a nail and a hammer?" – Yes, the cabin boy answers, I can find that for you. A moment later the cabin boy returned with nail and hammer... And then Myhrvold pulls up one trouser leg, and then the other trouser leg, places the nail upon his foot and hit it with the hammer ... At this point the cabin boy fainted".*[82]

In the summer Meidell and Myhrvold stayed at Antarctichavn, but when the trapping season started, Myhrvold moved to Kap Peterséns.

Here Myhrvold had a serious accident during the winter. It was serious enough, yet it resulted also in another good story. In 1991 Otto Lapstun remembered this: *"Myhrvold had a wooden leg, you know, and a wooden foot, assembled with a bolt in the ankle. One day, while Myhrvold was staying at Kap Peterséns, he splintered his wooden foot. So he took his dog sledge and drove to Mestersvig. The Danes knew Myhrvold, of course, but they had no idea that he had a wooden foot. When they saw that he appeared to have only one leg, they cried out: "Mercy, we must get you to the doctor as quickly as possible!" – "Oh no", Myhrvold answered, "but I would like to talk to a carpenter!" – – – And the following day Old Jakob, the master carpenter, made a very nice wooden foot for Myhrvold".*[83]

Returning to Kap Peterséns on the 23rd February 1953, Myhrvold had the company of the Danish trapper Hans Frederiksen, but once again Myhrvold was unlucky. He: *"developed frostbite in one leg yesterday, and it doesn't look good and since he has only one leg I cannot leave him"*, Frederiksen wrote in his diary.[84] However, in the event Myhrvold's frostbite was not so bad and Frederiksen was able to continue his own journey the next day.

1953-54

In 1953 Johan Laine, who had wintered at Kap Herschell in 1948-50, took over the territory together with a new trapper, Fjøsne (first name unknown). Johan Laine was of Finnish descent, according to Sverre Storholt, and stayed at Antarctichavn, while Fjøsne used Kap Peterséns as his base station. In 1992 Fredrik Sæterdal told the author that Fjøsne abandoned the station in the middle of the season, and went to Mestersvig to work in the mine.[85]

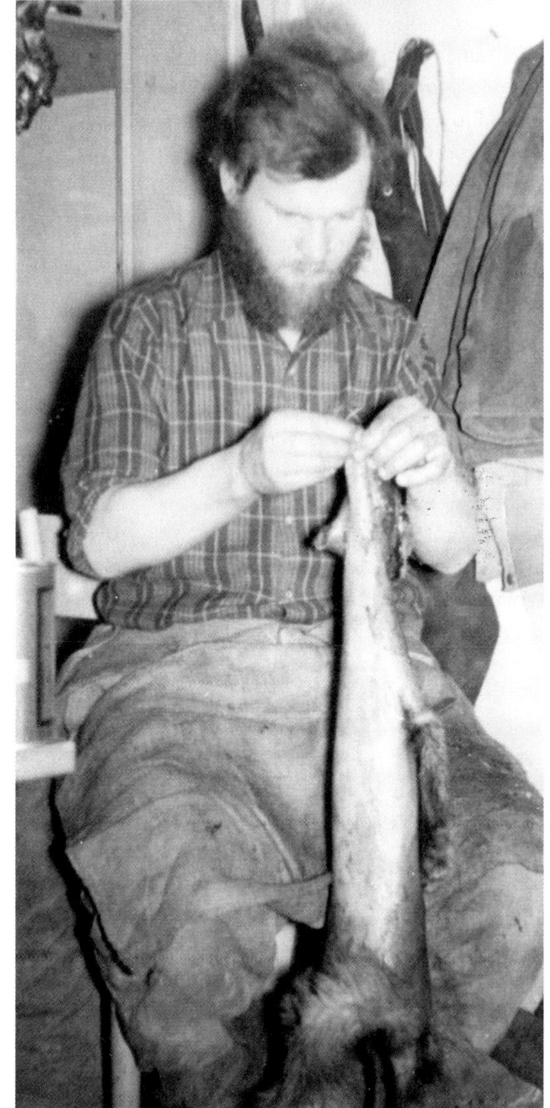

Trapper Otto Lapstun skinning a blue fox. © Otto Lapstun

1954-57

In 1954 Otto Lapstun returned to Greenland. He had previously worked as a trapper in 1952-53 at Kap Herschell. Now he had the entire Kong Oscar Fjord territory to himself. The first year he trapped from Antarctichavn, and in 1955-56 used the Kap Peterséns terrain. In 1956-57 he had intended to stay at Antarctichavn again, but broke his contract and went to work in the lead mine at Mestersvig instead.[86]

In the autumn of 1953 heavy swells had destroyed the trappers' hut Flatstranda [114-1], and in 1954 Lapstun moved the old Lavøira hut [208-1] from Hamna to Fleming Fjord, where it became known under the name "Lapstun-hytten" [114-2]. The following year another hut, Kåres-bu [109], was moved from Nathorst Fjord to Fleming Fjord; see "Fleming Fjord Nord" [114-3].

In the 1954-55 season, Lapstun caught 55 foxes and the following season about 35, but prices were low and there was little reward for his efforts. As mentioned above, Lapstun gave up trapping in the autumn of 1956, and "deserted" to work in the lead mine at Mestersvig. For Lapstun this was the first of several periods working for Nordisk Mineselskab A/S. Although Lapstun was elsewhere for several years, he spent a major part of the period between 1974 and 1987 in North-East Greenland. At first he wintered for several seasons at Nyhavn, but later on went to Greenland mostly during the summer period. He retired from his Greenland journeys in 1987, but has still many happy memories from these years.

1957-58

In the winter of 1957-58 Hermann Andresen had only one trapper, Ingvar Haga, wintering in Greenland. His three other trappers dropped out: one proved unfit for wintering and had to be sent home, while the two others immediately broke their contracts with Andresen and went to work at the lead mine in Mestersvig.

Ingvar Haga, who was to winter at Antarctichavn, was forced to give up in the summer of 1956 due to illness, and had to go back to Norway. In 1957 it went wrong again: *"In the autumn, after having caught 14 foxes, he fell ill. He managed to reach Mestersvig in a miserable condition. The Danes took care of him and arranged to send him to Iceland on an aeroplane. It turned out that Haga had a brain haemorrhage".*[87]

1958-59

"Anyone who has wintered in Greenland, leaves half of his heart there", Inge Sørlie said in 1992.[88] He grew up near Snåsa in Nord-Trøndelag and was to be the

The fall-trap or folding-trap was the most common trapping tool used during the trapper era in North-East Greenland. © Hans Madsen

last trapper in the Kong Oscar Fjord terrain. The desire to go to Greenland arose when by chance he learnt that they were looking for trappers: *"It was a winter with few foxes, but it was a magnificent experience"*, Sørlie recalled. His main station was Antarctichavn, but he also used Kap Peterséns, which he extended in the summer of 1958 with an annex. Originally, there were two men at Antarctichavn, Sørlie told me in 1993, but at Christmas time his partner (Sørlie could not remember his name) developed frostbite in his foot and had to be evacuated by plane via Mestersvig. When the Norwegian trapping finally closed down in 1959, Sørlie began to work for Nordisk Mineselskab A/S, and he also took part in the molybdenum prospecting at Malmbjerg. He returned to Norway in 1960 and has been a farmer ever since.

Giæver 1939; Orvin 1934; N034; N144; P132; R119.

Recent status

After the end of the trapper era, Antarctichavn station was used from time to time by the Sirius Dog Sledge Patrol. However, both use and maintenance was minimal, and by the 1970s the station had become more or less unusable.

In the summer of 2001 Antarctichavn was extensively renovated by Nanok. However, just a few months later the station was completely destroyed by an avalanche. In December 2001, the Kong Oscar Fjord region experienced a strong Foehn storm that raised temperatures to plus 8-9 degrees C. It is presumed that this relative heat led to the snow melting to form a thick layer of ice, on which subsequent snow layers could slide on all too well. No one knows exactly when the avalanche occurred, but in April 2002 the Antarctichavn station was reported destroyed by a passing Sirius patrol team.[89]

Antarctichavn visited by a Sirius dog-sledge patrol team on 25th March 1979. At this time, the house was already in poor condition. © Peter Schmidt Mikkelsen

Antarctichavn [201] was a Norwegian trappers' station built in 1930 for the Møre Expedition. It was used as a trappers' station until 1959, and subsequently as a travellers' hut until about the beginning af the 1970s. In 2001, it was completely renovated by Nanok, but destroyed by an avalanche the following winter.
(Left) Antarctichavn in the summer of 2001 after the station had been restored by Nanok. Only the side annex remained to be completed. August 2001. © NCN

(Right) The new "Antarctichavn" name plate placed on the house in 2001, and saved from the avalanche wreckage by Nanok in 2002, when a memorial plaque to Helge Ingstad was added. The text on the plaque reads (in Norwegian and English): IN MEMORY OF: This trapper station built by the Møre Expedition in 1930 was the residence of the Norwegian Sysselmann (Governor) in "Eirik the Red's Land" HELGE INGSTAD 1899-2001 from 01.08.32 to 05.04.33 when the Tribunal in Hague established that the Norwegian occupation of this part of North-East Greenland 71°30' – 75°40' was illegal and void. Norwegian Polar Club 2002" The memorial plaque was designed by and put up at the request of Ivar Ytreland, a lifelong friend of Helge Ingstad. Antarctichavn, 5th August 2004. © NCN

(Above) Antarctichavn after the avalanche that destroyed the station during the winter of 2001-02. In the background, close to the shore, the square contour of the original roof can be seen. 30th July 2002. © NCN

BASS ROCK
[461]

Wintering party
1911-12: Ejnar Mikkelsen, Iver P. Iversen
1920-21: Ferdinand Hansen, M.J. Larsen, Anker Hansen, N.J. Sørensen
1921-22: None
1922-23: Konrad Larsen, Svend Hansen
1923-24: Kristen Larsen

East of Lille Pendulum, at the margin of the Greenland Sea, is a small rocky island. In 1823 Captain Douglas Clavering named the island Bass Rock, because of its resemblance to Bass Rock in the Firth of Forth in Scotland (a steep-sided island that during the 17th century had been both a fortress and prison). This small island, barely one km^2 in area, was well known amongst the early whalers and sealers operating in the Greenland Sea. It was a prominent landmark, and is particularly well known for the two octagonal depot houses erected for the Baldwin-Ziegler Expedition in 1901.

1901
In 1898, the journalist Walter Wellman led an American expedition to attempt to reach the North Pole starting from Franz Joseph Land. However, the expedition had to give up and return.

Evelyn Baldwin, the second in command on Wellman's expedition, did not want to abandon the idea of reaching the Pole, and contacted William Ziegler, a German immigrant, who had become a multi-millionaire from selling baking powder with the catchy name: Royal Baking Powder.[90] Hoping to have his name immortalized in connection with the conquest of the North Pole, Ziegler offered to finance Baldwin's expedition. As a consequence, Baldwin in 1901 travelled to Franz Joseph Land with the "America". The same summer the expedition established two large depots in North-East Greenland, one at Kap Philip Broke and the other at Bass Rock, using the "Belgica".[91] Abundant provisions and equipment were placed in specially built houses at the depots, in case the Baldwin expedition returned from the North Pole via the east coast of Greenland.

Baldwin did not reach the North Pole, despite the immense amounts of money Ziegler invested in the project. Baldwin turned out to be a total disaster as an expedition leader, and the project ended with a lawsuit between him and Ziegler, who died in 1905 a disappointed man.[92] Thus, the Baldwin-Ziegler Expedition never used its depots and depot-houses in North-East Greenland. Ten years later, these depots proved to be of vital importance to the survival of the polar explorer Ejnar Mikkelsen and his companion Iver Iversen, when the "Alabama" sank in winter harbour on Shannon. Strangely enough, Ejnar Mikkelsen had also participated in Baldwin's unsuccessful expedition to Franz Joseph Land.

1911
In November 1910, Ejnar Mikkelsen and Iver Iversen had returned to Shannon after a dramatic journey from Danmark Fjord. They stayed for a year at

Bass Rock depot houses. About 1920. © Jonna Jensen

Alabamahuset, where they waited in vain for rescue, and then moved down to the Bass Rock depot where they hoped their chances of rescue would be better. They arrived at Bass Rock on the 21st November 1911, and discovered they had been desperately close to rescue. Iversen wrote: *"We found here a letter from the sealer "Laura", dated the 23rd July 1911. I cannot deny that it was hard blow, which at the same time diminished the joy of getting here. It could drive you mad to know that a rescue ship had been so close, and yet so far away. The houses here were in a mess, filled with boxes so that you could hardly enter the door. After a few hours work, we managed to move enough boxes outside so that there was just enough room for us. The stove did not work either; it had no pipe, but we found some next door. The stove had been placed on a box about 2 feet above the floor by the Danmark Expedition, because it lacked a pipe section. Tonight we will use it – as things are we have no alternative. We found some fruit preserves, so tonight feasted on pears, cherries and plums. Unfortunately many of the cans are unusable, most likely destroyed by damp".*[93]

It was not until the 18th July 1912 that the two men were rescued from Bass Rock by the Norwegian sealer "Sjøblomsten" of Ålesund. Eight years later, the Bass Rock houses were once again to serve as winter quarters for shipwrecked mariners.

1920-21

In August 1920 the seven shipwrecked men from the "Dagny" managed to travel about 30 nautical miles across the pack ice to reach the Baldwin-Ziegler depot at Kap Philip Broke. The space here became so crowded, that four men chose to move to the Bass Rock depot. The trapper Hans Nielsen wrote: *"On September 6th the ice conditions were sufficiently good that Captain Hansen, first mate Larsen, sailor Hansen and trapper Sørensen were able to depart for Bass Rock, where they planned to winter in the boat they had carried with them from "Dagny". On the 10th we rowed over to them with various items which we knew they needed badly, including a drum of kerosene. However, they had found the ice floe on which they camped when "Dagny" was crushed, and managed to save almost everything, so they had no need of our humble assistance".*[94]

By unbelievable fortune, the ice floe on which they had left the supplies rescued from "Dagny" one day came drifting by Bass Rock. With these supplies they were now able to face the winter at the Bass Rock with confidence. The wintering passed without any significant accidents.

On the 5th May 1921, they had unexpected visitors. The trappers Christian Ahlstrand and Ove Haaber Nielsen stepped through the door. A week earlier they had reached Germaniahavn from Dove Bugt. They knew nothing about the wreck of the "Dagny", and had only come to fetch a stove. On the other hand, the crew from "Dagny", who were actually on their way to visit the trappers in Dove Bugt when they were wrecked, had had no news from Dove Bugt, so now all uncertainties were cleared up.

In the middle of July 1921, the relief ship "Teddy" under the command of Gustav Thostrup arrived, and the involuntary wintering of the crew of "Dagny" came to an end.

1922-23

The summer of 1922 was a difficult year with respect to pack ice conditions. "Teddy" did not succeed in penetrating the pack ice at the first attempt, and had to return to Akureyri in Iceland to refuel. At the second attempt "Teddy" reached the coast, but the crankshaft broke and the damage took almost a month to repair. The planned visit to the northern Danish trapping stations in Dove Bugt had to be abandoned, and an attempt to reach them by motor boat also failed. The Germaniahavn station was becoming crowded, as seven men had "stranded" there. When the ice at last was safe, on the 31st October, the trappers Konrad Larsen and Svend Hansen therefore moved to Bass Rock using three dog sledges. Apart from a visit to Germaniahavn in January, the two men stayed at Bass Rock until the beginning of April 1923. Their catch was three bears and seven foxes.

1923-24

In the summer of 1923, "Teddy" once again had a problematic voyage, and shipmaster Henning Bistrup decided to supply all the stations using a motor boat. The trappers Viktor H. Stjernebo and Kristen Larsen found themselves almost constantly travelling from

The motor boat "Carl", c. 1923 © Jonna Jensen

On 8th August 1945, the 25th anniversary of the wreck of the "Dagny", survivors of the 1920-21 wintering met together. From left: Christian Ahlstrand, Broer Sandberg, M.J. Larsen, Ejnar Falsøe and Ferdinand Hansen. © Jonna Jensen

station to station using the motor boat "Carl". By the 1st September 1923 they had completed their supply transports, but during their return from Kap Philip Broke to their station at Germaniahavn, ice blocked the way and they were forced to seek shelter at the Bass Rock depot. Just after they arrived, a severe on-shore storm set in that lasted for a week. When the wind finally dropped, the small bay at the depot was completely blocked by a massive wall of ice. Further navigation was out of the question, and "Carl" was pulled ashore. This legendary motor boat, which had never given the company any problems, had now reached its last resting place; "Carl" is still there. Stjernebo and Larsen could not escape from Bass Rock until the 3rd October, when they walked across the ice to Germaniahavn, where their friend Viggo S. Lund was anxiously waiting for them.[95] Kristen Larsen had, however, decided to stay for the winter at Bass Rock, and returned there the next day taking with him a notebook and pencil, half a box of cigars and his rifle with cartridges. He arranged with Stjernebo and Lund that they should fetch him for Christmas.

When Christmas arrived, Kristen Larsen expected his friends to turn up, but nobody came and he spent Christmas alone: *"Christmas Eve I had peas and pork, which is the finest canned food I have, so this was my Christmas dinner. I sang a couple of hymns, and before I go to sleep I will say my evening prayers as usual as my dear mother taught me when I was a little boy. I hope that the good God will listen to me as well here, in my small humble house at Bass Rock, just as if I had been at home in Denmark".*[96]

As time went by the food and supplies available at Bass Rock steadily decreased, but finally on the 7th March 1924 Stjernebo and Lund arrived. Open water in Pendulumstrædet had hindered an earlier arrival. A few days later they all went back together to Germaniahavn and Larsen wrote: *"I have been in clover; my two friends are going out of their way to make me feel comfortable. I have checked all my gear, and tonight I have washed myself all over and put on some clean underwear and a shirt, and tonight I can sleep in a proper bunk".*[97]

During a 33 day long sledge journey later in the spring of 1924, Kristen Larsen, together with Viktor Stjernebo and Konrad Larsen from Sandodden, finally succeeded in fetching the fox furs they had left behind in April 1921 at Villaen in Danmark Havn. On this journey they also went to Hvalrosodden. The re-visit to the small living room made a deep impression on Kristen Larsen. Here his dear friend August Frederik Nielsen had died in great pain three years earlier: *"I believe that at such a moment, up here in the lonely and magnificent nature of North-East Greenland, the human mind is touched in a way that is rarely or perhaps never touched back home in civilization".*[98]

Edinburgh New Philosophical Journey 1830; Fiala 1907; Lauritsen 1984; Madsen 1963, 1989; Mikkelsen 1922, 1953, 1955; Ø046.

Recent status

The depot houses at Bass Rock have rarely been used since the 1920s. In 1930 ownership of the Bass Rock houses passed from American hands to the Norwegian state.[99] In 1969, all Norwegian stations and huts in North-East Greenland, including those at Bass Rock, were sold to Denmark.

While Bass Rock was a well-known landmark and a suitable site for a depot serving the pioneer arctic expeditions, it was less useful as a base station for trappers, or stranded mariners forced to winter in North-East Greenland. However, the two now more than one hundred years old house ruins, together with the legendary motor boat "Carl", make this an exceptional historic site in North-East Greenland.

Bass Rock [461], 23rd July 2004. Bass Rock is a former American travellers' station built 1901 for the Baldwin-Ziegler Expedition. In 1911-12 it was used for wintering by the Alabama Expedition and in 1920-24 by Danish trappers from the East Greenland Company. Bass Rock is one of the utmost desolate and barren places in North-East Greenland. Situated right next to the open waters of the North Atlantic Ocean the place is often covered with heavy fog and moist air. The two huts together with the legendary motor boat "Carl" today represent an exceptional historic site in North-East Greenland. © NCN

BESSEL FJORD
[601-2]

Wintering party
1932-33: Evald Rasmussen, Arne Philbert

1932-33
In the summer of 1932 the region between Wollaston Forland and Bessel Fjord – named after the German astronomer Franz Friedrich Wilhelm Bessel (1784-1846) – was practically invaded by Norwegian trapping companies. The Danish company Nanok, which had previously been alone in the area, decided to establish a new station at the entrance of Trumsdalen, where a "dummy hut", Bessel Fjord hytten [601-1], had been placed in 1931 to indicate their intentions. [100]

The material for the Bessel Fjord station was landed from "Gustav Holm" on the 13th August 1932: *"At 1.50 a.m. the ship cast anchor at the north side of Bessel Fjord off the locality where a trappers' station was to be erected, and the unloading of the goods for the station was immediately commenced. It was completed by 10.00 a.m., and at 11.05 a.m. the ship left Bessel Fjord to return southwards".* [101]

The operation of the station was entrusted to the Nanok trappers Evald Rasmussen and Arne Philbert, both then 25-years old. The first named, with the nickname "Evaldus", was already an experienced trapper. In 1924 he had participated in Ejnar Mikkelsen's founding of the Ittoqqortoormiit / Scoresbysund settlement. In 1929, he was contacted by J.G. Jennov, who offered him a job with the newly started Nanok trapping company. Rasmussen had accepted the offer, and 1932 was his third year with the company.

From left: Trappers Evald Rasmussen, Finn Kristoffersen and Arne Philbert at Hochstetter c. 1932. © Arne Philbert

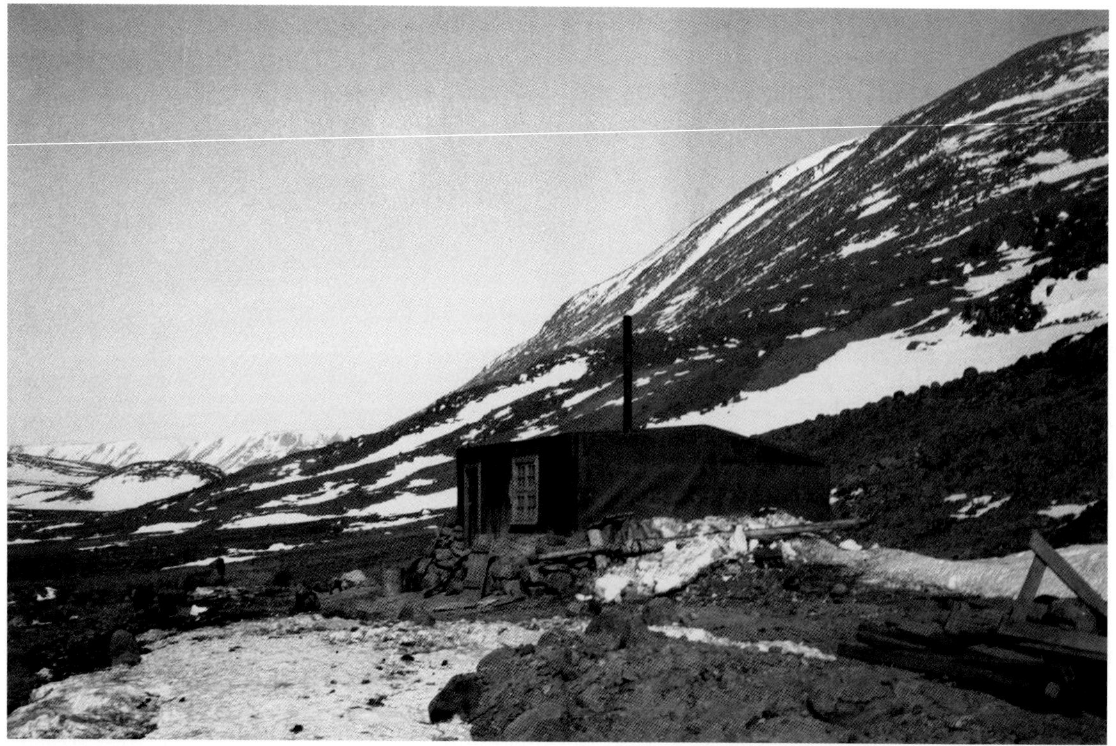

Bessel Fjord, 1932. © Arne Philbert

Arne Philbert, on the other hand, was a newcomer, and for him the contract with Nanok was the answer to a dream which went back to his childhood years on the Danish island of Fyn. As a young boy he had read everything there was about the Arctic, and in particular the books of Fridtjof Nansen.

On the 27th August 1932, Rasmussen and Philbert left the Hochstetter station to sail to Bessel Fjord: *"Building the station was done quickly"* Arne Philbert recalled in 1993, *"for Evaldus was a very skilled carpenter"*. [102]

Philbert also related that they had unfortunately received far too little building materials, as they also had to build trappers' huts, which were important to mark their territory. When the station was in order, they gathered what was left of the timbers, and there was just sufficient wood for a single hut, "Mundingshytten" [537-1], built on the south side of Bessel Fjord. However, there was almost nothing left with which to make the fox traps.

"We had good relationships with the Norwegians, especially our neighbours John Johnsen and Ole Sivertsen at Olestua. We sometimes visited each other, went muskox hunting together, and borrowed from each other when needed. Sivertsen was a heck of a trapper – a genuine trapper". Philbert recalled. But he also remembered that there were a few Norwegians who, due to the dispute over "Eirik Raudes Land", were hostile towards the Danes.

As a consequence of the expansion of Norwegian trapping, the territory available to the Danish trappers was very cramped. The Norwegians from Olestua trapped in Bessel Fjord, and Rasmussen and Philbert therefore placed their traps along the outer coast down to Kap Oswald Heer; however, the Norwegians at Ottostrand, Otto Johnsen and Ove Høeg, also trapped in this area. Hence, Philbert went out to Shannon in the winter, where he established himself at Kap David Gray: *"We caught about 30 foxes and a couple of bears that winter"*, he recalled.[103]

Some time in the spring of 1933, Philbert and Henning Nyholm-Poulsen from Hochstetter were given an interesting assignment, namely to save one of the old horse sledges used by J.P. Koch and Alfred Wegener during the Danish Expedition to Dronning Louise Land in 1913. The two sledges had been abandoned on the ice about 10 to 15 km from the front of Storstrømmen glacier. From here, the sledges had been carried slowly towards the front of the glacier, and when the glacier front calved the sledges stayed on the now detached floating ice floe without falling off. The ice floe with the sledges then drifted about 100 km eastwards through Dove Bugt towards Kap Peschel, where Nyholm-Poulsen found the sledges. Philbert and Nyholm-Poulsen succeeded in dragging one of the sledges down from the ice floe, and placed it on a small island near Kap Peschel, now known as "Slædeøen", where it still can be seen.[104]

In the summer of 1933, Philbert moved to the Hochstetter station, while Rasmussen went home to Denmark.

Hvidberg 1932; Koch 1913; Lauritsen 1984; Nyholm-Poulsen 1985.

Recent status

Bessel Fjord was not manned after 1932-33. It turned out to be a miserable place to stay in the winter, exposed to the cold northerly and often storm-force winds blowing out of Trumsdalen. Despite this, the Bessel Fjord station is still standing, although it has been unusable for many years.

Bessel Fjord station [601-2], 23rd August 2005. © NCN

Bessel Fjord [601-2], 23rd August 2005. Bessel Fjord is a Danish trappers' station built for Nanok in 1932. It is located at an exposed site on the east side of the entrance to Trumsdalen, on the south coast of Ad.S. Jensen Land. Bessel Fjord was only used as a trappers' station from 1932-33. Up to about the 1960s it had occasionally been used as a travellers' hut. (Top) The hut still contains a variety of old equipment. (Page 87) View towards Trums Ø (at the right side of the photograph) with the unmistakeable conical profile of Haystack visible c. 40 km to the south (just above the left edge of the station). © NCN

BORGANES
[421-1]

Wintering party

1908-09: Adolf Brandal, Johannes Dreyer Larsen, Mathias Lorentsen Hjellvold

On the 8th August 1823, when Captain Douglas Clavering placed his foot on Greenland soil for the first time, he was far from enthusiastic: *"I went ashore at night to examine the land. Never was a more desolate spot seen; in many places not a vestige of vegetation." ... "no reindeer, no birds, or whales" ... "Spitsbergen was, on the whole, a paradise compared to this place".*[105] Clavering named the place Cape (Kap) Borlase Warren after Sir John Borlase Warren (1753-1822), who in 1780 had married Caroline, a daughter of Sir John Clavering and a relative of Douglas Clavering.

1908-09

On a damp foggy morning in August 1908, seven young Norwegians were standing on the same godforsaken desolate spot. They made up the Floren Expedition, the first trapping expedition to winter in North-East Greenland. Three of the men probably scanned the surrounding area extra thoroughly, as they were going to winter at Kap Borlase Warren. These were Mathias Lorentsen Hjellvold 28-years old from Lofoten, Johannes Dreyer Larsen 27-years old from Helgeland, and Adolf Brandal 29-years old from Brandal. The latter wrote: *"Having finished our coffee and breakfast, we went ahead looking for a convenient location to build our house. On a slope, turning west close to a boulder, there was an eskimo earth-house. We found the place well situated, especially as there was a small pond between the sea and the house. We dug out the centre of the earth house, finding lots of animal bones. Our dugout is 8 feet wide and 14 feet long. Mathias and I started building the walls; the others dug out the earth house and quarried rocks from the piles of boulders which stood 6 feet from the place".*[106]

After a couple of weeks, their dug out, to which they gave the name "Borganes", was ready. Borganes is a place name from the Icelandic sagas. It was equipped with a coal oven, a couple of berths and a table - a primitive, yet functional home.

August was waning and September brought frosts both day and night. Brandal, Larsen, Hjellvold and their only dog, Viggo, were comfortable enough in

Borganes, 1937. © Will C. Knutsen

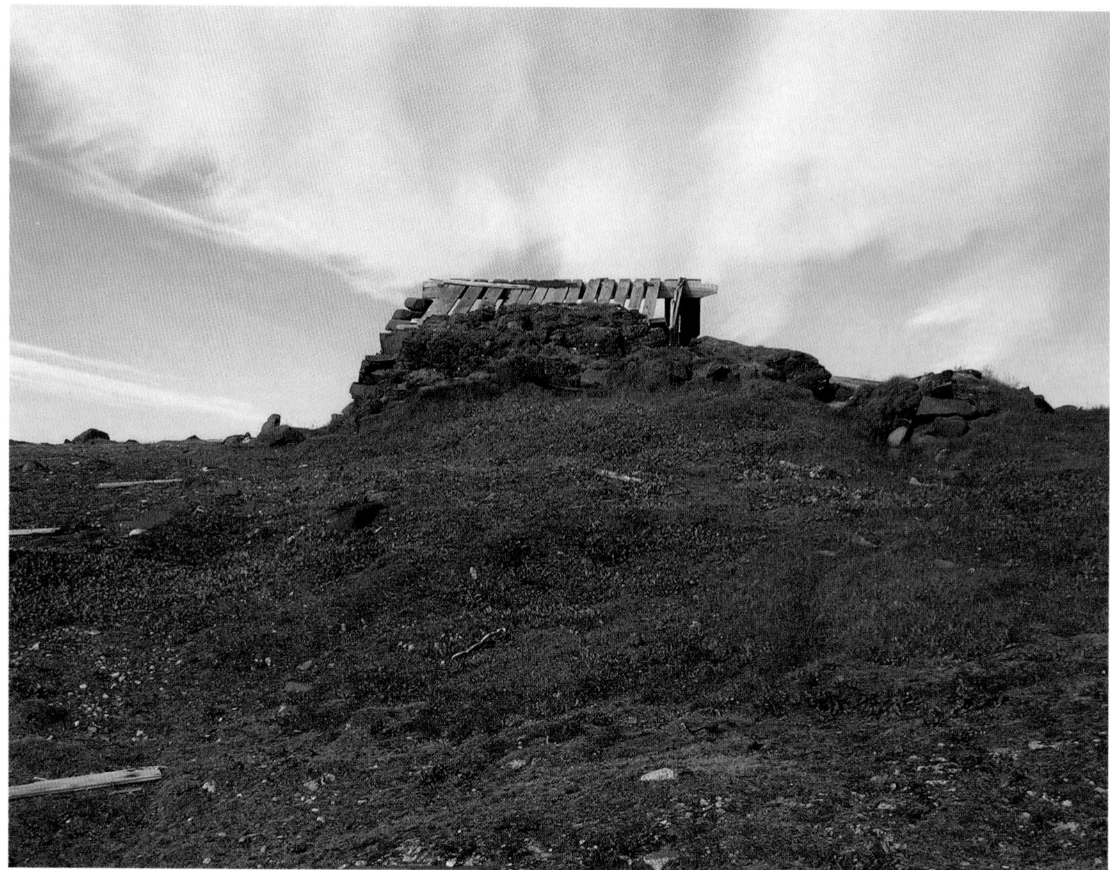

Borganes [421-1], 6th August 2004. © NCN

Borganes. They spent the autumn exploring their surroundings, hunted and became acquainted with the wildlife. Wolves were observed close by, and without knowing it they had landed in one of the best polar bear habitats in Greenland.

The trappers killed 28 polar bears during the winter, and in fact had more success with bear hunting than with fox trapping, which was the main object of their wintering. One reason was simply their lack of experience. To start with they had taken far too few traps with them; at the start they had only three, and two of these were swept away during a November storm so they then had to construct new traps. There was also a problem with the closing device on their box traps, which didn't function very well, so the foxes walked out of the traps as fast as they walked in. But the three pioneers refused to give up, and invented new closing mechanisms, each one shrewder than the other. However, all this took time and when the closing device eventually worked perfectly, the foxes gnawed their way through the wood of the box. Finally the hunters covered the box traps with thin sheets of metal, but at this point the trapping season was almost over. The expedition's catch was just 32 foxes, including three live animals.

After the polar night they were running low on firewood and then it became cold in Borganes. On the 15th March 1909 Brandal wrote: *"When we measure a temperature of 30 degrees at the roof we get the same result on the floor, with the difference that it is minus 30 degrees down there"*.[107] Without sufficient firewood and with a leaking roof, life in their dug-out was no longer a pleasure. Some time during the spring the three trappers therefore moved out of their dug out and went up to join their friends in Kopperneshuset at Kap Wynn.

Borganes was only used for wintering in 1908-09, but up to 25 years later it still served as an occasional shelter for trappers, mostly in emergency situations. It was still almost impossible to heat up this dug-out hut, and as a matter of fact, Hermann Andresen claimed that on a winter's day it was so cold inside that the grease on his steak would stiffen as he flipped the steak on the frying pan!

Brandal 1930; Giæver 1939, 1955; Description ... 1932; N032; N087

Recent status

Borganes today is a ruin. However, it is in surprisingly good condition and a unique example of the most primitive trappers' station in North-East Greenland.

Borganes [421-1], 6th August 2004. Borganes is a former Norwegian trappers' station built in 1908 by the Floren Expedition at Kap Borlase Warren. It was only used as a wintering station in 1908-09. Borganes station is still in surprisingly good condition, with all its walls still standing. Together with Germania-hamn [447-2], these are the only trappers' stations in North-East Greenland with a partly subterranean construction. © NCN

CARLSHAVN
[365]

Wintering party

1920-21: Viktor Hugo Stjernebo, H.A. Poulsen, Jens Yde Sindalsen
1921-22: Viktor Hugo Stjernebo, Peter Tutein, Jens Peter Carslund
1922-24: Niels Peter Andersen, Søren Peter Larsen

Tobias Dal, which divides Hold with Hope into northern and southern parts, opens into an east-facing bay. On the north shore of this bay, a few hundred metres from the shore, a heap of old, rusty metal items, including pots and pans, stove pipes and foot traps mark the site of a burnt-out trappers' station.

1920-21

The history of the Carlshavn station dates back to the 27th July 1920, when a few men came ashore on the flat beach. Their purpose was to find a suitable place to build a winter quarters; they had first tried further north, but the pack ice had blocked their way. So they decided instead to settle on the shore of the bay, where the land rises gradually to the heights of Home Forland. Their motor boat was called "Carl", and thus the station received the name "Carlshavn" (Carl's harbour).

The trappers, Viktor Hugo Stjernebo, H.A. Poulsen and Jens Yde Sindalsen, had arrived at Kap Broer Ruys in North-East Greenland on July 18th, where "Dagny" had unloaded the materials for their station. Stjernebo wrote in a report, that: *"we had to make four trips to move the material for the station from Kap Broer Ruys to Carlshavn; at times it was difficult navigating through the ice with our three boats, with the house materials sticking out in all directions. On the 11th August 1920, the house at station "A"* (Carlshavn) *was erected. We then returned to "B"* (Kap Broer Ruys) *to fetch the last load consisting of coal, all our firewood, kerosene, wood shavings, boards and much more".*[108]

Trapping for fox and wolf was begun on 1st October, but as they had no sledge dogs their hunting range was very limited. They used foot traps - a cruel trapping method that often damaged the furs. The first years' catch consisted of a little of everything, including. three wolves, 180 birds, 64 arctic hares, two lemmings, two ermines and: *"a part of a polar bear fur" ... "Of insects we collected two boxes in which the insects are pinned, and one box with wrapped up insects".* The wintering passed without any serious accidents, apart from a violent storm which crushed their motor boat "Carl" on the ground, and made a hole in the bottom.

Carlshavn at the beginning of the 1920s. © Jonna Jensen

1921-22

When the relief ship "Teddy" arrived at Carlshavn a summer day in 1921, the trappers at the station did not know that Peter Tutein was on board, and was going to be the new trapper at Carlshavn. He was a younger brother of John Tutein, who had been killed by a polar bear near Kap Broer Ruys in the winter. Those aboard "Teddy" had no knowledge of this tragic event. Peter Tutein writing about his reception, recorded that it was both: *"confusing and spooky. Every time I mentioned my name to someone, he would sort of shudder and hurry away; a strange fear crept up my spine".*[109] The truth came as a great shock to Peter Tutein, who had idealised his elder brother. Gustav Thostrup advised him to return home, but he nevertheless chose to stay.

Peter Tutein was born in Varde in 1902, and his experiences during the following two winterings provided him with the inspiration for a number of books about Greenland, as well as "Nordhavets mænd" (Men of the Arctic Sea) (1939), a film drama about the life of a fox trapper.

After his years in Greenland, he travelled widely and became well-known as an adventurer and writer. Although described as a versatile individual, he was also a troubled and disturbed person, so much so that he committed suicide in 1949.

In 1995 the largest Norwegian movie company selected Peter Tutein's semi-documentary novel "Larsen" (1930) for their film "Kjærlighetens Kjøtere" (Bastards of Love), with the international film title "Zero Kelvin". It gives a very convincing picture of three desperate trappers in North-East Greenland back in 1925. The famous Swedish actor Stellan Skarsgård plays one of the trappers. The film won several well-earned prizes.

Tutein wrote about Carlshavn: *"The house had only one living room measuring three by four metres, a small hallway one metre wide, an annex and an attic for provisions. Along one sidewall there were three berths, two upper and one lower. On the opposite wall, where the stove was placed, there was a window with a combined work- and kitchen table. The kitchen utensils hung on one end wall, and the door was placed at the other end; a square table with a kerosene lamp above was nailed to the berth pole. Three upside down boxes functioned as chairs".*[110] This quote is taken from his biographical book "Grøn ungdom hele livet" (A life-long youth) (1951), in which Tutein provides a very colourful account of life at Carlshavn in 1921-22.

Viktor Hugo Stjernebo. © Jørgen Nielsen

In addition to Peter Tutein and Stjernebo, another new trapper, 21-year-old Jens Peter Carslund from Nykøbing Mors, stayed at Carlshavn in 1921-22. Carslund did not take part in the trapping, but was employed to look after the motor boat. Tutein described Carslund as: *"of ordinary build, a talented accordion player, a skilled mechanic and a nice person".*[111]

The leader of the station, Stjernebo, was altogether a different kind of person. About 45-years old, he was in Tutein's words: *"short of stature, with long grey hair curling about his shoulders and held back from the face by a piece of wire, a full beard growing almost to his eyes, which had a tendency to become bloodshot when he got angry; he was definitely hot-tempered".*[112] The two fiery souls, Stjernebo and Tutein, soon fell out, and Tutein counted himself lucky that Carslund also lived at the station; otherwise: *"only one of us would have been alive the following year and the other one would have committed murder".*[113]

Tutein wrote that he and Stjernebo did everything in their power to annoy and harass each other, and eventually Tutein chose to desert: *"The last evening he* (Stjernebo) *took an unusually long time to fall asleep. I almost believed that he had guessed what I was about to do and would have caught me red-handed. It was more exciting than any bear hunt to write the note saying that I had left to live with the "Yankee" and the "Watchmaker" at Kap Mary* (Christianshavn), *and that if he followed me I would shoot him if he came within one hundred metres".*[114]

In spite of these quarrels, the catch at Carlshavn appears to have been satisfactory that winter. Both Stjernebo and Tutein were described as skilled trappers, and Hans Ludvig Jensen reported in the summer 1922 that the station was in excellent order.

1922-24

In the summer of 1922, Carlshavn was taken over by Niels Peter Andersen and Søren Peter Larsen. Niels Peter Andersen was a butcher by trade, and had wintered at Villaen at Danmark Havn and Hvalrosodden in 1919-21. Søren Peter Larsen, who went by the nicknames "the long" and "the big", was a game keeper and a newcomer in North-East Greenland. The catch in 1922-23 amounted to 25 foxes, four polar bears and 20 muskoxen.

In 1923 Andersen and Larsen had no relief visit from "Teddy", as the winter ice in the bay in front of Kap Kraus did not break up. They both returned to Denmark with "Godthaab" in 1924, after the East Greenland Company closed down its activities.

1926-27

There was no Danish trapping in North-East Greenland between 1924 and 1929, and thus no one to take offence when the Foldvik Expedition used Carlshavn as a travellers' hut in the winter of 1926-27; they were able to trap all the way around Hold with Hope. It was not until the summer of 1929, when Nanok arrived to resume the activities of the new East Greenland Company, that the Danes became aware that the Carlshavn station had burnt down to the ground after a Norwegian visit.

The Norwegian, Arnulf Gisvold, personally informed J.G. Jennov of the fate of the Carlshavn station when he met him at Germaniahavn. At the same time, Gisvold promised that the Norwegians would rebuild the station.[115] The incident was also slow to become known in Norwegian circles. In a letter Nils Foldvik wrote to Adolf Hoel, dated Tromsø 16th May 1929, he stated: *"Unfortunately the Danish house in Carlshavn has burnt down. Hallvard Devold had passed there in the autumn of 1927 and left the house without putting out the fire in the stove. When he returned in the spring, the house had burnt down. In my opinion it was very careless to leave a house like that. Devold said he would personally build a new house in Carlshavn. It is of course a big mistake that the right person in Denmark has not been notified about Carlshavn. I would be grateful if this could be sorted out in the best possible way. Should the Danes claim compensation, we may have to leave them some of what we have up there".*[116]

In spite of Gisvold's promise, and Foldvik's wish to grant the Danes compensation, this never in fact happened. The new Norwegian leadership abdicated any responsibility for the matter. As a result, Nanok built a new replacement station in 1930, Knudshoved [355], which was placed about seven km south of the former Carlshavn station.

Bistrup 1924; Dahl 1924, 1925; Devold 1940; N085; Ø060; Ø040.

Recent status

The ruins of Carlshavn appear to have remained almost unchanged since the station burnt down in the autumn of 1927. It is an interesting historic site, with many artefacts from the trapper era still present.

Carlshavn [365], 22nd July 2005. The site of the fire. © NCN

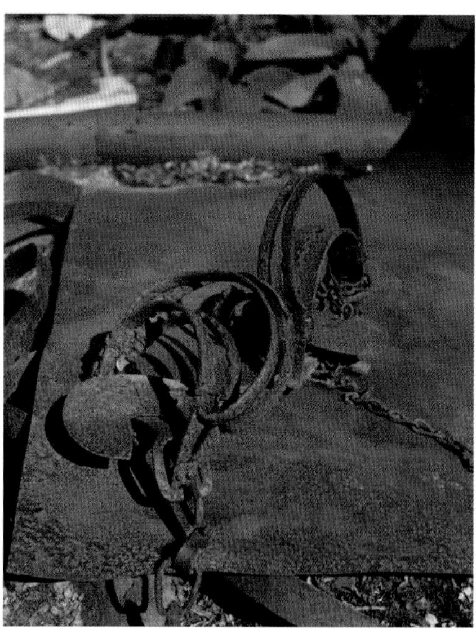

Carlshavn [365], 22nd July 2005. Carlshavn was a former Danish trappers' station, built in 1920 for the East Greenland Company. It was used as a trappers' station until 1924, and by Norwegian trappers as a travellers' hut until 1927; it was burnt down by accident in the autumn of 1927. Many artefacts from the trapper era are still present at the site. (Above, left). The old stove from Carlshavn. (Above, right) Foot traps at Carlshavn. 31st July 1989. View eastwards towards Kap Kraus. © NCN

CHRISTIANSHAVN
[410-2]

Wintering party
1921-22: Hans Givskov, Halvor Hansen
1922-23: Hans Givskov, Carl Georg Madsen

1921-22

In a small bay on the western side of Kap Mary, the East Greenland Company built a trappers' station in the summer of 1921, which they named "Christianshavn". The house was placed side by side with Kap Mary huset [410-1], the Norwegian house from 1909.

When the station was finished it was handed over to Hans Givskov, then 34-years old, from Hadsund, and Halvor Hansen, then 29-years old, from Grenå. The two men were known respectively as the "Watchmaker" and the "Yankee", and Peter Tutein wrote an amusing story about their visit to Carlshavn in the winter of 1921: *"By the way, Stjernebo burnt his fingers, much to my delight. He had never seen the Yankee and did not know that he had been in America and was fooled by the fact that he was named Hansen and spoke with a strong Jutland dialect. Stjernebo loved to tell stories, but applause had an unfortunate effect on his imagination. He was talking far and wide about life in the USA, where he had been a gangster, smuggled Chinese immigrants and so forth, and claimed he had also dug for gold in Dawson. I recognized some of his tales from the books of Jack London and others, but said nothing. He became more and more enthusiastic, but suddenly, when he had rescued twenty people from drowning and had been invited to stay at the White House for fourteen days while they prepared his medal, the Yankee had had enough. He jumped up with his 210 pounds of muscles, and yelled: " – Let me tell you one thing, Stjernebo, I have been in the States for nine years, and I'm fed up with you. Tell me one more lie and I will shove your nose up your ass! So shut up!"* [117]

In the summer of 1922 the "Yankee" went home to Denmark. Hans Ludvig Jensen wrote in his report: *"Halvor Hansen has asked to go home, which is convenient as he is unfit for the life in Greenland. The man has no idea of what trapping is about, and is said to be impossible to live with as a workmate; he is also a rather brutal person. He complained to me that there was too little milk, sugar, butter, flour etc., but the other trappers say that there is plenty, so his complaints in this matter are unfounded".* [118]

1922-23

Hans Givskov's new partner was Carl Georg Madsen, an engineer, and of him Hans Ludvig Jensen wrote: *"Madsen is alright, besides being a trapper; he has a passion for geology so he has probably found his vocation".* [119]

In the summer of 1923 the journalist Kai R. Dahl visited Christianshavn: *"It is strange to see how the life here sets its stamp on a man. When we brought Givskov up here in 1921, he was a pale, work-weary watchmaker who finally had said farewell to his workshop to follow his old love, the hunt. His body had become straight and elastic now, and there was a gleam like the ice blink in his eyes, while his coal-black full beard gave his gypsy face the look of a robber chieftain. He did not hesitate to confess that Clavering Island had never for a moment disappointed him, and as far as he was concerned his watch file was a prehistoric tool.*

In these two years Givskov had built up considerable of a record in hunting bears, musk-ox, wolves, and walrus, besides all the small game the country offered. It was the wolves he liked most to talk about. One time he was playing about with a whole pack of about seven, or, to be more correct, the wolves were playing about with him. He was home in the hut one day and looking out of the window he saw a team of unusually handsome dogs come dashing towards the house. He naturally went out to see what guests were approaching but was rather surprised at the actions of the strange dogs. They had surrounded him before he realized that they were wolves, and he had just about time to slip into the house to get his gun. When he came out again the pack had retreated a little towards the hillside with the exception of the

Kap Mary huset (left) and the Christianshavn station in the early 1920s. © Jonna Jensen

Peter Tutein (left), Hans Givskov and Kaj Jørgensen. © *Arctic Institute*

leader, a big, determined dog wolf. In a momentary nervousness he succeeded only in hitting this one wolf, which, badly wounded, fled towards the beach, while the others, howling loudly, disappeared among the hills. Shortly after, the wounded wolf fell on the new ice below the house, where Givskov and his comrades killed him later".[120]

On 23rd July 1923, one week after Dahl had been drinking coffee with Givskov and Madsen and listened to their stories about the events of the winter, the trappers started to tear down Christianshavn. During July the house was moved to Young Sund, where it was rebuilt as the station now known as Sandodden [425-1]. Both Givskov and Madsen left Greenland in 1923. Madsen later on became the owner of a concrete factory near Silkeborg.

Bistrup 1924; Jennov 1939; Møller 1939; Ø043; Ø060; P152.

Recent status

Christianshavn station, as well as the Kap Mary huset, were both long ago moved to other locations; see Sandodden [425-1] and Dahl Skær hytten [412]. Ice conditions off Kap Mary proved to be treacherous, and during the 1930s and 1940s no less than three drowning accidents were recorded. See Kap Herschell 1931-32 and 1932-33 and Sandodden 1945-46.

The Kap Mary huset (left) and Christianshavn in the early 1920s. © *Jens Mathiesen*

Danish bear hunters from the East Greenland Company at Kap Mary, c. 1922. Kap Mary huset and Christianshavn are just visible in the upper right corner of the photograph. © Jens Mathiesen

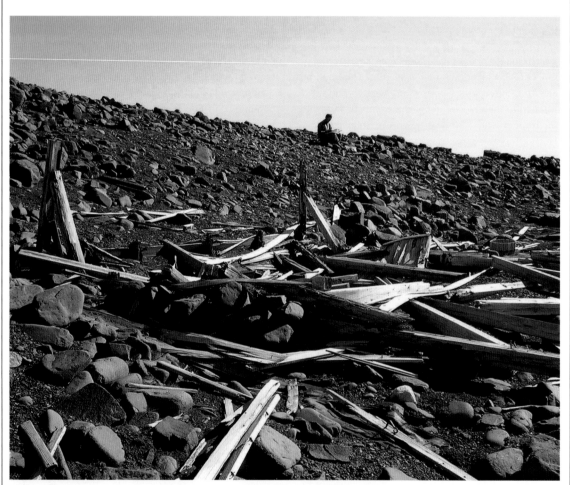

Kap Mary, 31st August 2007. Christianshavn [410-2] was a Danish trappers' station built in 1921 for the East Greenland Company. It was used as a trappers' station until 1923, when it was pulled down and re-erected as the present Sandodden station [425-1] at Daneborg. Kap Mary huset [410-1] was located at the same site as Christianshavn. Today only a few remains exist from the Kap Mary huset and Christianshavn station. Kap Mary huset was pulled down in 1948, and the materials were used to build the Dahl Skær hytten [412]. © NCN

ELVSBORG
[407]

Wintering party
1927-28: Jonas Karlsbak, Peder Sulebak, Jørgen Furnes.

1927-28

*"Farewell O mother Norway, now I leave thee,
I thank you for feeding and raising me.
You got too scarce with food for your fishing flock
You'll find us now in Greenland, were we get more than enough".*[121]

These were the words Jonas Karlsbak optimistically wrote on the first page of his diary. It was the 14th July 1927, the very day he and his five companions - Hermann Andresen, Peder Røbek, Peder Sulebak, Jørgen Furnes and August Hansen - left Ålesund with the small motor cutter "Hird".

The Hird Expedition safely crossed the Atlantic and reached land at Kap Mary on July 25th. Initially their plan had been to use the Germaniahavn station, and to anchor "Hird" in the natural harbour there for the winter. They abandoned this plan, however, following advice from the veteran Vebjørn Landmark, who happened to pass by with the sealer "Fangstmand", and warned them that the Danes might return.[122]

So they moved on to Kap Herschell, where they found a good location for their first trappers' station. On the 5th August they continued south-west into Gael Hamke Bugt, and on a broad sandy beach on the south coast of Clavering Ø, found their next good site. They immediately started unloading the materials, and already the following day held a topping-out ceremony - but with 24 hours daylight they were working rather more than an 8-hour day.

The 10th August 1927 it was: *"summer as you rarely find in Norway, +9 degrees in the daytime and in the evening +6 degrees in the shade, but it feels like when it is +20 degrees in Norway. We have now finished the house and baked the first bread in the stove, everything is working alright and we are all satisfied and happy". ... "We have named our house Elvsborg as a large river (elv) runs along some limestone cliffs – looking like old castle ruins – close to our house".*[123]

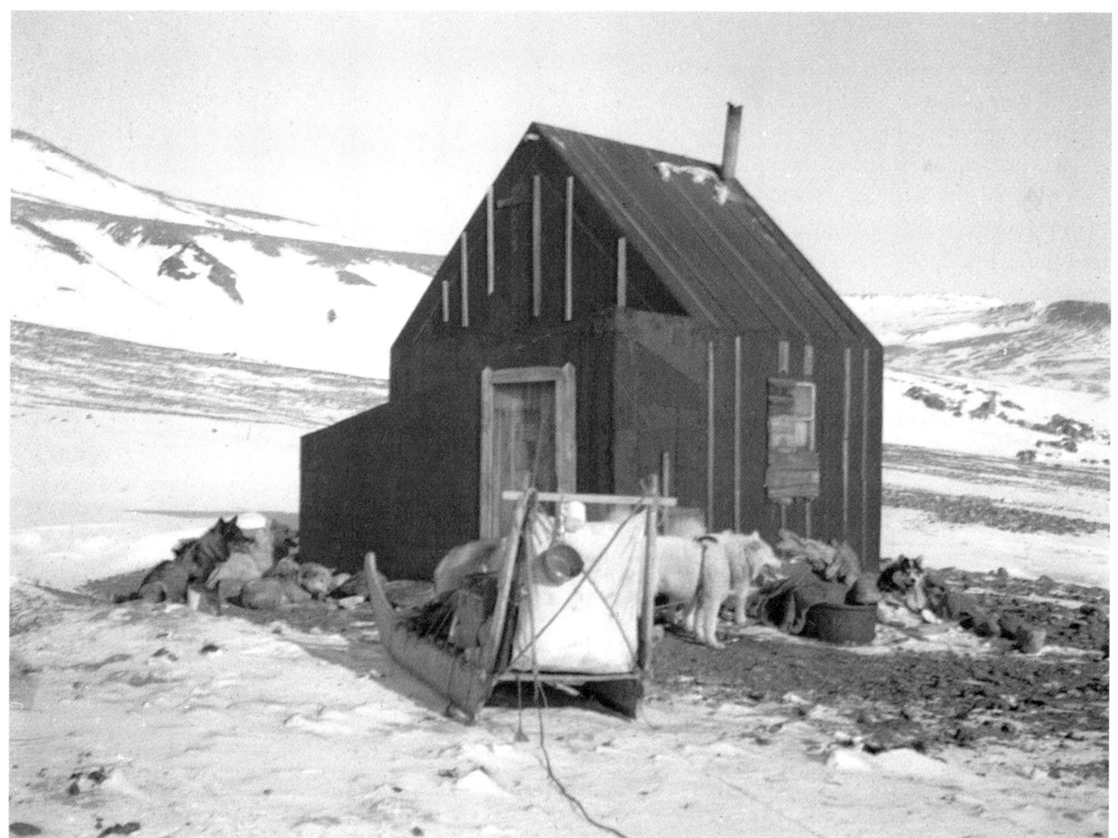

Elvsborg, c. 1939. © Niels Ove Jensen

The Hird Expedition now split up into two groups. One group moved to Kap Herschell, while the other - consisting of Jonas Karlsbak, Peder Sulebak and Jørgen Furnes settled at Elvsborg. Here they arranged themselves with practical routines and with a week's kitchen duty in turns. The menu was also put into a varied but regular system. On Sundays they had hare or ptarmigan, Monday was porridge day, Tuesday they had meatballs, Wednesday fish, Thursday salted mutton, Friday pancakes, and on Saturday the week closed with muskox steaks.

Old experienced shipmasters suggested a good natural harbour on the north-west side of Store Finsch might serve as a winter anchorage for their cutter "Hird", and here the ship was anchored for the winter. However, on the 26th August 1927 hurricane-force winds hit North-East Greenland. The storm grew in intensity hour by hour, and huge swells were driven ashore from the ice-free sea. For a time they feared that the sea would carry away the ground beneath the Elvsborg station; on the fourth day when the wind finally dropped, it looked like: *"a wild beast had gone berserk in the entire area"*.[124] The swells had reached so high that even the old grass-covered eskimo graves far up on the land were flooded and washed into the sea. All their fox traps had either been smashed into smithereens by the storm, or simply disappeared. The worst blow, however, was that "Hird" had been completely crushed and sunk in its harbour, in spite of being secured by double anchors, extra moorings and wires.

The trapping started quite well. Immediately after their arrival they had placed box traps around the station, and live foxes caught in the traps were transferred into cages; when the fox furs had reached optimal condition they could be killed and skinned. Fox trapping was carried out between Eskimonæs and Kap Mary; in total the catch amounted to 26 foxes and two polar bears, which was not quite up to their expectations.

They had regular contacts with their friends at Kap Herschell, and also with Meyer Olsen at Krogness. These contacts led them to the realisation, as they prepared for the next wintering, that three men at one station was one too many. Since it was important to expand their trapping territory as much as possible and establish a network of trappers' huts, they therefore decided to leave Elvsborg unmanned, and instead to place two men at Kap Herschell, two at Germaniahavn and one at Jackson Ø.

The wreckage of "Hird" at Store Finsch, c. 1939. © Niels Ove Jensen

Elvsborg station was only in fact used for wintering in 1927-28. Today it is almost unchanged, except that the "Hird" men pulled down the porch in 1928 to use it for Jackson-stua [371].

Giæver 1939; N032; P135.

Recent status

After 1928, Elvsborg was used only as a trappers' hut in the southern Kap Herschell territory. From the early 1950s it was used regularly as a travellers' hut by Sirius. About the end of the 1970s it was abandoned by the patrol, but despite the lack of any maintenance it was still in reasonable condition at the beginning of the 2000s. Nanok then placed Elvsborg on the agenda for renovation, but it was not until the summer of 2007, that a team was sent up to start the work. The Nanok team carried out a basic restoration in 2007 with support from Sirius and the National Environmental Research Institute.[125]

Elvsborg [407] before, during and after the renovation in 2007. Elvsborg is a former Norwegian trappers' station built in 1927 for the Hird Expedition. It was used as a trappers' station only in 1927-28, thereafter as a travellers' hut. © NCN

FRANKLIN-HUSET
[326]

---Wintering party
1922-23: The Johan A. Olsen Expedition, or "Anni I" Expedition (see also Myggbukta)

On the south side of Vestersletten there once stood a trappers' station, built in the summer of 1922 by the Norwegian "Anni I" Expedition. It was there just for a few years and was soon forgotten.

1922-23
At the end of July 1922, when "Anni I" left Tromsø, there were seven men on board. The leader was Johan A. Olsen from Skulsfjord in Tromsøysund, the wireless operator Helge Listerud of Toten, a mechanic and trapper, Alvin H.J. Olsen (brother to Johan A. Olsen) of Skulsfjord, cook and trapper, and Oskar Johansson of Halland in Sweden. The expedition was completed by the three trappers Olaf Olsen of Målselv, Jakob B. Andreassen of Lenvik and Edvard K. Løkvik, all from the Tromsøysund region.

The expedition carried enough materials to build two stations. The main station was built at Myggbukta, and the second house about 25 km south-west of Myggbukta, somewhere on the coast between Kap Bennet and Kap Franklin. Until 2004 the exact location of this second station was uncertain.

The "Anni I" Expedition vanished without trace during the voyage home in the bad ice-summer of 1923, and thus very little is known about the wintering, except that the catch consisted of 86 polar foxes, 11 polar bears, six wolves and seven live muskoxen.

In an attempt to solve the mystery of the missing "Anni I", the Norwegian government sent out a search expedition led by Gunner Isachsen in the summer of 1924. The expedition used the sealer "Quest", with Ludolf Schjelderup as master. They set out for East Greenland, but at the beginning of July it became known that the 21 persons on board the Danish ship "Teddy", wrecked in the ice off Liverpool Land, had managed to reach Ammassalik. "Quest" therefore altered course, and transported the men from "Teddy" from Ammassalik to Iceland before resuming the search for "Anni I".

They made landfall at Scoresby Sund and then sailed northwards along the coast. On the 15th August 1924 they approached Franklin-huset: *"We hurried eastwards to the Norwegian house at Kap Franklin, which stands between this cape and Kap Giesecke (Kap Bennet), and arrived at 12 o'clock noon. We rushed ashore and into the house. No one had been there since the "Anni" men left Myggbukta a year ago to the day. We had expected the worst, but even so we were greatly disappointed. Everyone was thinking what Schjelderup said: Well, I guess we can now write off Johan Olsen".*

"I stayed and examined the house while the others went hunting a herd of muskoxen in the hills. The house was in good condition and order. About 20 hectolitres of coal lay on the ground but there were no supplies in the house. In such trappers' huts it is normal to find messages or notes of some kind scribbled on the walls during the long winter, but here nothing was found. Nor were there any written accounts left by the trappers".[126]

Franklin-huset, 15th August 1924. © Gunnar Isachsen / Norwegian Polar Institute

1926-27

Franklin-huset was not used again until 1926, when the Foldvik Expedition took it over. Arnulf Gisvold from Myggbukta used the house for a while as his main base, but it was soon realized that if a decent catch was to be obtained, it was vital to build a large network of small trappers' huts. Franklin-huset was located at an awkward distance from Myggbukta, as it was not economical to heat up: *"We decided to pull down Franklin-huset and split it into two smaller huts and place these so that we expanded our territory"*, Hallvard Devold wrote.[127] In August 1927 the material was used to construct "Foldvik" [327] to the north and "Franklin Strand" [319] to the south.

N085; R135.

Recent status

The site of Franklin-huset was soon forgotten. Situated in the middle of the large, flat Vestersletten delta it was far off the beaten track. Nobody was likely to pass by, except perhaps dog sledge travellers in the wintertime when the site of the house would be hidden under the snow. It was not until the summer of 2004, that a Nanok party successfully located the remains of Franklin-huset.[128]

Franklin-huset [326], 27th July 2004. Franklin-huset was a former Norwegian trappers' station located in the middle of the Vestersletten delta, built in 1922 by the Johan A. Olsen Expedition. It was only used as a trappers' station in 1922-23, and as a travellers' hut until 1927. It was pulled down by the Foldvik Expedition and used to build two smaller huts, "Foldvik" [327] and "Franklin Strand" [319]. (Above) The remains of Franklin-huset. (Bottom) View from the site of Franklin-huset north-east towards Kap Bennet and Kap Broer Ruys. © NCN

GERMANIA-HAMN
[447-2]

Wintering party

1869-70: ("Germania") Karl Koldewey, Carl Börgen, Ralph Copeland, Adolf Georg Pansch, Julius Payer, Heinrich Sengstacke, Otto Tramnitz, Karl August Krauschner, Hermann Warkmeister, Johan Friedr. Büttner, Louis Ollenstädt, Georg Herzberg, Peter Ellinger, Theodor Klentzer, Wilhelm Mieders, Peter Iversen (from Haderslev in Jutland), Louis Wagner

1909-10: ("7de juni") Vebjørn Landmark, Johannes H. Brandal, Henning Idrevik, Gustav Abrahamsen, Hjalmar Høvik, Martin Bjørlo

1869-70

The coastal region around Germania Havn has been well known amongst seafarers since the early days of whaling and sealing. It was here, off the Pendulum Øer and Shannon, that the coastal pack ice could most easily be forced.

The name, Germania Havn, originated from the wintering of the German expedition led by Karl Koldewey in 1869-70. Their ship "Germania" had its winter harbour between the two peninsulas guarding the small bay on Sabine Ø. This was the first intentional wintering by Europeans in North-East Greenland, and Koldewey's expedition was the earliest to leave behind buildings as a witness to their activities: namely two observatories [447-1] on Vestre Havnenæs: *"one for astronomical, the other for magnetic purposes, raw from frozen rocks"*.[129] The site of Edward Sabine's pendulum observations in 1823 was a few hundred metres to the north-west: *"on the site of an Esquimaux village"*.[130]

1909-10

The next expedition to winter at Germania Havn was Vebjørn Landmark's "7de juni" Expedition 1909-10.[131] The Norwegians had originally intended to winter at Kap Mary huset [410-1], which they had recently built, but as Landmark could not find a good winter harbour for "7de juni" in Gael Hamke Bugt, he chose instead to winter at Germania Havn. One of the participants, Martin Bjørlo, wrote in his diary: *"We have now decided to anchor our ship there for the winter, as we cannot find a better harbour anywhere else. It is true that it is shallow water, but we intend to build a dug-out or hut on shore as a reserve, and then we will bring all our equipment ashore to lighten the ship as much as possible"*.[132]

They began to dig the dug-out mentioned by Martin Bjørlo at the end of August 1909. It measured 6 x 3 metres, was equipped with walls of rocks, a roof of zinc plates and a wooden floor. They also put in a window and sealed the walls on the inside with kneaded clay. Finally the walls were insulated with earth and turf, because: *"you never know if it will be needed to keep it as warm as possible"*.[133] They called their dug-out "Germania-hamn", but initially stayed on board "7de juni".

The expedition was struck by several accidents. In September, just as the sea started to freeze up, a violent storm broke "7de juni" loose from its moorings and it ran aground. With difficulty they managed to haul the ship back afloat again, and were relieved that

Germania-hamn, 1932. © Norwegian Polar Institute

the storm had not carried it out into the open sea instead. As the sea ice had broken up, Bjørlo, Idrevik and Brandal decided to row down to Kap Mary to check the house and the traps. It was meant to be a short trip, but then the pack ice returned and they were caught on their way back, and had to stay on Clavering Ø until early November.

The trapping that winter was more or less limited to Sabine Ø, because storms repeatedly broke up the fjord ice. The weather was worst around New Year 1910. When the wind finally dropped, they saw that the ice had broken in all directions and there was open water just 40 metres behind the ship. Afraid to stay on the ship, all but Landmark and Brandal moved into the dug-out onshore.

Shortly after New Year their worst hardships began. On the 18th January, Martin Bjørlo noted that Abrahamsen had pain in his legs and had difficulty walking. A few days later he had to stay in his sleeping bag, as his legs had turned blue and were badly swollen. During February, Brandal and Idrevik developed the same symptoms. Furthermore, Høvik for a period was incapable of working due to severe frostbite in his face.

At the beginning of March the sea finally froze, but only Landmark and Høvik were able to trap, because Bjørlo day and night was looking after his friends sick with scurvy. In the evening of 14th May 1910, Henning Idrevik passed away, just 33-years old. He was buried in an old eskimo earth house west of Germania Havn. The general despondency, which had been present for some time, now grew worse and the men began to doubt whether any of them would leave Greenland alive.

On 21st May 1910 they discovered they were not alone in North-East Greenland. At the Bass Rock depot Landmark had found a note stating that five Danes from the Alabama Expedition had wintered on Shannon, only 100 km to the north. The note asked anyone reading it for help in leaving Greenland, and Landmark in return left a letter in which he promised to assist if possible.

In the middle of July they were finally able to make "7de juni" ready for their home voyage. With great care, Brandal and Abrahamsen were carried from the dug-out to the ship, and on the 19th July they left Germania Havn. The following day they observed chimney smoke on the horizon, which proved to come from "Laura" of Tromsø. This was an especially lucky meeting for the sick men on "7de juni", because "Laura" had medicine and fresh fruit on board and a few days later the sick men were already on the road to recovery.[134] The possibility of rescuing the Danes from "Alabama" was now discussed, and "Laura" immediately set course northwards, until stopped by the pack ice. In the event it was "7de juni'" that picked up the stranded Danes.

On the 19th August 1910 the expedition arrived back in Norway and Martin Bjørlo ended his diary with the following words: *"Even though the journey has been unsuccessful for us with respect to trapping and in other ways, we have at least had the joy of saving five bold and brave men for old Denmark"*.[135]

The dug-out Germania-hamn station has not subsequently been used. The walls were still standing in 1919, when men from the East Greenland Company built their own station, but due to lack of maintenance the walls gradually collapsed, and today only the piles of rocks bear witness to the tragic wintering of the 7de juni Expedition.

Hareid 1984; Koldewey 1873, 1874; Description ... 1932; Ø046.

Recent status

The exact location of the Germania-hamn station is uncertain, because the collapsed walls of the dug-out may have been removed to be used for other purposes. It is likely that the dug-out was placed in one of the Inuit houses on the west side of the western peninsula at Germaniahavn, close to the site of the wooden cross that marks Idrevik's grave.

A wooden cross marks the grave of trapper Henning Idrevik at Germaniahavn, c. 1986. © Leif Vanggaard

It is likely that the "Germania-hamn" dug-out was placed in one of the Inuit houses on the west side of the western peninsula at Germaniahavn, 23rd July 2004. © NCN

GERMANIAHAVN
[447-3]

Wintering party

1919-20: Hans Nielsen, Johan F. Petersen, Ejnar Falsøe
1920-21: None
1921-22: Marius Madsen, Peder Vorre Thykjær, Carl Aage Knudsen
1922-23: Carl Aage Knudsen, Karl Kristensen, Viggo Riis, Hans Ludvig Jensen, Kaj Jørgensen
1923-24: Viktor Hugo Stjernebo, Viggo S. Lund
1924-28: None
1928-29: Jonas Karlsbak, Jørgen Furnes
1929-30: Carl Aage Knudsen, Andreas Hvidberg, Arne C.F. Schwarck, Evald Rasmussen
1930-31: Arne C.F. Schwarck, Hans Bruun

1919-20

After establishment of the East Greenland Company, the company decided to build its first trappers' station at Germania Havn.

On the 29th June 1919 "Dagny" reached Sabine Ø, and within a week the wintering station placed east of Østre Havnenæs was completed. Three trappers stayed here for the first winter: Hans Nielsen, carpenter, was leader of the group that included Johan F. Petersen and Ejnar Falsøe.

After completion of the station they explored in the vicinity, finding the remains of the 7de juni Expedition dug-out, Germania-hamn, and the grave of the trapper Henning Idrevik. Hans Nielsen wrote: *"The Norwegians have buried their dead friend in one of the eskimo winter houses west of Germaniahavn, which we discovered when we were examining the houses. I have made a wooden cross and put it on the grave".*[136]

The winter passed with hunting, with walrus as the main intended prey. They had three sledge dogs, and planned to start trapping in the middle of October, with possible excursions to Wollaston Forland and Shannon. However, like the "7de juni" trappers in 1909-10, the entire winter was characterised by bad ice conditions with the ice constantly breaking up without warning.
As a consequence the Danish trapping territory was very limited and the resulting catch was so poor they decided to give up trapping from Germaniahavn in 1920-21, and try from Shannon instead.

1921-22

On the 29th April 1921, life again returned to the house which was occupied by five weakened trappers

The crew of "Dagny" and trappers in front of the new Germaniahavn trappers' station in July 1919. Number six from left is the then 14-year-old ship's boy Broer Sandberg. He also participated in the 1920 expedition and had to winter in North-East Greenland after "Dagny" was wrecked. © Jonna Jensen

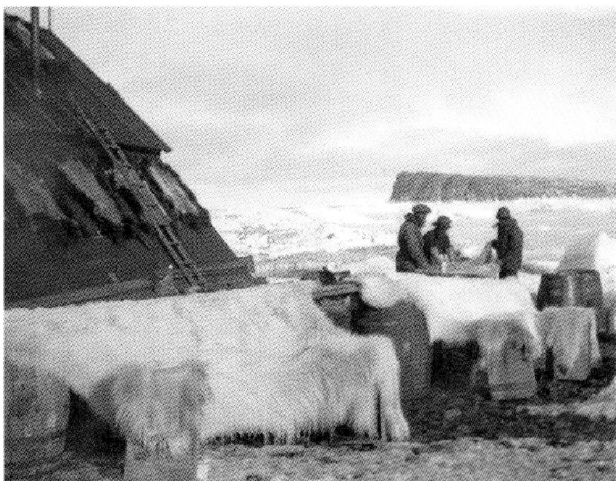

Cleaning and washing of bear skins at Germaniahavn c. 1922. © Jens Mathiesen

from the Dove Bugt stations of Hvalrosodden and Villaen, who after a long strenuous journey to Germaniahavn, planned to wait there for the arrival of their supply ship.

"Teddy" arrived on the 16th July, but the ship had to anchor at the edge of the fjord ice off the station to take onboard the men from Dove Bugt. Gustav Thostrup, captain of "Teddy", decided that the Germaniahavn station should be manned for the winter, and as temporary housing for the depot they built the "Hvalrosø depotskur" [442] on Hvalrosø, as well as a trappers' hut, "Kap Desbrowe hytten" [455], on Lille Pendulum.

Thostrup assigned the following men to Germaniahavn: Marius Madsen, 22-years old from Billund, Peder Vorre Thykjær, 23-years old from Rønde, and Carl Aage Knudsen, 26-years old from Ålykkeskov near Odense. The latter two were both trained gamekeepers and newcomers to Greenland, whereas Madsen had wintered at Kap Philip Broke the previous year.

One day in January 1922 the three men took a walk to "Teddys Udkig", a hill behind the station. As they stood there they caught sight of no less than five polar bears, two of these in the direction of Hvalrosø. The pursuit was immediately begun and one of the bears was killed out on the ice. They started skinning the animal and all was going well until they suddenly discovered that the ice beneath them was adrift. They were trapped on an ice floe that slowly but surely was moving: *"seaward, carried along on the ebbing tide"*.[137] It was freezing more than 30 degrees and black waters surrounded them. There was only one thing to do: jump into the water and swim 70 metres to solid ice. The swim was the least problem, whereas the seven km walk back to Germaniahavn almost killed them. They were soaking wet, and the cold chilled them to the bone. More dead than alive they finally reached the station, but after a month-long convalescence all three survived.

While Carl Aage Knudsen stayed on for another year, both Thykjær and Madsen went home in 1922. As late as 1950-51 Thykjær came back to winter for Nanok, but on this last journey he became ill and had to return with the ship.

After spending three years in Denmark, Marius Madsen emigrated in 1925 to Canada. He was lucky and discovered a large gold deposit, which according to himself made him one of the richest men in Canada.[138]

Walrus hunt at Germaniahavn c. 1922. © Jens Mathiesen

Germaniahavn station (left) and Hans Ludvig Jensens hus (right) in 1923. © Jonna Jensen

1922-23

On the 28th July 1922 "Teddy" arrived at Germaniahavn. Together with Carl Aage Knudsen the new wintering party consisted of Karl Kristensen, a gamekeeper, sergeant Viggo Riis and finally Hans Ludvig Jensen, who was going to be in charge. They were joined for the winter by Kaj Jørgensen, who planned to undertake mineralogical investigations. In order to house this large group, an extra house known as "Hans Ludvig Jensens hus", was built during the summer. This was pulled down the following year, as the Danish government had engaged the East Greenland Company to examine the possibilities of a colonization of Scoresby Sund. When "Teddy" had to give up the transport to Scoresby Sund, the materials from Hans Ludvig Jensens hus were instead unloaded at Kap Mary.

During the winter of 1922-23 the pack ice came and went as usual. A number of polar bears were shot but only few foxes were trapped. During a muskoxen hunt on Shannon at the end of April 1923, they caught a live muskox calf, which was brought back to Germaniahavn: *"The calf Båsse was put in one of the side sheds, but was somewhat stubborn and upset after the long drive, it fumed, wetted its horn and butted, but eventually calmed down, convinced that it was probably the first live muskox ever to have travelled about nine Danish miles (68 km) on a sledge".*[139] "Båsse" soon became tame and was allowed to wander freely.

Hans Ludvig Jensen (right) returns home with arctic hares. © Jonna Jensen

1923-24

"Teddy" arrived in North-East Greenland on the 15th July 1923, carrying two new trappers for Germaniahavn: Viktor Hugo Stjernebo and Viggo S. Lund. Stjernebo had previously wintered at Carlshavn in 1920-22, whereas Lund was a novice. At the start

Hans Ludvig Jensen – one of the driving forces behind Danish trapping in North-East Greenland. © Jonna Jensen

they had the company of Kristen Larsen, who later on moved to Bass Rock.

Lund later wrote an account of the wintering - his only one - in the book "Jægerliv og nordlysnætter" (hunting life and northern lights) (1926).

The motor boat "Carl" was a vital means of transportation: *"Stjernebo loved "Carl". Larsen admired it. "Carl" could not have had a better skipper than Stjernebo, and yet many considered him to be half-crazy; his biggest oddity was his peculiar tendency to convince people that he was completely crazy. As a seaman he had sailed the seven seas, knew the art of knots, how to set sail, and he could handle a boat between the drifting ice floes better than anybody. Like a hare he appeared to sleep with one eye open, and could spin a yarn worthy of any able-bodied seaman".*[140]

To Lund's great surprise, Stjernebo one day in the autumn prepared a grand dinner. The conversation went as follows: *"Well! It's my birthday"*, Stjernebo said with a superior attitude.

"Congratulations!" I sat down to enjoy the dishes and the wine and asked: "May I ask how old you are?"

"Forty five" he answered promptly.

"Well, what do you know; it's now the second time within six months you've celebrated that birthday".

"True! On board "Teddy" I also celebrated it and had myself a cigar from the Captain's box. A real cigar, you see – I celebrate my birthday as often as I want to. But today it is my birthday. Cheers, old sport!"

Then we touched glasses and for once I believed he was telling the truth".[141]

On Monday the 14th July 1924 "Godthaab" arrived. The East Greenland Company had been forced to give up trapping, and Julius Hansen, the master of "Godthaab", gave orders for the immediate evacuation of the station. The dogs were to be put down, and Stjernebo and Lund had to embark. Viggo S. Lund, who later on became a vet in Jyderup, wrote: *"I have been bored in Copenhagen, felt lonely in this desert of restless people running about on the paved streets in the city, but never, never was I bored in Greenland. Perhaps it was because that up there you have to think and act on your own and your ingenuity and resourcefulness are constantly put to the test".*[142]

1928-29

The next chapter in the history of Germaniahavn station began on the 13th September 1928, when two Norwegians went ashore. It was a stormy day, and they had barely reached the beach before their small boat was swamped by the foaming heavy seas. The two men, Jonas Karlsbak and Jørgen Furnes, were part of the Hird Expedition. Now that the Danish trappers were no longer active, the Norwegians were free to use Germaniahavn. During the summer the expedition had equipped the territory with trappers' huts, and had agreed between them that Karlsbak should trap on the Pendulum Øer while Furnes should have the mainland in the northern part of Wollaston Forland.

Christmas Eve they had a visit, and Karlsbak wrote in his diary: "(Hermann) *Andresen arrived here this morning bringing Christmas greetings from everybody. We also had a letter from Sulebak. He is fit and has a good catch and all is well for Christmas. We are very pleased with our catch and in our minds send a Merry Christmas and a Happy New Year to our friends and loved ones in Norway. The storm is howling and the house creaking, but we're smoking our pipes and have not a care in the world".*[143]

At the end of April, Karlsbak shot a female polar bear with two cubs. He brought the cubs with him to the station where they fell asleep at night on their mother's fur which Karlsbak had placed in a berth. "Kalle" and "Kitty", as the cubs were named, seemed to be doing alright and for the time being Karlsbak had to interrupt his trapping to take care of his pets. When Karlsbak and Furnes in the middle of June rowed to Kap Herschell to await the supply ship, they carried the cubs with them. They were taken back to Europe, and probably spent the rest of their days in a zoo.

1929-30

On the 19th August 1929 Danish trappers once again took over the Germaniahavn station. The director of the new company Nanok, J.G. Jennov wrote: *"We met three Norwegians here (to prevent any misunderstanding I must point out that they were sympathetic and nice people, who certainly would not have taken any material from the station). They were in the process of placing huts on the mainland from Kap Herschell, northwards through to Claveringstrædet and past Kuhn Ø. We negotiated on how to share the territory, as both parties realized that no one had any interest in trapping on the other part's territory. I made a deal with the leader Gjesvold* (Arnulf Gisvold) *that we would keep away from the mainland from Kap Herschell to around Borlase Warren, and from Lindeman and Fligely Fjords, as well as Ardencaple Inlet to a point on the north coast where the fjord split into two. Mr. Gjesvold committed himself not to trap on Sabine Ø, Pendulum Ø* (Lille Pendulum), *Kuhn Ø and the mainland north of the above mentioned point in Ardencaple Inlet. We have, by the way, agreed upon helping and supporting each other when possible.*

I have had to dispose of the stations differently than planned from home, partly because we have not been able to reach Danmark Havn, and partly because the station house at Carlshavn, presumably due to the carelessness of a Norwegian (Hallvard Devold) has burnt down. The house will be rebuilt next year and then put at our disposal".[144]

According to the plan, Andreas Hvidberg and Arne Christian Frederik Schwarck were to have stayed alone at Germaniahavn, but as Carlshavn could not be used, Carl Aage Knudsen and Evald Rasmussen were now also to winter at the Germaniahavn station. Andreas Hvidberg wrote in his book "Pelsjægerliv i Nordøstgrønland" (hunting life in North-East Greenland):[145] *"I am to stay here at Sabine Ø and have the responsibility for a station* (Germaniahavn), *that is a wooden house with a room four by five metres in two floors along the one wall, a pantry, same size, and two side sheds one metre wide and the length of the house, and an attic; it is the largest house in North-East Greenland".*

The choice of Andreas Hvidberg, 32-years old and from Middelfart, a newcomer to North-East Greenland as station manager, was not well received by Carl Aage Knudsen; he had earlier wintered for the East Greenland Company in 1921-23, and was to have been the station manager at the burnt down Carlshavn station. Jennov wrote later on that: *"Hvidberg is impulsive and talkative, while Knudsen is quiet, introvert and of the type who can go for ages brooding over a supposed insult. Knudsen and Rasmussen left Sabine Ø in January, and went to Sandodden, as the relationship during the polar night had become intolerable".*[146] Nevertheless, according to Hvidberg the Christmas had been extremely festive. The Norwegians, Eilif Herdal and Otto Johnsen, from the Liavåg station, had arrived in a snowstorm to celebrate Christmas with their Danish neighbours. They were men to Hvidberg's liking; full of juicy stories and crazy ideas. The house echoed from singing and toasting five days in a row and the party climaxed when Herdal gave lessons in ski jumping: *"With great difficulty we had balanced him with skis and everything on the upper bunk from where he was to jump over the stove to the floor. Schwarck lay behind on the skis as a counterweight and was supposed to roll away when told. I counted: '1' – '2' – but Cold-in-the-butt-Frederik-Schwarck became nervous and before I reached '3' our innocent stove had turned over on the floor together with a couple of broken skis and a cursing Norwegian. The ski points ended up sticking out through the window".*[147]

1930-31

On the 21st July 1930 the trapping season effectively ended, when the masts of "Godthaab" appeared behind Hvalrosø. Later the same day, the American schooner "Effie M. Morrissey" commanded by Robert (Bob) Bartlett, Peary's old ship's master, arrived.[148] A new Danish trapper, Hans Bruun, also arrived with the schooner. Bruun was then 31-years old, with a "live fast - die young" attitude, a playboy and gambler, who until his twentieth year had never known straitened circumstances. His father, Lars Emil Bruun (1852-1923), had made millions trading butter. The young Bruun had inherited this fortune, and within a few years had lost it all on gambling, fast cars and women. One day, at the fashionable Bellevue Strandhotel, he accidentally ran into the celebrated Danish polar explorer, Knud Rasmussen. They became friends, and Bruun was fascinated by Rasmussen's stories of Greenland. Eventually Bruun ended up in North-East Greenland with Nanok, where Jennov placed him and Arne Schwarck at Germaniahavn. In the summer of 1930 these two built the "Kap Buchenau hytten" [463].

Bruun left Germaniahavn in the spring of 1931, after J.G. Jennov learnt that the Norwegians were planning to establish a radio station in the inner part of Scoresby Sund. Jennov decided to report these rumours to Denmark, but as matters stood he could not send the telegram via the Norwegian radio station in Myggbukta. Hans Bruun, and James van Hauen from Hochstetter, were given the task of sending a telegram via the nearest Danish radio station, which in those days was located in Scoresbysund / Ittoqqortoormiit.

In 1931 Jennov summed up: *"Bruun and Schwarck have done a good job. The station has been put in complete order and during the trapping season 80 to 90 traps have been made and placed in the territory. Time after time during the winter the ice broke up in Pendulum Strædet, which made it difficult to use Hansabugthuset* (Ingrid Havn [456-1]) *and it was not possible to visit Pendulum Ø* (Lille Pendulum) *before the end of February. In spite of all that has been done, the catch has been extremely poor, namely eight foxes. I do not believe that Sabine Ø will ever provide a catch large enough to make it profitable to run it as an independent station".*[149]

This was effectively a death-sentence on the Germaniahavn station, which since 1931 has only been used as a travellers' hut.

In the summer of 1936, when there was no pack ice at all along the North-East Greenland coast, the heavy swells reached the house, smashing windows and doors.

In 1942-43 German forces from the Hansa Bugt station operated by Operation Holzauge used Germaniahavn as a hunting lodge, and it was here they were discovered by members of the North-East Greenland Sledge Patrol in March 1943.

During the following years the Germaniahavn station gradually fell into decay, due to lack of

Hans Bruun and James van Hauen en route to Scoresbysund. Maristua, 29th April 1931. © Sverre Sørensen / Norwegian Polar Institute

maintenance, and in the spring of 1947 the entire living room was reported to be filled up with a huge lump of ice. As a result, a Nanok team was sent up to Germaniahavn on the 29th July 1948, with orders to tear down the old house and build a new one from the same materials. For this task, Jennov had chosen Mogens Graae, Harald Mikkelsen, Erling Pedersen, Peder Klokker and Hans Thomsen. At the same time two new trappers' huts were built on Sabine Ø, namely "Hansa Bugt hytten" [456-2] and "Kroneberghytten" [449].

Giæver 1939; Jennov 1939; A138; Ø044.

Recent status

The new house at Germaniahavn was never used as a trappers' station. The location is not suitable for residence, unless you wish to study polar bears. Up to the 1980s Sirius occasionally used the house, but it was then abandoned due to its poor condition.

In 1999 Nanok decided to restore Germaniahavn. Parts of the woodwork and ceiling had become so moist, rotten and mouldy, that they had to be removed or replaced. A new coal stove was installed on the same occasion. Since then Germaniahavn has been maintained and is now used frequently.[150]

The original main house from 1919 at Germaniahavn, c. 1933. © Arne Philbert

The site of the original Germaniahavn trappers' station [447-3]; which was erected in 1919 for the East Greenland Company, 24th July 2004. (Above and centre, left) The foundation of the original Germaniahavn station main house is now close to being taken by the sea. (Centre, right and below) The foundation of Hans Ludvig Jensen's hus. © NCN

Germaniahavn [447-3]. The present hut at Germaniahavn was built in 1948 from materials taken from the old Danish trappers' station erected in 1919. At the end of the 1990s the hut had become so damp and mouldy that it was uninhabitable. Nanok therefore decided to restore the hut in 1999. (Above) Germaniahavn before restoration, 1999. (Centre, left) Inside walls and ceiling were rotted and mouldy. (Centre, right, top) The Nanok team repairing the roof, 1999. (Centre, right, bottom) Inside after restoration and installation of a new coal stove, 2003. (Bottom) Germaniahavn 12th August 1999. Hvalrosø in the background. © NCN

HAMNA
[208-2]

Wintering party

1939-40: Søren Richter, Magne Råum, Ole Andreas Bachke
1940-46: None
1946-47: Hjalmar Hanson
1947-48: Martin Larsen Lie
1948-50: Per Myrvold
1950-51: Halvor Bjørdal

A little north of Mesters Vig, on the south coast of Kong Oscar Fjord, is the small enclosed bay Noret, guarded by two peninsulas, Labben and Hovedet. On the east side of Hovedet there is a small bay, Hamna, and a trappers' station.

1939-40

One day in the beginning of 1939, Magne Råum received a letter with an Oslo postmark. The letter came from the archaeologist and trapper Søren Richter, and its contents presented Råum with a dilemma. Richter wrote that he was planning a wintering in North-East Greenland to catch live fox. The entire expedition would be financed by a ship owner, who had interests in fur farming and wanted live foxes from Greenland for breeding. The ship owner said he would pay 300 Norwegian kroner for each live white fox, and triple that for each blue fox. Richter had already made arrangements to use the Kap Peterséns and Antarctichavn territories in Kong Oscar Fjord, and had hired an experienced fox tender. The only thing he lacked was a skilled trapping partner – Magne Råum.[151] It was a tempting offer, taking into consideration that a forest worker had to work very hard in order to earn a mere 4-5 kroner a day. However, the problem for Råum was that after his return from his last wintering in 1937, he had married and taken over the family farm in Namdalen. He had also become a father. There had also been other good offers, because Råum was a much sought after expedition member. In 1938 Willie Knutsen had wanted him to join his Norwegian-French Polar expedition, but Råum had to decline due to a leg injury. Råum's wife, Ragnhild, however insisted that she would sacrifice one year of their life together for this opportunity, which might make them wealthy.

On the 14th August 1939, Richter, Råum and Ole Andreas Bachke, the fox tender, went ashore in a small bay in Kong Oscar Fjord that they named Hamna (or Havna), and immediately started to build a station house. It took them five days and they named the station "Trønderheimen". As they now had a home, Richter and Råum sailed off to make the trapping territory ready. It was already well provided with trappers' huts that had been built over the years by trappers from Kap Peterséns and Antarctichavn.

Ole Bachke remained at Hamna. He came from Fet near Akershus, and had his own fox fur farm back in Norway. Now he began to build cages at Hamna for the foxes they expected to catch.

On the 4th September 1939, the first signs of winter were apparent. By chance they turned on the radio and tuned in to the BBC. The headline news was that Hitler had not replied to the ultimatum proclaimed by France and Great Britain that German troops must be withdrawn from Poland. The Allies had therefore been at war with Germany for 24 hours.

Trapper Per Myrvold at Hamna, c. 1949. © Bjarne Myrvold

At an instant their dreams of prosperity and adventure had turned into a chaos of uncertainty and speculation. Indeed, Norway as a neutral country had not yet become involved in the war, but for how long? Surely Hitler and the German war machine would soon fix their eyes on the north? Would any ship return to pick them up the following summer? To these questions the radio had no answer.

On the night of the 16th April 1940, the Greenlander Lars Napatoq brought them a letter from Aage de Lemos, the Danish wireless operator at Ella Ø. This was the news they had dreaded most: Norway was now at war and had been occupied by Germany. The letter also reported that the German occupation had triggered off an allied blockade of Norway. Supplies would therefore now arrive from either Great Britain or Canada, and the trappers could not expect to return to Norway, which was now a German-controlled area. This letter naturally raised concern for their families at home, and was also a setback - for who would now buy the 40 or so live foxes they had caught during the winter?

On the 6th August 1940, the "Fridtjof Nansen", a Norwegian naval vessel, arrived in Kong Oscar Fjord.[152] The trappers were given a choice: they could either stay and carry on with their trapping, or return with "Fridtjof Nansen" to Iceland, where they would be given the chance to join the allied forces. Within a few hours the Hamna station was evacuated, and equipment dogs and catch - in all 34 live foxes and 46 fox skins - were loaded aboard the "Fridtjof Nansen". On arrival in Iceland the three men enrolled in the Norwegian ski squad, formed by seamen, whalers and other men who had escaped from Norway via Sweden.

In May 1941, thirteen members of the ski squad, including Råum, Richter and Bachke were ordered to Jan Mayen. In 1944 Råum was transferred to the Norwegian forces in Scotland in order to participate in the liberation of Norway. Fortunately, capitulation and peace soon came, and on the 12th May 1945 Magne Råum finally returned to Norway, to be welcomed by his wife and their now 6-year-old son.[153]

For the rest of his life Magne Råum lived in Foldereid, North Trøndelag, in Norway. He died in March 2003, 93-years old.

1940-59

In the years 1940-46 trapping was suspended due to the war, and Hamna was in this period used only as a travellers' hut.

Norwegian trapping was resumed in 1946, and between 1946 and 1959 the three trappers' stations Kap Peterséns, Hamna and Antarctichavn in the Kong Oscar Fjord region were manned by Hermann Andresen's Expeditions. During this period Hamna served as the main station in 1946-47 (Hjalmar Hanson), 1947-48 (Martin Larsen Lie), 1948-50 (Per Myrvold) and 1950-51 (Halvor Bjørdal). Some episodes from these winterings are described in the section on the Antarctichavn station.

Aune 1991; Nyquist 1945; Polarboken 1963-1964; Magne Råum pers. comm.

Recent status

After the end of the trapper era, Hamna has mainly been used as a weekend hut by the personnel stationed at Mestersvig Airfield, who have carried out essential maintenance. The house is still in good and usable condition.

Hamna, 22nd April 1979. © Peter Schmidt Mikkelsen

Hamna [208-2], 17th August 2006. Hamna is a former Norwegian trappers' station, built in 1939 by Søren Richter's Expeditions. It was used as a trappers' station until 1951, and subsequently as a travellers' hut. Hamna is still in good condition, thanks to regular maintenance by personnel from Mestersvig Airfield. (Top) View south-east towards Archer Øer. (Centre, left) Interior. (Centre, right) Fox cages from 1939 at Hamna. (Bottom) View eastwards towards Archer Øer and Kap Simpson. © NCN

HOCHSTETTER
[510]

Wintering party

1929-30: Hans Ludvig Jensen, Niels Hansen, James van Hauen, Knud Østergaard
1930-31: Niels Hansen, Berndt Jensen, Knud Østergaard, Andreas Hvidberg, James van Hauen
1931-32: Niels Hansen, Leander E. Emskær Larsen, Berndt Jensen, Bjarne Ludvigsen
1932-33: Niels Hansen, Henning Nyholm-Poulsen, Finn Kristoffersen
1933-34: Arne Philbert, Walther Povelsen
1934-35: Leo Hansen, Berndt Jensen, Christian Sørensen, Henry Larsen, Ole Winstedt, Arvid Waldenstrøm Petterson, Christian Jensen
1935-36: Berndt Jensen, Christian Sørensen, Henry Larsen, Ole Winstedt, Arvid Waldenstrøm Petterson
1936-37: Hans Ludvig Jensen, Georg Øksentjørn, Carl Henrik Schultz, Poul Hennings, Alfred Hansen
1937-38: Hans Ludvig Jensen, Georg Øksentjørn, Carl Henrik Schultz, Poul Hennings
1938-39: Alfred Hansen, Svend Aage Jespersen, Anders Kristian Østerlund Johannesen
1939-41: Alfred Hansen, Finn Kristoffersen, Mads Christensen
1941-46: None
1946-47: Orla Jensen, (Mogens Graae)
1947-48: Orla Jensen, Mogens Graae
1948-49: Harald Mikkelsen, Hans Thomsen
1949-50: None
1950-51: Erik Larsen
1951-52: Hans Frederiksen
1952-54: None
1954-55: Hans Frederiksen, Erik B. Larsen

1929-30

As early as 1921, Johan F. Petersen, who was a trapper in the East Greenland Company, had suggested that a trappers' station be built west of Kap Rink on Hochstetter Forland. On the 20th August 1929, the idea became a reality when the vessel "Birkild" anchored up, and the Nanok men aboard set about unloading materials for the station. When the ship left, Hans Ludvig Jensen, James van Hauen and Knud Østergaard remained behind to build the station under the leadership of Niels Hansen.

On the 30th August they raised the roof and Jensen recorded that: *"we wrote a letter, signed with the names of the participants and put it in the north-eastern corner of the house. We named the house "Nanok" in commemoration of our company".*[154] On September 17th they moved into the house which was: *"good and*

Nanok trappers in front of the Hochstetter station, summer 1932. Left to right: Finn Kristoffersen, Henning Nyholm-Poulsen (sitting on the doorstep), Evald Rasmussen, Bjarne Ludvigsen, Berndt Jensen, Niels Hansen, Leander Elias Emskær Larsen. © Arne Philbert

maybe the best of all the stations. It has side sheds along three walls, and faces towards the beach. From the two roof windows we have a wonderful view to Kuhn Ø, Kap Wynn, Sabine Ø and Pendulum Ø (Lille Pendulum). *Around the house we have build an earth wall".*[155] Still, Ludvig Jensen was not entirely content. It had taken valuable time to build the house and he estimated that if each man's board and wages amounted to 10 kroner per day, the company could have saved 145 kroner, had it instead bought a house for 1400 kroner: *"ready-made in modules, to be assembled and ready for occupation in two days".*[156]

At the beginning of November they caught their first fox, but then an accident occurred. They had prepared a trappers' hut which was to be placed at Kap Klinkerfues. On the 6th November, van Hauen and Jensen drove off with the first load, but while out on the ice in Peters Bugt they came to a crack. Jensen wrote: *"Two thirds of the sledge had passed the crack when I jumped upon the rear of the sledge, and my extra weight caused it to slide backwards into the crack with me sinking to my crutch and getting both kamiks filled with water".*[157] Van Hauen wanted them to return but Jensen insisted that they should continue. When they returned to Hochstetter late in the evening, six of Jensen's toes were found to be frozen stiff. Niels Hansen and Østergaard spend half an hour rubbing them with snow: *"and they succeeded in starting the blood circulation, but blimey, how swollen they are. The skin is torn to pieces, so it is bleeding and it feels as if they have broken every bone in my feet",*[158] Jensen wrote. He saved his toes, but had to remain at the station for the rest of the trapping season.

They never finished the hut intended for Kap Klinkerfues, and due to the lack of travellers' huts in the vicinity, trapping was mainly carried out close to the main station. On the 6th February 1930, van Hauen and Østergaard went to Ardencaple Fjord to investigate the trapping possibilities there, but two weeks later they returned from a fruitless trip. They had spent most of the time in a snow cave, held up by bad weather.

In the middle of March 1930, J.G. Jennov arrived together with the geologist Richard Bøgvad, and in May these two together with Hans Ludvig Jensen continued northwards to Danmark Havn in order to investigate an unconfirmed report of a cryolite deposit there. Unfortunately the rumour turned out to be a wild goose chase. Nevertheless, during their visit to Hochstetter Bøgvad located the coal seam that the Danmark Expedition had previously discovered on the east coast of Peters Bugt. This was good news. The coal lay exposed right down to the beach, and was only 12 km from Hochstetter, which meant that the station was self-sufficient with fuel. At the beginning of June 1930, Jennov and Bøgvad, together with van Hauen and Jensen, went southwards to the stations in the southern territory. Due to the problems with his feet, Jensen had to return to Denmark in 1930.

1930-31

During the summer of 1930, it was finally possible to equip the Hochstetter territory with trappers' huts. Niels Hansen had prepared the huts in advance, so that they would be ready to sail out when the ice broke up. Four were built: "Peters Bugt hytten" [522] "Kap Maurer hytten"[467], "Nordlige Fligely hytten" [474] and "Femdalhytten" [524-1].

The new trappers, under the leadership of Niels Hansen, were Berndt Jensen and Knud Østergaard. In December they were joined by Andreas Hvidberg and James van Hauen, who had given up a planned wintering on Shannon.

The new huts made it possible to expand the trapping territory. Niels Hansen spent two months in the hut at Peters Bugt, while van Hauen and Østergaard settled on Kuhn Ø. Hvidberg and Jensen chose "Femdalhytten" as their base for a period during

Greenlander sledge dogs in front of the Hochstetter station, summer 1932. © Arne Philbert

the spring, and it was on this trip that Hvidberg wrote his poem about the tribulations of the trapper, that was published in his book "Pelsjægerliv i Nordøstgrønland" (1932).[159]

One day at the end of April, J.G. Jennov arrived from the south. He wanted to expand the Nanok territory further northwards to Bessel Fjord, and in order to do so planned to build a series of trappers' huts. However, their few dogs had a limited carrying capacity, and with the materials available only three "dummy huts" were built: "Kap Oswald Heer hytten" [528], "Hundehuset" [535-3] and "Bessel Fjord hytten" [601-1].

In the summer of 1931, Østergaard, van Hauen and Hvidberg returned to Denmark. Of these three, only Hvidberg returned later for another wintering, as a participant in the Mørkefjord Expedition.

1931-32

The expansion of Nanok territory with new trappers' huts continued in the summer of 1931, when five more huts were built: "Koch Vig hytten" [515], "Kildedalhytten" [516], "Blåbærhytten" [469], "Sydlige Fligely hytten" [465] and "Kap Bremen hytten" [473]. The wintering party included Niels Hansen, Leander E. Emskær Larsen, Berndt Jensen and Bjarne Ludvigsen. The last-named was to have acted as wireless operator, manning the radio transmitter which had been installed at the station that year. However, the radio never came into use, as the batteries proved to be defective. In December, when Ludvigsen sledged down to Eskimonæs to fetch spare parts, he became so severely frost bitten that he had to stay there for the rest of the winter.

As in the previous winter, the trappers occupied different parts of the Hochstetter territory for several months. Larsen went to Kuhn Ø, and Hansen again stayed in Peters Bugt, where in the spring of 1932 using a foot trap he succeeded in catching: *"the old toothless female wolf, that had taken 17 foxes from the traps".*[160] This wolf was the only one ever caught by Nanok trappers.

In the spring, Berndt Jensen, who worked the Ardencaple Fjord district, developed blood poisoning from flensing a seal. He therefore had to travel home in the summer in order to receive medical attention for his hand. When he later returned to the east coast, he went under the nickname "Spækfinger" (blubber finger). Later, in 1943-45, he served as a member of the North-East Greenland Sledge Patrol. From this period, his friend Kurt Olsen wrote: *"Originally Berndt had played to dances in numerous village halls in Denmark. But he was calm natured and could not make himself play swing and jazz. As the gigs faded out he began to make his living in other areas. This is how he ended up as a trapper for "Nanok" in North-East Greenland. I guess he was looking for peace and quiet. And as he remained with "Nanok" for many years he probably found what he was looking for".*[161] Berndt Jensen worked for Nanok for a total of seven years. After WWII he returned to Denmark, where he from 1947 was manager of Randers Vandværk (Randers Waterworks) until he died of cancer in 1954.[162]

In the summer of 1932, Emskær Larsen and Ludvigsen also returned to Denmark.

1932-33

The wintering party at Hochstetter consisted of Niels Hansen, together with two novices, Finn Kristoffersen and Henning Nyholm-Poulsen. Thanks to their memoirs, "Jæger og fangstmand" (hunter and trapper) (Kristoffersen 1969), and "Fangstmand på Østgrønland 1932-33" (trapper in East Greenland 1932-33) (Nyholm-Poulsen 1985), the events of this season are well documented.

Niels Hansen, who was to celebrate his 55th

Left: Nanok trappers at Hochstetter 1932-33: Henning Nyholm-Poulsen, Niels Hansen and Finn Kristoffersen. Right: Henning Nyholm-Poulsen amongst the sledge dogs in the Hochstetter dog cages. © Arne Philbert

birthday on the 2nd November 1932: *"started in 1914 in West Greenland. Later he participated in the founding of Scoresbysund, and spent many years as a trapper in North-East Greenland. Greenland was his life, and when in the mood he would praise the land for us. He lived a simple life, but demanded strict order, so nobody was allowed to stagnate in his presence".*[163] The fact that "Old Niels" each summer could serve fresh radishes from his own vegetable patch contributed to making him a legend. He had in all nine winterings for Nanok, joined the North-East Greenland Sledge Patrol, and subsequently went to Julianehåb in West Greenland. After the war he returned to Denmark to enjoy his retirement.

Henning Nyholm-Poulsen, then 27-years old: *"was educated in the business world and had left a position as secretary of the board" ... "His reasons for taking this somewhat drastic step during the unemployment of the 1930s was probably his love of adventure, his loathing of the bourgeois life combined with an interest in the present Greenland dispute".*[164] However, he spent only one winter in Greenland.

Finn Kristoffersen described himself as a: *"17-years old hunting crazy gamekeeper trainee",*[165] who in spite of his youth had been permitted to sign a contract with Nanok. He spent a total of eighteen years in Greenland, including six winterings in North-East Greenland. As a big game hunter and trapper he was one of the few to whom, as he put it: *"it has been granted more or less directly to make a living from hunting throughout most of my life".*[166]

The year 1932-33 was characterized by an aggravation of the Danish-Norwegian dispute over the sovereignty of North-East Greenland. In the summer of 1932, the Hochstetter station - which previously had almost unlimited territory - became a Danish enclave surrounded by the three new Norwegian stations: Jonsbu, Sigurdsheim and Ottostrand. Despite the generally excellent relationships between ordinary Norwegian and Danish trappers, disagreements about sharing of the trapping territories could not be avoided. In the summer of 1932 the "Kap Buch hytten" [512] was built.

1933-34

When Denmark was finally granted sovereignty over all of Greenland, it was somewhat of an anticlimax that Nanok was only able to muster six trappers in the summer of 1933. Only two stations were manned. Hochstetter was taken over by Arne Philbert and Walther Povelsen. The latter was the brother of Povel Povelsen at Hvalrosodden, the only other station used this year. The first task of Philbert and Povelsen was to build the trappers' huts "Ailsahytten" [519] and "Langsøhytten" [532-1].

They had expected that the Norwegians would be prohibited from using poison for their fox trapping; however, on the 27th August they received information during a visit at Jonsbu where: *"Giæver told us that Dr. Koch had said, that with regard to the use of poison for trapping, as well as actions to protect the muskox, nothing would be done this year. This statement from Dr. Koch delivered by Giæver came as a big surprise for us; it would have been more appropriate if Koch had informed the Danish trappers directly".*[167] Philbert and Povelsen had no poison, so they definitely felt that they had been badly treated.

On the 29th October they split up in order to go trapping. Philbert worked the outer coast up to Bessel Fjord and the stretch to Peters Bugt. Povelsen tended the Kuhn Ø and the Ardencaple territories. When they met again on the 20th December, the result was 24 usable fox furs. Wolves had unfortunately ruined 16 furs. Both became ill at the beginning of January, but on the 8th of February 1934, they met once again, went their separate ways, and were reunited at Hochstetter on the 1st May. Philbert had then 37 furs and Povelsen 14, which they regarded as: *"a poor result considering the huge effort we put into it".*[168]

Amongst man's best friends. Left: Arne Philbert, 1932. Right: Walther Povelsen, 1932. © Arne Philbert

On June 11th they sledged down to Germaniahavn where they stayed until the middle of August. Jennov had ordered them to hunt seal and walrus, but the result was a few seals but no walrus. Arne Philbert later wintered at Ella Ø in 1936-37. He died in November 1995.

1934-35

In 1934 Nanok signed a contract with "Teatrenes Filmskontor" for the production of a film about trapping. The cine-photographer Leo Hansen was therefore on board "Gustav Holm" when it sailed for Greenland. However, difficult ice conditions raised problems. Firstly for Philbert and Povelsen, who were now back at Hochstetter, but had to be taken to Sandodden by motor boat, and then evacuated by plane so they could return home. Changes in manning of the stations also became necessary. Apart from Niels Hansen and Aage Hansen, all the newly arrived trappers had to take up temporary residence at Hochstetter, which then housed the following: Leo Hansen, Berndt Jensen, Christian Sørensen, Arvid Waldenstrøm Petterson, Henry Larsen and Ole Winstedt.

Leo Hansen, who was in charge of the party, told his story of the wintering in his book "Situationen er kritisk" (situation critical) (Hansen 1939). After a slightly chaotic start to the wintering, he signed contracts with the men on behalf of Nanok so that they: *"shall receive no salary but have 50% of the catch and "Nanok" the other 50%. The furs are all to be priced at 150 kroner each"*.[169]

The trappers, who were to receive equal shares of the profit, had to pay for their own equipment which amounted to 500-600 kroner per person as well as various expenses for transport and sale of the catch. In the autumn of 1934 two huts were built, "Ullahytten" [508] and "Grandjeanhytten" [503].

At the beginning of May 1935, the wireless operator Ole Winstedt and trapper Arvid Waldenstrøm Petterson went to Hvalrosodden to take over the station after Christian Jensen, who had arrived at Hochstetter from there at the end of November 1934.

In the summer of 1935 Christian Jensen became ill with scurvy, and when it became known that Captain Aage H. Vedel on "Godthaab" had announced on the 19th August that the supply visits to the stations of the north-east coast had been cancelled, something had to be done. Leo Hansen, Henry Larsen, Christian Sørensen and Christian Jensen decided to sail to Eskimonæs, where the chance of being rescued by air was still possible. However the drift ice in Hochstetterbugten caused so many difficulties that they did not reach Kap Berlin until the 25th August. Christian Jensen was by then very feeble. However, help was on the way. Vedel had asked "Buskø" for assistance, and as this proved impossible due to the pack ice four Norwegians sailed out from Kap Herschell. On the 27th August the rescue team was approaching Kap Berlin and: *"soon we recognized the Norwegian trapper* (Hermann) *Andresen, who, with a huge smile, welcomed us back"*.[170]

Leo Hansen and Christian Jensen went with "Buskø" to Norway while Christian Sørensen and Henry Larsen temporarily took up residence at Sandodden, the only Nanok station with sufficient supplies. Leo Hansen's film still exists and is played on festive occasions in Lyngby Bio, until recently owned by Leo Hansen's widow.

1935-36

After two years without resupply, the supplies at the Nanok stations north of Wollaston Forland were almost exhausted. This had an impact on the trapping,

Christmas Eve 1934 at Hochstetter. Sitting from left: Henry Larsen and Leo Hansen. Standing from left: Christian Sørensen, Christian Jensen, Berndt Jensen and Arvid Waldenstrøm Petterson. © Arctic Institute

as the men had to leave their stations and travel southwards. The situation was worst at Hvalrosodden, which Ole Winstedt and Arvid Waldenstrøm Petterson left in October 1935. They arrived at Hochstetter, where Berndt Jensen was staying on his own. Any clearer picture of where the trappers wintered this season is not available.

1936-37

In the summer of 1936, a supply ship finally succeeded in making a call at Hochstetter. However, once again Nanok had to change their plans. Originally two trappers, Georg Øksentjørn and Alfred Hansen, should have wintered at the station; but as the Captain of "Gustav Holm" had instructions not to sail north of Hochstetter, Hans Ludvig Jensen, Carl Henrik Schultz and Poul Hennings also went ashore here. They had signed a contract to take over the stations in Dove Bugt, but an attempt to go there by motor boat had to be abandoned. Øksentjørn then offered them lodgings at Hochstetter: *"and we accepted the offer with thankfulness"*, Jensen wrote on 1st September 1936.[171]

As soon as the first new fjord ice formed, the three men travelled northwards to take up residence at Ottostrand. They trapped here from the 3rd November until the 22nd December, when they returned to Hochstetter: *"as thunder and lightning with empty sledges. I got cramp in both my thighs and fainted, well, I'm getting too old for this shit"* the 62-year-old Hans Ludvig Jensen wrote.[172] Having celebrated Christmas with Øksentjørn and Hansen, the three once again returned to Ottostrand. In the period from the 8th March to the 25th May they were trapping north in Dove Bugt.

In the meantime, the two Hochstetter men had been hit by an accident. On the 20th February Øksentjørn and Hansen were heading for Grandjean Fjord. It was an unexpectedly hard journey, with very bad going and they finally reached Ullahytten at one o'clock at night. Here Alfred Hansen's: *"toes were frozen completely stiff. All through the night we rubbed them with snow, yet the two big toes developed large blisters"*.[173] A week-long blizzard delayed their return to Hochstetter. The pains were terrible and three weeks later Hansen went through a critical period with severe fever and loss of consciousness. From this point he slowly got better, but it was not until the middle of April that Øksentjørn dared leave his companion alone; one of his toes would not heal and they were running out of medicaments. At the end of May, Alfred Hansen was transported to Sandodden by Aage Hansen, who was stationed there. In the summer of 1937 Alfred Hansen was evacuated to Iceland with the "Quest" Expedition. When he reached Denmark, he underwent an operation to remove the outer joint of one of the big toes. However, this did not stop him from returning to North-East Greenland in the summer of 1938.

1937-38

It turned out to be another summer without a visit from any ship, and no fresh supplies, as "Gustav Holm" did not reach further north than Scoresby Sund. The sea ice never really broke up at Hochstetter Forland, and an attempt to supply the trapping territory using a motor boat also failed. On the 21st of September, Georg Øksentjørn wrote: *"Since no supply of the northern stations has been possible, and there is no food further north than Hundehuset* [535-3] *and only a few sacks of coal at Roseneath* (Ottostrand)*, the trappers Hans Ludvig Jensen and C.H. Schultz will remain here at the Hochstetter station this season – hopefully Poul Hennings is staying at Sandodden with all the dogs"*.[174] On the 30th October Poul Hennings finally turned up: *"as right as rain with 10 dogs, including four puppies. He had swapped his best dog "Smule" to the Norwegian trapper Tolløfsen for two puppies. I gave him quite a telling-off"*, Hans Ludvig Jensen wrote.[175]

And so the trapping could begin and it turned out to be the best fox year for ages. At Christmas the four men had caught 133 foxes, but unfortunately the missing supply ship in the summer led to unpleasant consequences. On the 8th May Øksentjørn wrote: *"Unfortunately I could not trap after Christmas as I developed scurvy in my legs, making it impossible for me to walk. As a consequence I missed a good catch this year, as I for sure could have counted on about 100 fox; well, the main thing is that I have recovered and my health is continually improving"*.[176] Øksentjørn could thank the British ornithologist Charles Bird for his recovery. Bird had come up from Myggbukta to stay at Jonsbu, and luckily had brought along some vitamin-C tablets; it was a dose of these that cured Øksentjørn.

The four trappers all went home in the summer of 1938. Hans Ludvig Jensen, who had participated in the founding of both the Danish trapping companies, closed his diary with the words: *"And so ended my final journey to Greenland"*.

1938-39

Alfred Hansen returned to take over the leadership at Hochstetter, where the trappers included Svend Aage Jespersen, then 28-years old and Anders Kristian Østerlund Johannesen. They built "Lindeman Fjord hytten" [458-2], but the events of the year were

Hochstetter 1938. From left: Carl Henrik Schultz, Georg Øksentjørn and Hans Ludvig Jensen. © Niels Ove Jensen

overshadowed by a tragic mystery.

In February 1939 Jespersen and Johannesen vanished, never to be seen again. Alfred Hansen was the last to see the two men alive on Friday the 17th February 1939. He noted: *"Fine weather. Jespersen and Johannesen have today gone to Ailsa with nine dogs and two puppies. Jespersen went as he was expecting mail and possibly telegrams".*[177]

The destination of their journey was Mønstedhus, where mail might have been brought from Hvalrosodden. If the mail required an answer, Jespersen was to travel on to Hvalrosodden, while Johannesen was to return immediately to Hochstetter. The distance between Hochstetter and Mønstedhus is only about 70 km, so Johannesen could have returned within a week, perhaps a little more if he stayed over a couple of extra days. However, the men did not return, and after three weeks had passed Alfred Hansen began to worry. Where could they be? Hansen himself could not start a search, as Jespersen and Johannesen had taken all the dogs with them, except for two bitches that had puppies.

On the 17th March 1939 (18th March according to the Hochstetter station journal) Alfred Hansen had a chance visit from a police patrol from Eskimonæs, Ib Poulsen and Christian Arke. Alfred Hansen reported his concern for the missing trappers, and asked Poulsen to instruct them to return to Hochstetter as soon as he met them. Poulsen and Arke continued their journey, arriving at Ottostrand on the 19th March, where Bjarne Jakobsen said he had not seen the two Danes. Both he and the trappers at Mønstedhus had been expecting their visit for a long time, as it had been arranged earlier. Of the further events, Ib Poulsen wrote in a draft for his "Årsberetning (annual report) for Eskimonæs 1938-39": *"Jakobsen told me, by the way, that the trapper Peter Nielsen at Mønstedhus, had found Johannesen's anorak on the 12th March at the Oswald Heer hytten. Nielsen had given it to Jakobsen, and he passed it on to me in order to return it to Hansen at Hochstetter; Hansen confirmed that it was Johannesen's anorak.*

The following day, the 20th March, I went to Mønstedhus, where I met Niels Hansen at home alone. Niels Hansen had written in his diaries the following relevant information: On the 27th February Peter Nielsen had been up the hill behind the Oswald Heer hut, and from there observed that the door of the hut was open; however as he was not going to use the hut on this trip, he had not taken the time to go down and take a closer look. On the 12th March on his next visit to the hut, Nielsen found Johannesen's anorak outside the still open door. As far as Nielsen could see, two men had stayed overnight in the hut and – judging from the consumption of the food – stayed there for about two days".

Peter Nielsen in 1988 wrote another slightly different account of this incident, that: *"somebody had been in the hut, but I could not tell whether some coal had been used and later on I found an anorak beneath the snow in the porch. They had possibly stopped for a few hours in the hut, but when they had realized that the weather was turning bad, they had continued and were taken by surprise by the snow, which blew with the force of a blizzard".*[178]

At Mønstedhus as well as at Ottostrand the trappers wondered why Jespersen and Johannesen had not turned up when they had been so close; but no one then considered the possibility of an accident let alone a search. However, assessing the information, Poulsen had to assume that an accident had occurred, and the following day he and Arke commenced the search along Hochstetter Forland. Poulsen wrote: *"Anything upright was carefully examined, but nothing of interest was found until we arrived at Ailsahytten, where we found Jespersen's sledge bag in the porch; in the bag we found a white fox together with some locking sticks for the traps."*
In the following weeks Poulsen and Arke searched the Hochstetter area as well as Shannon without finding any further traces. Later on a "Lauge Koch kamik" was found, presumed lost by either Jespersen or Johannesen between Oswald Heer and Ailsa, but this find did not provide any enlightenment as to the fate of the missing men.

Today - more than half a century later - the question remains: how could two men, two sledges and no less than 11 dogs, vanish without trace on a stretch with no open water?

The prevailing theory is that the men had been surprised by the blizzard and subsequently followed the coastline northwards from Oswald Heer. This way they might have entered the entrance of Agnetesøelven and continued further inland, where they succumbed. That not a single dog turned up later may have been because the hungry dogs had found poisoned bait intended for fox. Finally, the missing men's bodies and their sledges could have been washed out to sea by the river during the thaw. Another theory proposed by J.G. Jennov was that Jespersen and Johannesen could have died during a bear hunt out on frozen sea ice, where the two inexperienced trappers and their dogs may have been attacked and killed by a furious mother bear defending a wounded cub.[179]

A couple of incidents prior to the accident have provided ideas for other theories. In November 1938 Alfred Hansen pulled Jespersen out of the water, when he had gone through the ice. On this occasion Jespersen declared: *"If I ever find myself in a situation I cannot handle, I will shoot myself and the dogs."* Alfred Hansen did not believe him. There is also the fact that the relationship between the two missing was not without problems. In 1993 Alfred Hansen recounted that when the two trappers were in Iceland on their way to Greenland, they had got into a fight that resulted in a couple of loose teeth for Johannesen. At Hochstetter they had also quarrelled. Nevertheless, the fate of the two trappers is one of the major outstanding mysteries of North-East Greenland.

1939-40

No supply ship arrived at Hochstetter in 1939, and it was not until the 2nd September that Alfred Hansen's new partners Finn Kristoffersen and Mads Christensen arrived by motor boat from Sandodden. Kristoffersen had just completed his participation in the Danish Dog Sledge Expedition 1938-39. The trapping continued as planned, but unfortunately the 1939-40 winter did not live up to expectations.

On the 16th April 1940 Eivind Tolløfsen arrived at Hochstetter. He was homeward bound for Jonsbu after a visit to Niels Hansen and Peter Nielsen at Mønstedhus, where there was a radio receiver. Tolløfsen brought with him the alarming news that Denmark and Norway had been occupied by Germany. The trappers at Hochstetter decided to await events, and in anticipation of a new wintering gave the station house a thorough make-over. Rotten floor boards were replaced, the rustic walls were covered with roofing felt and a new kitchen was installed in the east-facing porch.

1940-41

On the 17th August, Finn Kristoffersen and Mads Christensen returned from a boat trip to Sandodden with the news that "Veslekari" could be expected within the near future. On the 23rd August they started on a depot trip to Ardencaple Fjord, and when they returned the following day, "Veslekari" had made a call at Hochstetter: "(Marius) *Jensen and* (Kurt) *Olsen, who were going to Mørkefjord were here, as the ship was unable to reach Mørkefjord. All supplies were unloaded here. There were potatoes and mail for us"*.[180]

Five days later Ib Poulsen arrived by motor boat from the south; he had also been with "Veslekari" to Greenland. On the 31st August the three Danes, who had newly arrived, made an attempt to sail further northwards to Mørkefjord; but they: *"came back at 11 p.m. They had been to Ailsa"*.[181] The day after the three men continued southwards for a temporary stay at Kap Herschell. In 1993 Alfred Hansen reported that he and the other men at Hochstetter had wondered at that time why the Germans had permitted these men to leave the occupied parts of Denmark and Norway.

On the 16th December Mads Christensen summarised the events of the autumn: *"During the autumn the station has been visited by Ib Poulsen and the wireless operator Olsen northward bound. Peter Nielsen from Roseneath has been here three times for supplies, which we had brought here from Sandodden." ... "Plentiful fox tracks have been observed in the trapping territories but the catch is poor, presumably because of the large numbers of small animals such as ptarmigan and lemming. On the 15th December we were all gathered at the station again with the following catch: Kristoffersen three white foxes, Hansen one white fox and one polar bear, I had three white foxes"*.[182]

On the 1st May 1941 Mads Christensen once again took stock: *"On the 11th January Hansen and I drove out into the trapping territories again. On the 10th April we were together again at the station and had a visit from* (Andreas) *Hvidberg southbound. After talking to Hvidberg,* (Alfred) *Hansen wanted to go with him to West Greenland as it had turned out that Kuhn Ø did not produce any catch. It ought to be mentioned that Hansen also found quite a lot of poison bait, which had not been removed. On his trip to Germaniahavn he found 12 poisoned ptarmigan set out as bait at Kap Berlin. These were brought back to the station. Furthermore, in the spring the station has been visited by* (Carlos) *Ziebell,* (Kristian) *Madsen and* (Kurt) *Olsen southbound. Ove Harder Jensen, Richard Nielsen and Peter Nielsen had visited the station on their way to Sandodden for supplies, and Marius Jensen on his way northbound. The catch this season has been as follows. The station territory, Peters Bugt and Ailsa, 34 white foxes, one blue fox. Ardencaple and Grandjean 13 white foxes, one ermine. Kuhn Ø and the Pendulum Øer six white foxes, one polar bear. These were mainly caught during the last two months of the season".*[183]

After a misty and rainy summer, Kristoffersen and Christensen prepared themselves for a new wintering; but on the 2nd August 1941 a stop was put to these plans: *"According to the express wish from the highest authority, we today close the station and sail with the motor boat to Eskimonæs, where we will be taken on board and transported to West Greenland by the American Coast Guard cutter, which in addition to 84 fox furs, one polar bear fur, three dog furs and six puppy furs now has our private luggage on board. All radio equipment belonging to the station will be taken to Eskimonæs; likewise, the motor boat will be put ashore there where it can be looked after. The dogs belonging to the station will be brought ashore, possibly at Eskimonæs or wherever there is room for them. Remaining at the station, besides the food and supplies listed, is a box with blown-out eggs, in all 26 specimens, and a box with stuffed birds.* (Signed:) *Finn Kristoffersen, station manager, Mads Christensen, trapper".*[184]

Hochstetter was to remain unmanned until 1946. Mads Christensen served in the North-East Greenland Sledge Patrol from 1941-42, while Alfred Hansen and Finn Kristoffersen went to West Greenland.

Alfred Hansen returned to North-East Greenland and served in the Sledge Patrol in 1944-45. After the war he returned to Denmark, where until his retirement he worked as a driver with the breweries.

In the period 1941-54 Kristoffersen worked at the sheep breeding stations in Julianehåb (Qaqortoq) and Godthåb (Nuuk). Subsequently he was employed at the Vildtbiologisk Station at Kalø in Denmark. Finn Kristoffersen died in 1990, 74-years old.

1946-47

On the 29th October 1946, the first post-war wintering trappers, Orla Jensen and Mogens Graae, arrived at Hochstetter, where: *"we went searching for some food. We can manage here, but are going to have to excavate a little coal, as there is almost nothing left",* Graae wrote.[185] They had tried to sail to Hochstetter at the end of August, but were stopped by the ice in Claveringstrædet. They stayed initially at Daneborg and Zackenberg, until they were able to sledge northwards on the new ice: *"It was a case of trusting one's luck"* Graae recalled in 1992. They brought along what they could carry on their sledges, hoping to find the rest along the way. After turning the station upside down to find usable supplies, they went exploring in the trapping territory. It was said that there were fox traps out there, but the problem was how to find them. Having prepared the territory in Peters Bugt, they took a trip northwards to Ottostrand.

On the 9th December they started on a planned Christmas trip to Daneborg Weather Station. They decided to try going via Albrecht Bugt and Kuppelpasset, but here they ran out of luck. The moon was waning and the going in Hochstetterbugten was almost impassable, filled with ice ridges and deep, soft and slushy snow. After struggling for almost a week they had only reached Albrechtsletten by December 15th, and so gave up the trip to Daneborg in order to return to Hochstetter. This was their toughest day. Graae wrote: *"We constantly wanted to lie down and give up. The dogs were almost impossible to drive forward, and our throats became hoarse from shouting at them. Afterwards we agreed that had there not been two of us to keep each other going, anything might have happened."* Finally they found the Kap

The Nanok trappers in 1946. From left: Orla Jensen, Mogens Graae, Kjeld Soelberg, Jørgen Andersen. © Mogens Graae

Maurer hytten, and: *"we agreed that this was the best moment of our lives"*.[186]

Five days later they arrived back to Hochstetter, and in spite of the disappointment of missing radioed Christmas greetings and Christmas dinner at Daneborg, they had a merry Christmas.

At the beginning of February, they decided to trap from separate stations, and drawing lots Graae got Mønstedhus and Jensen got Hochstetter. On the 12th February 1947 Jensen arrived at Kulhus where he met Harald Mikkelsen from Zackenberg: *"he had come to find out how we were getting on"*.[187] Jensen went along with Mikkelsen to fetch telegrams from Daneborg. He returned later together with Jørgen Andersen, who was to take over the trapping in Peters Bugt while Jensen tried his luck in Ardencaple and Grandjean Fjords. At the end of April, Graae returned from Mønstedhus and after having sorted out the catch the three men went south to spend the summer at Zackenberg.

In the spring of 1947, Graae and Jensen built "Slettehytten" [450] on Albrechtsletten.

1947-48

On the 20th August 1947, Orla Jensen and Mogens Graae returned to Hochstetter by motor boat. They had decided that this year the Hochstetter territory was to be prepared properly; but it almost went wrong. One day a storm broke loose just as they were going ashore at Hochstetter. Within a few seconds the boat was filled with water, and for the next two days Jensen and Graae had to endure watching the boat being slowly smashed into pieces at the mercy of the breakers. All they could do was walk along the shore collecting wreckage as it washed ashore. When the swells finally settled the boat had: *"3-4 holes in the bottom, the wheelhouse was smashed, the splashboard was knocked off and the motor was filled with sand to the end of the exhaust pipe"*.[188] There was not much hope, but they immediately started repairing the boat. Ingenuity knew no limits when it came to replacing ruined parts. Two days later: *"the motor worked perfectly and the boat was almost watertight"*.[189] On the 17th September formation of new ice hindered further sailing, but by that time their preparation of the Hochstetter territory was complete.

Following a two month Christmas trip to Daneborg, Graae and Jensen returned to Hochstetter on the 1st February to resume trapping. On February 27th they had an unexpected visit: *"It was Ivar* (Ytreland) *from Kap Herschell. It was a great experience to see a stranger all the way up here at Hochstetter. He came from the Danish hut at Kap Maurer and was exhausted. The wind is blowing and it is freezing 35 degrees. I gave him some food and coffee, and then we had a welcome-drink"*, Graae wrote.[190] Ytreland's visit lasted for two weeks, and then Graae and Jensen on the 12th March started on a long-distance sledge journey. Jennov had told them to go to Danmark Havn, trapping as they went. The journey lasted until the 29th April. They carried with them a memorial tablet that was to be placed at the old horse sledge of the J.P. Koch expedition 1912-13, discovered in 1933 and dragged ashore near Kap Peschel (see Bessel Fjord). They did not find the sledge on their way north, but found it on the 22nd of April on their way back: *"We put it upright and supported it with stones and mounted the memorial tablet"*.[191]

On the 19th May 1948 they closed down Hochstetter, and went southwards to Zackenberg to spend the summer.

In the summers of 1948-50 Orla Jensen took part in the Danish Pearyland Expedition. In 1950-51 he wintered at Danmarkshavn Weather Station. The following year he worked for the British North Greenland Expedition, for whom he purchased sledge dogs in West Greenland in the winter of 1951-52. Orla Jensen died in 1998.

1948-49

In 1948 it was finally possible to reach Hochstetter by ship again, when "Søndmøringen" arrived on the 13th August. Later on a team of trappers led by Jennov returned to supply the territory and to build a hut, "Mågenæshytten" [501], in Grandjean Fjord. In 1992 Harald Mikkelsen recalled that while the others were building the hut he remained at Hochstetter to find food for the 18 hungry dogs: *"First I put out a char net*

From left: Hans Thomsen, Ole Olsen and Harald Mikkelsen. Hochstetter, winter 1948-49. © Bjarne Myrvold

and within 20 minutes I had 22 char, which made the dogs very happy. Then I went inland behind the station and bumped right into an old muskox bull. I brought back a nice, large piece of meat and boiled a pot of soup with vegetables and dumpling, as the men from Grandjean Fjord might return soon. They arrived and ate well, but were in a hurry, as Jennov, Mogens Graae and Orla Jensen were to sail with the motor boat to Daneborg where "Godthaab" was waiting to take them home. Hans Thomsen and I were now finally alone and could start to prepare for our wintering. Building sledges, sewing dog harnesses and much more".[192]

Before the fjord froze up, Mikkelsen and Thomsen managed to build two huts on the west side of Shannon. They named these "Haraldsborg" [513] and "Tomsborg" [506], and Mikkelsen remembered that it was a tough home voyage: *"From the pack ice we could tell that there was a strong south-going current in Shannon Sund. We therefore set out due north for half an hour to gain some slack in the strong wind and current. The wind rose and it became foggy and the pack ice caused us much trouble, so it was difficult to stay on course and we could not see land. I realized that we were drifting but was nevertheless surprised when our first landfall turned out to be the north end of Kuhn Ø. Then we had two hours with our heads into the storm to reach Hochstetter. When we finally reached the station, we were very tired and chilled to the bone".*[193]

In 1948-49 the catch was a disaster for Nanok, with a total catch of only 33 furs altogether. After New Year the men tried to locate better trapping territories. Ole Olsen came up from Zackenberg to trap together with Hans Thomsen, and Harald Mikkelsen went north to Dove Bugt; but: *"there were no fox up there"* he recalled in 1992. He spent the summer at Mønstedhus and fished for char in the river, but: *"when I had caught and salted four barrels, I stopped the fishing, as the sea ice was unbroken as far as the eye could see, and I knew that Mønstedhus would not have any call from the supply ship".*[194] In the autumn of 1949 Mikkelsen went to Zackenberg. Hochstetter was unmanned in 1949-50.

1950-51

In 1950 the then 52-year-old Peder Vorre Thykjær, who in 1921-22 had been trapper for the East Greenland Company, had intended to winter at Hochstetter, but he became ill during the summer and had to return home again. However, before leaving he helped to build a new hut, "Jacks hytte" [452]. One consequence of Thykjær's returning was that Erik Larsen (actually H.E. Larsen), a newcomer and a former waiter, had to stay on his own at Hochstetter. At the end of October, Leo Ingwersen came down from Aalborghus to show Larsen his way about. On the 1st December the traps were put away and Larsen went south to spend Christmas at Zackenberg. The day after his arrival, December 17th, he went out to hunt musk oxen, but: *"at Pashytten my dogs ran away. They headed for Sandodden and we immediately went after them, but could not catch up. We arrived at Sandodden, but the dogs were not here.* (Hans) *Frederiksen and I afterwards went back to Zackenberg, but the dogs were not there either".*[195] They searched for days but with no result until the 30th December: *"Today we searched Kuppelpasset and found the sledge. Only two dogs were alive, the rest lay dead beside the sledge. They had killed each other. Have assembled a new dog team. Had two from Daneborg and two from Zackenberg".*[196]

On the 17th January 1951, when Larsen returned to Hochstetter, Hans Frederiksen went along. They had decided to join territories. After the trapping season they both went south to spend the summer at Sandodden.

1951-52

In 1951 Nanok built their final trappers' huts in the Hochstetter territory, namely "Birkedalhytten" [504] and "Vedethytten" [505]. On the 29th August 1951 after a busy summer Hans Frederiksen wrote: *"Today Larsen, Wind and I were set ashore here at Hochstetter, "Søndmøringen" has left tonight".*[197] The three trappers remained at the station until the ice was safe, then they split up. Ernst Wind went to Zackenberg, Erik Larsen to Mønstedhus while Hans Frederiksen remained at Hochstetter. Larsen and Frederiksen had some co-operation during the winter, and on the 23rd May 1952 they left Hochstetter to spend the summer at Sandodden. They brought along their catch, of which Frederiksen's numbered 32 foxes caught in Ardencaple and Grandjean Fjords. Hochstetter station was unmanned in 1952-54.

1954-55

In 1953-54 Hans Frederiksen had worked as handyman at Daneborg, but then he felt like living as a trapper again. His colleague at the weather station, the wireless operator Erik B. Larsen, was game: *"We applied for permission and received it right away"*, Frederiksen recalled in 1992, *"and we were allowed to use Nanok's huts and material".*[198]

On the 24th August Frederiksen arrived at Hochstetter. They went ashore from "Jopeter" that had fetched them at Mønstedhus, which they had participated in saving from falling into the sea the same summer. The first thing Frederiksen and Larsen did was to chop the motor boat free. It: *"lay in a small river bed, where Frederiksen and Larsen had placed it in 1951. The boat was completely packed in metre thick ice from deck to keel. Frederiksen cleaned the motor, and the very first time he pulled the handle, the Scandia started"*, Larsen wrote.[199] They were then able to sail to Daneborg to fetch sledge dogs and equipment.

They then undertook a major renovation of the Hochstetter station. On the 7th September 1954 Larsen entered in his diary: *"Tearing down wall, pantry, kitchen table and berths. Made new wall, laid the floor and made new berths." ... "Today we have made a new ceiling, that is, we have put hard masonite on top of the old. Furthermore made three large cupboards and a super large kitchen table, so there is space for a large washing-up. This saves time as well as soap"*.[200]

Trapping was undertaken alternately from Hochstetter and Mønstedhus, and Frederiksen and Larsen usually travelled together. On the 17th April they sledged south to Zackenberg and Daneborg, where they stayed for the summer.

On 21st August 1955 they boarded "Jopeter" to travel home. However, this journey turned out differently than expected. After the call at Danmarkshavn, "Jopeter" was caught in heavy pack ice off Store Koldewey, and on the 2nd September there were: *"large dents in the hull and the deck was bumpy as a roof of corrugated iron"*.[201] On 5th September "Jopeter" lost its propeller and drifted helplessly southwards, and on 13th September they were off Bontekoe Ø. In the meantime a rescue operation had been initiated, and "Kista Dan" had arrived. However, the: *"possibility for towing was not present. We have endured a minor pressure tonight. The ice is packed tightly. Have tonight unloaded our hand luggage and mail, and everyone except shipmaster* (Knut) *Nakken has left the ship"*.[202] On the 14th September 1955 they abandoned "Jopeter": *"Nakken came on board when "Kista Dan" was about one nautical mile away. When we came free of the ice we made contact with the Norwegian corvette "Andenes", and the Norwegians were transferred to her while Frederiksen and I remained on "Kista Dan"*. The following year "Jopeter" was found safe and sound in Mountnorris Fjord.

"I guess we had about 180 fox", Frederiksen recalled in 1992. *"We did not lose money, even though it took a long time before we were paid due to the Jopeter incident; but the price was good, a fine fox fur would fetch 200-300 Danish kroner. The auction took place at the fur auction near Børsen in Copenhagen, and due to the fine quality our furs sold for higher prices than the furs from West Greenland"*.[203]

Jennov 1939, 1945; A146; A150; A162; A164; A166; A167; A296; G117; N035; Ø048.

Recent status

After the last trappers left Hochstetter in 1955, the station was used and maintained by Sirius until 1980. The station then rapidly fell into almost total disrepair. In the summer of 1996 a repair team from Nanok gave Hochstetter main house a thorough renovation, and since then the house has been used and maintained on a regular basis.

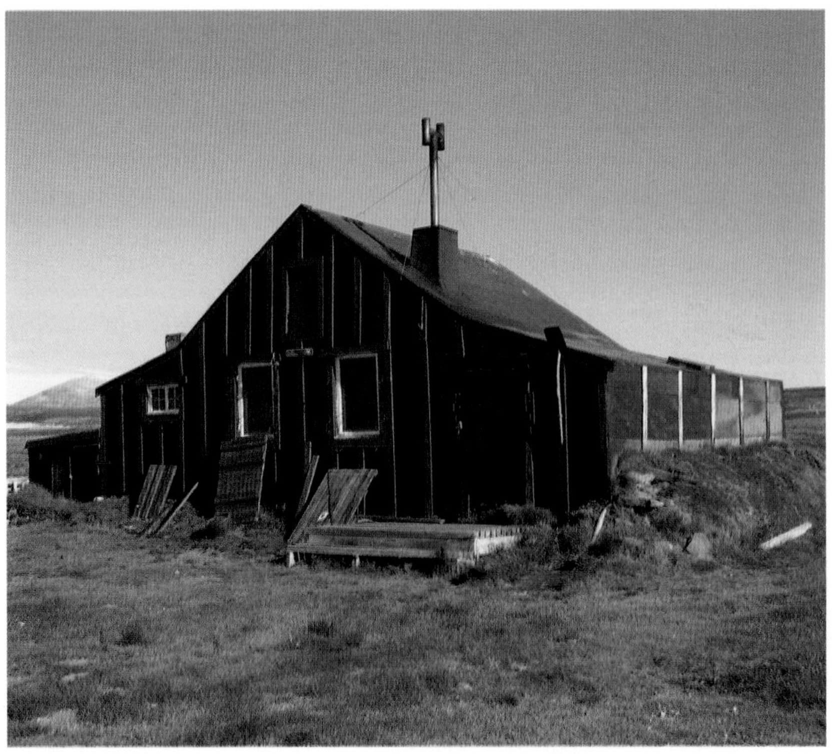

Hochstetter [510], 3rd August 2004. (Left and facing page) Hochstetter is a former Danish trappers' station built 1929 for Nanok. It was used as a trappers' station until 1955, and thereafter maintained and used by Sirius as a travellers' hut until 1980, when it was abandoned. In the beginning of the 1990s the condition of Hochstetter was very bad and the house had become unusable, but in the summer of 1996 it was renovated by Nanok. Today Hochstetter is used again regularly. © NCN

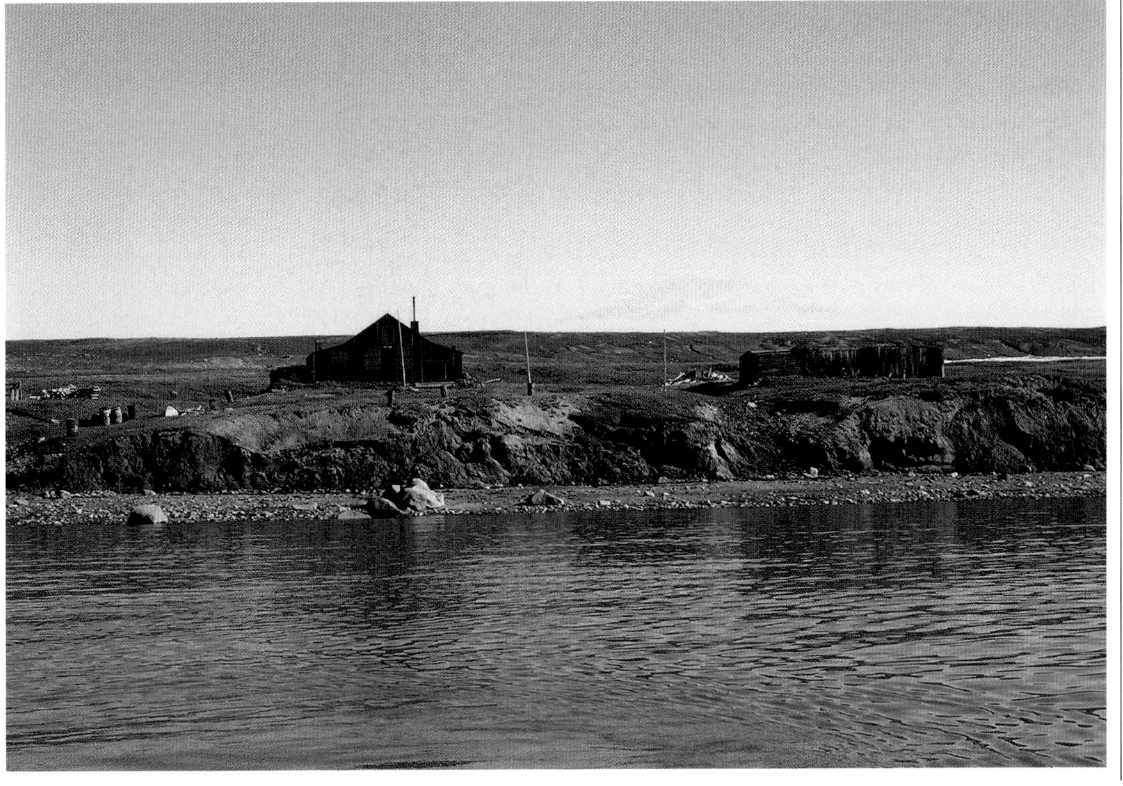

HOELSBU
[356]

Wintering party
1930-31: John Giæver, Otto Johnsen
1931-32: None
1932-33: Walter Molt, Knut Nakken
1933-34: Johan Listhaug, Knut O. Brandal
1934-35: Johan Listhaug, Walter Molt
1935-38: Levin Winther
1938-39: Arne Jacobsen
1939-42: Levin Winther, Petra Winther
1942-46: None
1946-47: Bjarne Akre, Egil Amsjø
1947-48: Trygve Havold, Paul Furuseth
1948-49: Trygve Havold
1949-50: Dagfinn Egeberg
1950-51: Harald Sverdsten
1951-52: Fredrik Sæterdal
1952-53: Helge Nesset, Odd Uthi
1953-56: Fredrik Sæterdal, Solveig Sæterdal
1956-58: Hilmar Gauteplass
1958-59: John Berg

In the morning of the 27th August 1899, "Antarctic" was sailing along the west side of Nordfjord heading for Waltershausen Gletscher. A.G. Nathorst wrote: *"We now headed towards the eastern side of the glacier and there discovered a new fjord trending eastwards, Moskusoksefjord, into which we sailed about 10.30 a.m. We expected it to end soon, but in fact we followed it the whole day." ... "We saw many muskoxen in this fjord, altogether sixty-seven animals, the reason for the fjord's name".*[204]

1930-31
Thirty-one years after Nathorst's visit, on the 4th August 1930, "Veslekari" sailed into Moskusoksefjord: *"and anchored in the morning on the north side of Moskusoksefjord about 10 km from Kap Kolthoff. Here we unloaded materials and equipment for a main station" ... "On the 5th August we had finished the unloading. Giæver and Johnsen went ashore here and immediately began building the house".*[205] It was the trappers John Giæver and Otto Johnsen who went ashore to build a new station for Arctic Commercial Enterprise: *"On the twelfth day the work was finished. The house stood there, shining red-painted, roofing felt on the roof, a metre and a half turf wall around it. And inside all the walls were wainscoted, a partition wall put up, benches, table and chairs in Muskox-fjord style were in place. In short: Hoelsbu was finished, and if I have to say it myself, then Adolf Hoel would not be sorry to lend his name to this station".*[206]

Adolf Hoel, (1879-1964) was at the time leader of Norges Svalbard- og Ishavs-undersøkelser (NSIU), and one of the driving forces behind the Norwegian occupation of "Eirik Raudes Land". He graduated with a mathematic-science teacher's degree in 1904. From 1905 he was employed at the Norwegian Geological Survey, and from 1907 took part in organising the annual research expeditions to Svalbard. In 1911 he received a university scholarship, and in 1919 became a reader in geology. He continued the arctic geology research - especially in Svalbard - which had been initiated by Gunner Isachsen, and this led to his interest in the Greenland sovereignty issue. In 1927 he suggested the establishment of a central institution for research in Svalbard and the Arctic Ocean. This institution, NSIU, was founded in 1928, and Hoel continued as leader until 1945, when he had to resign due to his involvement in the Nasjonal Samling (the Norwegian national socialistic party).
In his obituary, Søren Richter described him as: *"a gentleman who did not draw much attention to himself. He preferred to express his orders via an intermediary, but possessed a certain talent for following and knowing everything that happened on board".*
Hoel produced a number of publications, including a monumental account on Svalbard.[207]

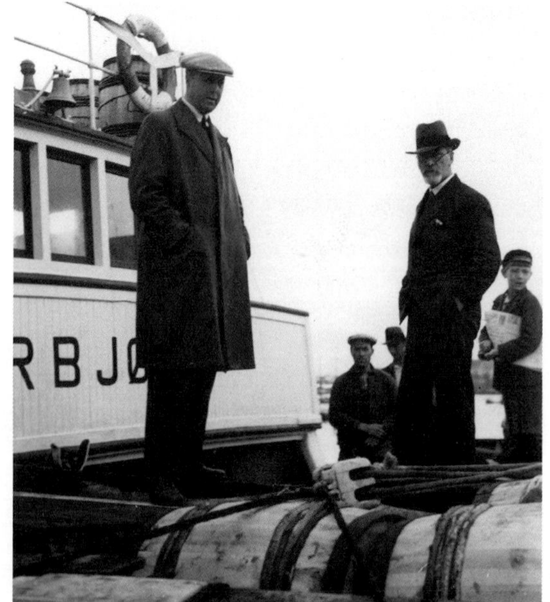

Anders Kristian Orvin (left) and Adolf Hoel in Tromsø, 1933. The two geologists were leaders of the Norwegian scientific expeditions to North-East Greenland 1929-33. © Carl Sæther / Norwegian Polar Institute

In 1930, when the Norwegians were still optimistic concerning the outcome of the Hague trial, the main task for Giæver and Johnsen was to annex and establish a new trapping territory on Gauss Halvø. Giæver described their wintering in his book "To mann i Moskusfjorden" (two men in the Moskusfjord) (1931). In 1930-31 a total of six trappers' huts were put up in the Hoelsbu territory: "Huttetu" [348], "Smedal" [320], "Dalheim" [336], "Von Krogh" [328], "Johnsenhytten" [357] and "Giæverhytten" [358-1]. The fox trapping came second to the annexing, and the catch at Hoelsbu amounted only to 15 fox furs.[208] Giæver and Johnsen both went home to Norway in 1931, and as Arctic Commercial Enterprise had only five trappers wintering, Hoelsbu was unmanned in 1931-32.

1932-33

On the 29th July 1932, Walter Molt and Knut Nakken, both from Sunnmøre and newcomers, took over Hoelsbu. In the autumn they used the materials for a planned hut "Herdal" [906] to build another hut, to which was later given the name "Petrahytten" [347].

Trapping began on the 22nd October, and they went together to Giæverhytten on Strindberg Land: *"The hut was in a good condition, but needed roofing felt which we put on as well as repairing a door. Then we prepared for the night, ate and talked a little. Then we saw that there were people in the Danish hut* (Nordfjordhuset)*, and decided to visit them. We introduced ourselves and were welcomed. "If you had not come here now, we would have gone to fetch you. Please sit down." We were invited for dinner, yes, we had already eaten, but that was no excuse and we tried to eat a little more." ... "It was the three scientists,* (T.) *Johansen,* (A.) *Jensen and* (V.C.) *Devantier. Very nice people".*[209]

On the 27th November 1932, Nakken left to tend the territory along Gauss Halvø. He planned to be gone for a week, but did not return until the 7th February, when Molt was awakened by the baying of dogs. He dressed in a hurry and opened the door, and: *"there stands Nakken before me, Well hello. You better believe I've been expecting you. Having been on my own now for 10 long weeks during the polar night, I finally have someone to talk with again. Have much to tell. Having started from here on the 27th November 1932, Nakken found that the weather was nice and wanted to visit the Humboldt trappers. One day turned into two and so forth. And then it started to snow and storm and of course he was held up due to bad weather. He had stayed with the people at Humboldt for no less than 10 weeks".*[210]

With scepticism Molt watched how Nakken treated his dogs, for instance on the 30th May: *"Nakken's dogs got quite a beating today, poor beasts, it doesn't take much before he goes at them with the whip. It almost looks as if he enjoys tormenting the poor animals. In return he was bitten in the chest by "Lauritz" who is now so mad that he attacks for no reason. Knut is a devil, beating the dogs".*[211]

One day at the end of May 1933, Knut Hofgaard from Myggbukta turned up; he: *"was glad to get away from Myggbukta. Glad to get away from a certain person, as he put it."* Hofgaard stayed for the summer at Hoelsbu. Both Walter Molt and the 20-year-old Knut Nakken went home in 1933, with a total catch of 69 foxes. Incidentally, it was Nakken who was master of "Jopeter" when she was abandoned in 1955 on the way home from Danmarkshavn.

1933-34

The night before the 18th September 1933, Johan Listhaug and Knut O. Brandal were finally able to sail back to Hoelsbu. The territory was ready for trapping. They had spent four long days and nights in Geologfjord, where they had built two new trappers' huts, "Kap Ovibos hytten" [340] and "Brandalhytten" [342].

Knut O. Brandal was 35-years old and had already spent a winter at Moskusheimen in 1931-32. The 23-year-old Johan Listhaug was also a Sunnmøring, from Ørskog. He was new in the trapping business, and expected to be able to rely on his partner's experience. Unfortunately it turned out somewhat differently.

One day Brandal suddenly began to complain about stomach pains. Hour by hour the pain grew worse, and before Listhaug could do anything about it he was alone. Knut Brandal died on the 30th September 1933, only twelve days after they had returned from Kap Ovibos. There was only one thing for Listhaug to do – bury his dead comrade. Johan Listhaug said in 1992: *"The tomb was made from stones in a river bed about 1 km west of Hoelsbu. The next summer it was covered with concrete. There I was, inexperienced and not at all happy, but I survived the winter with a decent catch (51 foxes). In May I went to Myggbukta and stayed there until the ship arrived".*[212]

In 1992 Listhaug recalled the old days when the country was still relatively unknown: *"When you* (this author) *arrived in East Greenland, everything was prepared for you. The huts were there and the land had been travelled regularly for many years. The huts were not so very inviting on a summer day, but on a winter day with snow and cold, they were just magnificent. The coal lay ready and when the stove had heated the hut you felt good right into your soul.*

Our equipment was minimal. We had a box on the sledge. It was not large, but contained what we needed to survive: a hammer, a few nails and rope, socks and mittens. There were three to four dried fish as a reserve for dog food. For ourselves there were two to three loaves, butter, cheese and coffee, and matches and candles. Dried vegetables served for the soup, which was standard on a sledge journey. We had some wooden sticks for the fox traps and of course a small axe. Canned food was only to be found on Danish sledges.

In our work we formed a team which could handle almost anything. We made stove pipes with folds as well as a professional. And we were proud of our work. We took good care of our dogs, and they always had their meal before we did. The result was good and faithful dogs".[213]

Even though it had been 60 years ago, and even though he had quite a different start from that he had hoped for, Listhaug's voice was filled with conviction when he said: *"Happy is he, who has once experienced this country!"*

1934-35

In 1934-35 Johan Listhaug had the company of Walter Molt: *"Well, here I am at Hoelsbu once again after one year of absence; nice to be back again in the old surroundings. Everything was as it used to be, the dogs have got their old places and the baying of the dogs echoes in the silence".* This Molt wrote on the 10th August, when he arrived at Hoelsbu with "Selbarden"[214].

Hoelsbu had until then appeared with a bright, red-painted façade; but in the winter it was unpleasant with many cracks in the walls. Molt wrote: *"Have put roofing felt on the entire front of the house. It seems a bit dull with black roofing felt, I think. But it is to stop the draught, so one has to ignore the appearance. Even though it was much nicer before when the house was painted red".*[215]

Before winter Molt also had another job to do: *"Today I have been busy carving a gravestone with an inscription for Knut Brandal. The stone is 1 metre high and 70 cm wide. I think it will be nice. A sad job, but I had promised to do it". ... "Then I made three buckets of cement and went out to Knut Brandal's grave. I put up the gravestone and arranged it as well as possible with a little cement between the stones. (The grave is situated near the moraine)".*[216]

In 1934-35 the total catch of Listhaug and Molt numbered in all 75 foxes. Unfortunately Listhaug was ill most of the time. He often had stomach pains, had to maintain a simple diet and to stay in bed for long periods.

For a few weeks in March they had the company of Magne Råum from Kap Humboldt. They had met him in Geologfjord, but just as he was about to drive on, a big stone unfortunately fell on his leg. He therefore went along with them to Hoelsbu and stayed there until the 1st April. Before they separated, they agreed to meet again with Råum and his partner, Ole Klokset, at the beginning of May at Strindbergelven on the west side of Nordfjord. Here they would all spend the summer fishing char.

The four trappers met as planned and it was: *"pure luxury, food in abundance. Walking meat* (muskox). *Char in the river, birds in the air. What more could we ask for. Good grief, I wonder what they would say at home if they saw that we feed the dogs with arctic char".*[217]

At that time the Norwegians only had a small hut, Giæverhytten, at the mouth of Strindbergelven. It was far too small for four persons, so they therefore decided to build a larger one. The new house, "Strindberghuset" [358-3], was subsequently often used by Norwegians fishing for arctic char.

Both Listhaug and Molt had their last season as trappers in 1935. Johan Listhaug died in April 1994.

Visit at Hoelsbu in the summer of 1936. From left: Nils Hanken, Søren Richter and Levin Winther. The latter stayed alone at Hoelsbu from 1935-38. In 1939-42 he was accompanied by his wife, Petra. *© Nils-Martin Hanken*

1935-38

In 1935, Levin Winther, then 40-years old and from Mo i Rana, took over Hoelsbu. He was already a veteran trapper, and had 10 years experience of wintering in the Arctic, mainly on Svalbard. He became the breadwinner of the family at a very young age after his father died, and had to find a way to provide for his younger siblings. First he worked at a mine on Svalbard; but this was not very rewarding from an economic point of view, and merely postponed his dream of having a farm of his own sometime in the future. So he decided to become a trapper instead. In 1928-30 he was a member of Finn Devold's Expedition to Greenland. At that time he wintered at Krogness, and it was his impressions from these years that prompted him to winter in Moskusoksefjord. He thought it was a promising trapping territory, and Arctic Commercial Enterprise had now given him exclusive rights to the area. Divided into two periods, Levin Winther stayed for a total of six years at Hoelsbu, which is the record for this station. He generally had very good catches, notably in 1936-37 when he obtained 142 foxes. It was presumably Winther who built the hut "Wintherheimen" [368] in 1936.

Winther became known for his quite special way of driving a team of sledge dogs that earned him the nickname "The singing trapper". John Giæver described this talent: *"He's singing for the dogs, and they like it. They work their buts off for him. He's like a God to them. A strange God if you ask me, but nevertheless the dogs like him as a soul-mate. He sings to them instead of shouting and commanding. He caresses them so hard that they purr like cats and wag their tails, and he never hits them. He feeds them before he feeds himself." ... "I myself have only heard Winther sing once, but it is still one of my brightest memories. We were three men and two dogs who were going to drive a muskox herd down from the hills to the Krogness station. We chased them part of the way, but then they stopped on a hill top as if nailed to the spot and we were unable to move them an inch by normal means. Then Winther got mad and began singing something he called "Hammerfossens brus"* (the sound of Hammer Waterfall). *That was more than the beasts could stand. They stampeded downwards in panic. Otto, the dogs and I panted along after them, but behind us, up in the hills, Winther stood and shouted ecstatically. – It never fails, he said later, and I for once believe him".*

"First of all his face is totally expressionless and can at best appear unapproachable. But it is just a mask, a cover-up for a pure devil-may-care spirit of helpfulness, which is highly renowned. Yet towards strangers Winther always appeared to be reserved. He needs no permission to express his straight-forward opinion. As when he some years ago arrived at Myggbukta and was introduced to some English scientists. He said coldly: – So this is what scientists look like in England? The scientists roared with laughter. Winther was a man to their liking. In the event Edward Bird stayed with him for most of the winter (1936-37). *And when I returned to Greenland the following year, Winther had somehow taught him Norwegian. Pure and unspoiled "helgelandsk"* (a Norwegian dialect) *with a twist of English to it. – That Winther, he is a jolly good sport, Mr. Bird said. – There can be none better in all of Norway. But Winther had not learned a single word of English. If someone wants to talk with me, he'll have to learn to speak Norwegian. That Edward speaks Norwegian fairly well now. But for a learned person you were a bit slow on the uptake in the beginning. Mr. Bird just laughed. – Yes, yes, that is completely true, he said".*[218]

1938-39

In 1938-39 Arne Jacobsen borrowed the Hoelsbu territory from Levin Winther, who was going home to Norway for a year. Jacobsen came from Tromsø and was just as experienced with trapping as Winther. On the 10th August 1938, Oscar Bang, from Myggbukta, wrote: *"Today Arne is 27-years old. When I woke up, my mouth was filled with reindeer hair and I had to spit out and swallow the rest, before I could congratulate the birthday child on his considerable age. It is remarkable to become that old, considering that Arne started to winter when he was just 16".*[219]

Of Arne Jacobsen's many winterings can be named: Jan Mayen 1928-29, 1930-31 and 1935-46, and in East Greenland, Kap Peterséns 1932-34, Kap Humboldt 1937-38 and Hoelsbu 1938-39. It was probably Jacobsen who built "Hastværkshytten" [354] in 1938.

"Arne said it was a splendid and unforgettable life", his widow Ellen Danielsdottir remembered in 1993. *"In 1939 Arne went to Tromsø and he was there when the invasion came. He participated in the war for two months until the Germans got the upper hand. Then in 1940 Arne went to North-East Greenland again, and Bjørn Western* (see Antarctichavn) *was also there trapping. They arrived at Myggbukta with "Veslekari" on the 12th August 1940. Arne and Bjørn Western were suspected of being "Quislings", and were taken to England with "Fridtjof Nansen" where they were imprisoned for three weeks in London. When their identity was cleared up, they were released. Arne went to Iceland with "Veslekari", which had now been attached to the merchant navy. Later on they were sent to Jan Mayen to establish a station. After three weeks there they returned to Iceland, and Arne Jacobsen lived in Iceland until his death on 29th May 1980".*[220]

1939-42

People shook their heads and friends at home said "goodbye for ever". Nobody could fathom what could persuade a young woman to go wintering in North-East Greenland. Petra, who was then 28-years old and born on Lofoten, had married the trapper Levin Winther in the winter of 1938-39, and now wanted to accompany him to Greenland. Arctic Commercial Enterprise was not dismissive of the idea, but Levin had to agree in writing to take full responsibility.

In 1992, Petra Winther related how the old trappers were amused: *"This is the end of Winther's record catches. He'll have to stay at home and tend the missus instead of trapping!"*[221] This was, however, only in the beginning as these dire predictions were soon laid to rest.

They went ashore at Strindberghuset: *"My life as a trapper began here. At Strindberg I met the dogs for the first time – seven in all. They soon became my best friends and remained so for many years".*[222] When the char fishing was over, they moved to Hoelsbu, where they were going to stay for the rest of the year.

The first winter was the worst. Levin had only one team of dogs, so Petra had to stay at home alone when he went out to check the traps. Each journey often lasted two to three weeks, and for this period Petra was on her own with only a domesticated dog for company. She made a weekly schedule so the days would not be too long: *"One day was for laundry, another for baking and so on. And I had the radio for entertainment. It was nice, listening to the news from Norway, and in addition I had plenty of newspapers, magazines and books. There was, of course, time to do needlework and to knit mittens, scarves and socks of muskox yarn. My husband had previously gathered muskox wool in the territory, and from animals he killed, and this had been spun in Norway".*[223]

The days went by fairly quickly, the 81-year-old Petra Winther recalled in 1992. The polar night was long, but fortunately she was not afraid of the dark. Yet she admitted that there were times when she felt not altogether safe: *"One evening I was going to bring inside our domestic dog. Boff! He was angry! I could hardly pull him in through the door. He would not lie down and the hairs on his back were raised. The dogs outside were howling, leading me to suspect that something dangerous was going on, but what? Two days later my husband came home and then the dogs were howling in a quite different manner".*

"So you are alive", were his first words when he saw me. *"Did you have any visitors? – Visitors?"* I answered, looking like a question mark. *"It turned out that a polar bear had been just 12-13 metres from the house. Levin had followed the tracks on his way home".*[224] Petra did have a rifle and could use it if necessary, but she did not do much hunting as she was far too fond of animals to shoot them.

Levin and Petra had planned to stay at Hoelsbu for only one year, but in April 1940 they learnt with dismay from the radio that Norway had been occupied. As a consequence they had to remain in North-East Greenland for three years.

As they began their second wintering, the dogs had puppies. So Petra soon had a dog team of her own, and for the next two winters she accompanied Levin around the territory. It went well, but: *"when it came to bringing them up, scolding them and making them obey by the crack of the whip, I was no good.*

Left: Petra Winther with her catch, a dead muskox. At the age of 28, Petra Winther became the first Caucasian woman to overwinter in North-East Greenland. In 1939-42 she stayed at Hoelsbu together with her husband, trapper Levin Winther. © Petra Winther. Right: Petra Winther in 1992 together with their son, Leif Bjørn Winther, who is holding a photograph of his father with his catch of foxes in front of Hoelsbu. Porsgrunn, 13th June 1992. © Peter Schmidt Mikkelsen

Hoelsbu, c. 1948. © Trygve Havold

No, then they flashed their teeth and growled. Bringing them up was Levin's business. Nobody objected – this was how it was meant to be".[225]

They had an argument the first time they were going out in the territory. Levin told Petra to put on woollen clothes. She objected, because the wool was so terribly itchy. Levin answered that if she did not put them on, she was to stay behind - and so Petra chose the wool.

Nevertheless it went wrong. On one of their journeys they came to Solstrand, a hut east of Waltershausen Gletscher. Levin was on a ski trip to see to the traps and meanwhile Petra was going to heat up the hut. Suddenly there was a riot amongst the dogs. It turned out that one of them had broken loose and a fight was well under way. Half-dressed Petra ran outside to part the dogs, but this was no easy task and in the severe cold she soon became chilled to the bone. A week later she developed pneumonia, and became so weak that she could not get up to keep the fire burning. It was a storm that had broken out the day before that saved her. Levin was supposed to have gone on a journey in the territory alone, but because of bad weather he had postponed his departure. Fortunately Levin was a good nurse and Petra soon recovered.

Petra Winther never forgot the wildlife and the nature in North-East Greenland. In particular the spring, when the nights became bright and the snow began to melt. However, in August 1942 the good days came to an end. The Americans arrived and demanded that the Norwegian trappers be evacuated from North-East Greenland. Their journey now went to Ivigtut in West Greenland, where the Winther's settled until the war ended. They both worked at the cryolite mine, - Levin in the office and Petra as house keeper. They had a good time and it was not until 1945, when they returned to Norway, that they learned the meaning of rationing. Unlike many others, Levin Winther also had a talent for keeping his money, and after 20 years "the singing trapper" said good bye to the Arctic and together with his Petra bought a farm in southern Norway.

Hoelsbu was unmanned from 1942-46.

1946-47

The summer of 1946 once again brought trappers to Hoelsbu, and the veteran Bjarne Akre was supposed to have stayed at the station alone. However, in the event he had the company of Egil Amsjø, a newcomer, because Amsjø's intended partner, Bjarne Myrvold, had been severely injured in a shooting accident and had to go home to Norway.

Akre did not describe this post-WW II wintering at Hoelsbu in detail in either of his two books "Fri manns liv" (life in freedom) from 1957, which mainly deals with his pre-war time in the Arctic and ""Heltene" i kald krig" (the "heroes" in cold war) from 1983 describing his arctic wartime experiences of 1942-45; however in the latter volume he does say that they: *"trapped in each their territory and met only once during the winter"*, and that Akre caught: *"140 foxes which was the best result in North-East Greenland that winter".*[226] Bjarne Akre returned to Norway in 1947 after his fifth and last wintering to Greenland, and later worked as a lumberjack and gamekeeper in his home county of Rendalen.

In 1946-47, materials for a hut were placed in "Brogetdal" [907] on Strindberg Land, but no hut was ever built there.

Hunting at Strindberg (Brogetdal) i 1947. From left: Egil Amsjø, Trygve Havold and Paul Furuseth. © Bjarne Myrvold

1947-48

Trygve Havold, from Svindal, was 32-years old when he took over Hoelsbu together with Paul Furuseth; who had been a trapper at Myggbukta in 1946-47. In his diary Havold noted on the 26th July 1947: *"I met Paul at Myggbukta. Today we are fishing char at Strindberg. Tomorrow we are going to Hoelsbu, and there Paul and I will leave the ship".*[227]

With a catch of 105 foxes, Furuseth and Havold produced a high score amongst Norwegian trappers that season. Paul Furuseth went home in 1948. The same year, Trygve Havold, during: *"a stormy day in Hallehytten"* wrote his well-known "Fangstmandsvise" (the trapper's ballad), also called the "Havold ballad":

Among the black mountains way up north.
Where giant glaciers glide into fjords
I sledge with my dogs and tend the traps
and once in a while a fox I catch.

From one hut to the next I go
on my way, often with soft, deep snow
but in the hut the stove is warm – it may reek in there
but when you're tired, do you really care?

When a bear has called at the hut I get so sad
remembering the good food I recently had
and I swear to myself that I will call the tune
but he's got a sixth sense that wicked loon.

Out on the ice the seal lies nice and fat
I slowly sneak forward sweaty and hot
when suddenly he looks up, laughs scornfully
two waving flippers is the last I see.

There goes an old muskox in a rug thick and long
and I'm short of meat and aim my gun.
He waves his head a bit and dies, the dark beast
and I drive home to the hut with one at least.

The dogs are carrying their load, that's for sure.
Now and then Blakken gives Juster a decent cure.
And all hell is loose when Svarta snaps his chain.
What a blasted job to catch him again!

When my mind goes back to Norway occasionally
It is people slaving for the clock I see
Though hard and rough life in Greenland may be
we are having a good time here and we are free! [228]

Trygve Havold

1948-49

Trygve Havold had the Hoelsbu territory to himself in 1948, as Paul Furuseth went home. Unfortunately, this was a poor year for fox trapping, and his meagre result was only 26 fox furs. In 1991 Havold explained how he: *"invented a new trick up there. I took the sticks for the traps and smeared them with honey. This was not a bad idea as the fox likes honey. I discovered that there were bumblebees and concluded that there had to be honey too. And I knew that foxes in Norway liked honey. Anyway, I caught a couple of foxes in the traps that I had smeared in honey".*[229] Havold, who died in November 1992, was one of the many former trappers whose kind encouragement and assistance and many conversations inspired the author to write this book.

"Quest" arrived on the 12th August 1949: *"I went aboard and my trapping adventure is over. It is sad to leave Greenland".*[230] You can also feel the melancholy in the poem Havold wrote shortly before his departure:

Way up north there is a land.
Home to a few Norwegian men.
They fight for Norway in snow and blizzards
for our right to the land that Eirik Raude gave us.

In winter and darkness they sledge along,
while the northern lights flame from above.
They struggle to make a living, they catch a fox,
Most often through much hard work and toil.

Once in Hague the world turned against us
stole from us our inheritance.
But as long as Norwegians in Norway live
we remember in sadness our rights to the north.[231]

Trygve Havold

1949-50

During the Second World War, the wireless operator, Dagfinn Egeberg, endured a terrible and traumatic experience. Sverre Storholt told the author in 1992 that Egeberg's ship had been torpedoed, and that for

72 days and nights he had drifted helplessly in the Pacific Ocean on a raft. The shipwreck had cost him an eye, and he had a glass eye when he came to Greenland.

Dagfinn Egeberg began as a wireless operator at Myggbukta in 1948, but soon after New Year 1949 he applied to Arctic Commercial Enterprise to become a trapper. He would have liked to have had Moskusheimen, but Normann Andersen had this for yet another year, so Egeberg instead got Hoelsbu.

On the 7th August 1949 he arrived there on board "Quest". Egeberg wanted to winter on his own - literally speaking. Apart from one accidental meeting in the middle of August 1949, when he ran into some Swiss scientists at Hastværkshytten - Erdhart Fränkl and Fritz Hans Schwarzenbach of Lauge Koch's expeditions: *"where the geologists served me a great dinner"*,[232] - Egeberg had no contact whatsoever with other people until the 30th April 1950. On this day, Stein Sørensen at Myggbukta was: *"awakened by the dogs and a sledge came into view. The time was only 4.30 in the morning and it was Egeberg from Hoelsbu in Moskusfjorden. He had caught 172 foxes and was very disappointed when he heard that Andersen had even more – he had obviously hoped to be number one that year"*.[233] While the other Norwegian trappers enjoyed the company of each other at Myggbukta for a week or more, Egeberg in his disappointment (and despite his fine catch) returned to Hoelsbu the next day.

It was not altogether without risk for Egeberg to have wintered alone. On 30th September 1949, he wrote about a muskox hunt: *"At the rear of the herd there were three bulls, constantly fighting each other. They were so pre-occupied that they did not take any notice of me. I walked up close to them and shot the nearest bull, and he fell. I walked up beside him and shot the other two bulls. The range was very close and they died at the first shot. I now had two cartridges left in the magazine, but as I turned around the first bull attacked me – I had not noticed that he had got up again, as I had been too busy with the other two. I had to shoot fast, but only hit the horns and had to run away to avoid being butted. As I stopped to reload the bull attacked again, furiously, getting very close. At last I finished reloading, and now the bull fell again and died. This was the only time I have felt any sort of excitement when slaughtering muskox"*.[234]

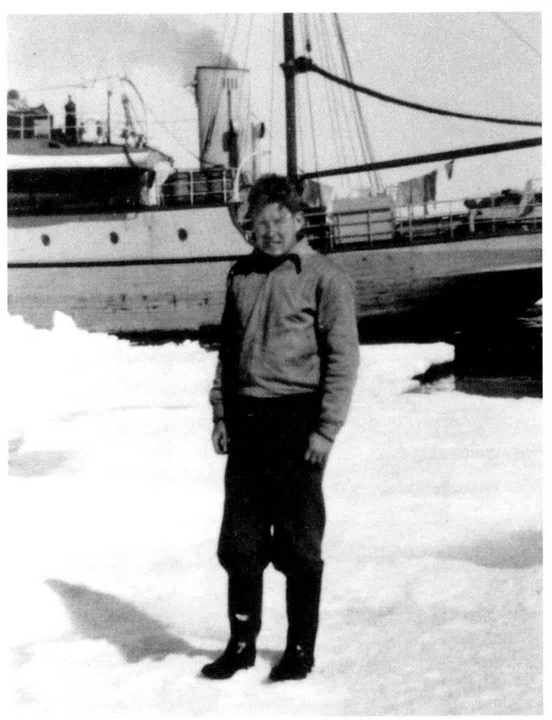

Dagfinn Egeberg, 1948. © Liv Berg

In 1950 Dagfinn Egeberg went home, but later returned to winter at Moskusheimen in 1951-52 and at Myggbukta in 1953-54.

It may have been his experiences in the war that made Egeberg such an unsociable loner. According to Birger Larsen, Egeberg was prohibited from wintering at all arctic stations after 1954.

1950-51

After wintering at Myggbukta, Harald Sverdsten moved to Hoelsbu in 1950. In 1992, Knud Erik Filskov recalled a visit from Sverdsten, who one day came to Loch Fyne to call on him and the other Dane, Hans Madsen: *"He had an enormous hirsute beard. What kind of man is this we wondered? And we hardly dared to let him in; but it turned out that he was the kindest person imaginable. And later on Stein Sørensen and I visited him at Hoelsbu"*.[235] Of this visit Stein Sørensen noted in his diary on the 6th of March 1951: *"Sverdsten is at home so we drink and talk until late in the night."* Unfortunately, Sverdsten was not entirely well, because: *"in January he went over a slope with a muskox on the sledge and sprained his foot and back, so he has stayed in bed for about three weeks and is still stiff as an old man. He had a hard time keeping himself and his dogs alive"*.[236]

Only a few days later Sverdsten had other visitors - this time soldiers of Slædepatruljen Resolut - and of this visit, former patrol member, Ole Lützhøft, wrote: *"We were cordially received, had coffee and for the first time we tasted home-brewed snaps. We had plenty of both. The Greenlanders soon saw their chance to leave and get some decent food from our own supplies. The rest of us had – out of politeness – to follow civilised practice which obviously was coffee and home-brew when it came to visitors. It tasted awful, but we had a great time and he told us about his joys and sorrows as a trapper at Hoelsbu, about his four years as a Norwegian sailor in the Canadian navy during the war, and about his catch of foxes".*[237]

In 1951, when Sverdsten was to travel home, "Polarbjørn" could not get through the ice to Hoelsbu. Sverdsten therefore had to leave his catch, 100 fox furs, and the replacement instead took place at the Danish Loch Fyne station, where his successor, Fredrik Sæterdal, came ashore with his equipment.

1951-52

Fredrik Sæterdal was one of the legendary personalities of the trapping era, when in 1951 he began his third wintering in North-East Greenland. Sæterdal had grown up in Mo i Rana, Norway, and was only 13-years old when he accompanied his father - an experienced trapper - to Hornsund in Svalbard in 1936-37. It was a good polar bear territory, and here Fredrik, at the age of 14, shot his first bear.

In 1941 he came to North-East Greenland for the first time, with the so-called "Buskø" Expedition, which also included the noted trapper Gerhard Antonsen, a relative of Sæterdal. However, Fredrik Sæterdal related in 1992: *"the thrill of arriving in Greenland was short-lived. The Americans would only allow those trappers who had been in Greenland before the occupation of Denmark and Norway to stay. "Buskø" was seized by the U.S. Coast Guard ship "Northland" off Myggbukta. They then sailed northwards and removed the trappers from our stations, one by one. The fact that a fully equipped Nazi wireless operator had been landed together with two trappers did not make matters any easier for us. It ended up as a trip to America for the ship, the crew and the trappers. At the Emigration Station in Boston we were held for about two months with enquiries and investigations in order to clarify that we were not Nazis. John Giæver came down from Toronto, and was one of the experts. We were all cleared, except for the Nazi wireless operator who was interned for the rest of the war. Hallvard Devold, the expedition leader, was sent to England, while the rest of us went to Canada Camp Norway in Lunenburg, about 40 km from Halifax. We worked in the camp during the winter until the spring of 1942, when everybody except Gerhard Antonsen joined the Norwegian forces, and were transferred to England. Some time later, after about three months in Scotland, I was transferred to Iceland to the Islandskompagniet, and went on two missions to Jan Mayen, where I shared a cabin with Magne Råum. Søren Richter was also there".*[238] After the war Sæterdal finally succeeded in getting to Greenland for a wintering. In 1948-49 he stayed at Kap Humboldt, in 1950-51 at Ottostrand and in 1951-52 and 1953-56 at Hoelsbu. The last three years he was accompanied by his wife, Solveig.

"The years in Greenland were the best time of my life. I loved the country and the freedom it offered me. It was a life that suited me better than anything I have tried – and that's quite a lot. The trappers I met there, Danes and Norwegians, were all the best friends I've ever had" Fredrik Sæterdal recalled. With respect to the small travelling huts, he said that: *"It is only someone who has used these primitive huts in the wintertime who can really appreciate them. When you arrive at one of them, frozen to the bone and with numb fingers, and manage to get the small stove and the coffee pot going, then you feel like a king and would not trade your little cabin for the largest castle in the world!"*[239]

> *"Put aside your sledge, ski and rifle, the journey now is over,*
> *go on and slave again for mammon in the world;*
> *But even if you get rich and find use for your skills, my friend,*
> *You will forever yearn for the north and your little cabin."*
>
> Fredrik Sæterdal

His Greenland friends remembered Fredrik Sæterdal not only as a skilled trapper and a good friend, but also for his sparkling temper. In 1992 Lauritz Storholt told an anecdote about Sæterdal, who was somewhat short of stature, and the steady Søren Richter, who was an unusually tall and stout man: *"At Myggbukta there was this home-made arm chair and Richter was so corpulent that the chair stuck to his backside when he got up! And then there was this story about Fredrik Sæterdal. He was a tough guy and when he got drunk, you should be careful with him. And they had this argument – Søren Richter and Fredrik – and Fredrik became furious, grabbed a large sheath knife and stabbed it into the table top right in front of Richter. Richter squeezed himself out of the arm chair and got up, grabbed Sæterdal by his chest, lifted him up against the wall and said: – Now you take it easy, you little troll! – And then Sæterdal turned pale".*

Sæterdal was also known for his quick remarks. In 1991 his old friend Birger Larsen recalled a winter's day, passing by Strømmen in Loch Fyne - a very dangerous place with open water all year round - and at the sight of the characteristic dark cloud hanging above the open water, Sæterdal exclaimed: *"Look, the Devil fires with coal!"*[240]

1952-53

Helge Nesset and Odd Uthi were almost the same age

– 37 and 35-years respectively – and from the same area in Norway, namely the Atna valley. The outdoor life, hunting and fishing had been a part of both their lives since their youth; but Greenland was something new: *"I guess it was mostly for adventure"* Uthi recalled in 1993; and Helge Nesset told the author, that: *"I got in contact with Gunnar Wefring* (a Norwegian painter) *who had been up there a bit. I visited him in Oslo and then we went to the Norwegian Polar Institute and talked to Giæver. And that went well"*.[241]

They divided the Hoelsbu territory between them, so that Nesset trapped along Gauss Halvø while Uthi had the territory around Strindberg Land and into Geologfjord. They had no experience with sledge dogs, but luckily: *"the dogs had been there before and they actually taught us how to drive"*, Uthi said.[242]

It was a year with much snow, and for the most part they had to ski in front of their sledges to break a trail for the dogs. Unfortunately, it was: *"a black year. We caught only 40 foxes between the two of us; but we caught a lot of char, 16 barrels, at Strindberg"*.[243]

1953-56

It was hardly surprising to anyone that Fredrik Sæterdal, after a year in Norway, returned to Hoelsbu in the summer of 1953. On the other hand, it probably came as a big surprise to most of them that he had married and was now accompanied by his wife, Solveig.

In North-East Greenland, where women were always a rare sight, it was quite an event for the tough trappers to meet Mrs Sæterdal. On the 4th May 1954, Stein Sørensen was visiting the Andersen's at Moskusheimen. Suddenly the dogs started howling – the Sæterdal's were arriving: *"I called to the others and Odd* (Bogholm) *and I went out to meet them. They have spent 4 days from Hoelsbu, today arriving from Villaen* (Norske Villa) *after a 10-hour trip skiing behind the sledge. Their faces are sun-tanned and they are in good condition. Solveig Sæterdal is 21-years old, a sweet and pretty girl in a red and white sweater and pixie cap, slim and agile. She looks as if she has stepped right out of Hollywood and does not appear to be bothered by the long and strenuous journey. This naturally calls for drinking and talking till late in the night and Odd and I of course have to postpone our start until tomorrow"*.[244]

Solveig Sæterdal was one of the three trappers' wives to winter in North-East Greenland, and like Petra Winther she also lived three years at Hoelsbu. Gudrun Andersen at Moskusheimen was also one of this exclusive group.

Like her husband, Solveig Sæterdal became a legend in North-East Greenland, and impressed everyone by taking an active part in the trapping. She had her own dog team and trapping territory, and in the summer participated in the char fishery at Strindberg. On the 15th January 1956, Stein Sørensen once again expressed his admiration: *"Today has been bitterly cold and the journey felt long. I take my hat off to Solveig Sæterdal who endures the cold without a word of complaint. She is a real trapper woman alright. Also caught three foxes today"*.[245]

Solveig also placed her mark on the huts in the territory. In 1992, Fredrik Sæterdal recalled: *"In 1954 my wife and I undertook a renovation of Strindberghuset, amongst other things the wainscoting of one of the rooms. We also put up a new provisions hut at Hoelsbu, as well as an annex at the back of the station as a bedroom. We also built a sauna at the end of the hallway"*.[246]

It is only natural that a number of stories and anecdotes about the Sæterdals arose. When they arrived in Greenland in 1953, Fredrik was asked what he had given Solveig for her wedding present. He

Stein Sørensen (left) visiting Solveig and Fredrik Sæterdal at Hoelsbu, 15th March 1956. © Fredrik Sæterdal

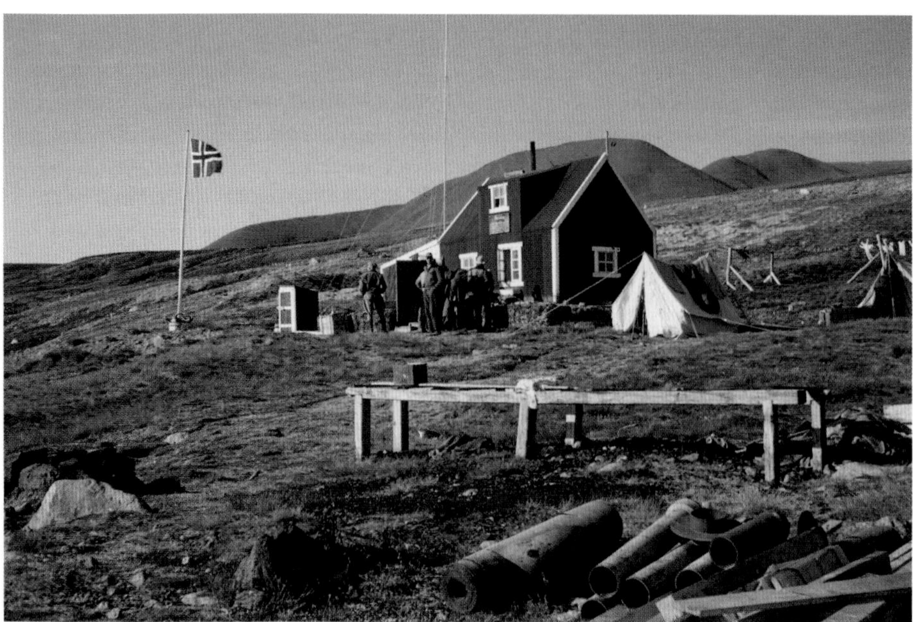

Hoelsbu, 1956. © Jørgen Rasmussen

is said to have answered: *"The biggest refrigerator in the world!"*

Another story, still remembered 30 years after Fredrik and Solveig had left the coast, recalls that a wireless operator at Myggbukta had referred to Solveig on the air in rather indelicate terms. Fredrik, listening to the radio at Hoelsbu, became absolutely furious. He burst out the door, harnessed the dogs and drove directly to Myggbukta, 75 km away, stopped outside the house and shouted: *"Come out here, you bag of shit!"* The operator came out; and Fredrik beat the hell out of him, got back on his sledge and returned straight home to Hoelsbu.

The Sæterdals went home in 1956, due to happy circumstances, as Solveig had become pregnant. A few years later they emigrated to Australia. Later on their paths separated.

Fredrik Sæterdal lived in Australia until his death in 1996.

1956-58

Hilmar Gauteplass from Geilo had arrived in Greenland in 1955 and spent his first year at Myggbukta. On the 13th August 1956 he took over Hoelsbu and on this occasion Stein Sørensen noted: *"We are unloading at Hoelsbu while I'm helping the Sæterdals to get their gear on board. At 6 o'clock in the evening everything is done and Hilmar goes ashore. He seems a bit uneasy and probably feels more like going back home again"*.[247]

In December 1955, Stein Sørensen added: *"Hilmar is somewhat of a little mischief maker so Knut* (Ødegaard) *and I are constantly targets of his teasing. I have been planning for some time now how to get even, and today I filled his pipe with gunpowder neatly covered with tobacco. It worked out brilliantly; after coffee tonight he lit his pipe which resulted in an impressive spurt of flame. Knut and I laughed hilariously and – having recovered from the shock – Hilmar laughed too"*.[248] However, Hilmar's ideas were not always equally bright. For instance, Sørensen recorded that on a day in February 1956, when it was: *"minus 22°C, cold and miserable outside. At 2 o'clock Hilmar set off, with the wind at his back, towards Kap Bennet. He has put up self-shooter traps at both Bennethytta and Franklinstranna in such a way that he has to remove them before Holger Madsen* (from Sirius) *arrives, in case he comes back this way. Hilmar has put up the self-shooters attached to the doors in the huts in such a manner that the shot goes off when the door opens – the bait is fastened to a hole in the door and is almost invisible to people who do not know it is there. What an idea! I asked him to get on with it right away and remove the self-shooters today, as soon as he told me*

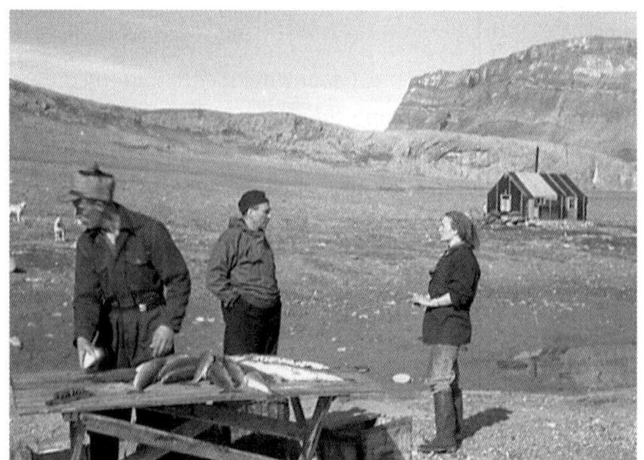

Lauge Koch talking to Solveig Sæterdal during a visit at Strindberg in 1956. © Jørgen Rasmussen

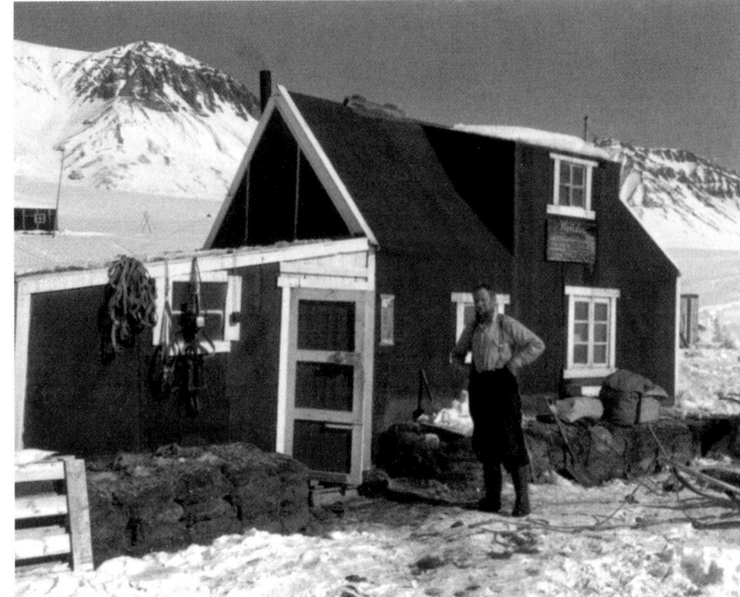

Left: Hilmar Gauteplass at Hoelsbu. Spring 1957. © Erik Jensen.
Below: John Berg – the last trapper at Hoelsbu. © Otto Lapstun

about them this morning. Perhaps he is now eating the bait himself at Bennethytta, while Holger meets his death at Kap Franklin".[249] Fortunately, Hilmar Gauteplass succeeded in disarming both his self-shooters before anyone got hurt. After three winterings, he went back to Norway in 1958.

1958-59

"The time I spent in Greenland was the best of my life and I have no reason to complain", former trapper John Berg related in 1991. He was from Nord-Trøndelag and just 21-years old when he arrived in Greenland. *"At the beginning I had the trapping territory in Myggbukta, but when Hilmar Gauteplass went home, I took over Hoelsbu and the territory there. However, I spent most of my time at Strindberg, and as there was nobody at Humboldt at the time I used that territory too. I travelled mostly in Moskusoksefjord, Nordfjord, Geologfjord and Dusén Fjord.*

The season of 1958-59 was a record year for fox trapping in the Franz Joseph Fjord area. I had 297 foxes plus 125 half-eaten. And I shot three bears and filled eight barrels with char. Having taken down the traps in the spring I took a vacation and drove down to Scoresbysund to visit the Greenlanders. I was well received by the manager and others, and have still pleasant memories from my visit there. On the 17th May I went northwards again and the going was fine, for I spent just six days sledging the 60 Norwegian miles (600 km).

I met a number of people from Daneborg, and occasionally sledged with them, and although I was invited to Daneborg I never actually got so far. I had been prepared for two more years, and it was very sad that it all unexpectedly came to an end in 1959 due to the end of Norwegian trapping in North-East Greenland".[250] John Berg was the last trapper at Hoelsbu.

Blom 1973; Polarårboken 1935; Rodahl 1946; P144.

Recent status

Up to the present-day Hoelsbu has remained one of the finest old trappers' stations in North-East Greenland. It has a large and comfortable main house and it is well placed along one of the main travellers' routes between Daneborg and Ella Ø / Mestersvig. As a result it has been in constant use, and after the end of the trapper era in 1960 was maintained by Sirius. However, by the 1990s the house was showing the need for a more thorough overhaul. In 1999 Nanok sent out a three-man team to renovate Hoelsbu, but it turned out to be too big a job for one summer and another four-man Nanok team went out the following year to complete the project.[251]

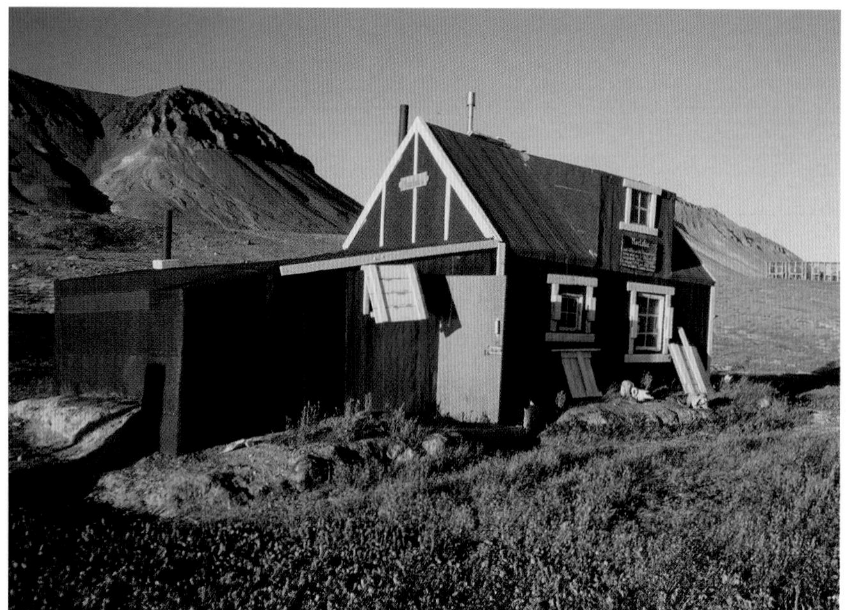

Hoelsbu [356] is a former Norwegian trappers' station built in 1930 for Arctic Commercial Enterprise. It was used as a trappers' station until 1959, and later as a travellers' hut by Sirius. By the end of the 1990s Hoelsbu was in need of a thorough renovation, and Nanok sent out repair teams in 1999 and 2000. © NCN

General cleaning of Hoelsbu by Sirius in the summer of 1979. (Above) All the furniture has been moved out of the house. (Far left) Cleaning and ... (Left) leaving three boards uncleaned for comparison. © Peter Schmidt Mikkelsen.

Hoelsbu and Moskusoksefjord seen from the east looking towards Nordfjord. Summer 2003. © NCN

HVALROSODDEN
[639-1]

Wintering party

1919-20: August F. Nielsen, Kristen Larsen, Ove Haaber Nielsen
1920-21: August F. Nielsen, Kristen Larsen, Christian Ahlstrand, Niels Peter Andersen
1921-32: None
1932-33: Henry V. Nielsen, Povel Povelsen, Christian Jensen, Gunnar Andersen
1933-34: Henry V. Nielsen, Povel Povelsen, Christian Jensen, Finn Kristoffersen
1934-38: None
1938-39: Christian Jensen, Carlos Ziebell, Henning Ørnlef
1939-40: Carl Henrik Schultz, Poul Hennings
1940-41: Poul Hennings
1959-60: Klaus Reindel

In the summer of 1906, when the Danmark Expedition had decided to establish their base camp at Danmark Havn, a boat expedition was sent westwards into Dove Bugt to hunt for dog food and to carry out scientific investigations. After a couple of days, the hunters reached a flat, sandy tongue of land (odde) where they observed some dark shapes that turned out to be a herd of walrus. A hunt was immediately initiated and eleven animals were killed. To the expedition this was a significant gain, as they now had close to 15 tons of dog food for their planned sledge journeys. The locality naturally became known as "Hvalrosodden".

1919-20

In 1919 the East Greenland Company was founded, and included two veterans of the Danmark Expedition 1906-08. As a consequence the management no doubt planned at an early stage the establishment of a trappers' station at Hvalrosodden. Unfortunately, activities in the inner part of Dove Bugt proved over the years to have one major disadvantage. This problem was encountered at the first attempt by "Dagny" in 1919 to transport materials for a new station to Hvalrosodden. As the fjord ice was unbroken in the inner part of Dove Bugt, the hut materials had to be unloaded at the edge of the ice somewhere between Stormnæs and Snenæs.

By the 19th August 1919, the ice conditions had improved sufficiently that Hans Ludvig Jensen, Robert Frørup, Christian Ahlstrand, Ove Haaber Nielsen and August F. Nielsen were able to transport the materials the remaining 25 km to Hvalrosodden with two motor boats. At Hvalrosodden, Jensen and Frørup levelled the ground for the house, which was finished on the

Picture taken at a shooting contest 17th May 1920 at Hvalrosodden. From left: Kristen Larsen, August Frederik Nielsen, Niels Peter Andersen, Hans Ludvig Jensen and Christian Ahlstrand. © Jonna Jensen

1st September 1919. A topping-out ceremony was held for the inhabitants of "Odden", who were: *"delighted with their station and territory"*, as Hans Ludvig Jensen expressed it.[252] Then it was time to say goodbye. Jensen, Ahlstrand and Frørup sailed in a dead calm sea back to their own station, Villaen, at Danmark Havn. It was at the last moment, for just a week later the bay froze up for the winter.

Remaining at Hvalrosodden were August Frederik Nielsen (a fisherman), Ove Haaber Nielsen (a butcher and cook) and Kristen Larsen (a gamekeeper) – and their five sledge dogs. In his diary, Kristen Larsen wrote that he was born in 1891 in Gjerlev near Randers. At the age of ten he went to stay with his uncle, who was the gamekeeper at the manor Overgaard near Mariager Fjord, and it was here he became interested in hunting; this interest endured. After completion of his military service he trained as a gamekeeper, and in 1918 took up a position at Hesselagergård on Fyn. The following winter he learnt that the newly established East Greenland Company was going to initiate trapping in North-East Greenland. He possessed the necessary qualifications, and got the job.

At Hvalrosodden, trapping started on the 1st October. It was carried out using foot traps placed at meat caches. On their first day they caught two white foxes, the next day none, but on the third and fourth days a total of 10 foxes. The fjord ice was now safe, and they were able to use their dog sledge.

On Christmas Eve: *"when dinner was ready, we dressed in as reasonable a Danish manner as possible. Our hair was fairly well combed, but all of us were more or less bearded. As a table cloth we used three pieces of white cloth from O.H. Nielsen's medicine box, and the dinner consisted of rice pudding, roast hare and apple pie, followed by coffee with liqueur. Afterwards we exchanged presents"*.[253]

After New Year, trapping was continued in the area between Spydodden and Snenæs. The winter passed without problems or illness. When the trapping season was over on the 30th April 1920, the catch was 45 white and 10 blue foxes, one arctic wolf, five polar bears and 37 hares. The summer was spent fishing in Lakseelven, the river that drains Sælsøen and enters Dove Bugt close to the station. Unfortunately their nets were torn apart by blocks of ice carried down by the river from Sælsøen. They also hunted for birds, which were skinned to be sent home for stuffing and sale.

1920-21

The supply ship "Dagny" was a long time coming, and one day in the middle of August the men from Danmark Havn brought alarming news: the fjord ice had not broken up. What the men did not know was that "Dagny" had actually been wrecked a week before in the pack ice east of Shannon; a new wintering was to become an unavoidable fact. A totally unexpected and critical situation had thus arisen. The company had optimistically considered navigation to be reliable, and had therefore only provided the wintering parties with supplies for one year. Flour, butter, sugar and milk were already running out, and even worse, there was not enough coal and paraffin. Ingenuity was essential for survival. Melted tallow substituted for butter, bones from walrus – crashed with a hammer – became "firewood", and the timbers from the Danmark Expedition hut at Pustervig ended that winter in the stove at Hvalrosodden. To survive the winter they lived at subsistence level, and to conserve energy stayed in their berths for 16 hours a day. They had only a few candles and one blubber lamp.

At the beginning of November the first signs of scurvy appeared. August Nielsen complained of severe pains in his knees. The parties at Danmark Havn and Hvalrosodden were reorganized, so that Haaber Nielsen swapped places with Christian Ahlstrand and Niels Peter Andersen. At Hvalrosodden, Christmas Eve was a spartan occasion. The culmination was that they were able to light the large paraffin lamp for a few hours.

On 14th January 1921, it was August Nielsen's birthday, but there was no festive atmosphere as his scurvy now affected his breathing. Continued breathing problems led to his death on the 28th January, only 45-years old. His companions later moved his body to Danmark Havn, where he was buried.

By this time everybody had become affected by symptoms of aching and swollen legs, and soon the scurvy claimed its next victim. On the 9th March 1921, Robert Frørup died at Danmark Havn, where he was also buried.

Trapping was carried out to the extent possible, but the catch was just 27 white and eight blue foxes, two ermines and five muskoxen.

The critical situation made it imperative to travel southwards to Germaniahavn, where the chances for rescue were greater. At the beginning of April 1921 the men from Danmark Havn arrived at Hvalrosodden. Their catch was brought to Danmark Havn and placed in Villaen. On April 14th they said goodbye to Hvalrosodden. The five men had about 300 km ahead of them, but Larsen and Andersen were already so weak they had to be carried on the sledge. On their way south they ran out of food, but after 14 days they reached Germaniahavn; all of them survived. Their deposited catch was not recovered until the spring of 1924, and apart from an inspection visit by Lauge Koch in 1927 and a visit by some Nanok men in the spring of 1930, Hvalrosodden and Dove Bugt were to be deserted for the following eleven years.

1932-33

In the summer of 1932, four Nanok men arrived at Hvalrosodden with the "Gefion". They were the trappers Henry V. Nielsen and Povel Povelsen, both 26-years old, and the wireless operators Christian Jensen and Gunnar Andersen. The station was supplemented with an annex, donated by the newspaper "Dagens Nyheder", where a radio station donated by "Ekstrabladets Østgrønlandsfond" was installed.

They were unfortunate at the start, losing their boat and all their dogs except one. To add to their problems, almost the entire supply of coal had been unloaded at Danmark Havn, so Povelsen and Jensen had to walk the 50 km back and forth three times pulling a sledge to fetch the coal. On the last trip, in March 1933, they had shot three bears in Stormbugt, and then - on the 8th April 1933 - the accident happened.

All four of them had gone to collect the skins from the killed bears, when they were surprised by a blizzard. Gunnar Andersen did not have the strength to walk back through the blizzard, and soon collapsed. Povelsen and Nielsen dragged him between them, while Jensen went ahead to fetch a sleeping bag for the exhausted man. Finally, Andersen refused to try to walk further and they were forced to leave him seven km from the station in order to save themselves. Soon afterwards Christian Jensen returned with blankets and hot coffee, but by that time Andersen had already died. He was buried beneath a large cairn at Hvalrosodden.

Despite the lack of dogs, the final result for the season was about 100 foxes, all trapped near the station.

At the beginning of May 1933, Henning Nyholm-Poulsen, Finn Kristoffersen and Arne Philbert arrived from the south to deliver some puppies. It was agreed that Kristoffersen should remain at Hvalrosodden to make up their numbers.

Greenland friends. From left trapper Arne Philbert, archaeologist Peter Vilhelm Glob and trapper Finn Kristoffersen, c. 1933. Glob (1911-1985), who overwintered at the Ella Ø station 1932-33, became the Director of the Danish National Museum in Copenhagen and Keeper of the national antiquities 1960-81. © Arne Philbert

1933-34

During the summer and autumn of 1933, the Dove Bugt territory was extensively built out with huts. In all, eight new trappers' huts were built: "Tvillingnæshytten" [703], "Mørkefjordhytten"[642], "Store Snenæs hytten"[632], "Vædderhytten"[635], "Hellefjordhytten"[636], "Port Arthur hytten" [629], "Pashytten" [618] and "Kap Stop hytten" [621].
In the spring of 1934 two further huts were built: "Bræfjordhytten" [615] and "Gefion Havn hytten" [613-1]. In 1933-34, Hvalrosodden was manned by Henry V. Nielsen, Povel Povelsen, Christian Jensen and Finn Kristoffersen. Kristoffersen wrote a description of the wintering in his book "Jæger og fangstmand" (hunter and trapper) (1969), which passed without any drama.

The grave of wireless operator Gunnar Andersen, who died during a blizzard on 8th April 1933. Hvalrosodden, 17th August 2005. © NCN

1934-35

The summer of 1934 brought an unpleasant surprise. Lauge Koch refused to let his expedition ship, the "Gustav Holm", call at the Nanok stations north of Sandodden. Koch's reason for his decision was that on the 10th August 1934 an aerial reconnaissance had shown the ice to be impassable.

As a consequence the wintering party at Hvalrosodden could not be brought home as promised. J.G. Jennov was furious with Koch. He was convinced that the ice was not the real reason that "Gustav Holm" was not sent northwards, and after his return to Denmark Jennov filed complaints with various authorities objecting to what he believed to be Koch's deliberate harassment of Nanok. The complaints did not help much, but Jennov unexpectedly received support from his Norwegian rival John Giæver, who wrote him a personal letter. In the letter, dated Oslo, the 3rd December 1934, Giæver told Jennov that he shared his views on Koch and added: *"And if there had been any possibility to pick up your men without an aeroplane, we would have done so with or without request"*,[254] – perhaps a rather bold remark from Giæver, who only a couple of months earlier at Jonsbu, on the 20th August 1934, wrote in his diary: *"Tonight I have learned that Nanok will try to have "Selbarden" fetch the four Danes at Hvalrosodden. At the first opportunity I will object to any transaction with the ship which may cause further delay to fetching our men up north* (i.e. Giæver's own party at Ottostrand)*"*.[255]

The failure to send a relief ship to Hvalrosodden had consequences for Nielsen, Kristoffersen and Povelsen, who had contracts only for 1932-33, and had expected to go home. Instead they were forced to stay for another winter. They would not stay without any contract at Hvalrosodden, and as soon as the ice was safe they went south to settle at Kulhus, kindly placed at their disposal by Lauge Koch. They stayed here until spring 1934, and then sledged on to Eskimonæs. At the end of the summer they were picked up from there by a Heinkel seaplane.

Povel Povelsen (1906-85) was a talented artist and his drawings and photographs have been reproduced in several accounts of the life of a trapper. He wintered at Ella Ø from 1947-49, and also participated in Lauge Koch's summer expeditions up to 1957. Subsequently he was employed as a photographer by Grønlands Geologiske Undersøgelse (GGU – Geological Survey of Greenland) from 1957-76.

Henry V. Nielsen (1906-90) subsequently wintered at Loch Fyne from 1945-46, and like Povelsen was employed by Geological Survey of Greenland (GGU); from 1952-76 he was equipment supervisor. He visited Greenland many times on summer expeditions, including the Scoresby Sund region of East Greenland.

After the departure of the three men to Kulhus, Christian Jensen was alone at Hvalrosodden as he still had a contract with Nanok; however, in November 1934 he went south to stay at Hochstetter. From here he carried out two trapping tours to Hvalrosodden at the beginning of 1935.

1935-38

In May 1935, the trapper Arvid Waldenstrøm Petterson and the wireless operator Ole Winstedt arrived at Hvalrosodden from Hochstetter. They were going to take over the station, and now awaited supplies. Unfortunately, ice conditions in 1935 turned out to be the most difficult in living memory, and for a second season the navigation to Hvalrosodden failed. Petterson and Winstedt now found themselves in a problematical position. Fortunately, they did not allow themselves to become depressed, and Winstedt replied to a telegram in which his father encouraged him to keep up his good spirits with: *"Why shouldn't I? – It is the only item we don't have to ration"*.[256]

"Syttenkilometernæshytten" [630-1] was probably built by Petterson and Winstedt before they left Hvalrosodden on the 6th October 1935 on their way southwards to Hochstetter.

In the summer of 1936, "Gustav Holm" had been instructed not to go further north than Hochstetter Forland. Paradoxically the ice conditions in 1936 were extremely favourable, but an order was an order, and as a result Hvalrosodden was unmanned from 1936-38.

1938-39

This became an entirely different year, with exciting activities all over the East Greenland coast. After a number of meagre summers living on hand-outs, Nanok had even succeeded in obtaining almost exclusive rights over "Gustav Holm", and after five years finally managed to land supplies at Hvalrosodden by ship. The station had one man in place, as Carl Henrik Schultz had arrived from Hochstetter in the spring of 1938; he had also built a new trappers' hut, "Trekronerhytten" [701]. However, Schultz was due to go home, and in his place two novices, Carlos Ziebell and Henning Ørnlef, were landed together with Christian Jensen, then 27-years old, who had returned for his fourth wintering.

To the trappers the first task of the season was to expand and improve their territory. A further two huts, "Midternæshytten" [705] and "Vindseløhytten" [633], were built. The trapping that winter took place in the triangle between Sælsøen, Kap Stop and Danmark Havn.

This was also the year when "The Danish Dog

sledge Expedition 1938-39" (Elmar Drastrup and Finn Kristoffersen) would make an attempt to travel north and then across North Greenland. They started from Sandodden in the autumn, but the expedition advanced only slowly, with a lot of time spent at Norwegian and Danish trappers' stations. It was not until the beginning of March 1939 that Drastrup and Kristoffersen reached Hvalrosodden. Here they spent a month, and in April they were assisted by Christian Jensen, who helped them continue northwards to Kap Amélie. Although the dog sledge expedition made new discoveries in the interior of Kronprins Christian Land, they failed to complete their mission. Drastrup and Kristoffersen turned back at Romer Sø (81°N) and returned to Sandodden.

Christian Jensen (1911-81), who was from Gellerup near Varde, never again wintered in North-East Greenland. During WWII he was a seaman, and subsequently became a fisherman in West Greenland. [257]

1939-40

On the 16th August 1939, "Gustav Holm" once again anchored at Hvalrosodden. The trappers Carl Henrik Schultz and Poul Hennings went ashore to take over the station, and "Gustav Holm" landed food and provisions for two years, including 22 tons of coal, seven barrels of paraffin, three and a half barrels of gas oil, four barrels of petrol and half a barrel of lubricating oil. Schultz and Hennings were both experienced trappers. In 1936-38 they had been partners at Hochstetter, and jumped at the chance of going to Hvalrosodden when Jennov contacted them in the spring of 1939.

One day at the beginning of September they visited the Mørkefjord station, where they received a depressing piece of news: war had broken out in Europe. Of course they had misgivings, but it was difficult for them to understand the significance of the announcement, especially when received in such a peaceful environment. However, there was nothing else to do but to carry on as usual. They built two new trappers' huts, "Lille Snenæs hytten" [637] and "Stormbugthytten" [631].

One day when heading by boat for Danmark Havn they discovered a walrus, sleeping on an ice floe near Bådskæret. They shot it and shouted with joy, but their pleasure was short-lived. While they were turning the boat another walrus climbed onto the ice floe and pushed its dead mate into the sea. The dead walrus sank immediately and was lost.

The winter catch that season numbered 72 foxes and two polar bears, and was the record for Danish trappers that year. During the season they occasionally visited their neighbours at Mørkefjord, only 10 km away. They had radio equipment, and were able to follow the developing situation in Europe.

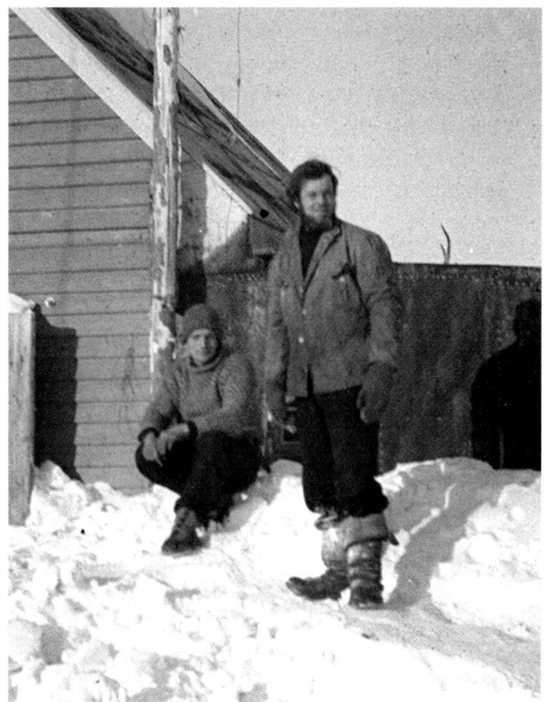

Carl Henrik Schultz (left) and Poul Hennings. Hvalrosodden 1940. © Niels Ove Jensen

On the 13th May 1940 Hennings and Schultz split up. Schultz and Niels Haarløv (1919-87),[258] a zoologist from Mørkefjord, had decided to make the 1000 km long journey south to Scoresbysund, in order to leave North-East Greenland from there. It was a long and exhausting journey, and they finally reached Scoresbysund on the 18th July. Schultz went on to America, joined the merchant navy and later settled in West Greenland. Haarløv went to Iceland with the "Fridtjof Nansen", and travelled on via Spain to Denmark, where he arrived on the 13th November 1940, six months to the day after his departure from Hvalrosodden.

1940-41

Poul Hennings, 28-years old, was now alone at Hvalrosodden, facing an uncertain future. In a letter to his family dated 13th April 1941, he wrote: *"It has been a good season and excellent snow conditions, and these two things have contributed to my substantial catch* (68 foxes). *Apart from my never ceasing to think of you and how you are, I have had only one worry, namely my beloved dogs. I have had much bad luck with them and lost four; one I lost to a bear, of which I have shot two this year. I now have two lovely puppies that were born on New Year's Eve, and they will soon learn how to run with the big dogs. What the future brings is hard to tell, but it is my hope that there will be a possibility for me to make a living here or in West Greenland. I think the easiest way to show you my different moods will be through a small selection of my new songs"*.[259] Hennings' songs were about walrus hunts, Christmas and farewells to colleagues going south. His declaration of love to Hvalrosodden he called "Oddens Pris" (praise to Odden).

"Praise to Odden"

Where the river runs from the lake to the sea
a station stands on the beach.
Built by Hans and his men so brave
in the year of two times 19.
It holds joy
it holds sorrow
from years gone by.
I hope it still stands
for a hundred years.
I think that Odden is great.

Now the char are jumping like silver from sea,
delightful in colour and taste
but with so many things to do
the summer goes by in haste.
But the heart has songs
as the sun has light
for twenty four hours a day.
May the song light up
in the winter's night.
I think that Odden is grand.

Poul Hennings; Hvalrosodden 1941[260]

One day in the beginning of August 1941 the American coast guard cutter "Northland" arrived. The war had reached North-East Greenland. The stations in Dove Bugt were to be closed down and the men evacuated. During the war Poul Hennings worked as a weather observer in Scoresbysund, and as a police assistant at the Ikáteq USAAF base (BE-2) north of Ammassalik. After the war he became a fisherman in West Greenland; from 1950-64 he was colony manager in Skjoldungen and from 1965-73 colony manager at Tiniteqilâq. Finally, he was employed by KGH in Ammassalik, where he lived until his death in October 1996.

Hennings was the last Nanok trapper to stay at Hvalrosodden. Apart from a brief intermezzo in 1959-60, the station has been unmanned.

1959-60

Klaus Reindel had started in East Greenland in 1950 as a weather service operator in Ammassalik. He stayed there for three years, went home for one year, then came to Danmarkshavn weather station where he worked from 1954-57 and 1958-59.

In the spring of 1959, Ib Palle Madsen and Viggo Block arrived by dog sledge from Station Nord. They had decided to quit their jobs there to become trappers. Strangely enough Reindel, at that time 31-years old, had the same idea: *"It was not just to make money; it was more to be on your own. But of course there should also be a purpose, as you could not just stare into space, so it was obvious to put up some fox traps"*, Reindel said in 1993.[261] Madsen and Block continued southwards, while Reindel settled first at Hvalrosodden and later on at Aalborghus.

An application had been approved by the authorities and: *"Jennov, the old director Jennov, wrote to me that he would be happy to lend me the territory and the station in return for two good quality fox furs – if I caught more than 100. And when I came home, I went to his office with two of my finest furs. He then asked me how many I had caught. I told him that I had caught 104. Damn! – He said, and laughed – then I should have asked you for some more.*

I even had a decent income from my catch, more than 10,000 kroner, and that was about the same as I could have earned at Danmarkshavn", Klaus Reindel continued. He has since lived most of his life in East Greenland: *"That year as a trapper was one of the best; but I had originally imagined that I could live on my own. I could, of course, but it turned out that I really missed having company. When you're alone with your dogs you begin to long for human company. It was quite a revelation to discover that you cannot live without the company of others"*.[262] Klaus Reindel died in 1996 at the age of 67.

Drastrup 1945; Friis 1909; Giæver 1939; Grønlandske Selskab 1983b; Haarløv 1941; Knuth 1942; Lund 1926; Nyholm-Poulsen 1985; Odsbjerg 1990; A144; A154; A155; A156; A157; A296; G132.

Recent status

Hvalrosodden is still well maintained, and is frequently used by the Sirius Dog Sledge Patrol and visitors from Danmarkshavn Weather Station. On several occasions, the flat terraces north of Hvalrosodden have served as a Twin Otter landing strip and the location of summer base camps for scientific expeditions.

Hvalrosodden [639-1] is a former Danish trappers' station built in 1919 for the East Greenland Company. It was used as a trappers' station until 1960, and thereafter as a travellers' hut, maintained by Sirius and Danmarkshavn Weather Station. Hvalrosodden is the oldest building still in regular use in North-East Greenland. (Left) Hvalrosodden, 29th May 1978. © Peter Schmidt Mikkelsen. (Below and Bottom) Hvalrosodden, 17th August 2005. © NCN

JACKSON-STUA
[371]

Wintering party
1928-29: Peder Sulebak
1929-33: None
1933-34: Johan Stordal

Jackson Ø lies in the southern part of the entrance to Gael Hamke Bugt, and is four km wide and twice as long. The island was named in 1822 by William Scoresby Junior after his brother-in-law, Captain Thomas Jackson of Whitby. [263]

1928-29

During the winter of 1927-28, it became clear to the Hird Expedition that they would have to expand their territory, and on the 23rd May 1928 the trapper Peder Sulebak walked to Jackson Ø: *"to have a look at the land, and if possible to use it next winter, as we are forced to expand the territory"*.[264] The walk from Elvsborg lasted twenty four hours, but Sulebak was happy, for he had seen numerous tracks of fox and bear, a sign that Jackson Ø was a promising trapping area. The "Hird" men therefore decided to build a winter house on the island, where Sulebak was to overwinter.

On the 6th August 1928 they began to gather building materials. Jonas Karlsbak wrote: *"Today we travelled with much effort to Clavering Ø, and further to Elvsborg, where we tore down the porch, which is to be used for the house at Jackson Ø"*.[265]

During the following days, Sulebak, Karlsbak, Jørgen Furnes and Peder Røbek built the house. As the materials from Elvsborg were not sufficient the house was partly built of drift wood, collected at Kap James and at Home Forland, supplemented by pieces of wreckage from "Hird". On August 14th the house "Jackson-stua" was finished. It measured 230 cm on each side and had a small porch. On the outside it was equipped with a turf wall, making it warm and tight. While a modest station, it was big enough for one trapper.

Trapper Peder Sulebak at Jackson-stua, 1929.
© Jonas Karlsbak / Norwegian Polar Institute

On August 20th it was time to say goodbye, and Sulebak wrote: *"My friends left this morning, for the last time this year, I guess. So now I have the rest of this year and a good part of the next to be alone, although I hope to have visitors from Kap Herschell over Christmas and then I will probably hear news from those at Sabine Ø. Although it is a long time to be alone, I'm not afraid as long as I am healthy. That is my hope, nothing more"*.[266] Peder Sulebak's modest wish came true. He lived alone on Jackson Ø, together with his dog Jack, until the end of May 1929, during which time he was spared any sickness or accidents. He was not entirely out of touch with the surrounding world. A couple of times he met with his neighbours at the Krogness station, and on the night before Christmas Peder Røbek from Kap Herschell arrived to spend Christmas with his colleague in Jackson-stua.

When the trapping season ended, Sulebak had a catch numbering five polar bears and about 60 foxes. The first foxes he caught live in box traps and placed them in a fox kennel. Later in the winter the trapping was carried out using folding traps. Peder Sulebak returned to Norway in the summer of 1929, together with the other "Hird" men. He came back for several winterings in North-East Greenland where his regular base was the Kap Peterséns station.

The Danish scientist Paul Gelting visited Jackson Ø in the winter of 1931-32: *"The walls are deck planks which for a time have served as skids. The spaces between the planks are stuffed with moss, paper and old, unravelled ropes. There is a berth for one man, but sufficient space for two more on the floor. There is a genuine small stove with two holes for kettles and suitable for baking bread. Beneath the south-facing window there is a square table measuring two feet across, a couple of chairs and the necessary kitchen utensils and tools." ... "The domestic utensils seem to have originated from many places. There were boxes with the Hudson's Bay Company brand and huge knives from the USA, that at one time had been in the depot at Bass Rock placed there by the Baldwin-Ziegler Expedition"*.[267]

1933-34

The trapper Johan Stordal, from the Sigurd Tolløfsen Expedition, used Jackson-stua as a base from November 1933 until the end of January 1934. No details from this wintering period are known.

Scoresby 1917; N026; N142; P134.

Recent status

After 1934, Jackson-stua was not used as a regular trappers' station. It was, however, used as a travellers' hut, as it was located at the southern limit of the Kap Herschell territory. After the trapper era it was used and maintained by the Sirius Dog Sledge Patrol until 1981, when it was accidentally burned down.

Jackson-stua [371] was a Norwegian trappers' station built in 1928 by the Hird Expedition. It was used as a trappers' station until 1934, and subsequently as a travellers' hut until 1981, when it was accidentally burnt down. (Above) A Sirius Dog Sledge Patrol dog team camping at Jackson-stua, 22nd May 1979. © Peter Schmidt Mikkelsen. (Left and below) The remains of Jackson-stua visited by a Nanok-team, 22nd July 2005. © NCN

JONSBU
[521]

Wintering party
1932-33: John Giæver, Johan Holm
1933-34: John Giæver
1934-38: None
1938-39: Sigurd Tolløfsen, Eivind Tolløfsen
1939-40: Eivind Tolløfsen

On the west bank of Peters Bugt, about eight km north-east of Kap Klinkerfues, there was once a Norwegian trappers' station. Today only the outline of the foundation is visible, covered by arctic willow and other slow-growing plants.

1932-33

The Jonsbu station was built in 1932. Its name and history is related to one of the best known characters of Norwegian trapping in North-East Greenland, namely John Giæver.

John Schjelderup Giæver was born in 1901 in Tromsø. He worked as a journalist from 1923-29, and as a trapper in North-East Greenland from 1929-31 and 1932-34. From 1935 he was secretary and expedition leader in NSIU, and from 1948 head of NSIU. He was leader of the Norwegian-Swedish-British Norsel-Expedition to the Antarctic in 1949-52.

In his younger years, Giæver wrote a couple of fictional novels, but he is best known for his numerous books about outdoor life and people in the Arctic. His books that deal with North-East Greenland include: "Fangsthyttene" (the trappers' huts) (1930), "To mann i Moskusfjorden" (two men in the muskox fjord) (1931), "Den norske fangstvirksomheten på Østgrønland" (the Norwegian trapping activities in East Greenland) (1939), "Dyretråkk og fugletrekk på

John Giæver – famous Norwegian expedition leader, trapper, journalist and writer. © Norwegian Polar Institute

The Jonsbu station at Peters Bugt, c. 1934. © Arne Philbert

74°Nord" (animal tracks and migration at 74°N) (1955) and "Hardbalne polarkarer" (tough polar lads) (1957).

It was originally Finn Devold who saw the possibilities of expanding Norwegian trapping northwards, during a sledge journey to Haystack in the spring of 1929. However, the company directors in Norway wanted Devold to lead a wintering expedition to the Skjoldungen area of South-East Greenland. As a result, it was John Giæver who carried out Devold's original plan for a trapping expedition to the area around Kuhn Ø and northwards: *"In 1932, at the same time as Sigurd Tolløfsen, I equipped an expedition of six men from Tromsø to establish a radio station in the area and transmit daily weather reports at the request of the Norwegian state."* ... *"For transport I hired together with Tolløfsen M/S "Isbjørn" of Tromsø".*[268]

On the 23rd July 1932, "Isbjørn" arrived in North-East Greenland, and having unloaded men and material for Tolløfsen, the ship continued with Giæver and his five men - Johan Holm, Otto Johnsen, Ove Høeg, Ole Sivertsen and John Johnsen - to the west side of Peters Bugt, where Giæver's first station was unloaded. Johnsen and Høeg went ashore here and started building the house. Having put out materials for trappers' huts in Ardencaple Fjord, "Isbjørn" headed for the outer coast of Hochstetter Forland, where Giæver wanted to place his main station with a radio some distance south of Haystack. However, the ice was unbroken, and "Isbjørn" therefore turned back. As a consequence Giæver decided to establish his headquarters at the station already put ashore at Peters Bugt. On the 8th August they began to unload the radio equipment and the 16 metre high aerial masts. In the meantime the ice north of Shannon had broken up, and "Isbjørn" was able to unload the two other planned stations, Ottostrand and Olestua.

When Giæver and Holm had finished building their station, the result was a nice, large house with two side sheds. Giæver initially named the station "Kolstad" (after the Norwegian prime minister, Peder Ludvik Kolstad), but on the 30th August he received a telegram from Norway to change the name to "Johnsbu". In time the spelling was changed to "Jonsbu". While Giæver worked with the house and the trapping, the wireless operator Johan Holm installed and operated the radio equipment; Holm did not take part in the trapping.

Fox skins hung for drying outside the fur shed at Jonsbu, c. 1934. © Arne Philbert

At the end of August, Giæver built two trappers' huts, "Holmsnes" [526] and "Skylstad" [514-1], in Ardencaple Fjord. The latter was built only a few km from the Danish "Kildedalhytten" [516], and on 13th September 1932 Giæver received: *"a telegram from Svalis* (NSIU) *concerning Danish criticism that my huts are too close to the Danish. Is that correct and why? Hoel asks. Of course it is correct and he knows it, and he also knows why. I answered that I had followed the plan regardless of the Danish huts, but that none of mine are closer to any Danish hut than the new Danish huts in the south are to ours".*[269]

The establishment of Jonsbu - in a territory where Nanok had previously had exclusive rights - inevitably led to conflicts, especially in the winter of 1932, when the Danish-Norwegian dispute in Hague entered its final phase. On the 29th October 1932, Giæver wrote: *"I found a Danish trap close to ours and saw traces of Niels Hansen. Later on, from the hills, I watched him drive across the bay. He had probably put up his small terrain yesterday. I am, of course, somehow sorry for old Niels, but I have to trick him by surrounding his entire territory with my traps."* And on the 31st October, Giæver continued: *"As far as I can see from here, the Danes have very deliberately put up two traps a few hundred metres from my station. All right, then tomorrow I will scatter a little pepper on their bait. No fox likes Norwegian spices".*

"I have wondered quite a bit what will happen to us if Denmark wins the trial in Hague," Giæver wrote on the 27th November 1932. *"I suppose we are done here then. In any case, as far as this station and the trapping in Ardencaple are concerned. Perhaps we will have to stop and go home. Then I'll be in trouble. This expedition was a 'to be or not to be' venture for me. And it may turn out as 'not to be', should it come to that".*[270] From his extensive diary it appears that he was deeply involved emotionally in the Hague trial and its possible outcome. Nor did he try to hide his great disappointment when the telegram with the Court's decision arrived at the beginning of April 1933: *"It feels as if the carpet has been pulled away from under me. Everything is so bloody meaningless. We are in Danish land".*[271]

1933-34

After the verdict at The Hague, the Norwegian

authorities decided to close down the weather service at Jonsbu, and move the wireless operator Johan Holm to Myggbukta. John Giæver was now alone at his station, but in the autumn of 1933 Otto Johnsen from Ottostrand helped him build two huts: "Tornøestua" [527] and "Bredruphytten" [529]. Materials left in 1932 at "Niflheim" [923] on the south side of Ardencaple Fjord were also used for Tornøestua.

John Giæver spent the entire winter in solitude, and had no contact with other people between the 14th August 1933 and 26th March 1934: *"The life here is like a spiritual hibernation. And as it has turned out it may at best be a waste of time. There is nothing new for me here anymore. I have tried, and know everything from mortal danger to baking bread, from the most wearing idleness to hard work, from intense excitement to unbelievable terror and fear. But that was in the beginning"*, he noted on the 4th December; but then - on the 6th January 1934 - the diary records: *"By the way, I write a bit every day now. I have already completed a collection of short stories. I guess they'll be rejected as usual, but I'm enjoying writing all the same. I should never have bothered writing novels. I realize that now. Short stories with a brief and sweeping characteristic, that's me. Novels bore me. I loose the thread, the interest as well as the excitement. And quin sabe, maybe I have found something"*.[272]

The disillusioned John Giæver really had found something, which later resulted in numerous entertaining books, exactly the kind of short stories written with "brief and sweeping characteristics".

Unfortunately the trapping also failed this year: *"And I who last year fantasized about a "fox year" and reckoned on 40-50 furs! If I get 30, I'll be lucky"*,[273] Giæver wrote on the 16th March 1934. In fact, the result was only 25 fox furs. Giæver and his men went home with "Selbarden" in August 1934, and Jonsbu was unmanned until 1938.

1938-39

In 1938 the 60-year-old Sigurd Tolløfsen, after an unsuccessful attempt the year before, managed to launch a new expedition. It consisted of himself, his son Eivind Tolløfsen and the two trappers Bjarne Jakobsen and Bjarne Dalsbø, all from Tromsø. On the 29th July 1938 they went ashore at Zackenberg, where they remained fishing until the 15th August, when "Polarbjørn" returned to transport them and their catch of 12 barrels of arctic char further north. Tolløfsen and his son disembarked at Jonsbu. They spent the following weeks repairing the station, and made a boat trip to inspect their territory and to deposit materials for a new hut at the head of Lindeman Fjord. However, this planned hut at "Svejstrup Dal" [911] was never built.

The winter of 1938-39 was filled with hardships and disappointments for Sigurd Tolløfsen. To start with, open water kept them imprisoned at Jonsbu. Eventually the fjord froze up and on the 9th November they were finally able to harness their dogs to the sledge and start on their way to Kap Buch; but the ice was unsafe. Sigurd Tolløfsen went through the ice and they lost five dogs. Fortunately, Tolløfsen's son had come along and they reached Arnljotstua safely. A couple of days later they were heading for Håkonshytten when suddenly a blizzard set in. At 10 o'clock in the evening they could continue no further: *"Completely wet through we built a shelter of snow to crawl into. A lot of snow is drifting in"*.[274] They were forced to spend three days and nights in their snow cave, only two km from the hut. The following days they were pestered by bad weather, deep snow and lack of food, but: *"we were fortunate to find a loaf which John Giæver had baked in 1932 or 1933. It was very hard, but it went down well as we are completely out of bread"*.[275] They did not get back to Jonsbu until the 12th of December, having spent seven days in the open air. This was truly a rough life for a 60-year-old man. They stayed at the station until January.

On the 19th January 1939, Tolløfsen had a visit from the Danish trapper Svend Aage Jespersen from the Hochstetter station: *"He tells me that my men up north* (Ottostrand), *Jakobsen and Dalsbø, on their first trip to Olestua had lost both boats, their sleeping bags, gun and some other equipment, materials etc. This was*

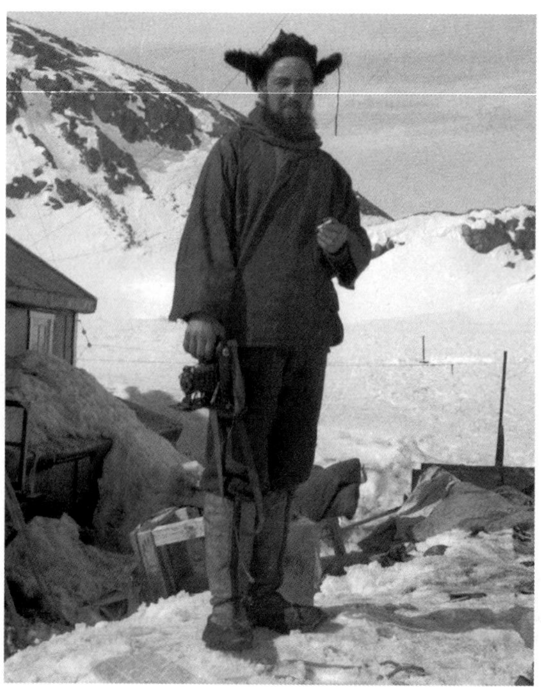

Eivind Tolløfsen in 1939. © Niels Ove Jensen

the worst piece of news I could receive now, when we have no catch here".[276] Even so, Tolløfsen's hardships were far from over.

The 8th February 1939 was a very cold day – minus 45°C. Late in the evening Tolløfsen and his son reached Sigurdsheim. They had been forced to leave their dogs 30 km behind at Kap Hamburg, as the dogs refused to walk further: *"We had to tug the puppies into the sleeping bag and leave the dogs and the sledge, as the dogs could not continue anymore. We each took our rucksack and rifle and alternately carried a sleeping bag containing two unskinned foxes. Despite the heavy load, and walking as fast as we could, we both developed frostbite in four toes, our thumbs and faces. We have now frozen our toes so much that the nails have come loose"*.[277]

Due to the weather it was five days before they could return to fetch the dogs and: *"it was a sad sight, that met us. "Bruno", who had a thin coat had frozen to death, and so had "Tia" and her five puppies.*[278] *They had crawled out of the sleeping bag"*. They now had only one dog left, and the three of them struggled on to finally reach Holmeslet hytten, but: *"as there is no firewood here, we had to break up the berth and a box we used for food. I have always been in high spirits, but lately I find my spirits are running low. First you borrow money to finance the expedition; then you have a poor catch in spite of hard work in the territory, and then all these misfortunes – losing the boats and the equipment in the north, and the accident with our dogs"*.[279] It was seven and a half weeks before they managed to return to Jonsbu from this trip, and Sigurd Tolløfsen was by then so plagued with arthritis that he had to stay home at the station for the rest of the trapping season.

At the beginning of May he was able to go to Eskimonæs, to radio for men to replace Jakobsen and Dalsbø, who wanted to go home; only to receive more depressing news: *"I had sent a telegram to Johan Stordal, who came here with me in 1932-34. I am so tormented by rheumatism that I cannot stay here for another year without medical treatment. The telegram from home reported that Stordal had been lost in the Vestisen in the spring. My son-in-law and his father died at Christmas, leaving my daughter with four children between the age of three and eight without any means of support"*.[280]

1939-40

Back home in Tromsø, Sigurd Tolløfsen's wife managed to arrange for a new trapper to go up to Greenland on "Polarbjørn". Tolløfsen negotiated with him about a contract, which: *"by the way was the same as the contracts my other men had last year. I decided to ask the company if they would accept such an arrangement. John Giæver, acting on behalf of the department, replied that it was not acceptable. I then offered a contract on the same terms as Arctic Commercial Enterprise, but such a contract was not acceptable to Giæver either"*.[281] As a consequence the trapper returned with "Polarbjørn" and Tolløfsen's son had to winter alone at Jonsbu.

Jonsbu in 1939. © Norwegian Polar Institute

Eivind Tolløfsen's catch was only 13 foxes. He had some contact with the Danes at Hochstetter, the last on the 29th April 1940, when he drove: *"south to Myggbukta to await the ship"*.[282] He left Greenland the same summer with "Veslekari" or "Fridtjof Nansen". Jonsbu was not subsequently used for wintering.

In the summer of 1941, the Buskø Expedition set ashore a pro-German wireless operator with a radio transmitter at Jonsbu, together with two trappers. When the Americans aboard the USCG cutter "Northland" heard the news they headed immediately for Jonsbu, which thus acquired a unique status in war history. The incident was published a year late on the 24th August 1942, in the American magazine "Life", with the headline: *"The first blow"* and the subtitle: *"Nazi radio station in Greenland is discovered and destroyed by Coast Guard in the fall of 1941"*. The article said that: *"The first American action in this war occurred on Sept. 14, 1941 when the Coast Guard Cutter "Northland", on routine patrol, destroyed a German-controlled radio station on the shores of a small bay in North-East Greenland. A few days before this, the destroyer "Greer" had depth-charged an attacking submarine in the northern waters but the Navy did not claim its destruction. Thus the burning of the station, which was almost ready to begin sending valuable weather information to German ports and submarines, was the first blow struck by our armed forces"*.[283] From the article you clearly get the impression that the Jonsbu house was burnt down on this occasion. However, this was not the case, as the fire and the smoke on the photographs in the article actually came from a large bonfire in front of house. In reality, Jonsbu was burnt down by a unit from the Greenland Patrol, but this did not happen until the 14th August 1943 when "Northland": *"stood up Ardencaple Fjord to Peters Bugt and anchored off Willspitze Mountain at 0700" ... "The landing force searched this area and burned a hunting station found here to prevent it being used by the enemy. (This station is off the track followed by the Sledge Patrol)"*.[284]

Polarboken 1963-1964; NSIU 1945; G109; N069.

Recent status

Jonsbu was never rebuilt at this location. Instead, Arctic Commercial Enterprise in 1948 established the "Ny Jonsbu" station [514-2] in Ardencaple Fjord about 16 km to the south-west of the ruins of Jonsbu.

Today, the foundation of the house and a few metal items mark the site of the Jonsbu station, together with the wooden framework of a fur shed.

Jonsbu, 30th July 2004. Jonsbu [521] was a Norwegian trappers' station built in 1932 by the John Giæver Expedition. It was used as a trappers' station until 1940. On 14th August 1943 it was burnt down by a US Coast Guard task force to prevent Jonsbu from becoming a Nazi-controlled weather station. (Above) The coal stove marks the exact location of the station house. (Facing page,top) The site of Jonsbu. In the background Barth Bjerge, c. 1200 m. (Facing page, centre) The framework of the fur shed. (Facing page, bottom) View over the Jonsbu station site towards Hochstetterbugten, between Hochstetter Forland to the left and Kuhn Ø to the right. © NCN

KAP BROER RUYS
[334]

Wintering party
1920-21: Alfred Ewers, Carl Meyer, John Tutein.

Traditionally, Kap Broer Ruys has been known as a place where it was always possible to reach land after the often dangerous voyage through the pack ice. Just north of the cape there is a small bay where ships can find shelter. Koldewey, Ragnvald Knudsen, Ryder and Nathorst all reached the coast here. However, as a matter of fact the locality is inhospitable, as the ice is always on the move and packs together here all year round. The place is often shrouded with a damp mist, and at times when the sea is open and waves are roaring, the rock walls are drenched with salt-saturated vapour. Once a house stood here, but it was taken by the sea a long time ago, and today only a few pieces of timber reveal that men once had their home here.

1920-21
In the summer of 1920 when the "Dagny" arrived in North-East Greenland, it was not only to set ashore trappers. The East Greenland Company wanted to expand their trapping territory and had brought along materials for two new stations. On their way, they had first gone ashore on Jan Mayen, but found that the territory here had already been taken over by Norwegians. The expedition therefore continued westwards to North-East Greenland. The pack ice was exceptionally heavy in 1920, and it was only with great difficulty that they reached the coast at Kap Broer Ruys on the 18th of July. According to their original plan, they should have gone ashore further north, but the way was blocked by unbroken ice and they therefore chose to land six men, a motor boat and the materials for the two stations on the spot. The trappers had planned to transport their goods further on when the ice broke up. On the 22nd July "Dagny" continued towards Germaniahavn - and her shipwreck.

At Kap Broer Ruys the trappers immediately began to build one of the stations, as they dared not wait for better ice conditions. On the 27th July the ice broke up at Hold with Hope, and three men - led by Viktor H. Stjernebo - sailed north to check out the ice conditions. It turned out to be impossible to pass by Kap Kraus due to the ice, so it was decided to build the other station at Carlshavn. The men then split up in two groups, with three men at each station.

The Kap Broer Ruys station was manned by Carl Meyer, John Tutein and Alfred Ewers. During August and September they made "fox depots", that is to say they shot some muskox and left them as bait to attract foxes. This procedure seemed promising at first. When the first snow fell in the middle of September, they could see a lot of fox tracks leading to and from the meat depots, but were unable to tell whether the tracks came from 20 or 200 foxes.

According to their instructions, their trapping season was to begin on 1st October. They put out foot traps and soon caught 15 fox: 10 white and five blue. However, the number of fox tracks subsequently decreased drastically. In November they only caught one fox and in December the catch was zero. Carl Meyer wrote: *"January has been just like December.*

Kap Broer Ruys, 1931. © Bernhard Luncke / Norwegian Polar Institute

Kap Broer Ruys, c. 1923.
© Jens Mathiesen

Occasionally I spotted a fox track and each time I did everything to catch it. As often as I put out the foot trap, just as often it became covered with snow, and it was not until the end of the month that another fox was caught. When I arrived at the scene there was neither fox nor trap; the chain had loosened from the mooring post and the fox had run off with the trap. I followed the tracks for about an hour, and at one point make an involuntary slide down a glacier wall. I was quite bruised and my rifle got bashed about too. I had to give up the fox that day and in the following days a blizzard set in; later attempts have proven unsuccessful. Nothing has been caught here since, and not a single fox track has been seen".[285]

On the 1st February 1921, the accident happened. John Tutein, who was an engineer and also a skilled painter, had agreed to paint illustrations of the fauna of the country for a publication which the director of the company, A.L.V. Manniche, was writing. That day Tutein had gone out to make some cartographic measurements at Kap Broer Ruys: *"He bent down to adjust his skis and did not notice the stealthy approach of a polar bear. His shotgun was on the ground a few feet away. When he realized the bear was nearly upon him, Tutein began to run. It was uphill, and the bear lumbered after him, much faster than most people realize they can travel. Tutein circled around and headed down the hill, presumably in the hope of getting to his gun before the bear overtook him. The bear increased its speed downhill and was close behind him when Tutein reached the gun. Picking up the shotgun, Tutein broke it open to insert a shell. But it was too late – there was no time to fire. The bear was upon him, and struck my friend a crushing, fatal blow on the head. Tutein's tiny poodle dog, with him to the end, must have defied the huge bear and came so close that it became the second victim. Badly injured, the poor dog made its way to the station, where Tutein's two companions had to shoot it".*[286]

John Tutein, who Madsen described as a tall, handsome man about 28-years old, has his lonely grave in a cairn close to the station at Kap Broer Ruys. He is the only person to have been killed by a polar bear in North-East Greenland in recent times.

In spite of the shock of Tutein's death, Meyer and Ewers continued trapping, but the result was depressing: 17 foxes for the entire season. On 24th August 1921, Meyer concluded: *"The amount of game I have seen here at Hold with Hope during the previous year is so little that there is no chance of a station at this location ever being profitable".*[287] His opinion was shared by many.

In 1922, the East Greenland Company ordered Hans Ludvig Jensen to move the station further into Mackenzie Bugt, and to man it; however, after a reconnaissance Jensen abandoned the project and returned to Germaniahavn with his men. In 1930 Nanok also attempted to move the station, but again had to give up due to the ice.

In the summer of 1936, there was almost no pack ice present off North-East Greenland, and the sea had free rein. The house was demolished by a spring tide in September, and was never rebuilt.

Asher 1860; Nathorst 1900; NSIU 1937; Payer 1877; A129; Ø040; Ø045; Ø046; Ø048; Ø055.

Recent status

The ruins of the Kap Broer Ruys station have remained almost untouched, as the location soon became a forbidden area due to the dangerous and unpredictable ice conditions both summer and winter. As a consequence, the site is seldom visited.

Kap Broer Ruys [334] was a Danish trappers' station built in 1920 for the East Greenland Company. It was used as a trappers' station only in 1920-21, and then abandoned. In 1936 it was destroyed by the sea. © NCN (Top and centre right) Ruins of the station house. © NCN (Centre left) Grave of John Tutein, c. 1923. © Jens Mathiesen. (Bottom) Grave of John Tutein, 28th July 2004. © NCN

KAP HERSCHELL
[417]

Wintering party

1927-28: Hermann Andresen, Peder Røbek, August Hansen
1928-29: Hermann Andresen, Peder Røbek
1929-30: John Giæver, Arnulf Gisvold
1930-31: Hermann Andresen, Peder Røbek
1931-32: Hermann Andresen, Knut Røbek
1932-33: Sigurd Tolløfsen, Haakon Karlsen
1933-34: Sigurd Tolløfsen
1934-36: Hermann Andresen, Nils Hanken
1936-37: None
1937-38: Hermann Andresen, Lars Vemøy
1938-39: Hermann Andresen
1939-40: None
1940-41: Marius Jensen
1941-46: None
1946-48: Ivar Ytreland, Odd Lindhjem
1948-49: Johan Laine, Karl Blindheim
1949-50: Johan Laine, Rolf Hauge
1950-51: Arne Grytten, Arvid Svoren
1951-52: Arne Ringstad, Olav Urke
1952-53: Arne Ringstad, Otto Lapstun
1953-54: Stein Sørensen, Odd Bogholm
1954-55: Arne Grytten, Halse (first name unknown)
1955-56: Herman Ingebrigtsen, Magne Kvernmoen
1956-57: Jørgen Løklien

Wollaston Forland was named by William Scoresby in 1822, out of respect for William Hyde Wollaston (1766-1828), one of the Commissioners of Longitude. Herschell Bjerg is the 682 m high mountain in southern Wollaston Forland, named by Scoresby in 1822 for Sir John Frederick William Herschel (1792-1871), a physicist, astronomer and inventor. On the coast at the foot of the mountain there is an old Norwegian trappers' station. For many years this was the first point of call for the annual supply ship.

1927-28

Hermann Andresen is particularly associated with the history of Kap Herschell. With the nickname the "Count of Herschell", he was a living legend, both as a trapper and because of his tall stories and humorous sayings, which could be like this: *"Never use motor boats. They are so heavy to row!"*[288]

Hermann Andresen, who described himself as a master-weaver, came from Melbu in Vesterålen, but settled in Langevåg near Ålesund. His first visit to North-East Greenland was in the summer of 1927 with the Hird Expedition, which besides himself consisted of Jonas Karlsbak, Peder Sulebak, Jørgen Furnes, Peder Røbek and August Hansen. Of his first trip to Greenland Andresen wrote: *"The "Hird" was a small 48 ft fishing boat. We were all pretty ignorant of the regulations for a voyage across the Atlantic, and started to load provisions and equipment as one used to. Then the authorities heard about it. By the time we were done loading, the deck was under water, and when the inspector came aboard he ordered the ship emptied, as it had to be taken ashore for inspection the following day. There was only one thing to do: to keep up appearances. We discussed the situation and agreed to clear out during the night. There was only one more thing we had to get aboard, the medicine box. When we went to the pharmacy to collect it, we found out that it had been impounded and was not to be handed over until further notice. We therefore sent out people to different pharmacies to buy the necessary items. At 2 o'clock on the night before Friday 13th July, we left. Much commotion arose in Ålesund the following morning when*

Legendary Hermann Andresen. Right: Andresen in front of Kap Herschell, c. 1935. © Nils-Martin Hanken

they discovered we were gone." ... *"We arrived at Jan Mayen after six days sailing. The weather was fine and we went ashore to send telegrams home. At the station an arrest warrant awaited us. We were ordered to go back – but in for a penny, in for a pound. We continued to Greenland"*.[289]

On 28th July 1927 they arrived safely and: *"as we reached Kap Herschell, Hansen, Røbek and I rowed ashore. We found a suitable place to settle for the winter"*.[290] Later on, they split into two teams. Three men were to winter at Elvsborg, while Andresen, Røbek and Hansen would stay in the station house that they built at Kap Herschell. August Hansen, with four seasons as a trapper on Jan Mayen, was the most experienced.

On 23rd August Hansen and Røbek rowed westwards to examine their territory, but then an unusually violent hurricane broke lose. Andresen wrote: *"Just once I dared to go out to fetch water, but the storm was so heavy that it caught both me and the water bucket, throwing us over. I sheltered behind a rock and waited there for a moment before crawling back to the house. The storm was now so intense that it had begun to blow over the oil barrels standing outside the house. I had to get out to tie them fast. I am now all dressed up in my polar outfit, ready to escape should the house blow down"*.[291] The storm lasted for three days, and finally Røbek and Hansen returned, on foot. The storm had taken their boat. It was the same storm that also wrecked the "Hird" at its winter harbour in the Finsch Øer. Perhaps Andresen had this very storm in mind when he later on explained his own definition of "stormy weather": *"When the grindstone flies over the roof, then it is storming at Kap Herschell!"*[292]

Winter arrived. They had not brought any sledge dogs, but even so the catch turned out quite well. Except for August Hansen, who wanted to go home, they decided to stay for one more year,

On 6th July, Andresen and Røbek visited Meyer Olsen at the Krogness station, and here they had a greeting from an old acquaintance: *"Hans Olsen came back today. He had a telegram for Røbek and great news for us all, namely that the chief constable in Ålesund has given Finn Devold power of attorney to send us home this summer. But this is not going to be so easy, as we have decided to stay here for another winter, never mind how many orders he sends"*.[293]

1928-29

The trappers from Sunnmøre had learnt a lesson from the Foldvik Expedition during their first wintering. They now realized that they had to have sledge dogs, and needed to cover a larger territory. Building materials were in short supply, but they obtained some timber by tearing down the ruin of the old Kopperneshuset [441-1]. During the summer of 1929 they built: "Augusta Dal hytten" [431], "Gåsneshuset" [441-2], "Falkberget" [448], "Sletta" [453-1], "Ingrid Havn" [456-1] and "Agnes-tufta" [460-1].

During their first winter the Hird Expedition trappers had been limited to the south-east coast of Clavering Ø and the south coast of Wollaston Forland; their expanded hunting territory extended from Jackson Ø, via Gael Hamke Bugt and the Pendulum Øer, to Kap Schumacher on the north side of Wollaston Forland. This was four times the size of their old territory. However, they had only been able to obtain a few sledge dogs and therefore still had to travel hundreds of kilometres on foot.

In May 1929, Andresen undertook the 140 km trip to Myggbukta, to arrange for their home voyage since they had lost the "Hird". They were offered a free voyage, in return for lending the territory to Arctic Commercial Enterprise. In the summer of 1929, the five "Hird" men went home with "Veslekari". They carried with them the catch from their two winterings, altogether 348 fox furs, four live foxes, 40 bear skins and two live bears, 30 ermine furs and two muskox calves. The sale brought in a total of 60,000 Norwegian kroner to share between them.

1929-30

In 1929, Arnulf Gisvold, a veteran of the Foldvik Expedition, returned to North-East Greenland with Arctic Commercial Enterprise. He was going to be in charge of the company's northern team and winter together with John Giæver at Kap Herschell. This was Giæver's first encounter with North-East Greenland, and during the winter he wrote the text for his book: "Fangsthyttene" (1930). In this he wrote: *"At Kap Herschell on the north shore of Tyrolerfjord a felt-covered hut lies in the shadow of the mountain. The "Kari"* (Veslekari) *drops her anchor here. Twelve hours later she leaves again. We wave goodbye. Most of us are looking for adventure. Here then our adventure begins, in the land behind the sea and the ice, far, far to the north-west"*.[294]

During the winter frictions arose between Gisvold and Hallvard Devold, the leader of the southern team. On 11th March 1930, at Kap Humboldt, the latter wrote: *"Gisvold from the northern team has not given any information about the situation there, but according to rumour in Myggbukta he has territory for only two men. It was agreed that he would meet me at Myggbukta this summer to make further arrangements about the distribution of the dogs that he has up north. However, due to engine failure he did not arrive. I then expected him in the autumn, but in vain. At Christmas I was sure I would meet him at*

Myggbukta. I waited there until New Year, as he was said to be on his way; but once again he did not turn up. I then sent word up north that he should come south immediately. We are now in the middle of March and he has not arrived. I therefore sent Søren Richter northwards on skies to fire him as the leader of the northern team, and to take the number of dogs that can be spared together with two men, Giæver and Herdal, southwards immediately".[295]

Søren Richter went north and on April 15th: *"Giæver, Johnsen* (Otto Johnsen from Liavåg) *and Richter returned from the north after a fine journey. Their reports of Gisvold's behaviour exceeded our worst expectations. From the rumours we had heard, anything could be anticipated; but that it was this bad was hard to imagine. The guy has an inflated idea of his own importance, and must be sent home".*[296] As a consequence, Arnulf Gisvold went home in the summer of 1930.

1930-31

In 1930, four veterans of the Hird Expedition returned with a new expedition, called the Møre Greenland Expedition (or the Møre Expedition). Once again there were six members, of which four went south to Kong Oscar Fjord to establish two new trapping territories (see Antarctichavn and Kap Peterséns).

Hermann Andresen and Peder Røbek resumed the trapping at Kap Herschell. As they wanted to trap between Jackson Ø and Kuhn Ø, they built three new huts: "Røbekstua" [369], "Hermannsbu" [424] and "Berlin Stua" [459]. In addition, they moved Agnes-tufta [460-1] from Kap Schumacher to a locality near Kap Hamburg on the south coast of Kuhn Ø, where the hut was known as "Furnes" [464]. One day in the autumn, J.G. Jennov was visiting from Sandodden, and Andresen wrote that: *"we had some debate concerning the rights to the territory, but finally we came to an agreement, however, only for the next two years".*[297]

Andresen and Røbek were usually on good terms with the Danish trappers. However, on 28th February Andresen discovered that some of his poisoned baits on Kuhn Ø had been removed by James van Hauen from Hochstetter, who had left the following note: *"Presuming you have not noticed our hut* (Kap Maurer hytten) *a few kilometres north of your poisoned baits, I have taken the liberty of removing them. In my opinion they were placed in our territory. Yours sincerely, James van Hauen, Nanok".*[298] Andresen was furious, and: *"speeded up my dogs to find out if I could meet the Danish devils and take them to task for their impudent behaviour. When I came to their house there was no one there, and it was their good luck as it could have turned into a hot day, despite the fact that it was minus 40°C outside".* The irate Andresen returned home. Then one day he went to Sandodden to complain to Jennov: *"We had an argument, but finally agreed not to make a big deal out of it".*[299]

Andresen and Røbek finished their season with a catch of about 110 foxes. In May, Andresen went south to meet his friends in Kong Oscar Fjord, a journey of altogether 600-700 km.

1931-32

In the summer of 1931, Peder Røbek wanted to stop as a trapper. His brother, Knut Røbek, was coming up from Kap Peterséns to take his place as a partner for Hermann Andresen at Kap Herschell. They already had a good, well-established territory and only really needed food for the dogs. At the beginning of September, they went hunting at Revet, where they immediately killed 23 muskoxen, so their dog-food problem was solved. Now they were ready to start trapping.

Arnulf Gisvold (left) and Eilif Herdal at Kap Herschell, 18th July 1930. © Adolf Hoel / Norwegian Polar Institute

Winter came late, and hardly any snow had fallen when they began trapping on the 26th October. Andresen went north to trap on Kuhn Ø and Bass Rock, while Knut Røbek went south to the Gael Hamke Bugt territory. This was the last time Andresen saw Knut Røbek alive.

When Andresen returned to Kap Herschell on the 22nd November, he noticed that: *"Røbek has been here, but has left again."* This gave no immediate cause for alarm, and Andresen went back to his territory from where he returned on the 17th December: *"It was late in the evening before I arrived here and it is no comforting message I'm facing. Knut has not been here since I went north"*.[300] Andresen now suspected that Knut Røbek had had an accident, and he made ready to start a search as soon as the weather had improved.

On the 19th December Andresen left. First he went to Sandodden to see if the Danes had had any contact with Røbek, but there was nobody there, except for a note that Elmar Drastrup had gone to Eskimonæs on 1st December. Andresen then continued to Kap Mary huset, and arrived late the same evening at Elvsborg - having found no trace of Røbek. The following day he went on to Breivikhytten, where he found a note from Røbek to Eilif Herdal at Moskusheimen. It said: *"Hello Herdal. I'm leaving today the 2nd December. I came here from Jackson Ø. When I arrived, I had no food left so I ate your oat meal. I have still not received any food. I'm not sure whether we're going to Myggbukta for Christmas. If I don't see you, I wish you a Merry Christmas. Best wishes, Røbek"*.[301] Having read Røbek's note Andresen continued to Eskimonæs, where the Danes could only report that Røbek had visited them twice, the last time on the 1st December when he had left for Kap Herschell.

Now only one possibility remained, namely that Røbek had fallen ill and was staying in Henningelvhytten. Evald Rasmussen from Sandodden accompanied Andresen on the way back. They spent the night at Elvsborg, and continued on the 23rd December: *"via Tennedalen to check in Henningelv; but found no one. Rasmussen then continued to Sandodden and I went on to Herschell. I don't know what more to do now. We must assume that Røbek has been lost, and the possibility is that he has gone through the ice, as there are no traces of him or the dogs. Rasmussen arrived to spend Christmas with me. He too is alone, as his partner* (Elmar Drastrup) *is staying at Eskimonæs with frostbite in his legs"*.[302]

It was not until the spring that Røbek was found. He had fallen through the ice and died near Elvsborg. The bodies of Røbek and his dogs were discovered frozen halfway into the ice, and only after the thaw had lasted a while; Andresen and Peder Sulebak managed to cut his body free. Røbek had had no chance of escape; his body was tangled up in the dogs' traces. He was buried initially at Kap Herschell, but his remains were later sent home to Norway in the summer of 1932 at his family's request.

After Knut Røbek's disappearance, Andresen trapped in the entire Kap Herschell territory, and regardless of the weather Andresen was almost constantly travelling between Jackson Ø and Kuhn Ø from New Year until May. He made a fine catch of about 135 foxes and 10 polar bears.

1932-33

On 23rd July 1932 it was time for change at Kap Herschell. The Sigurd Tolløfsen Expedition was going to take over the Kap Herschell territory from the

The coffin of Knut Røbek, a young Norwegian trapper who drowned at the beginning of December 1931 near Elvsborg on the south coast of Clavering Ø. Standing at right is Sigurd Tolløfsen, who later lost his own son, Arnljot, during another drowning accident in May 1933, not far from where Røbek had drowned. Kap Herschell, 17th August 1932. © Anders K. Orvin / Norwegian Polar Institute

Sunnmøre trappers for the two-year period 1932-34. Prior to departure some barter dealing was going on. Tolløfsen purchased Hermann Andresen's old motor boat, "Oljeoksen" (the oil oxen), for 400 kroner, and the six sledge dogs for 50 kroner each. The territory was already well equipped with trappers' huts, so Tolløfsen and Haakon Karlsen only needed to locate the traps. While Andresen had tended the entire territory in 1931-32, Tolløfsen and Andresen were on the whole content with trapping on the east coast of Wollaston Forland. The result was about 45 foxes.

During the winter some argument about the boundaries of the trapping territories around Sabine Ø and Kuhn Ø arose between Tolløfsen and Henning Nyholm-Poulsen from Nanok. The Dane also accused Tolløfsen of the reckless use of poisoned bait. Eventually Tolløfsen and Nyholm-Poulsen met at Sigurdsheim (see section on Sigurdsheim), where they reached a settlement.

On the 3rd June 1933, an entirely different issue began to occupy Sigurd Tolløfsen's mind: *"I'm so worried about Arnljot* (Tolløfsen). *He left for Myggbukta on the 13th May, and ought to have been back by the 25th May, at the latest. I hope he's alright and safe".*[303] Days and weeks went by without any sign of his son returning, and on the 20th July his hope had almost vanished: *"Dear God, have I lost my boy? He was the eldest of my children – if not the best of my trappers, Arnljot was surely one of the best. This is shown by his work and the catch this year, and this was his first wintering. We ate and went to bed, but I am so worried about the lad that I cannot sleep".*[304] The death of Arnljot Tolløfsen is further discussed in the Moskusheimen section for 1932-33.

1933-34

Despite the loss of his son, Sigurd Tolløfsen decided to stay for another year as planned. He wintered alone at Kap Herschell, as Haakon Karlsen was now to trap from Sigurdsheim. Sigurd Tolløfsen put up his traps in the triangular area between Breivikhytten in the south, the Gisvold hytten in the west and the Kap Wynn hytten in the north; a large territory for a man of 55 with only one sledge dog.

The loss of his son was naturally constantly in his thoughts, and it was a sad Christmas at Kap Herschell that year: *"Tonight I have played some Christmas carols, and my thoughts have been with my loved ones. I hope that both my wife and children have had a truly cosy Christmas. You can imagine how Christmas Eve has been for me, sitting alone at Herschell. Last year Arnljot had a merry Christmas Eve at Eskimonæs – this year he is celebrating Christmas Eve in eternity. How little we know of the future".*[305]

The catch for the winter numbered about 30 foxes and two polar bears. The Tolløfsen Expedition went home with "Selbarden" in summer 1934.

1934-35

The two veterans, Hermann Andresen and Peder Sulebak, returned to Kap Herschell with "Selbarden" on the 5th August 1934. They had equipped a four-man expedition: the Suløya Greenland Expedition. Andresen and Nils Hanken were to trap from Kap Herschell, while Peder Sulebak and his nephew Karsten Sulebak would trap in the territories in Kong Oscar Fjord.

Compared to the large catches of the Sunnmøre trappers in 1927-29 and 1930-32, the years 1934-36

From left: Johan Stordal, Sigurd Tolløfsen and Johannes Holmeslet at Kap Herschell, 17th August 1932. © Norwegian Polar Institute

were less profitable. The decline in the catch could have several reasons, but after a couple of months with poor results, Hermann Andresen believed he had found a specific cause. On the 14th January 1935 he wrote: *"This is the poorest trapping season I have experienced in Greenland. I have not wanted to write the reason why there are so few foxes before; but now I have to vent my anger. As soon as I went on my first trapping trip I realized what a poor state the territory had been left in by the damned Tolløfsen expedition. They have not collected their poisoned baits and nor have they taken down all the traps; on my first trip I found no less that 14 dead summer foxes".*[306]

Andresen's partner, Nils Hanken, then 23-years old, was from Borgund near Ålesund. After his confirmation he had followed his father to sea for several seasons. Due to his excellent shooting skills he was appointed first shooter, but after having been shipwrecked twice, he decided he had had enough of the sea and went to seek his fortune in Greenland instead.

Ice conditions in Gael Hamke Bugt, especially around Kap Mary and Basaltkap, were as dangerous as ever; the ice often broke up, and on the 27th January 1935 the trapping season ended abruptly for Nils Hanken. The night before he had arrived at Kap Mary huset: *"The storm woke me up tonight. I got dressed in a hurry to go out and check on the ice; but it had drifted out to sea. It is very difficult to leave Kap Mary when there is no ice. There are only two routes to try, but as things are now both are more or less impassable. The one leads across the mountain and the other across a glacier. I decided to try the route across the glacier. I used my axe to cut steps across the entire glacier, and the work took a long time as I was busy holding on so as not to be thrown into the sea by the gusts of wind. After five hours of work I finally passed the glacier, and soon after reached unbroken ice on the fjord.*

Shortly before Kvaderhuken (Basaltkap) *I spotted a sledge that had gone half through the ice. When I got there it turned out to be a Danish sledge. I checked a little around the sledge; but soon realized that both men* (Aage Hansen) *and dogs had managed to reach shore. When I reached Kvaderhuken it was my turn to be wrecked. I had just been ashore to check a trap, and when I jumped down from the ice foot I fell awkwardly against a sharp ice edge. I don't recall having seen so many stars and if I'm not mistaken I saw a couple of moons too. I crawled over to the sledge, and as I was trying to get up realized that one of my shinbones was broken. I tried to figure out what to do. I concluded that the best thing was to try and reach the Danish Eskimonæs station, some 35 km away. I tied my whip around my leg and then off we went. The storm had calmed down, it looked like snow was on its way, and it was dark too.*

The first 10 km went OK. But then we reached hummock ice. The sledge turned over time and time again. In Dødemandsbugten there was a lot of soft snow, and I had to leave behind some of my equipment. I took only my sleeping bag, the rifle, my diary and some chocolate with me. In the middle of Dødemandsbugten the dogs could not pull the sledge anymore. I then had to crawl in front of the dogs until we had crossed the worst part of the soft snow. When about 5 km from Eskimonæs, I fired my rifle a couple of times, and the dogs at Eskimonæs heard this and made a terrible racket. So my dogs just headed for the sound. At that time it was snowing so much that it was difficult to see land. However, I reached Eskimonæs safe and sound – the circumstances taken into consideration.

Eskimonæs was manned by Thorvald Sørensen, a botanist, and the wireless operator, Svend K. Espersen.

Arrived tonight at one o'clock. It was great getting indoors and having some food." ... "When I had finished eating I was put on the table. It is my left shine that is broken. They have now supported and splinted the leg according to the home first aid manual".[307]

His broken leg cost Hanken 2 1/2 months of convalescence, but this did not stop him from staying two more winters.

Nils Hanken, who broke his leg during a sledge journey in January 1935. Kap Herschell, spring 1935. © Nils-Martin Hanken

Hermann Andresen (sitting) and Nils Hanken in the living room at Kap Herschell. Spring 1935. © Nils-Martin Hanken

With Hanken out of action, Andresen had to manage the entire territory himself - just as in 1931-32. The outcome was about 55 foxes and five polar bears.

1935-36

In the summer of 1935, Andresen and Hanken extended the house with a couple of bays and a new porch. Ice conditions were so difficult that "Buskø" was unable to penetrate the pack ice until the 22nd August. A few days later "Buskø" received a request from the Danes to rescue the Nanok men, Christian Jensen, Leo Hansen, Christian Sørensen and Henry Larsen, who were stranded north of Kap Berlin. However, "Buskø" was unable to help due to the ice. Instead, Hermann Andresen, Finn Framnes-Hansen, Johan Johansen and mate Molskred set off to try and rescue them by motor boat, an attempt that succeeded. As a reward and thanks for their efforts, the Danish Government presented them all with inscribed silver cups.

With respect to the trapping, 1935-36 was a disappointment. Andresen, who was usually worth at least ten bears, shot only one, while Hanken managed to shoot three.

A lot of snow fell that winter, and the tough life began to leave its mark: *"The bloody rheumatism is going to kill me, if it goes on like this"*[308] Andresen wrote after a sleepless night with severe pain: *"Today I promised myself that this will be my last wintering up here."* That promise was not fulfilled, even though Andresen went home in 1936. Hanken, on the other hand, was in favour of a third overwintering. However he did not stay at Kap Herschell, which was unmanned in 1936-37, but moved south to Antarctichavn.

1937-38

In the summer of 1937, Hermann Andresen returned to Kap Herschell with his own two-man expedition: himself and Lars Vemøy. The catch that winter was very good and together they caught 340 foxes and 17 polar bears. Vemøy went home in the summer of 1938.

1938-39

Hermann Andresen wintered alone at Kap Herschell in 1938-39. In the spring he was joined by Bjarne Dalsbø, who had left Ottostrand due to poor trapping.

This was Andresen's last wintering, and his most successful with a catch of 642 foxes, the largest catch ever for a single trapper in the history of North-East Greenland trapping. Andresen later said: *"The summer of 1937 brought swarms of lemmings from the south, so there was plenty of food for the fox. In 1937-38 the largest catches were taken in the fjord areas. Gerhard Antonsen, who lived at Revet, got about 400 foxes, the largest catch that year. In the autumn of 1938 the lemmings disappeared and the foxes went out to the outer coast for food. This is why I have caught so many, as two thirds of the Herschell territory borders on the outer coast".*[309] In addition to the enormous fox catch, Andresen shot 21 polar bears, which was also a record for a single trapper on the coast of North-East Greenland.

Hermann Andresen now gave up working as a wintering trapper, but he was far from done with North-East Greenland. Between 1946 and 1959 he organized a series of trapping expeditions using hired trappers, and visited North-East Greenland every summer; here he felt at home, or in his own words: *"like a priest in an empty hell."* When the newcomers and the tourists stood on deck to admire the slowly appearing land, Andresen enjoyed coming up behind them and with an embracing gesture proclaiming: *"All you see here belongs to me!"*

Since the early 1930s, Hermann Andresen had become a living legend, and it is not possible to give a fair description of him without relating one of the countless stories that emerged in his wake. One of those who knew Andresen best, his apprentice so to speak, was Ivar Ytreland. He had come to Greenland as a member of Andresen's first trapping team after the war, and they became friends for life.

"It was a summer day and we were with "Polarbjørn" in Dødemandsbugten..." Ytreland began when re-telling one of his numerous stories in 1992: *"That day I experienced the absolutely biggest accidental shot there has ever been in Greenland. This Hermann was a legend, you know, and there were a lot of tourists onboard and many trappers too. And then we came into Dødemandsbugten. It was a pleasant and sunny day, and the sea was smooth as a mirror. Then we saw some geese swimming in the bay, and all at once someone began to shoot at the geese, but missed you know. Hermann watched this for some time, and then suddenly exclaimed: What lousy shooting, he said, and such a waste of ammunition. When you shoot geese you shoot two at a time, and through the head, so that you don't damage the meat!*

And I thought to myself: Well, Hermann, this time you're going to lose face. Now you've promised more than ... But all at once, all those gentlemen and tourists shouted to Hermann: You shoot, then!

Hermann just looked at them and said: Fetch me my rifle! I think we were five volunteers who rushed back to the cabin to fetch his old Krag-Jørgensen rifle. And I remember that then the master, Henrik Marø, and yes the entire crew turned up to watch. Hermann used his thumb to measure the distance, cleared his throat and said: One hundred and fifty metres!

And then he took his rifle, and at the same moment the entire flock of geese took off. He followed them with his eyes, fired one shot with the Krag and two geese fell into the water with a splash. Then he turned around and said: Fetch me my geese!

We jumped into the boat, and believe it or not, the one goose had been shot through the head and the second in the neck: stone-dead both of them. From that moment on the tourists believed everything Hermann said!" Ytreland finished his story with a roaring laugh, and then added: *"And that was actually the only time I ever saw Hermann use a rifle in Greenland".*[310]

Almost every Danish and Norwegian trapper was able to tell stories about Andresen, and they all agreed upon one thing: You never knew for sure whether he was telling the truth or not. He often said the exact opposite of what people expected. If, for example, someone asked: *"Tell me, is it true that the polar bear is such a terrible predator?"* he would answer: *"The polar bear? ... Oh no, he's a pussycat!"* And then he told a suitable story to confirm this theory. Whereas if anyone asked: *"Is it true that the polar bear is such a kind animal?"* then Andresen would answer: *"Oh no, he is the worst predator!"* Finally, there was the Danish trapper who asked why the Norwegians caught more foxes than the Danes: He got the reply: *"Well, you see, we place a little Norwegian flag at each trap".*[311]

1939-46

Kap Herschell was not manned in 1939-40. However, in the summer of 1940 the Dane Marius Jensen, who had arrived with "Veslekari", took over the unused Kap Herschell station and trapped from there until the spring of 1941. He then went north to the Mørkefjord station, and later the same year joined

Kap Herschell. c. 1939. © Niels Ove Jensen

the North-East Greenland Sledge Patrol. Kap Herschell was then unmanned until 1946.

1946-48

Hermann Andresen's first wintering party at Kap Herschell after the war consisted of Ivar Ytreland and Odd Lindhjem, both from Ålesund.

Ivar Ytreland was then just 20-years old, and in the years that followed demonstrated that a trapper can turn his hand to just about anything. A short biography of his life reads: Born 4th April 1926 in Kristiansund, Norway; grew up in Ålesund 1926-1946; trapper in North-East Greenland 1946-48; summer expeditions fishing in North-East Greenland 1949-52; served in the Norwegian Navy as a submariner 1948-49; qualified as a mechanical engineer 1950-52, supplemented by several technical engineering courses; research at the Norwegian Technical University in Trondheim 1952-54; product designer in the Norwegian metal industry and cast iron industry 1954-65; expedition leader in charge of oil exploration in Svalbard 1962-88; general manager of a cast iron foundry 1965-75; president of a Norwegian oil company 1975-84; board member of the University of Trondheim 1984-89; as well as president, chairman and director of several companies and organizations; deputy member of Parliament of Norway 1970-77; member of Trondheim City Council 1966-74; and governor and chairman of the County Council of South Trøndelag 1980-92.

You might think that Greenland had been forgotten, but Ytreland said in 1990 that: *"to me North-East Greenland is something special, it is my dreamland. Nothing compares to North-East Greenland"*.[312] Ivar Ytreland has also been a participant and leader of recent Nanok expeditions to North-East Greenland in 1997, 1999 and 2002.

For a number of years the Kap Herschell territory was not well maintained, and the neglect of the war years had resulted in the partial or complete destruction of many of the huts: *"in 1946 we had quite a job rebuilding them"*.[313] In 1947, the main station, Kap Herschell, was: *"moved about 60 m inland and enlarged. The house was about to be consumed by the sea that was eroding away the beach sand"*.[314] In the spring of 1947, Ytreland and Lindhjem built the "Blæsedalhytten" [430] (norsk/Sirius), and the following year the "Dahl Skær hytten" [412].

In the summer of 1947, Kristian Ytreland, Ivar's father, arrived with the "Polarbjørn". Together with Lindhjem, they went to the river at Zackenberg to: *"try out fishing for arctic char using two shabby, torn pre-war nets that we found"*, Ivar Ytreland wrote.[315] With this primitive and worn-out equipment they caught eight barrels of char in a few days: *"and we soon realized that we were on to something really special. My father, who was a fisherman by trade, was almost overwhelmed by this result and he immediately decided to return the next summer with more and better nets"*.[316] During the following summers the char fishing business was expanded, helped and financed by Hermann Andresen.

Ivar Ytreland and Odd Lindhjem went home in 1948, but Ytreland later returned each summer to fish together with his father. For a shelter during the fishing season they built the "Fiskerhytten" [438-4] at Zackenberg in 1949. Starting that year they began hiring three to five men each summer to assist with the fishing. This expanding business required much experience with respect to equipment, fishing season and fishing localities. Over the years they examined the entire coastal region between Hochstetter Forland

Trappers Odd Lindhjem (left) and Ivar Ytreland in front of Kap Herschell. Early August 1946. © Ivar Ytreland

in the north and Ymer Ø in the south, looking for good fishing grounds. Ivar Ytreland wrote that: *"I took part in the fishing until 1951, and both in 1950 and 1951 we had good results. My father carried on for several more years with favourable outcome. The char fishing continued until Norwegian activities in North-East Greenland closed down in 1959; however, during the last few years the fishing was in the hands of new and inexperienced people, and this was reflected in the catch".*[317]

Among the many memories from his life as a trapper, Ivar Ytreland in 1992 recalled a summer night long ago, when he had been hunting for seal. On his way back, near the Kap Berghaus hytten, the dogs discovered a flock of eiders swimming in an opening in the fjord ice. The dogs rushed off directly onto the thin ice and: *"before I could detach the whip from the upright, the ice began to break up beneath the weight of the sledge. And then I made the mistake which everyone knows never to make: I went in front of the dogs. And I had not walked more than 4-5 metres before I fell straight through the ice into the water, while behind me the ice collapsed beneath the dogs and the sledge. In the team I had a bitch that was quite a devil at biting over the traces in critical situations. Now she cut through all the traces except her own. I myself struggled to get out of the water, but the ice collapsed beneath me every time; I was wearing waders, and they were heavy as lead. Several times I was almost dragged under the ice; but when you fight for your life, then you fight!*

Finally I found some ice that held, and I crawled all the way to the Kap Berghaus hytten. The dogs followed, except for the bitch, which had climbed onto the sledge now drifting in the open water. The loose dogs rushed off towards Daneborg, and I myself followed behind breaking all speed records for the 4-5 km distance. It was the middle of the night and freezing, and as I came closer to Daneborg I became aware of hectic activity. The Danes were harnessing their dogs, for they had seen my loose dogs, and a Greenlander had seen the traces and thought they had been cut with a knife. So now Ivar perhaps is a dead man! Fortunately they then spotted me, and I was taken inside and given some dry clothes. After that we put a small rowing boat onto a sledge and drove back to Kap Berghaus. Although we had only been gone about a couple of hours, the patch of open water had grown huge, and out in the middle was my drifting sledge although the bitch had disappeared. She was all white, the bitch. Looking towards the hut I could see a white spot on the brown and open landscape, for the snow on the land had melted. The bitch had managed to cut through her own traces and had gone to lie down in front of the hut, not bothering to run to Daneborg. So then we rowed out to fetch the sledge".[318]

1948-49

In 1948 Johan Laine and Karl Blindheim took over Kap Herschell. There is only little information about their wintering. J.G. Jennov noted that while at the Kroneberghytten, he had a visit from the two Norwegians in a motor boat on the 18th August: *"It was the two new trappers from Kap Herschell. One of them was a kind and quiet man. The other one, who had been trapping on Svalbard for 12 years, held the somewhat arrogant opinion that he could trap wherever he liked. When we told him we were trapping around Sabine Ø, he declared that he would trap past the Germaniahavn station. When I asked him how he would feel if we were to trap past the Kap Herschell station, he answered that it didn't matter to him where we trapped. However, he did state that he would not use poison,*

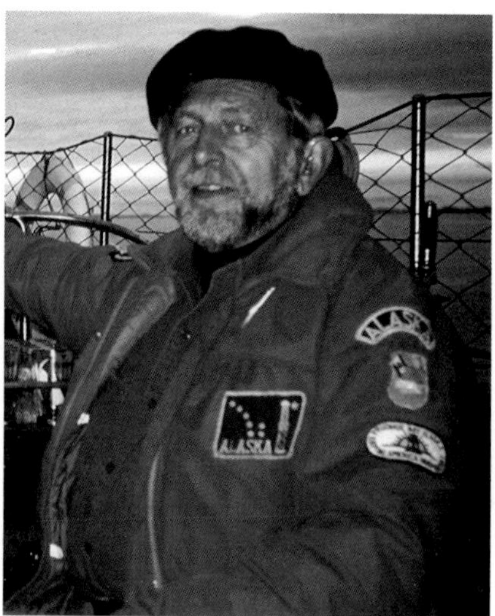

(Left) Ivar Ytreland, age 22, 1948. (Above) Ivar Ytreland, 2006. © Ivar Ytreland

Kristian Ytreland, who from 1947 and until the middle of the 1950s was in charge of the arctic char fishery at Zackenberg. *© Ivar Ytreland*

as it was prohibited in Norway and a most damaging way of trapping which destroyed the fox population".[319]

1949-50

In the winter of 1948-49, Rolf Hauge, Johan Laine's new partner, had worked as a trapper in Kong Oscar Fjord. In May 1949, when the season was over, he sledged northwards to spend the summer at Kap Herschell. According to Sverre Storholt, Rolf Hauge came from Drammen. Hauge was an aircraft mechanic and had been in Allied service during the war. He went home in 1950, and a few years later emigrated to Canada.

A few remarks about Laine's and Hauge's wintering are known from the diaries of Egil Amsjø and Stein Sørensen. On the 4th December 1949, Sørensen wrote that he at Myggbukta had spoken with: *"Hauge from Herschell, for the time being at Daneborg Radio, on the phone in the evening. Their catch was 26 foxes and one bear at Herschell. Everybody up north will be celebrating Christmas at Revet".*[320] On the 7th January 1950, Amsjø visited Kap Herschell: *"Hauge turned out to be quite an artist, and has made many splendid paintings of Greenland this summer".*[321]

On the 15th May, Stein Sørensen arrived at Daneborg, where he was greeted by a: *"grand reception with a long lunch table, set with 20 different courses like at a hotel" ... "Hauge from Herschell is also at Daneborg, and we enjoyed the reunion" ... "Late tonight Johan Laine from Herschell arrived, drunk as a lord. He and Hauge are to celebrate the 17th May at Revet and have brought plenty of home-brew. The dogs arrived first, and then two hours later Laine came staggering in. He had fallen off the sledge. We are having some drams at Daneborg too. I decide to go with them to Revet in the evening".*[322]

1950-51

Arvid Svoren, from Oppstrynn in Nordfjord, was 23-years old when he came to Kap Herschell, together with the slightly older Arne Grytten from Snåsa. In 1993, Svoren recalled that it was a longing for adventure that had brought him to Greenland. There was also hardship. He ran into trouble the first time he went to Jackson Ø. He crossed over from Dødemandsbugten, but the going was almost impossible as the water had been sucked up through the ice. After 17 hours of sledging, he was stopped by a huge embankment of snow only 50 metres from land. There he had to camp.

The following day he went back in his tracks, and now it went better: *"but I froze off three or four toe nails, because my feet were wet. I didn't feel anything until I took off my socks and discovered the loose nails lying there".*[323]

They had a good catch; but years went by before it was sold. Their first offer was 75-80 kroner per fur; but they thought that was too little; they wanted 85 kr. The furs then went into storage for three or four years; and eventually were sent to England to be auctioned at the Hudson's Bay Company: *"and there they went for 52 kroner"* Svoren laughed, *"but in those days money was not so important".*[324]

1951-52

In 1951-52 the party at Kap Herschell consisted of Arne Ringstad and Olav Urke, both on their first wintering.

Kap Herschell trappers Arne Ringstad and Otto Lapstun visiting Daneborg Weather Station in the summer of 1953. (From left) Arne Ringstad, E.B. Larsen, Hans Madsen, Villy Skovbjerg (standing) and Otto Lapstun. © Hans Madsen

Arne Ringstad was born in Madagascar, where his parents were missionaries. At the age of 11 he was sent to Norway to complete his schooling. After that he was employed at an office, but at the age of 30 decided he needed something different; so he became a trapper with Hermann Andresen and ended up in North-East Greenland. He stayed at Kap Herschell for two years, and after his home-coming took part in many fishing and trapping journeys to the Vestisen and Danmarkstrædet.

His partner, Olav Urke from Sunnmøre, was 26-years old when he first came to Greenland. He over-wintered only for one year; but came back each summer from 1952-57 to fish arctic char for Hermann Andresen. Later Urke worked on the construction of high-voltage systems, also in Greenland.

In 1992 both Ringstad and Urke recalled their time as trappers with pleasure. There was no money in it; but a wealth of good experiences.

1952-53

Otto Lapstun was from Oslo, but did not thrive in the shipping office where he was employed. One day a colleague from the bookkeeping department asked him if he would like go to Greenland as a trapper. This sounded like a good idea to the then 21-year-old Lapstun. Of course, they had only little knowledge of the conditions they could expect, but they quit their jobs straight away. Unfortunately, they were refused by Arctic Commercial Enterprise, and instead Lapstun went up to Østerdalen to work for a farmer there. One day in the spring of 1952 Lapstun had a phone call. The short conversation sounded like this: *"Hermann Andresen, Ålesund. I hear you want to go to Greenland? – Yes, I do. – Listen, I have two men who have cancelled at the last minute. Would you like to go instead? – Yes. – Do you have a rifle? – No. – Well, you can get one from me. Do you ski? – Yes. – Well, that's good, then I'll see you in Ålesund".*[325]

Greenland was a fantastic experience, Lapstun said in 1992, and especially to be alone at Kap Herschell for the first time while the others were fishing char at Zackenberg. Arne Ringstad was to trap northwards to Sigurdsheim while Lapstun had the southern territory; but it was a poor year for fox and they only caught 11 between them. Both went home in 1953, but Lapstun returned to North-East Greenland in 1954 after serving for one year as a UN soldier in Korea.

1953-54

In 1953, Stein Sørensen and Odd Bogholm took over Kap Herschell, and with a new employer, Hermann Andresen. They were very pleased, Sørensen wrote on the 19th August 1953, for: *"we have a lot of excellent equipment and the food is better than in Arctic Commercial Enterprise. For example, we have had a lot of boxes with canned fruit, such as pineapples and peaches. Hermann Andresen said that he had already allotted Kap Herschell to others when he received our application, but that he preferred master trappers from Ottostrand".*[326] In addition to the trapping, Sørensen and Bogholm had another interesting project, namely the recording of the last scenes of a film about the life of a trapper, which Sørensen and Hans Hvide Bang had begun making the year before. The film was later released as: "Pelsjægerliv at 76°N" (trappers' life at 76°N).

The short distance from Kap Herschell to Daneborg meant there were regular contacts between the trappers and the sledge patrol personnel and the staff at the weather station. They went to each other's parties and the relationships were fine; but: *"I find it much too boring here at Daneborg and Resolut, too civilized and too many people"* Sørensen wrote on the 5th November 1953. Still it was nice to be waited upon, as when Sørensen returned on the 26th February 1954 from a trapping journey to Ottostrand: *"I'm being cordially welcomed at Daneborg and drop right into a birthday party for Hans Frederiksen, so it's party time and drams until early morning. Odd is with the patrol and they are all coming down at around 9 o'clock".*[327]

In his diaries Stein Sørensen tells of good as well as sad experiences. The 5th April 1954 started as: *"a wonderful day, clear blue sky, nice and sunny,*

(Left) Otto Lapstun, age 22, in 1952-53 © Hans Madsen. (Right) Stein Sørensen, fishing char at Zackenberg. © Liv Berg

completely calm. It is just like the first day of spring, but still it turns out to be the saddest day in Greenland for Odd and me. We rise early and at 11.30 we set out for the Hansa Bugt hytten. From there we load up a stove, materials and a sack of coal and go directly across Pendulumstrædet to repair the Kap Desbrowe hytten on the south side of Pendulum Ø. It is a fine journey, the dogs are in top form, the going is good and the sun is shining so we can drive without mittens. It takes several hours to repair the hut, as it is filled with snow and ice. At 18.00 we return to Germaniahavn and drive along the edge of the ice, hoping to get a seal as we are out of dog food.

I'm driving some distance ahead of Odd, when I suddenly see his dogs running out onto the thin ice and Odd jumping off the sledge at the last minute. The dogs go through with the sledge and I turn around with my team in a hurry and drive back. When I get there the dogs try to join the others on the rotten new ice and it is hard for me to stop them. Together we manage to get the camera box and the film off the sledge and release the dogs. Odd's dogs are struggling for their lives in the water, and we are forced to watch them as they give up one by one and drown. We gather all the ropes and traces I have and try to get hold of the sledge or the dogs with a lasso, but we don't have enough rope. With a rope Odd tries to crawl out there; but goes through so I have to pull him back. It is a sad sight we are forced to witness, the dogs howling and screaming in their death struggles. Finally I take my rifle and shoot the last three – Storm, Thule and Don. Kabelius was the only survivor, as he managed to get himself up onto the thin ice and run to us when his snaphook opened. As well as the sledge and dogs, Odd lost his rifle, pistol, sleeping bag, some tools and other stuff. All we can see, as we harness my dogs to go home, is Odd's sleeping bag floating. Now we have only eight dogs left and it is a sad company that's heading towards Germaniahavn".[328] As a replacement for the lost dogs Bogholm was later given a new team by Sirius.

Both Sørensen and Bogholm went home in 1954.

1954-55

Arne Grytten, who had stayed at Kap Herschell in 1950-51, wintered in 1954-55 together with Halse (first name unknown), a newcomer from Nord-Trøndelag. No detailed information about their wintering is known, but Stein Sørensen gave a description of the change of guard on the 29th July 1955: *"Polarbjørn" dropped anchor at 2 o'clock tonight and we went out there at once. My friend Einar is standing at the rail together with a lot of familiar faces – Grytten, Nesset, Storholt and others. So there were handshakes and greetings all round and then we go down into the cabin to Hermann, who in the meantime has been awakened by the activity. All aboard are soon more or less drunk after a party at Herschell. Master Marø, still standing, steered the ship ahead. The rest are sleeping. Of course we have another party, a dozen men offering each other his bottle, so within a couple of hours the iron curtain is closing down on me. When I wake up at around 10, I am in my sleeping bag outside the hut, while the crew of "Polarbjørn" is unloading barrels and boxes. At noon "Polarbjørn" continues into Loch Fyne with two char fishers, Lars Vemøy and a newcomer. Old Ytreland, Urke and Einar are staying here with us, fishing at Zackenberg, so we are now five men. Grytten and Halse are staying for the day. They are bringing the dory to Herschell tomorrow while we borrow one of the boats from "Polarbjørn".*[329]

1955-56

Herman Ingebrigtsen and Magne Kvernmoen, from Østerdalen in Norway, were both on their first wintering in Greenland. *"Egil Grindflek moved to Østerdalen some years before me and we used to go hunting together and were neighbours too. He persuaded me to go to Greenland, and that was my reason for going there"*, the 73-year-old Herman Ingebrigtsen said in 1993.[330] Ingebrigtsen spent a large part of the winter in company with a Dane, Hans Madsen, for: *"Magne was a skilled mechanic and not particularly interested in hunting, so he swopped jobs with Hans*

Kap Herschell c.1955. © Hans Madsen

Madsen for most of the winter. Magne then stayed at Daneborg and repaired cars and motors, while Hans was trapping together with me at Herschell".[331]

On a couple of occasions Ingebrigtsen had some close encounters with the muskoxen: *"Once I was putting up a trap. It was in midwinter. And then I thought I felt something behind me. Suddenly a muskox attacked me. He came out of nowhere, and I had only one cartridge in my rifle because the chamber was broken. Somehow I got myself turned around and fired at him. That was all right, but as the muskox stumbled past me one of his horns scraped against the rifle trapping one of my fingers against the barrel.*

And there was another time at Daneborg. They had a muskox walking around the houses there, but we knew nothing about it. Suddenly the muskox was attacking the dogs, and I thought that I should try setting them loose. Then I set fire to an empty sack with kerosene and jumped out again to fetch the dogs, but the muskox came straight towards the flames anyway. Then he pushed me down in the snow and tried to attack me with his horns. I managed to keep my head clear, but he placed his hoof on my foot, so I could not escape. Fortunately Hans came by and shot him; if he hadn't done so it might have turned out really bad".[332]

1956-58

In 1956-57 Jørgen Løklien from Rena was supposed to have wintered together with another newcomer, Ingvar Haga, but Haga fell ill and had to return home. He came back again in 1957 and wintered at Antarctichavn. Jørgen Løklien became the last trapper at Kap Herschell, and went home in the summer of 1957.

The trapper who came up to stay at Kap Herschell in 1957, was picked up after 13 days, as:

Magne Kvernmoen (left) and Herman Ingebrigtsen after a successful seal hunt. Summer 1957. © Erik Jensen

"he found he could not endure being alone and was sent home again", Hans Oddvik recalled in 1993.

In the summer of 1958 it was not possible to land trappers at the station, as "Polarsel" could not force the pack ice: *"Sverre Storholt and Oskar Tørmoe who were going to Kap Herschell, were put off in a motor boat in Myggbukta with the most necessary equipment, in order to sail to Kap Herschell in the "land water". However, they did not get any further than Hold with Hope. Here they were taken aboard "Polarsel" again and had to go home, as it was not possible to go further northwards"*.[333]

Barr 1991; Giæver 1939; Hansen 1939; Orvin 1930, 1931, 1935; N026; N054; N142; N143.

Recent status

After the closure of the trapper era the Kap Herschell station was used and maintained by Sirius until about 1980. Lack of maintenance then led to a rapid decline in its condition until it was almost beyond repair. In the summer of 1999, Kap Herschell was visited by a Nanok team passing by on their way to Daneborg. On this occasion a close inspection led to the conclusion that a restoration of the station house would still be possible, but it would have to be done soon. As a result, Nanok sent out a team in the summer of 2002 to restore Kap Herschell. The leader of the team was the Norwegian Ivar Ytreland, who in 1946-48 had stayed at Kap Herschell as a trapper. Under Ytreland's supervision the station house was carefully restored back to its original appearance. After the restoration in 2002, a group from Sirius put in a new stove in September 2005, and completed the renovation by painting the interior. Kap Herschell is today a magnificent example of a trappers' station house.

Kap Herschell [417] is a former Norwegian trappers' station built 1927 for the Hird Expedition. It was used as a trappers' station until 1957, and then maintained as a travellers' hut by Sirius until about 1980. (Left) In 1999 Kap Herschell had become almost a total ruin due to lack of regular use and maintenance, 15th August 1999. © Peter Schmidt Mikkelsen. (Bottom) In 2002 Nanok decided to restore Kap Herschell. In charge of the project was Ivar Ytreland, who was a Norwegian fox trapper at Kap Herschell in 1946-48. Kap Herschell has today become a magnificent example of a trappers' station house. © NCN

The Nanok restoration team: Knut Ytreland, Ivar Ytreland, Otto M. Martens, Anders Bjerregaard. © NCN

Kap Herschell stripped of roofing felt during the restoration in 2002. © *NCN*

(Right) "Ivar's corner" at the Kap Herschell house. (Bottom) Ivar Ytreland in front of the restored house. This was actually the second time Ivar saved Kap Herschell. The first time was in 1947. Compare with photograph on page 169. © *NCN*

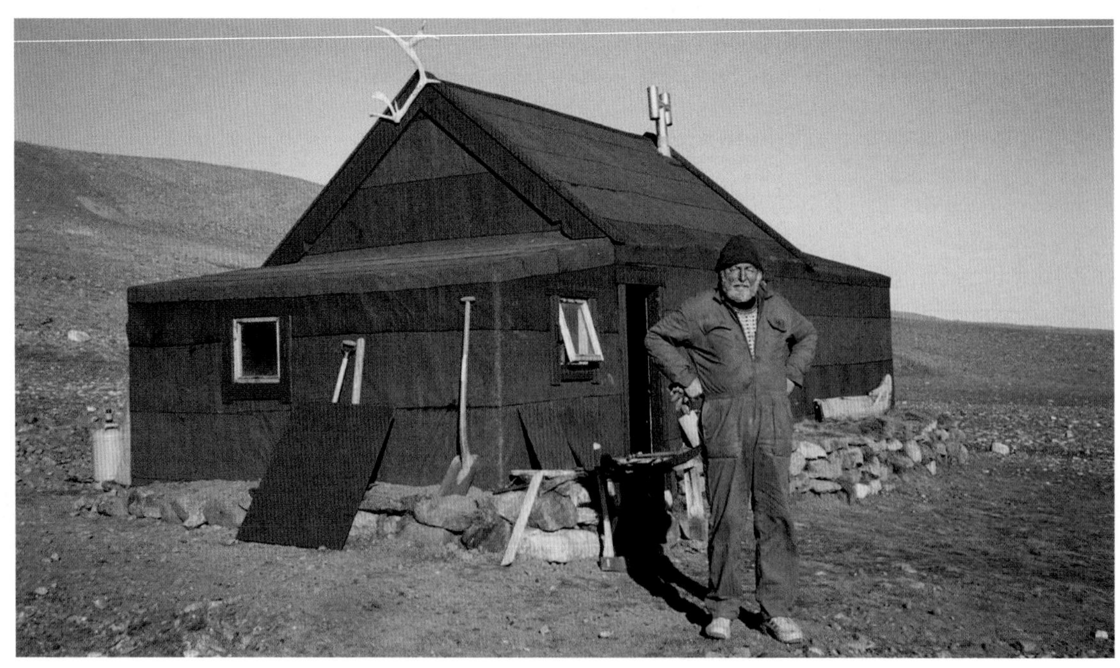

KAP HUMBOLDT
[308]

Wintering party
1929-30: Olav Kjelbotn, Hallvard Devold, Ingvald Strøm
1930-31: Olav Kjelbotn, Søren Richter
1931-32: None
1932-33: Bernt Marø, Hans Furland, Leif Brandal
1933-35: Ole Klokset, Magne Råum
1935-36: None
1936-37: Magne Råum, Ole Sivertsen
1937-38: Anders Godager, Arne Jacobsen
1938-41: Bjarne Akre, Oddvar Akre
1941-47: None
1947-48: Egil Amsjø, Bjarne Myrvold
1948-49: Fredrik Sæterdal, Trygve Slettemoen
1949-50: Birger Larsen, Sverre Storholt
1950-51: None
1951-52: Halvor Bjørdal
1952-53: Egil Grindflek, Lars Ellevoll

Kap Humboldt received its name in 1822, when William Scoresby junior named the cape after the German naturalist Alexander von Humboldt (1769-1859).[334]

1929-30

On the 3rd August 1929, "Veslekari" sailed along the coast of Ymer Ø: *"We were looking for a suitable location for a main station in the eastern part of Ymer Ø, and from the map it seemed that Kap Humboldt would be the best. From Nathorst's information we knew that there was also a good location for a station at Kap Graah; however, this was too far away from Sofia Sund and the coast of Geographical Society Ø, which seemed a promising trapping territory".*[335] About one kilometre north of the eastern entrance of Sofia Sund the Norwegians found what they were looking for: an excellent site for a station close to a small river and a spring. Remnants of an old eskimo settlement showed that others had also found the place to their liking. The following days were spent unloading materials for the trappers' station and supplies for three men for three years. On the 6th August they were done, and Olav Kjelbotn and Ingvald Strøm, both novices in North-East Greenland, remained there to build the station.

"The two of us stayed back at the place now called "Kjelbotn". We have worked until 9 o'clock and have put up a trappers' hut to live in temporarily until we have finished the main station", the 22-year old Olav Kjelbotn wrote.[336] He came from Namdalen, was a ski-maker and also an excellent skier. At the world championships in Oslo in 1926 he finished third in the 50 km race and fourth in the same discipline at the Olympic Games at St. Moritz in 1928. Ingvald Strøm was a skipper by profession.

In addition to Kjelbotn and Strøm, it was also planned that Hallvard Devold would stay at the new "Kap Humboldt" station. Devold was the architect of the Arctic Commercial Enterprise trapping company, and the leader of the wintering team. He was a busy man, so while Kjelbotn and Strøm built the station, Devold continued with "Veslekari" to Kong Oscar Fjord and Vega Sund to examine the trapping possibilities in these areas. On the 16th August he returned: *"At noon we arrived with "Veslekari" at Kap Humboldt where Kjelbotn and Strøm had already raised the house, now almost finished".*[337] It was a neat station, containing a living room of 3 x 3 m, a kitchen of 3 x 2 m and a porch of the same size. There was also an attic beneath the pitched roof. The outer walls

(From left) Hallvard Devold, Olav Kjelbotn, Ingvald Strøm and Thor Halle at the newly built Kap Humboldt house. 26th September 1929. © Sverre Sørensen / Norwegian Polar Institute

were painted red like Norwegian farm houses.

They now started on other necessary activities. Dog food had to be obtained and the territory was to be equipped with trappers' huts. "Veslekari" had already unloaded materials in Sofia Sund with which to build the huts, but in Dusén Fjord they had to transport the materials themselves. During the autumn they built a total of eight huts: "Strømhytten" [303], "Kikut" [311], "Brøggers hytte" [317], "Orvinhytten" [307], "Bødtkers hytte" [302], "Arentz hytten" [304], "Nørvehytten" [315] and "Devoldhytten" [318]. In the spring of 1930 they also built the "Varghytten" [324].

When the trapping season started, Strøm looked after the station while Devold and Kjelbotn went trapping, but: *"the winter was poor for trapping. It snowed and snowed, and the traps disappeared in the snow. In Dusén Fjord, where Kjelbotn was trapping, it was more or less all right. In Sofia Sund where I worked, it was bottomless snow everywhere, but we got some foxes anyway".*[338]

In the autumn of 1929, Olav Kjelbotn was harassed by a pack of wolves that followed him like a shadow during his journeys: *"I examined the track of the wolves I encountered yesterday and judging from the tracks there were 12 wolves".*[339]

On 15th April 1930, Søren Richter, John Giæver and Otto Johnsen arrived from Kap Herschell. They brought news that alarmed Hallvard Devold: *"The Danes are not doing well. They are already fighting amongst themselves – they have no nets for their fox cages and the 12 of them have caught only half of what we nine men have caught. They asked Giæver to take a long order list to Myggbukta to telegraph home: supplies the Danes wanted sent up in the summer. Finn* (Devold) *had decided that the telegram ought to be sent, as the Danes otherwise would acquire their own radio transmitter. This is foolish reasoning, and a total misunderstanding of his position as chief at Myggbukta. The Danes are already fighting amongst themselves – if they had enough money they would surely have brought a radio transmitter with them when they arrived last year. Giæver says that some foundation in Copenhagen will probably donate the company a radio transmitter if the trapping turns out to be profitable. Counting the 40 foxes which the Danes have caught so far, the "profitability" has to be questionable. On the other hand, should the Danes obtain nets for their cages and start breeding foxes, there is no reason to doubt that the trapping will be profitable. It is therefore crucial that they do not have the opportunity to order anything at all. Then they will lose a year and by then we can hope that the present trappers will become downhearted. If these people return to Denmark after a fiasco similar to the disaster suffered by the East Greenland Company, one may ask if the Danes might abandon the trapping up here".*[340] On the 17th April, Hallvard Devold went to Myggbukta and prevented the dispatch of the Danish telegram. In the summer of 1930 Hallvard Devold took over Myggbukta after his brother Finn.

1930-31

On the 19th August 1930, Olav Kjelbotn wrote: *"Today "Veslekari" arrived at Kjelbotn* (Kap Humboldt) *after a trip south, and was to leave immediately for Myggbukta and then home. We loaded all the live foxes that were to be shipped home, and also 65 fox furs. Ingvald Strøm left the station to become a fox tender at Myggbukta. Richter came ashore, so now it is up to the two of us to manage things here. I will be fine".*[341] At the end of August Eilif Herdal arrived. He was to look after the station while Richter and Kjelbotn went to maintain the territory. They built two new trappers' huts, "Svedenborg" [241] and "Dyrstien" [321], and moved Bødtkers hytte [302] from the south side to the north side of Sofia Sund where it was renamed "Stordalen" [306]. In the summer of 1931 "Stordalen" was moved once again, this time to Renbugten where it received the name "Renbugthytten" [325].

In the autumn of 1930, attempts were made to catch live fox using box traps. It worked out well, and on the 20th October they put 24 live foxes into cages and transported them to Myggbukta by sledge. The remaining catch was slightly smaller than the previous year. Both Kjelbotn and Richter went home to Norway in the summer of 1931, and Kap Humboldt was not manned in 1931-32.

1932-33

On the 28th July 1932, a new wintering party arrived. It consisted of Bernt Marø, 20-years old, together with Hans Furland and Leif Brandal, both 22-years old. Marø had experience from one year at Myggbukta, while the two others had just arrived with "Polarbjørn". One of their first tasks was to move "Strømhytten" [303] from Geographical Society Ø, in order to once again have a hut, "Stordalen" [306], on Ymer Ø.

Three men at Kap Humboldt was one too many, as there were only two proper trapping territories, Dusén Fjord and Sofia Sund. For part of the season Leif Brandal therefore stayed at Maristua, where he trapped on Ella Ø and in Vega Sund.

At the beginning of February 1933, Bernt Marø was surprised to discover that W. Holmboe's char fishermen - who had come up with "Isbjørn" in the summer of 1932 - had built a hut, "Noahytten" [322], in his territory in Dusén Fjord; they had even left an announcement that they annexed the area. All the same, Marø was: *"happy when I discovered the house, for it was cold and I had considered turning back".*[342]

In May Leif Brandal moved to Myggbukta to stay there for the summer. All three trappers went home in 1933.

1933-34

Ole Klokset and Magne Råum had first met in February 1933, when they were both aboard the sealer "Veslekari" in the White Sea (Beloye Mora). They became friends, and before the "Veslekari" returned home with a record catch of 11,500 seals caught in eight days, Råum (23-years old and from Foldereid in Nord-Trøndelag) and Klokset (22-years old and a Sunnmøring from Tennfjord) had hatched a plan to go to North-East Greenland. At first they had thought of equipping their own expedition, but there were no new vacant territories. However, the Arctic Commercial Enterprise station at Kap Humboldt was available.

On the 24th July 1933, they went ashore at Kap Humboldt, and had agreed between them a number of unwritten rules: they would never discuss politics, religion or the best way to do things. If it ever came to the point of disagreement, they had determined to discuss women instead of quarrelling.

The station needed a little gentle looking after, but the station's boat was in a poor state. The motor was worn-out and the hull was leaking. The company's promise of a new boat the next summer was of little help. However, they decided to make an effort with the motor as the alternative was rowing around their territory. This turned out to be quite an endurance test, but after a week of effort they succeeded in starting the motor. They shouted with joy and named the boat "Lappverk" ("patchwork"); the only thing the old boat carried without any problems. On the 25th September the territory was fortunately ready, as "Lappverk" barely managed to complete its last journey home to Kap Humboldt.

On the 7th November the two trappers parted company, Råum going to his territory in Dusén Fjord and Klokset a couple of days later heading for Sofia Sund and Vega Sund. Both had four fit dogs and a large puppy in their dog teams.

They met six weeks later in the Stordalen hut. The meeting was cordial and they talked until late in the evening. Both had made good catches; Råum already had 40 and Klokset 35 foxes. They agreed to go to Myggbukta, 70 km to the north, for Christmas.

On the shortest day of year, the 21st December, they both left for Myggbukta. Heading north and with no moonlight they groped their way forwards in the darkness; but finally found the hut at Kap Franklin. The next day, despite the heavy snow, they tried to follow the shore but soon lost their way and headed for land; it was almost a miracle that things turned out well. They could now feel the ice moving beneath them and starting to break up. Several times the dogs stepped into cracks, but as the going was slow, they managed to stop before they all fell into the water. At one point they had to ferry themselves on a small ice floe, pulling the dogs and the sledges behind them in the water. They drove and drove not knowing where they were, but finally good fortune came to their rescue as a mountain side loomed up before them. They followed the shore and a couple of hours later reached the Foldvikhytten at Kap Bennet - an immense struck of luck.

It was not until their return journey, after New Year, that they realized how lucky they had been on their travel from Kap Franklin to Kap Bennet. The route they had followed was now pitch-black open water, and they understood that they had been following: *"a lead of growler-ice which we had believed to follow the coast, but was actually a lead of hummocks*

Magne Råum (left) and Ole Klokset with some of their catch. Kap Humboldt 1934. © Ole Klokset

of old ice leading outwards into the bay. So in the blizzard and in good faith, we had travelled far out to sea until we reached the broken ice. At that time we believed that the ice had cracked and loosened due to the tide. Now we realized that it was the ice drifting into the sea".[343] They were only 25 km from Kap Humboldt, but the route was cut off, so they had to travel via Moskusoksefjord and Kejser Franz Joseph Fjord, a detour of 200 km.

The sun returns to Kap Humboldt on the 6th February each year, and from the 5th May there is midnight sun at the station. This was the main season for trapping, so neither Klokset nor Råum were much at home during this period. Occasionally they met for a few days, to hunt or to visit their Danish friends at Ella Ø. They travelled far afield, often to places where no trapper had been before them, and for both Klokset and Råum a day's travel of 70 to 130 km was not unusual. When the trapping season was over they were both well content. Their persistence had been rewarded with a combined catch of 180 foxes and five polar bears.

Then came the spring and the summer; others usually took a break during this period, but at Kap Humboldt there was never-ending activity. While Råum tended the furs, Klokset was busy planning and painting the floors and making furniture for the kitchen.

1934-35

On 11th August 1934, the "Selbarden" arrived with fresh supplies and mail - and best of all the promised new motor boat, which made putting out the supply depots almost effortless. Råum and Klokset expanded their territory with five new huts: "Festningen" [228], "Namdalshytten" [305], "Mineralbukta" [238], "Bjørnheimen" [310] and "Rimhytten" [230-1]. The "Rimhytten" was built on the east side of Kap Hedlund, as weather conditions prevented them finishing a hut [903] they had started to build on the west side of the cape.

On 27th October 1934, soon after the new trapping season had begun, Magne Råum had a serious accident. At Kap Mohn the ice appeared suspiciously thin: *"I left the dogs and walked a short distance to see where I could drive. Had to criss-cross a lot, and when I was about 50 metres ahead the dogs came running. It was the puppies that got the others going, and then they naturally crossed at a weak spot. The dogs went through first and the sledge followed. I thought the sledge would sink at once, but it floated quite easily, held up by a reindeer-skin anorak and the sleeping bag. It was heavily loaded with quite a lot of meat, chains, the rifle and other sinkable items. When I realized that the sledge floated so easily, I let the dogs work their way through the thinnest ice and then I crawled over and hauled one dog after the other out of the water. "Gamle" was almost done for. I had to cut the lashings as the load was now so heavy from all the water that it was impossible to drag it up all at once. Thought I would lose the rifle, but strangely enough I saved that too. Managed to grab the tent just as it was sinking. Using the whip I caught the reindeer skin anorak and the bread box before they disappeared below the water".*[344] Råum was lucky to get himself and the dogs ashore, but had to spend two cold days and nights here until the ice was safe and he could cross over safely to the Bjørnheimen hut.

As in the previous trapping season, Klokset and Råum covered a lot of ground during their trapping. At the beginning of March 1935, Råum was trapping in Geologfjord where he met Walter Molt from Hoelsbu. They teamed up for a few days, but then Råum was badly injured: *"Råum was putting up a trap of rocks. He was loosening a large boulder, when it suddenly moved. Råum lost his footing and tumbled down onto the ice, a fall of only about one metre, but the boulder followed hitting him on the shin, leaving a 2 cm deep and nasty wound that reached into the bone".*[345] The injury was so bad that Råum had to accompany Molt back to Hoelsbu, where he took a couple of weeks to recover.

Klokset had wondered what had happened to his companion, but on the 6th April they finally met in the Namdalshytten: *"Tonight we have talked a lot as it is now nine weeks since we last saw each other".*[346] The following day Råum went to Kap Humboldt. Two months had passed since he left the station: *"When I reached home I almost wondered if it really was Humboldt or some other place I had arrived at. Klokset has painted and cleaned up, so .... actually it is almost too tidy for a trappers' station. What a pity we are moving to Strindberg and not staying here for the summer".*[347] They had agreed to move from Kap Humboldt as soon as the trapping season was over, as they wanted to fish for char at the Strindberg river together with Walter Molt and Johan Listhaug from Hoelsbu. On 8th May, they loaded the sledges with their catch of 125 fox furs and drove to Strindberg. The fishing went well, but unfortunately problems now arose with respect to the homeward voyage.

The ice had become heavily packed along the east coast of North-East Greenland, and "Buskø" did not manage to reach the coast until the 22nd August 1935. Two days later they received a request from the "Godthaab" to go to Kap Berlin to try and rescue the four Danish trappers (see Hochstetter section). This rescue attempt was the reason that the "Buskø" was unable to carry through the planned supply of the stations south of Hold with Hope. On 2nd September, the four char fishers at Strindberg received a message to leave immediately for the head of Loch Fyne, where they would be picked up by "Buskø". They had to abandon the 80 barrels of char they had caught, but later received 8000 kroner, a part of the amount the Danish government paid out as compensation for the rescue attempt by "Buskø". Ole Klokset recalled in 1992 that the four char fishers had each received 2000 kroner, which was more than the fish were actually worth. Unfortunately, the lack of supplies meant that Kap Humboldt was not manned in 1935-36.

1936-37

After a year at home in Norway, Magne Råum once again went ashore at Kap Humboldt on the 20th August 1936, this time together with Ole Sivertsen, then 50 years old and on his sixteenth wintering in the Arctic; this was his last winter in North-East Greenland. Originally Sivertsen was supposed to have stayed on his own at Kap Humboldt in 1935, but as the ship was unable to re-supply the station that summer he wintered at Krogness instead.

Ole Sivertsen had worked together with many different trappers, but to him there was no doubt that Magne Råum was one of a special breed: *"It takes a lot to stop Råum once he has put his mind to something. He's a very lucky trapper too, who does not spare himself. Such men ought to be placed all over the Arctic, as they are born in the woods, and from childhood accustomed to hunting and fishing. Trapping companies in Norway should only hire such men, and would profit from it. Now he has just returned from his first trip with fox furs on his sledge and in his rucksack, and God knows where else. He is a very reliable man, and you can trust him in anything and everything".*[348]

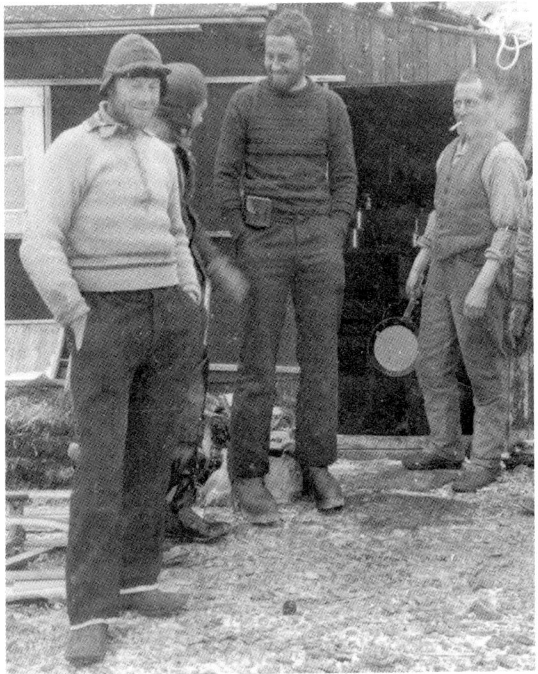

Visit at Kap Humboldt in 1936-37 by members of the Lauge Koch Expedition based at the Danish Ella Ø station. From left: Magne Råum, two unidentified visitors, Ole Sivertsen, holding a frying pan. © Arne Philbert

Ole Sivertsen was a very meticulous and stable man. The station had to be kept clean and tidy, and guests were always to be given the best possible treatment. His diaries are characterized by order, but also include many humorous passages that reveal the innovations a trapper has to possess: *"Råum has suffered from intestinal worms, which has put him in a bad mood. Yesterday evening he decided to get rid of this nuisance and mixed himself a dose of dog capsules and green soap. Unfortunately he had no hose, but had to use the thick rubber tube we normally use for filling paraffin. This turned out to be too wide in the opening, but Råum knew what to do so; he just cut through an empty Krag cartridge and placed it at the end of the tube, and this made an excellent tip. When the entire business was done with the cartridge had become stuck in his rectum. However, there was no reason to worry for the cartridge came out again at a furious speed. Today Råum is totally free of worms".*[349]

The ice froze up very late in 1936, and after New Year such huge masses of snow fell that even Magne Råum had to give up trapping for almost a month. On 13th February 1937, Sivertsen was passing through Kempe Fjord: *"I'm heading for a hard march tomorrow, but it will be even worse for the dogs. If the theosophy about us turning into other beings after death is right, then I will strongly request not to become a sledge dog. But if I am to be a dog, then I hope it will be a Pekinese. Then I shall surely be well off with some nice lady, and Ole Sivertsen will certainly have a good time. Imagine, to sprawl about in a lined basket and to be cuddled, not to mention when her ladyship takes me out for a stroll in the main shopping street".*[350]

It was a very tired Ole Sivertsen that returned to Kap Humboldt on the 22nd April 1937: *"I see that Råum has caught a lot of foxes, which is more than can be said for me. On this last trip I have travelled 400 km, and my entire catch amounts to only four white fox. No Ole, you will have to give up trapping – you are either too old or have just forgotten how to trap".*[351]
It was probably Råum's untiring energy that resulted in an excellent catch of about 200 fox furs.

Råum built the "Ragnhilds-hytten" [337] at the end of March 1937, and had originally planned to stay only one winter - but if he could have the entire Kap Humboldt territory to himself then he was ready for an additional year. A request was wired home to the company, but the reply was negative so both he and Sivertsen went home in 1937. At the end of July they packed their equipment and went to Strindberg to catch char. On the 14th August "Polarbjørn" arrived, and Råum and Sivertsen went aboard with their catch of foxes and 46 barrels of char, caught with nets and traps; each barrel weighed about 100 kg.

1937-38

On the 7th August 1937, the trappers Arne Jacobsen and Anders Godager took over the station. Jacobsen wrote in his diary that: *"Anders Godager from Hedmark and I, both employed by the company Arctic Commercial Enterprise, Oslo, are to winter here at Kap Humboldt probably for one year, but we are both determined to stay for two years".*[352] The catch was 225 foxes, but in fact they only had this one wintering together. In 1993, Ellen Danielsdottir, Jacobsen's widow recalled that: *"Godager had to return to Norway after one year because of appendicitis. In 1938-39, Arne stayed alone at Hoelsbu".*[353] Anders Godager later participated in the 1941 Buskø Expedition.

Arne Jacobsen (left) and Anders Godager. Kap Humboldt, Christmas Eve 1937. © Arne Jacobsen / Norwegian Polar Institute

1938-39

Up to WWII, most of the Norwegian trappers had come from the coastal areas of Norway, in particular from Troms and Møre, but woodsmen from eastern Norway were also tempted by the trappers' life. Of these the earliest were the cousins Bjarne Akre and Oddvar Akre, who in the summer of 1938 took over Kap Humboldt, planning to stay for two years. However, the war then started and they did not return to their home in Rendalen until 1945. From 1938-41 they were trapping at Kap Humboldt, and in 1941-42 worked in Ivigtut in West Greenland. Then in 1942-43 they served in the North-East Greenland Sledge Patrol before in 1943-45 joining the Norwegian forces in Canada. Bjarne Akre wrote two books about these years: "Fri manns liv" (life in freedom) (1957), an account of his experiences at Kap Humboldt, and ""Heltene" i kald krig" (the "heroes" in cold war) (1983), about the wartime period of 1942-45.

In the summer of 1937, Bjarne Akre had met Sigurd Tolløfsen who was on his way to North-East Greenland with an expedition. Akre was interested in a wintering and obtained from Tolløfsen the information he needed. As a result he and his cousin, Oddvar, came to Kap Humboldt the following year: *"Even if we were used to a bit of everything from years of living in the woods and mountains at home, this was nevertheless something different." ... "To a woodsman from eastern Norway this deep frozen Arctic mountain and glacier country seemed dead and deserted." ... "Here there was plenty to do. Amongst other things we had three huts to build about 150 km inland, and all huts in Oddvar's and my territories had to be equipped with coal, paraffin and dog food. Having prepared and stored the most important supplies and equipment we took off one day with "Humla", our motor boat".*[354] They now built two trappers huts, "Snaddheimen" [312] and "Rendalshytten" [309]. A third hut (Polarheimen) they had to give up, as strong winds and a rough sea stopped them getting ashore. "Polarheimen", however, was built after the war.

Then the trapping started: *"I opened up the trap so the stones tumbled off, and there was my first catch. A genuine blue fox, and a really fine specimen at that. I have to admit that my first fox in Greenland was treated with awe. I stroked it, blew on it, and stroked it again".*[355] Their catch in 1938 was about 120 foxes.

1939-40

In the middle of April 1940, Bjarne Akre returned from the last trapping journey of the season. Oddvar had arrived a few days before from a trip to Isfjord where he had built the "Isfjordhytten" [333]: *"I immediately saw that he was not the Oddvar I usually met after a long trip. He was silent and serious"* – but then it came: *"Norway is at war now, the Germans have invaded and there have been engagements in Østerdalen, all the way to Rendalen".*[356]

At the end of July they started the "Humla" and sailed off to Strindberg: *"Some days in advance we had had a visit from the Danish wireless operator, Aage de Lemos, and we agreed that we had to co-operate as best we could. By hunting and fishing, and using the remaining supplies at the stations sensibly, we should be able to keep going for several years without new supplies".*[357]

One day in the beginning of August a ship appeared in Nordfjord. It was the "Veslekari" with John Giæver on board: *"It was agreed that we should turn up at Humboldt in three days time to unload some supplies. In the meantime "Veslekari" was going south*

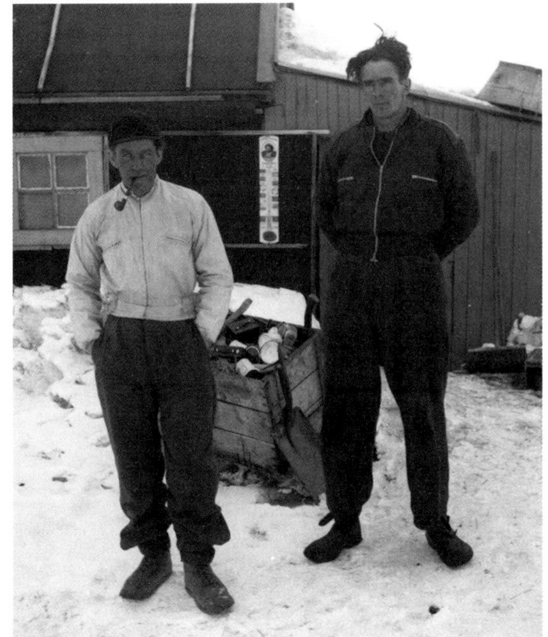

The two Akre cousins at Kap Humboldt. From left Oddvar Akre and Bjarne Akre. c. 1939. © Niels Ove Jensen

to "Havna" in Kong Oscar Fjord".[358] However, the "Fridtjof Nansen" then turned up and arrested "Veslekari" on her way. The trappers were given the choice of staying in Greenland, or going along with the ship to Iceland. The Akre cousins chose to remain at Kap Humboldt.

1940-41

In his book Bjarne Akre recounts that after New Year 1941 he developed sciatica, and while Oddvar went trapping, he remained limping at the station. Then: *"one day I couldn't get up anymore. I had feared this day, which I suspected would soon come. I had fed the dogs the previous day with so much that they would be alright for a couple of weeks if it came to the worse".*[359] The days went by, but on the 14th March voices were finally heard outside the house: *"Is anybody there?" someone shouted in a somewhat uncertain voice. "Yes, come on in" I heard myself answer. "But hell, are you sick?" It was the trapper Johansen from Myggbukta who came rushing in with the Danish wireless operator Kristiansen* (Leo Christiansen) *right behind him. Not much was said before the two of them were busy in the kitchen. The stove was lit, snow was melted and it was not long before I was served a warm meal, followed by a cup of strong coffee." ... "And now events took place one after the other. Johansen returned after a trip to Ella Ø, stayed at Humboldt and continued to Myggbukta. The following day, Hans Siewers who had heard that I was ill arrived at Humboldt to be nurse. A day or two later Siewers returned to Myggbukta to fetch an eiderdown for me together with various belongings, as he prepared for staying at Humboldt during the spring and the summer. Hans had promised to stay at Humboldt until I was well, and I knew him well enough to know that he was not one to break his promise".*[360] Siewers came back to Humboldt on the 28th April[361] and Bjarne Akre recovered during the spring. In the meantime Oddvar Akre had returned from trapping, but he was suffering from a gumboil and went to Scoresbysund to have a bad tooth pulled out. Later in the summer, Bjarne Akre also went to Scoresbysund, from where they both went to Ivigtut with "Gertrud Rask". The Kap Humboldt station was now unmanned until 1947.

1947-48

Egil Amsjø and Bjarne Myrvold were supposed to have taken over the station in 1946, but shortly after arriving in Greenland Myrvold had an accident.

Kap Humboldt, c. 1940. © Hans K. Siewers

Bjarne Myrvold (left) and Egil Amsjø. Christmas Eve at Kap Humboldt 1947. © Bjarne Myrvold

Kap Humboldt c. 1948. Egil Amsjø standing at the door. © Trygve Havold

A shotgun barrel exploded and his hand was badly injured. "Polarbjørn" at once headed for Iceland with Myrvold, where he received hospital treatment before returning to Norway. Despite the accident, Myrvold had not lost heart, and on 1st August 1947 he arrived at Kap Humboldt together with Amsjø, who in 1946-47 had instead been trapping from Hoelsbu. On their way to Kap Humboldt they had managed to build the planned hut "Polarheimen" [314]. The other old huts in the territory were also checked, and this was necessary as they had not had any maintenance for several years.

Amsjø and Myrvold were both in their mid-twenties, and their friendship went back to primary school in Myrvoll, Norway. Hunting and outdoor activities had been a shared interest. After the start of WWII, play suddenly became serious, and both Amsjø and Myrvold were amongst the young men of the resistance who received drops from allied aircraft and blew up railway bridges. After the war ended, life as a bookbinder soon became too boring for Myrvold, and Amsjø was also looking for a change from his job in a warehouse. The solution came from an advertisement in a newspaper, that Arctic Commercial Enterprise was looking for people to go to North-East Greenland. Although there were many applicants, they were both hired and spent three good years together as trappers in Greenland.

After their arrival Kap Humboldt went through a major renovation. On the 4th September they: *"burnt trash, old clothes and worn-out boots from the attic, where we have tidied up. It has probably not been cleaned for 5-6 years. Now it is very cosy at Humboldt. Outside the house has been re-covered with roofing felt. The new window frames are painted white, and it all looks very nice. Inside not much is changed, but we have agreed upon one thing: cleanliness".*[362] The agreement about cleanliness resulted in a so far unseen comfort: *"The sauna was opened today. It certainly exceeded our expectations. In a few minutes we were red all over – a terrible heat, and we had to make a quick retreat to the shower where we completed our bath at a somewhat more moderate temperature. It was a real pleasure to have a decent bath again. I don't know how I could have survived up here without a sauna".*[363]

On November 11th they left the station to go trapping. Amsjø had the northern territory and Myrvold the southern. On the 18th December Amsjø returned to Kap Humboldt where Myrvold had: *"arrived a couple of days ago and it was nice to come home to a heated house with roast and accompaniments for dinner. Bjarne had had a tiresome trip. The foxes had eaten all the dog food as well as the supplies in most of the huts in Vega Sund. So he had had to live on oatmeal and a little bacon for three or four days. Even so it had been a fine trip with a reasonable catch considering".*[364]

New Year of 1947-48 was celebrated at the station, and while Myrvold was occupied in the kitchen Amsjø made some notes of his impressions: *"The room in which we are celebrating was probably painted 8-10 years ago, and in some places we can even see what colour it was. The ceiling had been white; now it is an even grey everywhere except above the stove, where it is almost black. The walls were once green, but over the years the paint has worn away or faded. Where the paint has worn away the colour is more or less undefinable – something between grey and yellow, you might say. Where faded the walls are still dominantly green. The floor is scoured white as we have washed it today. But beneath the table and the berth and round in the corners a light brown paint is still visible. The furniture is a berth along each long wall. Along the short walls there is a table stretching from berth to berth. The table is very large and used for dining table, bedside table and working table, depending on the occasion. Right now it is – – – well, what can I say? At the table is a kettle of boiling water surrounded by two bottles, one containing home-brewed schnapps and the other*

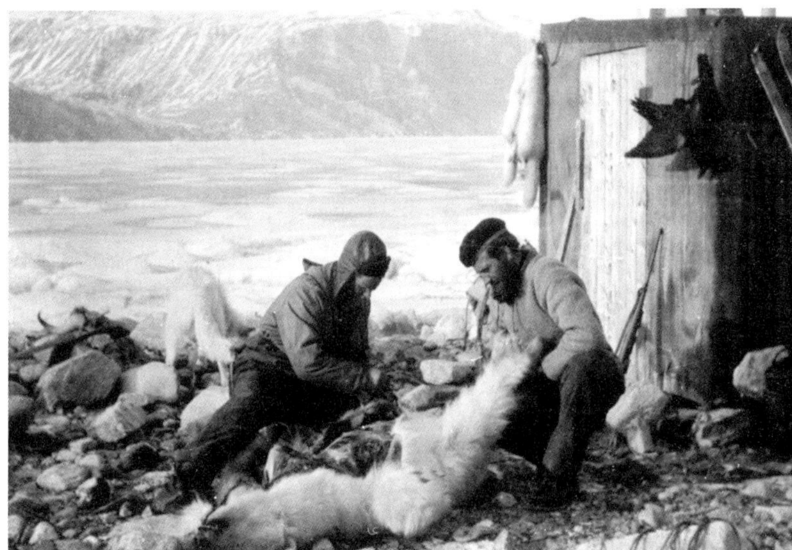

Birger Larsen (left) and Sverre Storholt skinning a polar bear at Polarheimen [314] 1949-50.
© Sverre Storholt

an imported bottle of old Brandy. And a tin box of brown sugar. At each end a half-filled glass of toddy. As the saying goes that good drinks are nourishing, you could say that its function now is as dining table. A bookshelf including a medicine cabinet is placed against the wall to the kitchen. The shelf is quite full of notebooks and scrapped issues from Deichmann (a public library in Oslo). *And also some weeklies and magazines. There is much good reading but we have been more or less through all of it. There are no stools and chairs. And in case we have guests someday, some empty boxes, stored behind the wall, will come in handy".*[365]

Amsjø and Myrvold finished the trapping season with a total catch of 60 foxes. On the 17th July 1948 they sailed from Kap Humboldt to fish char at Strindberg. In the summer of 1948, they built the Ny Jonsbu station, where they wintered in the years 1948-50.

1948-49

Fredrik Sæterdal and Trygve Slettemoen, both newcomers in North-East Greenland, took over the station in 1948-49. They had somewhat different backgrounds; Slettemoen was a law student from Oslo, while Sæterdal who came from Mo i Rana, was brought up in a family of trappers and had wintered in other Arctic areas since he was thirteen (see Hoelsbu section). Sæterdal and Slettemoen were to have moved to Ottostrand in 1949, but the pack ice hindered access and they both went home to Norway with the "Quest". Only Sæterdal later returned.

1949-50

Birger Larsen was 29-years old when he got the chance in 1949 to replace his office job with: *"the ultimate freedom."* It began by a coincidence, he recalled in 1993.[366]

One day he entered the Grand Café in Oslo to have a cup of coffee. All the tables were taken, but then a stranger waved at him. It turned out to be John Giæver, busy writing the supply lists for the Norsel Expedition to the Antarctic. They soon got talking about the Arctic, hunting and the trappers' life and it dawned on Larsen that North-East Greenland had to be the answer to his dreams. He talked a bit about himself, his interest in hunting and suddenly Giæver said: *"Listen, come with me to my office"*. Larsen went along and before they parted he was hired as trapper. The result was that he and Sverre Storholt took over Kap Humboldt in the summer of 1949.

Neither Larsen nor Storholt had any practical experience of trapping, let alone driving sledge dogs, and: *"for the time being it seems that driving with dogs is similar to an amateur circus performance. It was Storholt's debut today, and I had taken a seat in a soft snowdrift, but was ready to escape if necessary. The show turned out to be successful, at least seen from a humoristic point of view. Yes, now and then we are pleased that we have an eight-hour drive to Myggbukta and that the bookings are therefore slow. The performance will probably continue tomorrow"*, Birger Larsen wrote in his diary on the 6th October 1949.[367]

Storholt and Larsen were invited for Christmas at Ella Ø, and: *"it turned out to be an event, I shall never forget. No lack of Christmas spirits,"* ... *"The two Danes* (Aksel Jensen and Ove Barsted) *and the Swiss geologists* (John Haller and Emil Witzig) *had done a great job preparing for Christmas."* ... *"For Christmas presents we received telegrams from home, while the Greenlanders* (Elias Arke and Jon Brønlund) *had excellent presents, such as a new rifle, a watch etc. We gave one of them a white dog, which he liked very much, while the other received a box for cartridges. It was a joy to see how*

"Welcome to Kap Humboldt" (Velkommen til Kapp Humboldt). Sverre Storholt (left) and Birger Larsen testing their home distillery. Kap Humboldt 1949-50. © Sverre Storholt

their dark eyes shone with pleasure like those of children. For Storholt and me they had made each of us a dog whip".[368]

Tragically one of the young Greenlanders, Jon Brønlund, perished just one month later. Driven by home sickness he and Elias Arke had set off on the 27th January for Scoresbysund. They had almost no equipment with them, and were surprised by a snow storm in which Brønlund died (see Antarctichavn section).

In March-April Birger Larsen was trapping in the inner Kejser Franz Joseph Fjord complex. As his base he chose Polarheimen, a hut with: *"the usual interior, a muskox leg and a frying pan on the wall, a skin cap and a dog harness hung beneath the ceiling, and on the shelves, butter, cartridges, Danish oatmeal and Norwegian pork. On the "table" the coffee pot stands in the place of honour, flanked by the tobacco jar and a tin of liver pâté. On the berth is the sleeping bag, a muskox rug, some macaroni and 4-5 ptarmigans. This is how I will always remember a trappers' hut in Greenland",*[369] Larsen wrote in his diary on the 19th March 1950. The same spring he and Storholt built the "Brehytten" [313].

Birger Larsen should have wintered at Myggbukta in 1950-51, but developed problems with his appendix, and both he and Storholt went home in 1950. However, both of them returned for subsequent winterings. Kap Humboldt was unmanned in 1950-51.

1951-52

Halvor Bjørdal, who had wintered at Antarctichavn in 1950-51, had the Kap Humboldt territory to himself in 1951-52. He went home in the summer of 1952, and did not winter again.

Three new Norwegian trappers in front of the "Polarbjørn" going to Greenland. (From left) Odd Uthi, Helge Nesset, and Egil Grindflek. Ålesund 1952. © Egil Grindflek

1952-53

Egil Grindflek and Lars Ellevoll both came from Rendalen in eastern Norway, and took over the Kap Humboldt station in 1952; they were the last Norwegian trappers at Kap Humboldt.

In 1992, the then 67-years old Grindflek recalled that he had been living his entire life in the spruce forests of Norway, where hunting was a part of growing up. His interests in Greenland had developed from hearing about the adventures of the Akre cousins and: *"it was just such a life that fascinated me"*, Grindflek said; *"North-East Greenland – Oh, what incredible nature. I shall never forget Teufelschloss and Franz Joseph Fjord. It was fantastic country"*.[370]

When they arrived, they knew nothing about dog sledging, and Grindflek remembered that Ellevoll described his first attempt as: *"the worst experience ever in his life"*; later on he improved considerably.

Grindflek's most dramatic experience was when his dog team went through the ice in Dusén Fjord, at the narrowest point where swirling water currents stop ice forming. This was on his first trip: *"I sat on the sledge and suddenly the dogs went crazy. They had caught the scent of something. The dogs ran straight into the open water with the sledge, and I leapt off at the very last moment. There was a hut* (Dyrstien) *where I knew I could find some timber, so I ran there to fetch it so I could get out after the dogs. I thought I would never see them again. It was a terrible experience because without the dogs... So I ran out there, and when I arrived back they had managed to turn the sledge and were standing on the ice. It is impossible to understand how they suceeded in doing that. Then I laid out the planks and managed to pull the sledge up. But I got very wet as the water had splashed up onto the ice."*

"Unfortunately we had a very poor catch. 1952-53 was a "black" year", Grindflek recalled.[371] He only regretted one thing, namely that he had once shot a female bear to capture the cubs. It was wrong, he admitted, because man has no right to exterminate species of animals or lock up polar bears in a cage. Nevertheless, the two cubs were on board the ship when Ellevoll and Grindflek travelled home in 1953.

Aune 1991; Bang 1944; Giæver 1937a, 1957; Polarboken 1963-1964; Description ... 1932; NSIU 1945; Pantenburg 1944; N030; N064; N088; Ole Klokset pers. comm.; Bjarne Myrvold pers. comm.; Magne Råum pers. comm.

Recent status

After the end of the trapper era, the Kap Humboldt station was used and maintained by the Sirius Patrol. However, by the early 1990s the station was in need of a thorough overhaul. Sirius brought this to the attention of Nanok, and in the summer of 1997 the station house was renovated by a Nanok team, partly assisted by a team of Sirius men.

Kap Humboldt, 6th May 1979. © Peter Schmidt Mikkelsen

Kap Humboldt [308] is a former Norwegian trappers' station built in 1929 for Arctic Commercial Enterprise. It was used as a trappers' station until 1953, and thereafter as a travellers' hut maintained by Sirius. As Kap Humboldt eventually needed a thorough renovation, Nanok in 1997 sent out a team to restore the station. (Left) Kap Humboldt, 6th August 2006. (Centre) Interior of Kap Humboldt, 11th August 2003. (Bottom) View from Kap Humboldt towards east and Brochs Øer, 6th August 2006. © NCN

KAP PETERSÉNS
[218]

Wintering party
1930-31: Peder Sulebak, Knut Røbek
1931-32: Peder Sulebak
1932-34: Sverre Røstad, Arne Jacobsen
1934-37: Karsten Sulebak
1937-39: Peder Sulebak
1939-51: None
1951-52: Bakke (first name unknown)
1952-53: Lars Myhrvold
1953-54: Fjøsne (first name unknown)
1954-55: None
1955-56: Otto Lapstun

The name Kap Peterséns was given by the Swedish Nathorst expedition in 1899, probably for Carl Justus Frederik af Petersens [1851-1925], a contemporary of Nathorst at Lund University. A few kilometres south of the cape lies a trappers' station, which had originally received the name "Sunnmørsheimen", as the men who built it came from the Sunnmøre district on the coast of Norway. Nevertheless, over time the station became known as "Kap Peterséns", the name also used in this account. (The accent on the 'e' was added to the name in 1935 by the Greenland Place Names Committee, as an aid to correct pronunciation).

1930-31

The Norwegian family name Sulebak has a special connection with the Kap Peterséns station that began on the 9th August 1930 when Peder Sulebak noted: *""Veslekari" has now anchored at Kap Peterséns. This is the place we are going to build one of our main stations in a new region and claim the territory".*[372]

This territory on the 72nd degree of latitude may well have been a new region, but the 33-year old Peder Sulebak was in no way a novice to North-East Greenland or to trapping. From his youth the sea, fishing and trapping had been regular ingredients of his life. He had sailed in the Vestisen and around Newfoundland, first as a leading seaman and gunner, later as engineer and first mate. In 1927 he was among the pioneers that went to North-East Greenland with the "Hird", and founded the first "Sunnmøre territory" around Kap Herschell. Here they had been very fortunate with their catch, and now returned with a new expedition: the Møre Expedition. Two men had gone ashore at Kap Herschell, two others were going to build a station at Antarctichavn. Peder Sulebak and the 19-year old Knut Røbek were to team up, and build the Kap Peterséns station and trappers' huts.

The house at Kap Peterséns had a ground plan of 3.2 x 2.5 m plus a porch of about the same size. On the 15th August Sulebak wrote that: *"we have just about finished the house; only a bit of arranging is left, but this will have to wait as we have only a little time and still have trappers' huts to build"*. The materials for the trappers' huts had been laid out beforehand by the "Veslekari", and two weeks later Sulebak and Røbek had built four huts: "Beinhaugen" [223], "Kap Mæchel hytten" [216], "Raudberget" [215] and "Elveide" [213]. Each hut measured about 2 x 2 m and was equipped with an "oil barrel stove" made by Sulebak himself.

In the middle of September the first snow fell, and Sulebak and Røbek worked indoors to prepare for the trapping season, which started at the end of October.

The Møre Expedition bringing supplies ashore at Kap Peterséns, 9th August 1930. In front: Jonas Karlsbak. Rear from left: Knut Røbek and Odd Åmbak. © Norwegian Polar Institute

As a new trapper, Knut Røbek had to learn by experience. One day he had gone to the Elveide hut, but on the way home in the dusk a snowstorm set in. He drove for a while, but: *"then he came across his own tracks and stopped to drink coffee and think. At the end he had gone around in circles in the thick snow and could not see anything. Which way to go now was difficult to decide, as he could see nothing so had nothing to aim for, and he had left his compass at home".*[373] Røbek now stopped to await a clearing in the weather. In order to keep warm he began to walk back and forth, but he became tired and climbed into his sleeping bag. Wet as he was, he had a cold and sleepless night. From time to time the dogs were fighting, impatient from waiting in their harnesses. Fortunately the weather cleared up the next morning, and Røbek was able to continue to the station. He had been lucky: *"and learnt to take better care the next time"*, Sulebak wrote.[374]

The winter passed without any major incidents, but it was a tough job to work the territory as huge amounts of snow fell in Kong Oscar Fjord that winter. However, there were also pleasant times. One night at the end of May, Sulebak went into the beautiful Alpefjord to take down his last fox traps. The going was fine, so he sat down on his sledge and lit his pipe. He wrote: *"a fine sledge trip with fast dogs in a summer night into the fjord here in Greenland; you could not ask for a better life."*[375]

The result of their first year was a catch of 40 foxes, five polar bears and one wolf.

1931-32

As one man could easily manage the Kap Peterséns territory, it was decided that Knut Røbek should move up to Kap Herschell. On the 4th August 1931, Sulebak and Røbek said goodbye to each other - as it later turned out - for the last time. At the two stations in Kong Oscar Fjord, Kap Peterséns and Antarctichavn, only Peder Sulebak and Odd Åmbak now remained. They helped each other preparing the territory and built two more huts, "Bjørktun" [219] and "Polheim" [220] in the Kap Peterséns district.

They had limited materials for the huts and the roof of the Polheim hut was made of an old sawed-through boat.

In the middle of September Åmbak went south to stay at Antarctichavn. They did not meet again until the 10th November: *"Åmbak came from the south today. It is really nice to meet again after almost two months. He has had a good time this autumn, only like me a bit lonely".*[376]

Sulebak and Åmbak usually met about once every second month. The trappers were in general well informed of the situation elsewhere on the coast, thanks to the "kamik mail". Messages simply passed from mouth to mouth up and down the coast. On the 14th March, the Danish scientist S.O. Stenør from Ella Ø station arrived bringing sad tidings from Hermann Andresen at Kap Herschell: Knut Røbek had been missing since December and was presumed dead.

On May 14th Sulebak wrote: *"When I arrived from the north today, Åmbak had arrived from the south, so now the trapping season is over. We are not disappointed with the result which must be considered a good catch for two men, as we have caught 150 foxes between us. But then, we have trapped from 13 huts with an average distance between them of about 21 km plus the surrounding area; a total distance of about 325 km, which must be said to be a rather large distance for two men to cover".*[377] The following day Sulebak went northwards to Kap Herschell, to participate in the search for Knut Røbek.

1932-33

Anders K. Orvin, the leader of the NSIU's expedition in 1932, wrote: *"We went on through Antarctic Sund to Kong Oscar Fjord, unloaded coal at Maristua on Ella*

Knut Røbek (left) and Peder Sulebak at Kap Peterséns, August 1930. © Jonas Karlsbak / Norwegian Polar Institute

Ø and during the night built a house (Holm Bugt hytten) *in Holmbukta with materials, which had been unloaded there in 1929. On the 31st July we arrived at Sunnmørsheimen at Kap Peterséns where we met the trapper Oddmund Åmbak, who had lived here alone since May. Here Ingstad unloaded half of his equipment; the rest he brought ashore at Antarctichavn the next day".* [378]

In addition to the "Holm Bugt hytten" [222], two additional huts were built in 1932-34: "Alpehuset" [212] and "Kongeborg" [224-1].

In 1932-34 two of Ingstad's men, Sverre Røstad from Levanger and Arne Jacobsen from Tromsø, wintered at Kap Peterséns. One day in the autumn of 1932 they visited Ingstad at Antarctichavn: *"How it enlivens those in the Arctic to see new faces and hear new voices! One day the two other members of our expedition appeared – Røstad and Jacobsen, chugging in with their motor boat on a short visit from Kap Peterséns, their own headquarters. They were living apart from us, and this was the first time we had met since leaving the "Polarbjørn". They had things of their own to tell about – bear, seal, and much else – while the toddy came out and tobacco smoke lay thick beneath the ceiling. Muskoxen were scarce in their district, where the mountains are more often than not precipitous and impassable. But then they had shot seal in large numbers and were thus well stocked up for the winter.*

After some days' sojourn our guests departed. I stared after them as they thrust forward through a choppy sea, their motor boat half-laden with dogs. Fellows of that sort have no word for distress. Here one ceases to be mollycoddled. Young lads, of course, but with a lust for adventure in their blood and in no way squeamish about hard work". [379]

1933-34

Røstad and Jacobsen were not exactly successful in their fox trapping. So in the spring they decided to travel northwards. Ole Klokset, the trapper at Kap Humboldt, ran into them on 21st February 1934 in Maristua: *"Met here Røstad and Jacobsen who arrived half an hour ago. I had a bottle of cognac so we had a good time. They are going to Franz Joseph Fjord to trap, for there are no fox in their territory. They have only caught 22 foxes. Last year they caught 160: Røstad 110, Jacobsen 50."* [380]

Five days later Magne Råum - Klokset's companion - met Røstad and Jacobsen in Renbugthytten: *"Tonight I had a visit from Røstad and Jacobsen. They are on their way to Franz Joseph Fjord, but came up here to shoot muskoxen. It was nice seeing them, as it has been a long time since I have met anyone".* [381] On March 24th Råum met Jacobsen again, and: *"then learned that there were a lot of bears there and that Røstad and Jacobsen had shot four".* [382]

On the 22nd of April, Røstad and Jacobsen were on their way back to Kap Peterséns and once again Ole Klokset met them in Maristua. They had caught 24 foxes in Kejser Franz Joseph Fjord. The next day Klokset and Røstad went together to Kap Dufva and here they had an accident: *"We came to Kap Dufva at 8 o'clock. I decided to stay there for the night together with Røstad. However, our tent accidentally caught fire and burnt, because while we were both out the tent blew down onto the primus. That night was not at all cosy".* [383]

1934-35

""Selbarden" now headed southwards through Kong Oscar Fjord to Sunnmørsheimen at Kap Peterséns and to Antarctichavn, where the rest of the equipment belonging to the Suløya Greenland Expedition was unloaded. The trappers Peder and Karsten Sulebak went ashore here while the four men from Ingstad's expedition boarded with their catch and some equipment." [384] This time Peder Sulebak had brought along his 21-year old nephew Karsten. Karsten, who was from Mauseidvåg, was to stay alone at Kap Peterséns while his uncle mainly stayed at Antarctichavn.

The two men immediately went ahead preparing the territory. It was already late in the summer, and new ice could be expected any day. And the ice did begin to form in the first days of September, but then the weather suddenly changed. The weather turned mild and it rained heavily, in quantities Peder Sulebak could not recall ever having seen before in Greenland. At Kap Peterséns they had temperatures above freezing well into October and open water as late as October 20th when the trapping season usually started. Finally, on November 3rd, they could begin. Peder Sulebak wrote: *"Karsten has tested his dogs. I went along for a while and gave him the necessary instructions on how to drive with dogs. On this test drive he caught a blue fox, which is his first. I have finished my sledge and have baked some bread and cooked".* [385]

To Karsten Sulebak, the winter of 1934-35 was not an exciting trapping adventure. Judging by his diary, he only caught four or five foxes. Furthermore, there was a serious incident in December: *"When I woke up this morning I had only two dogs left, the other three had managed to get loose and I found them dead. Had they eaten something?"* [386]

In the beginning of May 1935, Peder Sulebak came up from Antarctichavn and together they spent the summer at Kap Peterséns. Time was used in repairing their motor boat "Triks" from end to end. It was a lot of work, but something that Peder Sulebak, who was clever with his hands, enjoyed in the long springtime days.

1935-36

Difficult ice conditions in the summer of 1935 meant that no supply ship visited Kong Oscar Fjord. However, the Sulebaks' had all the supplies they needed, and didn't hesitate to prepare the territory. In addition, they built a hut, "Nordborg" [231-1] on Traill Ø.

At the end of September, Peder Sulebak decided to sail back to Antarctichavn in the "Triks", but he had to give it up as the new ice was already too thick. Instead he left the boat at Noret, and walked back to Kap Peterséns. He waited there until the end of October, when the ice could carry the dog sledge.

To Karsten Sulebak, the year 1935-36 was very much the same as the year before. He returned empty-handed from one trapping trip after the other. In February he asked his experienced uncle for advice: *"Drove from Kap Peterséns at 11 o'clock and arrived at Alpehuset at 4.30. Peder has come with me to see why I can't catch any fox".*[387] None of them, however, wrote about whether they had found the cause of the problem.

1936-37

At the end of July 1936, Peder Sulebak went home to Norway with the "Selbarden". In his place Nils Hanken from Kap Herschell was to be Karsten Sulebak's partner. Hanken was due to travel with the "Isbjørn", but the ship was delayed and did not arrive until the 26th August. The supplies needed were unloaded, and there was another important matter Sulebak had to have fixed: *"Tonight I have had two teeth pulled out. There was a dentist on board and he offered his help when he saw my bad teeth".*[388]

Sulebak and Hanken chose to spend the autumn at Antarctichavn. Kap Peterséns was therefore unoccupied until the 19th November 1936, when Sulebak returned to the station alone.

Karsten Sulebak's third year was not much more successful that the previous two. He did not go out trapping in his territory until the middle of January, probably because he feared that the stomach pains he suffered from occasionally would turn out be appendicitis. His diary also leaves the impression that he was not very interested in fox trapping, as he rarely mentions it. At least Niels Hanken expressed his disappointment when he arrived at the beginning of May at Kap Peterséns: *"I cannot find more than eight foxes at the station. It really makes me angry, for as far as I can see there are plenty of foxes and it seems to be a fine territory."*[389]

Perhaps the lonely and unsuccessful trapper's existence had somehow extinguished the spark in Sulebak's 24-years old life early in his trapping career?

If Karsten Sulebak, or any other trapper, was to lose their courage at some point, it would certainly be understandable. Only very few people are able to relate to the physical and psychological stress a young trapper was exposed to. Weeks and months on their own in a wilderness require the utmost of their skills and resourcefulness. Hard work, sacrifice and hunger were his daily life. His contacts with home and family were limited to a few letters and telegrams, which could turn up once or twice a year. If he became disabled due to accident or disease, he was abandoned to his own stamina and the few medications that he might carry. It is one thing to endure such ordeals when you are a part of a team; it is altogether much more difficult to be alone with your doubts and fears.

Karsten Sulebak went home to Norway in 1937, and never returned to North-East Greenland. He died young, when the ship on which he was sailing during WWII was sunk by a torpedo.

1937-38

In the summer of 1937, Peder Sulebak returned to North-East Greenland together with Søren Richter and Ottar Årsvold on his fourth, and last, two-year wintering. They went ashore at Antarctichavn, where Sulebak stayed until the middle of November, when he moved to his old headquarters at Kap Peterséns.

New Years Eve of 1937-38 Sulebak spent alone in Kongeborg, a small hut on Traill Ø: *"So now I'm sitting here having a good time. The heat is crackling nicely in the stove so it is warm and comfortable even though the walls are packed with snow and there is a lot of snow inside. There are still two hours left of the old year, but I'm sure I'm not wrong when I say that the old year will end with a snow storm and the New Year will begin with one. Why should I be staring at these snow walls and a small candle; no, I would rather be in the sleeping bag and asleep, so to me the old year is already over, for I am tired. So goodnight, thank you for the old year and good luck with the new one".*[390]

One day at the end of April 1938, Sulebak returned from his round of Segelsällskapet Fjord with a huge catch: *"Back at Kap Peterséns again with the largest load of foxes I have ever had – 40 complete foxes and another three more or less damaged, so the sledge was full and very heavy and I had to walk all the way".*[391] Sulebak's total catch that season numbered 170 fox furs and it was: *"not that bad"*, he wrote. At the end of May 1938, Sulebak went to Antarctichavn to stay there for the summer. The new "Nordborghytten" [231-2] was possibly built in 1937-38.

1938-39

On the 10th August 1938 Peder Sulebak was: *"left on*

my own at Kap Peterséns watching the "Polarbjørn" leaving northwards, becoming smaller and smaller. Soon it will be out of my sight for this time. The "Polarbjørn" carries home my two friends, who have been my companions for a year, while I'm going to try my luck here for another year in solitude".[392]

Indeed it was a lonely year for Sulebak. The next time he had any contact with other people was on the 31st March 1939, when he visited the Danes at Ella Ø.

He had a winter with a disappointing catch and a lot of snow. On December 9th Sulebak wrote that: *"In all my years here I have never before seen so much snow as we have at the moment".*[393] Altogether Peder Sulebak had trapped in North-East Greenland for eight years and the wintering of 1938-39 was his last. He had been married since 1922, that is to say during all his winterings. During the war, and until 1948, Sulebak worked as a mechanic in a textile factory. Later he became a motor mechanic, and was for a period employed by the Fyrvæsnet. However, the Arctic was his life's passion until the end. He came home from his last voyage to the Arctic on the 5th May 1967, and died three weeks later. Karin Krogsæter, Sulebak's daughter, said in 1992 that he was: *"a man of few words who did not care to brag about himself, but he liked to talk about Greenland whenever anyone asked him".*[394]

1939-59

In 1939-40, the Søren Richter Expedition that had its main station at Hamna used Kap Peterséns as a trappers' hut. In the years 1940-46, all trapping in the territory was shut down due to the war, and during that period Kap Peterséns was only used as a travellers' hut.

In 1946 Norwegian trapping was resumed, and from 1946 to 1959 it was the Hermann Andresen Expeditions which manned the three trappers' stations in Kong Oscar Fjord – Kap Peterséns, Hamna and Antarctichavn. During this period Kap Peterséns functioned as a main station in the years 1951-52 (Bakke), 1952-53 (Lars Myhrvold), 1953-54 (Fjøsne) and 1955-56 (Otto Lapstun). These winterings are described in the section describing the Antarctichavn station.

In 1958 Kap Peterséns was extended with an annex built by the trapper Inge Sørlie.

Nathorst 1900; Polarboken 1963-1964; Description ... 1932; Orvin 1935; Ingeborg Grebstad pers. comm.; Otto Lapstun pers. comm.; Inge Sørlie pers. comm.

Recent status

After the trapper era, Kap Peterséns was maintained and used by the Sirius Dog Sledge Patrol. Over the years Kap Peterséns has also often functioned as a shelter for members of scientific and sports expeditions, as it is located on the normal routes from Mestersvig to Ella Ø or Alpefjord. A major goal of many sports expedition has been mountaineering in the Stauning Alper, the magnificent mountain range between Kong Oscar Fjord and Alpefjord. The Kap Peterséns station was still in good and usable condition up to the late 1980s thanks to minor maintenance carried out by the regular visitors.

However, eventually the house began to need a thorough overhaul, and in the summer of 1998 Nanok sent out a four-man team to restore Kap Peterséns. Following the recommendation of Ivar Ytreland, who had inspected Kap Peterséns in the summer of 1997,[395] the annex from 1958 was pulled down in 1998 by the Nanok team. As a result the station regained its original appearance, and stands today as a fine example of a Norwegian trappers' station.

Sirius dog sledge patrol camps at Kap Petersèns, 23rd February 1978. © Peter Schmidt Mikkelsen

Kap Peterséns [218], 28th July 2003. Kap Peterséns is a former Norwegian trappers' station built 1930 for the Møre Expedition. It was used as a trappers' station until 1956, and thereafter as a travellers' hut maintained by Sirius. Kap Peterséns is located on the south side of Kong Oscar Fjord, 31 km northwest of Mestersvig. In the summer of 1998 the house was restored by Nanok and on the same occasion brought back to its original appearance. Today Kap Peterséns is a fine example of an old Norwegian trappers' station. © NCN

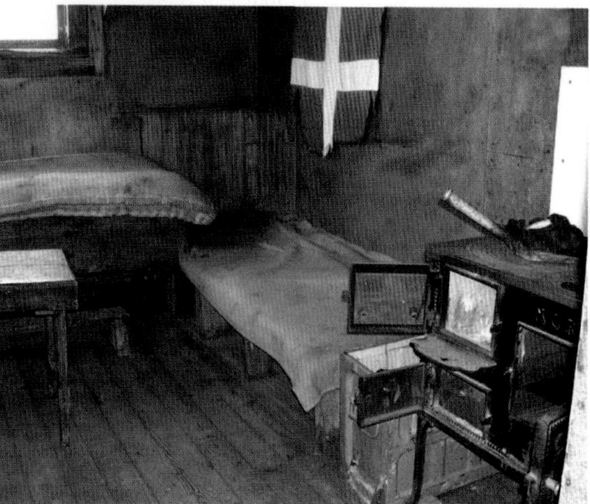

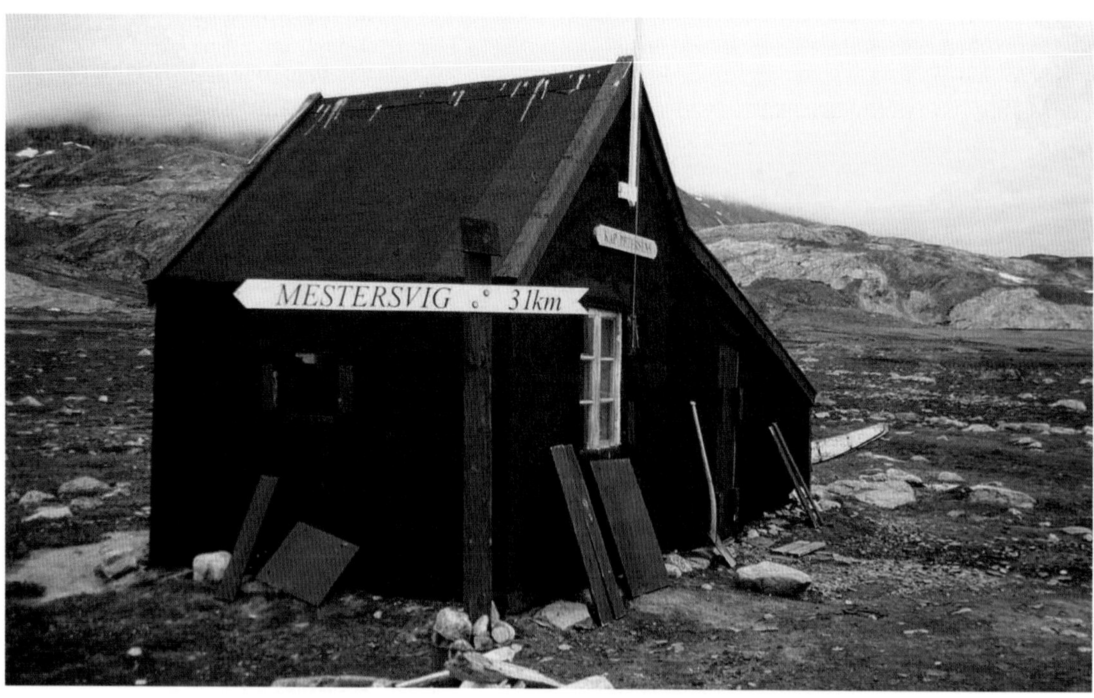

KAP PHILIP BROKE
[470]

Wintering party
1920-21: Hans Nielsen, Ejnar Falsøe, Marius Madsen, Broer Sandberg
1921-23: None
1923-24: Leander E. Emskær Larsen, Christian Rasmussen, Karl Richter

On 11th August 1823, Captain Douglas C. Clavering sailed his vessel the "Griper" northwards along the east coast of an unknown island at 75°N; but soon further advance was cut off by the pack ice and Clavering had to turn south again. Before doing so, he went ashore on the island on the 12th August: *"The island we were on being low and lying off the mainland 30 or 40 miles, I named Shannon Island, and the cape at its S.E. extremity Cape Philip Broke, from the ship it was formerly my good fortune to serve on board, and her gallant commander".*[396]

In the summer of 1901, probably the "Belgica" built an octagonal depot house at Kap Philip Broke, and also two identical houses at nearby Bass Rock. The depots were intended to support the possible line of retreat of the Baldwin-Ziegler Expedition, an imaginative but unsuccessful project to reach the North Pole from Franz Josef Land. The houses were sturdy and well equipped with supplies, but never came to serve their original purpose. Nevertheless, the supplies generously stocked in the houses by Ziegler were invaluable to several subsequent expeditions. Members of the Danmark Expedition on their winter sledge journeys found both shelter and food in the octagonal depot houses, and Ejnar Mikkelsen and Iver Iversen, the stranded members of the Alabama Expedition, made use of the depot at Kap Philip Broke on Shannon while awaiting rescue.

1920-21
In 1920-21, the Kap Philip Broke house served as winter base for the trapper Hans Nielsen of the East Greenland Company; he wrote: *"I moved from Sabine Ø* (Germaniahavn) *to Shannon for the following reasons. Fox trapping is and must be the foundation of our business, and the foxes were not numerous on Sabine Ø. We caught practically all we saw traces of. They were mostly old, toothless males, so there were poor prospects for the future. We reckoned that we could not expect a reasonable catch the next year. Ice conditions made it impossible for us to reach either Shannon or Dronning Augusta Dal. Our territory was as such very limited".*[397]

On the 5th August 1920, Nielsen arrived at Kap Philip Broke with the "Dagny". The plan was that he and Marius Madsen, a new trapper, would stay there for the winter. However, three days later the "Dagny" was wrecked in the pack ice and in the morning of the 14th August seven tired and exhausted men from the "Dagny" arrived back at Kap Philip Broke. After the shipwrecked men had recovered, they split up as it was impossible for nine men to winter in the small house. One man went to stay at Alabamahuset and four others rowed down to the Bass Rock depot. Four men were left at Kap Philip Broke: Hans Nielsen, Ejnar Falsøe, Marius Madsen and the 15-year old ship's boy from "Dagny", Broer Sandberg.

The catch at Kap Philip Broke that winter was disappointing, amounting only to two dozen foxes and a few bears, and existence was a constant search for

Kap Philip Broke, 25th August 1923. Christian Rasmussen is making a porch from an old Norwegian whaling boat.
© Jørgen Nielsen

food. They had only one sledge dog remaining, as the others had died from disease. On the other hand they had a black cat, "Pjevs". She had sneaked aboard the "Dagny" in Copenhagen and evaded all attempts to catch her and throw her overboard. Pjevs survived the shipwreck, wintered at Kap Philip Broke and in 1921 returned to Denmark with the "Teddy". This achievement is without doubt unequalled in the history of North-East Greenland.

1923-24

The poor catch of 1920-21 led to the trapping on Shannon being abandoned; however, the problematic situation with the ice in 1923, and with "Teddy", led to the East Greenland Company once more using the Kap Philip Broke house. Three men were placed there: Leander Elias Emskær Larsen; Karl Richter, a young German zoologist who had become a trapper on the condition that he could also undertake scientific investigations; and Christian Frederik Rasmussen, a 22-years old carpenter from Kirke Stillinge in Vestsjælland. After one year in North-East Greenland, Rasmussen returned to Sjælland in 1924, where he became known as "Tømrer Skrut" (carpenter Skrut) and lived at Næsbystrand until his death in 1970.

The three men at Kap Philip Broke added a porch made of the middle part of an old *"Norwegian whaling boat"*[398] to the Kap Philip Broke house, and also built the "Kap David Gray hytten" [472-1]. They remained on Shannon until May 1924, when they moved to Germaniahavn.

Shortly before they left the station they shot a female bear. Afterwards they discovered that the bear had a small cub. They adopted the cub, and named her "Grethe": *"Larsen had made a teat out of an old boot and bottle-fed the cub with diluted, condensed sweetened milk. Grethe had grown to like her "nanny" quite well, but the rest of us she detested, lashing out and spitting at us when we tried to pat her. When Larsen came she purred in a friendly fashion and accepted his stroking. Yes, she would even lie on her back so he could scratch her tummy".*[399] One morning Grethe's cage had been forced open and she was missing. They found tracks in the snow from another bear and at first they thought it was one of her fellow kin who had helped his imprisoned baby sister into freedom. A sympathetic thought, but then they found a fresh pool of blood and some fur tufts in the snow and realized that the old bear had only broken into the cage to eat the cub.

The Kap Philip Broke house was not used for wintering after 1923-24. In 1930 the house was donated to the Norwegian government[400] who later sold it to Denmark.

In 1930-31, the Nanok men Andreas Hvidberg and James van Hauen started a wintering at Shannon, but in December went for a Christmas visit to the Hochstetter station, where they remained for the rest of the season.

Dahl 1924; Fiala 1907; Hvidberg 1932; Madsen 1963, 1989; Mikkelsen 1953; P152.

Recent status

The Kap Philip Broke house has only rarely been used since the 1930s, and while more-or-less intact is in poor condition.

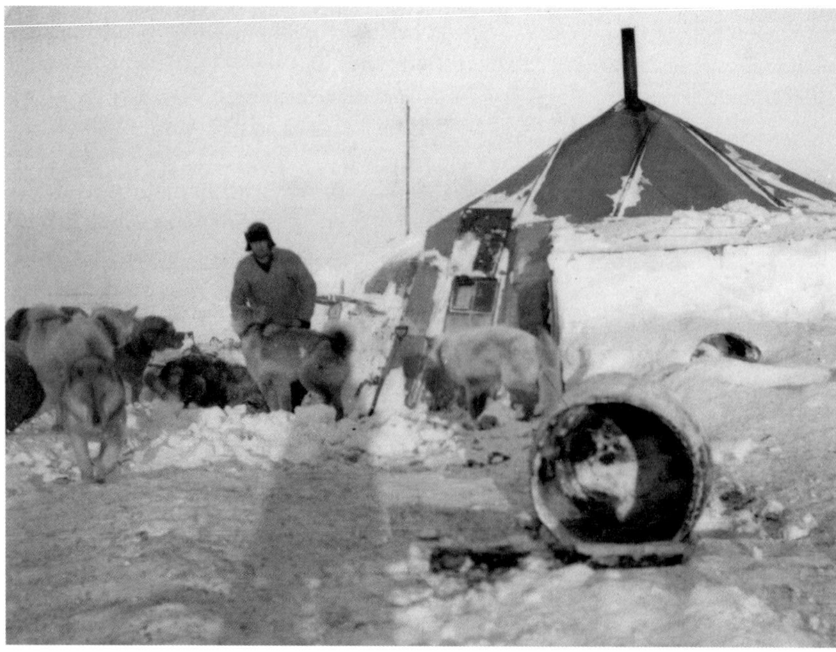

Kap Philip Broke, 1924. © Jørgen Nielsen

Kap Philip Broke [470], 8th July 2007. The house at Kap Philip Broke was built at the same time as the houses at Bass Rock [461] in 1901 for the Baldwin-Ziegler Expedition. Kap Philip Broke was used for overwintering in 1920-21 and 1923-24 by Danish trappers from the East Greenland Company. (Middle left): March 2004. © Erik Jochumsen. (Middle Right and bottom) In July 2007 the interior of the house was completely filled with a large lump of snow and ice. © NCN

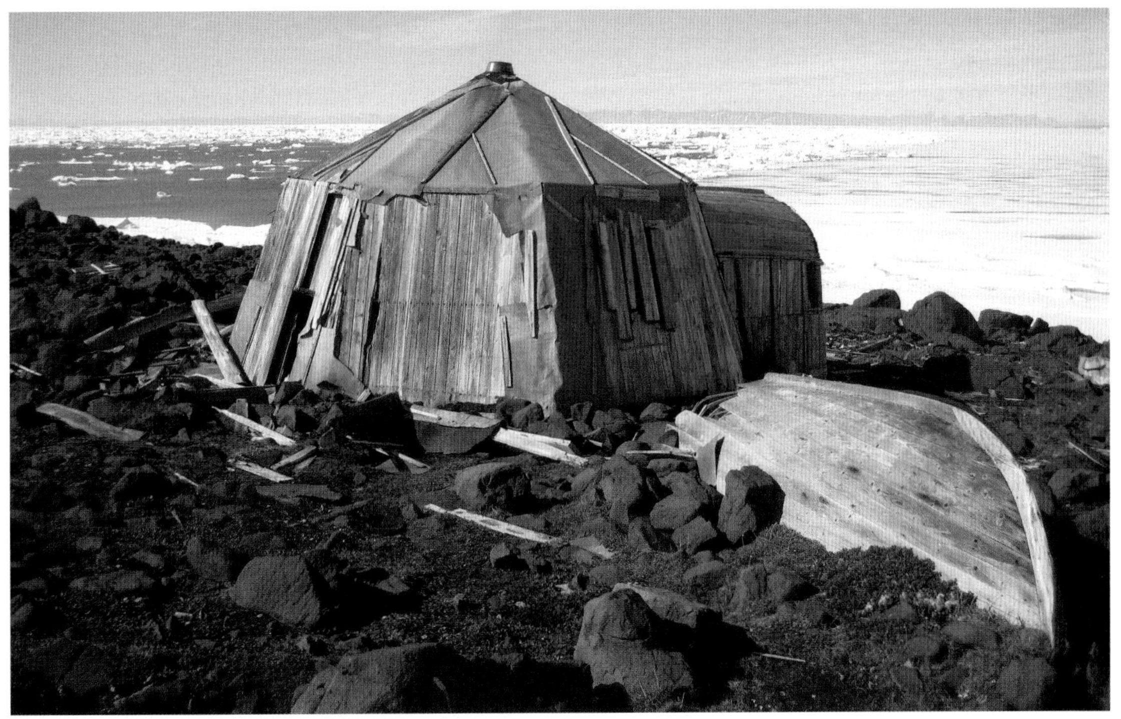

KNUDSHOVED
[355]

Wintering party
1930-31: Carl Aage Knudsen*, Evald Rasmussen*
1931-32: Evald Rasmussen*
1932-34: None
1934-38: Aage Hansen*
1938-39: Christian Petersen*
1939-40: Christian Petersen
1940-45: None
1945-46: Carl El'Vibe, Ib Bach Hansen
* Wintered in part at Sandodden

In the years 1920-24, the East Greenland Company used the Carlshavn station as a base for trapping, but after it was accidentally burnt down in 1927, Nanok built a new station at Knudshoved in order to maintain the Danish claim to the Hold with Hope territory.

On the 5th August 1930, the history of the new station began when the "Godthaab" dropped anchor at Knudshoved about 10 km south of Carlshavn: *"at a delightful place on an evenly ascending plain"* – as Hans Ludvig Jensen expressed it. When the building materials had been unloaded: *"the table was set, including schnapps, beer, coffee, brandy and cigars. There were a lot of speeches and we named the new station "Knudshoved". The party lasted until 7 o'clock in the morning".*[401] When "Godthaab" departed, responsibility was placed in the hands of Carl Aage Knudsen and Evald Rasmussen to build the house. In practice, Knudshoved never became an independent station. Instead it was run together with Sandodden and the trappers would winter at both stations for periods during the trapping season. Only in 1939-40 and 1945-46 was Knudshoved manned both in the autumn and the spring.

1930-31
Carl Aage Knudsen and Evald Rasmussen were supposed to have wintered at Knudshoved in 1930-31, but at Sandodden J.G. Jennov wrote that: *"on the 11th November Knudsen and Rasmussen arrived from Knudshoved because Knudsen was convinced that he had scurvy and dared not stay at the Knudshoved station. I examined Knudsen as best I could and concluded that it was unlikely he had scurvy. There was nothing wrong with his teeth, his stools were OK, and his appetite was excellent to put it mildly".*[402] Nevertheless, Knudsen and Rasmussen were allowed to stay at Sandodden. For part of February 1931 Jennov and Rasmussen stayed at Knudshoved while trapping.

1931-32
In 1931, Evald Rasmussen and Elmar Drastrup had the Sandodden and Knudshoved territories. Rasmussen was to have stayed at Knudshoved, but as Drastrup was severely frostbitten at the beginning of December and had to remain at Eskimonæs until April, Rasmussen mainly stayed at Sandodden. During the years 1932-34 Nanok had no trappers at Sandodden and there was therefore no trapping on Hold with Hope.

1934-38
In 1934-36 the Sandodden and Knudshoved territories were manned by Niels Hansen and Aage Hansen. The latter was going to work from Knudshoved and stayed there from the beginning of November until Christmas 1934, which was celebrated at Sandodden.

When Aage Hansen was returning at the end of January, an accident happened. Nils Hanken wrote:

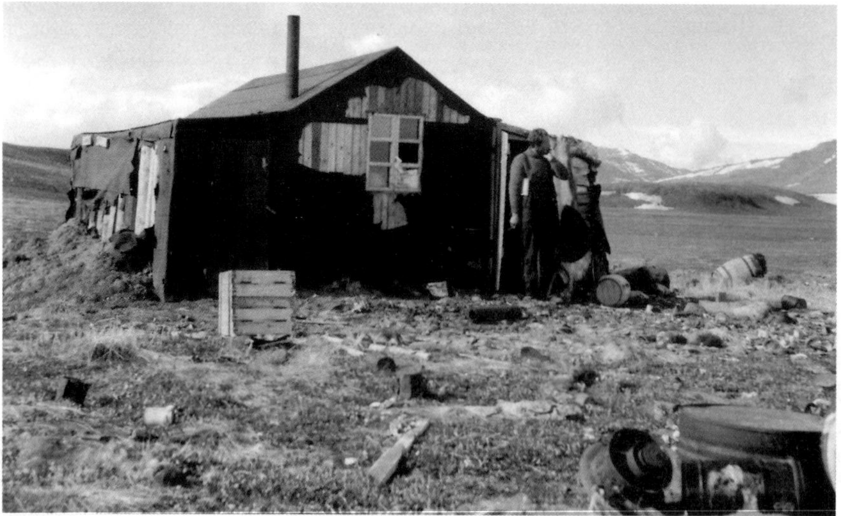

Knudshoved in 1937.
© Will C. Knutsen

"During his journey he ran into a snowstorm and went through the ice with his sledge. He had to abandon the sledge, and as the area was unknown to him it took about 20 hours before he managed to find my house at Elvsborg. When releasing his dogs from the sledge he lost his mittens, and developed some bad frostbite. He stayed at Elvsborg for two days, and then walked from here to Eskimonæs".[403] The frostbite forced Aage Hansen to stay at Eskimonæs until the beginning of March. He: *"escaped from all this without any permanent injuries apart from some deep scars on his face and hands; only few men could have endured what Aage Hansen suffered and lived to tell the tale"*.[404]

In 1935-36, Aage Hansen resumed trapping at Knudshoved, but it was a poor season where: *"there was no catch south of Clavering Ø"*.[405] In 1936-38 Aage Hansen had Sandodden and Knudshoved to himself. He lived at Sandodden in 1936-37, for it was: *"impossible to get to Knudshoved, as the pack ice blocked the entire route from Elvsborg and southwards"*.[406]

1938-40

Until 1938, Nanok had no trappers' huts in the Knudshoved territory. All the trapping therefore had to take place with the main station as starting point. In the summer of 1938 Nanok built the trappers' huts "Herjahytten" [361] and "Tobiashytten" [359] in Tobias Dal. At Knudshoved the old porch was replaced by a new one. Christian Petersen, who had the nickname "Ulvedræberen" (the wolf killer), was meant to have built a third hut during the winter of 1938, but when he, with some difficulty, located the materials beneath 1/2 m of snow, he discovered that: *"unfortunately there was not enough for a trappers hut"*.[407] Petersen did not build "Ulvedræberhytten" [346] until the 1939-40 winter. In 1938-39, Petersen only trapped from Knudshoved from January to April, and spent the rest of the time at Sandodden. In 1939-40, he probably stayed at Knudshoved during both autumn and spring.

Christian Petersen left North-East Greenland in 1940, and later fought on the Western Front as a soldier with the British Army. After the war he returned to Denmark.

In the summer of 1939, Nanok made several attempts to transport hut materials into Herjaelv and Tobias Dal using a horse-drawn carriage. Unfortunately, it was an unusually rainy season and the ground was soaking wet and impassable. The hut materials had to be abandoned; see "Herjaelv I" [920] and "Herjaelv II" [921].

1945-46

In 1945 when Nanok resumed its activities after the war, the company aimed at more extensive trapping in the Hold with Hope area. The Loch Fyne station was established, and three additional huts were built in the Knudshoved territory: "Kap Broer Ruys Nord" [338], "Kap Broer Ruys Syd" [331] and "Jordly" [362].

Of the season 1945-46, the former trapper Carl El'Vibe related in 1991: *"Jennov distributed the men at the stations. Ib Bach Hansen and I had Knudshoved, which meant the entire Hold with Hope area. This was the official programme, but we were everywhere. Due to the lack of sledge dogs it was decided that the men should travel two and two together. We did so at the beginning of the season, but in October we split up. Each man had only five dogs and it was only when we had long journeys, e.g. for Christmas at Daneborg, that we combined the dog teams. I went home in 1946, and in the autumn had a hernia operation. As I had a licence as a radio amateur, I decided to obtain a professional certificate so I could return to Greenland again. I was stationed at Daneborg in 1950, and stayed there for two years"*.[408]

Drastrup 1932; Jennov 1939.

Recent status

From 1946 Loch Fyne became the main station for Nanok in the territory, and Knudshoved was subsequently only used as a travellers' hut. Sirius used the station until 1982. It is currently in reasonable good condition, but is in need of renovation before it can be used again.

Knudshoved used as a travellers' hut by Sirius patrol team, 21st May 1979. © Peter Schmidt Mikkelsen

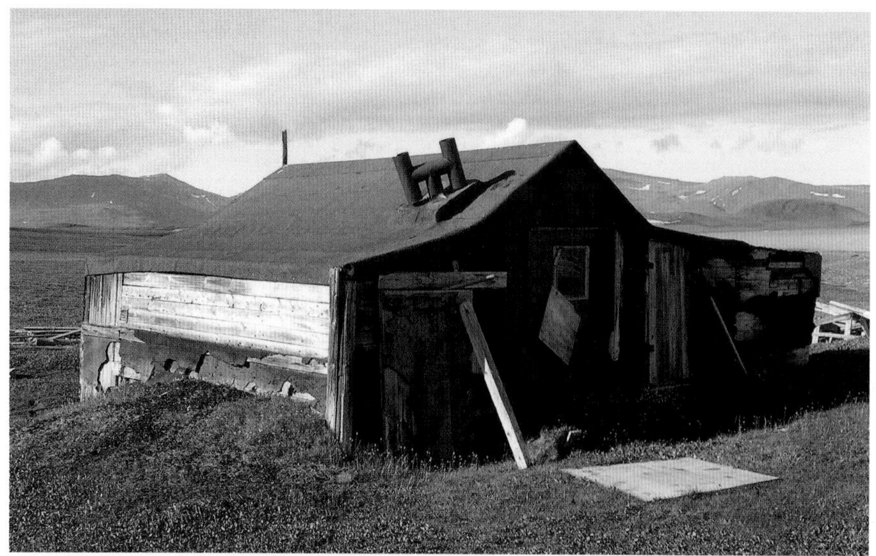

Knudshoved [355], 11th August 2003. Knudshoved is a former Danish trappers' station built 1930 for Nanok. It was the Danish main trappers' station at Hold with Hope until 1946, when the Loch Fyne station [350] was built to replace Knudshoved. Sirius maintained Knudshoved as a travellers' hut until 1982. © NCN

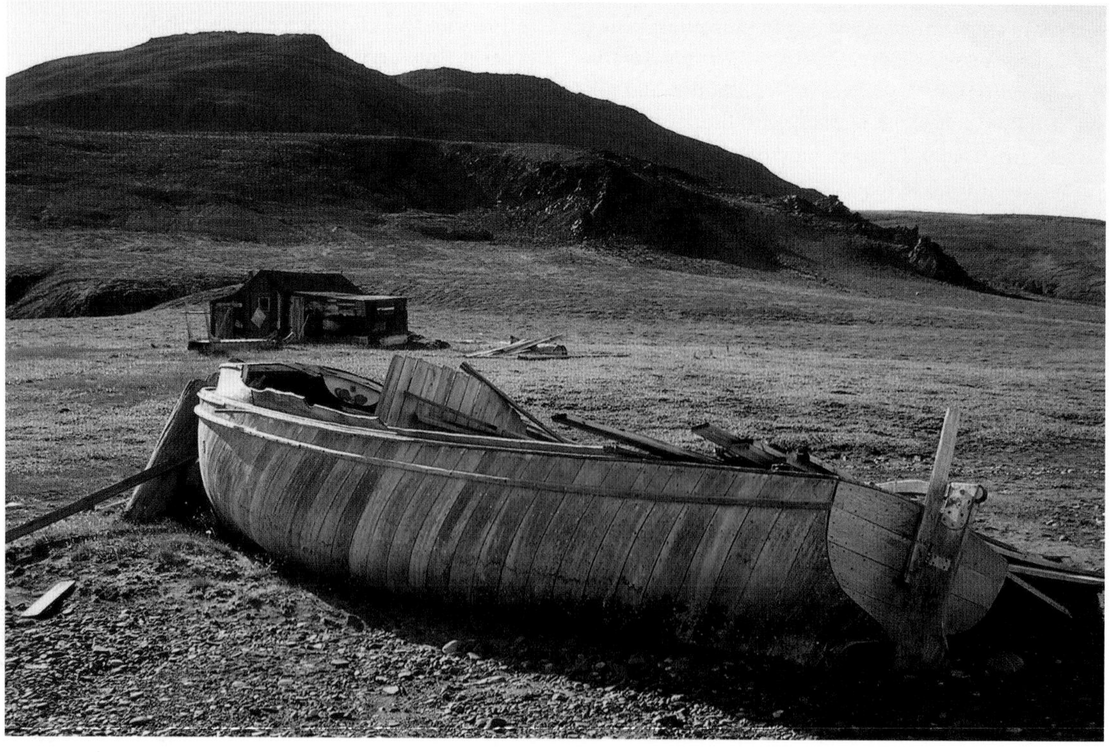

KOPPERNESHUSET
[441-1]

Wintering party
1908-09: Severin G. Liavåg, Peder E.P. Brandal, Baard I. Berge, Johan A. Hareide

1908-09
On the 3rd July 1908, the seven-man Floren Expedition arrived in North-East Greenland. They came ashore at Hvalrosø, and the very same day the leader, Severin Gåsnes Liavåg, rowed across Claveringstrædet to the mainland looking for a suitable location to build a winter house; however, these were pioneering days and no one knew what circumstances they would face during the winter: *"Immediately west of Kap Wynn there is a small clearing in the shadow of a high mountain. It looks inviting in the summertime, green and pleasant. The reason for the fertility is that during the winter the entire area is covered by large house-high snow drifts. The locality is dark as it faces north. The pioneers were not aware of its limitations, and built the house on the clearing near the beach".*[409]

The house was built by Liavåg and Adolf Brandal. It was built from wood, measured 4 x 4 m and on the south side had a stone-built annex: *"To me it looks just like the Norges Bank building back home in Ålesund – from the outside, of course"*, Brandal remarked dryly in his diary.[410] At the end of July "Kopperneshuset" was completed.[411] It was named after the Ålesund merchant Hans Koppernes, one of the sponsors of the expedition. They now split up in two groups: Severin Liavåg, Peder E.P. Brandal from Brandal (then 22-years old), and Baard I. Berge from Sogn and Johan A. Hareide from Leines near Bodø (both then 17-years old), who were to stay at "Kopperneshuset" at Kap Wynn; the other three, Adolf Brandal, Johannes Dreyer Larsen and Mathias Lorentsen Hjellvold, would spend the winter at a dugout, Borganes, constructed at Kap Borlase Warren.

At the end of August 1908 they caught some muskox calves, and discussed the unexpected possibilities. Four live muskox calves would undoubtedly bring in a good price, but it was already late in the year and the chances of gathering enough grass and hay for the winter were almost non-existent. Liavåg decided that he and three of the men should attempt to sail the calves to Iceland and sell them there, while the other three men would remain for the winter as planned. In haste they embarked on the "Floren", but after a few days in the ice had to acknowledge that they had left it too late. Hour by hour the new ice grew thicker and it was only with the greatest of difficulty they managed to reach shore again. When they later ran out of food they had to slaughter the calves.

The problem now was to find a secure winter harbour for the "Floren". Originally she was supposed to have been hauled ashore, but this was now impossible and they were forced to let her freeze in the ice of a small cove west of Germania Havn on Sabine Ø. Fortunately, they were able to keep an eye on the ship from Kopperneshuset using binoculars.

They now prepared themselves for the winter. The days went by without much happening. The fox trapping season began, but they had too little experience and their traps were too few and badly

Kopperneshuset c. 1920.
© Jonna Jensen

constructed. They were more fortunate with their bear hunting, but even here the pioneers had something to learn. At three o'clock one cold December night, Liavåg was woken by a low growl outside the door. He jumped out of his berth, reached for his Krag-Jørgensen rifle and cautiously opened the door. Four steps away from him stood a mother bear with two large cubs. He aimed and pulled the trigger, but the rifle misfired. He tried again with the same result. His colleagues had by then joined him, and handed him their rifles one by one, but all misfired. At last one rifle, Hareide's, worked. The bears were shot, but why had the rifles failed? Liavåg himself soon found the answer: in the severe cold the lubricating oil had become stiff and viscous. It has therefore become a vital rule in North-East Greenland that in the winter the rifles must be totally cleaned of all lubricating oil.

Claveringstrædet is a treacherous place for sledge driving, and the "Floren" men were the first to realize this. The day before New Year 1909, heavy swells from the rough sea began to beat against the shore beneath the house and within an hour the sea ice had broken up.

At the beginning of the New Year they expanded their trapping territory to Sabine Ø; however, as the winter waned Liavåg came to realize that the fox trapping had not lived up to his expectations. In his view the foxes had so much natural food available that they did not take the baits in the traps. He also recognized that he and his men had insufficient experience. Altogether he was content, for the bear hunting had been satisfying and none of the men had been seriously ill. After the fox trapping season ended, the three men at the Borganes hut moved up to Kap Wynn. Liavåg's diary ends abruptly on the 9th May 1909, as only three days later he died while bear hunting.

Severin Gåsnes Liavag. Leader of the Floren Expedition 1908-09. Drowned on 12th May 1909 during a bear hunt near Kap Wynn. © Årsskrift. Hareid Historielag 1984

It was one of those bright nights in May, the 12th May 1909, that five of the men were on their way home across the ice. It was foggy and the thaw had set in. They had been on Sabine Ø to tend their traps and check on "Floren"". A few hundred metres from the house at Kap Wynn they discovered the bear. It ran off across the ice towards Hvalrosø, and they started off in pursuit. Hareide shot it, but unfortunately the bear fell at a place with thin ice. The men went to the edge of the thicker ice, only two hundred metres from where the bear lay. Johannes Dreyer Larsen had gone to the house to fetch rope and a sledge. The others became impatient; first Adolf Brandal tested the thin ice, but it gave in even if he used his skis. Liavåg, however, thought that if two men had a rope between them and a long run-up it would be alright.

Liavåg and Hareide then ran-up and it worked until they were half way across. Then the ice broke and both went through into the water almost simultaneously. Peder Brandal rushed off for help while Adolf Brandal stood at the edge, helplessly witnessing his friends' struggle. The respite was short in the freezing water and after only a couple of minutes Hareide was gone. Just then Johannes Larsen came running up with the rope and for a few moments there seemed to be hope for Liavåg; but the rope was too short and soon the freezing water closed over Severin Liavåg as well.

The five remaining participants of the Floren Expedition returned safely to Ålesund on the 27th August 1909.

Brandal 1930; Giæver 1939; Giæver 1944; Description ... 1932; Orléans 1911; Orvin 1930, 1931; Vollan 1951; N032; N087.

Recent status

Kopperneshuset was never used for wintering again. When Adolf Brandal revisited it in the summer of 1927, it was already falling apart with only three walls standing. In the autumn of 1928, the Hird Expedition salvaged the remaining timbers to build four trappers huts: Gåsneshuset, Ingrid Havn, Sletta and Falkberget. Only a wall of stones now remains to mark the site of Kopperneshuset.

Kopperneshuset [441-1], 6th August 2004. Kopperneshuset was a Norwegian trappers' station built in 1908 by the Floren Expedition. It was only used as a trappers' station 1908-09. In 1928, all the remaining timbers of Kopperneshuset were salvaged to build four trappers' huts. © NCN

KROGNESS
[403]

Wintering party
1926-27: Meyer Olsen, Hans Olsen
1927-28: Meyer Olsen
1928-30: Gunnar Knoph, Levin Winther
1930-35: None
1935-36: Ole Sivertsen
1936-37: Willie Knutsen, Karl Nicolaisen

1926-27

In the summer of 1926, the Foldvik Expedition arrived in North-East Greenland Hallvard Devold wrote: *"a little south-west of Kap Stosch the landscape looked promising. The "Ringsel" anchored and we went ashore to take a closer look at the location. A few hares were jumping around and there were many geese. Meyer Olsen found the locality so attractive that it was decided to start unloading. The place was also strategically well placed as from here one could go south-west and south into Loch Fyne and eastwards along the south coast of Clavering Fjord* (Gael Hamke Bugt). *You could trap in two directions. We named the place Kap Krogness after the man who has done us the greatest favours and encouraged us to undertake this journey".*[412] Hallvard Devold was here referring to Ole Andreas Krogness (1886-1934), who was leader of the Haldde-observatory from 1912-18, director of the Geofysisk Institutt in Tromsø from 1918-28 and professor at Bergen Museum from 1928-34. He had many interests in the realm of geophysics and took a great interest in the Arctic. It was due to his initiatives more than anyone else that weather stations were established in the Arctic in co-operation with wintering Norwegian trapping expeditions, e.g. the station at Myggbukta.

Meyer Olsen (1880-1973) from Tennes in Balsfjord was a boat-builder and as early as 1923 had equipped his own wintering expedition to North-East Greenland.[413] It had been his plan to establish a trappers' station on the south coast of Gael Hamke Bugt, approximately where the Foldvik Expedition now built Krogness. He had also planned to transmit weather reports to Myggbukta using a small transmitter that the Geofysisk Institutt had placed at his disposal. Meyer Olsen's expedition sailed for North-East Greenland, together with the "Conrad Holmboe", aboard the motor cutter "Ørnen", a boat which Olsen had built himself; but the pack ice prevented "Ørnen" reaching the coast, and Olsen was forced to divert to Svalbard and winter there in 1923-24. "Conrad Holmboe" also had to return to Norway without reaching its destination Myggbukta.

Meyer Olsen did not give up North-East Greenland, however, and in the winter of 1925 Ole Andreas Krogness introduced him to Nils Foldvik, who was preparing an expedition together with Hallvard Devold. They joined forces and while Foldvik bought equipment and food, Olsen took care of the boat equipment and materials for the trappers' huts. They equipped the expedition for six men, and one of the last three chosen was Meyer Olsen's brother, who had sailed in the Arctic for many years as an engineer: *"Both brothers could do almost any trade".*[414]

When the Olsen brothers had built the Krogness station, they started to establish their trapping territory assisted by Frits Øien and Arnulf Gisvold. They built six huts: "Midtstua" [367-1], "Bunnhuset" [349], "Ørnereiret" [374], "Sandvik" [411-1], a hut [372] at Rødelv and one [369] at Kap James.

At the beginning of the trapping season, Meyer Olsen stayed at the Danish Carlshavn station; but as it turned out that there were no foxes in that area he moved back to Krogness.

1927-28

Experience from the first winter showed that the huts at Rødelv [372] and Kap James [369] were useless. They quickly got buried in snow and in addition the catch here was poor. The two huts were taken down in the summer of 1927 and rebuilt south and north of Kap Oetker on Clavering Ø. The southern hut received the name "Nes-odden" [414] and the northern hut "Kap Oetker" [420]. The hut "Sandvik" [411-1] was also moved to a better location. These huts later came to lie within the territory of the new station, Tyrolerheimen (see Moskusheimen), built at Revet. In the Krogness territory the hut "Norske Villa" [373] was built: *"Meyer Olsen was in charge of the building activity, and I do not hesitate to claim that the work carried out in the summer of 1927 is the best ever done by hut builders in East Greenland".*[415] The rapid expansion of the territory resulted in an acute lack of building materials. To remedy this, they also used the timber deposited by the East Greenland Company in 1923 at Kap Mary.

In the winter of 1927-28, only Meyer Olsen stayed at Krogness. The "Hird" trapper Jonas Karlsbak arrived on the 1st February 1928, after an exhausting journey from Elvsborg: *"Today I am resting after the difficult trip. I feel OK and am well treated by Meyer Olsen, for he is a man who understands what such a journey can do to you. I'm staying here for a few days to celebrate Christmas, a bit late perhaps, but we are not particularly strict about this here in Greenland"*.[416] Meyer Olsen's trapping experience was a considerable help to the "Hird" men, who also took over some of his equipment and dogs when he went home in 1928.

1928-30

Finn Devold chose two experienced trappers, Levin Winther and Gunnar Knoph, to take over Krogness in the period 1928-30. Both had several years of experience from Svalbard. The territory towards Kap James, which the Foldvik Expedition had abandoned, was taken into use again and a new trappers hut, "Knoph-stua" [372], was built at Rødelv.

Henry Rudi and Finn Framnes-Hansen, from Moskusheimen, stopped at Krogness shortly before Christmas 1928, and: *"here we saw Knoph by himself. He was nanny to a litter of new-born puppies. They had caught some live foxes. He could not leave his beloved animals and preferred to spend Christmas alone in their company. His companion had just left"*.[417]

John Giæver wrote that: *"Levin Winther is the only dog sledge driver I know who has had any benefit from using Alsatian dogs in the Arctic. In 1929 he had a team of five large, bat-eared pedigree dogs"*.[418]

It was at Kap Stosch that the Norwegians made their first annexation of an area in North-East Greenland on 25th July 1930. In the best Svalbard-style a board was erected with the inscription: *"The land around Kap Stosch is this day annexed by Arctic Commercial Enterprise Ltd, Oslo, for utilization of the deposits of coal. Borders: The coastline from Kap Stosch to a point in Loch Fyne. From here, due east to the coastline of Gael Hamkes Bugt. From here the coastline to Kap Stosch"*.[419] In the period 1930-35 Krogness was not used as a trapping station.

1935-36

Ole Sivertsen and Johan Johansen were to have wintered at Kap Humboldt in 1935-36, but as ice conditions made it impossible to call there, Johansen stayed at Moskusheimen while Ole Sivertsen went to Krogness. He arrived at Krogness on the 2nd September 1935: *"The day was spent tidying the house so that I can be here. This house was once used as a main station and it was surely a good house. In recent years it has been used only as a travellers' hut without any maintenance. It looks terrible, but now I'm going to throw out some surplus equipment and clean it throughout. Then I'm sure it will be fine"*.[420]

One day in October it became so cold in the house that it was necessary: *"to paste paper on the walls and ceiling. This, I believe, will make it considerably better. Of course it doesn't look good with all that paper, but if it becomes warmer in here that is not so important."* ... *"The walls are more or less like an art gallery, for there are hundreds of pictures from all over the place, so in my spare time I can imagine that I'm at the National Gallery or some other art collection. I have a number of Geographical Magazines that came from consul Carl S. Sæther and they are filled with illustrations from almost the entire world"*.[421]

Sivertsen's diaries are very informative and give a good impression of the everyday life of a trapper, and of the man Ole Sivertsen. He was 50-years old and had become a trapper more out of necessity than of desire. On the 22nd October 1935 he wrote: *"Today I have been married for 25 years and who would have thought that I would spend my silver wedding anniversary in a small hut in Loch Fyne in Greenland. So there you have it. Had anyone 25 years ago told me that today I would be in some hut in Greenland, I'm positive that I would have said to him that he was off his head. Looking back, a lot of things have changed*

The Krogness station, 26th July 1930. © Adolf Hoel / Norwegian Polar Institute

with me, and everything else for that matter. Then I looked at things differently. It was possible to get a job so you needn't be out of work. We got by on 18 kroner a week and could even afford clothes; but now it is totally different".[422]

Sivertsen was trapping in the area between Kap James and the head of Loch Fyne. On the 14th August 1936, "Isbjørn" arrived and Sivertsen went aboard for the journey to Kap Humboldt where he would stay for the next winter.

1936-37

Willie Knutsen was born in 1912 in Brooklyn, New York. His family originated from Tromsø in Norway and had for several generations a close attachment to the Arctic. When Willie was two years old the family moved back to Norway, where he grew up and also developed a keen interest in the Arctic. His ambition was to participate in a polar expedition.

In the summer of 1932 Knutsen met a French count, Gaston Micard, who became one of the most influential people in his life. Micard was then on his way to Tromsø to embark on a summer voyage to Greenland with the "Quest", Shackleton's old ship, which had been taken over in 1924 by Captain Ludolf Schjelderup from Bodø.[423] Knutsen was ready to go immediately, but even if Micard had agreed, it was not possible at such short notice.

In 1936, however, Knutsen succeeded. In the meantime he had completed studies of architecture, art and archaeology in England, and acquired a job with an architect company in Oslo. One day he read that Micard was preparing for a wintering expedition to North-East Greenland. Knutsen immediately sent a telegram to Micard in Tromsø. The brief reply arrived the next day, and read: *"Come, Micard"*.[424]

The Quest Expedition left Tromsø on the 6th August 1936, and comprised the following members: Count Gaston Micard, Paris; Captain Ludolf Schjelderup, Skånland; John Næss, mate of Tromsø; Ole G. Hansen, engineer of Lurøy; Ruben Goldmann, wireless operator of Hammerfest; Georg Eriksen, assistant engineer of Alta; Karl Skaugsvoll, steward of Gildeskål; Leif Lockert, cook of Tromsølund; Meyer Olsen, dog driver of Balsfjord; and the ship's crew Karl Nicolaisen (Tromsølund), August Jakobsen, (Lurøy), Egil Halvorsen (Bergen) and Willie Knutsen (Newcastle).

"It seems Schjelderup was something of an arctic buccaneer, helping himself to supplies from depots left by trappers who had gone back to Norway. His motto was, "Better that I get it, than the polar bears!" This might seem reasonable, Kalle said, except for the fact that these depots included building supplies and fuel intended for the next group of trappers to arrive. My new friend told me that the captain was a notorious skinflint, as well as a man who did not think that hunting conservation laws applied to him. Kalle added, "But he has the best arctic ship on the polar seas".[425]

The plan was to trap during the overwintering and for this purpose the expedition had rented a territory at Loch Fyne from Arctic Commercial Enterprise. On the 17th August 1936 "Quest" called at the Krogness station, a well known place to Meyer Olsen. Knutsen and Nicolaisen went ashore to winter here. The rest of the expedition members continued to the head of Loch Fyne, where "Quest" was to serve as their trappers' station during the winter. The territory was more or less well equipped with huts; however they built the following huts: "Schjelderup-hytten" [344], "Kalles hytte" [402], "Tobias Dal (vest)" [360], "Provianthus (Quest)" [351] and possibly

The Quest Expedition hunting walrus in Young Sund, 1937. Karl Nicolaisen (left) and Willie Knutsen. © Will C. Knutsen

"Quest" in winter harbour at the head of Loch Fyne 1936-37. © Will C. Knutsen

Gaston Micard (left) and Ludolf Schjelderup with Micards' unique palanquin sledge in front of Waltershausen Gletscher, spring 1937. © Will C. Knutsen

"Tobias Dal (øst)" [363]. The Provianthus (Quest) hut [351] was taken down in 1937 and used as fuel on the expedition's home voyage.

Egil Halvorsen was the expedition photographer. He had just returned from Spain where he had worked as a photographer during the Spanish civil war. In 1992, Halvorsen said of his first encounter with Gaston Micard: *"I was at the time working in a shop in Bergen selling sports equipment. I was then 21 or 22 years old. On a glorious summer day a foreign-speaking gentleman stepped into the shop, a neat little man. In English he said that he would like to purchase a pair of ski boots. This was somewhat remarkable, the weather and the season taken into consideration. So I asked him: – For what purpose? Where was he going to go skiing? Well, he answered, he was going to Greenland. I was curious and asked for a little more information. He told me that he had hired the "Quest" and Captain Schjelderup. I answered that it sounded very interesting and that I would like to come along. Well, it was not up to him to decide, but he gave me the address of Captain Schjelderup with whom I should get in contact. And I did, and I was permitted to come along – A year with no pay, but room and board included. But this was more than enough for an adventurous youth".*[426] Thanks to Egil Halvorsen a lot of film was recorded during the winter, and a good part of this still exists. Halvorsen also worked as a trapper, with the area from "Quest" towards Myggbukta as his territory.

"Karl "Kalle" Nicolaisen was a lad from Tromsø. When just 15-years old he had sailed on board a sealer to Spitsbergen and learnt to hunt and trap. The year before we met he had wintered there again. He had been a ship's master, but was hired as trapper on the "Quest". Kalle became a close friend and my companion during three expeditions to the Arctic." ... "During our breaks at Krogness, Kalle spent the time baking and tidying the hut. He had an unshakable spirit, and he would often hum to himself or sing one of his favourite tunes".[427] Willie Knutsen spent his free time on the local archaeology, and during the course of the winter produced quite a collection of paintings and drawings.

Knutsen and Nicolaisen celebrated their Christmas on "Quest", which was ice-bound a few kilometres from the head of Loch Fyne. This was where count Gaston Micard was living. Micard was a quiet character, introvert and thoughtful. He loved the Arctic, its vast stillness and indescribable beauty; here he felt at ease. He had a daily routine of walking around the ship, saying hello to each and every dog, following the snow track to the shore and then straight back to his cabin: *"In the cabin I keep my favourite biscuits, canned pears and my beloved detective stories. What more could I wish for?"*[428]

Gaston Micard (1879-1961) was raised in the aristocratic upper-class. His family included Ferdinand

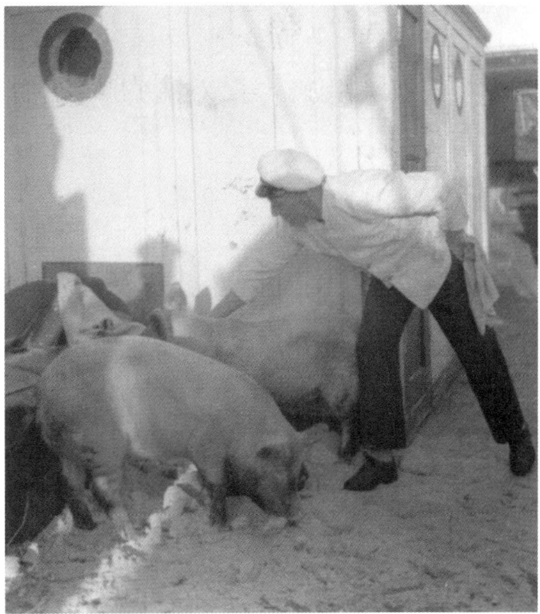

Fresh food supplies. Leif Lockert, cook of the Quest Expedition 1936-37, taking care of the pigs, which were kept on the "Quest" to be used for food during the overwintering © Will C. Knutsen

de Lesseps (1805-1894), who developed the plan for and was in charge of the construction of both the Suez Canal and the Ethiopian railway. Another relative was Pope Pius IX (1792-1878). Micard himself was extremely wealthy and had travelled widely. This journey to North-East Greenland was part of a plan to establish the northernmost all-year scientific station in the world.

Micard was well-liked, and his little eccentricities were accepted; for example he never travelled anywhere without taking along a French-educated chef, and never went outdoors - summer or winter - without his multicoloured parasol. He was quite a strange sight. The parasol was a symbol of his Ethiopian title of 'Count' that the Micard-family had received from the Ethiopian emperor, the grandfather of Emperor Haile Selassie; Gaston Micard was in fact both a French and Ethiopian count. His "palanquin sledge" was another remarkable arrangement - in principal this consisted of an ordinary dog sledge equipped with an armchair that could be turned through 180° as required. Seated in this, Micard could watch the passing scenery while his men carried out the hard work. In this way he even let himself be transported on some long trips, including a journey to Strindberg Land.

The fox trapping during the Quest Expedition amounted to about 160 fox furs. In July 1937, preparations were made for the return to Norway, via Ammassalik where he had promised to pick up the Frenchman Paul-Émile Victor, who had crossed the Greenland ice cap from west to east together with Eigil Knuth, Robert Gessain and Micha Perez.

Willie Knutsen and Karl Nicolaisen were the last to winter at Krogness. In 1938-39 they both went back for another wintering with Gaston Micard (see section on Micardbu [704]).

Bang 1944; Vervarslinga for Nord-Norge 1945; N032; N085; P134; R135; Willie Knutsen pers. comm.

Recent status

Krogness is located alongside the main north-south dog sledge route, and the station house is still maintained and used by the Sirius Dog Sledge Patrol today. The construction of the main house is unique, as it is largely built from local driftwood.

Krogness. The living house (left) is quite unique, made from driftwood. The provision shed (right) was made from several sections prefabricated in Norway. © NCN

Krogness [403], 9th August 2003. Krogness is a former Norwegian trappers' station built 1926 for the Foldvik Expedition. It was used as a trappers' station until 1937, and thereafter as a travellers' hut maintained by Sirius. (Left and Below) The living house, inside and outside. (Bottom) View across Godthåb Golf towards Blosseville Bjerg, Copeland Fjord and Clavering Ø. © NCN

LAPLACE
[301]

Wintering party
1938-39: Ole Klokset, Yngve Friberg

1938-39
Ole Klokset, a 37-year-old trapper from Tennfjord, longed to be back in North-East Greenland, and he had a plan. He intended to charter a ship in order to penetrate the pack ice as far north as possible in North-East Greenland. Having arrived at his destination, he planned to build a station for wintering and from there travel northwards by sledge towards Peary Land.

Klokset chartered the "Grande" of Sandshamn. This was one of the smallest ships in the Sunnmøre arctic fleet, only 80 gross tons. The master was Bernt Hide. On the 18th July 1938, "Grande" left Ålesund with 14 people on board, including some of Klokset's family as well as Einar Sverre Pedersen, who later became the chief navigator in Scandinavian Airlines System (SAS) and one of the originators of the SAS north polar routes. In his book "Polarbasillen" (the polar germ) (1969) Pedersen describes the summer journey with Klokset.

"Grande" reached the Greenland coast during the last days of July. They then tried to go north, but were stopped by pack-ice off Bass Rock. Klokset decided to make another attempt in the middle of August and in the meantime fish arctic char at Zackenberg. At the entrance to Young Sund they met the "En Avant" with Willie Knutsen and Gaston Micard, and learnt of their plans to establish a station on the coast of Germania Land. "Polarbjørn" and "Veslekari" were already at Zackenberg. It was becoming crowded, and Klokset's private initiative was not welcomed by the established trapping companies such as Arctic Commercial Enterprise: *"John Giæver, the leader of the relief expedition, was not at all gentle. He told me straight out: "You should have come with us instead of that pirate ship you have come with." I answered that I was doing fine amongst my friends, the pirates on board the "Grande", and that was the end of that discussion".*[429]

One day the char were gone and the fishing was over. They now loaded twenty barrels of sugar-salted char onto the deck of "Grande", but their plan to go north had been abandoned. Instead they sailed south to hunt for muskox in Dusén Fjord. Ole Klokset wondered where to build his winter house; Bontekoe Ø was one possibility as he anticipated it would be good polar bear terrain. However, in the event he chose to build his station at the foot of Laplace Bjerg on the north side of Geographical Society Ø. The surroundings were well known to Klokset, as it was only 18 km from Kap Humboldt station where he had wintered for Arctic Commercial Enterprise in 1933-35. He had now become a rival to his old company, which later claimed that he had placed his "Laplace" station too close to the Kap Humboldt territory.
The place name "Laplace" derives from William Scoresby Junior's 1822 voyage, and was given for Pierre Simon, Marquis de Laplace (1749-1827), a French astronomer and mathematician.

"As soon as we had arrived we started unloading

Laplace c. 1940. © Hans K. Siewers

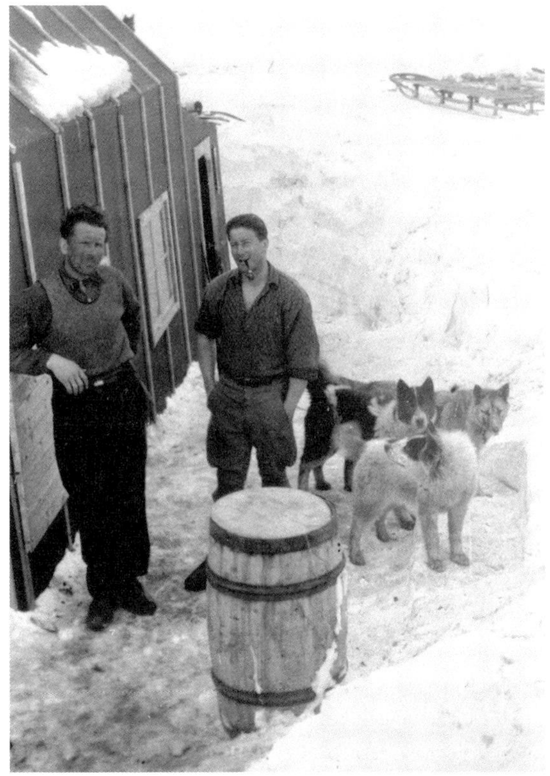

Ole Klokset (left) and Yngve Friberg at Laplace, spring 1939. © Jørgen Tvermose

materials and supplies. It was quite hard work as it was rather shallow water at the coast below Laplace Bjerg. First of all we had to load the goods into the trappers' boats and row ashore. As the boats could not go all the way to the beach we had to carry the load on our backs the final distance. Twenty-four hours a day we staggered through the breakers until everything was finally ashore. The wintering party were going to build the station themselves later in the autumn".[430] Having landed the materials, the expedition sailed northwards to Moskusoksefjord to hunt muskox. After they returned they built "Kloksethytten" [323] and possibly "Solstrand" [366], and: *"when we were off the Laplace foreland, the two winterers climbed down to their little green motor boat, started their engine and disappeared towards land".*[431]

When "Grande" had left for Norway, Klokset and his Swedish partner, Yngve Friberg, started to build their station: *"and it became a good and warm cabin"*, the 81-year-old Ole Klokset recalled in 1992. With a laugh he then added: *"But one day it got a large hole in the roof."* Friberg was cleaning the house one day and a couple of guns were in his way: *"I was sitting in the living room"*, Klokset said. *"Then there was a shot followed by silence. Not a sound. And I thought: – Hell, he has shot himself. So I jumped up to see what had happened, and there he stood gazing up through a hole in the ceiling. And the brim of his cap – Friberg had a cap with a long brim – the bullet had gone right through it".*[432]

Klokset trapped along the outer coast of Traill Ø as well as in the valleys in Hudson Land, which was a fine territory with many muskoxen. Unfortunately it was more than 100 km from Laplace. A trip to Hudson Land would take Klokset more than a month. During this time he lived in a tent. He carried with him only the most important items on his sledge - tent, sleeping bag and primus: *"And I had plenty of sugar and margarine. Then I shot muskox. I lived on muskox meat all the time, you know"*, he recalled.[433]

Regrettably, Klokset later lost his diaries, but he remembered it as a winter without major incidents. The catch consisted of 58 foxes, two bears and 15 ermines.

Norwegian Greenland veterans meeting at Ålesund Museum, Norway. From left: Henrik Landmark (leader of Ålesund Museum), Johan Listhaug, Ivar Ytreland and Ole Klokset. 20th July 1991. © Peter Schmidt Mikkelsen

Laplace, 5th May 1979. © Peter Schmidt Mikkelsen

The Laplace station was only used for wintering that one year, and Klokset said that he sold the station in the spring of 1940. Shortly after the outbreak of war he had a call from the Dane Jørgen Tvermose (of the Furenak Expedition), who purchased Laplace for 1000 kroner. However, Tvermose never had an opportunity to use the house. Ole Klokset died in December 1996, at the age of 90.

Recent status

In 1950, Laplace was acquired by the Danish government for use by Operation Resolut. Use of the house probably ceased in the 1960s, and today it is in such poor condition that it would be difficult to renovate.

Laplace, 7th August 2006. © NCN

Laplace [301], 7th August 2006. Laplace is a former Norwegian trappers' station built in 1938 for the Ole Klokset Expedition. It was used as a trappers' station only in 1938-39. Afterwards it was neither used much nor maintained. It is therefore today in a poor condition. *© NCN*

LIAVÅG
[441-3]

Wintering party
1929-30: Eilif Herdal, Otto Johnsen

1929-30
In the summer of 1929, Arctic Commercial Enterprise managed to establish trappers' stations in the area south of Myggbukta. However, plans to build a station on Kuhn Ø were not implemented because of unbroken winter ice between Shannon and Kap Wynn. The materials for the planned Kuhn Ø station were therefore landed at a small valley about three km south of Kap Wynn, which subsequently became known as Landingsdalen. The plan was that the four trappers who were going to stay in the northern territory should transport the materials to their destination by motor boat. However, mishaps and other circumstances meant that this plan was never initiated. The only house built was a new station at Kap Wynn: *"and even this could not have been done, had not director J.G. Jennov of "Nanok" been kind enough to transport the materials there,"* John Giæver wrote.[435]

Eilif Herdal and Otto Johnsen erected the house, and called it "Liavåg" in memory of Severin Gåsnes Liavåg, who had built Kopperneshuset in 1908 - the first house at Kap Wynn. In 1928, the Hird Expedition had used the remaining timbers from Kopperneshuset to build a smaller hut they called Gåsneshuset, and the Liavåg house was placed beside it. Herdal and Johnsen wintered here in 1929-30.

On the 20th November 1929, Andreas Hvidberg wrote: *"Their house was 6 feet wide and 14 feet long* (190 x 440 cm) *with a door and a stove at the one end and two berths at the other. The house was completely buried by snow and they had dug the passage through which we entered. From the outside the snowdrift with its round entrance looked like a polar bear's winter lair, but inside it was nice. What a reception we got. A joint of muskox was produced and the whole leg was put in the oven; while it roasted we had fresh lemons in water for soft drinks, and a lunch with herrings, liver pate, sardines, cheese and coffee, something we had not enjoyed for ages. Even the dinner, rare roast of young muskox with cranberries, and the dessert, preserved apricots with whipped cream, was a meal you would die for! When the six of us had eaten our fill of that roast there was not much left, and we were so full that we were swollen close to bursting. Johnsen, what a great story teller he was – although his language is unfortunately not reproducible and certainly not in print. Cigarettes, tobacco, lemon juice, red-currant juice was still offered as time went by. We were about to go home and started to get ready when* (Evald) *Rasmussen came in, saying that it was snowing and blowing heavily outside. We could hear nothing beneath all that snow; and yes, we could not leave in the darkness in the blizzard with all the gaps in the ice. "That's great" Johnsen said, "I just had another story to tell".*[436]

Liavåg was only used for wintering in 1929-30. The house was later used as a trappers' hut, but despite the inevitable decay over the years it still stands at the location where Herdal's and Johnsen's modest catch was loaded on board the "Veslekari" on the 20th July 1930.

Description ... 1932; Orvin 1930, 1931.

Recent status
Liavåg has probably not been used or maintained since the 1950s. The house is today in a poor state, but might still be renovated as the woodwork is in a reasonable condition.

Gåsneshuset (left) and Liavåg c. 1930.
© Svein Torske

Liavåg [441-3], 6th August 2004. Liavåg is a former Norwegian trappers' station built in 1929 for Arctic Commercial Enterprise. It was used as a trappers' station only in 1929-30, and thereafter as a travellers' hut until the 1960s. (Left) View south-eastwards towards Kap Wynn. (Centre) Interior of Liavåg. (Bottom) View north-west towards Claveringstrædet. Kronebjerg is the mountain with the characteristic flat top right above the hut. © NCN

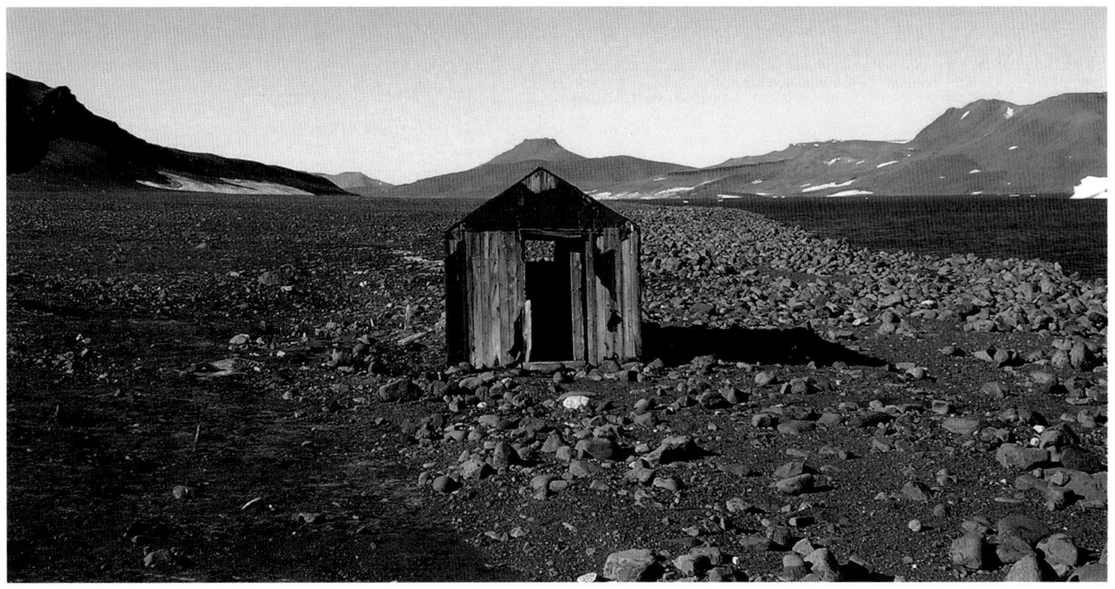

LOCH FYNE
[350]

Wintering party
1945-46: Henry V. Nielsen, Svend Søegaard
1946-47: Ib Bach Hansen
1947-48: Kjeld Soelberg, Erling Pedersen *
1948-49: Johannes Sørensen, Steen Egon Petersen
1949-50: Hans Egede Jacobsen, Iver Carsten Iversen
1950-51: Hans Madsen, Knud Erik Filskov
1951-52: Hans Madsen, Svend Olsen
* Wintered partly at Sandodden

On the 22nd August 1821, Captain Douglas Clavering and his crew reached the entrance of an unknown fjord: *"Proceeded up the inlet, the head of which we soon reached: it terminated in low marshy land, about eighteen miles from its entrance from the bay; named it Loch Fine"*.[437]

Loch Fine (and other places named by Clavering) was named after a location in Scotland. J.M. Wordie's Cambridge Expeditions to East Greenland in 1926 and 1929 modernised the spelling to "Loch Fyne" on their maps, and this spelling was later adopted by the Greenland place names committee.

1945-46

In the afternoon of the 9th August 1945: *"the "Godthaab" quite unexpectedly ran aground at the head of Loch Fyne where the depth according to the sea chart should have been more that 50 metres. The ship is stuck on a bottom of clay and sand. Unfortunately it happened at high tide. In the evening I went ashore to look for a location for the Loch Fyne house and found a well suited place with a natural harbour for motor boats"*.[438] These words come from J.G. Jennov's diary, and mark the establishment of the new Nanok station, "Loch Fyne". The following day "Godthaab" came afloat again, and: *"sailed to the place on the west bank, where the Loch Fyne station will be placed. They anchored in about 20 metres of water"*.[439] The house was built on the 11th and 12th August and was: *"more or less finished by the morning of the 13th. The trappers have been working 16 and 24 hours respectively for the last two days"*.[440]

It would be wrong to characterize Jennov's decision to build the Loch Fyne station as a signal of reconciliation towards the Norwegians, who in 1945 had not yet been allowed to enter Greenland. The matter also caused quite a turmoil and was discussed at the Nanok board meeting on the 12th October 1945: *"Already prior to "Godthaab"'s return, engineer Tuxen had informed the board that the Greenland Administration had received a report from Captain Ib Poulsen, in which Nanok's decision to place a station in Loch Fyne was harshly criticized, as it was pointed out that it was a matter that could provoke the Norwegians. At this time – when there was so much talk about Danish-Norwegian co-operation – this is even more unfortunate. Director Oldendow* (of the Greenland Administration) *was said to be rather alarmed by the incident"*.[441] Jennov justified his actions by saying that Nanok had needed a replacement for the Knudshoved station, where it was often difficult to get ashore and that he did not wish to force the Norwegians away from the east side of Loch Fyne, but only use the west side of the fjord and the valleys beyond where the Norwegians had never undertaken any serious trapping. How the Norwegians would react was uncertain; but the station was now a fact and after a long debate the board decided to wait and see. Norwegian criticism did come, but only from Arctic Commercial Enterprise. Neither the Norwegian nor Danish authorities apparently wanted to make this incident a national matter.

Later Danish as well as Norwegian trappers have

Loch Fyne c. 1954. © Hans Madsen

characterized the Loch Fyne station as one of the best-built trappers' stations in North-East Greenland. In 1945-46 it was manned by Henry V. Nielsen and Svend Søegaard. The 39-year-old Nielsen, who had also wintered in 1932-35, was leader of Nanok's wintering team. Søegaard, nicknamed "Fup", was a metalworker and a novice in North-East Greenland. They both went home to Denmark in the summer of 1946.

1946-47

Ib Bach Hansen, who was at Knudshoved in 1945-46, demanded the entire Loch Fyne territory to himself if he was going to continue trapping in Greenland – and he got it.

The same summer, the Norwegian trappers returned to North-East Greenland, and even though Nanok had wedged the Loch Fyne station into what had been Norwegian territory, there were apparently no hard feelings between Danish and Norwegian trappers. Bach Hansen had a distance of about 120 km to his nearest countrymen at Zackenberg and Sandodden, and he presumably was pleased to have a visitor on the 29th November 1946, when: *"a Norwegian from Bundhytten came to visit me. He was a nice chap and invited me to spend Christmas at Myggbukta".*[442]

After the Christmas visit at Myggbukta, Bach Hansen often stopped off to visit the Norwegians when returning from his territory on the east side of Hold with Hope. Only twice, in February and May, did he briefly visit his countrymen at Young Sund. On both occasions Bach Hansen made the journey in one long stretch, taking only a couple of hours rest for himself and the dogs at Moskusheimen.

Bach Hansen did not trap west of Loch Fyne in the Stordal area, but during the spring of 1947 he took several loads of material into Stordal and built the "Arvehytten" [353]. His catch numbered 101 foxes.

On the 12th August 1947, the "Gustav Holm" arrived and Bach Hansen realized that: *"he had lost two days in his calendar during the winter, and discovered that it was his birthday, which of course called for an extra schnapps and later a rum toddy. Kjeld Soelberg and Erling Pedersen went ashore after having been introduced to the conditions by Bach Hansen".*[443] Bach Hansen, who was originally a carpenter, returned with "Gustav Holm" to Denmark. Later he went to Canada where he once more became a trapper.

1947-48

On the 31st August 1947, there was a curious incident at the Loch Fyne station of which the news soon spread along the entire coast during the winter. The Norwegian Ivar Ytreland, who was at Kap Herschell at the time, recalled in 1991: *"Director Jennov, who by the way was a charming fellow, had some fixed ideas about transport. He had the obsession that it was possible to trap inland, for example in Stordalen that lay west of Loch Fyne. Jennov had purchased in Copenhagen a three-wheeled carrier cycle. In front it had a sign saying "Christianshavn Budcentral", and he expected that Kjeld Soelberg and Erling Pedersen* (who were at Loch Fyne in 1947-48) *would use it for carrying equipment and materials into Stordalen – a hopeless project ... But Kjeld had stayed the year before at Sandodden, and knew what the terrain was like, so the tricycle just stood parked behind the station house.*

Anyway, one day in the early autumn, they had shot a muskox behind the station – it was good muskox territory at Loch Fyne you know. And so Kjeld Soelberg thought of using the "Alpe-gondola" – which they had named the tricycle – to fetch the muskox. While Erling watched with mouth wide open he harnessed their ten sledge dogs to the trike. Kjeld told me this story:

The dogs scowled suspiciously at the apparatus;

J.G. Jennov (facing camera) had new ideas about transport using different types of vehicles. The photograph shows one of his prototypes, used in 1951 to transport hut materials into the Hold with Hope area. © *Hans Madsen*

The wreckage of "Alpe-gondola", 1990. © *K. Cowan*

but I mounted the trike, loosened the handbrake, rang the bell and cracked the whip. The dogs looked back now and then; but we got to the muskox alright. I then turned the trike so it was headed towards the station, pulled the handbrake and put a rock under the wheels.

We then cut up the muskox, and loaded half of the meat on the carrier at the front of the tricycle. Erling removed the rocks, I rang the bell, cracked the whip and let go of the handbrake. The dogs rushed off in fear and terror, for the trike bounced violently. I stood on the brake, but...there was this big rock...and then the dog team divided into two around the rock. One of the front wheels hit the rock, the trike stopped abruptly and I was thrown what seemed like twenty metres into the air and over the dogs and crashed head first into the ground. When I came to, I heard hysterical laughter. It was Erling – he thought I had died. We laughed – but Erling laughed most".[444]

From Erling Pedersen's note in the station journal it appears that: *"the trike is repairable. We will fetch the remaining meat later on by sledge"*.[445]

At the beginning of February, Erling Pedersen left Loch Fyne to stay at Sandodden. In May Soelberg went to Zackenberg to spend the summer, taking with him the year's catch, only 11 foxes. Both Soelberg (from Copenhagen) and Pedersen (from Køge) returned to Denmark in the summer of 1948.

1948-49

In 1948, the Loch Fyne station was once again handed over to two men from Sjælland, namely Steen Egon Petersen, a motor-mechanic from Ringsted and Johannes Sørensen from Copenhagen. Neither had any experience with trapping and according to the station journal the major problem of the autumn was: how does one build a dog sledge? *"As we have no experience, we don't really know how to do it; but we are going to make a sledge each the way we think it should be done. Then, when the snow falls, we will see which one is the better"*.[446] After their first journey through their trapping territory and a visit to the Norwegians at Myggbukta, Petersen and Sørensen had learnt one thing, that: *"our sledges are far too heavy, so we will have to rebuild them and will try to make a couple of ski-sledges using some large skis we have here at the station"*.[447]

The trapping was not going well. They had not caught a single fox when at the beginning of February they returned to Loch Fyne after a Christmas visit to Zackenberg and Daneborg. Sørensen decided to go north to Danmarkshavn and try his luck there, while Petersen remained at Loch Fyne. Sørensen's trapping success is unknown, but according to the station journal, Petersen had caught only two foxes when he left the station at the beginning of April 1949 to spend the summer at Zackenberg. Sørensen returned to Denmark in the summer of 1949, whereas Petersen took employment at Danmarkshavn Weather Station.

1949-50

After the record low catch in 1949-49 the: *"catch in the Loch Fyne territory in 1949-50 was fair, the conditions taken into consideration"*.[448] Hans Egede Jacobsen and Iver Carsten Iversen had a total catch of 41 foxes, mainly caught along the west side of Loch Fyne.

In the spring of 1950, the two trappers - both novices - tried out bear hunting from Knudshoved and "Arundelhytten" [364], which had been built in 1949. Early one morning, on the 12th April at Knudshoved: *"one of the dogs, Splint, gave his well known signal: vof, vof, vof. We both rushed out. A magnificent sight met us, a large, old female bear with two cubs coming straight towards the dogs, and now it was showtime. All the dogs pulled and dragged at their*

Loch Fyne c. 1954.
© Hans Madsen

chains. We let a couple loose and they raced to the bear that was now on the warpath. One dog came too close and was thrown several metres into the air; it ran wailing back to the station. We soon reached the bear and I shot and killed it with a single bullet. We had some difficulty with the two large cubs, but eventually managed to get them into the living room of the station, although Hans received a few scratches on his behind".[449] One of the cubs had to be put down the next day, because the dogs had injured it too badly. The other cub they took back to Loch Fyne, but it became ill and died three weeks later.

Jacobsen and Iversen stayed for the summer at Loch Fyne, and on the 2nd August their replacements arrived. Jennov arrived by motor boat with the two new trappers, Hans Madsen and Knud Erik Filskov: *"The station is in excellent condition and the furs were well-treated. After Iversen and Jacobsen had packed their clothes we left Loch Fyne on the 3rd August at 7 o'clock".*[450] Iversen returned to Denmark the same summer, while Jacobsen was taken on as cook at Danmarkshavn Weather Station. Subsequently he made his career in the shipping department of the Royal Greenland Trading Company (KGH).

1950-51

Hans Madsen was a 29-year-old night watchman in Copenhagen, when he heard that Nanok was hiring trappers, so: *"then I took my bike and went out to see Jennov. He lived at Store Møllevej 5"*, Madsen recalled in 1992.[451] Jennov immediately hired the even-tempered Madsen, originally from west Jutland, who had been hunting and fishing since his boyhood days near Agerbæk. His salary was 1000 kroner per year plus 50% of the catch, and fox-furs were then selling for an average of 70 kroner each. Madsen wintered in North-East Greenland for five years altogether. The first two were for Nanok, followed by one year at Daneborg Weather Station. After a year back in Denmark in 1953-54, he returned in 1954-56 for another spell at the weather station. He has no regrets, for: *"you could not be better off anywhere else. It's as simple as that. You had everything. You had a motor boat in the summer, you could go hunting and fishing, and nobody interfered with what you were doing".*[452]

Hans Madsen c. 1951. © Hans Madsen

Knud Erik Filskov, Madsen's partner, was from southern Jutland, 20-years old and the youngest member of the Nanok team. By profession he was a grocer: *"but since childhood I had loved nature in the wintertime"*,[453] and it was a dream come true when his application for Nanok was accepted with very short notice. Yet Filskov had only one winter as trapper.

One of the tasks that autumn was to build a new hut, "Danske Villa" [370] at Strømmen in Loch Fyne. While Madsen and Filskov were there, they had a strange experience. They spotted some white dots in the water that at first they thought was foam. Then they realised that it was a fox that: *"swam across the fjord – a swim of about 1500 m in the freezing water. During the six days we have been there, we have seen five foxes crossing, three at the same time. Today another one crossed; but as we were hunting seal at the same*

Knud Erik Filskov, 1950-51. © Hans Madsen

Loch Fyne, 9th August 1978. © Peter Schmidt Mikkelsen

time we followed the fox and caught it just before it came ashore. We lifted it up by its tail, washed it and took a couple of pictures while Filskov held it. However, when we put it back in the water, it swam back across the fjord again, although it was only 100 m from its original destination. All the other foxes crossed over to our side, but then we have also been treating them well".[454]

The 2nd February was always a special day at Loch Fyne, for that was the day the Polar Night ended and: *"the joy you feel and the feeling you have when you see the sun again after a night lasting 2½ months cannot be described. We both stood outside for a long time, enjoying the sight, even though only half the sun was above the horizon"*, Madsen wrote in the diary.

1951-52

"I have got a new partner, Svend Olsen from North Sjælland, 27-years old and a fisherman by trade. He seems to be a nice fellow and a keen hunter", Hans Madsen wrote on 1st September 1951.[456] It had been a busy summer with little time to maintain his diary. One of their many tasks was to build a new hut, "Vulkanhytten" [401]. They had also put out materials at "Kap Kraus" [908], but neither this hut nor the planned hut "Dybendal" [909], where Svend Olsen deposited materials for a new hut in the spring of 1952, were built before Nanok suspended its trapping activities the same summer.

Among the major incidents of their wintering was the encounter Madsen and Olsen had with an unusually robust polar bear. It took place at the beginning of November, when they were trapping from the Knudshoved station. One evening Svend Olsen came back and said he had found a bear's lair in a large snowdrift near the station. The bear had looked out, and he had fired a couple of shots at it, but did not dare to investigate whether the bear was dead.

The next morning they both walked over to the lair, and it turned out, that: *"there wasn't any dead bear in it, but on the contrary a large bear, very much alive and kicking"*.[457] Madsen shot at a distance of 75 m and the head of the bear again disappeared in the opening. They approached cautiously, and: *"when we came closer, we could see that blood had splashed onto the snow, so we assumed it was now dead and walked a little closer; but when about 10 m from the opening the bear once again looked out and stared at us"*. Madsen fired again twice, and the bear again disappeared. Now it had to be dead; but when Madsen arrived at the opening he could see the bear in the lair: *"it began to turn its head. But that was the end – it got a bullet between the eye and the ear"*. Both trappers were a bit shaken, mainly Svend Olsen, because: *"yesterday when Svend shot at it, he was standing only four steps from the lair, and had he walked two steps further he would have been right above the lair. If the snow had then collapsed he would have fallen right into the arms of the bear"*.[458] At the beginning of May 1952, they received the message that Nanok had suspended trapping, and as they could not expect any ship to call at Loch Fyne, Svend Olsen went to Daneborg to collect the motor boat. Hans Madsen: *"mostly lived on char these days. It is easy and quick to row out and drop a net. In a matter of minutes you have more char than you can use. Those I don't need, I let go and they are not hurt from being in the net. Today the whole operation lasted only 20 minutes. I caught three large char and let two go again; the third is simmering now at 00.30 and it's time to eat – boiled char with potatoes in white sauce and stewed prunes".*[459] On the 28th July, Svend Olsen returned with the motor boat and the following day he and Madsen went to Daneborg. This was the end of Loch Fyne as a manned Nanok station. However, it should be mentioned that Birger Larsen, a Norwegian trapper (see Myggbukta), stayed at the station for a period in 1953-54.

"Slædeposten" No. 75; A158; A159; A160; A170; A171; A172; P144; Nanok 1993.

Recent status

Loch Fyne is one of the best known stations in North-East Greenland. After the trapper era, it was used and maintained by Sirius. Eventually the old station needed a more thorough renovation, and Nanok sent out a three-member team in 1993 to restore Loch Fyne.[460] In the summer of 2002 the station house was further improved when a team from Sirius repaired the rotting roof.[461]

In 2007, a Nanok team gave the station house a new makeover: repairing the foundations, and tarring and painting the outside and inside.[462]

In the summer of 2002 the roof and the interior of the Loch Fyne station was repaired by a team from Sirius.
© Erik Jochumsen

Summer 2002, the roof of the Loch Fyne station being repaired by a team from Sirius. © Erik Jochumsen

(Right) Loch Fyne station and view eastwards to Hold with Hope. (Below). Loch Fyne main house. © NCN

Loch Fyne [350], 9th August 2003. Loch Fyne is a former Danish trappers' station built in 1945 for Nanok. It was used as a trappers' station until 1952, and later as a travellers' hut maintained by Sirius. (Left). Interior of Loch Fyne, one of the finest trappers' stations in North-East Greenland. (Below). The carriage used by Nanok in 1951 to transport hut materials in the Hold with Hope area. (Bottom) Loch Fyne station from the south. © NCN

MARISTUA
[236]

Wintering party
1930-31: Sverre J. Sørensen, Gustav Lindquist

1930-31
In the summer of 1929, Arctic Commercial Enterprise established a new trapping territory with Sverresborg as the main station. Experience from the winter of 1929-30 had shown that trapping in the eastern part of Vega Sund was impossible due to the thick layer of soft snow that accumulated in that area. However, the territory had to be maintained, and in haste it was decided to build a station on Ella Ø. On the 8th August 1930, "Veslekari" anchored about three km south of Kap Elisabeth and here the materials for the station were unloaded.

Sverre J. Sørensen, who had been leader at Sverresborg the previous year, was given the responsibility of building the station. Before the work could begin he had to wait at Myggbukta for the return of the motor boat from a long voyage to the north. When Sørensen and his partner Gustav Lindquist finally arrived at Ella Ø on the 1st September, they: *"were disappointed to find so little. There is not even material enough for a trappers hut".*[463] As a result they decided to sail to Sverresborg for extra materials: *"It will be a huge load and we may not be able to carry it all. We do not have much time to travel with the boat and we will not be able to get done half of what has been agreed. But that is how it is when the best month of the summer is wasted. It's a bloody nuisance that it has not been better prepared. In Myggbukta there are materials for a small church, whereas here on Ella Ø only some unusable wooden strips and hickory boards have been put ashore. And this is supposed to be a main station, ha, ha".*[464]

Finally, on the 9th September, they were able to start building the house - or rather hut - as the materials were not sufficient for anything larger. At first they called it "Camp Lindquist", but later named it "Maristua".

Sørensen and Lindquist did not find any muskoxen on Ella Ø and there was soon a shortage of food for themselves as well as their six dogs. They therefore had to hunt for muskoxen at other places, but the new ice and problems with the motor boat engine made the task difficult. Eventually they decided to move to Sverresborg, in case the conditions had miraculously improved there; but they only stayed at Sverresborg for a few days: it was a hopeless place for trapping.

Gustav Adolf Lindquist - nicknamed "Pusten" (the puff) - was from Tromsø and an experienced Svalbard trapper, and he was at a relatively high age when he came to North-East Greenland. He was known to have a quick and sometimes disrespectful temper. But he was also known for developing an effective version of the "self-shooter" in 1927, subsequently used by all trappers: *"It consists of a small square box with three legs which is placed in the snow. Inside the box is a shooting mechanism and a slice of blubber. When placed correctly at the right height above the snow, these self-shooters are 100% efficient. They are easy to erect – not like the old ones that could take an entire day to set up".*[465]

To Lindquist, Greenland was a huge disappointment. He wrote in his diary on the 24th December 1930: *"Well, this is Christmas Eve 1930, my 15th Christmas in the Artic. From my first wintering I had wanted to come here, as I believed there must be plenty to catch here, but this is the worst I have ever experienced. Would you believe only two foxes and*

Gustav Adolf Lindquist – nicknamed "Pusten". One of the pioneers and a colourful character amongst the trappers in North-East Greenland. *© Gustav Lindquist/Norwegian Polar Institute*

a bear before Christmas - it's almost unbelievable that it could be so bad here in Greenland. The worst place in Spitsbergen is better than this." ... "And this company (Arctic Commercial Enterprise) *does not even remember its men with a Christmas present; they have not sent as much as a cigar, and a bottle of liquor is of course taboo. I have worked and wintered for many different employers, and they have always sent a Christmas present to their men; but this company does not think of anything else but the money and annexing the land".*[466]

It was a continuous problem to obtain food for their dogs, and on the 28th February Lindquist wrote: *"Today we have travelled here and there looking for hare and ptarmigan, but without any result. Bloody hell, and then they say that East Greenland is one of the best hunting territories in the world. No, all we can do is to get out of here to other hunting fields and look for meat. At this location it is impossible to stay alive. It is hopeless – no fox, no bear and only a few hare and ptarmigan".*[467] All the same, Lindquist and Sørensen stayed at Maristua until the end of the trapping season, but the catch was only one bear and a few foxes.

Despite his disappointment over the trapping and the leadership in Arctic Commercial Enterprise Lindquist let himself be talked into staying for another winter, but at Myggbukta. He went home in the summer of 1932, and the following year wintered in Augustabukta in the south-western part of Nordaustlandet in Svalbard together with another trapper. Sadly it ended tragically. When the summer arrived two bodies were found in the ruins of the cabin: their powder supply had exploded.

After 1931 Maristua was not used as an independent trappers' station. However, Leif Brandal took up residence here during February-April 1933, after the Vega Sund territory had been combined with the Kap Humboldt territory.

Giæver 1957; Orvin 1931; N084; N088.

Recent status

After the trapper era Maristua was used and maintained by Sirius as a travellers' hut until about 1980. Although it has not been maintained for many years it is still in quite good condition.

Maristua, 5th August 1931. © Thor Askheim/ Norwegian Polar Institute

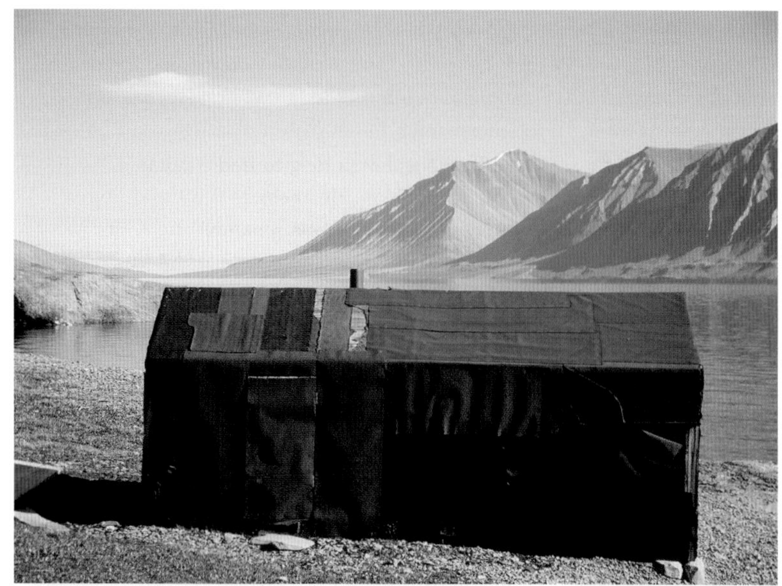

Maristua [236], 13th August 2003. Maristua is a former Norwegian trappers' station built in 1930 for Arctic Commercial Enterprise as a replacement for the Sverresborg station in Vega Sund. Maristua was only used as a trappers' station in 1930-31. It was later used as a travellers' hut until c. 1980. (Left) View over Kong Oscar Fjord looking north-east. From left: Fladedal, Rødebjerg, the entrance to Sofia Sund and Svedenborg Bjerg. (Centre). Interior of Maristua. (Bottom). Maristua seen from the north-east. © NCN

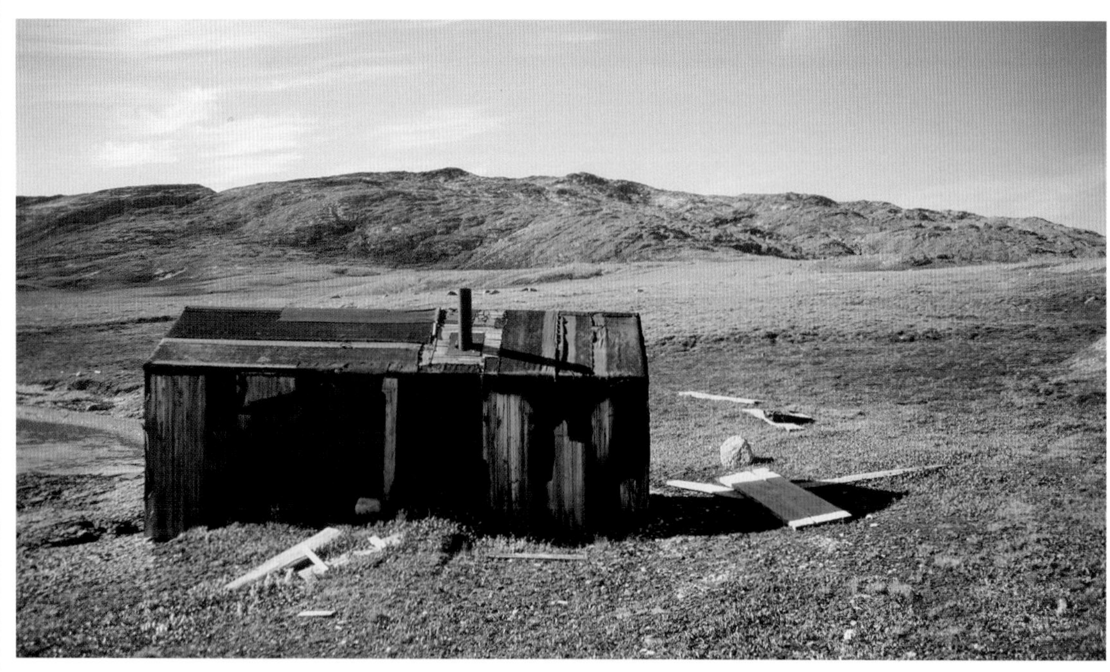

MICARDBU
[704]

Wintering party

1938-39: Gaston Micard, Willie Knutsen, Karl Nicolaisen, Kristian Hatlevik, Sigbjørn Aamodt, Ingvald Ingebrigtsen, Kristian Nielsen, William Jakobsen, Jess Tillier, Sigmund Snarby, Leif Olsen, Nils Nøis, Edvard Wilhelmsen.

1938-39

In the autumn of 1937, when Willie Knutsen came back to Norway with the "Quest" Expedition (see Krogness), he considered going to Svalbard to hunt polar bears together with his friend Karl Nicolaisen. However, on a train journey between Bergen and Oslo he met Arne Høygaard, who a few years earlier had crossed the Greenland ice cap. Høygaard suggested that Knutsen should instead undertake research work in unexplored parts of North-East Greenland, and soon Knutsen was deeply involved in planning a wintering expedition to Peary Land. Various Norwegian polar experts praised his plans and there was only one problem - the usual one - financing the expedition. Knutsen had no capital, but he knew someone who might be able to help, namely the French polar enthusiast Count Gaston Micard.

Knutsen went to Switzerland to meet Micard, who picked him up at the station. Five minutes later, Micard said: *"I'll buy the expedition!"* Thus "The Norwegian-French Polar Expedition" was a reality and with the millionaire Micard as guarantor it did not take Karl Nicolaisen long to find a suitable ship for the expedition. He chose the "Ringsel", which in honour of Micard was renamed "En Avant".

Knutsen himself had designed the expedition's winter house, which measured 7.5 x 6.5 metres. It was built from panels made by students from Statens Fag- & Forskole (a college) in Oslo, where Knutsen had previously studied to be an architect.

In July 1938 the expedition members gathered in Tromsø. Amongst the thirteen men there were three veterans from the Quest Expedition 1936-37, namely the leader Willie Knutsen, second in command Captain Karl Nicolaisen and Gaston Micard. The others were Edvard Wilhelmsen (mate), Ingvald Ingebrigtsen (engineer), Sigmund Snarby (engineer), Kristian Hatlevik (geophysicist), Sigbjørn Aamodt (wireless operator), Kristian Nielsen (wireless operator), William Jakobsen (cook), Leif Olsen (trapper), Nils Nøis (trapper) and Jess Tillier (wireless operator). Tillier was originally meant to be the pilot of the expedition's airplane, but he crashed it before the departure from Norway. He came along anyway, but as a third wireless operator.

"En Avant" safely reached Danmark Havn, where they were stopped by the pack ice. At the end of August a storm broke up the ice and they were able to continue northwards to Syttenkilometernæsset, where they were again stopped by the ice. During the journey to Greenland they had fed the dogs with margarine, and from the empty boxes they built the

Micardbu almost buried under the snow in May 1956. © *Erik Jensen*

hut "Margarinecentralen" [638] while waiting for improvements in ice conditions. A new storm again provided some open coastal water and "En Avant" succeeded in reaching 77°04'N, where on the 24th August they were stopped by solid ice. It was decided to build the winter house here. Ingolf Fjord, the original destination of the expedition, is several hundred kilometres further north, and would have to wait until next year.

While the other members of the expedition built the winter house, Knutsen and Leif Olsen went northwards to build "Thomas Thomsen Næs hytten" [707]. When they returned a couple of days later they were met by an encouraging sight: *"The station was almost finished. The three high antenna poles were up, the weather measuring equipment was ready and the house, large and spacious, was almost complete. The kitchen had a huge stove to make it easy for us to melt snow to water and a tank in the next room held several litres. Micard's room was next to the kitchen, and had French lace curtains and a good library. The rest of the men slept two in each room. Aamodt had a radio room, in which he could also organize his studies of the stars and the northern lights. All in all, a really civilized weather station and the northernmost in the world. The new house was named Micardbu".*[468]

The station was named after Count Gaston Micard (1879-1961), the generous Frenchman who financed the expedition. Micard was educated at École Polytechnique and was a "Docteur en droit". He had travelled widely, and visited Norway as a tourist for the first time in 1914. In the summer of 1927 he made a hunting expedition to Nordaustlandet and the sea around Franz Joseph Land with the "Quest". In 1931 he was back in the same areas with the "Isbjørn". In the summer of 1932 he went to North-East Greenland with "Quest", which he also used for wintering in 1936-37 in Loch Fyne (see Krogness).

The Norwegian-French Polar Expedition had several purposes. Firstly Micardbu was to be a weather station and transmit weather reports four times daily. Furthermore, Kristian Hatlevik (the geophysicist) was to undertake research of cosmic radiation and photograph the Aurora Borealis - the Northern Lights. The photography of the Northern Lights achieved a scientific breakthrough during the winter. Through co-operation with the Danish Mørkefjord Expedition they had altogether three observation locations: Micardbu, Mørkefjord and "En Avant". As these were located about 50 km from each other and formed more-or-less an equilateral triangle, it was possible on the 9th January 1939 to carry out the first ever triangulation of the Aurora Borealis, with the photography synchronized using radio connections between the three stations.

The expedition also had a commercial purpose,

Gaston Micard (in front) and Georg Eriksen visiting the Kap Mary station at Clavering Ø in 1936.
© Will C. Knutsen

namely fox trapping. They trapped between Micardbu and "En Avant", which had its winter harbour at the north point of Store Koldewey. Karl Nicolaisen and some of the crew stayed at the ship during the winter, and two trappers' huts were built on Store Koldewey: "Bergfjordhytten" [619] and "Dagmar Havn hytten" [620]. However, the total catch of the winter was only 12 foxes.[469]

At the beginning of April 1939, Gaston Micard became seriously ill and as his condition rapidly became worse, they began to check out the possibilities of an emergency flight from Norway. One of Widerøe's Stinson floatplanes was loaded on board the "Veslekari", which immediately set course for North-East Greenland. After six days they were near Shannon, and on May 19th the seaplane took off heading for Micardbu, about 300 km to the north. Off Micardbu there was a large opening in the sea ice that allowed the plane to land. Micard was carried on board, and the seaplane's pilot Erik Engnæs and wireless operator Helge Bjørnbu flew back with Micard and Willie Knutsen to "Veslekari". Knutsen went along at Micard's request.

In Oslo Micard was operated for kidney stones and prostate problems, and soon recovered: *"They removed almost a cup of stones. He shook it cheerfully. Officially it was said that he would have died within two days if the catheter had not been inserted as soon as he received treatment",*[470] Willie Knutsen wrote (1992). Knutsen and Micard kept in contact until Micard's death in 1961.

The successful air rescue of Micard was the first of its kind in North-East Greenland. Altogether, the Norwegian-French Polar Expedition had cost Micard about 200,000 kroner, including 50,000 kroner for the rescue. "En Avant" and the remaining expedition members returned to Norway under Karl Nicolaisen's leadership in August 1939. The homecoming was overshadowed by the tense political situation in Europe, which also put a definitive stop to Willie Knutsen's plans for a new wintering expedition.

In the summer of 1940, Knutsen went with "Ringsel" to Ammassalik, and from there onwards to the USA where he regained his American citizenship. During the first years of the war he worked as an architect in Alaska and other places. In 1942 he was asked to join the US Army Air Force as an instructor in arctic survival. He spent the major part of the war at Baffin Island in Canada, attached to the search-and-rescue service. After the war he worked for a few years as a civilian architect, but in 1948 again joined the American military forces and for the next 21 years was employed on different assignments helping to establish arctic defence systems for the USA. He was involved in establishing the Thule Air Base and the DEW-line radar stations. In 1957-58 he was in command of the floating ice island, T-3.

Willie Knutsen retired in 1969 and settled in Norway making paintings and sculptures of his arctic memories. By the summer of 1991, his summer residence at Vågå was filled by numerous paintings that witnessed his long and active life in the Arctic. One of his latest paintings showed an Inuit drum-dancer, whose soul in a trance visits the moon. The multitalented Willie Knutsen had this interesting explanation of this picture: *"The white man came to the moon for the first time in 1969, but the Inuit have been there for thousands of years"!*[471] Willie Knutsen died in July 1992. Shortly before his death he published his memoirs in: "Mitt Arktis" (1992). The book was later republished in English by his son, Will C. Knutsen, as "Arctic Sun on My Path" (2005).

Knuth 1942; Polarårboken 1939; Gerhardt Blaase pers. comm.; Egil Halvorsen pers. comm.

Recent status

Micardbu was not manned after 1939, and the house went into rapid decay. In 1960, Gerhardt Blaase and John Madsen from Danmarkshavn Weather Station pulled down the original house and built a smaller hut from the usable materials a hundred metres further inland. This hut was used by Sirius as a travellers' hut up to the 1980s.

Micardbu [704], 28th July 2006. Micardbu was a Norwegian scientific and trappers' station built in 1938 for the Norwegian-French Polar Expedition. It was used as a station only in 1938-39. Later it was used as a travellers' hut. In 1960 the original house was taken down and used to build a smaller hut further inland. (Top) In the foreground remains of the original Micardbu station from 1938, with the new, smaller hut from 1960 in the background. (Centre and Bottom). The hut from 1960.
© NCN

MOSKUSHEIMEN
[429]

Wintering party
1927-28: Hans Olsen, Arnulf Gisvold
1928-30: Henry Rudi, Finn Framnes-Hansen
1930-31: None
1931-32: Eilif Herdal, Knut O. Brandal
1932-33: Gerhard Antonsen, Arnljot Tolløfsen
1933-35: Gerhard Antonsen
1935-36: Gerhard Antonsen, Johan Johansen
1936-38: Gerhard Antonsen
1938-39: Gerhard Antonsen, (Oscar Bang)
1939-40: Henry Rudi, Schjølberg Nilsen, Kåre Rodahl
1940-42: Henry Rudi
1942-46: None
1946-47: Normann Andersen
1947-49: Normann Andersen, Gudrun Andersen
1949-51: Normann Andersen
1951-52: Dagfinn Egeberg
1952-54: Normann Andersen, Gudrun Andersen
1954-55: Sverre Storholt
1955-56: Asbjørn Tøndell
1956-59: Harald Sverdsten
1959-60: Viggo Block

1927-28
The story of Moskusheimen at Revet began one day in the summer of 1927. During the winter of 1926-27, the pioneers of the Foldvik Expedition had gained some experience. The Norwegian trapping territories had to be expanded, and while certain areas had turned out either to lack wildlife or to be impassable due to snow, other areas such as the western part of Clavering Ø seemed promising. There were foxes and snow conditions were generally favourable. Revet was in the centre of this area and they decided to locate a trappers' station here. Nils Foldvik described it this way: *"Main station. Name "Tyrolerheimen". House of planks covered with roofing felt and turf. Wooden floor. Size 2.80 x 2.30 m. Porch size 2.30 x 2.00 m. Stove with oven. One window in the living room and one in the hallway. River close by. The house is situated at a very pleasant spot. The sound between Revet and Clavering Ø dries out at low tide".*[472]

The same summer they built several trappers' huts around the station: to the north "Bakkehaug" [435], "Meyer-hus" [439] and "Gisvold" [436], and to the south "Jordan-stranda" [409-1], "Nes-odden" [414] and a hut north of Kap Oetker [420]. Few details are known about the winter of 1927-28 when Hans Olsen and Arnulf Gisvold lived at the station. In Myggbukta Nils Foldvik wrote on the 3rd April 1928: *"Øien and I went from Loch Fyne at noon. Tail-wind but slow going. Gisvold was here when we arrived. He tells us that he and Hans have 46 foxes, five of them blue".*[473]

1928-29
When Finn Devold's expedition took over the territory in the summer of 1928, they built a new station house and named it "Moskusheimen". The house from 1927, Tyrolerheimen, was subsequently used as a depot shed.

"Moskusheimen" was built and manned by Finn Framnes-Hansen and Henry Rudi, men with totally different backgrounds.

Framnes-Hansen was then 27-years old, and it was his first wintering. In 1927 he had completed his training as an engineer, but with no immediate prospect of employment at home, he accepted an offer to go to Greenland. This was the first of a total of seven winterings, including two in South-East Greenland.

The 39-year-old trapper, Henry Rudi (1889-1970), had already twenty years of experience in the Arctic, although this was his first trip to Greenland. So far Svalbard had been his world. His parents had given him a commercial education, but by the time he was 18 he had had enough of being a shopkeeper in his home town of Tromsø. He wanted to be a trapper like his older brother Olaf. Luckily as it turned out, his first ship sailed without him, as the following year the

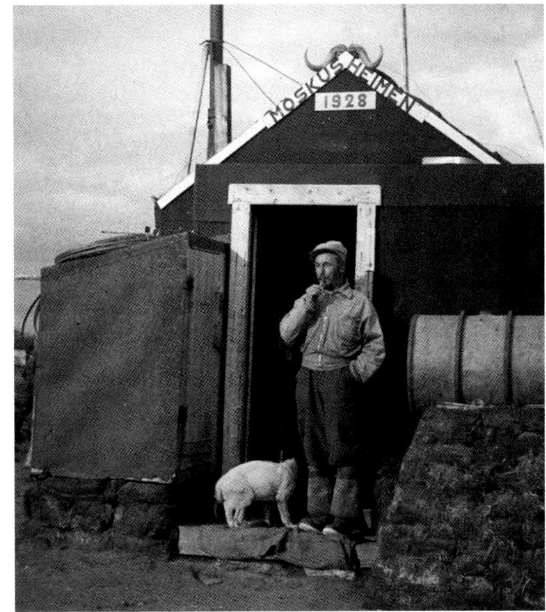

Henry Rudi – "The Polar Bear King" – at Moskusheimen in 1941. © Niels Ove Jensen

captain and the three crew members were found dead next to their hut in Nordaustlandet. However, in 1908 Rudi had his first wintering on Hopen, one of the islands in Svalbard. His companion was a Swedish trapper, who taught him the duties and serious aspects that came with the trapping profession: *"When you take on killing, you must do it humanely, painlessly. It is the only way you can defend being a human and a trapper." ... "The devil who would torment a creature to death, – I will personally kill!"* the Swede swore.[474] After this first wintering many winterings followed. Rudi had also breaks between his trips and winterings when he stayed at home in Norway; and: *"the toughest wintering a trapper can endure is a winter in Tromsø"*, Rudi believed, for the dust from the wintering was flushed with beer – a lot of beer.

"Greenland? The possibility had not occurred to me, so to speak", Rudi recalled; not until the day he accepted Finn Devold's offer in 1928: *"But what a country! Old Svalbard is nothing compared to this; here everything is so much more spacious, both the plains and mountains. Wide open vistas and unknown valleys lay magically before our eyes."* Rudi and Framnes-Hansen were set ashore near Revet, where: *"we built a new station, a fine and solid building, into which we put all our efforts. It was quickly done in the summer weather. While we were working a herd of muskox approached, strolling around as if they belonged here and would like to enter the house. We therefore agreed to call our station "Moskusheimen". Yes! That was the name for it, now and forever"*.[475]

Even though the territory was already well supplied with huts they also built "Skrænthytten" [440] and moved "Kap Oetker" [420] to Breivik [404-1].

Rumour has it that there was one thing the legendary Henry Rudi never really learnt to manage, namely sledge dogs: *"We had taken over twenty-four dogs from the Foldvik Expedition, four for each man to be responsible for. This was new to me and I must say that these animals made a hell of a racket"*.[476] In Svalbard most trappers considered it was stupid to bring dogs, as they scared off the foxes. Nevertheless, the trapper Hilmar Nøis had used sledge dogs on Svalbard with good results and probably inspired by his example the Foldvik Expedition took along sledge dogs. Even Rudi came to see their advantages because: *"when the winter came and we were going to travel in the territory, I immediately realized that without sledge dogs, it would be impossible. The land is so vast, the distances so immense, one would get nowhere without a well-trained dog team"*.[477]

In the middle of April 1929, Rudi and Finn Devold went northwards to look for traces of Roald Amundsen who had disappeared in 1928 during a flight from Tromsø to Svalbard, with the purpose of solving the disappearance of the airship "Italia". Rudi and Devold had intended going as far as Danmark Havn, but when they reached Haystack they found that their paraffin drum was leaking. They were forced to give up and return south again.

1929-30

To Henry Rudi the winter of 1929-30 was just another one in the line; but in March 1930 something remarkable happened. One day he stumbled across a lot of tracks in the snow. Polar wolves! – and a whole pack too: *"It took me only one hour or so to place a poisoned bait and I sincerely hoped that they were as hungry as a wolf is supposed to be. And yes, the following day eight of them lay in the snow, stone dead and frozen stiff"*.[478] Eight wolves at the one and same bait – a sensation! He put one of them on the sledge and went off home, now Framnes-Hansen was going to have a surprise: *"We had got visitors. Winther and Knoph* (from Krogness) *had arrived. Great, even more to surprise. They didn't believe me when I told them, that I had a bunch of wolves, which I was going to fetch in the morning. So I didn't want too much to drink tonight, – it could wait until later, hm! Just two-three glasses, the right amount for a wolf hunter. The guys came along to my wolf spot and their faces fell. I was delighted there in the snow"*,[479] Rudi said. It was also Henry Rudi, who got the nickname "The Polar Bear King", as he in his long life as a trapper had killed no less than 713 polar bears. An unequalled record in world history.

Rudi and Framnes-Hansen went back to Norway in 1930; but both followed Finn Devold to South-East Greenland in 1931-33 and both later on came back to North-East Greenland; Framnes-Hansen in 1935 and Rudi in 1939. Moskusheimen was unmanned in 1930-31.

1931-32

In the summer of 1931, Arctic Commercial Enterprise could barely manage to assemble a full wintering team. Of the trappers who had arrived in 1929, only Hallvard Devold and Eilif Herdal wanted to continue for another season. However, in the event Gustav Lindquist was also persuaded and: *"instead of two trappers who had originally intended to stay for another year but changed their minds at the last moment and went home, I got hold of two men, Knut Brandal and Bernt Marø, who were on board "Polarbjørn","* Hallvard Devold wrote.[480] Well done – the two sailors from Sunnmøre who had just come along for the summer trip and stayed on for the winter.

It was Eilif Herdal and Knut O. Brandal who were to take over Moskusheimen. On the 12th August they went ashore and immediately began to make ready the territory for the winter. On the 30th August

1931 Herdal wrote: *"Since the 22nd we have been out with the boat laying depots of food and coal from Clavering Ø to Krogness. We have erected new traps all the way and found some old ones. At Krogness we have taken down the old porch and built a smaller one, and taken the surplus material to Granta Fjord".*[481] This surplus material was used to build "Granta-botn" [426]. Brandal worked the northern territory from Revet to Tyrolerfjord and Zackenberg. Herdal's trapping territory was bounded by the huts Breivik, Ørnereiret, Krogness and Jordanstranda; he also trapped in Loch Fyne, an area that normally belonged to Myggbukta. On the 17th November Herdal returned from his first trip: *"My entire trapping territory is prepared and ready. I'll only need a few more traps in addition to the 174 traps already put up. In Brandal's territory there are just 60 traps".*[482]

At Christmas it was traditional to visit one's nearest neighbours. Although Norway and Denmark were now at "war" over "Eirik Raudes Land" this was not sufficient reason to miss out on a delicious Danish Christmas dinner. So Herdal, together with Gustav Lindquist and Bernt Marø from Myggbukta, went on the usual Christmas visit to the Danes at Eskimonæs. They arrived at just the right time: *"24/12. Went to Eskimonæs. Terrible going but arrived more or less as the Danes were preparing Christmas dinner. We were well received and will stay here for a few days".*[483]

On 21st May, Herdal drew up the result of their fox trapping: *"It was 89 for me and 40 for Brandal".*[484] He and Brandal went home in 1932, but both returned for another season with Arctic Commercial Enterprise in 1933.

1932-33

In 1932, Sigurd Tolløfsen borrowed the Arctic Commercial Enterprise territory at Revet, where his 23-year-old son Arnljot was to be partner with the 9-years older Gerhard "City" Antonsen.

They were put ashore on the 25th July, and started to prepare the territory; this was a tough job to carry out with only a rowing boat. On the 7th September Sigurd Tolløfsen visited his son: *"He and City are two work horses. They have rowed out with everything for their huts and built a new trappers' hut "Fjordbotten"* [454]. *They have collected a lot of drift wood from which they have constructed and put out 200 fox traps in the territory".*[485] Another hut was built in the territory that summer at the mouth of Store Sødal, namely "Bjørnnesstua" [437], which was built by Holmboe's fishing expedition.

On the 19th October they started trapping. Arnljot Tolløfsen was going to trap along the south coast of Clavering Ø as far as Kap Mary. This took him past Eskimonæs where the young Norwegian soon became a welcome guest. On the 14th December 1932 he noted in his diary: *"Would have left today but Johansen, the manager here, persuaded me to stay on as there are dark water clouds over Kap Mary, Breivik and Finsch Øerne, and it looks like snow".*[486] The weather became so bad that Tolløfsen had to stay at Eskimonæs until the beginning of January. On the other hand, when it had to happen, Eskimonæs was not a bad place to get stuck.

It was a year with difficult conditions, and the large amounts of snow were not the worst. In Gael Hamke Bugt the ice conditions were directly lethal and time and again Tolløfsen had to turn back at Elvsborg due to open water in the bay. Frequently the ice broke up at Kap Herschell, and it probably never froze up at Kap Mary. No one could have anticipated it would end as badly as it did.

Skins of arctic fox being dried outside Moskusheimen. Note the difference between white fox and blue fox skins, c. 1932. © Nils-Martin Hanken

The Sigurd Tolløfsen Expedition at Moskusheimen, 25th July 1932. Standing from left: Sigurd Tolløfsen and Johannes Holmeslet. Sitting from left: Johan Stordal, Arnljot Tolløfsen, Gerhard Antonsen and Haakon Karlsen. © Sigurd Tolløfsen / Norwegian Polar Institute

On one of the last days of May 1933, when the trapping season was over, Arnljot Tolløfsen decided to take a quick trip down to Myggbukta to celebrate the "17th May" - Norway's independence day. He was a well-liked guest and for a week held everyone's attention with his cheerfulness and inexhaustible supply of good stories. When the party was finally over he intended to go to Kap Herschell where his father was staying. The route went along Loch Fyne and via his Danish friends at Eskimonæs where he arrived on the morning of the 25th May. He slept for a couple of hours and went on towards Kap Herschell the same evening. The night was bright as day but the outer coast was covered in thick fog. No one knows exactly how or where the accident happened, but Arnljot Tolløfsen undoubtedly drowned on this trip probably quite close to his destination of Kap Herschell. Sigurd Tolløfsen searched in vain for traces of his missing son the entire summer, until finally, on the 30th September 1933, he found: *"the frame of Arnljot's rucksack about 500 m from the house.* (see also Kap Herschell). *This suggests that his accident happened between Henningelv and Herschell"*.[487] It was a terrible blow to Sigurd Tolløfsen to lose his son, and it was of course no comfort that Arnljot and Antonsen had caught a total of 168 foxes.

1933-39

Moskusheimen is well situated on the west side of Clavering Ø, where it is sheltered from the bitter wind and fog of the outer coast. The fertile land provides a rich wildlife and from a fox-trapping point of view the territory is amongst the best in North-East Greenland.

Gerhard "City" Antonsen (1900-1945) became a living legend among trappers for his "seven years in a row" (1932-39) at Moskusheimen, five of them alone; evidently it was difficult for him to leave such an ideal location. God only knows how many years he might have stayed if he had not been injured during the seventh year, and if war had not broken out in 1939. Admittedly other trappers stranded in North-East Greenland who became members of the sledge patrol might have equalled the "King of Revet" - but seven years wintering without a break is an outstanding record.

Gerhard Antonsen came from Mo i Rana in Norway, and when he arrived in North-East Greenland in 1932 he had already experienced several winterings in Svalbard. From the beginning he stood out as an excellent trapper. When Sigurd Tolløfsen went home in 1934, Antonsen took hire with Arctic Commercial Enterprise provided that he could keep Moskusheimen. This proved to be a good deal for the company. The territories had now become fully developed and the company now aimed at maintaining a group of experienced trappers. Antonsen put down roots at Moskusheimen. It became his home, from where he could go fox-trapping in the winter and fishing for char at Zackenberg river in the summer. Once every summer the ship would bring in new supplies, and take away the winter's fox furs.

The catch in the years 1933-34, 1934-35 and 1937-38 was 93, 100 and 412 respectively. Antonsen built "Antonsens hytte" [444] in 1937 and "Breivikhytten (yngre)" [404-2] in 1938. A third hut, "Hansen Havn hytten" [413] was built in 1935, probably by Ole Sivertsen from Krogness.

In 1935-36 Antonsen unexpectedly had a partner.

Gerhard "City" Antonsen - the "King of Revet" in 1939. © Nils-Martin Hanken

Johan Johansen should have wintered at Kap Humboldt, but ice conditions made it impossible to call at the station. Instead it was decided that he should stay with Antonsen.

It was also unintended that Antonsen should have company for a large part of the winter of 1938-39; but this was due to a bad accident. Antonsen: *"was in Granta Fjord while the ice was still unsafe. The hut in which he stayed during one of the worst snow storms ever lacked the handle on the inside of the door so it was difficult to close. To secure it behind him when he went to sleep, he (as so many times before) stabbed his knife into the door and pulled it shut. However, on this occasion the knife was loose and flew out straight into his eye. He stayed there for the night. In the meantime the fluid drained out of his eyeball and his sight slowly diminished. The pupil was fortunately not damaged, but it was bad enough. Strangely enough, the sight of the other eye also diminished little by little. He became afraid of going completely blind and wanted to get back to his station before it went that far. Outside it was still a blizzard, but in the afternoon he started off and walked, partly crawled, across the mountain until after more than 24 hours he reached Revet the following night. What this walk really entailed in terms of endurance and suffering can only be understood by someone who knows Greenland".*[488]

To go for help was out of the question, because the bandage he had tied around his head froze to ice as soon as he went outside. Fortunately some Danes had just then decided to pay a visit to Moskusheimen. When they realized the seriousness of Antonsen's situation, they immediately set off to Eskimonæs for medicine and advice, and via the weekly radio contact also contacted the trappers at Myggbukta. It was here decided that Oscar Bang should go to Moskusheimen to help Antonsen, but the weather was very bad and it was not until the 3rd January that Bang arrived at Moskusheimen: *"A strange fellow came out of the door when I arrived. Pale, bearded and with a large bandage around his head, Antonsen was unrecognizable from last summer".*[489] Unfortunately Antonsen's eye became gradually worse and one day he and Bang discussed the future: *"We agreed that I should stay and trap in his territory, for he is not able to do it himself. He suggested that I should have the entire income for the foxes I caught, although he would skin, scrape and clean the fur.*

This of course I did not accept. So we agreed to share the entire catch equally, an arrangement I think is more satisfactory for both parts".[490]

Time and again Oscar Bang was impressed: *"Antonsen is an excellent host, a tremendously nice fellow. But he spoils me. I'm served coffee and cookies when I wake up in the morning. Then after I have had a smoke and got out of my sleeping bag, he serves a splendid breakfast. Today he brought me lemon tea and all sorts of goodies." ... "Antonsen knows more about the wildlife here than any professor and he talks vividly about it".*[491]

As Antonsen's eye showed no signs of improvement by the end of February, Bang decided to go to Myggbukta to try and contact doctors in Norway. A telegram was transmitted and medical advice arrived promptly. It was a matter of closing the hole in the eye so that the fluid could build up again, and then the pressure in the fluid of the undamaged eye would also increase. The treatment was so successful that Bang was able to leave Antonsen at the beginning of May.

As a consequence of the eye damage, Antonsen reluctantly had to return home to Norway in the summer of 1939. He had an eye operation and kept his sight. Alas, he was less fortunate in other ways. His seven years of trapping had earned him a substantial fortune, but rumour had it that in Oslo he had become acquainted with a famous actress. One day he bought seven suits and seven coats, a bowler hat and a silver mounted walking stick. He lent money to everyone who asked, and drank champagne out of beer glasses - in spite of the fact that he had been a teetotaller in Greenland. Three months later he was broke.

Gerhard Antonsen never wintered again in his beloved Greenland. In 1941 he came close, as he was part of the so-called Buskø Expedition and was to have wintered together with Henry Rudi. However, the expedition and their ship were seized by the US Coast Guard, and all on board taken to America. In 1992 Fredrik Sæterdal recalled: *"Antonsen spent some time in Little Norway, Toronto, and then went to the Pacific Coast, where he obtained a job as a lumberjack. There in 1945 a tree fell upon him, and he died from loss of blood on the way to the hospital. He was just 45-years old.*

There are numerous stories you could tell about Antonsen; but there is one that illustrates his stubborn streak and iron will. He hated motors, because he could never get them started – I'd rather row than have to work with a motor, he said. One day in the middle of Claveringfjord (Godthåb Golf) *he had had enough. He threw the motor overboard and refused to accept a new one from the company. After that he delivered all supplies to the huts around Clavering Ø and into Tyrolerfjord by rowing boat".*[492]

Another story recalls that when the supply ship arrived at Moskusheimen one year, the crew was met by a peculiar sight. Towards them came a human with a large hirsute beard and tangled long hair, and if they had not recognized Antonsen's cheerful eyes, they would have taken him for a madman: *"Well"*, Antonsen said, *"the growth of hair is nothing special this year. That's how it is with me; when there are plenty of foxes my hair and beard grow well, and when the foxes are few, very badly".*[493] Nonetheless he had an excellent catch, so people not familiar with his sense of humour have wondered how he would have looked if he had been content with the catch.

1939-40

In 1939, when Antonsen went home, Moskusheimen was handed over to Henry Rudi and Schjølberg Nilsen. These two experienced trappers were going to have the company of a 22-year-old medical student, Kåre Rodahl: *"In 1937 I accidentally started working with arctic nutritional issues and later planned a wintering expedition to North-East Greenland in order to examine the vitamin content in arctic animals used as food. This was to take place in a laboratory which I intended to arrange at the trappers' station at Revet".*[494]

However, at about Christmas time, Rodahl learnt that professor Hans W:son Ahlmann, the director of Geografiska Instituttet in Stockholm, was planning to carry out glaciological surveys on Clavering Ø. These surveys were the last in a series started by Ahlmann in 1918, and were intended to clarify whether global climate changes were in progress. It was agreed that Rodahl should assist Ahlmann in the summer of 1939, and continue his surveys throughout the winter of 1939-40. In addition, Rodahl wanted to determine whether it was enrichment of vitamin A in polar bear's liver that made it so dangerous for humans to eat: *"But the real reason that I was willing to spend a whole year in the arctic wilderness was that I wanted to find out whether my girl at home could remain faithful without a chaperone".*[495]

The glaciological measurements, in which the meteorologist Backa Eriksson also participated, lasted a couple of weeks and took place at the glacier "Frøyabreen". The glacier drains into Skilledal and reaches the fjord at Lerbugt on the north side of Clavering Ø; at the bay they built the hut "Leirvågen" [434] as a base while surveying.

On the 20th August 1939, Ahlmann and Eriksson were picked up and: *"the three of us stood in front of the hut watching the "Polarbjørn" weigh anchor and steam up the fjord back to Norway".*[496] ... Rudi: *"could do anything, or at least a little of everything. He was smith, joiner, and quack doctor, all in one. He was an expert in the art of baking bread and home brewing, and above all well versed in cooking problems. His speciality was ptarmigan with game sauce and whortleberries, aqua vitae and fruit jelly with cream. This sweet I have never tasted the like of before or since."* ... *"There was one thing, however, that Rudi could not do, and that was to drive dogs".*

"Schjølberg Nilsen was a sturdy, solid, conscientious fellow, the kind who never says more than he can prove. He had great experience after six years' of winter in the Arctic, was an efficient team driver and an excellent companion, always helpful and kind, calm and level headed. He was exactly the kind of man one likes to meet in the Arctic".[497]

Moskusheimen in the late 1930s. © Niels Ove Jensen

In his book "Isbjørnkongen" (the polar bear king) Henry Rudi wrote: *"It was cosy to have a doctor* (Rodahl) *in the house. I had never experienced that before. But the first patient he treated happened to be himself. He ought to be happy that he survived the accident alive, the good Dr. Rodahl. He was going up a glacier to do some survey for professor Ahlmann. Merrily he rowed away across the fjord, but just as he was going to pull the boat ashore his revolver, an 11.5 mm weapon, fell out of the holster and a shot went off. The bullet went through his upper arm, not far from the heart and only one millimetre from the bone".*[498] It took Rodahl two days using one arm to row the long way back to Revet. Fortunately it was only a flesh wound and: *"it didn't take long until he was working full time in his "office", where he had all kinds of peculiar instruments and glasses."* ... *"He would sit there day after day looking for vitamins in everything living or dead: Grass, seaweed and rushes, offal – nothing escaped being examined in the "office". But I did not envy him this life. When we took off with the dog sledges along the fjords at full pelt, he stayed inside as if in a prison".*[499]

In April 1940 Rodahl went on a sledge journey to collect materials and undertake a nutritional survey amongst the trappers at different Norwegian trappers' stations. After visiting Myggbukta he had the company of Hans Siewers, and when they came to Hoelsbu: *"Winther came rushing out of the door. He waved his arms and seemed very agitated. He shouted something about Germans having attacked Norway and that battles were taking place. We thought he was mad, left the dogs in front of the sledge and ran inside with Winther to listen to the radio. Petra stood there, her ear close to the radio, tuning the knobs, but caught only bits of a sentence each time she tuned into a station. Then everything went quiet because the battery was running down. We weren't much wiser after that".*[500] The next morning Rodahl and Siewers were again back in Myggbukta, and here all doubt was dispelled: war had come to Scandinavia

The catch in 1939-40 was not the best: *"When we took down the traps, the counting of the catch was quickly done: 28 foxes between two men. Schjølberg swore that he would not stay here one day longer than he had to. I comforted him that there might be many reluctant days ahead".*[501]

The summer came and up to the beginning of August they had still not heard news of any ship coming to North-East Greenland; but just before midnight on the 11th August they spotted a ship. It was the "Veslekari". With a mixture of wild enthusiasm and curiosity they jumped into the motor boat to meet the ship. They had misgivings too, for they had no idea who was on board. Could it be that a German machine gun was pointing at them from the deck? But as they came alongside the ship, they were met by familiar faces with John Giæver at the front. After the supplies were unloaded, "Veslekari" went back through Young Sund and headed south for Kejser Franz Joseph Fjord. Rodahl, Rudi and Nilsen remained at Moskusheimen.

In the middle of August they went to the Danish radio station at Eskimonæs to follow events by listening to the radio. Soon they received a cryptic announcement from the station at Ella Ø. They were to expect a pleasant surprise, it was said. They waited for several days, and then "Fridtjof Nansen" turned up and they were given the same choice as the other trappers: stay in Greenland or accompany the ship to Iceland. Rudi stayed, but Rodahl and Nilsen went along with "Fridtjof Nansen". In 1949-50 Nilsen, who originated from Risøyhamn in Vesterålen, became a member of the Norwegian-British-Swedish Antarctic Expedition (NBSAE).[502]

Five years passed before Kåre Rodahl saw his home country again. The long route home went via Iceland to England, where he was able to continue his research into vitamin A and its enrichment in the livers of arctic mammals. Partly based on Rodahl's work, it was later demonstrated that polar bear liver contains up to 20,000 units of vitamin A per gram; consumption even in very moderate quantities may result in vitamin-poisoning. From 1942-45 Rodahl served in a Norwegian paratrooper company, and was stationed at various places in Great Britain.

Rodahl took his medical doctorate in 1950. For the following 15 years he lived in the USA, where he held a number of leading positions linked with the Arctic. Later, from 1965-87, he was head of the Arbeidsfysiologisk Institutt (Work Physiological Institute) in Oslo and in 1966-87 he was professor at Norges Idrettshøgskole (Norwegian School of Sport Sciences) in Oslo. In addition to scientific publications concerning nutrition, climate, athletics and work physiology, Rodahl published several travellers' books. In "Nytt land under vingerne" (new land below the wings) (1948), he describes his participation in the Danish Peary Land Expedition of 1947.

1940-41

Henry Rudi, now 51-years of age, had chosen to remain in North-East Greenland: *"Greenland now had a new meaning to us. It became the land of peace. In the crazy western world hell had broken loose. Here in the fjords peace prevailed – and when in my motor boat some time later I was going home to my solitude at Revet, I wondered why people really wanted to leave. Why would they want to take part in the terrors. Here I sat with half a beer, the motor ran like clockwork and the nature was beautiful – yes, here I would like to stay until the madness out there had come to an end".*[503]

The place had become empty after the summer's evacuation, but the loneliness brought people together: *"Eli Knudsen arrives from Sandodden, asking if it wouldn't be cosy to go together to Eskimonæs and celebrate Christmas there. There is plenty of room, and they have lots of food and supplies. Well, things are not that bad at Revet either, my famous muskox rolls are ready. Jensen from Kap Herschell arrives outside the hut, it's getting quite crowded. He agrees with Knudsen, Eskimonæs it is.*

But I have a sore mouth. I have a gumboil which is killing me. I haven't slept properly for several nights and I'm yawning and moaning, and can't eat anything – I'm starving to death. It is as if my entire jaw is one huge swollen finger. They can go to Eskimonæs for Christmas and ... it hurts when I speak. They take off and wish me well." ... "Just before New Year I had recovered so much that I was able to harness the dogs and set out for Eskimonæs – I took along two special muskox rolls as Christmas presents and on top of that a real desire to have a late Christmas party. High-spirited I went ahead to good friends and good company. Together we would meet the year of grace 1941".[504]

1941-42

"The ship is coming! 8th September – the ship is coming! I have felt it for a long time and heard it too"[505] Henry Rudi wrote. It was the "Buskø" that had arrived with people and supplies. At Moskusheimen, Gerhard Antonsen and his spartan equipment was put ashore; but then the US Coast Guard vessel "Northland" unexpectedly turned up. All the recently unloaded supplies were seized and taken on board "Northland", and "Buskø" was arrested. Rudi and Antonsen were told that they would be evacuated: *"There was a long parley back and forth, back and forth. The commander patiently listened to all my arguments. Finally he gave in. I could stay for another year, but Antonsen had to come along. No prayers helped here, although I think Antonsen was on the verge of tears".*[506]

So Henry Rudi was allowed to stay at Moskusheimen for another year. One day in the summer of 1942, when he arrived with the motor boat at Eskimonæs, two US Coast Guard ships were waiting there. The commander offered Rudi a choice: *"Either come along to West Greenland or join something he called a "sledge patrol" which was going to have headquarters here at Eskimonæs".*[507] As there was no third alternative, Rudi chose the sledge patrol and moved to Eskimonæs, where he served in "the North-East Greenland Sledge Patrol" until the autumn of 1943. He then sailed with "Polarbjørn" to West Greenland, where he lived at Ivigtut until the end of the war. After the war Rudi once again wintered at

Normann Andersen, Norwegian trapper, who had 9 over-winterings in North-East Greenland. © Lauritz Storholt

Svalbard. The "King of Polar Bears" died as a 81-year-old pensioner in 1970 in his native town of Tromsø.

Moskusheimen was not manned again until 1946.

1946-51, 1952-54

In the summer of 1946 "Polarbjørn" arrived at Moskusheimen and Normann Andersen, one of the most qualified trappers in Norway, went ashore to take over the station. Andersen spent a total of nine years in North-East Greenland, the most years of any Norwegian trapper - and he was the only one to live there in the 1930s, 1940s and 1950s. Like Gerhard Antonsen, Normann Andersen spent seven winters at Moskusheimen, 1946-51 and 1952-54. During four of these years he was accompanied by his wife, Gudrun, and for a number of years "Andersen at Revet" was a well-known phrase amongst people in North-East Greenland. Andersen's skill as a trapper was the main reason, as he usually had the largest catch. During the years 1947-51 his catch was 47, 55, 201 and 240 foxes respectively. The territory was so well equipped with huts that Andersen only needed to build two, namely "Jordanhill hytten" [409-2] and "Norma hytta" [411-2].

Normann Andersen (1896-1982) was the youngest of 10 children born at the farm Øijord in Lenvik, Troms fylke. As usual in that part of Norway, the property extended far into the mountains and down to the sea. It was a good farm, the time and location taken into consideration. With the fjord so close, Andersen soon became used to boats, and the sea was the main means of transport during the summers.

Yet Normann Andersen did not feel a vocation for farming or fishing. At the age of 17, he obtained work establishing the iron mine in Kirkenes for I/S Sydvaranger. The age limit was 18, but he was tall and strong and got the job anyway. From time to time he came home and worked at the farm. Later he worked on Bjørnøya and at mines in Svalbard. These years stimulated his interest in the Arctic. In 1925 he settled in Tromsø, took employment at the power plant, married Gudrun and they had a daughter.

However, in 1932 his life as a townsman was interrupted. Helge Ingstad needed a good man for his expedition in 1932-34. Norma Larsen - Andersen's daughter - said in 1993 that: *"it was actually these two years in Greenland that created the "trapper" Normann Andersen".*[508]

After that period with Ingstad followed several years at Prins Karls Forland in Svalbard. Gudrun Andersen wintered together with her husband in 1936-37, and Norma Larsen recalled in: *"the summer of 1941 they went up again together. By then Norway was occupied, but neither of the warring parties had reached as far as Svalbard yet. And we were naïve enough to think that Svalbard would be kept out of the war. However, the very day after my parent's arrival a plane flew over the station, dropping a message saying that they should prepare themselves to be picked up by a large English passenger ship, the "Empress of Canada" in a day or two. Then followed five long years in England".*[509]

In the autumn of 1945, Normann Andersen went to Bjørnøya to work at the new radio station. The manager of the station was Bjørn Western, Andersen's companion at Antarctichavn in 1932-34. In the summer of 1946, Andersen returned to North-East Greenland where he stayed until 1951. Gudrun Andersen went up to join him at Moskusheimen for the years 1947-49. After a year in Norway, he returned to the station in 1952 and stayed there for two further years. That was the end of the Greenland years: Normann Andersen was then 57-years old.

"Later he went with an Ålesund sealer to Newfoundland. It was the first and last time he participated in that kind of sealing. He never talked about the trip, but I don't think he liked it.

My mother died in 1959. Soon after my father was employed as an engineer at a small power plant outside Tromsø, and worked there until he was 72. Here in Sunavik there were good opportunities for leisure-time activities like hunting and fishing. He fished a little on the fjord for his own needs, but he never hunted. People wondered a bit about that – with his background – but he once said to me that he "had killed enough".[510]

Gudrun Andersen, who spent 4 years at Moskusheimen together with her husband, Normann Andersen, c. 1952. © Hans Madsen

Normann Andersen reached the age of 86, and Norma Larsen was grateful that her father died: *"with his hat and boots on".*[511]

A detailed description of Normann Andersen's winterings is not possible, as his diaries no longer exist; but in "Polarboken 1961-62" he wrote an article with the subtitle "Four years at Revet with Gudrun". The story begins in the summer of 1947 when he was awaiting his wife's arrival: *"For the occasion the house here at "Revet" has been thoroughly cleaned from floor to ceiling and is barely recognizable. The kitchen has acquired new and simple cupboards for pots and plates, I have made an extension to the sink and above the washbasin is a mirror with a glass shelf. I have made two comfortable chairs, stuffed in seat and back and upholstered with muskox skin. They will be nice and warm when the snow from the north is whirling around the corners on a winter's day. The workshop has been emptied, and with great care turned into a light, cosy bedroom with a sleeping sofa, a cupboard and bedside table for each of us. Both rooms are newly painted from top to bottom, including doors and windows. On one side of the hallway is a small sauna, with an oven built from stones and clay, simple and efficient. The oven heats up the room to 60 degrees with a minimum consumption of coal and time. The water tank on the roof has a device to allow showers in the summer. It is small, but not altogether primitive.*

Gudrun is enthusiastic about this little home and its furnishing here in the wilderness and I'm no less content with my work"....

"Actually we had planned to drive together in the winter, but "Mikki"'s romancing in the summer had the result she was going to have puppies. Driving around with an expectant bitch at the busiest time of the year is not to be recommended and we discussed the situation back and forth until Gudrun came up with the solution: she would stay at the station alone with the patient and two other dogs. I admire the women who have travelled together with their husbands on winter journeys and endured the weather and hardships as they came. But I know that it is an even greater challenge to be alone in a hut for days and weeks in the darkness of the winter, and to be self-reliant whatever happens. One has to be well-balanced in mind and spirit. We agreed to try it, at least for one trip and I promised to be back within two weeks. We parted, and I was a bit anxious when

Visitors at Moskusheimen. E.B. Larsen (left) visits Gudrun and Norman Andersen, c. 1952. © Hans Madsen

I arrived home two days ahead of schedule, but everything was just fine. "Mikki" had had her puppies, and Gudrun had caught three white fox in the traps. We had much new to talk about – and then it was time to prepare for a new trip. Gudrun wanted to keep one of "Mikki"'s puppies, that was white and named "Suak" ...

"For four years we were together in East Greenland – four years that passed all too soon. We belonged there at "Revet", and both celebrated our anniversaries there. We both turned 50, and in all modesty we celebrated not only our 25th wedding anniversary but our 30th anniversary as well. I remember with gratitude Gudrun's years with me in the wilderness and the home she made with great courage and a will that never failed – and for her hospitality towards passing travellers who visited us".[512]

1951-52

Dagfinn Egeberg began his third wintering in 1951 when he took over Moskusheimen for one year. Hans Madsen and Knud Erik Filskov from Loch Fyne stayed with Egeberg on 17th December, on their way to the Christmas visit to Daneborg: *"We arrived at around 9 o'clock this evening after a 7 hour bitterly cold journey with strong headwinds. We are now listening to the radio, having a good time with the Norwegian trapper Egeberg".*[513]

On 2nd May 1952, Madsen and Filskov had a return visit from Egeberg, who was on his way to Myggbukta. He had with him a fancy new cinecamera: *"and filmed us, while we washed and stretched a bear skin".*[514]

In the summer of 1952, Egeberg returned to Norway, and Norman and Gudrun Andersen came back to Revet and stayed there until 1954.

1954-55

Sverre Storholt had just turned 38 when he came to Greenland on his second and last wintering: *"I think that North-East Greenland was a great place to be"* he recalled in 1992, *"and if I was still twenty, I would go there tomorrow".*[515]

Storholt came from Solør in Norway. Having qualified as a carpenter he joined the military forces, and was an officer when Germany attacked Norway in 1940; Storholt took part in the heavy fighting in Gudbrandsdalen, refused to capitulate and immediately joined the resistance movement. He went to Sweden where he was employed at the Norwegian intelligence service in Stockholm. From here he also acted as a border guide and courier and in the last years of the war made 24 secret missions across the Swedish-Norwegian border: *"Once went 28 Norwegian miles* (280 km) *on ski in two days to help a man out"*, he remembered.[516] It was at great personal risk, as Storholt had a death sentence hanging over his head.

The war ended, but his health had suffered, both physically and mentally. Tuberculosis, nine months in a sickbed and a broken marriage followed. It took years for him to recover, but then North-East Greenland came into the picture. In 1949 he came to Kap Humboldt, and: *"that was a good place to recuperate".*[517]

In 1991 Birger Larsen, Storholt's partner in 1949-50, said: *"I have never experienced a man so skilled with his hands as Storholt."* Larsen was here referring particularly to an accident he had on the 22nd November 1949. At the time he wrote in his diary: *"Almost killed myself with my rifle today. Stood outside, target practising when a shot twisted the barrel into a semicircle. There was probably something wrong with the cartridge. Usually that's the reason, but often the lock also breaks – so I was lucky this time".*[518]

"I figured that rifle was lost", Larsen recalled: *"but Sverre was sure he could fix it. We had no forge, but we had the stove in the kitchen, and there he started working with the rifle. First he cut a small piece off the barrel. Then he began heating up the barrel in the stove, and took it out to the vice in the small workshop we had in the hallway in order to align the barrel. I think he had to go in and out to re-heat the barrel about fifty times. After that he removed the foresight from the piece he had cut off and put it back on the barrel again. At the end of the day that rifle shot perfectly at one hundred metres. It was incredible".*

At the beginning of August 1954, Storholt built the trappers' hut "Storholts hus" [414-2]. Apart from two winterings he had also made summer journeys to East and West Greenland. When his Greenland days were over he worked for 10 years at Norsk Folkemuseum (Norwegian Folk Museum) rebuilding old log cabins. Sverre Storholt died in May 1993, at the age of 76.

Harald Sverdsten, the last Norwegian trapper at Moskusheimen, 1959. © Bent Zwergius

Viggo Block, the last trapper at Moskusheimen, 1960. © Bent Zwergius

1955-56
Asbjørn Tøndell, who in 1953-55 had been a radio operator, decided in 1955 to try his luck as a full-time trapper at Moskusheimen: *"He is a man of few words"* Stein Sørensen wrote.[519] One day in October 1955 Tøndell was almost killed when he went through the ice in Godthåb Golf. After three winterings Tøndell went home in 1956, but returned, and in 1958-59 he was the last station manager at Myggbukta.

1956-59
Harald Sverdsten, who in 1949-51 had wintered at Myggbukta and Hoelsbu, was the last Norwegian trapper at Moskusheimen. Originally he had planned to go home in 1958, but ice conditions were so difficult that "Polarsel" could not call at Revet, so Sverdsten had to stay for another year. In 1959 "Polarsel" managed to navigate the entire coast, and on 15th August the ship arrived at Moskusheimen. Sverdsten went aboard and so ended the Norwegian trapper era.

1959-60
Viggo Block was born in 1927 in Vendsyssel, Denmark. In 1952 he went to Greenland as a weather service operator at Kap Tobin. He intended to stay only for a few years, but the country and travelling with sledge dogs fascinated him, and the years went by one after the other. In 1956 he went back to Denmark, but returned the following year to Station Nord, as leader of the weather service in 1957-59. One day, he and a colleague, Ib Palle Madsen, decided to quit their jobs to become trappers: *"We wanted to see if we could do it"*, Block explained in 1993, *"and so we sent an application to the Ministry of Greenland asking if we might take some dogs from the station and go south. We also applied to J.G. Jennov, the director of the trapping company, to see if we could borrow some of Nanok's huts and boats. And he allowed us to do so"*.[520]

On the 14th April 1959 they left Station Nord, and dog sledged via Daneborg to Zackenberg: *"We stayed there for the summer, fished for char, some of which we dried and used as dog food during the winter. We also salted some char for ourselves. At the beginning of September we sailed to Revet. I had bought a dinghy with an outboard motor from the cook at Daneborg. Originally we had planned to go to Hochstetter to trap; but at Daneborg in the spring I had met Sverdsten, the Norwegian trapper at Revet. He said right away: "Well, then you are welcome to take over my station with dogs and sledge and everything!" – I thought a bit about that; but it was a good idea, because then we would get a territory each. So I took over everything from Sverdsten"*.[521]

Block used the autumn to paint and renovate the station, and when the trapping season began he put out more than 100 traps. He and Madsen had a total catch of about 120 foxes: *"and as we stayed each at our own trappers' station we were allowed to shoot 10 muskoxen each. We sold a few of the muskox skins at Mestersvig and actually made a decent profit when the entire fox catch had been sold"*.[522]

In April 1960, they travelled southwards to Scoresbysund. Block continued south to Ammassalik and then to Egedesminde and did not return to Denmark until 1963. He stayed there only for a few months, before he was once again back working at different places in East and West Greenland until 1977, when he returned home for good.

Giæver 1939, 1957.

Recent status
Moskusheimen - or "Revet" - is one of the best known hunters' stations in North-East Greenland. Since the end of the trapper era it has been maintained by Sirius. In 1994 it was inspected by a Nanok group,[523] and in the autumn of 2001 was thoroughly renovated by a Sirius team.[524]

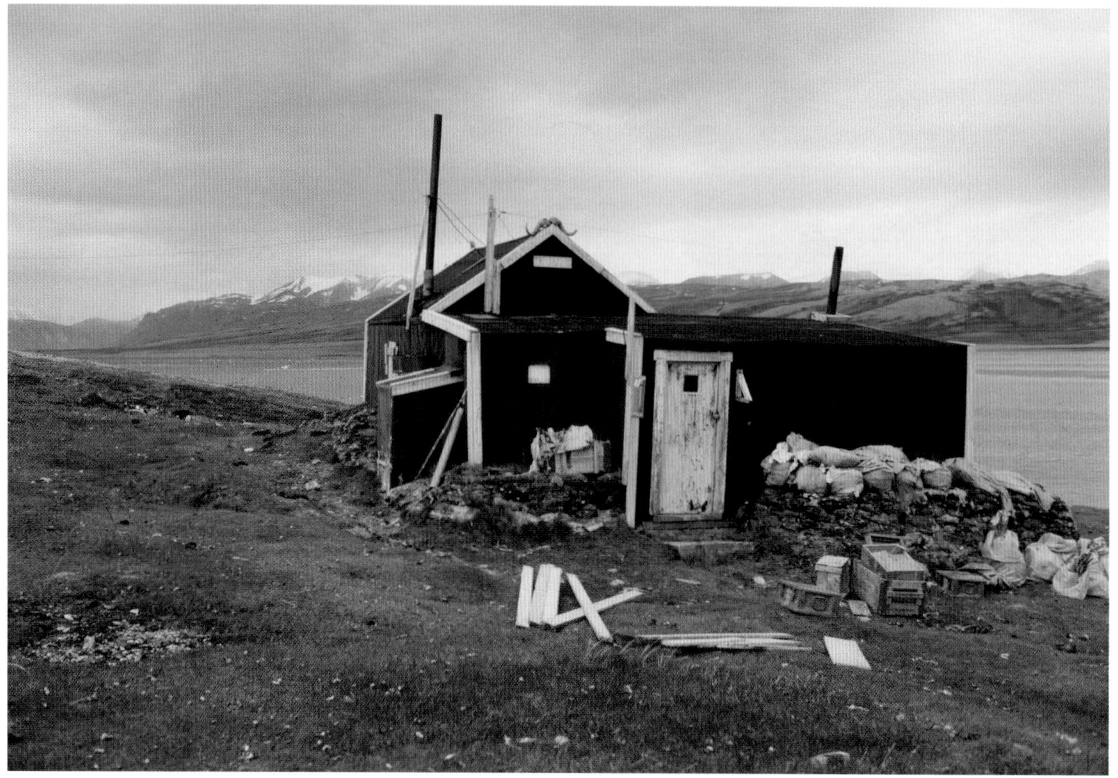

Moskusheimen, 5th August 1977. © Peter Schmidt Mikkelsen

Moskusheimen [429], 25th July 2003. Moskusheimen is a former Norwegian trappers' station originally built in 1927 for the Foldvik Expedition. The present house was built in 1928 by the Finn Devold Expedition. Moskusheimen was used as a trappers' station until 1960, thereafter as a travellers' hut. (Opposite page, top). The foundation of the original 1927 house. (Opposite page, centre) Fox cages. (Opposite page, bottom) Moskusheimen seen from east. © NCN

MYGGBUKTA
[335]

Wintering party

1922-23: Johan A. Olsen, Helge Listerud (T), Alvin H.J. Olsen, Oskar Johansson, Olaf Olsen, Jakob B. Andreassen, Edvard Løkvik
1923-26: None
1926-27: Nils Foldvik (T), Hallvard Devold (T), Fritz Øien (T), Arnulf Gisvold
1927-28: Nils Foldvik (T), Hallvard Devold (T), Fritz Øien (T)
1928-30: Finn Devold, Leif Brox (T)
1930-31: Hallvard Devold (T), Thor Halle, Eilif Herdal, Ingvald Strøm
1931-32: Hallvard Devold (T), Bernt Marø, Gustav Lindquist
1932-33: Sverre J. Sørensen, Knut Hofgaard, John Thorsteinsen (T)
1933-34: Eilif Herdal, Johan Holm (T)
1934-35: Eilif Herdal, Henry Haug (T)
1935-36: Finn Framnes-Hansen, Søren Richter, Øivind Holm Johnsen, Johan Holm (T)
1936-37: Finn Framnes-Hansen, Sverre Røstad, Henry Haug (T), E.G. Bird, C.G. Bird
1937-38: Finn Framnes-Hansen, Johan Johansen, Johan Holm (T), C.G. Bird
1938-39: Eilif Herdal, Oscar Bang, Egil Rogstad (T)
1939-40: Johan Johansen, Hans Siewers, Andreas Skaanevik (T)
1940-41: Johan Johansen, Hans Siewers
1941-42: Johan Johansen
1942-46: None
1946-47: Peter Melleby, Paul Furuseth, Jan Jansen (T)
1947-48: Peter Melleby, Helge Strand (T), Lorang Larsen (T)
1948-49: Dagfinn Egeberg (T), Stein Sørensen (T), Nils Haugmo
1949-50: Henry Olsen (T), Stein Sørensen (T), Harald Sverdsten
1950-51: Henry Olsen (T), Stein Sørensen (T)
1951-52: Nicolay Nicolaysen (T), Amundsen (first name unknown) (T), Alf Rustøen
1952-53: Nicolay Nicolaysen (T), Finn Jensen (T), Lauritz Storholt
1953-54: Dagfinn Egeberg (T), Asbjørn Tøndell (T), Birger Larsen
1954-55: Asbjørn Tøndell (T), Finn Jensen (T), Helge Nesset
1955-56: Stein Sørensen (T), Knut Ødegaard (T), Hilmar Gauteplass
1956-57: Knut Ødegaard (T), Anund Amundsen (T), Hans Oddvik
1957-58: Knut Ødegaard (T), Raftevold (first name unknown) (T)
1958-59: Asbjørn Tøndell (T), Bjørn Hylen (T)

(T) = telegraphist, radio operator

Greenland plays a significant role in the movement of global air masses in the Arctic and North Atlantic region. Not only does the country hinder the free movement of air masses between the Arctic Ocean and the temperate zones, the large ice-covered landmass also affects the air temperature and winds. Meteorologists became aware early in the 20th century that the weather in Greenland controlled the weather in western Europe. At a meeting in London on the 22nd-27th November 1920, the International Commission of Weather Telegraphy passed the following resolution: *"It was unanimously decided that the establishment at the earliest possible date of a high-power radio-telegraphic station in Greenland is of the utmost importance to the meteorology of Western Europe, and further, it is of such importance as to warrant the international provisions of funds for maintaining it"*.[525]

In September 1921, this statement was discussed at a meeting with the International Meteorological Committee and led to a corresponding resolution: Europe wanted weather reports from Greenland.

As early as the summer of 1918, the Geofysisk Institutt had been founded in Tromsø. The purpose of the institute was to establish an efficient weather service for northern Norway. This was, however, difficult since most of the storms affecting northern Norway originated from the region between Iceland and Svalbard, a region totally lacking weather stations. Negotiations with Denmark and the United Kingdom to establish wireless weather services in Greenland and Jan Mayen were unsuccessful. In 1921, Norway established a weather station at Jan Mayen on her own initiative, the first in the large open space between Iceland and Svalbard.

Yet a single station was insufficient, as it could only register that a storm was approaching, but not determine its location, velocity or direction. The Geofysisk Institutt therefore began to examine the possibilities of establishing a weather station in North-East Greenland. In the winter of 1921-22, the institute became aware that Johan A. Olsen from Skulsfjord was planning a trapping expedition to North-East Greenland. The institute consulted Olsen, and it was agreed that for a fee of 3500 kroner the expedition would transmit weather reports. The Geofysisk

Institutt provided a radio station and a radio operator, but was not itself involved in the trapping.

1922-23

In the summer of 1922, Johan A. Olsen's Expedition went to North-East Greenland with the "Anni I". On the lowlands on the north side of Mackenzie Bugt they found a suitable location for their main station. It soon became evident that the place was pestered by huge swarms of mosquitoes, and they consequently gave the place the appropriate name of Myggbukta (mosquito bay).

On the 14th October 1922, the wireless operator Listerud transmitted not only the first weather report, but the first wireless communication ever between Greenland and the rest of the world. The weather reports were subsequently transmitted three times a day with virtually no interruptions until the 15th August 1923, the day the expedition began their home voyage to Norway.

It was planned that the weather service would be taken over by "Mikal Olsen's and B.H. Tolløfsen's Expedition" which had been sent out with the ship "Conrad Holmboe". However, due to very difficult ice conditions the ship did not reach land and had to return, while "Anni I" disappeared without trace during her home journey. To investigate the mystery of the loss of "Anni I", the polar explorer Gunnar Isachsen visited Myggbukta with "Quest" in the summer of 1924. It was discussed whether to man the radio station, but the idea was dropped. However, the director of the Geofysisk Institutt, Ole Andreas Krogness, subsequently purchased the radio station at Myggbukta from the estate of the deceased Johan A. Olsen on behalf of the Norwegian state; in the meantime he had to accept that Greenland was once again a blank spot on the weather chart.

1926-27

One day at the beginning of 1925, two of his radio operators at the Geofysisk Institutt, Nils Foldvik and Hallvard Devold, approached Ole Andreas Krogness and provided him with a solution to his problem. They wanted to equip a two-year trapping expedition to North-East Greenland and at the same time volunteered to take over the weather service in Myggbukta. It was agreed that the expedition would be ready for departure in the summer of 1926.

Both Foldvik and Devold had arctic experience. The 34-year-old Nils Foldvik had wintered as a radio operator on Jan Mayen in 1922-23, and had taken part in Gunnar Isachsen's summer search expedition in 1924. He returned enthusiastic about North-East Greenland and the hunting possibilities, and this brought him in touch with Devold.

Hallvard Ophuus Devold (1898-1957), had left the University of Oslo with a degree in economics in the spring of 1920, but monotonous work behind a desk in a bank was not his cup of tea, and when an assistant job at Haldde Observatory became vacant, he took it. However, Devold wanted to go to the Arctic and after a summer expedition to Svalbard and a course in radio telegraphy, Krogness offered him a position as wireless operator in Svalbard at Quade hoek station in the spring of 1923, where his brother, Finn Devold, was manager. The regular contacts with trappers in the area that winter provided the Devold brothers with a thorough knowledge of trapping methods. Hallvard Devold had, furthermore, found himself a destination – Greenland. Svalbard was OK, but: *"if I were to go ahead with a trapping expedition, it had to have a certain size otherwise it would be of no interest".*[526] In October 1924, Hallvard Devold returned from Svalbard and joined the weather service for northern Norway in Tromsø – here he met Nils Foldvik.

The Quest Expedition repairs the roof at the original Myggbukta house. Summer 1924. © Norwegian Polar Institute

On 17th July 1926, the Foldvik-expedition left Tromsø. The expedition had six members, including three radio operators, namely Nils Foldvik, Hallvard Devold and 27 year old Fritz Øien. Øien father was the skipper Jens Øien of Tromsø, who had sailed tourists to North-East Greenland for a number of years and was therefore familiar with the Arctic. In 1925-26, Fritz Øien had wintered together with Hallvard Devold on Jan Mayen. Arnulf Gisvold, who was 23-years old and the youngest participant of the expedition, had wintered no less than eight seasons as a trapper and miner in Svalbard. The two brothers Meyer Olsen and Hans Olsen, both well experienced with the Arctic, completed the expedition.

The expedition arrived at their destination on the 28th July 1926: *"As you sail towards Myggbukta you see large green plains dotted with lakes in front of you. Geese and divers are cackling and quacking. Herds of muskox are grazing on the plains; you can hear the ptarmigan on the slopes while the hare is easily spotted, white all year round. There is life everywhere. Myggbukta certainly deserves its name. There are mosquitoes everywhere in Greenland, but nowhere in such vast numbers as at Myggbukta. It's a terrible plague. I have never seen such incredible numbers of mosquitoes as there"*, Nils Foldvik wrote.[527]

After their arrival they started making Johan A. Olsen's old house liveable: *"The house is made of 3 x 3 inch beams with two layers of panelling and one layer of roofing felt on the outside. There is a floor and a ceiling. The living room is 2.8 m long by 3.2 m wide. Adjacent to the south wall is a small room for the radio station, 1 m wide by 3.2 m long. Along the north wall is a porch, 3 m long by 3.2 m wide but without floor or ceiling. The roof of the entire house is made from rough planks. Outside there are two radio masts 100 m apart; they are electroplated pipes 18 m high and 3 inches in diameter"*.[528] From a trapping point of view Myggbukta had an ideal location. You could trap in three directions; southwards towards Kap Franklin, eastwards to Kap Broer Ruys and northwards and westwards towards Loch Fyne and Moskusoksefjord. For overnight stays while trapping they only had Franklin-huset, while the Danish Kap Broer Ruys station lay about 40 km away. They therefore built a hut, "Geisha" [330].

"It was now decided that Meyer Olsen and Foldvik should go to Carlshavn, east of Kap Krogness, and trap from there, while Øien was to trap in Loch Fyne. Hans Olsen kept the home territory, and the hut (Sandvik) *at Clavering Ø. Gisvold and I would take care of Myggbukta and the territories to the south-west and east from there. I was to transmit weather reports for the time being"*.[529] In mid-November Foldvik came back. He and Meyer Olsen had stayed some weeks at Carlshavn, and caught a few foxes, but now there were none left. For the rest of the winter Foldvik, Devold, Gisvold and Øien all trapped from Myggbukta.

In May 1927, the Foldvik Expedition was able to count up the results of the first year's trapping. It was disappointing - just 100 foxes - and: *"we had to make a considerable effort in order to come home with that many"*,[530] Devold wrote. They concluded that the trapping territories would have to be dramatically expanded.

1927-28

The Foldvik Expedition men had a busy summer. As soon as the ice broke up they started building trappers' huts, although they were short of building materials. "Gamvik" [343] and "Skandalen" [339] were made of driftwood, and the men had to tear down Franklin-huset [326] in order to have enough wood for "Foldvik" [327] and "Franklin Strand" [319].

Arnulf Gisvold had moved to the new station at Revet (see Moskusheimen), and at Myggbukta the remaining three shared out the trapping territories between them. Foldvik had the territory towards Kap Franklin, Øien the area around Loch Fyne and Devold made his base at the Danish station at Carlshavn, which he accidentally burned down.

On the 10th August 1928, "Terningen" arrived and Finn Devold's expedition took over the station and the trapping territory, and by the 20th August the Foldvik men were back in Tromsø. Nils Foldvik summed up: *"The economic outcome of the expedition was not large. When all expenses were paid not much was left. We went there with great expectations, as it was unknown ground and new to us. We had no experience to build on. You have to be acquainted with the country before optimal results can be achieved. However, in one respect we can be content with the journey. We came home safe and sound and we had built 19* (18) *huts in a territory covering more than 300 km. It was an enormous work to build all these huts, due to the heavy loads and long transport of the materials before you got them to the building site. Trappers going to Greenland can now benefit from our experiences. Perhaps one can go to East Greenland again and once more roam across the vast plains, where there is no discussion of mine or yours. You never have to worry about trespassing"*.[531] After the expedition Foldvik became a scientific assistant at Vervarslinga (weather service) for northern Norway in 1929. He never had the opportunity to use his experience in another wintering in North-East Greenland.

1928-29

The Finn Devold Expedition had six members: Finn

Devold, Leif Brox, Levin Winther, Gunnar Knoph, Finn Framnes-Hansen and Henry Rudi, who described the group as: *"a handsome bunch if I may say so myself. No wimps here"*.[532]

"I knew Finn Devold from when he was a boy. He was one of those lads who climbed in the rigging and into the crow's nest, and was called down and promised a good beating on the spot; nevertheless he would have pea soup with the crew as soon as he was on deck".[533] Finn Devold (1907-79) was born in Bergen, the son of a vicar and brother to Hallvard. He grew up in Ørsta and Tromsø, and passed his exams in 1921. He became an assistant at the Haldde-observatoriet and the Geofysisk Institutt in 1922-23, and became manager at the Quade hoek radio station on Svalbard in 1923-24. He studied at the Sorbonne, Paris, in 1924-26, and was manager at the Jan Mayen weather station in 1926-27 and assistant to Fridtjof Nansen in Oslo in 1927-28. Then began his Greenland adventures as leader of the Finn Devold Expedition to North-East Greenland in 1928-30. He was employed by NSIU from 1930-31. Then came the Finn Devold Expedition to South-East Greenland in 1931-33, when at the request of the Norwegian government he declared the occupation of the area between 60°30′ and 63°40′N on 10th July 1932. That was the end of his arctic winterings. In 1940 he took his doctorate in marine biology, was employed by the Fiskeridirektoratet (fisheries control) and led a number of research expeditions to the Arctic. In 1956-57 he was sent out by the FAO of the United Nations to Brazil. Finn Devold became one of the world's leading experts on the herring fishery and wrote a number of scientific publications.

Finn Devold wintered at Myggbukta together with the wireless operator Brox, then 23-years old and from 1925 employed by the weather service for northern Norway. Hallvard Devold expressed his disappointment with his brother: *"Finn had brought much less building materials than I had expected. It seemed to me obvious that the most important thing now was to build huts and to take the land into effective possession in accordance with article 4 of the Østgrønlandsavtalen. I thought this so obvious that I had not even sent Finn any specific request"*.[534]

An attempt was made to catch live foxes. The population that winter was large, and before Christmas they had gathered almost 100 in the fox cages at Myggbukta; however a large number of them died, and most were killed for skinning.

1929-30

In 1929-30, Moskusoksefjord was annexed into the Norwegian trapping territory with the building of the huts "Halle" [341] and "Bråstad" [345] in the summer of 1929. The Finn Devold Expedition went home in 1930 with a total catch of 329 foxes including 17 live foxes, as well as skins from 11 bears, eight wolves and 24 ermines.

1930-31

In the summer of 1930, Arctic Commercial Enterprise took over the trapping territory as well as the operation of Myggbukta Radio. "Veslekari" arrived on the 29th July, carrying two carpenters, Kristian Nakken and Kristian Ellingsæter. A completely new house was to be built as a replacement for Johan A. Olsen's house from 1922. The new house had an area of 11 x 3.5 m and had two storeys. The radio equipment was also replaced by a new shortwave station, a gift from consul Lars Christensen of Sandefjord to NSIU. "Veslekari" revisited Myggbukta on the 20th August before starting the homeward voyage: *"The radio station was completely reconstructed with four rooms. The shortwave equipment was working and they had already been in direct connection with Bergen"*.[535] When the ship sailed, Hallvard Devold, Thor Halle, Eilif Herdal and Ingvald Strøm remained at the station to overwinter.

December was a tiresome experience for Hallvard Devold and Thor Halle. They had been on a visit to Hoelsbu and started their home trip on 7th December. The going was terrible. The further they went in Moskusoksefjord, the softer the snow became and it took them no less than 12 hours to reach Halle-hytten. Here they were stuck for five days due to bad weather. On the sixth day they struggled onward to Bråstad-hytten, where they became stranded again. For how many days they did not know, as they had lost all sense of time. Despite rationing, their food began to run out, and they had to make an attempt to reach

The Finn Devold Expedition 1928-30. From left: Henry Rudi, Finn-Framnes-Hansen, Leif Brox, Levin Winther, Finn Devold and Gunnar Knoph, 20th August 1930. © Adolf Hoel / Norwegian Polar Institute

Bunnhuset in Loch Fyne; but: *"despite the sledges being loaded only with the sleeping bags, we realized after 200 m that we would have to abandon them. We continued with just our rucksacks, but after five hours we had only covered about one third of the distance to Bunnhuset in Loch Fyne. At the same time it started to get darker and the fog set in. We barely managed to get back to the hut."* The day after the last food was gone. *"We have today slaughtered a fox and shared it with the dogs. Fox legs are not all that bad. It could have been better; but still, it was all right because we are now very hungry".*[536] The days went by and they had to kill a dog for food, but: *"the dog meat was not as good as the fox meat"*, Halle pointed out.[537] At last the weather cleared and on the 23rd December they finally reached Myggbukta.

It was a year with a catch below average. As the territory was well equipped with huts, only one, "Flata" [332-1], was built in the spring of 1931, the year that Myggbukta hit the headlines of newspapers around the world.

On 26th June 1931, Hallvard Devold received a coded telegram: *"Lauge Koch on his way to annex the land north of Scoresbysund. In Norway strong opinion for Norwegian occupation. However, the state is hesitating and an encouraging act from the Norwegians in East Greenland is therefore essential given the present situation. I strongly urge you without delay to hoist the Norwegian flag in the presence of your colleagues and declare that in the name of King Haakon, you occupy the land from Carlsberg Fjord to Bessel Fjord and name it Eirik Raudes Land. Then you must immediately send a telegram to the prime minister, informing him of the act of occupation, and requesting the government to accept this and to incorporate the area into Norwegian sovereignty. State as a reason for the occupation, that due to the turn of events occupation is the only means of securing Norwegian business interests in East Greenland. Transmit telegrams to Tidens Tegn, Dagbladet and Sjøfartstidende* (newspapers) *two days before you transmit the telegram to the prime minister. Your friends. Telegram strictly confidential".*[538]

Such were the instructions from Adolf Hoel and Gustav Smedal to Hallvard Devold requesting him to take action. The following day Devold drew up a document stating:

"Today, at 5 o'clock p.m., we have hoisted the Norwegian flag and in the name of H.M. King Haakon VII annexed the land from Carlsberg Fjord in the south to Bessel Fjord in the north, and named this area Eirik Raudes Land.

Myggbukta, the 27th June 1931.

Signed: *Hallvard Devold, Ingvald Strøm, Søren Richter, Eilif Herdal, Thor Halle".*[539]

It is difficult to determine how many of the trappers knew of the occupation plans in advance. It was probably only Hallvard Devold. Thor Halle wrote in his diary: *"As such an act has to be acknowledged by the government, Hallvard required that a document was drawn up, where the five of us at present at Myggbukta share the responsibility for the act; or as Hallvard said: I'm not taking the blame alone if things go wrong".*[540]

Things did not go wrong, even if the Norwegian government did not accept the private occupation until the 10th July. Meanwhile telegrams of congratulation came pouring in from people and organizations in Norway. On 30th June: *"Telegram from Tidens Tegn. Professor Skeie and all the experts in international law express their support. In the Danish press we are presented as three young Norwegians playing cops and robbers up here."* And on the 3rd July: *"tonight a telegram from Haugesunds Mål og Fedrelandslag. Quite bombastic, of trappers' vigilance over the flag in Eirik Raudes Land. Well well, they sure know how to put it".*[541]

On the 17th July, the first ship of the year arrived, "Veslekari", hired by the Louise A. Boyd Expedition. Miss Boyd came ashore and made quite a fuss of having Hallvard Devold - who had been appointed police authority - stamp their passports. On the 1st August the "Polarbjørn" arrived. On board were no less than three Norwegian reporters. Myggbukta had become interesting news.

1931-32

Arctic Commercial Enterprise had only five men wintering in 1931-32. Bernt Marø, Gustav Lindquist and Hallvard Devold stayed at Myggbukta. Devold was the only one remaining of the 1929 party: *"At first I knew we were heading for a fine trapping winter. I could tell from the presence of the many lemmings and birds of prey. The broods of ptarmigan were large and ermine were regularly seen. Furthermore, I wanted to try out another year with the fox cages, which I had decided to take care of myself. Above all, I wished to see Arctic Commercial Enterprise Ltd. succeed. We have had two poor years; the third should bring a good result".*[542]

One of the first days in December they had a visit from the archaeologist Helge Larsen and the geologist Curt Teichert, both part of the Danish Three-Year Expedition. They arrived from the south and were exhausted. A couple of days later, the botanist Paul Gelting, the zoologist Alwin Pedersen and the wireless operator Axel Henry Nielsen arrived: *"The Danes were friendly and witty fellows and it was cosy to have them as guests. It is true that officially we were enemies in the ongoing dispute between our countries, but in the wilderness you cannot really bother with such considerations. It is so rare that you see a new face that you are more than happy for a visit. They stayed with us for a week or so, until the dogs were properly fed again. Then they put skis under their narrow sledge runners and continued northwards to Clavering Ø, where they lived".*[543]

The catch at Myggbukta was about 100 foxes. Neither Hallvard Devold nor Gustav Lindquist, who both went home in 1932, returned to winter again in North-East Greenland.

1932-33

The summer of 1932 became one of the busiest in the history of Myggbukta; at least as far as the airspace above the station: *"We arrived at Myggbukta on the 24th and prepared a landing strip on the large sandy plain north of Kap Bennet Hill. In the evening the Spartan machine was taken ashore a bit south of the station and immediately after Aagenæs set off and scampered about with the silver-painted plane against the blue sky. When he landed, after having completed the first Norwegian flight in East Greenland, he was greeted with three cheers"*, Anders K. Orvin wrote.[544]

It was consul Lars Christensen of Sandefjord, who had lent out his Lockheed Vega plane "Qarrtsiluni" (in the Inuit language meaning: while waiting for something to burst) for NSIU's aerial mapping. As a reserve, a Spartan biplane had been rented. The purpose of the aerial mapping was to supplement the NSIU surveys from previous years with aerial photographs, which were subsequently used to make topographical maps. The flights took place between the 30th July and the 18th August from "Balås Flyveplads", a landing strip established on the large sandy plain five km south-west of Myggbukta station. The aerial photography was carried out in co-operation with professor Otto Lacmann from "Deutsche Versuchsanstalt für Luftfahrt" and "Hansa Luftbild" in Berlin.

On the 21st August, when "Polarbjørn" left Myggbukta, three men stayed behind to trap and run the station: Sverre J. Sørensen, 33-years old, Knut Hofgaard, then 29-years old, and the wireless operator John Thorsteinsen. Originally Realf Berg, a doctor, was to have wintered, but he became ill and returned to Norway.

The wireless operator was to have a share of the catch in return for helping out, but this arrangement became a nuisance to Sørensen: *"Thorsteinsen is looking after his main job, but needs help all the time, and this is not what was meant with the contract. He receives 2% of the catch in return for helping us but we receive nothing for helping him with his radio transmissions".*[545] The atmosphere amongst the three men - especially between Sørensen and Thorsteinsen - was badly strained that winter. It was Sørensen's third and last year in North-East Greenland, while for Hofgaard and Thorsteinsen it was their only wintering.

From a trapping point of view, something new was tried; seven silver foxes had been imported from Norway. Knut Hofgaard who was from Halden, was an experienced fox tender, and was to take care of the animals that it was hoped would produce better quality fur under arctic conditions. With the aim of catching live polar foxes, another 39 fox cages were built and: *"the entire line is about 100 m long".*[546] A fair number of animals were caught, but on New Years Day 1933 a blizzard hit Myggbukta, and when the storm was over the men were met by a sad sight: *"the fox cages, in which the live animals had been were thrown about 25 m away, and had knocked down one of the radio masts. The fox cages were smashed to pieces and all except three silver foxes are gone".*[547] Despite the aggravating losses, Myggbukta's total catch amounted to 104 foxes.

"17th May gathering" at Myggbukta, (17th May is the Norwegian independence day). In front from left: Knut Hofgaard, Hans Furland, Knut Nakken, Arnljot Tolløfsen and Leif Brandal. Rear: Sverre J. Sørensen. This is the last known photo of Arnljot Tolløfsen. Just one week later he drowned on his way north to Kap Herschell. Myggbukta, 17th May 1933. © Norwegian Polar Institute

1933-34

"Polarbjørn" arrived at Myggbukta on the 22nd July 1933. Supplies for Arctic Commercial Enterprise were unloaded, after which the ship continued to the other Norwegian stations. On the 3rd August the ship was at Jonsbu in Peters Bugt. The meteorological station there was to be closed down and: *"wireless operator Holm, who was going to Myggbukta the next winter, went along southwards with the ship in the evening".*[548] Apart from Johan Holm, the trapper Eilif Herdal wintered at Myggbukta in 1933-34. Herdal's catch was 58 foxes.

With respect to Johan Holm, and the job of a radio operator in general, John Giæver wrote: *"Holm's enemy and best friend was his alarm clock. It was an extremely unpleasant specimen with a cheeky and snarling Nazi-buzz. An utterly hated but necessary piece of clockwork. It brutally forced poor Holm out of his warm bed and into a freezing cold room. Groggy and sleepy he had to go out in the dark night in all kinds of weather with a paraffin lamp in order to read the instruments. With chattering teeth and frozen fingers he then sat down to prepare the weather report." ... "All I know is that if a trapper, chilled to the bone, arrived at Myggbukta one evening, then Johan Holm would dish up the best meal an arctic chef could prepare. Nevertheless, if that damned alarm clock started ringing, then he would let the guest be a guest and leave the waffles to burn to coal in the oven. Head over heels, he left everything, such was the snarling command of duty, just as it simultaneously would snarl in six other Norwegian radio stations in the Arctic".*[549]

1934-35

In 1934 the "Selbarden" reached Myggbukta on 8th August. Henry Haug came ashore to relieve Johan Holm as radio operator, while Eilif Herdal continued as trapper.

Henry Haug, born in 1907 at Halden, had been station manager of the Norwegian weather station Storfjord Radio at Kangerdlussuaq in South-East Greenland in 1932-33. He was already well acquainted with trapping and the polar regions, for: *"I had previously been on board a whaler in the Southern Ocean for three years"*, Haug said in 1993.[550]

"I sailed with British whalers around South Georgia. Then I worked as radio operator, but was still one of the crew and had to help with the whaling".

Haug thus became wireless operator at Myggbukta and: *"it was not just out of love of adventure. The times were hard and it was difficult to get a regular job in Norway. Those who were used to the Arctic went along with that. But it was no gold mine and no great adventure, but hard daily work, yet interesting. The years between 1930 and 1940 were exciting in many ways, for these were still pioneering times. And it was fun because we worked in areas practically untrodden by man".*[551] Haug was also radio operator at Myggbukta in 1936-37. After his retirement he lived in Oslo, where he died in 1994.

1935-36

In 1935 the ice conditions were the most difficult and dangerous since the fatal summer of 1923. "Buskø" left Ålesund on the 27th July, and after many difficulties succeeded in reaching the coast; but on the 31st August they were forced to give up calling at Myggbukta and the southern stations. Fuel was running low and on the 4th September "Buskø" sailed to the head of Loch Fyne and unloaded the supplies for Myggbukta there. The winter catch and the trappers who were going home came on board there too.

A young student of engineering, Øivind Holm Johnsen, had been allowed to come along with "Buskø" on a summer voyage, but the difficult ice conditions now gave him an unexpected chance: *"The problem was how normal trapping could be carried out at the stations which had not received their supplies, and this is where I came into the picture. I was asked to stay over the winter in order to transport food and equipment by dog sledge to the stations, so that the trappers could trap in as normal a way as possible"*, Johnsen wrote.[552]

Johnsen, who stayed with Finn Framnes-Hansen, Søren Richter and Johan Holm at Myggbukta, summed up his experiences as follows: *"The outcome of my wintering, financially speaking, was sufficient to cover the expenses of my studies the following year at University. In the meantime I gained something else, the value of which cannot be measured in money, but which has meant a lot to me – a sort of life philosophy, that I will try to explain further. The welfare state offers us a number of easy fundamental blessings. By this I mean such things as always having a roof over your head, not being cold, always having food and drink when you need it. Rarely if ever do you need to call on your body's last reserves. These things are taken for granted and are not much appreciated. If something has to be measured or evaluated, you need a standard of reference, a zero. My stay in Greenland in my youth gave me the opportunity and ability to appreciate what life has since offered me. All young people ought to have such a chance".*[553]

1936-37

Apart from the trappers, the "Isbjørn" in 1936 carried up two British ornithologists from Cambridge, the brothers Edward and Charles Bird, who were to winter at Myggbukta. The other wintering personnel consisted of the station leader Finn Framnes-Hansen, the radio operator Henry Haug, and Sverre Røstad who had early participated in Helge Ingstad's Expedition of 1932-34: *"I went up there to experience the freedom of the hunter's life in one of the finest wildernesses in the world"*, Røstad wrote. *"There were good and bad years for trapping; but when it was really good you could sit out on a hill in the moonlit nights and hear the foxes sing in a playful and crazy way. Then we had good catches. The furs of course would be of slightly different quality as is usual with wildlife furs; but there were always a number of furs of such brilliant quality that any ordinary fox farmer would turn green with envy. Such years we had money to burn when we came home"*.[554]

Of a visit in the summer of 1937, the German journalist Vitalis Pantenburg wrote: *"It is crowded in the radio room. No more space than Haug can barely squeeze himself past the wires, the insulators, switches etc. to get to his simple table, made of rough planks. Normal standards do not apply here. It is solely the performance and sense of duty that count.*

With all his notes in front of him, the wireless operator takes his seat at the radio and puts on his headphones. There are still a few seconds before the exact time. Now it's time – Haug eagerly switches on the various equipment and the small room is filled with buzzing and sparking. There's a smell of ozone – "Myggbukta radio here – Myggbukta radio here. Weather report." Haug transmits the different results of his readings and emphasizes each number carefully. It is important to speak as clearly as possible in order to eliminate misunderstandings. After the official part follows the usual entertainment of news and gossip".[555]

1937-38

In 1937, "Polarbjørn" did not reach Myggbukta until 5th August. It was another summer with difficult ice conditions, and to add to her troubles "Polarbjørn" was delayed by some days when she ran aground at Zackenberg. The summer was unusually cold and rainy.

At Myggbukta Finn Framnes-Hansen continued for his third year in a row, while Johan Johansen took over from Sverre Røstad; Johan Holm was radio operator. Charles Bird stayed for another wintering while his brother Edward went home. During the autumn Framnes-Hansen and Johansen built the hut "Funkis" [316].

It was the best fox year ever: *"Until Christmas the men had an ordinary and good catch; but during January large numbers of fox began flocking through the territory. They were migrating but I do not know from where they came. The trappers say they came from the south and were going north, but even in the summer of 1938 there were swarms of foxes everywhere. As a result of this invasion the company's men made an excellent catch"*.[556] The total catch of Arctic Commercial Enterprise's trappers was 1400 foxes.

1938-39

In 1938 Myggbukta had a completely new crew. Eilif Herdal was taking his sixth and last wintering, while Oscar Bang and the radio operator Egil Rogstad both wintered for only this one year in North-East Greenland. In October 1938, Herdal and Bang built a new trappers' hut, "Stormbu" [332-2].

In the summer of 1938, Arctic Commercial Enterprise experimented with canning char directly on site. Previously they had just salted the char and packed it into barrels. Now, with the more modern methods available they were hoping to make higher returns. Eilif Herdal had visited the tinning industry (Hermetikkindustriens Laboratorium) to learn the special technique, and the laboratory had lent out suitable machines for the experiment, which took place on Strindberg Land at the mouth of Brogetdal. Oscar Bang wrote about the canning process: *"First we clean the fish, then they have to be scraped and brushed before we cut them open and put them into the tins. The tins are then filled up with brine or jelly. This is done quite quickly with a bit of training. Finally the tins are boiled for 45 minutes under eight atmospheres of pressure. That is, the temperature of the water rises to about 112°C"*.[557] Although the experiment went well it was never repeated.

The wireless operator Rogstad came from Vinger, and was said by John Giæver to be: *"the happiest "spark" in the world. I don't believe that Egil Rogstad cried when he was born – no matter what his mother says. But even if he did so, I'm sure he has not cried since. There is no other "spark" with such a spark on earth"*.[558] During the war, Rogstad went via Canada to Jan Mayen, where he served in the Norwegian defence forces. Later he went with John Giæver on the Norwegian-British-Swedish Antarctic Expedition (NBSAE) to the Antarctic.

Oscar Bang, a law student, described his overwintering in his book "Blant fangstfolk og bikkjer i Eirik Raudes Land" (among trappers and sledge dogs in Eirik Raudes Land) (1944): *"But how difficult it was to convince old polar veterans that a law student, coming from the inland town of Kongsberg, could take on the job as trapper in North-East Greenland"*;[559] but Bang was thrilled with his job as a trapper and: *"in just one month I have had more practical experience than for the last five years"*.[560]

The ice froze up late, and Bang was not able to go trapping until the middle of November. At about the same time news reached Myggbukta of Gerhard

Myggbukta c. 1940.
© Niels Ove Jensen

Antonsen's injury to his eye at Moskusheimen. In the middle of December, Bang decided to go north to help the injured trapper, and stayed with Antonsen until May 1939. At Myggbukta Herdal's catch was 113 foxes.

1939-40

Myggbukta once again had a new team in 1939. One was Johan Johansen, who had had two previous winterings in North-East Greenland. The two others were Hans Kleinsorg Siewers and the radio operator Andreas Skaanevik, both newcomers to Greenland.

For Hans Siewers the job as a trapper was the realization of a dream going back to his childhood in Drammen. Then he had become interested in the Arctic, outdoor life and dog sledge driving. In 1933 he was one of the founders of "Drammens Trekkhundklubb" (Drammen dog sledge club).

In Myggbukta he took over a good team of 12 dogs: *"In my first winter "Kalle" was the leader of the pack. He was old, wise and calm and totally dominated the other dogs in the team, as he should – but at first he also dominated me. I soon found out that dog sledge driving in the backyards of Drammen was not the same as in Greenland. It was Kalle and not me who decided if the bitch I brought with me from Norway was going to be accepted in the team" ... "After much cursing and beating I finally had the dogs harnessed. They resolutely lay down and curled up again. I jumped onto the sledge with a "left march" and let go of the reins. Nothing happened. More beating and cursing. This was too much for Kalle. He looked at me with a reproaching glance, got the team up and in a wild gallop they went "right march" around the station buildings, the fox cages and the radio antennas until Kalle spotted the open porch door. We all ended up there, dogs, sledge and me. Kalle looked at me, wagging his tail. In the station door the old trapper stood and glared. That's how I learnt that when it is minus 40 degrees outside, both men and dogs "stay in." Kalle and I eventually became good friends. He showed me where each and every trap in my territory was, and many times during that winter he saved me from driving across thin ice when I wanted to take a short cut".*[561]

At the end of December 1939, Johan Johansen summed up the trapping: *"Will not go out again before New Year, as there are no foxes. Have only caught 10 foxes in two trips around the entire territory and Siewers had none. Christmas Eve, fine weather and good mood, muskox steak and toddy, good entertainment on the radio*

The new over-wintering crew 1939-40 on board the "Polarbjørn". Sitting in front from left: Helland (christian name unknown), Levin Winther and Hans K. Siewers. Rear from left: Ole Andreas Bachke, Schjølberg Nilsen, Magne Råum, Søren Richter, Johan Johansen, Kåre Rodahl and Henry Rudi. 1939. © Ebbe Arneberg / Norwegian Polar Institute

etc." ... "The year that went by was probably the poorest year ever for Norwegian trapping in Greenland, equally disappointing at all stations, but we hope for better times; so farewell and thank you 1939".[562] The outcome of that year was 31 white foxes and three live foxes.

When the trapping was over, Siewers went out to lay down the traps. He was accompanied by Kåre Rodahl from Moskusheimen. On the 15th April 1940, they arrived at Hoelsbu where Levin Winther told them that war had broken out in Norway: *"He had a battery radio, but the batteries were almost used up. We turned on the news from Oslo, but the only thing we understood from the radio was: He who....gets shot. That day we drove for 20 hours in one stretch to Myggbukta, in order to find out what was happening in Norway".*[563]

1940-41

The war in Europe was the source of much anxiety for the trappers during the summer of 1940. Would they get their supplies? Would there be any attacks from the enemy? On the 24th July Johansen and Siewers started fishing char from Strindberghuset. Here they met the trappers from Hoelsbu and Kap Humboldt and the Danes from Ella Ø. It was important to gather as much food as possible for the coming winter.

On the 12th August Johansen and Siewers sailed back to Myggbukta: *"13th to 25th August: Came to Myggbukta on the 13th. "Veslekari" arrived in the afternoon of the same day. We have our own motor boat in tow and follow "Veslekari" to Strindberg on the 14th. Stay at Strindberg until the 17th when we go back to Myggbukta. Arrive there on the 18th, finding the station occupied by British marines, with Captain Dennis in charge. On the 21st the naval vessel "Fridtjof Nansen" arrived with "Veslekari". Both ships stayed for some hours and then continued to Eskimonæs. On the 22nd "Polarbjørn" arrived from Saint John's in Canada, bringing provisions and coal for all stations, but nothing is taken ashore. "Fridtjof Nansen" and "Veslekari" came back in the night of the 24th. All three ships then depart in the afternoon of the 25th. Our radio operator Hannestad, who arrived with the "Veslekari", went along with them so now we are two men again.*

26th August to 4th September: Siewers and I take the motor boat up to Claveringfjorden and Loch Fyne to supply the huts with provisions for the winter, return on the 4th September.

5th to 6th September: "Fridtjof Nansen" returns in the night of the 5th to destroy the radio equipment and remove various instruments. They leave again on the morning of the 6th".[564]

Johansen and Siewers were now alone at Myggbukta. The latter said in 1993: *"After the "Veslekari" had been seized in the summer of 1940, Ullring for a time had orders to evacuate everyone from North-East Greenland. John Giæver and Søren Richter – as senior Norwegian representatives – suggested that it might be a "good idea" if some of us stayed back to protect Norwegian interests, something which Ullring finally accepted on condition that officially we were going to maintain the trapping. Unofficially, we were to stay here at his orders to patrol and observe, and to report any hostile activities through Niels Ove Jensen at Eskimonæs and Aage de Lemos at Ella Ø".*[565] Yet the winter of 1940-41 passed by without any dramatic events. Late in the winter, Bjarne Akre at Kap Humboldt developed sciatica and on 28th April Hans Siewers went south to look after his sick fellow-countryman.

In the summer of 1941, Hans Siewers joined the North-East Greenland Sledge Patrol: *"I moved to Ella Ø and from there I patrolled in the Kong Oscar Fjord and Kejser Franz Joseph Fjord areas until the summer of 1942".*[566]

In the summer of 1942, Hans Siewers went to West Greenland with the USCG cutter "North Star". He went to Godthåb (Nuuk) where he applied for permission to join the Norwegian forces in Little

British soldiers from the "Fridtjof Nansen" with their officer in front. Myggbukta, August 1940. © Hans K. Siewers

Norway in Canada. While his case was being processed, he worked together with Niels Ove Jensen and others on the Danish naval vessel "Ternen". On Christmas Eve of 1943, something unexpected happened. He met Bernt Balchen, who at that time was in charge of the Bluie West 8 air base in Søndre Strømfjord: *"He asked me whether I would stay in Greenland to help him organize a Search & Rescue squadron for rescuing air crews which had made emergency landings on the Inland Ice".*[567] Siewers accepted the offer, stayed in Greenland until the end of the war and participated in numerous rescue operations in and around Greenland.

In the autumn of 1945, Siewers returned to Norway, but in 1947 settled in the USA as arctic consultant with the Strategic Air Command (SAC), US Air Force. For the next 32 years the main theme of his work was arctic survival and aircrew life support equipment. He became one of the founding members of the SAC Survival School at Fort Collins, Colorado. Thanks to their efforts, thousands of aircrews learnt how to survive under extreme conditions. His last four years before retirement in 1973 were spent working on the design of an escape system for the advanced B-1 bomber. Hans Siewers lived out his last years in Fort Collins, Colorado, where he died in March 1996 at an age of 77 years.[568]

1941-42

In the summer of 1941, American naval forces took over patrol of the Greenland coast, and in North-East Greenland the main question was whether the trappers would be forced to be evacuated. From Johan Johansen's diary it appears that Myggbukta had several visits from US Coast Guard ships. First the "North Star" arrived on 2nd August. Johansen was supplied with some provisions and: *"at the same time was asked if I would leave Myggbukta. I turned down the offer, and was told that all of us might be forcibly evacuated".*[569]

On the 13th August Johansen had a lift with the "Bear" to Gael Hamke Bugt, from where he continued on his own to Henry Rudi at Moskusheimen to discuss the situation. They went together to Eskimonæs: *"The following morning "Northland" arrived and we were asked to come aboard to meet Commander Smith. Commander Smith told us – on behalf of the Greenland Administration* (Governor Eske Brun) *– that we would get a good job in Ivigtut or other places in Greenland, and that they would do anything to satisfy us as long as we were willing to leave the East Coast".*[570] Commander Smith made several attempts to convince the trappers, but Johansen, Rudi, and Levin and Petra Winther at Hoelsbu, all refused to be evacuated and were eventually permitted to stay.

On 24th August Johansen came back to Myggbukta. Two days later a floatplane from the "North Star" arrived with a letter for Johansen. The letter was from Commander Ernst Ullring and was dated Reykjavik, 23rd August 1941: *"It is hereby announced that Dr. Rodahl has discovered huge quantities of vitamin A in the liver of polar bear and bearded seal, and that their organs are possibly rich sources of vitamin D, from which vitamin-rich oils can be produced. The gall bladder of the polar bear is also very valuable and should be stored in bottles. John Giæver says: "Trapping in 1941-42 must as far as possible be focused on polar bear and bearded seal. First of all you must preserve the livers from the animals, so that they can be stored in brine in ordinary wooden barrels. Walrus and ringed seal are also of value." ... "The men must be strictly ordered to give fox-trapping second priority and first and foremost focus on trapping seal and bear, no matter the season".*[571] Vitamins were now of greater military importance than fox furs.

After a final visit from "Northland" on 26th September, the area once again became peaceful, secure behind the impenetrable masses of pack ice. Johansen carried on with his trapping and lived as a hermit. Christmas 1941 was celebrated with Rudi at Moskusheimen.

Then came spring and summer of 1942, and Johansen was prepared for another wintering. However, on the 10th September 1942: *"the American USCG cutter "North Star" arrived in the bay and anchored. Lt. Conby came ashore with orders to take me onboard. I objected as he had no orders concerning where to set me ashore, but when he told me that it had been arranged with the Norwegian Legation in Washington, I went aboard. Soon after we sailed to Moskusoksefjord and took Winther and his wife on board".*[572]

Johan Johansen went into allied service: *"The Americans needed experienced dog sledge drivers for their forces in Greenland, so I was able to stay up here in the north." ... "There were many and interesting assignments; aircraft that disappeared, and sometimes managed to send emergency signals so we knew where to look for them – other times they didn't and then it was like looking for a needle in a haystack"*, Johansen wrote.[573] After the war, Johansen joined the Norwegian merchant navy.

1946-47

Myggbukta had been unmanned from 1942 until the summer of 1946, when Peter Melleby and Paul Furuseth arrived to resume the trapping. At the station they were accompanied by the wireless operator Jan Jansen.

"The two years I spent in East Greenland, were a wonderful time", Peter Melleby recalled in 1992. He was 29-years old when he came to Greenland, but already had comprehensive experience of the Arctic.[574] Melleby, who was born in 1917 at Halden in Østfold, had interrupted his studies in 1939 to become a surveyor so he could go to Svalbard. His job was surveying the mines and it was well paid. Then war broke out, and everyone was evacuated in 1941; Melleby went to Scotland. In May 1942, the ships "Selis" and "Isbjørn" set course for Svalbard and Melleby was on board. In Grønfjorden they were discovered by German planes and attacked. The two ships sank, but Melleby was one of the 69 Norwegian soldiers who survived and managed to reach shore. For the rest of the war he was part of the Norwegian garrison on Svalbard.

Peace came, but the Arctic did not let go of Melleby. One day he read in the newspaper that Arctic Commercial Enterprise was looking for people to go to Greenland and contacted John Giæver. Melleby was an obvious candidate, as in addition to his arctic experience he was also a qualified radio operator: *"and besides he was a formidable skier"*, Ivar Ytreland, one of Melleby's friends from his Greenland days, recalled.[575] With such a background, it is understandable that Melleby in 1992 looked back on his Greenland years of 1946-48 as a special sort of holiday.

In 1949-52 Melleby went to the Antarctic with John Giæver and the Norwegian-British-Swedish Antarctic Expedition (NBSAE), also known as the Norsel Expedition or the Maudheim Expedition, where he was in charge of the sledge dogs. He revisited Greenland briefly in 1952, when he participated in an Arctic Commercial Enterprise summer expedition. From 1955 until his retirement Melleby, who had also been a ski instructor in Scotland, was employed by Norges Geologiske Undersøkelser (the Geological Survey of Norway).

In 1947 Paul Furuseth moved to Hoelsbu, while Jan Jansen went home to Norway after one wintering.

1947-48

As from the summer of 1947, Arctic Commercial Enterprise changed its manning system at Myggbukta. So far there had been two trappers and one radio operator, but now it was reversed. It was simply too tiring for a single man to run the weather service as he never had a day off. Furthermore, one trapper could easily manage the entire territory. Jan Jansen was therefore relieved by the radio operators Helge Strand of Sandefjord and Lorang Larsen from northern Norway.

In 1947 Peter Melleby had trapped in the territory along the south side of Gauss Halvø, but this area was now taken over by Hoelsbu. Instead he trapped towards Kap Stosch and caught 37 foxes. Melleby, Strand and Larsen all went home in the summer of 1948.

1948-49

The new overwinterers at Myggbukta consisted of the radio operators Dagfinn Egeberg and Stein S. Sørensen, and the trapper Nils Haugmo.

Stein Sørensen (1922-1987) was born in Oslo. He was to have six winterings in North-East Greenland as radio operator and trapper: Myggbukta 1948-51, Ottostrand 1952-53, Kap Herschell 1953-54 and Myggbukta 1955-56. From 1957-59 he was chief radio operator in the Antarctic in connection with the International Geophysical Year of 1957-58. Subsequently he was employed at Norsk Meteorologisk Institutt (the Norwegian Meteorological Institute) from 1960-87, and as manager at Bjørnøya 1963-64 and Hopen 1972-73. Stein Sørensen's Greenland diaries have survived, and provide vivid descriptions of his experiences.

On 22nd October 1948, Sørensen summed up his

"17th May gathering" 1948 at Myggbukta. From left: Trygve Havold, Bjarne Myrvold, Lorang Larsen, Gudrun Andersen, Peter Melleby, Egil Amsjø, Normann Andersen, Helge Strand. © Trygve Havold

first impressions of Greenland: *"We have now been here for about 2 1/2 months and during that time you build up quite a number of impressions. You might think that the days would seem long for three men, isolated from the world, but I have not been bored for one single minute. There is always lots to do apart from your daily job, which of course takes up most of the time. Preparations for trapping, making traps, locks, sledge, cooking, heating, washing, cleaning, maintenance of the station, the instruments, clothes and shoes – we have so far had a 10-hour working day. Books there are in plenty, many good; they will probably last for a year in spite of frequent use. The atmosphere amongst us is good, some arguing and irritation is of course unavoidable, but it helps to keep up our spirits. Nature, climate and wildlife here is without exaggeration heavenly"*.[576]

Life at Myggbukta followed a steady routine, where the radio operators in turn had one week on and one week off. Weather reports were transmitted at 7 - 10 - 13 - 16 - 19, that is five times each day. The radio operators shared a dog team and a trapping territory, stretching from Myggbukta eastwards to Kap Broer Ruys. Haugmo's territory extended south, west and north, that is between Kap Franklin and Kap Stosch.

It was a poor year for trapping. In April 1949 Sørensen wrote: *"The trapping is terrible at all stations this year, total failure, so the trappers are devastated. We assume that the unusual abundance of ptarmigan and small game is the cause; the foxes have so much food that they don't care about dried baits. Those we have caught are so fat that it's a mystery that they have gone into the trap – it must have been pure laziness"*.[577] The wireless operators had their fixed salary so it was worst for Nils Haugmo, the trapper, who came from Sjøåsen in Nord-Trøndelag: *"Poor Haugmo has this winter travelled a distance the same as from Oslo to Kirkenes and back again. He has caught seven foxes and one bear, that is he has earned 500 kroner; so a trapper's pay here now is almost nothing. He is married and has three children and has saved money for years to be able to spend a year here. This has been his dream. He is a forester and keen hunter. An altogether 100% great guy"*.[578]

On 14th July Sørensen said goodbye to Nils Haugmo, who: *"started his trip to Hoelsbu, to take the motor boat from there to fish char at Strindberg"*.[579] Dagfinn Egeberg also left Myggbukta in the summer of 1949, to become a trapper at Hoelsbu.

1949-50

The "Quest" arrived at Myggbukta on 3rd August 1949. Two new men arrived with the ship, both on their first wintering, the radio operator Henry Olsen and the trapper Harald Sverdsten.

During the autumn an engine room for various radio- and engine equipment was built. A new radio room was also furnished in which: *"Olsen has painted the walls and ceiling. It looks as if the room will be quite good, it is three times the size of the old one and warm and comfortable"*, Stein Sørensen wrote on 7th September 1949.[580] They continued the renovation and gave the rest of the house an overhaul: *"Sverdsten has painted the sitting room green. It's becoming very nice with a white shiny ceiling, apple green walls and new linoleum on the floors, and most of all electric light, which I installed before the polar night began"*.[581]

On 3rd November trapper Per Myrvold arrived. He had fallen ill at his station in Kong Oscar Fjord, and wanted to stay at Myggbukta for Christmas and take over the cooking in return for five fox furs.

The fox catch was much better than in 1948-49, also for the radio operators. Henry Olsen was not particularly interested, but Stein Sørensen's catch of 31 foxes was a quantity, which: *"offends the trappers. They think it's too much that we radio operators are allowed to trap at all. What's annoying them is of course that in such a small territory as we have, we take a larger percentage of the catch than any of them. The reason is that I have made 60 traps and exploit the territory much better than ever before. And finally, I'm off in my territory in all my spare time, so the traps are always set up"*.[582]

Harald Sverdsten left Myggbukta on 8th July to fish char at the Strindberg river, and in 1950-51 took over the Hoelsbu station.

1950-51

The "Polarbjørn" arrived on 4th August 1950: Stein Sørensen wrote: *"At the rail are, of course, Hermann Andresen and Sæterdal, who is coming back. The film-maker Høst is also greeting us. We have beer and drinks in the lounge together with Andresen, Høst and Søren Richter. Then a hectic unloading begins, and I tell the others that there will be plenty of drinks in the evening. And so there are, probably the biggest polar party in the history of Myggbukta. Olsen has to be carried to his bed early on and a hell of riot is developing bit by bit. I know many of the crew, who worked on the old "Polarbjørn", and all of them can stand a few drinks. Some play the accordion, some the guitar and others the mouth organ. The rest of us sing our songs, dance, yodel and stamp our feet while Høst is filming. Eventually he has to be carried away too. Finally – at 04.00 in the morning – there are only three of us left, Sæterdal, the second engineer and myself. It looks terrible everywhere, empty bottles, broken chairs and windows. But we go ahead with washing and cleaning and in the morning everything is hunky-dory again"*.[583]

Soon peace again settled at Myggbukta, and the ever busy Stein Sørensen built a: *"porch in front of the front door to prevent the hallway from filling up with snow once again in the winter".*[584] Sørensen also had ideas. He wanted to try out a bear hunt at Kap Broer Ruys and on the 12th September 1950 he went there to build a hunters' hut, "Gnisten" [329]. He had just finished and was on his way down to the shore to pick up a sack of coal: *"when suddenly my blood turned into ice, I got shivers down my back and cold sweats. There, right next to the coal sack, stands a huge bear, sniffing and scratching the sack only a few metres in front of me (afterwards measured to 5½ metres). At the same moment the bear spots me and I think we stood there, staring at each other for at least a minute. He sort of crouches down, ready to jump, tightening all his muscles. I'm just waiting for him to attack and crush my skull. The hut, where I keep my rifle, is about 50 metres behind me, so I have little chance should he attack. It occurs to me that a bear can jump up to 10 metres so I'm right in his line of fire. But he is probably just as scared of me as I am of him – we both want to run away but each of us is afraid to turn our back on the other. Eventually I make the decision, throwing myself backwards and running as I have never run before, at the same time yelling for Peik. He comes rushing towards me from the hut. I hear a loud splash behind me, turn around and see the bear swimming full speed towards the pack ice about 200 m from the shore, so he didn't hesitate to follow my example. I grab my rifle and have him right in my sights there in the water, but he spared me so I spare him – and have myself a well-earned cigarette, while I watch him until he reaches the ice, climbs it, shakes himself and disappears at a gallop between the ice hummocks. This was my first encounter with the king of the pack ice – a little different from what I had hoped for".*[585]

Everything indicated a good year for fox trapping and: *"Olsen and I have agreed that I can go trapping whenever I want, then he'll take care of the radio station and we will split 50/50"*, Stein Sørensen wrote on the 31st October 1950.[586] It did turn out to be a good year for trapping and Sørensen, who still minded his radio watch, had a total catch of: *"128 foxes, nine without tails, 90 part-eaten and four bears".*[587]

That winter was not altogether idyllic however. When Sørensen returned from a trapping trip on 1st April, he realized that his partner had: *"made home-brew again and is drunk. When I arrive back, he is lying drunk in the attic. The stoves have gone out and the house looks like a pigsty. No paraffin or coal are available and no observations have been noted in the logbook. So from tomorrow there will be another tune here at the station, as surely as my name is Stein Sørensen. In the evening when I turn in, he wakes up and I call him a drunken carcass, chicken, an old hag etc".*[588] After this telling off the relationship improves, judging from Sørensen's notes. Both of them returned to Norway in the summer of 1951.

1951-52

The wintering party in 1951-52 consisted of the radio operators Nicolay Nicolaysen and Amundsen (first name unknown), and the trapper Alf Rustøen. Both radio operators were newcomers to Greenland, although Nicolaysen had previously wintered at Jan Mayen.

Alf Rustøen had been a trapper for the Hermann Andresen Expedition in Kong Oscar Fjord the year before. In November he was lucky and shot a bear at the Foldvik-hytten at Kap Bennet. The Danish trapper Hans Madsen told the story: *"It was a 2-year-old male that had broken into the hut and eaten all the muskox*

Danish Sirius patrol visiting Myggbukta, 7th May 1952. From left facing camera: Nicolay Nicolaysen, Verner Andersen, Flemming Carlsen, Mathias Aasen, Finn Jensen, Bakke and Fredrik Sæterdal, Knud Bernt Andersen, Alf Rustøen and Halvor Bjørdal. Odd Bogholm is standing with his back to camera. © Folmer Berthelsen

meat that was intended for his dogs. Afterwards the bear had dragged a muskox skin from the berth outside and laid himself down on it to rest. It was here Rustøen surprised it – the dogs had bear meat instead of muskox".[589] Rustøen went home to Norway in 1952, and later emigrated to Canada.

1952-53

Nicolay Nicolaysen continued as station manager in 1952-53, and had the company of two newcomers: the radio operator Finn Jensen and trapper Lauritz Storholt. The latter was a younger brother of the trapper Sverre Storholt.

Lauritz Storholt, who was from Solør, had just turned 22-years old when Germany invaded Norway in 1940. Like his brother Sverre, he was an active member of the resistance throughout the war. In 1940 he had taken part in the battles at Stryken. Later he worked as a courier and border guide for the resistance. From Oslo he often made the journey to the Swedish border to exchange courier mail with Sverre, who during the war operated from Stockholm. The Storholt brothers kept this important channel of information open at the risk of their own lives. Sometime after the war Greenland came into the picture: *"I had read so much about Greenland and being a bit of an adventurer I wanted very much to go there. My brother Sverre had been there in 1949-50 and he came back and told about the trip – but you must not go there, he said, you'll never make it. Never mind, I said, I'll apply for it. And then I sent my application with certificates from the doctor, the rifle club, the ski club and the military – and that they had removed my appendix in 1947. I was told that I could have the job at Myggbukta, but I was going to be the only trapper there – and I accepted"*, Lauritz Storholt said in 1992. He added with a smile: *"I would probably have accepted anything".*[590] Lauritz Storholt died in December 1998, at the age of 80.

On the night of the 5th December 1952, the station house at Myggbukta was almost burnt down. Storholt recalled in 1992 that: *"the manager, Nicolaysen, had poured petrol into the stove and then lit it. The wind was in the east, and the flames hit the roof, melted the snow and set fire to the entire attic. And Finn Jensen was at Daneborg at the time. We had nothing but snow to put out the fire, so we went up on the roof, made a hole and pushed in snow through it. Nicolaysen stayed up there pouring in snow while I stood below and cut out big blocks of snow, which I threw up to him. Half the roof burned. Luckily I was there at the time, for if Nicolaysen had been alone, he would never have made it".*[591] Storholt, Nicolaysen and Jensen all went home to Norway in 1953.

The Myggbukta crew 1952-53. From left: Lauritz Storholt, Nicolay Nicolaysen and Finn Jensen. © Hans Madsen

1953-54

In 1953, Birger Larsen returned to Myggbukta to winter with the radio operators Dagfinn Egeberg and Asbjørn Tøndell. Egeberg was on his fourth and last

Norwegian trapper Lauritz Storholt before and after his "spring" shave. © Hans Madsen

wintering, while Tøndell was a newcomer to North-East Greenland.

Although Larsen made the largest catch of the year, 143 foxes, his winter passed very differently than he had hoped for. The worst problem was the situation at Myggbukta where Egeberg was causing problems. Towards the end of the year the situation became so bad that on 24th December, Christmas Eve, Larsen had had enough of the never ending harassment. He loaded up his sledge to go the Loch Fyne station, and: *"when Tøndell understood that I was leaving Myggbukta he packed his sledge too and went along. Quite understandably. There will be no big Christmas party here. We haven't made any preparations, but at least we will have some peace and quiet"*.[592] From then on Birger Larsen stayed at the Loch Fyne station, which the Sirius Dog Sledge Patrol had allowed him to borrow. In 1992, Birger Larsen said that after that year Dagfinn Egeberg was banned from wintering at arctic stations.

Unfortunately, even more unpleasant experiences were in store for Birger Larsen: *"This winter ended in a somewhat sad way for my part. I went northwards to my father-in-law Normann Andersen's station at Revet in Tyrolerfjord. It was an easy trip with rested dogs. The previous summer we had made a deal with Fredrik Sæterdal, who wintered south at Hoelsbu in Moskusoksefjord together with his wife, Solveig, that they too should come to Revet around the 1st May.*

As we came closer to mid-May, and they had still not arrived, we began to wonder whether something had gone wrong during the winter. Andersen and I agreed that it would be best to go to Moskusoksefjord and we set off with two dog teams.

Then it happened. I was sitting on the sledge and became annoyed that one of the dogs had its trace wrapped around his neck. So I stopped the sledge and walked forward to unwind the trace. After two weeks of rest the dogs were playful and frisky, and started fighting while I was standing between the dogs. I was hit by the sledge trace just above my left knee and both ligaments were torn. I remained sitting, covered by dogs and traces, realizing that I could not get up. I was soon picked up by Andersen, who was driving a short distance behind me. He tied me to the sledge and then we went off back to Revet.

It turned out to be a serious injury that we normally could do nothing about under these primitive conditions. Something had to be done however, and Normann Andersen again climbed onto his sledge and drove to the Danish weather station at Daneborg. They contacted the doctor in Mestersvig, who according to Andersen's description diagnosed: double torn ligaments and severe internal bleeding requiring hospitalisation and two months in plaster. However, there was no hospital available, nor plaster, and the doctor indicated that at best the leg would be ruined for life. Just as Andersen was leaving, the Danes had a telegram from Keflavik in Iceland asking about landing conditions east of the station at Revet. Keflavik had heard about the accident from the doctor in Mestersvig and planned to send a Catalina plane to fly me to Iceland. It could probably have been done, but we considered the risk for the air crew to be so great that we declined the offer. Instead Normann went back with instructions received by telegraph from the doctor in Mestersvig. (After my homecoming in September the diagnosis turned out to be correct.)

Then Normann started an hour-long surgery on my injured knee. And this is one of the things I will always remember about my father-in-law, how skilled he was with his hands.

Hopefully it is the last time that such an injury will be treated using a ruler, sensitive hands, sealskin straps and butter-boxes soaked in water. Eventually the knee was braced solidly at a special angle and then two months on the back followed.

This was a sad way to end an otherwise successful trapping season. When I was back on my feet again in July, the leg had fixed itself in a kind of upright position, but was clearly intact. Two things have to be said in connection with this story: I came home in September and was hospitalized, and on the second day the doctor came to me and said – "We are aware of the circumstances of the accident and what happened afterwards, and I can only say that the world has missed out on a first class surgeon. We could not have repaired the damage any better here at the hospital. You can go home, and a physiotherapist will help you regain full ability in your leg." The other thing was that the Sæterdals were alright and arrived at Revet approximately a week after our unsuccessful expedition".[593]

Birger Larsen, who ended his professional career as a personnel manager of a large company, has written several articles and given radio talks about his experiences in Greenland.

1954-55

Asbjørn Tøndell continued as radio operator in 1954-55, together with his colleague Finn Jensen and the trapper Helge Nesset, both of whom had wintered before.

It was very good fox year, Helge Nesset recalled in 1992. The foxes became so tame that they would eat from your hand and: *"the first day I thought the fur to be usable I had about 15 to 20 foxes about the house that I had fed since they were cubs. So I just opened the*

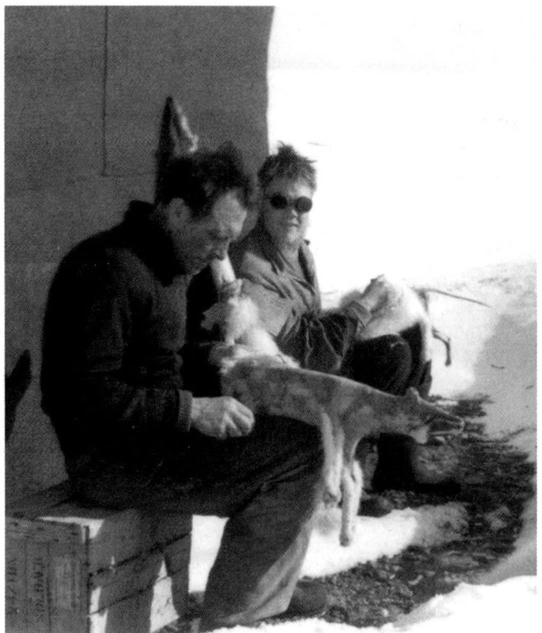

Skinning of polar foxes. From left: Helge Nesset and Asbjørn Tøndell. © Helge Nesset

door and let them into the porch, picked those with the finest fur and let the others out again. I took about 28 foxes this way".[594] Helge Nesset also remembered how the foxes once had their well-deserved revenge. He had baited about 300 bait-sticks that were stacked in a shed ready for use; but then a storm blew open the door to the shed. The foxes immediately took advantage of this opportunity, ran into the shed and ate all the bait; he had to start all over again.

Once a bear had visited one of Helge Nesset's huts and made a terrible mess. It had thrown out the stove and lamps, and eaten all the food as well as three unskinned foxes that he had stored there. The hut seemed to have been systematically emptied of everything - except for a box of pepper: *"and there the bear had stopped"*.[595]

In the summer of 1955, Nesset went together with Sverre Storholt to fish for char in Loch Fyne: *"We had nets in the fjord and caught enough for five or six barrels."* It was on this occasion that they rebuilt "Norske Villa" [373] and "Mellemhuset" [367-2].

1955-56

In 1955 Stein Sørensen came back for his sixth and last wintering in North-East Greenland. He was going to be station manager and winter together with two newcomers, the radio operator Knut Ødegaard and the trapper Hilmar Gauteplass.

It had been four years since Sørensen had last stayed at Myggbukta, but: *"the station looks more or less exactly as before. However, the radio equipment is better. We now have two usable German 100 W transmitters installed in addition to the one I brought with me. In the living room we have a good radio, a Radionettes Frihetssuper. The power plant is also improved, two Petter diesel engines and one petrol engine, all fully operational as well as two spare generators. The battery situation seems satisfactory too. Knut Ødegaard and I have already completed our first weekly turn on the radio, and he has now started his second week. Hilmar Gauteplass, the trapper, is at present in Loch Fyne to rebuild a hut* (Bunnhuset)*"*, Stein Sørensen wrote on 22nd August 1955.[596]

With Sørensen as the driving force, the station had a thorough overhaul and on the 18th September it started to: *"look presentable at the station, both indoors and out. The radio room is all white – walls and ceiling, while the floor is painted brown. The living room has a white ceiling, cream-coloured walls and brown mouldings, doors and window frames. The kitchen has the same colour scheme"*.[597]

The year went by and on 6th August 1956, just as Stein Sørensen had gone aboard "Polarbjørn" to return home, they received an unexpected message: "Jopeter" had been discovered.

In the summer of 1955, "Jopeter" had sent out distress calls to the Danish weather stations in the area; it had been caught in the ice and was eventually abandoned by the crew in the vicinity of Bontekoe Ø. Everyone thought that the ship had sunk, but now one of Lauge Koch's Norseman floatplanes had accidentally spotted the ship in Mountnorris Fjord in east Traill Ø.

Danish and Norwegian ships immediately rushed towards the abandoned ship. The Danes arrived first, as "Polarbjørn" was delayed by fog and did not arrive until 9th August: *"We arrived in the evening to find Jopeter guarded by a Danish naval vessel – a small wooden ship named "Teisten" – they have hoisted the Dannebrog* (the Danish flag) *on Jopeter and tell us that we have no business there and will be shot at if we try to board the ship. Giæver and Marø are absolutely furious and transmit urgent telegrams to shipping company and newspaper agencies and Svalis* (the office of the Norwegian Svalbard- & Arctic Ocean Survey). *We leave at once. Jopeter looks fine, with its bow on the sandy beach and no leaks worth mentioning or water in the bottom. Marø thinks that "Polarbjørn" would have been able to repair and pull loose the ship without any problem. But the Danes have taken her as a prize, it would seem"*.[598] In the meantime the sealer "Melshorn" had been called from Norway in order to pull "Jopeter" free. It was easily done and when "Polarbjørn" returned to Mountnorris Fjord on 19th August, Sørensen noted that: *"Jopeter is the ship that looks the best, although is has been in the ice for a year. It is completely tight and had only an insignificant amount of water in the hull which Melshorn has long since pumped out".*[599] The "Jopeter" affair gave rise to a variety of complications, diplomatic as well as insurance.

1956-57

In 1956, the 37-year-old Knut Ødegaard was promoted to station manager, and had trapper Hans Oddvik and radio operator Anund Amundsen as wintering companions. Hans Oddvik from Nord-Trøndelag was on his first wintering: *"It all began quite traditionally. I had read about the famous expeditions by Nansen, Amundsen and Sverdrup, and it made me dream of going to the Arctic to experience some adventure myself. It might have stayed as a dream as with so many others, but by chance I met the famous trapper Magne Råum from Foldereid. I had just turned 19 that winter and Magne thought that I was old enough to go trapping"*, Hans Oddvik said in 1993.[600]

On 21st January 1957, Oddvik and Amundsen drove to Kap Bennet to hunt polar bear and muskox. The weather was fine and the temperature minus 40°C. It was easy going and they were soon far from land: *"Suddenly, without any warning, it starts to blow. We sense the danger and head for the nearest land. But the storm soon rises to an inferno and as we don't have the strength to continue we decide to make a shelter. We had left Myggbukta for a one-day trip, without food or sleeping bags and we realized that this might be a close call; it could even kill us. We pulled the dogs around us and held on while the hours crept away. The following evening we both believed we could see land. Sizing up the direction we crept forward metre by metre. I don't know how long it took, but we reached the land and immediately began digging into a snow drift. It was not cold inside the snow, but after a while the ice on our clothes began to melt and we were soon soaking wet. Anyway, this night was at least better than the previous one, but hunger was beginning to be painful so we decided to try finding the hut at the cape. It was desperately hard work and we used up our last strength to get there. I'm not sure we would have survived one more night in the open. Once again the dogs saved the situation as we drove right into the hut. It was an indescribable feeling to have the warmth filling up your body again".*[601] While the blizzard continued Oddvik and Amundsen had to stay in the Kap Bennet hytten, where they took turns sleeping and keeping the stove burning. Luckily a passing muskox saved them from starvation. It was not until the 30th January - after a day-trip that lasted nine days and nights - that they arrived back at Myggbukta.

When Oddvik and Amundsen went home to Norway in 1957, they witnessed the end of the "Polarbjørn". It was the 24th August when the ice masses off Kejser Franz Joseph Fjord crushed the ship. Everyone left the ship and: *"it was decided to call the American Base at Keflavik in Iceland for help. A helicopter was dismantled and put into a cargo plane, which flew to Mestersvig in North-East Greenland. With*

Fox skins drying in the spring sun at Myggbukta. © *Helge Nesset*

this helicopter we were picked up in an orderly manner and flown to Sophia Sund, at the mouth of Kejser Franz Joseph Fjord, where we were taken aboard a Danish naval vessel and brought to Mestersvig. From Mestersvig we flew with the cargo plane to Keflavik and from there by boat to Bergen".[602]

In 1964, Oddvik participated in Bjørn Staib's North Pole Expedition. In 1967 he travelled by dog sledge with a friend around the entire Svalbard archipelago, a journey that lasted three months.

1957-58

Knut Ødegaard continued for his third wintering, in the company of a new radio operator, Raftevold (first name unknown). After this summer Arctic Commercial Enterprise gave up hiring trappers for Myggbukta.

1958-59

Asbjørn Tøndell and Bjørn Hylen were the last to winter at Myggbukta. It was Tøndell's fourth wintering in North-East Greenland. Hylen was on his first wintering, 24-years old, and managed to fulfil his dream of a trip to Greenland before Arctic Commercial Enterprise stopped all activities.

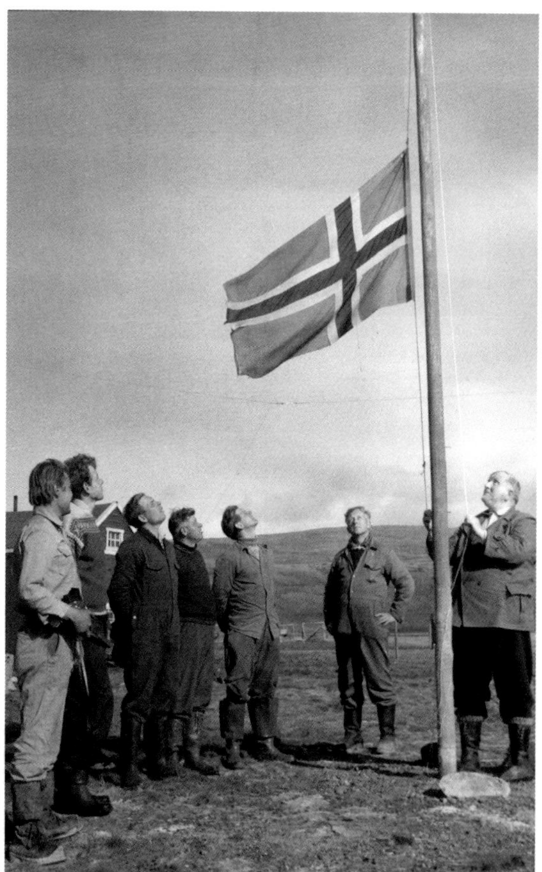

Veteran Søren Richter striking the Norwegian colours in Myggbukta for the last time on 22nd August 1959. Richter was one of the five men, who on 27th June 1931 hoisted the Norwegian flag in Myggbukta. From left: Asbjørn Tøndell, Bjørn Hylen, Bjørn Richter, Søren Richter. © Torbjørn Torkildsen / Norwegian Polar Institute

On 22nd August 1959, the veteran Søren Richter lowered the Norwegian flag at Myggbukta for the last time. This was undoubtedly a sad moment for Richter, as he was one of the five men who had hoisted the Norwegian flag at the same place on 27th June 1931. A certain degree of indignation can be sensed in his short note in "Polarboken": *"In 1959 the station was shut down for good. The Norwegian Meteorological Institute could not recommend the continued manning of Myggbukta. The first radio weather station in Greenland, a station with fine polar traditions and a certain glory of adventure was removed at the stroke of a pen." ... "I guess it is presumptuous for an unschooled arctic veteran to justify Myggbukta's existence as weather station, but anyway – Old Norway stuck her head out in a new arctic area. A large part of our own coastal population lives adjacent to the Arctic Ocean and makes their living from it. The Arctic Ocean means more to Norway than to any other country. Why must we retreat? Myggbukta was more than a weather station; it was a fortress, an outpost of the greatest importance to Arctic Norway. Was this retreat necessary?"*[603]

Arnesen 1932; Barr 1991; Blom 1973; Ellefsen et al. 1957; Luncke 1933; Polarboken 1983-1984; Smedal 1930; Vervarslinga 1945, 1970; N048; N061; N085; N089. Dennis Carter pers. comm.; Per Michelsen pers. comm.

Recent status

Since 1960, the Myggbukta station has gradually decayed for want of maintenance, and might have become a ruin. Fortunately, Myggbukta lies in an attractive area with a rich and interesting fauna, and this historically important station has regularly been used as a base by scientific summer expeditions, e.g. by Swedish ornithological expeditions in 1979 (Magnus Elander and Sven Blomqvist) and 1982 (Magnus Elander and Mats Ericson),[604] and also private groups and individuals. Many of these expeditions have made repairs to the Myggbukta main building on their own initiative, notably Dennis Carter who in 1992 made repairs to the roof to stop the rain from coming in.[605]

In the summer of 1999, Nanok sent a three-man team to Myggbukta to undertake a more thorough renovation. With the support of a Sirius team, they also installed a new large coal stove. In 2002 another Nanok team replaced the floors in the kitchen and the living room.[606]

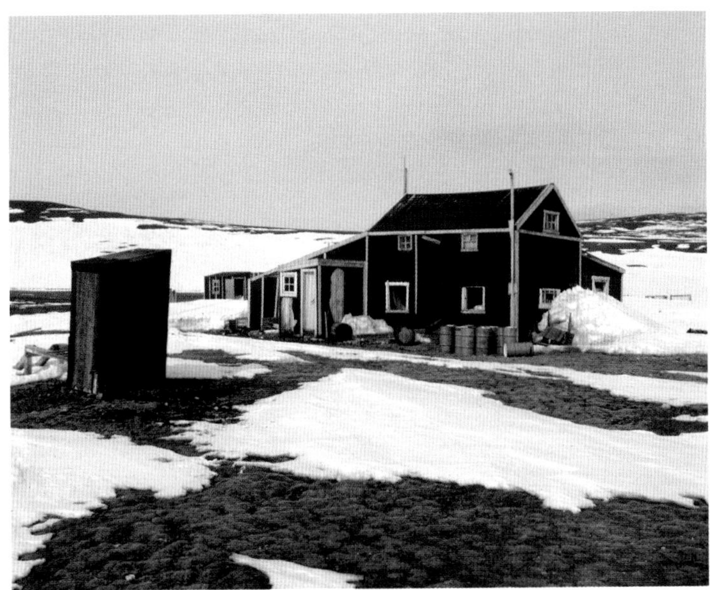

After the Norwegians left Myggbukta in the summer of 1959, the historically important station fell into decay. Luckily private expeditions and individuals, not least the Englishman Dennis Carter, made crucial repairs to Myggbukta during the 1980s and early 1990s. Then in the summer of 1999 Nanok made a more thorough renovation of the Myggbukta main house. In 2002 another Nanok team replaced the floors in the kitchen and living room.
(Top) Myggbukta, 16th May 1979.
(Centre) Myggbukta, 4th August 1989. © Peter Schmidt Mikkelsen.
(Bottom) Myggbukta in 1999 with the Nanok team (from left): Thor Melhuus, Ivar Ytreland, Øystein Killie. © NCN

Myggbukta [335], 29th July 2004. Myggbukta is a former Norwegian trapper's and weather station originally established in 1922 for the Johan A. Olsen Expedition. The present house was built in 1930 by Arctic Commercial Enterprise. Myggbukta was the main Norwegian station in North-East Greenland until 1959. Since then it has been used only as a travellers' hut, and more recently as a summer base for scientific expeditions. © NCN

MØNSTEDHUS
[532-2]

Wintering party
1938-41: Niels Hansen, Peter Nielsen
1941-46: None
1946-47: Mogens Graae *
1947-51: None
1951-52: Erik Larsen
* Wintered partly at Hochstetter

In 1938, Otto Mønsteds Fond made a grant of 40,000 kroner to Nanok, spread over three years. The money was to support establishment of a mink and arctic fox farm at the mouth of Langelv, one of the major char rivers in North-East Greenland. On 13th August, "Gustav Holm" arrived at the chosen location, where Nanok had already built the "Langsøhytten". Jennov went: *"ashore to check things out. The station will be located in an excellent place where the mink cages will be free of snow. The conditions for loading and unloading are good. Furthermore, at the small bay at Haystack there is a good sheltered harbour for ships if it starts to blow or the ice sets in. Last, but not least, there are plenty of excellent quality char in the river".*[607]

They immediately started to build the station. The veteran trapper and carpenter Hans Ludvig Jensen helped: *"make the floor. We are in all six men hammering away. The chief engineer is installing the radio, and it's working fine".*[608] While this went on other Nanok men built the "Gåseholmhytten" [539] in Bessel Fjord. On 16th August "Gustav Holm" departed, and the station was left in the hands of Niels Hansen and Peter Nielsen. There was still a lot to do, for: *"when the ship departed, there were neither walls nor roof on the house",*[609] Peter Nielsen recalled in 1988.

Police patrol from Eskimonæs visiting Mønstedhus. April 1940. From left: Petrus Arke, Niels Hansen, Peter Nielsen, Niels Ove Jensen. © Niels Ove Jensen

1938-39
Niels Hansen, a veteran trapper with six winterings for Nanok, was the envy of some of the other trappers as he had a fixed salary of 100 kroner per month for looking after the mink farm, as well as his own trapping territory extending for five km on each side of the station. Peter Nielsen was a newcomer. He had been on board the "Gustav Holm" in 1937, but as the ship met difficult ice conditions and only just made it to Scoresbysund, he had to return to Denmark. In 1938, the then 25-year-old farmer's son from Illerup near Skanderborg succeeded in reaching Mønstedhus, where he was to be the assistant of "Old Niels". He was to trap along Langelv and the outer coast between Kap Oswald Heer and Bessel Fjord. This was the beginning of a seven year stay in North-East Greenland, as from 1941 to 1945 Peter Nielsen was amongst the men who made up the North-East Greenland Sledge Patrol. From this period his friend Kurt Olsen gave the following characteristics of Nielsen: *"He was an idealist, and characterized by the strong sympathies and antipathies of the idealist. He was a farmer with all of a farmer's best qualities, including an unbreakable loyalty towards everything he believed in and had faith in. In his relationships with the rest of us he was one of the team's most unshakable supporters, but he could not really tolerate that the sledge patrol from time to time had to use things which rightfully belonged to the trapping company Nanok." ... "As a travelling companion he was lively and entertaining; one could hardly believe where he had the inspiration for all the practical jokes buzzing around him".*[610] In 1949 Peter Nielsen emigrated to Canada, where he lived at Pass Lake in Ontario until his death in August 1997 at the age of 84.

It was Peter Nielsen who kept the station journal, that was brief and down-to-earth. New Years Day 1939: *"Wind and snow drift. Have a visit from the Norwegians* (Bjarne Dalsbø and Bjarne Jakobsen from Ottostrand)*".*[611] In 1988, Nielsen gave a more detailed account of the Norwegian visit: *"The lunch lasted three hours. We had to put Dalsbø to bed before we had finished, as he could not stand more than half a bottle of aquavit. Jakobsen, on the other hand, had emptied two whole bottles and he wasn't even drunk. We sent him to bed when Niels was about to make supper and in the heat the aquavit began to work, so there was absolutely no desire for a rum toddy. On 2nd January the Norwegians went home and we gave them the rum they couldn't face the night before".*[612]

The experiment with the mink did not turn out as hoped. On 1st November there was a storm and: *"so much snow that we are almost drowning in it. We have spent several hours digging out the minks and moving them"*.[613] Of the 12 breeding animals that had come up with the ship, three died during the first winter and the cubs born during the summer of 1939 also died. The climate was simply too cold.

1939-40

In the summer of 1939, pack ice blocked the route to Mønstedhus and the supplies were instead unloaded at Sandodden. Jennov was not worried: *"Last year the station was supplied with provisions for two men for two years, and there were as well a considerable amount of older provisions from Hochstetter. There can be no doubt that Niels Hansen has economized on the provisions, so the station will be well supplied for the entire coming season"*.[614] At Mønstedhus they also did not anticipate any problems. At any time they could obtain fresh meat from muskox and the river was rich with char that could be smoked or salted and dried. They built a new provisions hut during the summer.

The fox trapping started well: *"Niels Hansen caught a few straight away, but I drove 1200 km before I got my first"*, Peter Nielsen wrote in 1988.[615] It was a lonely life. From 10th April 1939 until March 21st 1940, they only saw other people twice. Once was in October, when Finn Kristoffersen arrived with the mail bag. The other occasion was in November, when Peter Nielsen drove to Hochstetter to fetch the 300 pounds of potatoes, lemons and miscellaneous private items that had been brought up from Sandodden.

In April 1940, Mønstedhus was the only station between Eskimonæs in the south and Mørkefjord in the north to still have a usable radio receiver. At the other stations, where the trappers were often away trapping for days or weeks, the batteries had been destroyed by the frost, but at Mønstedhus they still functioned as Niels Hansen was never so far away from the station that the fire in the stove went out. It was on the radio on the 9th April, that he and Nielsen learned that Denmark had been invaded by the German Wehrmacht. The news was disturbing, but he stayed calm and the entry in the station log that day simply read: *"Quiet, clear. Have been brewing beer"*.[616]

Niels Hansen tending the cage foxes. Mønstedhus, April 1940. © Niels Ove Jensen

In the middle of May, Niels Haarløv and Carl Henrik Schultz from the Mørkefjord station passed by on their way to Scoresbysund as they wanted to leave North-East Greenland. Hansen and Nielsen, however, chose to stay. Old Niels would make sure they could manage yet another year without fresh supplies.
In the beginning of June they made a kitchen garden where they sowed vegetables beneath glass, and on 11th July they were able to eat home grown salad and radishes for the first time.

1940-41

No ship arrived at Mønstedhus in 1940 either. The summer was spent with char fishing and different work at the station. After a mild autumn, Niels Hansen and Peter Nielsen started trapping at the end of October. On 1st November there was a little more to write about than usual: *"Drove to Påskenæsset to see if there were any messages in the hut from the men up north. The hut was full of snow and no one had been there. On my return, I saw two bears at Carl Ritter, galloping towards Koldewey. A little south of Carl Ritter I drove into a crack and had a lot of work getting the sledge out of the water again. I got some huge blisters on my hands. Fortunately I had dry mittens in my pocket, for everything on the sledge had become soaked. Shortly after my return to the Bessel Fjord station, Ib Poulsen and radio operator Kurt Olsen arrived. They were heading for Mørkefjord"*.[617]

It was a winter with little snow and only one real blizzard. The trapping ended on the 22nd April with a total catch of 86 foxes. A few days later Richard Nielsen and Ove Harder Jensen arrived. They were heading south for supplies and Peter Nielsen went along with them. First they went to Sandodden and Eskimonæs and then back to the station at Aalborghus. Then Nielsen returned to Mønstedhus to stay there for the summer.
The station log abruptly ends on the 25th July 1941 – a US Coast Guard ship had unexpectedly arrived. By order, Hansen and Nielsen were evacuated, but both remained on the coast as members of the North-East Greenland Sledge Patrol. Mønstedhus was then unmanned until 1946.

1946-47

"Mogens Graae is one the most versatile human beings, I have ever met", the former Norwegian trapper Ivar Ytreland recalled in 1992.[618] Ytreland was here referring to his long-time Danish friend Mogens Einar Work Graae, who originally came from Østerbro in Copenhagen.

In 1992, Graae himself recalled: *"One of my friends had been with the "Godthaab" to Greenland in the summer of 1945 and when he came home, he enthusiastically told me about North-East Greenland. One day I ran into a childhood friend, Kjeld Soelberg, and we soon started talking about Greenland. After the war both of us needed to get away from everything at home, preferably out on an adventure"*.[619] One day they went to see J.G. Jennov to find out about the possibilities. Soelberg could be hired at once, as he was a carpenter and had: *"'half' a mate's certificate"*.[620] It was a different matter with Graae: *"I was merely escaping from a shop-keeper's counter"* as Graae expressed it. Even though he had been working on a farm and tried a lot of other things, Jennov hesitated; but things worked out anyway. Graae came along when someone else cancelled, and in 1946 his versatility and dexterity were much needed. The available equipment was very poor, and he therefore had to make everything himself: anorak, sleeping tent, and so forth.

"I actually got the Mønstedhus territory as a trade off", Graae recalled. *"I had teamed up with Orla Jensen. We spent the summer at Daneborg and Zackenberg, but at the end of October 1946 we drove to Hochstetter. We had no idea what supplies there might be north of Wollaston Forland, as they had not been supplied after the war. Right from the start Orla and I decided to share like brothers. Everything we found – food, clothes and so on – we put into two equal heaps, which we traded with. When we decided to trap from each our station, we bargained about that too. Orla got Hochstetter and I got Mønstedhus"*.[621]

Graae drove to Mønstedhus in the beginning of February. On 19th April he closed down the territory and went south again. He also trapped in the territory in 1947-48, but without any real supplies Mønstedhus was only usable for short stays.

Mogens Graae's connection with the Arctic was far from over when he returned to Denmark in 1948. In the summers of 1949-51 he took part in the Peary Land Expeditions, which needed a man experienced with provisions and equipment: *"The equipment we had there was far better than what we had in 1946"*, Mogens Graae said in 1992, *"and I had had quite a few ideas for improvements and thought there might be a market for good expedition equipment"*.[622] These ideas brought him in touch with P.E. Hansen, who was employed in the company that had delivered equipment for the Peary Land Expedition. When Hansen started his own company, "P.E. Hansen & Co./APA-Outfit", Graae joined him and designed the "Muskox", which later became the name and logo of the company.

Graae's experiences were extremely valuable, whether it concerned the design of anoraks, parkas, tents, sleeping bags, survival suits or other expedition equipment. He knew the importance of detail and: *"I simply made the things the way I would have liked them myself"*, Graae recalled.[623] The number of customers grew steadily and amongst others included Lauge Koch, the Geological Survey of Greenland (GGU), the Lauritzen shipping company and the Danish air force. As well as the "Muskox" company, Graae co-operated with his old trapping companions Peder Klokker and Orla Jensen to produce sledges for expeditions; initially for the British North Greenland Expedition in 1952, and later the Hillary and Fuchs Commonwealth Trans-Antarctic Expedition 1955-58; other expedition orders followed.

To Graae the customer's satisfaction was everything. Often the design was made in close collaboration with the customer; thus much of the equipment for Sirius - tents, sleeping bags, anoraks etc - was developed by Graae to almost classical perfection based on the experiences of the patrol.

In 1970, Graae left his job as managing director of "Muskox" in order to establish his own company at Frederikshavn. For a fee of 10 øre per item of clothing, he purchased the right to call his company "Nanok". Graae's interest in the old trapping company had not faded. In 1976 he took over the management of Nanok after J.G. Jennov, and in 1989 when the company had no more capital he acquired Nanok and its rights in North-East Greenland. Although he sold the "Nanok" textile company in 1980 - which amongst its customers counted KGH - the name Mogens Graae is in more than one sense synonymous with the name Nanok.

Even after his 75th birthday, Mogens Graae still manufactured equipment for demanding customers, although now in more modest surroundings in his "Mallemuk" workshop. He was a modest man, who made no fuss about his work or claims that his equipment had saved several arctic travellers. Graae's efforts were widely known, and he was awarded "Thor's Hammer", a mark of recognition from "Danish Arbejde" (Danish handicraft).

Mogens Graae died on 28th February 1999, at the age of 82.[624]

1951-52

Mønstedhus had been unmanned since 1947, but on 11th October 1951, was taken over by the trapper Erik Larsen. For the first couple of weeks he had the company of Hans Frederiksen and Ernst Wind, who helped to transport his equipment from Hochstetter. On the way they stayed overnight at Ottostrand. Here there was: *"a new man,*[625] *Odd Bogholm. He is to be here on his own this year"*, Larsen wrote.

As the distance between Mønstedhus and Ottostrand is only 10 km it was only natural that Larsen and Bogholm soon agreed to help each other and keep each other company. On 17th November 1951: *"Bogholm and I set out for Aalborghus. After about one kilometre we saw two dark spots on the ice in Roseneath Bugt. Assuming they were seals we drove towards them, stopped about 200 m from the first one and took a shot at it. At this point we could not hold back the dogs any longer and drove right up to the seals. Too late we realized that they weren't seals, but walruses, so to save some of the dogs from being killed, we had to shoot the other walrus too as it attacked. We looked for possible blowholes or cracks in the ice, but found none. The animals were very skinny, so I assume they had crawled up onto the ice at new moon, when it was spring tide and there was probably open water around the icebergs in the bay".*[626]

Bogholm celebrated Christmas with Larsen at Mønstedhus, together with Hans Frederiksen from Hochstetter with whom Larsen also had joint activities. During the spring of 1952, they put out materials for two huts in Langelv. However, the huts - in this book called "Langelv" [914] and "Langsø" [915] - were never built. At the end of May, Larsen and Frederiksen went south to stay at Sandodden for the summer. Erik Larsen left Greenland in the summer of 1952.

1954

After 1952 Mønstedhus was not used for wintering as Nanok had given up its trapping activities. However, it became known that during the summer of 1953 heavy swells had eroded a large section of the shore so that the station was now barely two metres from the coastal cliffs. Nanok initiated a rescue mission, and in the summer of 1954, J.G. Jennov and Mogens Graae arrived with the "Kista Dan" that was calling at Daneborg. From Daneborg the two men together with Hans Frederiksen and Erik B. Larsen were airlifted by Catalina to Mønstedhus: *"It wasn't particularly difficult to lift the house onto rollers on top of planks that we had brought along, and others we found by the provisions shed. It turned out to be considerably easier to push the house using a jack and then tightening it up with tackle. When we finished the work in the evening the house had been moved 6.1 metres"* Jennov wrote on the 20th August 1954. The following days they moved the house further inland, so finally it was some 20 metres from the cliff. After a job well done the four men were

As the sea in the summer of 1953 had taken a large part of the shore, it became necessary in 1954 to move Mønstedhus further inland. © Mogens Graae

picked up by the ship "Jopeter" on the 24th August.
Jennov 1939; A161; G102; G133.

Recent status

Erosion on this coastal stretch is not a new phenomenon. After the 1954 move Mønstedhus stood solid and stable for many years. It was a good building and much used - a good place to spend a rest day. The station was frequently used by Sirius and other travellers, because there is only one north-south route worth taking on this particular stretch of coast - you simply could not miss Mønstedhus!

In the four consecutive summers of 2001-2004 ice conditions along the east coast of Greenland were rather unusual. There was almost no drift ice along the coast and the huge Atlantic swells made tremendous cuts into the coast. In November 2001, a Sirius sledge team gave the first alarm, that the distance between Mønstedhus and the coastal cliff was now only three metres. It was obvious that something would have to be done urgently if Mønstedhus was to be saved. Unfortunately, Nanok at this time was unable to help as the ownership of the old Danish stations and huts in North-East Greenland was unresolved. As a consequence, all that Nanok could do was to urge Sirius and other relevant parties to act as soon as possible.

Sirius undertook the task, but unfortunately there were delays and when the "removal" team from Sirius finally arrived at Mønstedhus on 14th September 2002, the historic building had fallen over the cliff. Only four days earlier an aeroplane had reported that the station was still intact at the cliff edge! Sirius saved all that was possible, and built a smaller hut "Ny Mønstedhus" [532-4] out of material from the old station. There was nothing else to do - but the loss of Mønstedhus was a disaster that should never have happened![627]

Mønstedhus [532]. Mønstedhus was a Danish trappers' station built in 1938 for Nanok. It was used as a trappers' station until 1952, then as a travellers' hut until September 2002, when it was taken by the sea. (Left) Mønstedhus [532-2], 5th June 1978. © Peter Schmidt Mikkelsen. (Below) Mønstedhus [532-2] as it appeared shortly after it had fallen over the cliff, 14th September 2002. © Søren Rysgaard. (Lower, left) Ny Mønstedhus [532-4] was built of materials from Mønstedhus by a Sirius team, September 2002. (Lower, right) Ny Mønstedhus [532-4], 4th August 2004. (Bottom) View north-east towards the Haystack mountain. © NCN

NY JONSBU
[514-2]

Wintering party
1948-1950: Bjarne Myrvold, Egil Amsjø

1948-49
In 1948, Arctic Commercial Enterprise received financial support from the Norwegian government to re-establish the northernmost Norwegian trapping territories, which had earlier been used by John Giæver and Sigurd Tolløfsen. As a replacement for the old, burnt-down Jonsbu station, a new station was to be built, but rather than rebuilding it in Peters Bugt where there was often a lot of snow the house was placed on the south side of Ardencaple Fjord, at the mouth of Kildedal.

It was Bjarne Myrvold and Egil Amsjø who built Ny Jonsbu, the last trappers' station to be established in North-East Greenland. The previous year they had stayed at Kap Humboldt. In 1991 Myrvold recalled that: *"Amsjø and I started building at once. Ny Jonsbu was partly pre-fabricated, that is the walls were shipped to Greenland as sections ready for mounting, while the floor and roof were made on site. John Giæver's hut* (Skylstad) *was at the same place, and we lived in it while we built Ny Jonsbu and used it afterwards for fur storage".*[628]

In connection with the re-establishing of the Jonsbu territory they also built a trappers' hut, "Myrvoldhytten" [523] in Peters Bugt. This was carried out by sledge in the autumn, as they had unfortunately lost their motor boat "Humla". Bjarne Myrvold said about this accident: *"When we prepared the territory we used the motor boat, placing a box with provisions at each trappers' hut. It was on one such trip that we lost "Humla" outside Sigurdsheim. It was late in the evening and dark. As there was no pack ice off the coast and the wind was blowing we had huge swells and the waves were hitting the boat. It was really nasty weather. I was operating the motor and Egil was steering, and then we made a turn. It was shallow water off Sigurdsheim, and as it was so late in the autumn there was a bulwark of ice along the shore. Egil turned the boat so that we could get on top of a wave and ride on it to the shore; but we didn't make it. The boat caught the bottom, turned halfway around and hit the icy bulwark. There it got stuck and was smashed to pieces. Fortunately we had a small boat in tow, filled with traps that we had made at Ny Jonsbu to be placed in the territory".*[629]

While Amsjø was trapping in Ardencaple Fjord, Myrvold had the territory extending towards Sigurdsheim. It was here that one day in the beginning of 1949 he had a visit from two Danes: *"I had just arrived in the afternoon when they crossed the shore, coming from the south. I didn't hear them coming as I was not expecting any visitors. It was Hans Thomsen and Ole Olsen. They entered, and as I had just made soup for supper we began eating soup. There was a paraffin lamp above the table and from time to time a drip fell in Ole's soup. I didn't notice, and it was the first time we met, and he said nothing. He ate the soup!... But later on we had a party at Hochstetter and became better acquainted and then he told me; but he had not dared say anything at Sigurdsheim".*[630]

1949-50
At the beginning of June 1949, Egil Amsjø and Bjarne Myrvold, together with Hermod Sætre and Erling Juell Ramberg, went to Ottostrand to fish for char. The

Egil Amsjø (left) and Bjarne Myrvold have been set ashore with all material and equipment at Kildedal to build Ny Jonsbu. In background: "Polarbjørn". August 1948. © Bjarne Myrvold

outcome, however, was disappointing. They were all supposed to return to Norway, but as the summer came to an end, the ice was still unbroken as far as the eye could see. It was obvious that there would be no ship, so at the end of August they all went south.

Myrvold and Amsjø returned to Ny Jonsbu at the beginning of September, and then got busy preparing for the unexpected wintering. This work included building the following huts: "Femdalen" [524-2], "Amsjøhytten" [517] and "Barth Bjerge" [525]. Naturally, the missing supply ship caused certain problems. As soon as the ice was safe Myrvold therefore went to Daneborg. On 31st October he returned: *"in the afternoon having a lot of news to tell. And the most important things he brought along were various foodstuffs including potatoes, milk and eggs. And vitamins – we need those now having had such a poor diet for the last six months".*[631]

Myrvold reported that their supplies had been deposited at the Krogness station, and on 14th December they and Erling Juell Ramberg started southwards to collect the supplies. It turned out to be quite a journey. Christmas was celebrated with Normann Andersen at Moskusheimen, and on the 27th December they continued to Kap Stosch: *"We had expected to find a note from the company, but there wasn't anything. And we cursed John Giæver, as the potatoes, vegetables, eggs and most of the milk had been taken back to Norway. Even the small quantity of liquor we had ordered was missing. All the barrels and boxes were outside, covered with snow. There was no packing list. It is hard to believe that this was carried out by adult people"*, Amsjø wrote.[632]

On 16th January 1950, they were back again at Ny Jonsbu, but: *"Amsjø and I find the Ny Jonsbu territory too small for two men. Furthermore, there were very few foxes so after we had been south for Christmas and fetched provisions, Amsjø went north to Olestua at Bessel Fjord to trap there for the rest of the season"*, Myrvold said in 1991.[633]

Bjarne Myrvold building a trappers' hut, Autumn 1948. © Bjarne Myrvold

In the summer of 1950, Bjarne Myrvold and Egil Amsjø went home after three and four winterings respectively. Egil Amsjø died in the late 1980s and Bjarne Myrvold in 2005.[634]

Norsk Polarklubb 1964; Fredrik Sæterdal pers. comm.

Recent status

Ny Jonsbu was not regularly manned after 1950. However, Trygve Saga from Ottostrand used the station for a part of the season 1950-51.

After the end of the trapper era, Sirius maintained Ny Jonsbu as a travellers' hut. However, the station eventually needed a more thorough renovation, and in 1995 a Nanok team took the opportunity to undertake this task. As a consequence Ny Jonsbu is today in good condition.[635]

Egil Amsjø on the roof of Ny Jonsbu, August 1948. © Bjarne Myrvold

Ny Jonsbu [514-2], 27th July 2004. Ny Jonsbu is a former Norwegian trappers' station built in 1948 for Arctic Commercial Enterprise. It was used as a trappers' station until 1950, then as a travellers' hut. (Top) Ny Jonsbu. (Centre, left). A copy of the Norwegian newspaper "Østlandets Blad" for 14th May 1948, still on the bookshelves at Ny Jonsbu. (Centre, right) Interior of Ny Jonsbu. On the table, lamps and matches are carefully made ready for the next visitors as the custom demands. (Bottom) Ny Jonsbu seen from the north-west. © *NCN*

Østlandets Blad

Minnesteinen for de falne fra Soon.

17. mai 1948.

Men Rocambole var ikke død.

Også Vestby går inn for interkommunal yrkesskole i Follo.

OLESTUA
[603]

Wintering party
1932-34: Ole Sivertsen, John Johnsen

1932-33
On 14th July 1932, the "Isbjørn" of Tromsø arrived at Kap Carl Ritter, the easternmost point of Ad.S. Jensen Land. In a small cove behind the cape, materials for a station and provisions for two men for two years were unloaded.

On the same occasion, Ole Sivertsen and John Johnsen from Tromsø went ashore to establish a new trapping territory for the John Giæver Expedition. Sivertsen, then 46-years old, was an experienced trapper with 12 winterings in Svalbard to his credit. John Johnsen, a brother of the trapper Otto Johnsen, was about 25-years old and a newcomer. They immediately started to build the house, which John Giæver later on named "Olestua" after Sivertsen, and on 20th August they could celebrate their moving in with some good muskox steaks: *"So far we have only the attic to sleep in, we'll take care of the furnishing later on. I've always been in favour of the 8-hour working day, but that's out of the question here"*.[636] When the station was ready, Sivertsen and Johnsen built four trappers' huts in Bessel Fjord: "Botten" [541], "Johns hytte" [540], "Fredhaug" [538] and "Sætherhytten"[602].

In 1932, the result of the Hague sovereignty trial was still pending and Olestua was located in an area where so far only Danes had been trapping. On 22nd August, they had a: *"visit from the Danish motor schooner "Gefion". Went down to the beach to greet the crew. There were five men, including Mr. Jennov. They had come to object to our building a house here. They informed us that they had built a house* (Bessel Fjord station) *in Bessel Fjord, as well as huts from Danmark Havn and southwards. I answered that we intended to build the huts we had been told to build, and furthermore referred Mr. Jennov to my leader at Peters Bugt* (John Giæver at Jonsbu)*"*.[637] Yet this disagreement did not affect the good relationships between the ordinary Norwegian and Danish trappers.

One day, Sivertsen and Johnsen to their disappointment discovered that they hadn't brought enough yeast, so they had to use sourdough for baking. Then one day in September they had a visit from their neighbours Evald Rasmussen and Arne Philbert from Bessel Fjord. They started talking and agreed to help each other: *"John went along with the other two and they promised that we could borrow some yeast from them. In return, they accepted some meat from us as it turned out that they were out of dog food"*.[638] After that the four men would often meet, among other things to hunt muskox in Bessel Fjord. On one occasion they shot 18 muskox, enough meat for several weeks.

The Norwegian trapping was carried out using both fall-traps and poisoned bait, but using strychnine

Olestua, 1933. © Arne Philbert

had its costs. In February, a dog died from poisoning and in March it almost went wrong again: *"John cleaned the sledge box of snow. Unfortunately a bit of the poisoned bait fell out, and one of the puppies ate a little and became very ill. Luckily I became aware of this in time. We took the puppy inside and immediately gave it plenty of water and milk. After 1 1/2 hours continuous work the puppy, to our relief, started to improve. We barely managed to save it, half a minute more, and it would probably have died. It was already becoming stiff in its neck and all its limbs when we started working on it. Tonight it is fresh again, just a bit limp and scared".*[639]

The catch the first year numbered 60 foxes and 11 bears. After the thaw the time was spent with the usual work at the station, such as building a hut of stone for storing meat.

1933-34

During the first year Sivertsen and Johnsen only trapped in Bessel Fjord. Now they intended to expand the territory towards Dove Bugt. They had only materials for two regular huts, but by dividing up the wood they had sufficient for four small huts. The main thing was to have a roof over your head. In the middle of August the ice in Dove Bugt finally broke up, and while Johnsen was at Ottostrand to fish char, Sivertsen went north and built "Kap Niels hytten" [614], "Sjelnan" [609], "Kroken" [611] and "Strømsbukta" [607].

The year 1933-34 was not the good trapping year that Sivertsen and Johnsen had hoped for. The result was only 45 foxes and a few bears. In particular, their northern territory did not live up to expectations and Ole Sivertsen made many trips in vain. In the middle of March 1934, he wrote: *"So far I have almost believed that the good Lord would see to it that I caught a fox from time to time; but now I believe that it is "Old Nick" himself. If only I could sell my soul for 200 foxes, then never mind the soul – it would probably find its way anyhow".*[640]

Then came spring and the mosquitoes: *"Last year I used frost ointment to keep them away and it worked as long as the smell of the ointment lasted. This year I will try some carnation oil. If only I had a drugstore, then – – . Should have brought lavender oil, for they hate that, but the smell clings to your clothes for an awfully long time. In my childhood the farmers used lavender oil instead of perfume and they smelt like death and the devil from far away".*[641] The mosquitoes could be annoying, but it was even worse when toothache set in: *"I have been tormented by a tooth the entire winter and nothing has helped. On top of that I have a huge gumboil – I hope the gumboil will burst soon so that the pain will go away. I have even tried hydrochloric acid in desperation, but I won't do that again as I became raw in the mouth and couldn't taste anything for a long time".*[642]

When the trapping season ended, Johnsen went south to spend the summer at Ottostrand and Jonsbu. At Olestua, Sivertsen waited for the ice to break up. He waited for a long time, and barely managed to get himself down to Ottostrand where he was picked up by "Selbarden" on 22nd August.

North-East Greenland did not fulfil the

John Johnsen, Otto Johnsen and Ole Sivertsen, 1933. © Arne Philbert

Ole Sivertsen, 1937. © Norwegian Polar Institute

expectations of Ole Sivertsen. He had hoped that these two years would make him financially independent so he could give up being a trapper. This wish did not come true, and he was back again in 1935-36, not at Olestua - as it was not used again for wintering - but at Krogness. In 1936-37 he wintered at Kap Humboldt. At the end of the 1930s, Sivertsen was killed in an accident working in the mines on Svalbard. A steel wire broke and killed him on the spot.

John Johnsen did not return to North-East Greenland. He died of tuberculosis in the 1940s. In the spring of 1950, Olestua was used as a base by Egil Amsjø.

Nyholm-Poulsen 1985; N076; Arne Philbert pers. comm.

Recent status

After the trapper era, Olestua was maintained by Sirius as a travellers' hut until 1982, when it was accidentally burnt down.

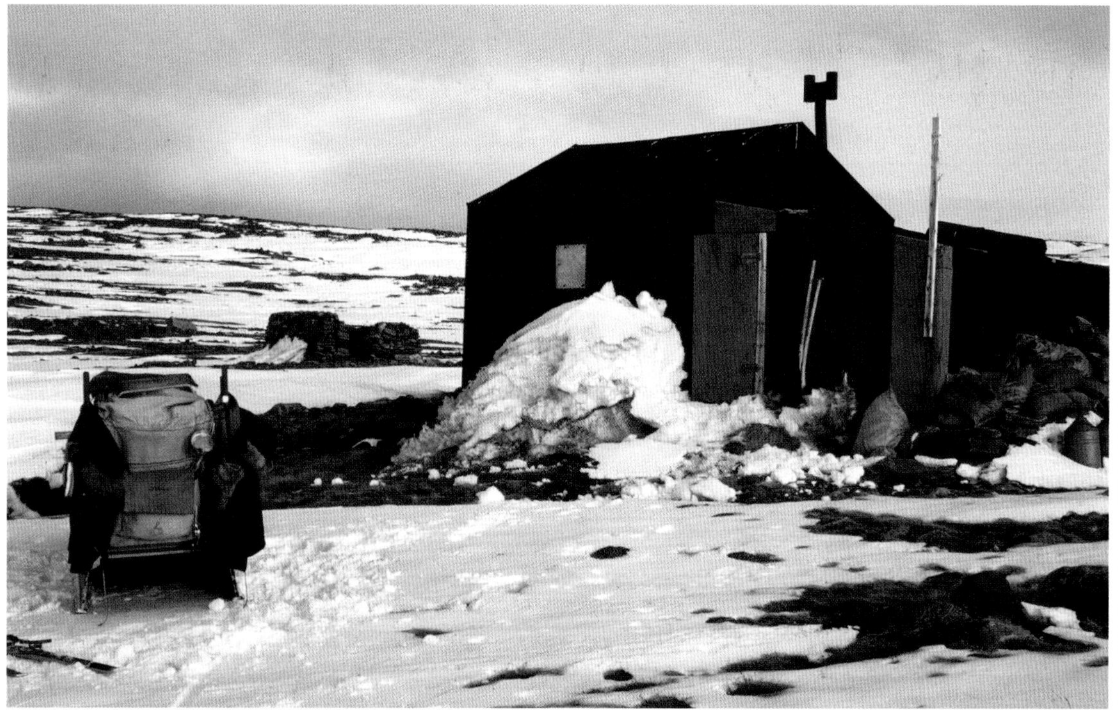

Olestua used as a travellers' hut by Sirius, 3rd June 1978. © Peter Schmidt Mikkelsen

Olestua [603]. Olestua was a Norwegian trappers' station built in 1932 for the John Giæver Expedition. It was used as a trappers' station until 1934, and then as a travellers' hut until 1982, when it was accidently burnt down. (Above and left). Remains of Olestua, 25th July 2005. (Bottom) View north-east from the Olestua ruin across Dove Bugt towards Store Koldewey with the remains of the depot stone house at left, 25th July 2005. © NCN

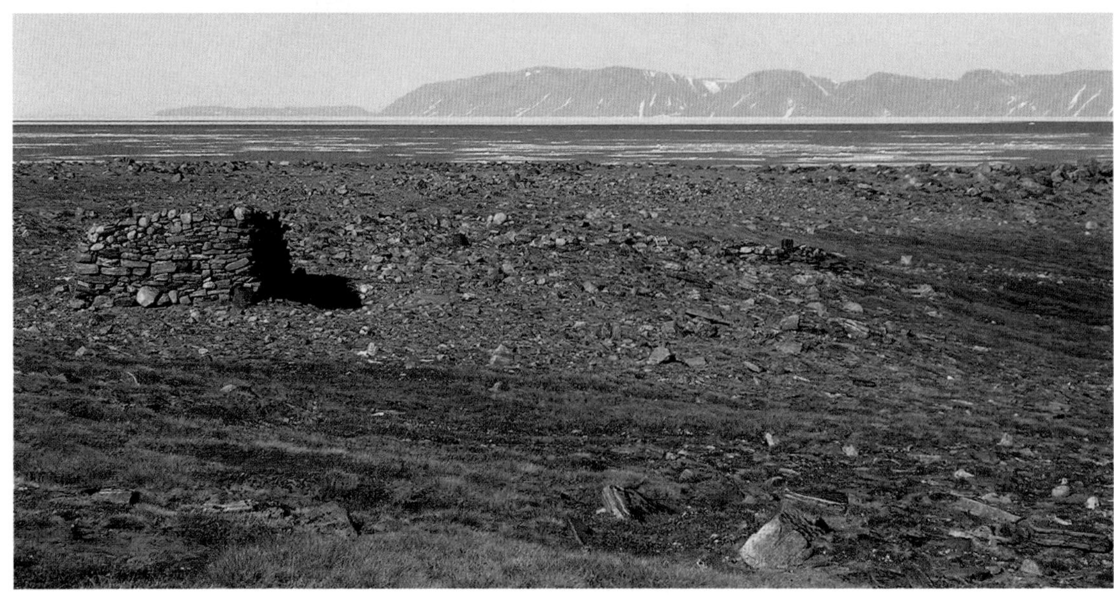

OTTOSTRAND
[531]

Wintering party
1932-34: Otto Johnsen, Ove Høeg
1934-38: Part of 1936-37 only
1938-39: Bjarne Jakobsen, Bjarne Dalsbø
1939-48: None
1948-50: Hermod Sætre, Erling Juell Ramberg
1950-51: Fredrik Sæterdal, Trygve Saga
1951-52: Odd Bogholm
1952-53: Odd Bogholm, Stein Sørensen,
Hans Hvide Bang

1932-33

A few kilometres north of the mouth of the Agnete Sø river lies an old Norwegian trappers' station named Ottostrand. It was established in 1932 by the John Giæver Expedition.

Ottostrand was planned to be the main station of the expedition, but the pack ice caused trouble. Twice "Isbjørn" made an attempt to approach the coast of Hochstetter Forland, but on 10th August Giæver had to initiate a contingency plan. This meant that the radio equipment together with Giæver and the radio operator Johan Holm would be placed at the Jonsbu station in Peters Bugt. Furthermore, the other two stations of the expedition would have to be placed far to the south in the inner part of Kejser Franz Joseph Fjord and at Eleonore Bugt respectively. However, first of all "Isbjørn" was going to make a third and last attempt. On 31st August Giæver received a telegram, saying that "Isbjørn" had managed to unload the stations Ottostrand and Olestua at the originally planned locations. Giæver was very relieved: *"I had feared that they would have to go south to Kejser Franz Joseph Fjord, but everything has now gone better than we had dared to hope. I have sent a request to the social department on 16th August for annexation of the land between the south point of the entrance to Ardencaple Fjord and the south coast of Germania Land".*[643]

Instead of John Giæver, it was now the 31-year-old Otto Johnsen from Tromsø who was to be in charge of the station at Roseneathbugt [Ottostrand] for the next two years. Giæver and Johnsen knew each other from Arctic Commercial Enterprise. In 1929-30 they had been neighbours on Wollaston Forland, and in 1931-31 they built the Hoelsbu station together. Johnsen was going to have Ove Høeg, a newcomer, as partner. The station at Roseneathbugt was at first called Kolstad - named after the Norwegian prime minister - but one day Giæver received a: *"telegram from the prime minister. He "thinks the naming policy unfavourable." Well, perhaps?! He ought to know best. To me it doesn't matter what the station is called"*, and so Giæver named it Ottostrand after Johnsen.[644]

On 15th December 1932, Giæver's men visited

Otto Johnsen – holding the skin from an arctic wolf – and Ove Høeg, 1933. © Arne Philbert

Jonsbu for Christmas: *"At 1 o'clock tonight Otto and Ove arrived from the north. They had driven for 14 hours without stopping, but both were in good shape. During the autumn they have built three huts:* "Kaphytten" [537-2], "Haystackhytten" [533] and "Pollenhytten" [536], *"and have materials for three more in stock."* ... *"Otto and Ove have had the pack ice up to the shore the entire autumn so they have not been able to use the motor boat at all. They built the huts after the ice froze up in November".*[645]

Johnsen and Høeg stayed at Jonsbu until February. Their next meeting was in the middle of May 1933, when Giæver visited Ottostrand: *"Here they have 37 foxes including one blue. We have altogether about 100 foxes including 20 blue. They have unfortunately lost their foxes in cages – 12 white. The cages were snowed down over Christmas".*[646]

1933-34

During the summer of 1933, Johnsen and Høeg built "Agnetehytten" [530] and "Langelv-hytten" [534-1]. A third hut that should have been placed close to the mountains on Hochstetter Forland was never built. At the end of November, John Giæver had news from Ottostrand through the Dane Arne Philbert, that Johnsen and Høeg had built a new hut, "Sønderelv" [535-1] between Haystack and Bessel Fjord and that their catch so far numbered 17 foxes and 11 live foxes in cages.

There were only few foxes at Ottostrand that winter; the catch was 40 each. One day a muskox attacked their dogs while they were chained up and before the men could get out of the house, three dogs had been badly injured. They survived, but one had a punctured lung and never really recovered. Johnsen and Høeg stayed at Ottostrand for the summer until the 22nd August 1934, when they were picked up by "Selbarden". Neither of them wintered again in North-East Greenland.

1934-38

The Norwegians did not use Ottostrand during the years 1934-38, although in the winter of 1936-37 three Nanok men, Hans Ludvig Jensen, Carl Henrik Schultz and Poul Hennings, used the station for a good part of the trapping season (see Hochstetter).

1938-39

In 1938 Sigurd Tolløfsen returned to North-East Greenland with a new expedition, that apart from himself and his son Eivind included the trappers Bjarne Jakobsen and Bjarne Dalsbø; all were from Tromsø. Jakobsen and Dalsbø were to stay at Ottostrand.

The expedition had poor results and was dogged by bad luck. Ebbe Munck, who the same summer had initiated the Mørkefjord Expedition together with Eigil Knuth, said: *"We were the last ship homeward-bound from the coast. It was cold and stormy, about 10 o'clock in the evening as we sailed in the dusk somewhere in Dove Bugt, when we suddenly became aware of a bright bonfire on the shore a few kilometres north of Påskenæsset. There was no doubt, someone on the shore wanted our attention. We put a boat into the water and I rowed together with the first mate and one of the sailors. It was a long row in a strong off-shore wind. It was a rather pathetic meeting. In the dusk stood two soaked and exhausted trappers. They were Bjarne Jakobsen and Bjarne Dalsbø, both from Tromsø in northern Norway. I asked if they had been calling us and if we could be of any assistance. At the beginning they were reluctant and answered only in monosyllables. I asked again if anything had happened?*

– Not really.

Whether they wanted to come on board?

– Well, alright.

If they were not freezing in their wet clothes?

– Not so much that it hurt.

Ottostrand c. 1949.
© Bjarne Myrvold

We had brought a bottle of rum with us and when it had been passed around the conversation became a bit more coherent. We now learnt that they had lost their motor boat as well as a dory and almost all of their equipment, rifles, sleeping bags, provisions etc. On the 20th August they had been set ashore from "Polarbjørn" in order to winter on the coast with their main station about 15 kilometres south of Haystack (Ottostrand). *The same day they had sailed to Bessel Fjord to repair the trappers' hut "Ullestuen"* (Olestua), *where we now were. During an off-shore storm on the 24th August the high tide had taken their boats that were lying on the shore. When they discovered what had happened, both boats had already drifted well away amongst the ice floes. Even though Dalsbø had cut his hand to the bone earlier that day, he immediately threw himself into the ice-cold water to swim after the boats. It was suicidal and he soon had to give up the attempt to avoid cramp, so the boats with their valuable cargo drifted further and further out to sea. He then tried to make a boat from some empty paraffin barrels and a door from "Ullestuen". But Dalsbø was powerless in the storm. When he disappeared behind a small peninsula Jacobsen thought he had drowned, but he had managed to come ashore. Deeply depressed the two men went up to the hut to make a cup of coffee. The only things they had brought ashore were coffee beans".*[647]

Dalsbø and Jakobsen came on board the "Gamma", where they replaced most of their lost equipment and provisions. The next day they were set ashore at the Danish station of Mønstedhus, about 10 km north of Ottostrand.

The trapping at Ottostrand was disappointing. Dalsbø and Jakobsen therefore decided to follow the Dane Christian Jensen from Hvalrosodden on a journey into Dove Bugt. They went northwards on 1st March and the trip lasted well over a month. A few days after their return, Dalsbø and Jakobsen decided to abandon Ottostrand. They went to Jonsbu, where Sigurd Tolløfsen on 19th April 1939 wrote: *"Today both the Bjarne's arrived from the north. They have spent seven hours on the journey from Ottostrand to here. Their entire catch is 13 white foxes. They were determined to go home this year".*[648] Dalsbø and Jakobsen continued southwards to stay with Hermann Andresen at Kap Herschell and Gerhard Antonsen at Moskusheimen respectively. Later in the summer they went home with the "Polarbjørn". Ottostrand was then unmanned until 1948.

1948-50

In 1948, when Arctic Commercial Enterprise had support from the Norwegian state to re-establish the Norwegian trapping territories north of Wollaston

Hermod Sætre (left) and Erling Juell Ramberg. Ottostrand, 1949. © Bjarne Myrvold

Forland, Ottostrand was manned by Hermod Sætre and Erling Juell Ramberg, both from Vesterålen in northern Norway. The catch at Ottostrand in 1948-49 was the worst in the history of the company, just three white foxes; but in general it was a very poor year for fox.

In the summer of 1949, Sætre and Ramberg went fishing char together with Egil Amsjø and Bjarne Myrvold from the Ny Jonsbu station. They tried out Agneteelv as well as Langelv, but it turned out to be: *"a waste of effort with little to show for it. We had altogether about eight barrels"*, Amsjø wrote.[649] He believed that: *"the main reason so few char went up the rivers is that the sea ice was intact as far as they could see. For this reason there was only fresh water in the sea next to land. It didn't taste salty until the middle of August".*[650]

For the fishing they built "Langelv fiskerhytte" [532-3]. Another hut, "Astralhytten" [535-2] was also built in 1948-49.

The four Norwegians awaited the ship's arrival, but: *"as we had passed the 20th August and the winter ice was still unbroken, we were worried that there would be no ship at all. Together with Ramberg and the Dane* (Harald) *Mikkelsen I climbed to the top of Haystack on 23rd August. Then we could see the winter ice was unbroken from land to Store Koldewey and all of Dove Bugt southwards to Shannon and the outer Ardencaple basin. There was no open water anywhere. In the night of the 27th August the four of us, with 12 dogs and necessary equipment, took off in a dory with an outboard motor. We went southwards in the land water and arrived late in the day of the 28th at Kap Rink. We had spent 30 hours on that trip"*.[651]

The missing supply ship meant that Sætre and Ramberg had to go south for fresh supplies. On 9th December 1949, Egil Amsjø at Ny Jonsbu noted that: *"Ramberg and Sætre had arrived from the north"*.[652] On 14th December Ramberg, Amsjø and Myrvold continued further southwards to fetch some of the supplies that had been left for them at Kap Stosch. The three trappers returned to their stations after New Year.

Hermod Sætre and Erling Juell Ramberg, who in 1949-50 had a total catch of 110 foxes, both went home in the summer of 1950.

1950-51

Fredrik Sæterdal and a new trapper, Trygve Saga from Hvittingfoss, had the Norwegian territories north of Kuhn Ø in 1950-51. They stayed at Ottostrand that was to be Sæterdal's territory, and from here Saga went up to his territory at Ny Jonsbu when the trapping season began.

In the autumn they built "Fjellborg-hytten" [534-2] as a replacement for Langelv-hytten that had disappeared: *"This of course was not welcomed by the Danish trappers, which is understandable"*, Sæterdal said in 1992.[653] *"Erik Larsen didn't mind since we were the best of friends and he only had traps 5-6 kilometres into the valley, but it did not end there"*.[654] On 15th April Sæterdal visited his neighbour Erik Larsen at Mønstedhus, and he met there the Sirius patrol men Holger Jørgensen and Eli Kristiansen: *"They had shot three bears on the trip and I tasted bear steak for the first time this winter. They came with me and are leaving tomorrow. Jørgensen brought a telegram from Dr. Orvin. It said that Danish trappers had complained to Nanok that I had been trapping from Haystack to the bottom of Bessel Fjord and that I had built a hut in the Langelv valley. Nanok assumed that I used Danish traps. It should be added that it was not Erik Larsen who had filed the complaint, but the two trappers* (Leo Ingwersen and Knud Nielsen) *at Aalborghus"*.[655] The incident of the Fjellborg-hytten did not have any significant consequences.

Odd Bogholm, trapper 1951-54. © Bendt Nielsen

Trygve Saga went home in 1951, and Sæterdal moved to Hoelsbu leaving the following remark on the wall of a hut somewhere in Ottostrand territory:

"A trapper slaves day and night,
to Satan's great delight".[656]

1951-52

Odd Bogholm, then 25-years old and from the Narvik area of Norway, came up in 1951-52 to winter alone at Ottostrand. Originally he should have had a partner, another trapper - who on the way to Greenland received the nickname "Ursus Olsen" - but when the "Polarbjørn" came to Mestersvig: *"Ursus Olsen got hold of some aquavit and he and Bogholm got into a fight. And then Olsen – they were big guys both of them – took a beating. The next day Olsen claimed that he had been so injured that he was pissing blood – he claimed his kidneys had been damaged. And then he asked to go home"*, Ivar Ytreland recalled in 1992.[657]

As Bogholm was now alone at Ottostrand with 5-6 days journey to his nearest countryman, he went into a sort of partnership with Erik Larsen at Mønstedhus and they agreed to share the catch in certain areas.

1952-53

In 1952-53, Odd Bogholm had the company of Stein Sørensen and Hans Hvide Bang. After three winterings at Myggbukta, Sørensen had been home in Norway where he had met Hans Hvide Bang, a friend from school. They agreed to go to Greenland to become trappers for Arctic Commercial Enterprise and at the same time make a film about the trappers.

The 30-year-old Hans Hvide Bang from Oslo had until then worked as a surveyor in his father's company. The desire to go to Greenland partly came from Stein Sørensen's stories and partly from his uncle, Oscar Bang, who had wintered at Myggbukta in 1938-39. To Hans Hvide Bang - a descendant of the old Danish 'Hvide' family (c. 1100-1600) - the stay in Greenland was the beginning of a lifelong career as a cameraman. After his trip to Greenland he was contacted by the filmmaker Per Høst, who wanted him to make a film about the Sami (Laplanders). In addition to a number of his own nature films, Hvide Bang has been a photographer for Helge Ingstad in "Vinland" (Newfoundland) and David Attenborough amongst others.

Sørensen and Bang should have gone ashore at Ottostrand, but the ice blocked access and instead

"Polarbjørn" had to leave them at Kap David Gray on Shannon. Here they built "Tåkeheimen" [472-2], that served as their base until it became possible to sledge across to the mainland.

They had not had any contact with Bogholm, but on the 12th October they had: *"our so far greatest experience since we annexed Shannon. While I'm tidying up inside, the dogs start to howl and bark. I assumed that it is only because Hans is returning, but look out of the window anyway. And then – right down at the shore – I see a dog team and two men, the first visitors this winter. Hans comes towards land from the ice. I rush outside and welcome the visitors as is only proper. It is the trapper Bogholm from Ottostrand together with an Englishman, John Oakley, from a British expedition; there are four men with eight weasel tractors at Kap Rink on Hochstetter Forland, who are to continue to the main base of the expedition on the inland ice west of Dove Bugt* (Dronning Louise Land) *later in the winter. We have a small party that evening, as we have all Bogholm's aquavit in stock"*, Stein Sørensen wrote.[658]

They then moved in with Bogholm at Ottostrand: *"Odd is to trap northwards in Dove Bugt and Bessel Fjord, I am going southwards to the Jonsbu territory. Hans is to stay at Ottostrand and trap in the home territory and around Agnete Sø inland"*.[659]

The three trappers now went to each their territory, a lonely job. On 27th November Sørensen wrote: *"The solitude is beginning to hurt, it is fine to be on your own for about fourteen days, but then you begin to long for someone to talk to. To me it results in restlessness – I sleep badly at night and smoke far too much."* ... *"When it is a good trapping year you become so caught up in obtaining a large catch that you forget about the polar night, like last year at Myggbukta. But this year has reached rock bottom – I know that even if I put up traps everywhere, the result will be next to nothing and the eagerness and the desire is gone"*.[660] However, it turned out not to be a particularly lonely wintering, for now and again people from the Sirius Dog Sledge Patrol and the British North Greenland Expedition would pass by. The three trappers made several long journeys together, e.g. a Christmas trip to Danmarkshavn and in March a month-long trip to build "Stormheimen" [507] on Shannon.

During the wintering Sørensen and Bang continuously worked with their film. In the summer of 1953, Bang went home, but as more filming was needed Sørensen decided to take another wintering at Kap Herschell together with Bogholm, who then joined the film project.

In the summer of 1953, Arctic Commercial Enterprise decided to stop trapping in the northern districts; Bogholm, Sørensen and Bang thus became the last trappers to winter at Ottostrand.
A244; A296; G123; N076; N080.

Recent status

As Ottostrand was close to Mønstedhus, which later on became the preferred depot locality of the Sirius Dog Sledge Patrol, Ottostrand was not maintained and fell to decay. As Mønstedhus was taken by the sea in the autumn of 2002, it is now likely that Ottostrand will be renovated by Nanok in the near future.

Ottostrand [531], 4th August 2004. © NCN

Ottostrand [531], 4th August 2004. Ottostrand is a former Norwegian trappers' station built in 1932 for the John Giæver Expedition. It was used as a trappers' station until 1953. It has probably only been used as a travellers' hut on very few occasions since 1953.

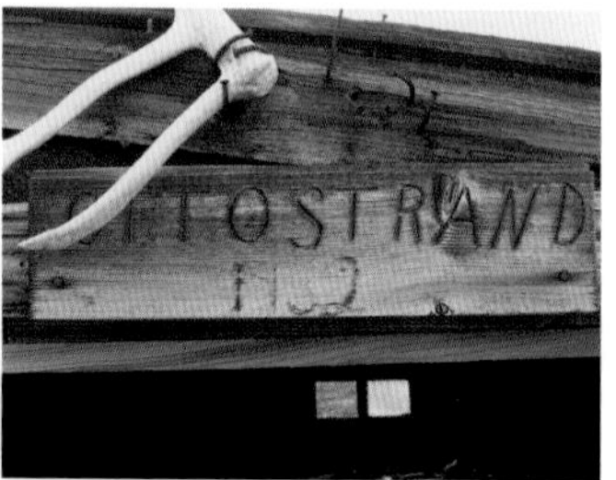

Ottostrand remains almost unchanged since it was used as a trappers' station. It consists of four individual buildings, the main house and three provision huts. © NCN

SANDODDEN
[425-1]

Wintering party

1923-24: Konrad Larsen, Christian Fischbech, Axel Christensen, Jens Jensen
1924-29: None
1929-30: J.G. Jennov, Berndt Jensen, Leander E. Emskær Larsen, Richard Bøgvad
1930-31: Leander E. Emskær Larsen, J.G. Jennov, Carl Aage Knudsen*, Evald Rasmussen*
1931-32: Elmar Drastrup, Evald Rasmussen*
1932-34: None
1934-36: Niels Hansen, Aage Hansen*
1936-38: Aage Hansen*
1938-39: Berndt Jensen, Christian Petersen*
1939-40: Berndt Jensen, Eli Knudsen
1940-41: Eli Knudsen
1941-45: None
1945-46: Aksel Nielsen
1946-47: Kjeld Soelberg
1947-48: Erling Pedersen**
1948-49: None
1949-50: Leo Ingwersen, Jack Engelbrecht Christensen

* Wintered partly at Knudshoved
** Wintered partly at Loch Fyne

1923-24

Young Sund was named by William Scoresby Junior after Thomas Young (1773-1829), a physician, egyptologist and secretary of the Board of Longitude 1818-28.[661] Daneborg is a settlement of low houses on the north side of Young Sund approximately opposite Basaltø - a short distance from the other buildings and close to the beach stands a small green house with a pitched roof, "Sandodden" (sand point). It is the oldest building in Daneborg. It may seem a bit quaint that the East Greenland Company's old trappers' station carries this name, for there is no sand or point; however, along the beach about 4-5 km to the south, there is a flat sandy point. This locality, Kap Berghaus, which Ragnvald Knudsen had called "Heklas Hvalrosnæs" in 1889, was mentioned by Hans Ludvig Jensen in connection with a successful walrus hunt on 2nd August 1922: *"At a closer look we saw a large number of walrus skeletons showing that this is one of the places where the Norwegians made their big catches. The bones have all been gnawed, which indicates that it is a good place for fox trapping." ... "I recommend that we place a station where we shot the walrus".*[662] As a result, the locality became known to trappers as Sandodden. On the 16th July 1923, Hans Ludvig Jensen at Germaniahavn ordered his men to pull down the Christianshavn station: *"so that "Carl" can immediately begin the transport of the house to Sandodden".*[663] In the meantime, "Teddy" had arrived and the master Henning Bistrup personally decided to take charge of the transfer of the materials from Christianshavn. The journalist Kai R. Dahl noted on 28th July 1923: *"Captain Bistrup returned to the ship about midnight. Sandodden, where the new station was established, had fulfilled all expectations".*[664] In reality the house was placed a few kilometres north of the sandy point. Although the house was officially named "Ny Valdemarshaab", in practice it has never been called anything else but Sandodden.

Sandodden was to be main station for the

Sandodden c. 1923. © Jørgen Nielsen

Known and unknown Danish trappers gathered at Sandodden, c. 1923. Sitting on ground to the left: Viktor Hugo Stjernebo. Standing above: Christian Rasmussen and L.E. Emskær Larsen. © Jørgen Nielsen

trapping territory that had earlier been shared between Christianshavn and Valdemarshaab. It was Konrad "Fynboen" Larsen and the new men Christian Fischbech, Axel Christensen and Jens "Sibirie" Jensen, who were to stay at Sandodden; but they had barely settled in before a serious accident occurred.

On 21st August 1923, they were on a trip to Kap Borlase Warren. On their return they discovered a seal and 23-year-old Axel Rasmus Christensen resolutely reached for his rifle, which was leaning against the rail. He grabbed the barrel near the muzzle, but as he pulled the rifle the trigger caught against the rail and the rifle went off. The bullet travelled along the length of his left arm and became stuck in his shoulder; it was a terrible wound. They rowed back to Borganes hytten and dressed the wound as best they could. At home the doctors might have saved him, but up here the chances were vanishingly small. The only person who might be able to do something, due to the fact that he had participated in WWI, was Dr. Karl Richter, a German scientist, who had arrived that summer. But Richter was at Kap Philip Broke. While Fischbech took care of the injured man, Konrad Larsen and Jens Jensen at once set off to row the 40 kilometres to Germaniahavn. Here Victor Stjernebo and Kristen Larsen immediately started the motor boat "Carl", and headed for Shannon. They found Richter and sailed back to Kap Borlase Warren, but just as they came around the last point they saw Fischbech walking outside the house. Two days had passed since the accident, and as they feared it was too late. Axel Christensen had died from loss of blood the day before, on 22nd August 1923, at 1 o'clock in the afternoon.

An hour later they sailed their dead colleague back to Sandodden. Here they made a simple coffin, dressed with a mattress on which the body was placed. A blanket was pulled over and the lid was nailed down. As the coffin was lowered into the grave – a few metres behind Sandodden – Konrad Larsen said a few words and the Lord's Prayer and the grave was filled up.[665]

Of his visit to Sandodden in the spring of 1924, Viggo S. Lund said: *"The house is encircled by side sheds to the north and the east and is completely covered with roofing felt outside and with coarse felt paper on the inside. It is the warmest hut in North-East Greenland. Jensen had rebuilt the stove with granite boulders and with fireclay the Siberian way. It could stay warm all night and in the morning you could get up in a living room not below zero degrees C. It sounded like a fable to those of us from Germaniahavn, where the temperature in the living room once went down to minus 16 degrees C.*

It wasn't for nothing that Jensen had lived 23 years in Siberia. There was no doubt about that when you

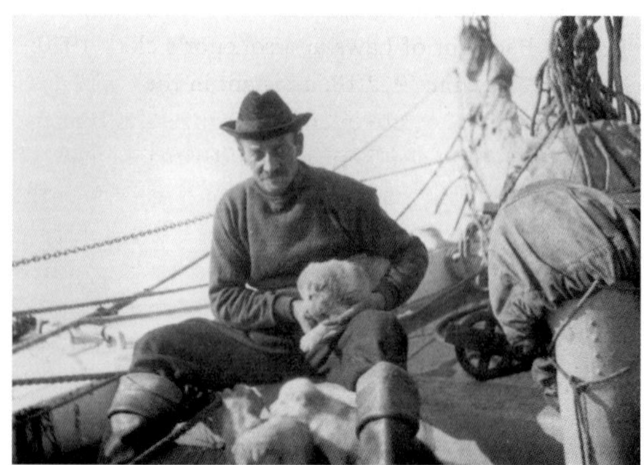

Leander Elias Emskær Larsen, c. 1923. © Jørgen Nielsen

Axel Rasmus Christensen's grave at Sandodden, Daneborg, July 1999. © Peter Schmidt Mikkelsen

tasted his home-brewed Kyrgyz beer. I made him give me the recipe: a couple of unleavened hard-baked loaves of rye bread, some yeast and hops, sufficient water and sugar and a few raisins. It was the raisins that made the difference".[666]

Sandodden was unmanned from 1924-29.

1929-30

On the 25th August 1929 the "Birkild" of Ålesund anchored at Sandodden: *"The main house is somewhat damaged, and there is some fungus on the floor, but not more that we can deal with",*[667] J.G. Jennov wrote. Together with Leander E. Emskær Larsen, Berndt Jensen and Richard Bøgvad, Jennov went ashore to take possession of the station. Only three months earlier, on 20th May 1929, Jennov and Emskær Larsen had met with the lawyer Svend Engelhardt at Nørregade 4 in Copenhagen; this was the occasion that "Nanok" was founded.

Johannes Gerhardt Jensen was born on 27th January 1886 in Copenhagen, the eldest of seven children. About 1900 the family moved to Horsens, where his father Christian Jensen became manager and Swedish vice-consul. In 1912 the family changed their name to Jennov.

J.G. Jennov's biography can be summarized as follows: Bachelor of Laws and solicitor's clerk 1910; second lieutenant 1912-13; assistant in the Generaltolddirektoratet (general customs department) and lieutenant in the Fæstningsartilleriregimentet (fortress artillery regiment) as well as a teacher in the Corporal- and Non-Commissioned officers School 1914-17; Managing director for the Baltica Shipyard in Copenhagen 1917-25, and member of the board 1922-25; assistant in the Inspectorate for Tobacco taxation 1926-29; co-founder of Nanok 1929, and managing director 1929-76; wintered in North-East Greenland 1929-31, and leader of Nanok's summer expeditions 1932-52. Jennov, who died in 1980 – wrote a number of articles on East Greenland, particularly about its zoology.

Of his interest in Greenland, Jennov wrote: *"In 1927 I accidentally came in contact with the trappers by reading the book "Jægerliv og nordlysnætter", written by a former trapper Viggo S. Lund. I had always been interested in the Arctic and especially Greenland subjects, and like many others I had a strong and clear feeling that there was an urgent task waiting to be undertaken in North-East Greenland, not least for national reasons".*[668]

With respect to the competing Norwegian trapping companies, Jennov in 1929 started with a positive attitude. He wrote: *"At that time I wished to do what I could to make sure the relationships between us were as good as possible in all respects".*[669] However, after a couple of disappointing experiences, such as the incident when the Carlshavn station was burnt down and not replaced, Jennov's attitude hardened. Nevertheless, most of the disputes with the Norwegians concerning rights to trapping territories were solved amicably.

It was on the home front that Jennov had his most bitter struggles. Different Danish authorities and influential people regarded Jennov as a somewhat difficult gentleman. Captain Ejnar Mikkelsen called him: *"a strange idealist"*[670] and believed that he had sent out too many unqualified trappers to North-East Greenland and that this was the main reason for Nanok's disappointing results. Jennov's controversies with Lauge Koch are legendary – in Jennov's opinion, Koch did everything he could to make life difficult for Nanok.

Officially it cannot be denied that Jennov and the Danish trapping activities played a considerable part in Denmark's winning the trial at The Hague,

Mogens Graae (left) and Johannes Gerhardt Jennov, 1954. © Mogens Graae

and: *"in recognition of the work done by Nanok in East Greenland in the benefit of Denmark's interests",*[671] Jennov obtained employment at the National Bank of Denmark. As late as 1949 Jennov was awarded the Knight's Cross of the Order of the Dannebrog.
It is impossible to say how the Danish trapping enterprise might have developed without J.G. Jennov, but one has the impression that he usually acted more like a lawyer than as a businessman.

Leander Elias Emskær Larsen was, with Jennov, a co-founder of Nanok. In 1922-24 he had worked for the East Greenland Company, and based on this experience he was in charge of Sandodden in 1929-31. Berndt Jensen - a brother of trapper Jens "Siberia" Jensen - was a newcomer, but later became one of the company's most experienced men. Richard Bøgvad, who was an engineer and mineralogist did not take part in the trapping, but instead carried out geological surveys for Øresunds Chemiske Fabriker. In May-June 1930, Bøgvad, Jennov and Hans Ludvig Jensen made a sledge journey to Danmark Havn.

Due mainly to lack of experience, it was a disappointing year: *"In all we have caught 15 white foxes and five bears. The reason for this poor catch is partly that the Norwegians use poison for trapping which has had an extremely damaging effect on the fox population, and partly because this season we have had unusually heavy snow falls in the territory, so the foxes tend to move to areas with less snow. Furthermore, the lack of sufficient trappers' huts has also been a drawback for the trapping".*[672] In order to remedy the latter, the following huts were built in July 1930: "Henningelvhytten" [416], "Djævlekløfthytten" [427], "Zackenberghytten" [438-1] and "Grønlænderhuset" [419].

In the summer of 1930, Berndt Jensen moved to the Hochstetter station, whereas Richard Bøgvad went home.

1930-31

In the summer of 1930, Knudshoved on Hold with Hope was built and only two men were needed at Sandodden; these were Emskær Larsen and Jennov, but they had a variety of problems.

To start with, Emskær Larsen and Jennov lost their motor boat and were unable to take out sufficient supplies to the trappers' huts: *"In addition to this, in September Larsen managed to push a knife through the middle finger of his left hand while cutting up a muskox, and in October Larsen was tormented by a gumboil which for a while seemed like it would develope into a dangerous jawbone inflammation".*[673]

One day in the middle of November Carl Aage Knudsen and Evald Rasmussen arrived. Knudsen thought he had scurvey and dared not stay at Knudshoved. An examination showed that it was probably far less serious, but he was allowed to stay anyway. Jennov decided then to go to Knudshoved together with Rasmussen, but for various reasons they did not not leave until the end of January.

To Jennov it became yet another disappointing year: *"The trapping at Sandodden has been poor; 18 foxes in that part of the territory where we trapped last year and only one fox in the Zackenberg territory".*[674] Jennov had other problems: *"The atmosphere at the Danish station is very bad as it is no fun staying there with Jennov present, because everybody is cross with him. However, several of his men are alright".*[675] This was what Hermann Andresen from Kap Herschell wrote after a visit to Sandodden in the beginning of March. While Jennov went home in the summer of 1931, Leander E. Emskær Larsen moved to Hochstetter.

1931-32

In 1931, Evald Rasmussen and Elmar Drastrup took over Sandodden, a wintering described by Drastrup in his book from 1932: "Blandt danske og norske

L.E. Emskær Larsen (standing) and Arne Philbert fishing arctic char at Zackenberg, July 1932. © Arne Philbert

Afternoon light inside Sandodden. Sitting at the table L.E. Emskær Larsen (left) and Evald Rasmussen. 26. July 1932. © Arne Philbert

fangstmænd i Nordøstgrønland" (among Danish and Norwegian trappers in North-East Greenland): *"There are two berth beds along each wall. In the middle of the living room there is a stove. It's not very big but heats well. There is plenty of space for cooking the little food we need. It has an oven and everything, and the flue goes straight up through the ceiling. On the other wall hang our rifles, pistols, carbines, cartridge belts and hunting knives. In the corner stands a large pot with fresh water, surrounded by pots and pans and other kitchen utensils. In the other corner we have a small kitchen table, and there is a shelf for plates (tin plates of course), coffee tins, cups and such like. Above the table by the window is a paraffin lamp with a porcelain globe and golden chains hanging from the ceiling. On the wall above the table is the tobacco shelf. Pipes, cigarettes, paper and tobacco. We have also chairs, of course, although they are strange species made of old boxes and boards. A single sea chest, Icelandic sweaters, anoraks, mittens and socks on the line in the ceiling, rubber boots and sea boots. On the stove the blue coffee pot is simmering cosily"*.[676]

Drastrup's career as a trapper was brief. On 27th November 1931, Bjarne Ludvigsen, the radio operator at Hochstetter arrived. He was going to Eskimonæs to pick up spare parts for a defective radio receiver and Drastrup decided to go with him.

They left Sandodden on 1st December, but when they had crossed Henningelv they discovered that the ice had broken up in Gael Hamke Bugt. This forced them to sledge on land, but on their way to Elvsborg the sledge skidded down a slope and their skis were crushed. They now had to wade in deep, loose snow, first to Elvsborg and then towards Eskimonæs. Off Dødemandsbugten they had to leave their sleeping bags, but there were cracks beneath the snow and they both went through and got wet feet. In the intense cold the water froze to ice instantly. They had to turn around and luckily found their sleeping bags. The following day they finally reached Eskimonæs. They both had serious frostbite in their feet. As a result of this accident Drastrup had to return home in the summer of 1932, and was hospitalized for months. It eventually became necessary to amputate some of his toes.

Drastrup later wintered for the Lauge Koch Expedition in 1933-34 and in 1938-39 was leader of the Danish Dog Sledge Expedition. Elmar Drastrup (1909-1981) was born in Copenhagen. He wrote several travel books, novels and articles based on his experiences in North-East Greenland.

Evald Rasmussen moved to the Bessel Fjord station in 1932.

Even though Sandodden was unmanned in 1932-34, a new trappers' hut, "Pashuset" [433], was built in the territory.

1934-36

In 1934, the 53-year-old veteran Niels Hansen, who in 1929-33 had wintered at Hochstetter station, returned to Greenland to take over the Sandodden/Knudshoved territory together with a new man, Aage Hansen.

It was a tradition that the Danes at Sandodden and the Norwegians at Kap Herschell were in regular contact with each other. On 20th October 1934, Nils Hanken at Kap Herschell wrote: *"When I woke up this morning, I started to melt ice for washing. I have cleaned all over so the place is shining now. When I had finished Andresen arrived from Sandodden together with the two Hansens from there. We boiled and fried and have had a really nice evening. It's like at Grand Hotel"*.[677] The two newcomers, Nils Hanken and Aage Hansen, agreed to go together to their trapping territories at Jackson Ø and Knudshoved respectively.

On 28th December Aage Hansen returned from

Niels Hansen (left) and Aage Hansen visiting Kap Herschell. In the background in the door Hermann Andresen is visible. c. 1935.
© Nils Martin Hanken

Knudshoved, and went to Kap Herschell to invite his neighbours to celebrate New Year's Eve at Sandodden. They accepted the invitation and on 31st December 1934 Hermann Andresen wrote: *"We have had a really nice time. Have been drinking aquavit and beer all day and toasted the New Year with a nice rum toddy, but we're not drunk"*.[678]

Both Aage Hansen and Nils Hanken had serious accidents in January 1935 (see Knudshoved and Kap Herschell).

In the summer of 1935, ice conditions prevented the Danish supply ship from reaching North-East Greenland. No fresh supplies were delivered to the trappers so: *"conditions at the stations in the trapping season 1935-36 were the most difficult imaginable" ... "that there could be no decent trapping results under these circumstances is obvious"*.[679] As Sandodden was the only Danish station with sufficient supplies, some of the other Danish trappers also stayed at this station during part of the 1935-36 season.

1936-38

When Niels Hansen went home in the summer of 1936, Aage Hansen had the Sandodden/Knudshoved territory to himself in 1936-38. He wrote that: *"foxes taken in 1936-37 were all caught at Sandodden, mainly at Pashuset, as it was impossible to get to Knudshoved because pack ice blocked the entire way from Elvsborg and southwards; it was impossible to get there until the beginning of April"*.[680]

In the summer of 1937, the "Godthaab" did not reach Young Sund and: *"as there was no transport, Aage Hansen at Sandodden station, who was supposed to go home after three years, had to stay for another year, something he was at first very unhappy about. That a man who has lived three years in the wilderness, and who has been looking forward to going home does not exactly sing with joy when he is told that he has to stay one more year is really quite understandable, but when his disappointment had settled he started his fourth year in a good mood"*.[681] Aage Hansen had probably no kind words to say about Jennov, because in reality he could have gone home with "Polarbjørn": *"Aage Hansen sent a telegram via "Polarbjørn"s radio to Jennov, but was refused the chance to go home with the Norwegian ship"*.[682]

Fortunately, 1937-38 was an extremely good year for trapping, thanks to a boom in the lemming population. Aage Hansen wrote that: *"the lemmings are everywhere, inside and outside, in the porch, the meat house and in the provisions shed. It is as if there's not room enough for all of them beneath the snow. They started to migrate northwards as soon as there was new ice. In Tyrolerfjord thousands of them had frozen to death, simply because the ice was so wet that they had frozen to it. But for the foxes and the owls it is an Eldorado. Yes, even "Dot" feeds herself and her puppies with lemming and in the spring when the snow disappears, it's like walking in hay in front of the house so many are the nests, although the lemmings themselves have disappeared". ... "The foxes were all well fed, but still willing to go into the traps presumably because they wanted a change in their diet. The major problem with these 'lemming foxes' – as we called them – is that they are difficult to clean, as the fat is red, very tough and watery, so when removing the fat the skins sometimes became so dirty that they have to be washed with soap. A 'muskox fox' has a fine white and solid layer of fat, easy to remove in large flakes"*.[683]

In 1938, Aage Hansen finally went home after

Aage Hansen (left) and Alfred Hansen at Sandodden. Summer 1937. © Will C. Knutsen

Berndt Jensen (left) and Elmar Drastrup at Sandodden. 1938. © Niels Ove Jensen

four years. He qualified as a radio operator and in 1945 after the war returned to North-East Greenland - not as a trapper - but as the first station manager of Daneborg Weather Station.

1938-39

In the summer of 1938, Nanok built the "Blæsenborghytten" [443], that brought Lindemansdalen into the Sandodden territory. The station was taken over by two experienced trappers, Berndt "Spækfinger" (blubber finger) Jensen who was on his sixth wintering for Nanok, and Christian Petersen who had spent six years as a trapper in Canada, earning himself the nickname "Ulvedræberen" (wolf killer).

Until the 26th November 1938, they had Elmar Drastrup and Finn Kristoffersen at the station - the two men formed the Danish Dog Sledge Expedition that intended to make an attempt to travel westwards across North Greenland. Neither Jensen nor Petersen showed any great enthusiasm for their guests as Drastrup's expedition included 16 sledge dogs that were in constant need of food. Christian Petersen wrote that: *"it's a shame that the muskox must be killed in this way just because a writer is loafing about here on the coast. It may be in Danish interests that Drastrup is doing this trip, but as hunters we do not want our muskox exterminated".*[684] It was an autumn with many snow storms and the idleness told on their nerves. One day Petersen got into: *"a quarrel with Drastrup about his dogs, as we have a bitch on heat and do not want her mated yet. I told him twice to chain them, but he answers that he'll be in charge of that decision. So I said that if they got near her, they'd be shot. – Is that so? Then you'll get a bullet too, he answered".*[685]

On the other hand, Petersen's relationship with his trapping companion was good, because Berndt Jensen was: *"quite a genius when it comes to cooking. We live well from muskox steak and soup and stew and liver. I have never lived better than during the time Jensen has been doing the cooking".*[686]

On 8th January 1939, Petersen went to Knudshoved and stayed there until 10th May when he went northwards again. At Eskimonæs he met Berndt Jensen. Their total catch was only 37 foxes, a miserable result compared to Hermann Andresen's record catch of 642. After their return to Sandodden, Jensen and Petersen built "Sødalhytten" [446], thus expanding the Sandodden territory with Store Sødal.

1939-40

The name of Eli Knudsen will for ever be associated with Sandodden. It was here he lived as a trapper and later - in March 1943 - met a violent death: *"A cheerful guy he was this young man from Copenhagen, with his short-cut dark hair, full of funny stories from his time as a carpenter in his Amager home and other places. He had a noticeable preference for the exceptional and for foreign countries. When he was hired for a summer job with Nanok he had just returned from a trip to Argentina".*[687] This characterization was given by Knud "Silvanus" Bavngaard, a journalist who visited Greenland in the summer of 1939. He had been hired as an unskilled labourer as the area was then forbidden territory for journalists.

The 26-year-old Eli Knudsen had only been hired for the summer as a carpenter, but on 26th August when the "Gustav Holm" was homeward bound, he asked J.G. Jennov whether: *"there was any chance that he could stay on. I offered him a place at Sandodden where he could help by building huts using the four horses we had there, and furthermore assist Berndt Jensen. In return, Knudsen had board and lodging and work for the following year if he wanted to. In the*

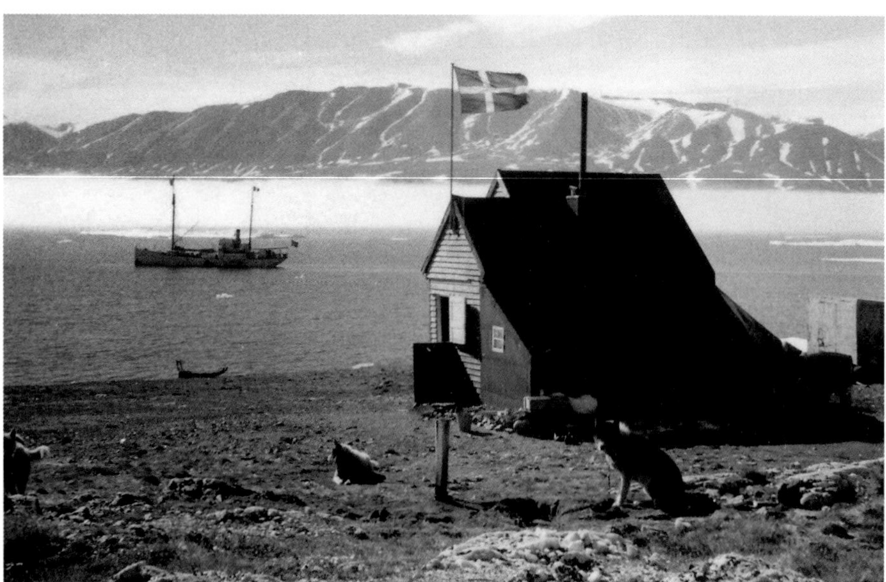

Sandodden, 1937.
© Will C. Knutsen

morning he cleared his gear and around 9 o'clock the ship departed".[688] That is how Eli Knudsen came to stay in Greenland. However, they did not manage to build the huts that were planned for Blæsedalen and Kuppelpasset.

1940-43

In the summer of 1940, Berndt Jensen and Christian Petersen left North-East Greenland with the "Fridtjof Nansen", and Eli Knudsen therefore wintered alone at Sandodden. Henry Rudi at Moskusheimen was in a similar situation, and visited Sandodden in November 1940: *"It was cosy to meet another person. Eli Knudsen was a straight guy, small and slight, but brave and quick-witted, with a light and cheerful temper. He was OK, but had no catch. We were in the same boat".*[689]

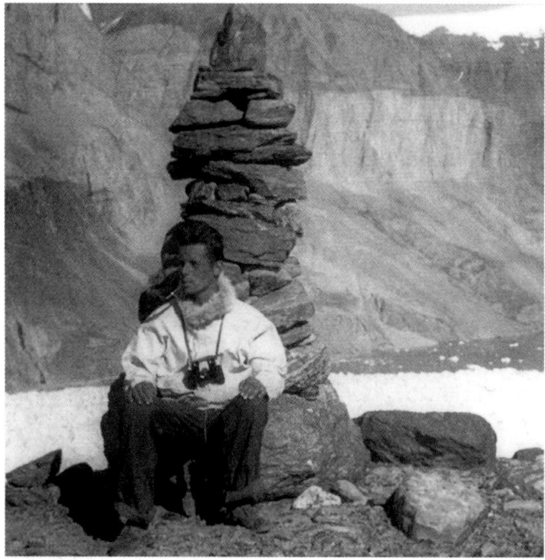

Eli Knudsen sitting by a cairn on the south side of Hisinger Gletscher 1941-42. © Hans K. Siewers

In the summer of 1941, Eli Knudsen, like the other trappers, had the choice between going to West Greenland or joining the North-East Greenland Sledge Patrol. Knudsen preferred the latter alternative, left Sandodden and moved to Ella Ø, where the first year he was just a member of the patrol, but in 1942-43 the group leader.

Sandodden was unmanned from 1941-45.

In March 1943, Eli Knudsen was staying at Eskimonæs. It was here, on the 13th March, that they received the news of a German presence at Sabine Ø. On 18th March, Knudsen and Marius Jensen went northwards to find and warn Peter Nielsen, who was believed to be staying at Hochstetter. They found him and set out together southwards. On 26th March, they reached Kuppelpasset, unaware that the Germans from Hansa Bugt in the meantime had attacked Eskimonæs and - what was worse - at that very moment were staying at Sandodden. Jensen and Nielsen put up their tent, but: *"Eli absolutely had to go down to Sandodden"*, Peter Nielsen recalled in 1993.[690]

It was late in the day of 26th March 1943, that Knudsen approached his old station at a great speed. The Germans had seen him coming, and when he was about 100 metres from the house they stepped out and challenged him. No one knows exactly what went on in Eli Knudsen's mind for the next few seconds, but the Germans later said that when he didn't stop they tried to stop him by shooting his sledge dogs. It was an accident, they explained, that Knudsen was hit in his chest by a bullet and severely injured fell off the sledge. They immediately took him into the house, where their doctor treated him, but

Eli Knudsen's grave at Sandodden, July 1999. © NCN

there was nothing they could do. Eli Knudsen died half an hour later.

The Germans placed the fallen man in Sandodden's provisions shed, and in front of the entrance placed a simple cross with the inscription: *"Er starb für sein Vaterland"* (he died for his country). He was later buried behind Sandodden.

In April 1943, the sledge patrol achieved military status and Eli Knudsen was posthumously promoted to corporal and awarded the American "Legion of Merit" medal for his services.

1945-46

The first Nanok men at Sandodden after the war were to include Aksel Nielsen, a brother to Henry V. Nielsen who was overall leader of the Nanok party. Originally there had been eight men, but one of them, Kjeld Nielsen, had second thoughts and went back home with the "Godthaab"; Aksel Nielsen then had to winter alone at Sandodden. However, he did not lack company as there were four men at Daneborg Weather Station only a short distance away. As the Norwegians did not return to North-East Greenland until 1946, Aksel Nielsen was also able to trap in the Norwegian territory on the south side of Clavering Ø, an area with dangerous ice conditions that had already claimed two victims. An accident led to Aksel Nielsen becoming the third.

Harald Mikkelsen, the trapper at Zackenberg, spoke to Aksel Nielsen for the last time on 17th January 1946 at Moskusheimen: *"Henry Nielsen, Svend Søegaard and Aksel Nielsen set out for Eskimonæs today".*[691] When six weeks had passed and no one at Daneborg had heard from Aksel Nielsen, Mikkelsen started to worry. On 27th February 1946: *"Today I will go to Revet to look for Aksel Nielsen, from whom we have heard nothing since the 17th January."* On 1st March: *"I have met Aksel Jensen who came along with me to Eskimonæs. We found a note that on 13th February Aksel Nielsen left from there to go towards Dødemandsbugten."* On 3rd March: *"Last night I arrived at Dødemandsbugten. Jensen has returned to Revet. Nielsen left here on 15th February".*

On 4th March: *"I drive towards Sandodden. On the way I visit Elvsborghytten. There is a note from Nielsen that he left for Sandodden on 15th February. I myself continue towards Sandodden. When I get there, there is no sign of Nielsen. Later in the evening his lead dog shows up at Sandodden and now we know that an accident must have occurred."* Later on 4th March 1946: *"Aage Hansen, Gustage* (Gustav Hansen) *and I today drive across Henningelv around Kap Mary and find Nielsen's sledge partly beneath the ice. It looks like he went through the ice and has drowned when about one hour from Sandodden".*[692] In 1992 Mikkelsen added that they found three dogs alive by the sledge, while four others had died and were frozen into the ice. The body of Aksel Nielsen was never found. It is assumed that on the 15th February the dogs had run away from Nielsen, who in pursuit had fallen into the water and drowned. In memory of his brother, Henry V. Nielsen later built a cairn at Sandodden.

1946-47

In 1946, Kjeld Soelberg, a 30-year-old carpenter from Copenhagen, took over Sandodden. The Norwegian trapping at Kap Herschell was resumed the same summer and the Sandodden territory then stretched between Blæsedalen, Henningelv, Djævlekløften and Isdal. Three huts were built: "Kap Berghaus hytten" [423] in the autumn of 1946, and "Grønnedalshytten" [418-1] and "Blæsedalhytten (Nanok)" [428] in the spring of 1947.

The area was becoming crowded, as there was

only about twenty kilometres from Sandodden to the stations at Kap Herschell and Zackenberg. Soelberg spent the Christmas at Zackenberg: *"On the 3rd day of Christmas I was back at Sandodden, and took turns in my territory. I caught no fox"*.[693] From a trapping point of view it was a major disadvantage that Daneborg was so close to Sandodden, for the men at the weather station often spent their free time fox trapping. In 1946-47 they caught about 20 foxes, and when you compare this to Soelberg's catch of 57, it is understable that Jennov complained to the new station manager at Daneborg, Jens Martin Andersen, in the summer of 1947. Andersen explained to Jennov that: *"the station crew were told by the Greenland Administration that the fox trapping from Daneborg was to be carried out so it would not harass the trappers and he believed that there would not be much trapping at all"*.[694] This reply did not reassure Jennov, for: *"as far as I know the new radio operators had a different view. It was rumoured that Captain Ejnar Mikkelsen had specifically instructed the Daneborg personnel to trap as much as their time allowed"*.[695]

The trapping from Daneborg Weather Station continued unaffected in the following years, and eventually Nanok gave up using Sandodden as an independent trappers' station.

1947-48

In 1947-48, Nanok had only five trappers wintering. Jennov therefore told Peder Klokker at Zackenberg to take care of his own as well as the Sandodden territory. However, on his own initiative Klokker allowed the men at Daneborg to continue trapping in the Sandodden territory. When Mogens Graae heard about this arrangement he became worried. He spoke to Klokker privately and: *"made him aware that he should tell Andersen not to mention this to Jennov (who would probably have a stroke), and Daneborg had to abandon trapping in the territory the following season"*.[696]

In 1947, Sandodden was host to the trappers' traditional Christmas get-together. Originally it was one of the Norwegians at Kap Herschell, Ivar Ytreland, who: *"suggested that when we were going to Daneborg we should tidy up Sandodden so we could stay there for Christmas. Then we could sleep there and eat there on the days we did not eat at Daneborg"*.[697] The Danish-Norwegian trappers Christmas gathering lasted for about two months that year, and is said to have been extremely festive.

Shortly after New Year 1948, one of the Loch Fyne men, Erling Pedersen, decided to settle at Sandodden and trap from there for the rest of the winter. Sandodden was not manned in 1948-49.

1949-50

"The dogs are dying. I'm freezing and sweating and feel bad. My feet, especially the left one, are somewhat damaged and my toes are black with huge badly swollen blisters".[698] These words are from the diary of trapper Jack Engelbrecht Christensen, and were written on 27th February 1950 in the Norwegian trappers' hut Sletta at Albrecht Bugt. Originally Engelbrecht was to have stayed at Zackenberg, but in November he chose to move in with Leo Ingwersen at Sandodden.

As the fox trapping continued to be disappointing, Engelbrecht decided to go bear hunting on 10th February. At first he went to Germaniahavn, but the hunt failed and on 24th February he continued towards Hochstetter via Albrecht Bugt. The going was fair until Falskebugt, but then: *"it was deep soft snow and was very bad for the dogs, so as it got dark I had just passed Falkebjerg and had driven about 20 km. I dug a hole, lit the primus, made some tea and prepared for the night. Then I discovered that my lead dog had broken loose from its snap hook and disappeared; I figured that he would be back in the morning. I crept into the sleeping bag after having fed the dogs half a loaf each. The weather was fine and calm and I slept well"*.[699] The next day Engelbrecht only travelled about eight km before he once again had to dig himself into the snow: *"the weather was still fine, but rather cold"*.[700]

In the morning of 26th February, Engelbrecht decided to continue: *"my kamiks were frozen stiff and the primus was empty. The dogs were unwilling. We got started, but "Kvik" kept dragging so at last I shot him and split him up in four parts for the last four dogs. They didn't like the food very much, but nevertheless ate so*

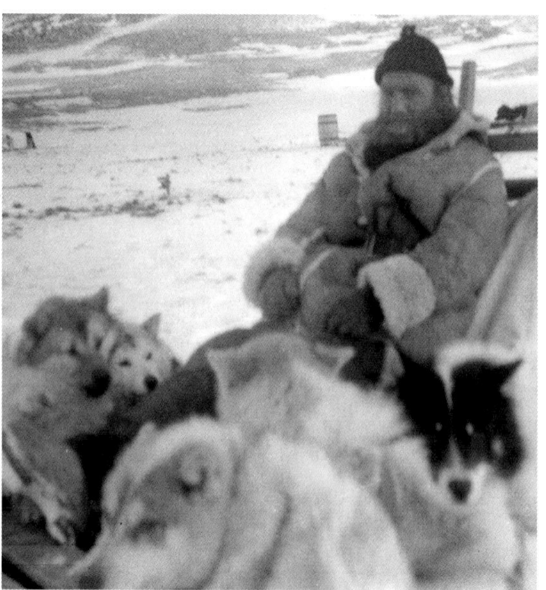

Jack Engelbrecht Christensen, 1949-50.
© Bjarne Myrvold

much that they gained some strength and by united efforts we arrived long after dark at the hut (Sletta)*".*[701]

Engelbrecht had developed severe frostbite and had to stay in the Sletta hut. On 2nd March: *"the two dark blue blisters on my left foot burst".*[702] Nevertheless, he walked back in his tracks to fetch the sledge box that he had abandoned on the way.

On 13th March, the coal was used up and Engelbrecht had to try somehow to get to Germaniahavn, but he: *"only got to the Norwegian Falkebjerghytte* [448] *after a tough trip. 3½ dogs are too few to pull a sledge with equipment and one man. I couldn't help the dogs much as my feet hurt and my socks were frozen to them".*[703]

The following day, Jack Engelbrecht finally managed to reach Germaniahavn where the Norwegian trappers Bjarne Myrvold and Johan Laine happened to be staying: *"We agreed that they should take me to Daneborg"*, Engelbrecht wrote in his diary as a final remark. He stayed at Daneborg until he returned home in the summer of 1950. The accident cost him a couple of toes. In 1950, Leo Ingwersen moved to Aalborghus.

Bistrup 1924; Drastrup 1945; A148; G103; G112; G127; N090; Ø044; Ø054.

Recent status

Sandodden was not used as a trappers' station after 1950, but the old house was not allowed to fall into decay. Sirius used and maintained the station from 1951 until the beginning of the 1960s, and have continued to keep it in good condition ever since.

From the beginning of the 1990s Nanok has taken over much of the repairs and maintenance. However, in 1999 Nanok arranged with Sirius that they could use the Sandodden station and the three associated buildings (Hotel Karina, Sorte Skur and Skindskuret) as summer headquarters. In 2000, on the basis of this agreement, Nanok converted Hotel Karina into a small museum to house a collection of historic trapping equipment and other items dating from the trapper era.

Sandodden with "Skindskuret" and "Sorte Skur" seen from Young Sund. August 2000. © Peter Schmidt Mikkelsen

Sandodden [425-1], August 2000. Sandodden is a former Danish trappers' station built in 1923 for the East Greenland Company, and used as a trappers' station until 1950. It then became living quarters for Sirius until the 1960s. (Left and bottom). "Hotel Karina" that since 2000 has been home to historic items from the trapping era. © Peter Schmidt Mikkelsen

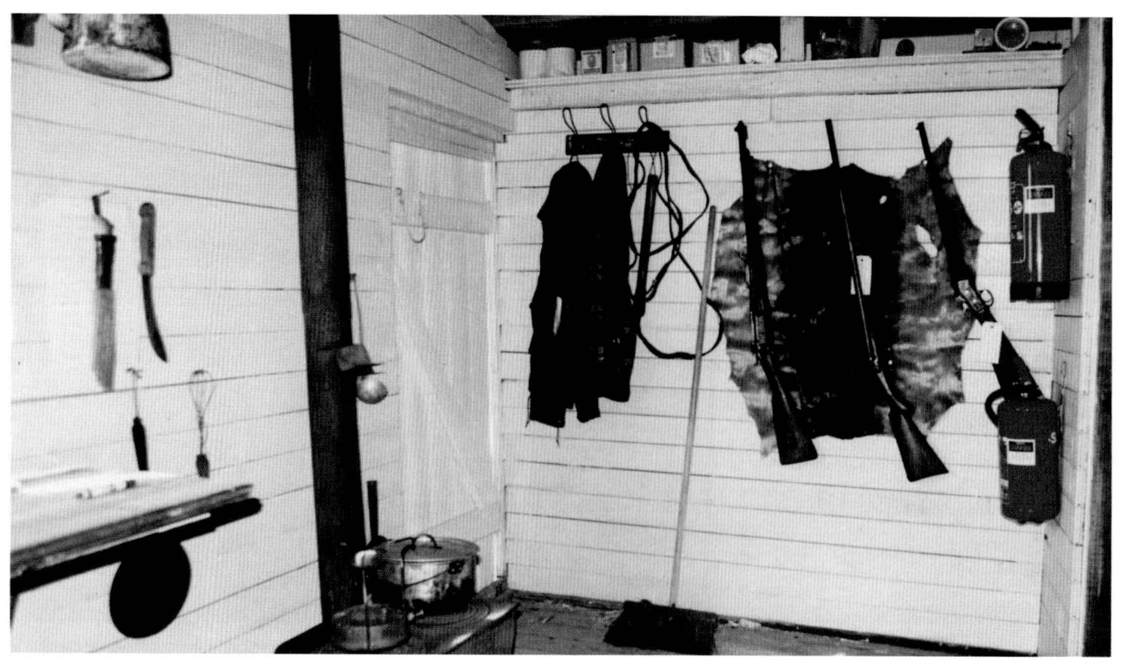

SIGURDSHEIM
[468]

Wintering party
1932-33: Johannes Holmeslet, Johan Stordal
1933-34: Johannes Holmeslet, Haakon Karlsen

1932-33

In 1932, Sigurd Tolløfsen made agreements with Arctic Commercial Enterprise and the Møre Expedition to take over the Moskusheimen and Kap Herschell territories for a two-year period. Tolløfsen himself intended to establish a new trapping territory around Kuhn Ø.

Tolløfsen, who came from Målselvdalen near Tromsø, was a bit of an outsider compared to the established trapping companies. He had tried a little of everything, been a civil servant, had his own grocer's shop and then in 1932 - at the age of 54 - went to North-East Greenland on his first wintering. His interest had started years previously. In 1923, a very unfortunate ice-year, he had been part owner of the Conrad Holmboe Expedition, but the expedition never reached Myggbukta. However, Tolløfsen was an unfailing optimist: *"of the lean, tough sort"*, in John Giæver's words.[704] Tolløfsen also fathered a large family, and according to an anecdote O.A. Krogness, the director of the Geophysical Institute in Tromsø, once asked him: *"Do you really have 11 children, Tolløfsen? – Yes, Tolløfsen answered, that I have. – Then I suggest that you have one more to have the full dozen, otherwise I'll have to call you Ellefsen"*.[705] - And Sigurd Tolløfsen did as suggested, so he could rightfully bear his name.

"As we were leaving for Greenland, Mr. Orvin pointed out the locations where I should build my huts in the Kuhn Ø territory", Sigurd Tolløfsen wrote;[706] but when he arrived in North-East Greenland he discovered that Nanok had already built several huts in the Kuhn Ø area in 1930 and 1931. He consulted Orvin, who answered: *"that I should establish the territory as planned, which I did"*.[707]

The expedition ship, "Isbjørn", reached the east coast of Kuhn Ø on 27th July 1932, and Tolløfsen: *"went ashore to select a location for the main station". ... "This is pure and simple an ideal spot in the summer. At 4 o'clock we began unloading materials, provisions and equipment for the main station. We kept working until we had unloaded everything"*.[708] Tolløfsen built the new station - Sigurdsheim - together with the trappers Johannes Holmeslet and Johan Stordal. When the house was finished it was handed over to Holmeslet and Stordal, as Tolløfsen himself wanted to winter at Kap Herschell.

That same summer, six trappers' huts were built in the Sigurdsheim territory: "Holmeslet" [460-2], "Svendsby" [458-1], "Håkonshytten" [466], "Bolettestua" [471], "Arnljotstua" [509] and "Citystua" [502]. Originally seven huts had been planned, but when Stordal and Holmeslet arrived at Kap Buch, the materials deposited there for the planned "Alidastua" had vanished into thin air: *"Somebody was here and helped themselves"*,[709] but who "somebody" was, was never cleared up.

The Nanok hunters, were the first to trap in the Kuhn Ø territory and considered it as theirs. The Dane, Henning Nyholm-Poulsen from Hochstetter, was quite surprised when on 3rd November 1932 he found some of his traps equipped with Norwegian bait: *"And while I was replacing the baits with my*

Haakon Karlsen at Sigurdsheim in 1934. © John Giæver / Norwegian Polar Institute

Sigurdsheim, 21st August 1939. © Norwegian Polar Institute

own, what do I see 100 metres away but the roof of a Norwegian hut".[710] In the hut Nyholm-Poulsen found an announcement: *"This station "Håkonshytten" belongs to Sigurd Tolløfsen – Tromsø – Norway, and the land in 40 km circumference is on this day hereby annexed as my property for all kinds of trapping, fishing, mining and/or any other sort of exploitation".*[711] Nyholm-Poulsen did not agree, and left a note saying: *"The above announcement must be due to a misunderstanding. The land is Danish and the trapping territory already annexed".*[712] However, Stordal and Holmeslet acted in good faith. They had not been thoroughly informed about the situation, Holmeslet's diary shows this. Undoubtedly they felt what Nyholm-Poulsen wrote: *"What a shame having to fight in the dark, but I guess there is no alternative, especially now when I realize that there are only few foxes this year".*[713]

On 24th February 1933, Nyholm-Poulsen decided to sort things out with Stordal and Holmeslet: *"They have found my letters in Håkonshytten* [466] *and were very sorry for having trespassed on my territory and said that they would have to remove their traps.*

However, to entirely clear up the problem I suggested that they could have the territory including my – I think – three traps with any catch south of Håkonshytten. In this way they could still have some benefit out of this hut. In return they should hand over their eight traps with any catch north of the hut and commit themselves not to trap there. With respect to the areas between Blåbærhytten [469] *and their Citystua* [502] *and between our huts at Kap Buch* (Arnljotstua [509] and Kap Buch hytten [512]) *it would be appropriate to place the border half way between the huts. Their hut at Kap Bremen* (Bolettestua [471]) *south of our Kap Bremen hytte* [473] *would not cause any trouble if only they trapped inwards towards the bay, away from our hut. They appreciated this suggestion which we then agreed upon. How our companies will react is another matter; I am prepared for a strong objection from our side. The three of us however agreed that it was more than enough to allow them to quarrel back home. Up here we wanted peace and quiet".*[714]

After this, relationships between them were good, and on 24th March 1933 Nyholm-Poulsen wrote: *"After a short break I went to the Norwegians at Sigurdsheim and stayed there for the night. When you have not seen another person for three weeks, it's rather cosy to be able to talk with someone for a single night – and refreshing to have food you have not cooked yourself." ... "They've had a visit from Tolløfsen, who had left a bitch that had just had puppies. It was quite moving to see this coarse trapper* (Johan Stordal) *who has been trapping around the Arctic Ocean since he was 14 take care of the small puppies. "Guri" did not have milk enough for all seven so he had made a teat out of a rubber glove from the medicine chest and fed them with diluted warm condensed milk".*[715]

In 1932-33 the catch at Sigurdsheim numbered about 30 foxes.

1933-34

In the summer of 1933, Haakon Karlsen arrived to take over from Johan Stordal, who was going to overwinter at Jackson-stua.

Holmeslet and Karlsen left Kap Herschell for Sigurdsheim on 21st August 1933. As a means of transport they had the infamous motor boat that went by the name of "Oljeoksen" (the oil ox), which Sigurd Tolløfsen had purchased from Hermann Andresen for the bargain price of 400 kroner in 1932.[716] It is very likely that Andresen's experiences with "Oljeoksen" gave rise to one of his best known quotations: *"Never use motor boats. They are so heavy to row!"*[717] After much trouble with "Oljeoksen", Holmeslet and Karlsen arrived at Sigurdsheim on 3rd September, only to discover that their four dogs: Bamse, Labb, Signe and Bobby, had disappeared. The dogs fortunately turned up again after some time but gave rise to other problems. The main cause was the widespread use of poison bait by the members of Tolløfsen's expedition. The trappers always had to be very careful that the dogs could not get to the baits, as the strychnine was lethal. Unfortunately this wasn't always possible. On 26th January 1934, Johannes Holmeslet wrote in his diary: *"I'm sorry to say that we have lost our best dog – Bamse. Karlsen had tied him with a rope when they came back yesterday, but this was probably too light for Bamse. Shortly after I arrived we could hear that one of the dogs was loose. Both of us rushed out, and saw Bamse running towards the house with a poisoned bait in his mouth. About 100 metres from the house he dropped the bait and fell over. We gave him a whole kettle of black coffee, and twice he got onto his feet, but the third time he didn't get up again. So he will never again chase over the Greenland plains. He was probably the best sledge dog of the expedition. Andresen – whom we got it from – said that it was the best dog in Greenland. We now just have Labb and Signe left"*.[718]

From Sigurd Tolløfsen's diary it is known that up to 14th February 1934 Holmeslet and Karlsen had caught only six white foxes and one blue fox.

Giæver 1939; Norsk Polarklubb 1964; A153; N026; N082; Fredrik Sæterdal pers. comm.

Recent status

Sigurdsheim was only used as a trappers' station in 1932-34. The territory was not large enough to support an independent trappers' station, and was later split up between Kap Herschell, Hochstetter, Jonsbu and Zackenberg. Nevertheless, in 1941 it was planned to man the station again. Fredrik Sæterdal and another trapper who had arrived to North-East Greenland with the Buskø Expedition, were set ashore at Sigurdsheim; but they were soon picked up by the American Coast Guard and taken to the USA.

After 1934, Sigurdsheim was only used as a trappers' hut and until about 1980 was maintained by Sirius; after that it was abandoned. In August 2003, Sigurdsheim was renovated by a combined team from the Sirius Dog Sledge Patrol and the crew of the Danish Navy vessel "Vædderen".[719]

In 2003 Sigurdsheim was renovated by a team from the Sirius Patrol and the Danish Navy vessel "Vædderen", August 2003. © Tommy Pedersen

Sigurdsheim [468], 24th July 2004. Sigurdsheim is a former Norwegian trappers' station built in 1932 for the Sigurd Tolløfsen Expedition. It was used as a trappers' station until 1934, and then as a travellers' hut maintained by Sirius until about 1980. (Top) Sigurdsheim. (Centre, left) Interior of the living room. (Centre, right) Interior of the provision room. (Bottom) View west from Sigurdsheim. © NCN

SVERRESBORG
[232]

Wintering party
1929-30: Sverre J. Sørensen, Søren Richter, Thor Halle

In the morning of the 17th August 1899, the Nathorst Expedition ship "Antarctic" was in Kong Oscar Fjord: *"We had not sailed far from Sofia Sund before another fjord was seen extending eastwards; this later turned out to be a sound. I have named this Vega Sund in memory of the "Vega", just as the name Sofia Sund commemorates the steamer "Sofia" that carried successful Swedish expeditions to Spitsbergen in 1868 and Greenland in 1883. The large island between these two sounds I have named after the Royal Geographical Society in London, which is always interested in arctic exploration and made a contribution to this expedition".*[720] They now continued into Vega Sund and later in the day reached a group of islands, which was named after Scott Keltie, the secretary of the Royal Geographical Society. It turned out that the sound at this locality was shallow and filled with skerries. To avoid running aground, Captain Forsblad decided to take the "Antarctic" back to Kong Oscar Fjord.

1929-30
In the morning of 17th August 1929, exactly 30 years after the Nathorst Expedition's discovery of Vega Sund, three Norwegians spent their first night in a new wintering station they had built by a small river on Geographical Society Ø, a few kilometres north-west of the Scott Keltie Øer.

The three trappers had been hired by Arctic Commercial Enterprise and were all newcomers, with very different qualifications: Sverre J. Sørensen from Tromsø, was 30-years old and a ship's carpenter; Søren Richter from Narvik was 26-years old and an archaeologist; Thor Halle, aged 28, was from Elverum and was a surveyor.

When the house was finished - painted red with white window panes and roof edges - it was reminiscent of a fisherman's house on the Norwegian south coast. The ground floor consisted of three rooms: a living room measuring 3 x 3 m, a kitchen 2 x 3 m and a hallway 2 x 3 m. Upstairs there was an attic beneath the pitched roof. Not a large house, but sufficient for three persons and with furniture consisting of a table, three chairs and three bunk berths. In honour of the head carpenter Sørensen, the station was named "Sverresborg"; experienced trappers considered it was the most handsome trappers' station ever built in North-East Greenland. Unfortunately, it was placed in an entirely unsuitable location.

Sverre J. Sørensen (left) and Søren Richter at Sverresborg, 5th September 1929. © Sverre Sørensen / Norwegian Polar Institute

From left: Sverre J. Sørensen, Søren Richter and Thor Halle at Sverresborg, c. 1929. © Sverre Sørensen / Norwegian Polar Institute

When they had finished the main station, Sørensen, Richter and Halle started to build trappers' huts. Materials for three huts had already been put out by "Veslekari" at selected locations towards Kong Oscar Fjord. The remaining huts were to be placed east of the station, and in this area they had to transport the materials by motor boat themselves. The first three huts, "Nils Hermans hytte" [237], "Solveigs hytte" [233] and "Traill hytten" [234] were soon built, but then the motor boat began giving trouble, and as the eastern part of the sound is very shallow it was with great difficulty they managed to build the next three huts "Jomfruen" [229], "Richter-hytten" [227] and "Vogtshytten" [225]. They put out materials for a seventh hut [904] on Traill Ø due south of Sverresborg on Traill Ø, but it was never built. At the end of September the fjords froze up, and on their way back from a visit to Kap Humboldt they had to leave the motor boat on shore at the entrance of Vega Sund.

In October winter set in, and the fox trapping could begin. Thor Halle was to have the territory towards Kong Oscar Fjord, Søren Richter the home territory and Sverre Sørensen, the station manager, was to trap towards the ocean in the east. It was all a huge disappointment. Day by day thick fog shrouded Sverresborg and the snow fell endlessly from the skies. The snow fall was a part of the winter season, but the problem was that at Sverresborg they never had a decent storm to blow the impassable morass of loose snow into a solid surface. It was depressing because the traps disappeared in the loose snow and Sørensen began calling Sverresborg the "Grødstationen" (the porridge station). No muskox were visible for miles around so they had to live on porridge and bread - an unworthy diet for a trapper.

In the middle of March they capitulated. They left the station and settled in with their friends at Kap Humboldt. Sørensen and Halle returned later in the spring, but the conditions were unchanged and it was now obvious to them that the outer part of Vega Sund was completely unsuited for trapping.

The consequence was that in the summer of 1930 Arctic Commercial Enterprise built the Maristua station on Ella Ø. During the winter of 1930-31, they also tried to trap in Vega Sund but gave up on 6th November, when Gustav Lindquist wrote: *"We have stayed at Sverresborg for a month and not seen or caught anything except three hares and 30 ptarmigan. Sverresborg is the deadest place I have ever seen, so I am really glad to get out of here".*[721] The destiny of Sverresborg was hereby sealed, and the usable western part of the territory was subsequently annexed by Kap Humboldt. Ever since it was only the most persistent trappers who dared to go trapping further into Vega Sund. On 8th April 1935, Ole Klokset wrote: *"I went to Sverresborg. It looks terrible. The porch is filled with snow, the kitchen almost filled and the living room half filled with snow".*[722]

Giæver 1959; Orvin 1930; N054; N056; N084.

Recent status

With no maintenance Sverresborg soon fell into decay, although today the structure of the house is still mainly intact.

Sverresborg [232], 31st July 2004. Sverresborg is a former Norwegian trappers' station built in August 1929 for Arctic Commercial Enterprise. It was used as a trappers' station only until 1930, and then abandoned. (Top) Sverresborg. (Centre, left) The station includes a provision shed. (Centre, right) The attic of the main house. (Bottom) View southwards across Vega Sund towards Traill Ø. © NCN

VALDEMARSHAAB
[421-2]

Wintering party
1922-23: Arthur Andersen, Peter Tutein,
Leander E. Emskær Larsen

1922-23
On 24th August 1922, when Captain Gustav Thostrup began the home journey to Denmark with the "Teddy", he left the trappers with the task of building a trappers' station of the materials that had been put ashore in the summer at Kap Borlase Warren.

At the beginning of September, the trappers started to build "Valdemarshaab", as the station was to be called after the leader of the East Greenland Company, Arner Ludvig Valdemar Manniche (1867-1957).

Three men were chosen to winter at the station: Arthur Andersen, the station manager, was born in Copenhagen about 1882. He was a former sergeant in the Danish army and had worked for six years as a sheep boy in Patagonia. Then, in 1922, he came to North-East Greenland. In the summer of 1923, he started the journey home with "Teddy", but the ship was wrecked in the ice and the trappers and crew of "Teddy" did not get back to Denmark until 1924. A few years later Arthur Andersen went to Canada, and vanished. He had left his luggage in a hotel in Edmonton, but never returned to pick it up. Two years later the Royal Canadian Mounted Police found his bones in the wildernes outside Edmonton. The cause of his death was never discovered; robbery was unlikely as his wallet and silver watch lay together with the bones. The watch was a school prize awarded for diligence according to the engraving on it.[723]

The second trapper at Valdemarshaab that winter was Leander Elias Emskær Larsen, born in 1883, a fisherman and the driver of the station's motor boat. Larsen was a skilled baker and confectioner and like Andersen had tried out South America. In 1913 he and his family had emigrated to Argentina; but after four years there had had enough of primitive life on a large ranch and returned to Denmark. In the spring of 1922, he was in contact with the East Greenland Company, and went to Greenland. Larsen returned to Denmark in 1924. In May 1929 he was one of the founders of Nanok, and returned to North-East Greenland for his second period as a trapper from 1929-32. He ends his account of his time in Greenland with the following thoughts, as from the quarterdeck of "Gustav Holm" he watched Greenland pass by astern: *"... this land, which has given me so many joys, disappointments and hardships. I sat there until it became dark. I watched the land disappear in the distance, and it was with bitter sadness I watched the mist cover the land and the mountains that have created the framework for the best years of my life, and which I was never to see again. But in all those years since we first went to East Greenland it is with the greatest joy, that the hope we took up with us and fought for finally came through. East Greenland remained Danish and in this Nanok played its part".*[724] Larsen died in 1971, 89-years old.

Both Andersen and Larsen were on their first wintering in North-East Greenland, while the third man at the station, Peter Tutein, had wintered the previous year at Carlshavn.

To build the house they had help from the trappers from Germaniahavn, but as the risk of being trapped by the pack ice was significant the men from Germaniahavn returned to Sabine Ø after a couple of days.

Valdemarshaab, 1922-23.
© Jonna Jensen

Christmas Eve at Valdemarshaab 1922. From left: Arthur Andersen, Peter Tutein, L.E. Emskær Larsen. *© Jens Mathiesen*

Peter Tutein wrote that: *"the year at Borlase Warren became somewhat cheerless. Andersen and Larsen did not get along very well, but I had learned so much from my previous year* (see Carlshavn) *that I kept my neutrality, which perhaps isolated me, but on the other hand was preferable to the endless bickering about historical dates that we could not get clarified for a year, or other trivial matters."* ... *"The snow last midsummer had reduced the fox population, so we only caught 17 foxes altogether, although it was a new and unused territory"*.[725]

In 1923, Henning Bistrup was the master of "Teddy". Unfortunately they had an engine breakdown just as they reached the coast, and the ship remained at Kap Borlase Warren for most of the summer. On 30th July, they began tearing down Valdemarshaab, which – according to plan – was to be rebuilt in Scoresby Sund. When the house had been taken down the materials were loaded on board "Teddy" together with the materials from another house, Hans Ludvig Jensens hus, that had stood at Germaniahavn.

On 4th August 1923, "Teddy" had reached Kap Mary, but due to problems with the ice, the motor and the crew it became necessary to have a ship's council. Bistrup wrote: *"I am not going to report the ship's council negotiations, only the conclusion: The journey to Scoresby Sund is abandoned, a station will be established on Shannon* (Kap David Gray hytten), *the ship is made ready to sail and the home voyage is commenced as we head for Kap Borlase Warren and from there outwards into the ice, partly by engine as long as possible, partly by sail"*.[726] The following day they started unloading the materials from the two houses at Kap Mary.

In principal the story of Valdemarshaab ends here, but when Nanok started trapping in 1929 they discovered that the materials at Kap Mary had disappeared. After an investigation, the Danish trappers concluded that the Foldvik Expedition had used the materials for trappers' huts in the Clavering Ø area. This was later confirmed by a declaration – dated Myggbukta 21st August 1931 – in which Hallvard Devold announced: *"The undersigned hereby declares that all huts built by the Foldvik Expedition at Clavering Ø and in Tyroler Fjord with the exception of the main station "Revet"* (Tyrolerheimen), *have been made from timber deposited at Kap Mary and removed by the participants of the Foldvik Expedition in the summer of 1927"*.[727]

The issue soon became politicized. The Danes claimed that the Norwegians had no rights to take the materials, but members of the Foldvik Expedition maintained that Lauge Koch had allowed them to use the timber. In a statement – dated Tennes, 17th September 1932 – Meyer Olsen wrote that one day in the summer of 1926 he walked along the north coast of Hold with Hope: *"Not far from Kap James I began finding wooden boards and soon in such large quantities that I began to use them for fox traps. One place I found an entire section so I knew it came from a house."* ... *"All the materials are worn at the edges from lying in the water. The fox traps show clear evidence of this, even today, evidence that I'm telling the truth. We had not been at Kap Mary so we didn't know that the materials came from there. From the materials that we picked up, we built a hut at Jordan Hill* [409-1]*"*.[728]

Meyer Olsen continued that on 27th April 1927 he had a visit from Lauge Koch. The following day they went out to look for fossils in the vicinity of Krogness

A bearded seal killed. From left: Arthur Andersen, L.E. Emskær Larsen and Peter Tutein. c. 1923. © Jens Mathiesen

at Kap Stosch: *"While we're sitting there, each on our stone, Mr. Koch suddenly remarks as follows: Do you need anything in the Danish huts? I answer that I believe we have sufficient equipment for the next two years, but after a little talk back and forth I say that perhaps we may need a stove and Mr. Koch says: Why not take the stove at Carlshavn? I answer that we cannot take that one, because we plan to use the house the coming winter. Koch says that the stove at Sandodden may be broken, because it was built from bricks. We then agree to take to stove at Hold with Hope* (Kap Broer Ruys) *as we later did. Mr. Koch encouraged me to take all that I needed in the Danish huts and said that at Sandodden there was half a barrel of sugar and asked me to take it before it got ruined. When we had finished I asked Mr. Koch what to say if the Danish authorities complains that we have taken the stove and other things. I asked if I could say that I had permission from Lauge Koch. And I remember clearly that Mr. Koch looks down and thinks for a while and then he looks me in the eyes: Yes, he answers, say that you have permission from me and he adds: I am in charge of the Danish huts in East Greenland you know. It never entered my mind at the time that Mr. Koch would be the first to make complaints. Any other gentleman would admit the truth of this. And as God is my witness, it is true and I hope that Mr. Koch is enough of a gentleman that he will admit this, even if it is against his claim.*

On 26th July 1927, my brother Hans, Øien and I took the motor boat to Kap Mary. There are some boards and other materials along the shore and we are then certain that the materials we had found the previous years about 30 km away, came from here and had been taken by the sea. We also took some of what was left. You know, we had permission to take everything we needed. And naturally we did not think that the man who gave us the permission would be the first to blame us for taking some materials which were so exposed and in part had been taken by the sea and carried 30 km away from where they had been deposited".[729]

In the years around 1930 it was often one person's word against another's, but with today's recycling point of view one should be pleased that Valdemarshaab lives on in a few small huts that later on gave shelter to many a tired traveller.

Dahl 1924, 1925, 1926; Thomsen et al. 1988; Tutein 1945; P152; Ø040; Ø043; Ø044.

Recent status

The exact location of Valdemarshaab at Kap Borlase Warren is still not established with certainty.

Kap Borlase Warren, 6th August 2004. Valdemarshaab was a Danish trappers' station built in 1922 for the East Greenland Company. It was used as a trappers' station only until 1923, when it was pulled down to be moved to another location. Today there is no real evidence of the exact location of Valdemarshaab. The photograph (left) shows the present Borlase Warren hytten [421-3]. The square of white stones around the hut probably marks the former site of the Valdemarshaab house.

VILLAEN / DANMARKS-MINDE
[628-1]

Wintering party

1906-08: Participants of the Danmark Expedition
1919-20: Hans Ludvig Jensen, Robert Frørup, Christian Ahlstrand, Niels Peter Andersen
1920-21: Hans Ludvig Jensen, Robert Frørup, Ove Haaber Nielsen

1906-08

On 16th August 1906, the Danmark Expedition anchored the expedition ship "Danmark" in a south-facing bay close to Kap Bismarck. This bay was named Danmark Havn and became the base of the expedition, and the centre of their travels and activities during the next two years.

The expedition numbered 28 participants: Ludvig Mylius-Erichsen, Niels Peter Høeg Hagen, Jørgen Brønlund, Peter Hansen, Knud Christiansen, Hendrik Olsen, Carl Johan Ring, Johan Peter Koch, Alfred Wegener, Johannes Achton Friis, Andreas Lundager, Frits Johansen, Christian Bendix Thostrup, Tobias Gabrielsen, Aage Bertelsen, Harald Hagerup, Johannes Lindhard, Jens Gundahl Knudsen, Hans Ludvig Jensen, Henning Bistrup, Alf Trolle, Andreas Koefoed, Charles Poulsen, Gustav Thostrup, Arner L. V. Manniche, Peter Freuchen, Ivar Weinschenck, Hakon Høeg Jarner. When not on journeys by boat or sledge, most of the participants had their living quarters on board the ship, but four men - Bertelsen, Lundager, Koch and Wegener - lived ashore where a winter house, "Villaen", had been built.

"Danmark" was to have taken along materials for two prefabricated houses, but the space aboard the ship was insufficient and the largest house had to be left in Iceland, to where the materials had been shipped by freighter. Even the elements for the smaller house had to be taken apart in order to find room for them on the already fully loaded ship.

In Danmark Havn, Jens Gundahl Knudsen, who was a joiner, had the task of assembling the house. It was erected about 70 m from the shore and had only one room, measuring 5 x 5 m. The first winter the house was warm and tight, but by the second winter snow had begun to drift in through the cracks in the corners. In the autumn of 1907, attempts were made to make the house warmer by building a stone wall around it. The attic and two smaller provision sheds were used for storing equipment, instruments, plant collections, paintings, tools etc.

Villaen was equipped with different scientific measuring instruments, and also had a telephone connection to the ship.

In the autumn of 1910, Ejnar Mikkelsen and Iversen P. Iversen arrived at Villaen in an exhausted state on their journey back to Shannon and their ship "Alabama". The provisions at Villaen left by the Danmark Expedition and the shelter the house provided undoubtedly saved their lives.

1919-21

In 1919, the East Greenland Company was permitted to use Villaen as a trappers' station. Four trappers were to winter there: Hans Ludvig Jensen, Robert Frørup, Christian Ahlstrand and Niels Peter Andersen. To the then 45-year-old Jensen it was a return to the region he had come to know and love from the Danmark Expedition.

Villaen, c. 1907.
© Arctic Institute

Inside Villaen / Danmarks-Minde, c. 1920. From left: Hans Ludvig Jensen, Robert Frørup, Niels Peter Andersen, Christian Ahlstrand. © Jonna Jensen

Hans Ludvig Jensen was born in Skibshuse near Odense on 3rd April 1874. He came from an old sailing family and travelled the seven seas himself before he signed on the "Godthaab" in 1898, which would carry the Carlsbergfondets Expedition to the Ammassalik region. When Mylius-Erichsen in 1905 began to look for participants for the Danmark Expedition, Jensen was hired as cook and steward. After the return to Denmark in 1908, Hans Ludvig Jensen participated as a cook in Adolf S. Jensen's Expedition to West Greenland in the summer of 1909. After that he worked in the restaurant business for a number of years, e.g. in Russia - but, as the saying goes, "once Greenland, always Greenland". During the Danmark Expedition Jensen and his friends had discussed the possibilities of running a trapping business in North-East Greenland. Now he brought up the idea again. In the spring of 1919 the East Greenland Company was founded and Jensen became the trapping supervisor on the first expedition. In the five years the company existed he wintered himself in 1919-21 and 1922-23.

In 1929, partly through Hans Ludvig Jensen's initiative, the old trapping company was revived as the East Greenland Trapping Company Nanok Ltd. (Nanok). Here he again participated in the first wintering, but after developing bad frostbite in his feet he had to go home in 1930. He wintered for the last time in 1936-38, and then settled in Herringløse near Veksø, where he spent his retirement. Hans Ludvig Jensen died on 8th September 1948.

To Hans Ludvig Jensen and the three trappers who arrived at Danmark Havn with the "Dagny" on 1st August 1919, the two winterings did not live up to their expectations: *"It was a depressing sight that met us. Our lovely house, which we left in 1908 in excellent condition full of provisions was now a sad sight. Windows and doors were broken. The roof was lying about 30 m away. We could see that the roof had been on fire and had been cut into with an axe. Inside the house was one metre of snow. Outside the house lay a large pile of various canned food, indeed a depressing sight ... It took us three days to clear up the house and eight days to build a new roof, but then it was again the good old house, which became the home of three men for two years".*[730] Jensen and his men renamed Villaen as "Danmarks-Minde". It was never established, who had caused the damage to the house.

They had other frustrations. Lemmings, the most important food for the polar fox, were few, and that contributed to the poor result. Their catch was only 30 foxes the first year and 20 the following season.

In 1919-21, a total of 145 foxes, 11 bears, two wolves, four ermines, 40 muskoxen and 300 hares were taken at the two stations in Dove Bugt: Villaen and Hvalrosodden. In addition 400 birds and 350 butterflies were preserved.

In the summer of 1920, there was no resupply of Danish stations due to the shipwreck of "Dagny", and the year 1920-21 became a struggle for survival. They had hardly any necessities, and had to cease trapping at Christmas because Robert Frørup and Ove Haaber Nielsen had become ill with scurvy. On 20th February 1921, their friends from Hvalrosodden arrived with the body of August F. Nielsen, and on 9th March Robert Frørup also died of scurvy. The two men were buried at Danmark Havn. On 1st April 1921, the remaining five men left at Villaen drove to Hvalrosodden, from where the weakened men set out for Germaniahavn. They all survived.

Villaen / Danmarks-Minde has not been used for wintering since.

Amdrup et. al 1913; Grønlandske Selskab 1983a; Ø040.

Recent status

In 2006, Nanok made an agreement with the Greenland National Museum and Archives (GNA) in Nuuk to report on the present condition of Villaen – or Danmarks-Minde – to mark the 100 years since the arrival of the Danmark Expedition at Danmark Havn. While the present day Danmarks-Minde differs somewhat from Villaen, it is in every relevant respect identical to the house that Hans Ludvig Jensen and his men rebuilt in 1919 – as a trappers' station.

The Nanok men were authorized to make a drainage system around the house in 2006, in order to remove melt water from beneath the floor, but did not have permission to carry out a thorough renovation before the report had been analyzed by GNA.[731]

(Top) Villaen / Danmarks-Minde [628-1], 20th July 2006. (Bottom left and right) The grave of Robert Frørup and August Frederik Nielsen, two Danish trappers who died from scurvy during the winter 1920-21. Danmarkshavn, August 2005. © NCN

Villaen / Danmarks-Minde [628-1], 20th July 2006. Villaen is a former Danish scientific station built in 1906 for the Danmark Expedition. In 1919 the house was restored by the East Greenland Company, which used it as a trappers' station, "Danmarks-Minde" until 1921. Since 1948, Danmarks-Minde has been maintained by Danmarkshavn Weather Station. (Left) Villaen / Danmarks-Minde with Danmarkshavn Weather Station in the right background. (Centre right) The graves of Robert Frørup and August Frederik Nielsen. (Bottom) Villaen / Danmarks-Minde. © NCN

ZACKENBERG
[438-2]

Wintering party
1945-46: Harald Mikkelsen, Aksel Jensen
1946-47: Harald Mikkelsen, Jørgen Andersen
1947-48: Peder Klokker
1948-49: Peder Klokker, Ole Olsen
1949-50: Harald Mikkelsen, Christian Andersen
1950-51: Hans Frederiksen, Ernst Wind
1951-52: Ernst Wind
1952-53: Hans Frederiksen
1959-60: Ib Palle Madsen

On A.P. Olsen Land at the mouth of Tyrolerfjord is a jagged mountain, to which the Koldewey Expedition in 1869 gave the name Zackenberg.

On 30th July 1930, Nanok built a trappers' hut at the foot of Zackenberg: *"It was placed on the left side of the large river at Zackenberg. There was a lot of vegetation in the area – even polar birch. I shot a char in the river – so there are certainly some char".*[732] It later turned out that the river was one of North-East Greenland's richest char rivers, and it was here in particular that Norwegian trapping companies for many years carried out concentrated char fishing in the summer months.

1945-46

In 1945, Nanok decided to build a station at Zackenberg. The newspaper "Horsens Folkeblad" announced that it would: *"support Nanok by donating the financial means for establishing a trappers' station".*[733] With the promise of this donation Nanok ordered the materials for the station, which was to be named "Horsnæs". On the 14th and 15th August 1945, the materials were unloaded and when the "Godthaab" sailed on, the trappers Aksel Jensen, Ib Bach Hansen and Kjeld Nielsen were left behind to build the station; However, while the ship was still in Greenland, J.G. Jennov was contacted by a member of the Nanok board, H. Tuxen, who reported that the promised donation had not been paid, and if it was possible: *"to avoid naming the station Horsnæs".* The trappers' station therefore received the name "Zackenberg", and on 23rd August 1945 Jennov was able to state that: *"the house in there was almost finished, only a part of the interior panelling was lacking".*[734] Before his departure, Jennov appointed the trappers Harald Mikkelsen and Aksel Jensen to stay at Zackenberg and complete the station.

"I wanted to go out and see the world!" Harald Mikkelsen (1915-2002) explained in 1992.[735] Originally he had thought of going to Canada, but then an acquaintance told him that Nanok was hiring trappers. It was in the spring of 1945, shortly after the liberation of Denmark. Mikkelsen went to see J.G.

Trappers' station Zackenberg, c. 1952. © Hans Madsen

Jennov at his office and told him something about himself and his background. Mikkelsen was 29-years old, from Tappernøje in southern Sjælland and had been a fisherman since his youth. When he added that he had worked as a carpenter for a couple of years, Jennov was satisfied: *"But it was more or less impossible to obtain clothes and equipment in 1945"*, Mikkelsen recalled, *"so we had to make it all ourselves, when we arrived in Greenland"*.[736]

Neither Mikkelsen, nor his partner Aksel Jensen, knew anything about fox trapping, but they had a lot of good advice from Aage Hansen - the station manager at Daneborg Weather Station - and a former trapper.

The first year they trapped in the Norwegian territories as well as Zackenberg, and Aksel Jensen spent a lot of his time at Moskusheimen. In the autumn of 1946, they built "Kuppelpashytten" [432]. Aksel Jensen returned home in 1946, but wintered again at Ella Ø in 1950-51, when he helped to build the Maria Ø station [239-2].

1946-47

In the summer of 1946, the Norwegians resumed their trapping activities and according to the station log book, on 25th August the men at Zackenberg had a: *"visit from the Norwegian from Revet, who thought that a Norwegian hut should be here"*.[737] In 1992, Harald Mikkelsen recalled his first meeting with Normann Andersen quite well: *"We were sitting in the house drinking coffee when he arrived by boat. Well, we went outside to greet him, but the first thing he did after landing was to carry two sacks of coal to the small hut next to our station. – Well, I thought, he's got a nerve.*

- So I went to him and said: – You don't have to supply our station with coal.

- But it's my hut, he said.

- No, it isn't, I said. – You are welcome to visit us, but this is our hut and our trapping territory.

- That he could not understand, as Hermann Andresen had told him that this was Norwegian territory. And I also have a hut (Gisvold) *down there in the bay, he said.*

- Yes, that's correct, I said, but we have a fine hut (Pashuset) *right next to it, and we consider it our territory.*

Well, he was kind enough. Let's talk about it, I said to him. There's no reason for us to fall out over each others traps, and he agreed. Then we agreed how to split the territory between us".[738]

Jørgen Andersen, a carpenter from Ringsted, became Mikkelsen's new partner at Zackenberg. They started trapping at the end of October, at the same time as Orla Jensen, who was staying at the station, set off for Hochstetter together with Mogens Graae who had had been staying at Sandodden. As there was no news from the two by Christmas, Mikkelsen went north in January to check they were OK. On his return, Jørgen Andersen drove to Hochstetter, and in May came back with Graae and Jensen to spend the summer at Zackenberg. In the spring of 1947, "Svejstrup Dal hytten" [462] was built in the territory. Harald Mikkelsen went home in 1947, while Jørgen Andersen took a job at Daneborg Weather Station.

Walrus hunt, 1947. Orla Jensen (left) and Harald Mikkelsen. © Mogens Graae

1947-48

In 1947, Peder Klokker took over Zackenberg. He had just qualified as a carpenter and was 22-years old, but Denmark soon became too small for this adventurous youngster from Kerteminde. So what brought him to Greenland?

Probably the same thing that years later led him to sail halfway around the world from New Zealand to Denmark, all alone in a small home-made boat. The morning after his departure, he woke up to a clear horizon and with 3000 km to Australia, he entered in his diary: *"It's a wonderful uncertain feeling. It is not without risk travelling so far on your own without any safety net at all. To take a risk and to save your neck that's a joy."*

In 1993, Peder Klokker explained: *"I have always been fond of being out in the wilderness and have had plenty of opportunities all my life. It's not just for the hunt, but to be out in nature under different conditions. Not only when it's idyllically beautiful and nice weather; the tempest can also be breathtaking. To manage everything yourself and reach your destination no matter the weather, to do without – to make everything yourself – that is a tremendous satisfaction"*.[739]

Three Danish trappers. Peder Klokker (left), Kjeld Soelberg and Mogens Graae. Zackenberg, summer 1948. © Mogens Graae

1948-49

In the summer of 1948, Peder Klokker had the company of Ole Olsen, a new trapper. Unfortunately it was the worst year for fox trapping for many years, and the five Nanok trappers had a total catch of only 33 foxes. After New Year, the men spread out hoping for better luck elsewhere. Ole Olsen went northwards to try out the Hochstetter territory, while Peder Klokker decided to try his hand with bear hunting.

"It was in February or the beginning of March. We had bad weather, but I left Zackenberg anyway, went through Kuppelpasset and across Albrechtsletten",[740] Peder Klokker recalled in 1993. A few days later, and after an exhausting trip, Klokker was approaching the Germaniahavn station when he suddenly saw three bears close by. He killed them all, but had to leave them as the weather was so bad he was forced to seek shelter at the station.

The next day he went out to fetch the bears, and while he was skinning them two more bears turned up. They ran off, but Klokker's dogs stopped one of them and it was shot. As he was dragging the dead bear down to the shore, he caught sight of another three bears on the ice: *"and off we went over the ice"*.[741] Klokker released some dogs and the three bears were run down and shot.

The following day Klokker wanted to drive on, but suddenly yet another bear turned up. It was also brought down and Klokker decided to spend the night at Germaniahavn. In the evening - as he was sitting by the lamp, writing about the bear hunt - the dogs suddenly began to bark. Klokker had no doubts - another bear. He took his rifle, placed himself in the doorway in order to let his eyes get used to the darkness. After a while he sensed in which direction the bear was: *"and that's thrilling, a mere joy, to be so close to a bear without being able to see it"*.[742] Klokker took a few steps forward and now the bear seemed to attack the dogs. In the darkness it was impossible to take aim, but the distance was short and Klokker quickly fired some shots. The bear was hit and fell: *"I left the bear until next morning. It was really a huge bear, 2.65 m from nose to tail"*.[743] It was Klokker's ninth within three days.

Both Peder Klokker and Ole Olsen went home in 1949. Klokker tried out different jobs, including building 38 sledges for the "South Georgia Survey" expedition and later on for the Hillary and Fuchs Commonwealth Trans-Antarctic Expedition 1955-58. He later went sealing with Norwegians, worked as a craftsman in Greenland and as a forest worker in Sweden. In 1957 he emigrated to New Zealand and became a state-employed hunter; then one day he was badly injured in a fall and that was the end of it. He decided to make a solo trip back to Denmark and designed and built "Tiki", a small boat with a 6 hp diesel engine. He worked his passage home and the trip lasted several years. In 1970-72 he was in Kenya as a development aid worker, but then his health began to fail and he returned to Kerteminde in Denmark to take up an old passion, painting. He gave exhibitions and his paintings sold well, but after a few years he decided to settle in Southern Europe: *"I could not live in Denmark. I feel much better out there, in the "free" world"*,[744] he said in 1993. In particular, Klokker was unhappy with the social and taxation systems in Denmark. He thought they were not leaving any space for artists, freaks or other individualists. On Midsummer Eve of 1986 he undertook a dramatic protest action burning 140 of his paintings on a bonfire on the Nordstranden beach at Kerteminde.[745]

Peder Klokker died in May 2002, at the age of 76.[746]

1949-50

Originally two new trappers, Jack Engelbrecht Christensen and Christian Andersen, were supposed to take over Zackenberg in 1949-50, but in November 1949 Harald Mikkelsen moved in. Then Engelbrecht preferred to go to Sandodden: *"It was intolerable to live in such a negative atmosphere"*,[747] Engelbrecht wrote and in 1992, Harald Mikkelsen openly admitted that relationships between him and some of the other trappers were not particularly good.

Mikkelsen had spent the summer at Mønstedhus, but neither this station nor Hochstetter, where he arrived at the beginning of August, had received any supplies by ship in 1949. Food was running out and as his teeth started to loosen - due to undernourishment - he decided to go south. He never forgot the trip across the thin ice of Hochstetterbugten. For the last 10 km the ice was so thin that it made waves beneath the sledge. Then followed a hard trip up through the stony Lindemanspas, but he managed to get to Zackenberg alive. A few days later he went to Daneborg to send a telegram to Jennov and the very next day the answer came: *"Go north at once with the new men!"* – *"But I didn't do anything that winter"*, Mikkelsen recalled in 1992. *"I simply couldn't. My health was ruined and I really didn't care. I didn't earn a single penny the first year, so I can afford to earn nothing the last year as well!"*[748] To Harald Mikkelsen his Greenland era ended in 1950 when he left the coast on board one of the Catalina airplanes used by the Danish Peary Land Expedition. Christian Andersen also went home that summer.

Harald Mikkelsen died in 2002, at the age of 87.

1950-51

Hans Frederiksen from Frederiksværk was attracted to the trapper's life through his friendship with Harald Mikkelsen. In 1947-48, they were fishing together in Denmark and originally he had hoped to go up with Mikkelsen in 1948: *"but then one of the guys up there didn't want to go home"*, Frederiksen explained in 1992. *"And as I was only 18 and the youngest, I had to stay back home. I didn't mind, as Jennov promised that I would get my chance later on, and so I came up in 1950"*.[749] To Hans Frederiksen this was the beginning of a total of eight winterings in North-East Greenland. First he was two years with Nanok, but in the summer of 1952 when the company ceased hunting he was allowed to stay for another year. After that he worked for one year at Daneborg Weather Station, but in 1954-55 was a trapper again, this time on his own account at Hochstetter. In 1955-56 he was home in Denmark, but then returned for three more years at Daneborg until 1959, when he said a definitive goodbye to Greenland.

In 1950, Hans Frederiksen had another new man as partner. It was Ernst Wind (K.E.P. Wind) and during the summer: *"a new shed was built in connection with one of the old ones and now there ought to be enough buildings at the station"*.[750]

At the beginning of December, Erik Larsen came down from Hochstetter to spend Christmas and New Year at Zackenberg. In 1992, Hans Frederiksen recalled that the relationships between the three of them and the men at Daneborg were not particularly warm.

On 15th January 1951, Hans Frederiksen went northwards with Erik Larsen. They had decided to merge the Hochstetter and Zackenberg territories. Wind stayed at Zackenberg until Frederiksen and Larsen returned at the beginning of April. During the spring, the three trappers built "Lindemanspashytten" [451] and "Kuhnpashytten" [445].

On 25th June, the first 20 char went into the trap they had placed in Zackenbergelven as an experiment; but after a couple of days they caught no more fish and the attempt was dropped.

1951-52

After spending the summer at Hochstetter, Ernst Wind returned to Zackenberg on 6th November 1951. He was going to have the territory for himself. Unfortunately, his entire catch was lost on 7th July 1952 when: *"the fur shed caught fire. We lost 14 fox furs, 30 sacks of salt, four fishing lines, a sack with about 200 corks for char nets, a coil of rope, five trays for nets and some extra nets. This is what I can remember was in the shed. It happened like this. I was on my way to the river and had reached the slope when I turned around and looked back at the station – there was smoke coming out of the open window in the shed. By the time I got back, there were flames everywhere. I tried to put out the fire with water, but it was hopeless as the fire had already reached the roofing felt and was quite intense. I used up all my energy in preventing the fire from reaching the station building, and this was not an easy task because the wind was from the south-west and blowing the flames directly towards the house. There was so much heat that the roofing felt on the station began to melt, but luckily I managed to keep the fire away by throwing water all over the roof. I'm not sure how the fire started, but it may have been a cigarette that caused it. I was in the shed before I went to the river and as far as I remember, I then had a cigarette in my hand"*.[751]

Ernst Wind, who left North-East Greenland in 1952, died two years later in a drowning accident in West Greenland.

1952-53

In the summer of 1952, when Nanok withdrew its trappers, Hans Frederiksen, Svend Olsen and Erik Larsen had intended to stay for another year. However, when the ship arrived without the cigarettes, clothes and provisions they had ordered: *"then Erik and Svend quit and I stayed back on my own"*, Frederiksen recalled in 1992. *"However, everything went quite well, for the men in the sledge patrol said: – We have more than enough, you're not going to lack anything. – And I didn't. Apart from that – at that time – there were still a lot of provisions at the trappers' stations"*.[752] Frederiksen settled at Zackenberg, but trapped all the way up to Mønstedhus. Unfortunately, it was a poor trapping year.

"I spent Christmas with the sledge patrol and then we sat there New Year's Eve, well plastered and figured out that it would be nice to send mail back home. – And then I said: OK, I'll go to Mestersvig with the mail. – But it turned out to be a tough trip, with a lot of bad weather and bad going".[753] Nevertheless, he managed to get the mail bag there, even though he went through the ice the day before he arrived at Mestersvig. Fortunately it happened near Skeldalhytten [213]. On 16th March 1953, Frederiksen returned to Daneborg where: *"they threw a big party because they had received mail. There were actually about 1200 letters"*.[754]

1959-60

In 1953, a desire for adventure brought the 19-year-old wireless operator Ib Palle Madsen to Danmarkshavn, where he spent the next two years. After one year back in Denmark, he was at Station Nord in 1957-59. It was here that he and Viggo Block had the idea of trying their luck as trappers: *"It was in the good old days, when you could ask whether you could leave – and we could"*, Madsen recalled in 1993.[755] They loaded their dog sledges and travelled southwards to Daneborg.

"Finally my life as trapper has begun" Madsen wrote on 31st May 1959.[756] He and Block had arrived at Zackenberg that same day, where they would stay for the summer. They spent the summer fishing char and fixing up the station, which had been empty since the summer of 1953. At the beginning of September, Block moved to Moskusheimen. Madsen enjoyed his life at Zackenberg and on 10th September he wrote: *"Fine weather, feels like 30 degrees in the sun just like a good summer day in Denmark, but it's freezing when the sun goes down. All morning I have been trying to get the boat onto the bridge, but failed. On the other hand I managed to move a barrel of paraffin up onto the bench in front of the house. The river is still running beneath the snow. Fried eggs, potatoes, pork and a serving of preserved prunes, followed by coffee and cognac; who could ask for more?"*[757]

Madsen put out his traps in the area between Blåbærhytten [469], Lerbugt [434] and Pashuset [433]. Now and then he had visitors from Daneborg. On 23rd December, Block arrived from Moskusheimen dressed: *"in his bear outfit. We enjoyed roast and pudding and what the house could offer of liqueurs, and with the candles lit we listened to Christmas greetings. We sat there until 6 o'clock in the morning"*.[758] They spent the Christmas at Daneborg, and then went their separate ways.

In the middle of April, they stopped trapping, packed up their private belongings and made ready for departure. They set off on the 18th April 1960, when Madsen wrote: *"A last farewell and then we're off southwards tonight, hopefully to end up in Scoresbysund"*.[759] They arrived safely in Scoresbysund, and from here they went on to Denmark: *"We had about 120 fox skins and some muskox skins, which we sold for about 12,000 kroner altogether, that fully covered our expenses for the trip, the stay and the home voyage. We even had a couple of thousand over for each of us"*.[760]

Ib Palle Madsen subsequently spent a number of years in East Greenland, including a period as station manager at Danmarkshavn from 1989-93.

Norsk Polarklubb 1966; A162; A163; A173; G101; G102; G116.; Nanok 1992.

Recent status

After 1960 Zackenberg was maintained and often used as a travellers' hut by Sirius.

In the summer of 1991, a seven-man scientific team was sent out to examine whether the Zackenberg area would be suitable site for a permanent research station. The outcome was the present-day Zackenberg ZERO station, which opened in 1997.[761]

The same summer of 1991, another team arrived at Zackenberg, namely the first of the Nanok expeditions of recent years. The Nanok team included the 75-year-old former trapper Mogens Graae, on his last visit to North-East Greenland. Graae and Henning Schwegler Poulsen carried out the first thorough renovation of Zackenberg for many years that summer.[762]

Zackenberg, 4th August 1977. © Peter Schmidt Mikkelsen

Zackenberg [438-2], 27th July 2003. © NCN

Zackenberg [438-2], 27th July 2003. Zackenberg is a former Danish trappers' station built in 1945 for Nanok. It was used as a trappers' station until 1960, and then as a travellers' hut maintained by Sirius. In the summers of 1991 and 1992, it was given a thorough restoration by Nanok. Since 1997 the station has also been frequently used by personnel from the nearby ZERO station [438-5]. © NCN

AALBORGHUS
[613-2]

Wintering party
1938-39: Franz Dalskov, Marius Jensen
1939-41: Richard Nielsen, Ove Harder Jensen
1941-50: None
1950-52: Knud Nielsen, Leo Ingwersen

1938-39
To Nanok, the year of 1938 was characterized by optimism. The company had almost exclusive right to the ship "Gustav Holm" and had succeeded in obtaining financial funding from several different sources. In the cities of Aalborg and Nørresundby the newspaper "Aalborg Stiftstidende" had arranged a collection for Nanok. The result was an amount sufficient to support establishment of a new trappers station. The plan had been to place it in Skærfjorden. Unfortunately the ice conditions that summer prevented sailing so far north, and when informed that the ice in Skærfjorden was unbroken, J.G. Jennov had to divert "Gustav Holm" to the alternative, Gefion Havn on Godfred Hansen Ø, where Nanok already had a trappers' hut. Here the new station was to be built.

"We arrived at Gefions Havn at 2 o'clock in the morning of the 20th August." ... *"During the day the wind started to blow, but not so much that it delayed the unloading and the building of the house"*, Jennov wrote.[763] The veteran, Hans Ludvig Jensen, also took part in the building: *"I am painting a large sign saying "Aalborghus". It is meant to be mounted on the station. The sign is red with black letters and quite impressive"*.[764]

On the 23rd August 1938, Jennov could state that the: *"station was practically finished. The roofing felt has been put on and we have put up the sign "Aalborghus", the two metal plates with the inscription and the mark of Aalborg Stiftstidende, and also, of course, the window pane with Mrs. Levin's poem"*.[765] The pane in question has an unusual story. A glazier named Levin in Aalborg had donated the windows for the station, and on one of them he had engraved a poem written by his wife:

"A pane may experience much on Earth
I was made in a Belgian hut,
By ship to Denmark I later went
In a building I was to be put.
Soon a course to the north I set again
To Aalborghus I was sent,
Here I will shield from frost and snow
And capture the sun when I see its glow.
From Aalborg greetings, warm and kind,
I bring to all who this trappers hut find".
(signed) *Mrs. Jenny Levin, Aalborg 5/7-1938.*

For many years this pane had its place in one of the windows of the station, but to help preserve and protect it, was later dismounted and placed on a wall in the living room.

The wintering team was made up of Franz Dalskov and Marius Jensen. Their first task was to build some new trappers' huts and with the assistance of the Hvalrosodden men, Christian Jensen and Henning Ørnlef, five new huts were built: "Rechnitzerhytten" [612], "Påskehytten"[604], "Nørresundbyhytten" [617], "Hasseriishytten" [608] and "Majhytten" [610]. At Aalborghus, Dalskov and Jensen also built a tall rack intended for drying walrus meat. Franz Dalskov and Marius Jensen were both newcomers as trappers and went home to Denmark in the summer of 1939.

Marius Jensen, however, returned to Greenland in 1940, hired by the Mørkefjord expedition, and also served in the North-East Greenland Sledge Patrol from 1941-45. From this period, Kurt Olsen wrote the following about Jensen: *"Originally he was a farmhand. However, the eight hundred kroner he usually earned during a winter meant that his dream of having a farm of his own was many, many years into the future, so he had looked for a quicker way to acquire the necessary capital."* ... *"He spoke rarely, and only if there were practical reasons for talking; but you did not have to watch him or his work for long, before you could see that everything he did was carefully thought out"*.[766] Marius Jensen died in April 2001.

Kurt Olsen (left) and Marius Jensen. Eskimonæs 1941-42. © Niels Ove Jensen

1939-41

In 1939, Aalborghus was taken over by Richard Nielsen and Ove Harder Jensen.[767] They were both 25-years old, from Copenhagen, and had for a number of years lived almost parallel lives. Both were mechanics, trained at the same place. Both had been to Greenland with the Three-Year Expedition in the summer of 1934, and from 1936 to 1938 they had served in the police service, where Nielsen had been stationed at Ella Ø, while Harder Jensen worked from Eskimonæs. After a year in Denmark the two friends became restless and needed new challenges; but this time the road to North-East Greenland went via Nanok and the office of J.G. Jennov.

"Jennov was a bit of a conman", Richard Nielsen said in 1993. *"You had to sign a contract, and he had this trick that it always had to be on the very day the ship departed. Well, we went to see him and I brought up different issues mentioned in the contract. As an example, it said that he had the right to make use of any photographs we took up there. And there were some other issues we did not want to sign either.*

– Well, it is just something mentioned in the contract, Jennov said, it is not important.

– OK, then let's remove it, I answered and struck it out.

It also stated that Nanok was to receive 60% of the catch, while we only got 40%. – I'm not too happy about that. I would prefer fifty-fifty, I said to Jennov.

Well, that's something we can always negotiate, Jennov answered.

Great, then I'll write 50% now, I said and did so. This way we had a contract acceptable to us. But there was no money in it anyway. We went up entirely for the adventure".[768]

In the summer of 1939, Nielsen and Harder Jensen built the provisions shed, placed next to the main house: *"It was much bigger than planned"*, Nielsen explained, *"but that was practical, because*

Richard Nielsen (left) and Ove Harder Jensen.
© Knud Bavngaard

then we could run the sledge directly inside when we came home from a trapping trip and could stay inside when unloading or loading the sledge".[769]

The provisions shed was equipped with a small annex, which functioned as toilet and sauna.

The adventure ended abruptly a summer day in 1941. Harder Jensen, who had gone for a trip to Hvalrosodden, returned on board a Grumman Duck aircraft from the US Coast Guard cutter "Northland". The message was not negotiable: All trappers were to be evacuated. No objections did any good and: *"we went aboard under protest"*, Nielsen recalled.[770] Ove Harder Jensen went with the Coast Guard to West Greenland where he worked as an engineer at the radio station in Julianehåb during the war. Richard Nielsen went to Ammassalik to become a weather observer for the US Army Air Corps: *"And I knew nothing about that"*, Richard Nielsen said in 1993, *"but then vice-admiral Smith – Iceberg Smith – said that they would teach me, and so they did"*.[771] Richard Nielsen died in February 1995.

After the evacuation, Aalborghus remained unmanned until 1950.

Mogens Graae (left) and Orla Jensen at Aalborghus, 23rd March 1948.
© Mogens Graae

1950-51

On the 23rd August 1950, the "Søndmøringen" anchored at Aalborghus. The trappers Leo Ingwersen and Knud Nielsen went ashore to take over the station, which Jennov noted: *"was in good condition"*.[772] Leo Preben Ingwersen was from Copenhagen, and usually known as "Leo Ludwig" or "Sonny Boy". In 1949-50 he had wintered for Nanok at Sandodden. His partner Knud Nielsen, born in Tønder in 1924, was a journalist by profession and a novice, but over the years was to become a living legend amongst the trappers under the name "Sylte" (jam).

Prior to departure, Jennov instructed them to: *"trap in a territory as large as they could manage, preferably from Mønstedhus to Hvalrosodden"*,[773] and the two men split the territory so that Nielsen would have the northern area with his base at Hvalrosodden while Ingwersen would trap southwards from Aalborghus.

1951-52

In the summer of 1951, ice conditions prevented the "Søndmøringen" from reaching Aalborghus, and the supplies for the station were unloaded at Ailsahytten [519] on Hochstetter Forland.

When Ingwersen and Nielsen realized that they would not receive fresh supplies, they began to ration some provisions such as oat meal, dried milk and coffee. Otherwise they did not worry, and although they lacked coal there was plenty of wartime German paraffin. On September 14th they hauled their motor boat ashore. Their territory was now more or less ready and a new hut, "Fiskerhytten" [606], had been built in Syttendemajfjorden. On the 20th October 1951, the ice was safe and they set out into their territories. On December 12th they counted their autumn catch, 31 foxes, and then left for their Christmas visit to Danmarkshavn.

In February they resumed trapping, but neither Ingwersen or Nielsen could have foreseen the announcement that unexpectedly arrived on Saturday 10th May 1952: *"I have today via our radio communication received the news that Jennov has not received the necessary financial support from the State and is forced to withdraw all Nanok trappers"*,[774] Ingwersen wrote. It was discussed whether "Sylte" would stay for another winter using up their remaining provisions, but the idea was dropped and both he and "Sonny Boy" returned to Denmark in the summer of 1952.

Knud Nielsen, who took his certificate as a radio operator in 1956, later became station manager at Daneborg Weather Station and Danmarkshavn Weather Station. In 1965, he was employed in the Telecommunications Department of Grønlands Tekniske Organisation (GTO) and participated in the establishment of a chain of radio stations in West Greenland. Until shortly before his death in September 1987, he was coordinator for the GTO

Aalborghus, 31st May 1978. © Peter Schmidt Mikkelsen

weather stations in East Greenland.

For Aalborghus its existence as a trappers' station ended on the 20th August 1952; J.G. Jennov was on board the "Polaris" which: *"left after we at 2.30 p.m. had closed down the station"*.[775]

Jennov 1939; Lauritsen 1984; A134; A141; A152; G110; G115; Bendt Nielsen pers. comm.

Recent status

After 1952, Aalborghus was maintained by Sirius as a travellers' hut until 1988, when the patrol built a modern Sirius hut in the south-west corner of Dove Bugt. Aalborghus was without any maintenance until the summer of 1999, when a Sirius team carried out a thorough renovation.[776]

In September 2002 a joint team from Sirius and the Danish Navy vessel "Vædderen" visited Aalborghus and made various improvements.

In August 2006 another joint team, from Sirius and the Navy vessel "Hvidbjørnen", made further improvements at Aalborghus and installed a new coal stove sponsored by HM Queen Margrethe II of Denmark. The Queen had in 2005 visited Aalborghus together with HRH Crown Prince Frederik, and at the time the old Scandia stove was leaking and producing a lot of smoke - not an altogether pleasant experience. The Queen therefore decided to have the old stove replaced[777]

Aalborghus, interior including the old Scandia coal stove. 31st May 1978. © Peter Schmidt Mikkelsen

A joint team from the Sirius dog sledge patrol and the Danish Navy vessel "Vædderen" at Aalborghus checking and making various improvements. September 2002. © Søren Rysgaard

Aalborghus [613-2] is a former Danish trappers' station built in August 1938 for Nanok. It was used as a trappers' station until 1952 and thereafter maintained and used as a travellers' hut by Sirius until 1988. In 1999 it was restored by a party from Sirius. (Top, Centre left, Bottom) 4th August 2005. © NCN. (Centre right) "The Queen's stove". In 2006 the old stove at Aalborghus was replaced by a new one on the personal initiative of Her Majesty Queen Margrethe II of Denmark. © Thomas Hansen

OTHER STATIONS

In alphabetical order this chapter deals with category IB buildings/settlements, which are buildings erected for weather observations and scientific purposes etc. - never used for wintering in connection with trapping.

ALWIN PEDERSENS HUS
[639-2]

Wintering party
1938-39: Alwin Pedersen

The zoologist Alwin Pedersen, had been preparing his own expedition to North-East Greenland when in 1938 he heard about plans for an expedition to Mørkefjord by Eigil Knuth and Ebbe Munck. Pedersen wanted to continue his biological research especially with respect to muskox, and was permitted to join the Mørkefjord expedition as a "freelance" participant: *"At Hvalrosodden the zoological member of our expedition, Alwin Pedersen, built his own private house that he had brought along on the "Gustav Holm".*[778] "Alwin Pedersens hus" was erected during August 1938 by Pedersen with the help of the Nanok trappers Christian Jensen, Carlos Ziebell and Henning Ørnlef: *"The house was situated immediately north of the "Nanok" hunting station* (Hvalrosodden). *It was built of two layers of boards, the innermost of which consisted of matched boards. Like all Danish hunting stations it was covered on the outside with tar roofing. It contained only one room with a floor area of 3 x 3 1/2 m, and a porch was fitted in front of the entrance".*[779]

Alwin Joseph Hermann Pedersen was born in 1899 at Osnabrück in Germany, and had wintered in Scoresbysund in 1924-25 as a participant of Ejnar Mikkelsen's expedition to establish the Scoresbysund settlement. In 1927-29, he wintered at the same place with his own expedition. In 1931-33, he was a wintering member of Lauge Koch's Three-Year Expedition. In addition to a number of publications in "Meddelelser om Grønland", he wrote several books about arctic fauna, e.g.: "Polardyr" (polar animals) (1934), "Et naturens reservat" (a nature sanctuary) (1940), "Rosmarus" (walrus) (1951) and "Polar Animals" (1962). Alwin Pedersen strongly advocated the protection of wildlife through establishment of a national park in North-East Greenland: *"A totally preserved area, a so-called national park or a reservation, will be the only real solution here".*[780] In 1974, Pedersen's vision became a reality.

Pedersen 1951, 1962.

Recent status
Alwin Pedersens hus has probably not been used, if at all, since Alwin Pedersen left it. Inside it remains essentially unchanged. With the addition of some new roofing felt, it would last for many more years.

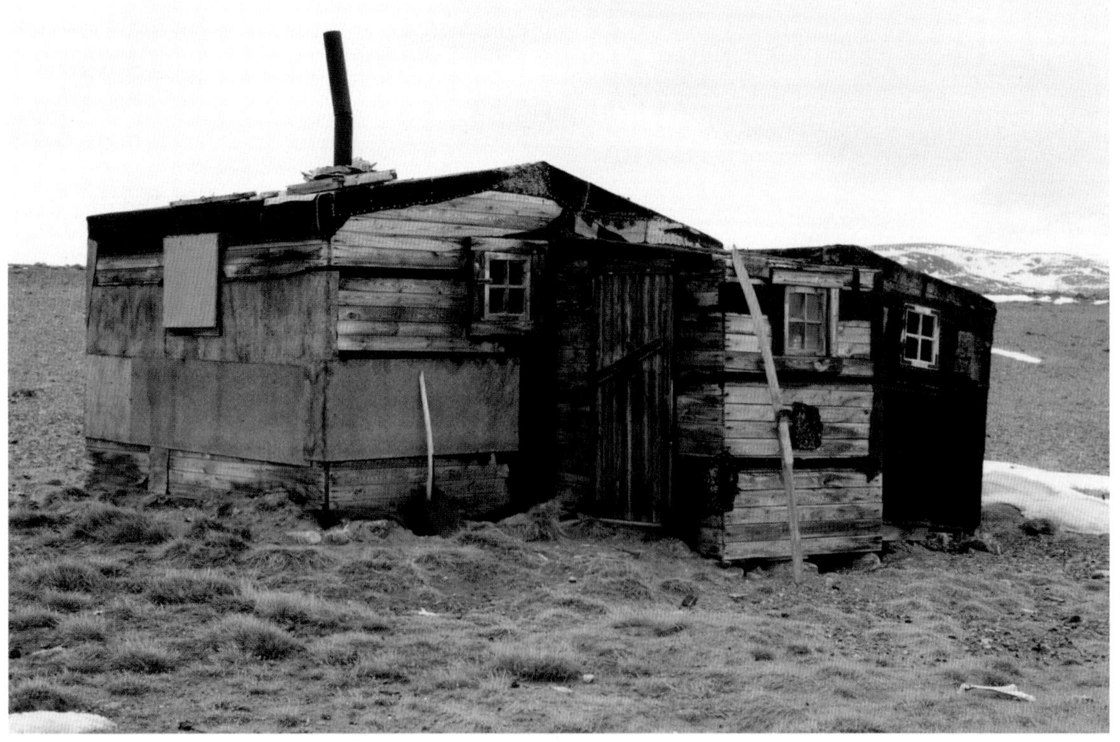

Alwin Pedersens hus, 29th May 1978. © Peter Schmidt Mikkelsen

Alwin Pedersens hus [639-2], 17th August 2005. Alwin Pedersens hus is a former Danish scientific station built in 1938 for Alwin Pedersen. It is situated next to the Hvalrosodden station [639-1]. © *NCN*

BRITANNIA SØ
[706]

Wintering party

1952-53: C.J.W. Simpson (leader), J.S. Agar, M.E.B. Banks, S.P. Boardman, R. Brett-Knowles, F.R. Brooke, C.B.B. Bull, G.F. Cadd, H.R. Dean, A.B. Erskine, R.A. Hamilton, H.A. Jensen (Danish), E.O. Jones, H.E. Lewis, H. Lister, J.P. Masterton, R.W. Moreton, J.W. Oakley, J.D. Peacock, G. Rollitt, C.G.M. Slesser, K.E. Taylor, P.F. Taylor, J.D. Walker, P.J. Wyllie

1953-54: C.J.W. Simpson (leader), K.C. Arnold, M.E.B. Banks, R. Brett-Knowles, F.R. Brooke, R.J.M. Bruce, C.B.B. Bull, H.R. Dean, A.B. Erskine, G.R. Fletcher, D.E.L. Homard, E.O. Jones, H. Lister, J.P. Masterton, R.W. Moreton, J.W. Oakley, S. Paterson, G. Rollitt, K.E. Taylor, P.F. Taylor, P.J. Wyllie

In the summer of 1950, the Royal Navy commander C.J.W. Simpson was invited to visit North-East Greenland as a guest of Eigil Knuth's Danish Peary Land Expeditions. Observing the largely unexplored nunataks of Dronning Louise Land (76°-78°N) from a distance, Simpson considered the region a possible site for a British Joint Services Expedition. In 1951 he led a reconnaissance expedition to Dronning Louise Land, which is guarded by two 30 km wide glaciers, Storstrømmen and L. Bistrup Bræ. The reconnaissance expedition had four members, and was assisted by the former Danish trapper Orla Jensen.

In 1952, the British North Greenland Expedition 1952-54 became a reality, and Simpson returned to Greenland as leader of the 25 participants. For transport the expedition had chartered the "Tottan", a Norwegian sealer. The equipment was unloaded at Zackenberg Basen [438-3], and during a period of three days about 150 tons of building materials and supplies were airlifted from Zackenberg to Britannia Sø on Dronning Louise Land using five Short Sunderland flyingboats. The expedition also had eight weasel tractors with trailers, and these were unloaded at Kap Rink on Hochstetter Forland, as "Tottan" was unable to reach Dove Bugt due to ice conditions. In the winter the weasels were driven under their own power across the glacier Storstrømmen to Britannia Sø.

The wintering station consisted of two buildings (c. 16 x 8 m and 9 x 7 m) connected by an unheated and fireproof passage.[781] In the summer of 1953, some of the participants were replaced and the following season 21 participants wintered. During the two years of the expedition, extensive topographical, geological and glaciological surveys were undertaken in the region. A geophysical traverse of the Inland Ice was carried out using the weasel tractors.

Banks 1957; Hamilton 1958; Lister 2005; Simpson 1957; Tusaat 2 3/93 pp. 33-35.

Recent status

The Britannia Sø base no longer exists. During the 1980s the base houses were crushed by the advance of Britannia Gletscher.

The base hut at Britannia Sø. The frozen lake is seen beyond the bank of moraine c. 1953. © Stan Paterson/ British North Greenland Expedition

DANEBORG
[425]

DANEBORG WEATHER STATION
[425-2]

Wintering party 1944-60:

1944-45: Niels Ove Jensen (L/T), Malekalet Arke (D), Alibak Cortsen (D), Berndt Jensen (P), Marius Jensen (P), Peter Nielsen (P), Kurt Olsen (P/T), Carlos Ziebell (P)

1945-46: Aage Hansen (L/T), Johannes Eriksen (T), Gustav Hansen (H), Walter Olesen (M)

1946-47: Aage Hansen (L/T), Mikkel Brønlund (H), Møller Madsen (first name unknown) (T) Mikkelsen (first name unknown) (T)

1947-48: Jens Martin Andersen (L/M), Jørgen Andersen (H), Mikkel Brønlund (H), Carl Edingsborg (C), Verner Hansen, (T), Børge Haagensen (T), Ludvig Weischer (T)

1948-49: Jens Martin Andersen (L/M), Verner Hansen (T), two wireless operators (T), a cook (C), two Greenlandic assistants (H)

1949-50: Arne Hammer (L), Wang Dinesen (C), Henning Groth (T), Otto Jørgensen (T), Jørgen Svendsen (T), S. Weber Nielsen (M), Abraham (surname unknown) (H), Boas (surname unknown) (H)

1950-51: Harry Erlander (L), Aage Bendixen (C), Carl El'Vibe (T), Villy Hansen (T), Søren Jensen (T), Johannes Sørensen (H), S. Weber Nielsen (M)

1951-52: Jens Martin Andersen (L/M), Carl El'Vibe (T), Gert Schou Frandsen (T), Erik B. Larsen (T), Hans Anker Nielsen (R), Gunnar Petersen (W), Knud Petersen (W), Ole Petersen (W), Villy Skovbjerg (C), Laurits Hansen (H)

1952-53: Jens Martin Andersen (L/M), John Durbahn (T), Erik Crillesen (R), Hans Madsen (H), Erik B. Larsen (T), Ernst Trier Skakke (T), Villy Skovbjerg (C)

1953-54: Erik B. Larsen (L/T), John Ahlgreen (M), Frits Conradsen (C), John Durbahn (T), Hans Frederiksen (H), Erik Crillesen (R), Ernst Trier Skakke (T)

1954-55: Tage Jørgensen Thure (L/T), John Ahlgreen (M), Helge Andersen (T), Niels Birkelund (R), Frits Conradsen (C), Hans Madsen (H), John Sjørslev (T)

1955-56: Tage Jørgensen Thure (L/T), Helge Andersen (T), Niels Birkelund (R), Svend Børge Hansen (M), Hans Madsen (H), John Sjørslev (T), Bent Søndergaard (C)

1956-57: Erik B. Larsen (L/T), Helge Andersen (T), Niels Birkelund (R), Hans Frederiksen (H), Svend Børge Hansen (M), Leo Wolsing (T), Adam Østergaard (C)

1957-58: Erik B. Larsen (L/T), Bossen (C), Hans Frederiksen (H), Orla Jensen (W), Erik Koch (R), Børge Rasmussen (M), Gert Steen Svensson (T), Leo Wolsing (T)

1958-59: Erik B. Larsen (L/T), Hans Frederiksen (H), John Hancke (T), Erik Koch (R), Knud Nielsen (T), Børge Rasmussen (M), Per Sørensen (C)

1959-60: Knud Nielsen (L/T), John Hancke (T), Hans Dinsen Hansen (T), Harly Åberg Hansen (H), Erik Koch (R), Per Sørensen (C), Anton Johan Thomsen (M)

1960-75: About 7 men/year.

(L) = leader, (T) = telegraphist, (R) = radio operator, (M) = mechanic, (H) = handyman/assistant, (D) = sledge driver, (P) = North-East Greenland Sledge Patrol, (C) = cook, (W) = labourer etc.

1944-45

In the summer of 1944, the head-quarters of the North-East Greenland Sledge Patrol was established at Young Sund on American initiative. In the annual report of the patrol for 1944-45, written by the leader, Niels Ove Jensen, it appears that the Americans had originally planned to establish a station manned by five American soldiers: *"Prior to arrival Captain Strong had indicated the west bank of Loch Fyne as a suitable location for his station. When he asked my opinion regarding this location, I could only reply that if it was his intention to stay out of the danger zone the spot was well chosen, even if it would be difficult to unload the ship due to shallow waters in that part of Loch Fyne. In my view he would do better to build his station close to ours* (Dødemandsbugten) *as our forces separately were too small to put up an effective defence – or alternately a more northern location such as Young Sund; at present it probably would not be possible to go further north. As the ship* (USCG Cutter "Storis") *was anxious to start unloading as soon as possible, they chose to build the station a few hundred metres north-west of the Sandodden trappers' station"*.[782]

In the meantime the idea of American soldiers wintering was dropped, and Governor Eske Brun in West Greenland considered that the sledge patrol could take over: *"the materials and provisions brought along by Captain Strong. As we at this point had already built the main building, a hut of 20 x 50 feet, close to Sandodden, I decided to transfer the headquarters of the patrol to this location".*[783]

The Daneborg station initially had the call sign "OYK", but: "after the war it turned out that Thorshavn Radio used the same call sign OYK*, so in order to avoid misunderstandings I changed our call sign to OYA, and at the same time the station was named "Daneborg". Out of the remaining materials left over after the station was built and additional materials from the German station* (Tyskerdepotet [917]) *at Lille Koldewey, we built two provisions sheds during the spring. The station thus consists of a main building of 20 x 50 feet, a garage including a repair shop of 16 x 16 feet, one provisions shed also 16 x 16 feet and a second provisions shed of 13.5 x 19.5 feet".*[784]

During the winter the patrol men also built "Blæsedal retrætedepot" [422].

1945-75

In 1945, after the war, it was decided to maintain Daneborg as a weather station. During the summer of 1947, the buildings were significantly expanded to house the weather station and the staff was increased to 7-8 men. On 26th November 1947, trapper Mogens Graae wrote: *"Major changes have taken place at Daneborg. We could hardly recognize the station. A new hut has been built, larger than the previous one. At the station there is now a power plant with two large diesel engines running the power generators. The workshop and the radio station in the old building are now used as temporary living quarters".*[785]

Daneborg Weather Station was rebuilt in 1952 and again in 1961. The main house is known as "Kystens Perle" (pearl of the coast). For hunting and other trips the station crew built "Kap Breusing hytten" [415] in 1951. Furthermore, a so-called pump-shed was built at "Lille Vandsø" [425-4].

Daneborg Weather Station, 1956. © Jørgen Rasmussen

Daneborg Weather Station and Sirius Daneborg worked side by side for 24 years. In 1970 the Ministeriet for Grønland (Greenland Department) appointed a committee to consider rationalization of the government operations in East Greenland, including the possibility of Sirius taking over the weather service at Daneborg. The committee concluded that this was possible, provided that the patrol crew was supplemented by professional radio operators. However, the final decision was to close down the weather service, and when Daneborg Weather Station transmitted its final weather report on 31st July 1975, Sirius took over the buildings.

Recent status

In the summer of 1994, a new era started when the Danish biologist Søren Rysgaard and his group arrived at Daneborg to make studies of climate changes in the Young Sund area, and used Sandodden as their base. During the summer they also visited the former weather station "Kystens Perle" near Daneborg: *"As no one seemed to own the building, we started to clean it up and undertake repairs as it could accommodate a quite large research team".*[786] Rysgaard continued: *"Staying in the area that summer, I realized that it would be the perfect place for integrated ecosystem studies and that we could greatly increase existing knowledge of high arctic marine ecosystems by including diurnal, seasonal and interannual variability studies at a relatively low cost compared to working from an icebreaker".*

On his return to Denmark Rysgaard applied for additional research grants, and the project "Nutrient dynamics in Northeast Greenland waters and sediment" was funded for three years; after one year of preparation 15 scientists from different scientific disciplines worked together in Young Sound during 1996-97. This "baseline" study was followed by the project: "Changes in Arctic Marine Production" (CAMP), which focused on the coupling between climate and the marine ecosystem and involved 30 scientists.

Alongside the research activities, Rysgaard and his team started to repair Kystens Perle, and in the summer of 1998 the house was thoroughly renovated. Initially, they received support from the Danish Polar Centre (DPC), the Danish National Research Institute and Sirius. During the field campaigns, members of DPC together with a carpenter and some of the scientists continued to repair and rebuild Kystens Perle whenever they had time in between experiments, and rooms were converted into laboratories, a kitchen and bedrooms: *"There was a fantastic team spirit and everyone worked for weeks without much sleep".*

Then, in close co-operation with the terrestrial program "Zackenberg Ecological Research Operations" (ZERO), a long-term marine monitoring programme "MarineBasic" was implemented as an integrated part of the Zackenberg Basic monitoring programme. MarineBasic has now collected data since 2002. Together with the monitoring programmes in the terrestrial environment, it will provide important data on this remote region for which there was very little data before 1994.

Daneborg Weather Station [425-2] is a former Danish weather station originally built in 1944 for the North-East Greenland Sledge Patrol. The present buildings date from 1947 and were used until 1975, when the weather service closed down. The buildings were partly abandoned and partly used by Sirius for storing provisions until 1998, when the main building was renovated for marine research investigations. (Top) "Kystens Perle", the main station house [425-3], 8th July 2007. (Centre) Daneborg Weather Station overview, 8th July 2007. (Bottom) Daneborg Weather Station, 6th August 2000. © NCN

SIRIUS DANEBORG
[425-3]

Wintering party 1951-60:

1951-52: Holger Jørgensen (H), K. Bernt Andersen, Verner Andersen, Folmer Berthelsen, Flemming Carlsen, L. Magnus Jensen, A. Krag-Jakobsen, Ole Lützhøft, Holger Madsen

1952-53: Ole Lützhøft (H), K. Bernt Andersen, Folmer Berthelsen, Hans Borring, Flemming Carlsen, P.E. Diernisse, Svend Henckel, L. Magnus Jensen, Holger Madsen, Vagn Kaalø Petersen, Oluf Schifter-Holm

1953-54: K. Bernt Andersen (H), Folmer Berthelsen, Frede Bille, Hans Borring, P.E. Diernisse, Mogens Guldbrandsen, Svend Henckel, Steen Malmquist, Anders Busk Petersen, Vagn Kaalø Petersen, Ivan H. Rasmussen, Oluf Schifter-Holm

1954-55: Svend Henckel (H), Frede Bille, Mogens Guldbrandsen, Frede A. Hansen, Frede Korsgaard, Holger Madsen, Steen Malmquist, Mogens Mathiesen, Anders Busk Petersen, Henning Schwegler Poulsen, Ivan H. Rasmussen

1955-56: Henning Schwegler Poulsen (H), Frede A. Hansen, Erik Jensen, B.W. Jørgensen, Frede Korsgaard, Holger Madsen, Mogens Mathiesen, A. Smith-Andersen, Jens Sonne-Harild, Claus Vahlkvist

1956-57: B.W. Jørgensen (H), Erik Jensen, Folke Møller Jensen, Ebbe Korsgaard Pedersen, Martin Reenberg, Poul Adam Sihm, A. Smith-Andersen, Jens Sonne-Harild, Claus Vahlkvist, Peter Hofman Wistisen

1957-58: Poul Adam Sihm (H), Friits Arbs, Einar Gade-Jørgensen, Axel Hansen, Carl Heydenreich, Folke Møller Jensen, Ebbe Korsgaard Pedersen, Martin Reenberg, Poul H. Stab-Nielsen, Peter Hofman Wistisen

1958-59: Axel Hansen (H), Hans Carlo Clausen, Poul Erik Damkjær, Einar Gade-Jørgensen, Carl Heydenreich, Tonny Zangenberg Jakobsen, Ebbe Korsgaard Pedersen, Poul H. Stab-Nielsen, Claus Vahlkvist, Bent Zwergius

1959-60: Poul Erik Damkjær (H), Hans Carlo Clausen, Tonny Zangenberg Jakobsen, Hans Ladefoged, Kurt Pedersen, Egon Ivar Petersen, Marius Rich, Poul Ringsmose, Claus Vahlkvist, Bent Zwergius

1960-94: About 12 men/year

(H) = Head of the Sirius Dog Sledge Patrol

In 1950, a military dog sledge patrol called Operation Resolut was established. The first year the patrol had its headquarters at Ella Ø station, but in the summer of 1951 the patrol moved to Daneborg, where a new headquarters was built a few hundred metres south of the weather station. At the same time, the patrol changed its name to Slædepatruljen Resolut. In 1953, the patrol acquired its present name from Sirius, the "dog star" and the brightest star in the night sky. The patrol and its buildings became "Sirius Daneborg".

In 1951, the station at Daneborg consisted of a mess building, "Sirihus", designed like many old expedition houses, with a large mess in the centre, surrounded by the personnel rooms, a radio room and a kitchen. Five to six men had their quarters here. In another building, "Lemmingbo", two to four men were housed. The remaining patrol members lived at Sandodden, the old trappers' station. The "Krumtap" housed the power plant and functioned also as a workshop for sledge building. "Flådemagasinet" was used as a storeroom for clothing, provisions and sledge equipment.

In 1952, a shed for ammunitions was built, and given the appropriate name "Krudtmaren" (powder Mary). It was made from elements taken from the house at Dødemandsbugten [408]. During the winter of 1953-54, a new workshop and garage, "Syndikatet", was built to house a patrol jeep and a pigsty - the patrol kept live pigs until 1962, when large freezers for storing meat were acquired. A carpenter's shop was also built, and in 1958 a provisions house, "Proviant" later renamed "Nordre Magasin", was added.

There were several serious fires in the 1960s. In 1960 Daneborg Weather Station was badly damaged, in 1961 the workshop at Sirius Daneborg caught fire, and finally "Sirihus" burnt down in 1962: *"After the fire in 1962 three new houses were built the same summer, namely a new "Sirihus"* (also called the Parliament) *on top of the ruins of the old one, a new workshop also on top of the old "Syndikat" and finally new living quarters, "Overhuset"* (the House of Lords). *Overhuset had six bedrooms – a darkroom – a sledge room, a boiler room that provided central heating, and a bathroom. The new Sirihus has a kitchen with a refrigerator, a food mixer, electric stove, gas cooker, and all the things the modern housewife cannot do without." ... "The new workshop has a heated room for provisions (for beer and other blessings), a room for paint and similar items and finally a 20 kw generator.*

"Lemmingbo" is now exclusively used for storage of sledge equipment and as an armoury. "Krumtappen" still has a radio workshop and power plant. "Sandodden" is used as storeroom for 'second year' provisions. In 1963, another living quarters was built, "Underhuset" (the House of Commons), *almost identical to the first one, namely with six bedrooms, an office and a boiler room with shower".*[787] Since 1964, most of the buildings have been replaced with new and more modern buildings.

From 1950 and up until the middle of the 1960s the patrol built: "Kap Hedlund hytten" [230-2], "Kap Mac Clintock hytten" [226], "Kap Simpson hytten" [204], "Borlase Warren hytten" [421-3], "Albrechtbugthytten" [453-2], "Thors Café" [709-2] and "Grønnedal" [418-2]. Furthermore, some huts were enlarged, e.g. "Blæsedalhytten (norsk / Sirius)" [430]. All these huts had a basic construction similar to the old trappers' huts. From the middle of the 1970s the patrol has exclusively constructed strong, bear-proof, prefabricated, travellers' huts. These special military huts are not included in this account.

J. Bjerre 1980; Claus Birkbøll pers. comm.; Carl El'Vibe pers. comm.; Erik Birger Larsen pers. comm.; Erik Jensen pers. comm.; Bent Zwergius pers. comm.; Erik Koch pers. comm.; Ivar Ytreland pers. comm.

Recent status

The Sirius Daneborg station has been enlarged several times, and none of the original buildings from 1951 now exist. During the 1990s and early 2000s several new and more modern houses have been built.

(Left) Sirius Daneborg, c. 1955. © Ivan H. Rasmussen. (Bottom) Sirius Daneborg. July 1977. © Peter Schmidt Mikkelsen

Sirius Daneborg [425-3] is a station established 1951 for the Sirius Dog Sledge Patrol. The station has been enlarged several times, and today there are none of the original buildings from 1951 left. (Left) 26th July 1999. (Centre) 6th August 2000. (Bottom) 8th July 2007. © NCN

DANMARKSHAVN WEATHER STATION
[628-2]

Wintering party 1948-60:

1948-49: Ib Poulsen (L), Frode Andersen (W), Otto Andersen (W), Villy Andersen (T), Kaj Brandt (R), Erik Christiansen (W), Gert Schou Frandsen (T), Hannibal Gylden (W), E. Heering-Hansen (M), Kasper Karlsen (H), Eli Kristiansen (H), Erik Lehmann (T), Julius Nissen (W), Erik Palsby (O), Frede Munck Petersen (W), Villy Skovbjerg (K), Kristen Sørensen (W)

1949-50: Hans Thomsen, (L/T) Kaj Brandt (R), Gert Schou Frandsen (T), E. Heering-Hansen (M), Erik Palsby (O), Steen Egon Petersen (H), Knud J.O. Sørensen (T), Villy Skovbjerg (K)

1950-51: P.O.C. Johansen (L/O), John Ahlgreen (M), Hans Egede Jacobsen (K), Orla Jensen (W), Poul Gluud Larsen (O), H.O. Lauridsen (R), Steen Malmquist (T), Ejvind Olsen (T), Steen Egon Petersen (H), Knud Søgaard Rasmussen (O), Knud J.O. Sørensen (T)

1951-52: P.O.C. Johansen (L/O), John Ahlgreen (M), R. Danielsen (K), Knud Ernø (T), Hans Egede Jacobsen (H), Karl Holm Jakobsen (T), Steen Malmquist (T), Knud Søgaard Rasmussen (O), Poul Gluud Larsen (L), H.O. Lauridsen (R)

1952-53: Arne Neergaard Nielsen (L/T), R. Danielsen (K), Knud Ernø (T), Ove Hermansen (O), Hans Egede Jacobsen (H), Arne Holm Jakobsen (M), Karl Holm Jakobsen (T), Axel Kidal (O), H.D. Larsen (W), Knud Søgaard Rasmussen (O), Knud J.O. Sørensen (T), Larry Sørensen (R)

1953-54: Vivian Bille Fritz (L/T), Ove Almtoft (O), Niels Chr. Bahnson (T), R. Danielsen (K), Ove Hermansen (O), Hans Egede Jacobsen (H), Arne Holm Jakobsen (M), Poul Gluud Larsen (O), Ib Palle Madsen (T), Knud J.O. Sørensen (T), Larry Sørensen (R)

1954-55: Vivian Bille Fritz (L/T), Niels Chr. Bahnson (T), Gerhardt Blaase (O), Aage Eigil Christensen (W), Anker Hansen (M), Leo Ingwersen (H), Carl Georg Jørgensen (K), Erik Hjortenberg Knudsen (O), Harry Ingvard Larsen (W), Ib Palle Madsen (T), Carl Erik Pedersen (T), Ole Herman Petersen (W), Verner Poulsen (R), Klaus Reindel (O)

1955-56: Knud Ernø (L/T), John Alfred Andersen (T), Gerhardt Blaase (O), Leo Ingwersen (H), Carl Georg Jørgensen (K), Leif Klintmann (R), Bertel Møhl-Hansen (O), Carl Erik Pedersen (T), Mogens Bloch Poulsen (T), Klaus Reindel (O), Anton Johan Thomsen (M)

1956-57: Knud Ernø (L/T), Gerhardt Blaase (O), Leo Ingwersen (H), Leif Klintmann (R), Bertel Møhl-Hansen (O), Carl Erik Pedersen (T), Chresten Vilh. Petersen (K), Mogens Bloch Poulsen (T), Ove Poulsen (T), Klaus Reindel (O), Anton Johan Thomsen (M)

1957-58: Tage Jørgensen Thure (L/T), Erik Andersen (T), Harry Andreasen (O), Tonny Bøgh (T), Jens Andreas Jensen (T), Ib Lorentzen (O), Christian R. Nielsen (R), Dan Eivind Pedersen (O), Chresten Vilh. Petersen (K), Anton Johan Thomsen (M), Helge Vich (H)

1958-59: Tage Jørgensen Thure (L/T) Børge Andersen (W), Erik Andersen (T), Gerhardt Blaase (O), Tonny Bøgh (T), Jens Andreas Jensen (T), Erik Lykke Larsen (O), Christian R. Nielsen (R), Dan Eivind Pedersen (O), Poul Poulsen (M), Klaus Reindel (O), Evald Sonne (W), Adam Østergaard (K), Helge Vich (H)

1959-60: John Madsen (L/T) Gerhardt Blaase (O), Jens Andreas Jensen (T), Conny Knop (R), Karl Chr. Mathiesen (T), Poul Poulsen (M), Bent Ramsberg (O), Leif Rasmussen (H), Adam Østergaard (K), Frank Aabak (T)

1960-94: 10-12 employees/year

(L) = leader, (T) = telegraphist, (R) = radio operator, (M) = mechanic, (H) = handyman/assistant, (K) = cook (O) = radiosonde operator, (W) = workman, labourer.

On 25th July 1948, KGH's new polar ship, the "G.C. Amdrup", anchored in a small bay on the south coast of Germania Land. The ship was carrying 400 tons of building materials and the task for the 31 passengers was to build a modern weather station within 2-3 weeks. The station was to be financed by the International Civil Aviation Organisation (ICAO) and the construction work was under the supervision of

Captain Ib Poulsen, who was also appointed leader of the 17 men who were to run the station the first year. On the 6th November 1948, the weather station "Danmarkshavn" was reported ready for regular operation.

For both coastal navigation and the rapidly growing intercontinental air traffic, the establishment of a radiosonde operating weather station in North-East Greenland was considered highly desirable: *"The new weather station Danmarkshavn was placed on the Greenland Administration construction program for 1947, but then had to be postponed due to difficulties in procuring materials and limited opportunities for sailing to North-East Greenland"*, Ib Poulsen wrote.[788] *"However, ICAO expressed a definite wish that the new weather station should be established in 1948. The project now had the highest priority and other scheduled activities in North-East Greenland were postponed. Even the establishment of the military sledge patrol Sirius had to be deferred"*.[789] The Ministry of Defence had placed Poulsen at the disposal of the Greenland Administration that - through the Grønlands Radio- og Vejrtjeneste (Greenland Radio- and Weather Service) - was responsible for the project.

"As was so often the case in North-East Greenland – and probably still is – it was a rather mixed group that populated Danmarkshavn the first year", journalist Erik Palsby, one of the first winterers, wrote. *"Carpenters, more or less skilled radio operators, mechanics, Greenlandic hunters, a dairyman, a journalist, a radio technician, a bookseller, a baker/cook, a navvy. The age distribution ranged from the early 20s to a little over 40. Military men – present or former – ordinary civilians, people from Fyn, Sjælland, Copenhagen ... – People who had year-long experience on the East Coast and people who had never seen Greenland before. – That the 17 of us could work together and create a well-functioning society, may seem incredible – but maybe that is exactly the reason why it worked"*. It was only during the first year that Danmarkshavn had 17 men. From the summer of 1949, the manning has numbered 10 to 12.

The first weather report from Danmarkshavn was transmitted on 5th November 1948, and by 1st January 1949 the full scale operation included weather reports every third hour, 24 hours a day, all year round. The radiosonde service began simultaneously and since 1950 a radiosonde has been launched twice a day. A radiosonde is a small electronic device, which measures the temperature, pressure and humidity of the air and transmits these to the radiosonde station. The radiosonde is lifted into the air by a hydrogen-filled balloon. By following the radiosonde's ascent through the atmosphere using a radio direction finder, it is possible to calculate

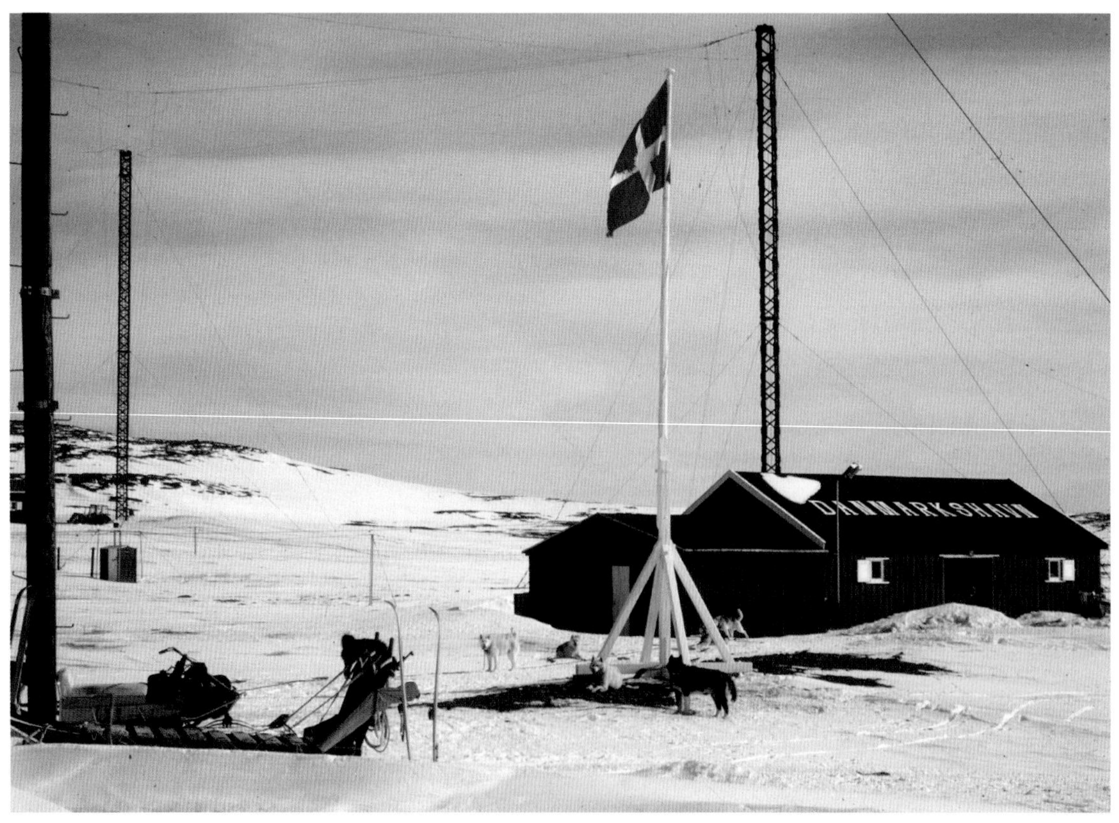

Danmarkshavn Weather Station. 21st May 1978. © Peter Schmidt Mikkelsen

windspeed and direction at different altitudes. When launched the balloons, each containing about 2 m^3 hydrogen, are about 1.7 m in diameter, but at an altitude of 30 km have expanded to 7 m.

Since the start of operations, the various station members at Danmarkshavn have used their off-duty time on shorter or longer excursions along the coast. Over the years the personnel at Danmarkshavn have built no less than 12 travellers' huts: "Heeringhus" [626] in 1949, "Kap Quist hytten" [624] in 1951, "Weaselhytten" [622-1] in 1953, "Trækpashytten" [605] in 1958, "Syttenkilometernæsset" [630-2] in 1959, "Kap Helgoland hytten" [625] in 1965, "Syltekrukken" [634] in 1966, "Den ny hytte" [616] in 1966, "Kradshytten" [627] in 1968, "Germania Land hytten" [702] in 1979, "Kap Bismarck hytten" [623] in 1979, "Åndehullet" [622-2] in 1991 and "Ny Store Snenæs hytte" [632-2] in 1999.

Brandt 1995; Fischer 1983, 1993; Nuna-Tek 1988; Thomsen 1966; Allan Nielsen pers. comm.; Bendt Nielsen pers. comm.

Recent status

Danmarkshavn is still an oasis, a home to a very special breed of people who thrive best far from "civilisation". The place has a strange and lasting attraction for its personnel: several have a seniority of 5-10 years and many have returned for new winterings after decades of absence.

Danmarkshavn Weather Station. 21st May 1978. © Peter Schmidt Mikkelsen

Danmarkshavn Weather Station. 8th July 2007. © NCN

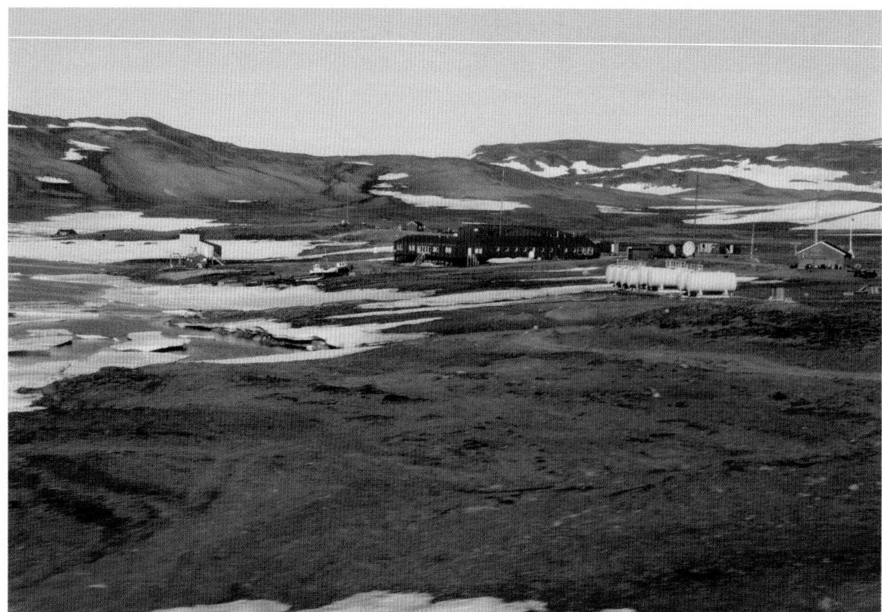

Danmarkshavn Weather Station [628-2] is a Danish weather station built in 1948 for Grønlands Radio- and Vejrtjeneste. Since the beginning several buildings and installations have been added to the station, August 2006. *© NCN*

DØDEMANDSBUGTEN
[408]

Wintering party
1943-44: Niels Ove Jensen (leader), Berndt Jensen, Marius Jensen, Peter Nielsen, Kurt Olsen, Carl Henrik Schultz, Carlos Ziebell

In the summer of 1943, Niels Ove Jensen returned from West Greenland to resume the leadership of the North-East Greenland Sledge Patrol. When in West Greenland he had heard that Eskimonæs had been lost. He therefore signed off the navy cutter "Ternen" and went to the American air base Bluie West One (Narsarsuaq) in order to obtain reinforcements. The outcome was new weapons, provisions, fresh dogs and two new Danish patrol members, as well as materials for a new patrol station. Jensen chose to place this new staion at Dødemandsbugten, about 12 km east of the burnt down Eskimonæs station: *"The station was situated on the eastern side of the bay, at the same location as an old Inuit settlement. The station house was just a rectangular wooden hut, surrounded by turf walls to the height of a man. In the cold of the winter the turves froze together into a hard and compact mass which turned the hut into an almost bullet-proof fortress. In the hut there was a large room, used as a living room. In addition it contained a kitchen of almost the same size, but this was filled with provisions in tall stacks along the walls so that the cook barely had space enough to fry our muskox steaks on the big, black stove. In addition there were two four-berth rooms along the two walls and one single-berth room for the boss. Plus a room where the radio station was installed. About fifty metres from the house was a wooden hut used as a workshop and storeroom. During the autumn yet another hut was built, an engine room to house a heap of spare parts we had succeeded in collecting from many different places on the coast, that were used to make a paraffin-powered motor that could supply the radio station with electricity. This enabled us to resume the weather service that had been disrupted when the Germans destroyed the Eskimonæs station six months earlier".*[791]

On 21st October 1943, two dog sledge patrols drove north, and when they returned on 17th December Peter Nielsen reported that he had discovered traces of a German presence at Kap Sussi on Shannon. At the beginning of February 1944, a reconnaisance revealed the exact location of the German base. The Americans said that they would land eight soldiers in Dødemandsbugten by plane, to take part in a joint attack on the Germans. At the very last moment this was cancelled, and it was left to the sledge patrol to carry out the attack themselves. Niels Ove Jensen was in charge of the attack that took place on 22nd April 1944 (see Kap Sussi).

In the summer of 1944, the station at Dødemandsbugten was evacuated and the sledge patrol moved to its new headquarters, which was later named Daneborg.

Recent status
Today Dødemandsbugten has fallen into decay. The provision huts noted above no longer exist and the main house has become one section shorter. In many ways the house is much changed from the original. Materials taken from the station have been used to build the Kap Breusing hytten [415] and for buildings at Sirius Daneborg [425-3]. On the hills behind the station there are still remains of the defences that the patrol established during the war.

Dødemandsbugten, 27th July 1989. © Peter Schmidt Mikkelsen

Dødemandsbugten [408], 6th August 2003. Dødemandsbugten is a former Danish military station built in 1943 for the North-East Greenland Sledge Patrol. It was used as a station only until 1944, when the patrol moved its headquarters to Daneborg Weather Station [425-2]. (Top) The main house was built from prefabricated materials. (Centre) View eastwards. (Bottom) View south across Gael Hamke Bugt towards Store Finsch and Hold with Hope. © NCN

ELLA Ø
[235]

Wintering party

1931-32: S.O. Stenør (L/E), Aage de Lemos (T), Arne Noe-Nygaard (G), Jørgen Petersen (D), Benjamin Samuelsen (D), O. Simonsen (E), Thorvald Sørensen (B), Gunnar Thorson (Z)
1932-33: S.O. Stenør (L/E), Jørgen Barnabas (D), P.V. Glob (A), Aage de Lemos (T), Jørgen Petersen (D), Benjamin Samuelsen (D), O. Simonsen (E), Eugen Wegmann (G)
1933-34: Aage de Lemos (L/T), Frode Søgaard Andersen (Z), Jørgen Barnabas (D), Heinrich Bütler (G), Jørgen Petersen (D)
1934-35: Ib Poulsen (L/T), Allan Lind (H)
1935-36: Ib Poulsen (L/T), Aage de Lemos (T)
1936-37: Leo Christiansen (L/T), Konrad Arke (D), Th. Heinrichson (G), Richard Nielsen (H), Arne Philbert (H), Hans Peter Schaub (G), Jakob Senimoinaq (D), Hans Stauber (G)
1937-38: Aage de Lemos (L/T), Karl Andersen (D), Malte Andersson (G), Wilhelm Bierther (G), Richard Nielsen (H), Th. Heinrichson (G), Jakob Senimoinaq (D)
1938-39: Aage de Lemos (L/T), Jonas Brønlund (D), Jørgen Tvermose (H)
1939-40: Aage de Lemos (L/T), Lars Napatoq (D)
1940-41: Aage de Lemos (L/T)
1941-42: Aage de Lemos (L/T), Arparte Høegh (D), Eli Knudsen (P), Hans Siewers (P), Evald Simonsen (D)
1942-43: Eli Knudsen (L/P), Bjarne Akre (P), Oddvar Akre (P), Arparte Høegh (D), Evald Simonsen (D)
1943-47: None
1947-48: Aage de Lemos (L/T), Silvio Eha (G), Walter Huber (G), Kristian Kunak (D), Eba Olsen (D), Pavia Olsen (D), Povel Povelsen (H)
1948-49: Aage de Lemos (L/T), Erdhart J. Fränkl (G), Rudolf Katz (G), Eba Olsen (D), Pavia Olsen (D), Povel Povelsen (H)
1949-50: Aksel Jensen (L), Elias Arke (D), Ove Barsted (T), Jon Brønlund (D), John Haller (G), Emil Witzig (G)
1950-51: Aksel Jensen (L), Peter J. Adams (G), John W. Cowie (G), Emil Piki (D) Holger Jørgensen (L/R), Verner Andersen (R), Flemming Carlsen (R), Eli Kristiansen (D/R), Ole Lützhøft (R), Eba Olsen (D/R) Kristen Sørensen (R)
1951-52: Alfred Christensen (H), Jørn Riel Eierst (T), Åge "Ugge" Simonsen (D)
1952-53: Janus Arke (D), Wagn Kromann (H), Max P. Sommer (G)
1953-54: Wagn Kromann (H)

(L) = leader, (T) = telegraphist,
(H) = handyman/assistant, (G) = geologist,
(E) = geodesist, (Z) = zoologist, (B) = botanist,
(A) = archaeologist, (D) = sledge driver,
(P) = North-East Greenland Sledge Patrol,
(R) = Operation Resolut.

Ella Ø, named by A.G. Nathorst in 1899 after his wife, is located in the middle of some of the most magnificent and breath-talking scenary of North-East Greenland. The western cape of the island, Bastionen, is a near vertical cliff that towers 1367 m above the fjord. However, it was not the scenary that inspired Lauge Koch to establish a large scientific station on Ella Ø. The locality possesses a sheltered safe harbour with good anchoring conditions, a good climate with many sunny days, a dry and slightly sloping terrain, well-suited for building houses and a small lake that supplies fresh water directly to the station.

The Ella Ø station was established in August 1931 by members of the Three-Year Expedition. Gunnar Seidenfaden, the equipment manager, wrote that: *"the eight scientists must have worked enormously hard. They could now show us an almost finished home, the stove was lit and they could offer us coffee and rum toddies. On the evening we went ashore they had a couple of well-deserved hours off for the first time. We spent a very cozy night ashore where the gramophone for the first time played the records for the winter and the cheerful wireless operator de Lemos gave a preview of his stock of incredible stories that were going to maintain spirits high at the Ella Ø station all through the winter".*[792] Aage de Lemos became a legend on the coast, and his name is particularly associated with Ella Ø, where he wintered no less than 11 times in the period 1931-49.

The station house, *"Ørnereden" (the Eagles Nest), is: "built of masonite plates on a timber construction made in Denmark. Their area was 66 m² (external measure). The roof and the side sheds were covered with tared boards. The walls consisted on the outside of two layers of hard masonite and on the inside of one layer of semi-hard masonite; the interspace between the outer and the inner layers was 12 cm, and the insulation was air. The floor consisted of two layers of boards with an intermediate layer of insulite (calcium silicate insulation).*

The ceiling consisted of masonite divided by wooden ridges".[793]

During the years 1931-43, Ella Ø and its sister station Eskimonæs on Clavering Ø, functioned partly as main stations for the Lauge Koch's geological expeditions, and partly as headquarters for the Danish government authorities in North-East Greenland. During the Three-Year Expedition of 1931-34, Ella Ø was manned by 5-8 men in the winter, comprising scientists, assistents and Greenlandic sledge drivers. During this period Lauge Koch, who in 1931 had been appointed police authority, handed over the authority to the station manager when he left the coast each autumn.

In 1934, Ejnar Mikkelsen had been appointed Inspector of East Greenland. As such he was the head of the police service in North-East Greenland (mainly formed by radio operators with police authority). The police district of Ella Ø covered the region between Storefjord in Liverpool Land to the south and a line through Teufelsschloss and Dusén Fjord to the north. In 1934 the police service moved a hut formerly used as a photographers darkroom from Ella Ø to Maria Ø; "Maria Ø (østhavn)" [240]

In August 1941, the North-East Greenland Sledge Patrol was established and Ella Ø became the headquarters of the central of the three patrol regions. In 1941-42 the Sledge Patrol built "Eli Knudsens hytte" [239-1] on Maria Ø.

In the spring of 1943, after Eskimonæs was attacked and burnt down, the patrol evacuated the Ella Ø station and retreated to Scoresbysund.

During the years 1947-54, Ella Ø was once again manned by members of Lauge Koch's Expeditions. After WWII, police authority was given to the station managers at Daneborg and Danmarkshavn. In 1950, this authority was transferred to the newly established military sledge patrol, Operation Resolut, which in 1950-51 had its temporary headquarters at Ella Ø before moving to Daneborg in 1951. However, the patrol maintained a seasonal manning at Ella Ø until 1963, after which the station was only used during the summer.

Ella Ø, in addition to Ørnereden, consists of several buildings built since 1931: "Pynten", "Kokkens hus", "Pisa", a workshop, a provisions shed, two living quarters and a generator hut.

Koch 1955; Mikkelsen 1986; Schwarzenbach 1993.

Recent status

After Lauge Koch's Expeditions were brought to a close after the summer of 1958, Sirius took over the maintenance of the Ella Ø Station. Sirius still uses Ella Ø as a summer base when supplying their travellers' huts and depots in the large interconnected fjord complex between Hold with Hope in the north and Scoresby Land in the south. Sirius normally has a team of 4-5 patrol members stationed at Ella Ø during part of the summer.

Thanks to the continuous maintenance undertaken by Sirius, the Ella Ø station is still in excellent condition. It is a beautiful station located in some of the most magnificent scenery in North-East Greenland.

The main building "Ørnereden" (the eagle's nest) at Ella Ø, 1936. © Arne Philbert

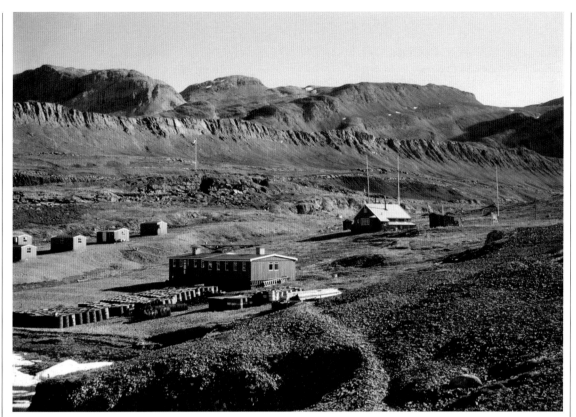

Ella Ø, 1955. © Jørgen Rasmussen

Ella Ø, 16th August 1989. © Peter Schmidt Mikkelsen

Ella Ø [235] is a Danish scientific station built in 1931 for the Three-Year Expedition. It was used as an overwintering station until 1954; subsequently it has been used and maintained by Sirius, that uses Ella Ø as a summer base station. (Top and Bottom) Ørnereden, 29th July 2003. © NCN

ESKIMONÆS
[405]

Wintering party

1931-32: Thyge Johansen (L/E), Johan Davidsen (D), Paul Gelting (B), Helge Larsen (A), Axel Henry Nielsen (T), Alwin Pedersen (Z), Arne C.F. Schwarck (A), Curt Teichert (G)

1932-33: Thyge Johansen (L/E), Johan Davidsen (D), Valdemar Carl Devantier (E), Alexander Jensen (T), Axel Henry Nielsen (T), Eigil Nielsen (G), Holger Madsen (Z)

1933-34: Thyge Johansen (L/E), Johan Davidsen (D), Elmar Drastrup (I), Olaf Eklund (G), P. Halfdaner (E), Birger Malmberg (G), Axel Henry Nielsen (T), Benjamin Samuelsen (D)

1934-35: Thorvald Sørensen (L/B), Svend K. Espersen (T)

1935-36: Svend K. Espersen (L/T), Evald Rasmussen (I)

1936-37: Niels Ove Jensen (L/T), Karl Andersen (D), Th. Gideonsen (D), Ove Harder Jensen (I), Wolf Maync (G), Eigil Nielsen (G), Andreas Vischer (G)

1937-38: Niels Ove Jensen (L/T), Konrad Arke (D), Th. Gideonsen (D), Ove Harder Jensen (I), Wolf Maync (G), Andreas Vischer (G)

1938-39: Ib Poulsen (L/T), Christian Arke (D), Peter Bachmann (G), Niels Ove Jensen (T), A. Mittelholzer (G), Jakob Senimoinaq (D)

1939-41: Niels Ove Jensen (L/T), Petrus Arke (D), Leo Christiansen (T)

1941-42: Niels Ove Jensen (L/T), Mads Christensen (P), Niels Hansen (P), Marius Jensen (P), Peter Nielsen (P), Kurt Olsen (P/T), Carlos Ziebell (P)

1942-43: Ib Poulsen (L/T), William Arke (D), Marius Jensen (P), Mikael Kunak (D), Peter Nielsen (P), Kurt Olsen (P/T), Henry Rudi (P)

(L) = leader, (T) = telegraphist,
(H) = handyman/assistant, (G) = geologist,
(E) = geodesist, (Z) = zoologist, (B) = botanist,
(A) = archaeologist, (D) = sledge driver,
(P) = North-East Greenland Sledge Patrol.
(I) = assistant

"In the summer of 1930 during our second ship expedition to East Greenland, when Lauge Koch visited the place and while he was still planning for the Three-Year Expedition, it seemed natural to him to name this place Eskimonæs. It struck him that a locality that the Eskimos had found attractive, and where they with their vast experience of weather and climate, of winter storms and summer thaw, had built their primitive dugouts; this also had to be a good site for the large wintering station that he dreamed of".[794] Lauge Koch's own explanation was as follows: *"Before establishing a permanent station it is desirable to acquire intimate knowledge of various conditions in the place, first of all the harbour conditions. Thus a station should be placed near a sheltered natural harbour with good holding ground and fairly free of drift-ice and icebergs during the period of navigation. The only suitable place on Clavering Ø was its southernmost point, Eskimonæs".*[795] Furthermore there had to be sufficient supply of fresh water for the station personnel.

"On the 4th August 1931 we were all on deck when "Gustav Holm" carefully and with continuous soundings glided into the bay", Gunnar Seidenfaden wrote.[796] The next morning the work began and it was: *"most exciting working for the building team. Supervised by the two capable ship's carpenters, we found in the piles of material the wood that we had to use first. It had all been numbered at home". ... "After a couple of days it really starts looking like a house. The roof is barely finished before we go ahead with the roofing felt. All through the day you can hear the hammer strokes across the bay, while thousands of nails are driven in, only interrupted by curses, when a botanist or zoologist has hit his fingers instead of the nail". ... "The engine that is to supply the station with light and power for the radio installation is a smart little thing from the Delco-Light factories". ... "After a fortnight the building activity is so advanced that we can safely leave the rest of the work to the wintering party".*[797]

As a scientific station Eskimonæs had its great period during the Three-Year Expedition 1931-34. In the summer of 1933, a mining team made an excavation east of Breivik on Clavering Ø, that went by the optimistic name of "Guldminen" (the gold mine) [922].

The station house was identical to the house on Ella Ø known as "Ørnereden". At the end of 1941, six smaller houses also existed at Eskimonæs. The history of the two stations was almost identical from 1931-43. Ella Ø and Eskimonæs functioned both as bases for the Lauge Koch Expeditions and as headquarters for the Police Service. The Eskimonæs station was in the northern police district, that had its southern border along a line through Teufelsschloss and the middle of Dusén Fjord. In 1938 the Police Service built "Kap Ruth hytten" [406].

From August 1941, Eskimonæs was used as the headquarters for the northernmost group of the North-East Greenland Sledge Patrol. For a good

18 months the patrols were carried on without any drama, but on 11th March 1943 members of the patrol unexpectedly came across men from a German weather station near Hansa Bugt (see Hansa Bugt and Sandodden). This resulted in a German attack on Eskimonæs - led by Hermann Ritter - shortly before midnight on the 23rd March 1943. The patrol men escaped by fleeing from Eskimonæs in some disorder. Eskimonæs was destroyed, but there is still some controversy as to when and how this took place:

1) David Howarth wrote in "The Sledge Patrol" that: *"Ritter and his party smashed the radio, shot some of the dogs because they could not take all of them away, and poured petrol in the wooden house and set it on fire. It blazed furiously, and soon there was nothing of Eskimoness left except its ashes, glowing in a pit which the heat had melted in the snow"*.[798]

2) Gottfried Weiss - who participated in the attack - wrote in "Das Arktische Jahr": *"Ritter liess die schöne Station zerstören, da er das für unsere Sicherheit notwendig fand"*.[799] (Ritter allowed the nice station to be destroyed as being necessary for our safety).

3) Franz Nusser wrote that the station: *"wurde zerstört. Die gefüllte Pelzkammer mit dem Besitz der dänischen Fänger, die zugleich Hilfpolizisten waren, blieb unversehrt"*.[800] (was destroyed. The house filled with furs and containing the belongings of the Danish trappers, who were also police assistants, remained unharmed.)

4) Franz Selinger stated: *"In the morning of March 24th the main station and the storage hut were set on fire. The fur hut was undamaged, as Ritter ordered that private property such as personal belongings and the furs should be protected" ... "There is no German report of the amount of destruction caused by burning the main station and the storage hut"*.[801]

5) On 13th May 1943 - barely two months after the German attack - Eskimonæs was, for unknown reasons, bombed by aircraft from the US Army Air Corps under the leadership of Bernt Balchen: *"We made several preliminary passes at low altitude to orient the bombardiers with the target. We could see how completely the Germans had destroyed the station: doors swung open, windows were broken and vacant, there was no sign of life around the half-burned and wrecked buildings. Scratches made by sled-runners were still discernible on the ice, leading both north and south, but in the Arctic it is difficult to tell how old a sled-track may be. Although we assumed the station was deserted, we carried out our orders, dropped our bombs, strafed the buildings, and left them burning as we headed back to Iceland"*.[802]

It is obvious that Balchen's and Howarth's descriptions differ, and none of the other sources give any definitive picture of the destruction of Eskimonæs. "Zerstört" means destroyed or inhabitable, but not necessarily burnt down. It is, however, a fact that one hut was intact after the destruction.

Recent status

The hut that survived the war was, shortly after the war, moved a short distance away to another site at Eskimonæs. This can be concluded by comparing photographs taken at Eskimonæs in the late 1930s and the early 1950s.

Ever since the 1950s, Sirius has maintained the surviving travellers' hut at Eskimonæs that is still frequently used by Sirius as well as scientific and sporting expeditions.

In the summer of 1998 the traveller's hut was renovated by a Nanok group supported by a Sirius team.[803]

The site of the burnt down main station is marked today by a miscellaneous collection of rusty metal objects, a stove, canisters, metal boxes and the metal parts of a row of rifles; these relics of a once handsome building have remained essentially undisturbed since the station was destroyed in 1943.

Historical Eskimonæs [405]. At the end of the 1930s Eskimonæs was an important Danish scientific station. The main building was identical to the sister station at Ella Ø [235]. (Opposite and Top) Eskimonæs c. 1938. (Bottom, left) From left: (Unknown), Marius Jensen, Niels Ove Jensen, Berndt Jensen (with violin), Kurt Olsen (facing camera), (unknown), Henry Rudi. (Bottom, right) Christmas Eve at Eskimonæs 1938. From left: Jakob Senimoinaq, A. Mittelholzer, Ib Poulsen, Christian Arke, Peter Bachmann, Niels Ove Jensen. © Niels Ove Jensen

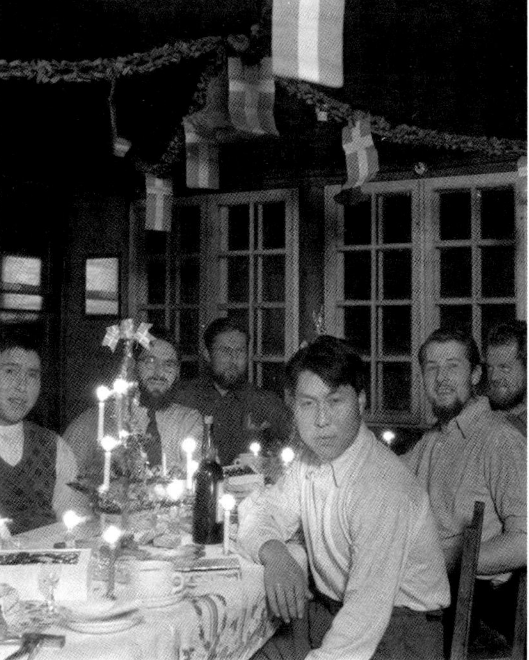

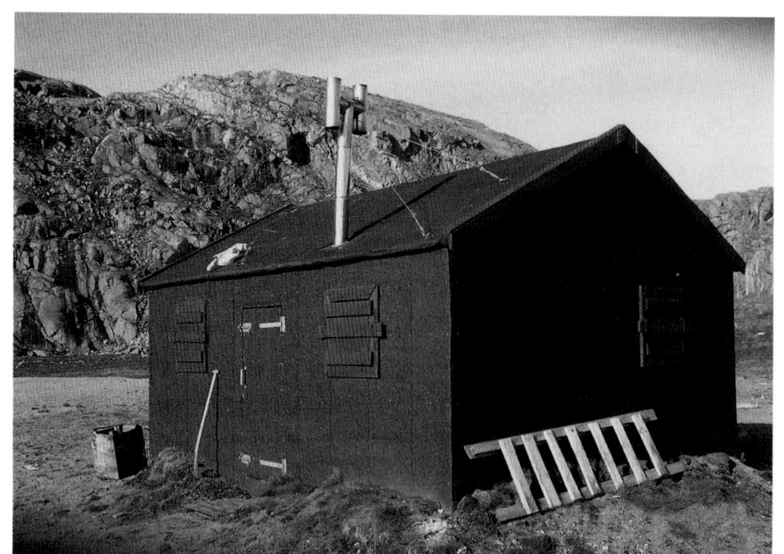

Eskimonæs [405] was a Danish scientific station built in 1931 for the Three-Year Expedition. It was used as an overwintering station until 23rd March 1943, when Eskimonæs was attacked by a German task force, which destroyed the station. The present hut at Eskimonæs was left undamaged, but by comparison between old and new photographs was moved to its present location after the war. (Top, Centre left, Bottom) 11th August 2003. © NCN (Centre right) 28th July 1989. © Peter Schmidt Mikkelsen

HANSA BUGT
[457]

Wintering party

1942-43: Hermann Ritter (leader), Heinz Hardt, Hermann Henning, Heinz Hofmann, Karl Kaiser, Rudolf Kasper, Fritz Koch, Friedrich Littmann, Norman Müller, Otto Möller, Günter Nawroth, Wenzel Novotny, Alfred Pretzsch, Hans Röttger, Helmut Scherer, Rudolf Sensse, Heribert Wenglorz, Gottfried Weiss.[804]

At the beginning of WWII Germany avoided activities close to the American continent that would appear threatening to the USA (the Monroe-doctrine). When the USA actively entered the war against the Axis Powers in December 1941, this policy became obsolete and the Germans began to activate their plans to establish a German manned weather station in North-East Greenland. The German Naval Weather Service (Marinewetterdienst) initially appointed Dr. Rupert Holzapfel as head of the project that was given the name "Operation Holzauge"; however, when Holzapfel became occupied with other tasks the duty was instead passed on to Captain Hermann Ritter, with Dr. Gottfried Weiss in charge of the scientific aspects. The plan was for the "Sachsen" WBS 1 (Wetterbeobachtungsschiff) - renamed as the "Hermann" - to carry personnel and equipment as far north as possible on the East Greenland coast, preferably to Kap Bismarck. On 10th July 1942, a 15 hour reconnaissance flight was undertaken from Trondheim in Norway over the area between Kong Oscar Fjord and Bessel Fjord by a Focke-Wulf Fw 200 Condor; its task was especially to check for any activities around the stations of Ella Ø, Myggbukta and Eskimonæs.

On the 13th August 1942, the "Sachsen" left Kiel and via Tromsø reached the pack ice at the latitude of Shannon on 25th August. Compact masses of ice to the north forced the Germans to sail to Hansa Bugt on Sabine Ø, where "Sachsen" was anchored. On 30th August, weather observations began and weather balloons were sent up; weather reports were transmitted daily to Tromsø via a German radio station on Svalbard.

During the autumn, two houses, "Alte Hütte" and "Neue Hütte" [457], both measuring about 4 x 5 m were built in the innermost part of Hansa Bugt. Ten men - meteorologists and engineers - remained aboard the ship while the other eight men settled in Alte Hütte that was located about 100 m inland. The houses had double wooden walls covered with canvas and roofing felt, and were supplied with electricity from "Sachsen". There was also a telephone line between the shore and the ship. Fearing the ship would be an easy target if spotted from the air, the meteorologists on the ship moved ashore in February 1943 to Neue Hütte - which was built behind a small hill about 200 metres inland.

During the winter of 1942-43, the Germans undertook various scientific explorations and it was a peaceful time without any dramatic situations. Any spare time was spent by the men hunting locally, and little by little it became common that a couple of men would stay for short periods at Germaniahavn, the old Danish trappers' station, to hunt polar bears. It was during such a "vacation", that the Germans peaceful daily routine was threatened.

For more than half a year, the Germans had remained unseen on Sabine Ø, but on 11th March 1943 Hermann Ritter ordered his men to an immediate assembly, dressed for departure. The reason was that two Germans has just returned from Germaniahavn with the message that their presence had been discovered by three sledge drivers approaching from the ice. This may have been an enemy patrol, but the two hunters explained that they had been unable to make themselves shoot the people. Instead they had tried to escape unseen, but in vain. From a strictly military point of view their conduct was extremely reprehensible, but according to Arctic ethics quite understandable. On the other hand, there would be catastrophic consequenses if the three sledge drivers were allowed to report their observations.

Ritter immediately ordered a pursuit and the Germans almost succeeded in capturing the three sledge drivers - Marius Jensen, Mikael Kunak and William Arke - who were on their way to Eskimonæs. Strangely enough the three patrol members had chosen to stay overnight at the Liavåg-hytten at Kap Wynn, only eight km south of Germaniahavn. However, warned by their dogs they escaped under shelter of darkness abandoning everything, even their dogs. The Germans gave up their pursuit and returned to Hansa Bugt with the captured sledges and dogs. From the diaries left at the Liavåg-hytten by the patrol men, the Germans gained a good knowledge of the sledge patrol and its whereabouts. A report on the situation was transmitted to Germany, from where they were given the order: *"Attack and destroy Eskimonæs"*.

The attack took place late in the evening of 23rd

March 1943. After some shooting Ritter and his five men – Weiss, Sensse, Nawroth, Littmann and Novotny – captured the station, while the members of the sledge patrol fled. Ritter then had Eskimonæs destroyed. On his way back to Hansa Bugt, the Danish patrol member Eli Knudsen was killed at Sandodden (see Sandodden section). At the same place two other patrol members, Marius Jensen and Peter Nielsen, were captured and taken to Germaniahavn. The killing of Knudsen affected Hermann Ritter so much that at Germaniahavn he gave Peter Nielsen five dogs and a well-equipped sledge so that Nielsen could drive back to Sandodden and bury Eli Knudsen. The Germans did not really expect to see Nielsen again, and they didn't. Later on, Ritter decided to go on a long sledge journey with his prisoner Marius Jensen. Along the way, they exchanged roles, and Marius Jensen with Hermann Ritter as his prisoner undertook the long journey to Scoresbysund, where Ritter surrendered to the Danish authorities.

After Ritter's disappearance, the command at Hansa Bugt was taken over by Gottfried Weiss, who with a force of four men made a sledge journey to Ella Ø in the beginning of April. On 25th April they reached the deserted station and stayed there for a week. It may seem strange that Weiss did not take the opportunity to destroy the Ella Ø station, but this may indicate that the trip was made more for pleasure than as a hostile act. After a leisurely return journey, Weiss's group arrived at Sabine Ø on 13th May, the same day that American air aircraft commanded by Bernt Balchen bombed Eskimonæs.

On 25th May, Balchen led another air raid. This time the target was the German base at Hansa Bugt. Two B-17 "Flying Fortress" and two B-24 "Liberator" bombers participated and from a high altitude dropped a total of 16 bombs, without doing much damage. Afterwards they made low-pass attacks and raked the area with machinegun fire. During the two-hour long attack, the Alte Hütte was burnt down completely, but without major damage elsewhere and without hitting "Sachsen". Although the radio station at Alte Hütte was destroyed, the Germans had been prepared for such an eventuality and had an alternative transmitter and survival depots placed around in the area.

There were no further air raids, but the Germans decided to to give up their plans for another wintering at the location. On 7th June 1943, evacuation began when a large Dornier Do 26 seaplane landed in an opening in the ice. The last Germans were picked up on 17th June. Prior to departure all installations were destroyed or burnt, and the first engineer sank "Sachsen" by opening the seacocks.

The Germans had no casualties, but apart from Hermann Ritter another man, Dr. Rudolf Sensse, was left behind. At some point Sensse had left Hansa Bugt for unknown reasons in order to go south by dog sledge. He did not return in time for the evacuation, and was found by an American commando force from the USCG Cutter "Northland" that stormed the abandoned German base on 21st July 1943. Both Sensse and Ritter became American prisoners of war.

Balchen et al. 1947; Balchen 1958; Nusser 1979; Selinger 1991; Thomas 1951; Weiss 1949; Franz Selinger pers. comm.; Leif Vanggaard pers. comm.

Recent status

Various remains of the German wintering on Sabine Ø are still present around the burnt down Hansa Bugt station and in the surrounding terrain.

The ruin of "Alte Hütte at Hansa Bugt, 23rd July 2004. © NCN

Hansa Bugt [457], 23rd July 2004. Hansa Bugt was a German meteorological station built in autumn 1942 for the German Naval Weather Service. It was used as a wintering station until 25th May 1943, when it was attacked by American air forces that destroyed the "Alte Hütte". The remaining buildings were destroyed later in 1943 by other American military forces. (Top and Centre) The location of "Alte Hütte". (Bottom) Location of "Neue Hütte". © NCN

KAP SUSSI
[520]

Wintering party

1943-44: Heinrich Schatz (leader), Hermann Ackermann, Hugo Busch, Heinz Carlsen, Erich Helms, Hermann Helms, Wilhelm Kleffmann, Martin Klein, Kurt Koos, Walter Machulla, Helmuth Marks, Eugen Müller, Franz Mushalek, Kurt Pritsch, Max Richter, Robert Riedl, Johann Rodebrügger, Heinrich Schmidt, Friedrich Schewe, Karl Schweitzer, Rudolf Stephan, Richard Sternberg, Alfons Stickling, Hans-Georg Sturm, Günter Triloff, Gerhard Zacher, Johann Zima

Due to the evacuation of the Hansa Bugt station, following its bombing by American forces, the chief of the German Naval Weather Service decided that a new, manned weather station should be established in North-East Greenland. Dr. Heinrich Schatz was appointed leader of this operation that received the code name "Bassgeiger". Lieutenant Gerhard Zacher was to be in charge of the military operations in the event of acts of war.

The expedition left Rostock on 14th August 1943 with the "Coburg" (WBS 2). Johann Rodebrügger was master of the ship and the plan was to land a wintering crew as far north as possible in East Greenland. On 31st August they reached the limit of the pack ice at 76°51'N and 2°50'W. "Coburg" immediately became stuck in the ice and attempts to blast the way to the shore were unsuccessful. When the "Coburg" eventually reached a distance of 20 nautical miles from the coast, it began to drift south in the pack ice. They therefore prepared themselves to function as a floating weather station during the winter, but on 2nd October they reached unbroken ice about 12 km east of Kap Sussi on Shannon. The drift of "Coburg" stopped here, and the Germans began their synoptic weather service from a hut called "Eislager" (ice camp) built on the sea ice about three km from the ship on the landward side.

On 18th November, a severe storm blew up and "Coburg" collided with an iceberg and developed a list of 31 degrees. At the same time much of the weather service equipment was destroyed, and the planned radiosonde launches had to be abandoned.

After the collision, twelve men moved from the ship to the "Eislager" station. As a result of the damage to the ship a "snow cave station" was excavated in a large snowdrift onshore at Kap Sussi on 23rd November. On 4th January the snow cave station was ready, with radio equipment etc. installed, and 11 men settled there.

A foehn storm in the middle of January made "Eislager" unusable, and the party split up with 13 men in the snow cave station and 14 on board the ship. The wireless operators moved their radio equipment from the remains of "Eislager" to a "Funkhütte" (radio hut) built on shore.

The North-East Greenland Sledge Patrol had discovered the German activity at Kap Sussi in November 1943, and on 22nd April 1944 at 11 o'clock precisely, six men attacked the snow cave station. However, the attack force was spotted by lieutenant Zacher and thus lost the element of surprise. Zacher was killed during a brief exchange of fire and the Danes withdrew. Apart from a short engagement near Alabamahuset the Germans and the sledge patrol had no further encounters. Zacher was buried at Kap Sussi.

Oberkommando der Kriegsmarine (The High Command of the German Navy) decided to evacuate the Bassgeiger Expedition and on 3rd June 1944, a Junkers Ju 290 landed on the sea ice south of Alabamahuset. The Germans blew up "Coburg" that was in a sinking condition anyway, and destroyed the snow cave station. The plane evacuated the 26 men to Trondheim. In the period between 13th September 1943 and 3rd June 1944 the expedition had transmitted 619 weather reports.

Some time in the summer of 1944, an American commando force from the "Northland" went ashore at Kap Sussi. Niels Ove Jensen wrote: *"The nest was empty of course, but it was noted that the station had been left in a hurry from the fact that leftovers from a meal were still on a laid table and that machineguns, radio material and other items were found undamaged. The station consisted of a hut of about 3 x 5 metres, and some snow caves in the snow drift around the station." ... "In their haste the most valuable things were taken with them and the rest were burnt".*[805]

Nusser 1979; Olsen 1965; Schatz 1951; Selinger 1991; Thomas 1951; Franz Selinger pers. comm.

Recent status

Various remains from the German wintering are still present at Kap Sussi and in the surrounding terrain. A new white-painted cross has been set up by the Sirius Dog Sledge Patrol on Gerhard Zacher's grave.

Kap Sussi [520], 2nd August 2004. Kap Sussi was a German meteorological station built in 1943 for the German Naval Weather Service. The site was used as a base station until 3rd June 1944, when the German personnel were evacuated by air. (Top) Site of "Funkhütte" (radio hut). (Centre left) The grave of Gerhard Zacher. (Centre right) Various remains spread over the area at Kap Sussi. (Bottom) An observation post at Kap Sussi. © NCN

KULHUS
[511]

Wintering party
1932-33: P. Halfdaner, Alwin Pedersen, A.B.C. Madsen, Arne C.F. Schwarck
1933-34: None
1934-35: Finn Kristoffersen, Henry V. Nielsen, Povel Povelsen

In May 1908, Hakon Høeg Jarner, the geologist of the Danmark Expedition, discovered a deposit of coal on the east side of Peters Bugt on Hochstetter Forland. The place was named "Jarners Kulmine" (Jarner's coal mine). Later on the good "Hochstetter coal" was burnt in many stoves at huts and stations on the coast, and was used in larger quantities by several expedition vessels.

The presence of the coal was also the main reason that Lauge Koch decided to build one of his expedition houses at this place: *"In 1932 the station Kulhus was erected on Hochstetter Forland. It was built there, because the surface of the ground was strewn with coal fragments, so sufficient coal to heat the house could be picked up in the immediate neighbourhood of the station".*[806]

"Seen from the house end the house is triangular with an attached sleeping annex towards the east. The sleeping annex is divided into five small rooms. Furthermore, there is a large living room, a hallway, a kitchen and a utility room. Behind the house there is a large square provisions house. In the rock exposures around the bay the coal layers are clearly visible. Further south, along the 250 m high mountain "Negeren" the coal layere are even more distinct".[807]

Originally Kulhus was intended to be a travellers' station, but during the winter of 1932-33 four members of the Three-Year Expedition wintered here. They were the geodesists A.B.C. Madsen and P. Halfdaner together with the zoologist Alwin Pedersen and the archaeologist and former trapper, Arne C.F. Schwarck.

Ornithologist Charles G. Bird at Kulhus in 1938. © Niels Ove Jensen

Kulhus was also used for wintering in 1934-35, when Hvalrosodden did not get any supplies in the summer of 1934. The trappers Finn Kristoffersen, Povel Povelsen and Henry V. Nielsen, who were supposed to have returned to Denmark refused to stay at Hvalrosodden without a contract or provisions. As soon as the ice was safe they therefore went south to Hochstetter: *"and we continued the journey to the nearby station Kulhus, one of Dr. Lauge Koch's stations which he kindly had placed at our disposal".*[808] The three men moved to Eskimonæs later in the winter.
Amdrup et al. 1913; Koch 1955; Nyholm-Poulsen 1985.

Recent status
Despite the excellent location close to supplies of coal, Kulhus was seldom used after the 1930s, and already in the 1970s the house was reported as in poor condition. Inside the house is damp everywhere.

Kulhus, 1938. © Niels Ove Jensen

Kulhus [511], 30th July 2004. Kulhus is a former Danish travellers' station built in 1932 for the Three-Year Expedition. It was used for overwintering in 1932-33 and 1934-35. It was occasionally used as a travellers' hut until the 1950s og 1960s, when it was abandoned. © NCN

MESTERSVIG
[207] [209-1] [209-2]

Wintering party
The mine:
1951-52: 4 employees
1952-63: About 50 employees in the winter and 150 in the summer

Mestersvig Airfield:
1952-85: About 10 employees per year
1985- : 2 employees per year

In the summer of 1948, geologists of Lauge Koch's expeditions discovered lead-zinc bearing quartz veins in the region west of Mesters Vig. The next three years were spent on a comprehensive and systematic survey of the entire area. The practical work was led by the engineer Carl Koch, the son of Lauge Koch, and prospecting teams and mining specialists were brought in, notably from Sweden. From 20 men in 1948, the work force increased to 50 in 1951.

In 1949, "Ekspeditionshuset" [206-1] was built in the south-west corner of Mesters Vig to support the prospecting teams. In 1950 the exploration headquarters were moved to Blyklippen where the richest occurrences of ore had been located. Living quarters, canteen huts and storage facilities were built here. In 1951, about 35 tons of ore were sailed to Europe to establish the grade of the deposit, and four men wintered in order to carry out observations of water occurrences, snow- and ice conditions, with respect to any future exploitation of the deposits.

NORTHERN MINING COMPANY LTD.

In the spring of 1951, the framework of the Northern Mining Company was outlined through a co-operation between the permanent secretary Eske Brun and the managing director of Kampsax, Per Kampmann. A so-called "lead committee" was established comprising four prominent Danish top executives who through the Department of Greenland encouraged Per Kampmann to draw up a recommendation for further exploration and exploitation of the ore deposits. The recommendation, that was ready in the autumn of 1951, proposed establishment of a private company that on the basis of a concession from the government would take over the project. The terms of the concession led to formation in 1952 of Nordisk Mineselskab A/S (Northern Mining Company Ltd), usually known as "Nordmine", with a share capital of 15 million kroner. The Danish government held 27.5% of the shares and a number of major Danish companies another 27.5%. The remaining 45% were owned by two Swedish and a Canadian mining company with 15% each. The company was granted a concession in East Greenland between 70°N and 74°30'N, corresponding to the region between Scoresbysund and Daneborg, for a period of 50 years. Per Kampmann became the chairman of the board of directors.

In the summer of 1952, a mining camp, "Minebyen" [207] was built in Blydal adjacent to Blyklippen with permanent accommodation for 100 persons. Aksel Mikkelsen, a son of the famous polar explorer Ejnar Mikkelsen, was in charge of the construction work.

By 1954, a resource of about 560,000 tons of mineable ore had been proven, and Nordmine decided to start the actual mining. Minebyen was expanded, and on the coast of Kong Oscar Fjord at "Nyhavn" [209-2], about 12 km north of the mine, an open-air site for storing the lead-zinc concentrate on pallets was established. The first consignment of lead-zinc concentrate was shipped out in 1956. Mining continued for the following five years, with about 50 employees at Minebyen in the winter and 150 in the summer.

Lauge Koch's geologists had reported molybdenum mineralisation in 1954 at a locality known as Malmbjerg. Diamond drilling was carried out in 1959-60, and a small mining camp "Malmbjerg" [118] was erected on an adjacent moraine. Unfortunately, the grade of the ore was too low, and it was not profitable to start mining given the molybdenum price of the time.

In 1961, about 534,000 tons of lead-zinc ore had been mined at Blyklippen, but lead prices had then hit rock bottom and as no additional profitable ore had been located, mining operations closed down on 21st August 1961. Minebyen was, however, still manned until August 1963.

Nordmine subsequently undertook extensive investigations in their concession area in North-East Greenland. In 1983-84 negotiations with the Atlantic Richfield Oil Company (ARCO) to explore for and exploit oil and gas in the Jameson Land basin led to granting of an exclusive concession. At the same time the original Nordisk Mineselskab concession rights were relinquished, and replaced by six exclusive mineral concessions and one concession for hydrocarbons. However, these concessions lapsed when Nordisk Mineselskab closed down in 1990. The mining camp area at Blyklippen was cleared during the 1970s and the 1980s. Some of the houses were moved to Nyhavn, and today only two of original buildings remain at the site.

MESTERSVIG AIRFIELD

Part of the concession agreement to undertake mining at Mesters Vig was that the Danish government would establish an airfield, and according to the law of "Nordisk Mineselskab A/S" (law no. 431) the Ministry of Public Works was authorized to build the airfield. The law was dated 17th December 1952, but by then the construction work had long been completed.
In the summer of 1952, at the same time as Minebyen was expanded, the construction company Monberg and Thorsen Ltd. built the airfield at the expense of the Danish Civil Aviation Administration (Statens Luftfartsvæsen). The work began on 30th July and ended on 22nd September 1952 when the ground froze up. The same day "Mestersvig Airfield" [209-1] was taken over by the Danish Civil Aviation Administration.

The airfield was used for the first time on the 8th September 1952, when an Icelandic Catalina airplane - "TF-ISK" flown by Captain Johannes Snorrason - landed on its own initiative. The formal opening did not take place until 26th September 1952, when a SAS DC-4, "Sigtrygg Viking", arrived with the vice president of the Department of Aviation and his guests.

At first conditions at the airfield were spartan. The only buildings were a combined radio station / power plant, a living quarters, a garage / provisions house and accommodation for summer guests at "Grand". Drinking water was obtained by melting ice, heating came from paraffin stoves and the toilet facilities were an unheated privy. The personnel included an air traffic controller, a radio operator, a meteorologist and a cook's assistant. For snow clearing and maintenance work it was planned to hire equipment and manpower from the mine and to use other facilities at the mine, such as baths, laundry etc.

It soon became necessary to increase both manning and facilities at the airfield. Machinery for snow clearing was acquired. Further living quarters, "Olympos", and a workshop were built in 1954. The workshop was expanded in 1955, burnt down in 1961, and was rebuilt in 1962. Additional living quarters, "Millionæren" and "Hilton", were built in 1958, partly to house the crew of the Catalina aircraft that the Danish Air Force stationed at the airfield every summer until the late 1960s.

Although Nordmine reduced its activities at the beginning of the 1960s, it was decided to maintain the airfield that therefore had to become completely self-sufficient. In 1963, a garage / laundry and a new living quarters, "Blåtårn", were built, central heating was added to the buildings and new toilets with water flushing were introduced.

In 1965, another living quarters, "Rødull", and a canteen building "Valhal" were built. In the following years storage buildings and a separate power plant were erected. In 1977 construction of a control tower was commenced, as the existing radio building lacked a clear view of the runway and apron; this provided space for a post office and an office for the Greenlandair representative. The control tower was the last major construction work on the airfield, and with the appropriate name "Luftkastellet" (castle in the air) was taken into use in April 1979.

Mestersvig was for many years the most important gateway into North-East Greenland. The staff numbered 10 persons. The nature of the air traffic gradually changed, from flights when needed and transport for passengers to Scoresbysund by dog-sledge, to more regular air traffic. At first Mestersvig was mainly served by Icelandic planes, such as the DC-3, that when mounted with skis could also could land on the sea ice at Scoresbysund in the winter. In the summers smaller aircraft would transport transit passengers from Mestersvig to an airstrip in Jættedal west of Scoresbysund. In 1974 Greenlandair began more regular flights to Mestersvig. In the summer there was a scheduled weekly flight and a helicopter was stationed at Mestersvig. Originally it was the Ministry of Public Works that covered the running costs of the operation, but public cut-backs led to a new agreement, with the Ministry of Greenland paying 5/9, the Ministry of Defence 3/9 and the Ministry of Public Works 1/9. It was the Ministry of Public Works that took care of maintenance and operations until 1st January 1985, when the airfield was transferred to the Ministry of Greenland.

While the individual buildings at Mestersvig, Nyhavn and Minebyen are not described in detail in this volume, a number of huts and stations are included. Nordmine built the following: "Sorte Hjørne" [203] in 1952, "Lomsøhytten" [113] in 1957, "Jakobsbo" [202] in 1960 and "Stresshytten" [106] in 1976. Personnel from Mestersvig Airfield have built "Skida" [211] in 1965, "Bådhytten" [217] in 1968, "Vælddalhytten" [214] in 1970, "Nyt Ekspeditionshus" [206-2] in 1974-75, "Sporvognen" [221] in 1976 and "Kokkens Lyst" [103] in 1977.

Astlund et al. 1957; Brinch; Fischer et al. 1958; Blyklippen ... 2005; Kampmann 1953; Lassen 2005; Tusaat 1992; Finn Kløve Lassen pers. comm.; Aksel Mikkelsen pers. comm.

Recent status

On 15th October 1985 Mestersvig Airfield was officially closed, and air traffic was transferred to the Constable Pynt airfield north of Scoresbysund. However, there was a broad desire to keep Mestersvig open to serve scientific exploration activity by state organisations and private scientific and sports expeditions. Up to 1988 two men were employed by Råstofudvalget, and responsibity then passed to another two man party from "Forsvarets Vagt Mestersvig" (Defence Guard Mestersvig), reporting to "Patruljetjenesten Nord- og Nordøstgrønland" (The North- and North-East Greenland Patrol Service). The men employed were usually former members of the Sirius patrol.

From 1997 to 2003, Danish Polar Center (DPC) operated a logistics platform service in Mestersvig. each summer, again drawing on former members of the Sirius patrol. Their task was to handle the increasing numbers of civil passengers using Mestersvig in summertime. In 2004, the logistics platform service was moved to Constable Pynt.

About 2000, the Danish military announced their desire to leave Mestersvig, but a new ownership has yet to be established, and the full time guard is still (2007) provided by Forsvarets Vagt Mestersvig.

In 2005, a new Danish logistics service company entered the scene in North-East Greenland, when the Polar Logistics Group (POLOG) was founded by former members of the Sirius Dog Sledge Patrol. In 2005 POLOG was responsible for a large-scale air transportation task in connection with new field investigations of the molybdenum deposit at Malmbjerg. About 40 flights (carrying 400 tons of equipment) were made between Iceland and Mestersvig with a chartered Ukrainian AN-12 (Cub) heavy aircraft.

Mestersvig has three main locations:

1) Minebyen [207], a Danish mine built in 1950 to exploit lead-zinc ore deposits. Minebyen was closed in 1963.

2) Mestersvig Airfield [209-1], a Danish airfield built in 1952 for Statens Luftfartsvæsen. The airfield was officially closed in 1985.

3) Nyhavn [209-2], a harbour facility established in 1954 to export lead-zinc ore concentrates from the mine.

(Above) The airport terminal at Mestersvig Airfield, August 2006. (Opposite top) Mestersvig Airfield, August 2006. (Opposite centre) Minebyen, August 2006. (Opposite bottom) Nyhavn, August 2006. © NCN

MØRKEFJORD
[641]

Wintering party

1938-39: Eigil Knuth (L/A), Kurt H. Bæk (T), Paul Gelting (B), Eli Kristiansen (D), Eigil Nielsen (G), Svend Sølver (G), Ove Rossbach (D), Zackæus Sandgreen (D)

1939-40: Andreas Hvidberg (L), Niels Haarløv (Z), Kristian Madsen (T), Carlos Ziebell (H)

1940-41: Andreas Hvidberg (L), Kristian Madsen (T), Kurt Olsen (T), Ib Poulsen (T), Carlos Ziebell (H)

(L) = leader, (T) = telegraphist, (G) = geologist, (Z) = zoologist, (B) = botanist, (A) = archaeologist, (D) = sledge driver, (H) = handyman/assistant

"A snow ball rolls down the slope, growing bigger and bigger; this is how an expedition is born, and so did ours. In 1935, as participants in August(ine) *Courtauld's British expedition to East Greenland on board the "Quest", Ebbe Munck and I discussed whether the situation was ripe for our generation to make an effort in the Danish exploration of Greenland".*[809] These words were written by the polar explorer Eigil Knuth in his preface to "Under det nordligste Dannebrog" (1940), a book about the Danish North-East Greenland Expedition of 1938-39, known as the Mørkefjord expedition. *"First of all it was important to ensure the initiative of Danish science in areas where we could look back on its proud traditions. The object had to be something real. After consulting leaders within different branches of science, our attention was drawn to the large region of North-East Greenland between 76° and 82°N, the old activity field of the Danmark Expedition. Since the days of Mylius-Erichsen and his men it had been largely untouched, and there was still much research to do".*[810]

Throughout his life the multi-talented Eigil Knuth had proved that he could put action behind his words. The "grand old man" in Danish arctic research lived an adventurous life, and on the 8th August 1993 when he was once again on a summer expedition to North-East Greenland he celebrated his 90th birthday. Eigil Knuth died in March 1996, 92-years old.

In the summer of 1938, the Mørkefjord Expedition sailed to North-East Greenland aboard the "Gamma": *"Before the "Gamma" left us on August 22nd it was decided to call our new station "Mørkefjord"; this seemed to us a good name with a phonetic sound – three distinct, equally stressed syllables, easily understandable over the wireless. Alwin Pedersen built his own house on Hvalrosodden near the "Nanok" hunting station, and we, the eight other members of the wintering party, began to build and lay out the Mørkefjord-station near Gravelven".*[811]

The house was prefabricated in Denmark and measured about 8 x 7 m with side sheds in addition. A provisions shed 2.5 x 4 m was also built. The station was equipped with a generator and radio equipment and had the call sign: OYY. During the winter of 1938-39, three sledge teams (Sølver, Knuth and Nielsen) carried out exploration journeys as far north as Kap Prins Knud (81°50'N). Furthermore, the expedition worked together with the Norwegian-French Polar Expedition based at Micardbu with

Mørkefjord, 18th August 1939. © Knud Bavngaard

Mørkefjord, visited by the author as a member of the Sirius patrol, 29th May 1978. © Peter Schmidt Mikkelsen

observations of the Northern Lights (aurora borealis).

In the spring of 1939, it was decided to continue the manning of Mørkefjord for another year. Eigil Knuth had plans to return with a new expedition in 1940-41, but the Meteorologisk Institut wanted the weather reports to continue without interruption. A new team was hired for 1939-40 while Knuth and the old wintering party went home. However, the scientific research party due to come up in 1940-41 was prevented by the German occupation of Denmark. Niels Haarløv left Mørkefjord, while the rest of the party remained for another winter. In November 1940, the team was expanded with Ib Poulsen and Kurt Olsen, who had arrived in Greenland in the summer with "Veslekari": *"because we had promised the previous party that it would be replaced, and because we still wanted to keep the station going in the hope of better times and a renewal of the expedition"*.[812]

In 1940-41, the party at Mørkefjord built two huts, which later received the names "Knuthsminde" [708] and "Kap Amélie hytten" [709-1]. In April 1941, Hvidberg, Ziebell, Madsen and Olsen left the station to go south. Ib Poulsen then had the company of Marius Jensen, who had also arrived with "Veslekari" but had wintered at Kap Herschell. The two men were evacuated by "Northland" in the summer of 1941, and the manning of the Mørkefjord station ended.
Andreassen 2003 pp. 143-180; Bæk 1943; Knuth 1995; Eigil Knuth pers. comm.; Allan Nielsen pers. comm.

Recent status

The Mørkefjord station has not been used since the war, and without any maintenance the station is today in a very poor condition. In 1981, personnel from Danmarkshavn converted the small provision shed into a travellers' hut.

Mørkefjord [641], 13th August 2005. © NCN

Mørkefjord [641], 13th August 2005. Mørkefjord is a former Danish scientific station built in 1938 for the Mørkefjord Expedition. It was used as a wintering station until the summer of 1941, when the station personnel were evacuated by US Coast Guard forces. © NCN

PUSTERVIG
[640]

Wintering party
1907-08: Peter Freuchen

When and where did the "automobile" make its entrance in Greenland? Answer: In 1907 on the route from Danmark Havn to Pustervig. The Danmark expedition had brought along a: *"motor vehicle with accessories"* - modified from an American Waltham Orient. On several occasions serious attempts to use the vehicle as a means of transportation had been made, but the rough terrain, the snow and the cold were overwhelming obstacles. The automobile was therefore degraded to a "steam winch", and only used for hauling down weather balloons and kites; however, at the end of September 1907 an opportunity for yet another bold experiment arose.

Alfred Wegener, the meteorologist and geophysicist of the expedition wanted to establish a manned meteorological observatory near the Inland Ice to enable comparisons with those at Danmark Havn, and thus obtain a better knowledge of local weather conditions. Wegener had already selected the head of Mørkefjord as a suitable location for the observatory.

At the end of August an attempt to transport the materials to the destination by boat was prevented by the fjord ice. As a consequence, the materials were temporarily stored at Snenæs. For the automobile this was the last chance to prove its worth as a vehicle: *"It had been so impossible that only a disaster could save it from laughter"*, Achton Friis wrote. *"Thanks to Weinschenck's skilled hands the automobile was chosen to transport two men and a load to "Pustervig". The sea ice was smooth and good when they started, and to our undivided admiration and amazement we watched it disappear with its cargo in an elegant curve around Havnenæsset"*.[813]

Eventually they got there, not to the head of Mørkefjord for the water was still open there, but to Pustervig where they unloaded the materials and started to build the house. A couple of days later Weinschenck was going to drive back; but it started snowing heavily, and at Snenæs the automobile became hopelessly stuck in a snow drift. Weinschenck had to walk the rest of the way to Danmark Havn. At the end of November, a party went out to fetch the automobile, but it had already gone through the ice and could not be saved.

In the meantime the Pustervig station had become operational. It was manned by Wegener's assistant, Peter Freuchen, the almost two metre high adventurer from Nykøbing Falster: *"We were short of wood, so the house had to be small. Even so it measured three times five metres inside when it was finished. But the space shrunk when the winter and cold set in. A thick layer of ice covered the walls and floor, because moisture from cooking and breathing in there immediately froze. At last the room had become so small that it became a regular wrestling match when two men tried to pass each other. Still, it was cosy in Pustervig, as the place was called"*.[814] Freuchen lived most of the time alone in Pustervig until the end of April 1908. The name Pustervig derives from an alley with the same name in Copenhagen.

The Pustervig house ended up as firewood. The reason was that the trappers at Hvalrosodden did not have a visit from a supply ship in the summer of 1920, and the shortage of supplies became disastrous. Trapper Kristen Larsen wrote: *"We tore down a small house, standing in Pustervig from the days of the Danmark Expedition, and drove it back as firewood. It was a minor supplement to our supplies, but when the living room was to be heated by wood alone, it took a lot of wood"*.[815]

Only the stone walls now remained of the hut: *"at half their height and the ruin looked exactly like one of the old Norse ruins on the west coast of Greenland"*.[816]

Amdrup et al. 1913; Grønlandske Selskab 1983a; Meddelelser om Grønland, bd. 42 Nr. 6 p. 450-460.

Recent status
There are today only very few remains of the Pustervig station; all woodwork was removed in 1920, as mentioned above, and the abandoned stove is one of the few indications that someone once lived here.

The meteorological station at Pustervig, where Peter Freuchen spent the winter 1907-08. 18th August 1912. © Arctic Institute

Pustervig [640], 13th August 2005. Pustervig was a Danish meteorological station built in 1907 for the Danmark Expedition. It was used only in the winter of 1907-08, when Peter Freuchen, who was assistant to Alfred Wegener, stayed here, most of the time alone. There are today only very few remains of Pustervig, as all the woodwork was removed by trappers from the East Greenland Company in 1920 to be used as firewood at Hvalrosodden [639]. © NCN

ZACKENBERG ZERO
[438-5]

The Zackenberg ZERO station was established in 1995-96 and officially opened in 1997. The station is located about 25 km north-west of Daneborg, on the east side of the main Zackenberg river and about 2 km inland. The Zackenberg ZERO station has its own runway where helicopters and STOL aircraft like Twin Otters can land. The station can house up to 25 persons. It is designed for year-round use, but is usually staffed for about 100 days from late May to early September. In addition to research projects, an extensive environmental monitoring programme is operated from Zackenberg. The station is owned by the Greenland Home Rule authorities.

Originally the Zackenberg ZERO station had five houses, and the scientists were accommodated in sturdy, heated 'Weatherhaven' shelters. In 2006, new accommodation houses were erected, financed by the Danish Aage V. Jensen Charity Foundation. Today the station comprises nine buildings, including a wet laboratory, dry laboratory, computer room, kitchen, mess, seminar room, toilets, showers, communication room, office, food storage room and workshop.

Zackenberg Station has a diverse long-term monitoring programme, Zackenberg Basic that consists of four elements:

1) ClimateBasis: monitoring climate and river water discharge;
2) BioBasis: monitoring the dynamics of selected biotic ecosystem parameters;
3) GeoBasis: monitoring the dynamics of the abiotic environment that is not covered by ClimateBasis;
4) MarineBasis: monitoring the dynamics of selected parameters in the marine environment.

The permanent monitoring is designed to provide a long-period series of background ecosystem data from a high arctic area. Data from the monitoring programme can be used free of charge by scientists working at Zackenberg. More than 350 individual parameters are measured by Zackenberg Basic.
www.dpc.dk/sw5397.asp

Zackenberg-basen [438-3] in 1956. The old Zackenberg base, situated on the west side of the Zackenberg river, was used as a base station by the Danish Peary Land Expedition 1947-50 and the British North Greenland Expedition 1952-54. The adjacent bay was the starting point for airlifts to Peary Land and Dronning Louise Land using seaplanes. © Jørgen Rasmussen

*ZERO, 9th July 2007.
The Zackenberg ZERO station was established in 1995-96 and officially opened in 1997. The station can house up to 25 persons. Designed for year-round use, it is usually staffed only for about 100 days from late May to early September. In addition to research projects, an extensive environmental monitoring programme is operated at Zackenberg. © NCN*

REGISTER OF STATIONS, HOUSES & HUTS

This register provides a description of 376 buildings at 322 locations in North-East Greenland, including 59 stations and houses used for overwintering (category IA - IB), 295 stations, houses and huts not used for overwintering (category IIA), 17 material sites (category IIB) and 5 doubtful building locations (category IIC).

This English edition includes the following locations not found in the original Danish editions published in 1994 and 2001, that have been identified or erected subsequently: MELLEMHUSET [367-2], STORHOLTS HUS [414-2] ZACKENBERG ZERO [438-5], NY MØNSTEDHUS [532-4], NY STORE SNENÆS HYTTE [632-2], HERJAELV I [920], HERJAELV II [921], GULDMINEN [922] and NIFLHEIM [923].

Explanation of register:

Location number* / geographical position (latitudes & longitudes GPS) / region

PRIMARY NAME, alternative names
The primary name is often the original name, sometimes the name by which it is most commonly known.

■ Description	Nationality, type, date of erection, for whom, by whom, in which station territory.
■ Location	Description of location
■ Characteristics	Preservation List Code:** A: Protected B: Maintainable C: No maintenance D: Manned station Category (IA - IIC). Dimensions of building. Stove. Make or type is included in order to identify ruins of buildings. In some cases the original stove may have been changed later to another make.
■ History	Quotations, explanation of names, use, special conditions, etc.
■ Status	Latest known status of the hut. The description is usually illustrated by a photograph, recorded during the 2003-2007 Nanok site survey. Historical photos are included to illustrate the original or earlier states of the building, as well as to show recent changes or decay.

* in the entire register the number in brackets [ ] refers to the hut identified by this number.

** a Preservation List Code (PLC) describing the protection / preservation level of each building has been added in accordance with an agreement with the Greenland National Museum & Archive (GNA) in Nuuk.[817]

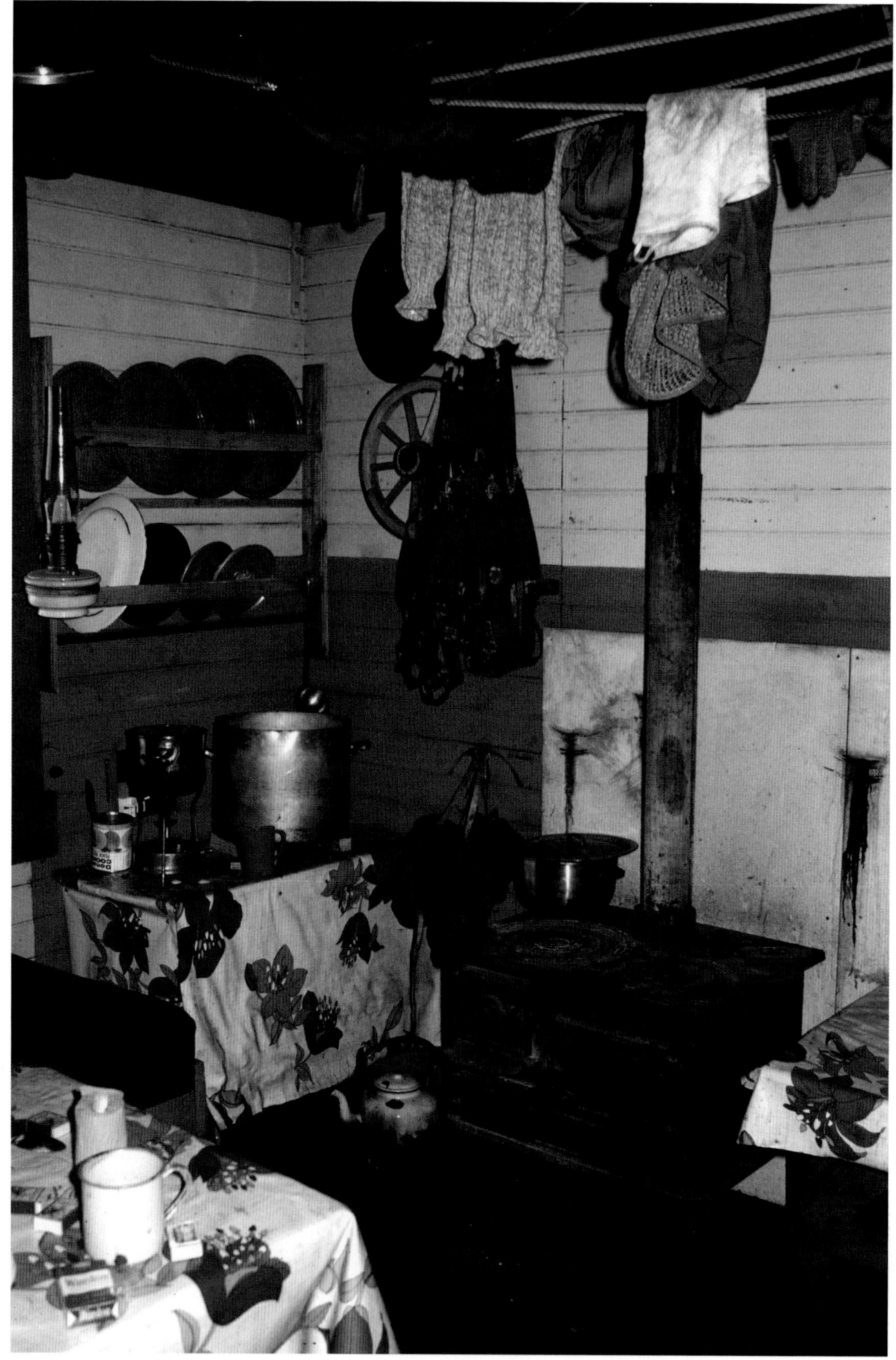

The living room at Hvalrosodden, 18th November 1977 © Peter Schmidt Mikkelsen

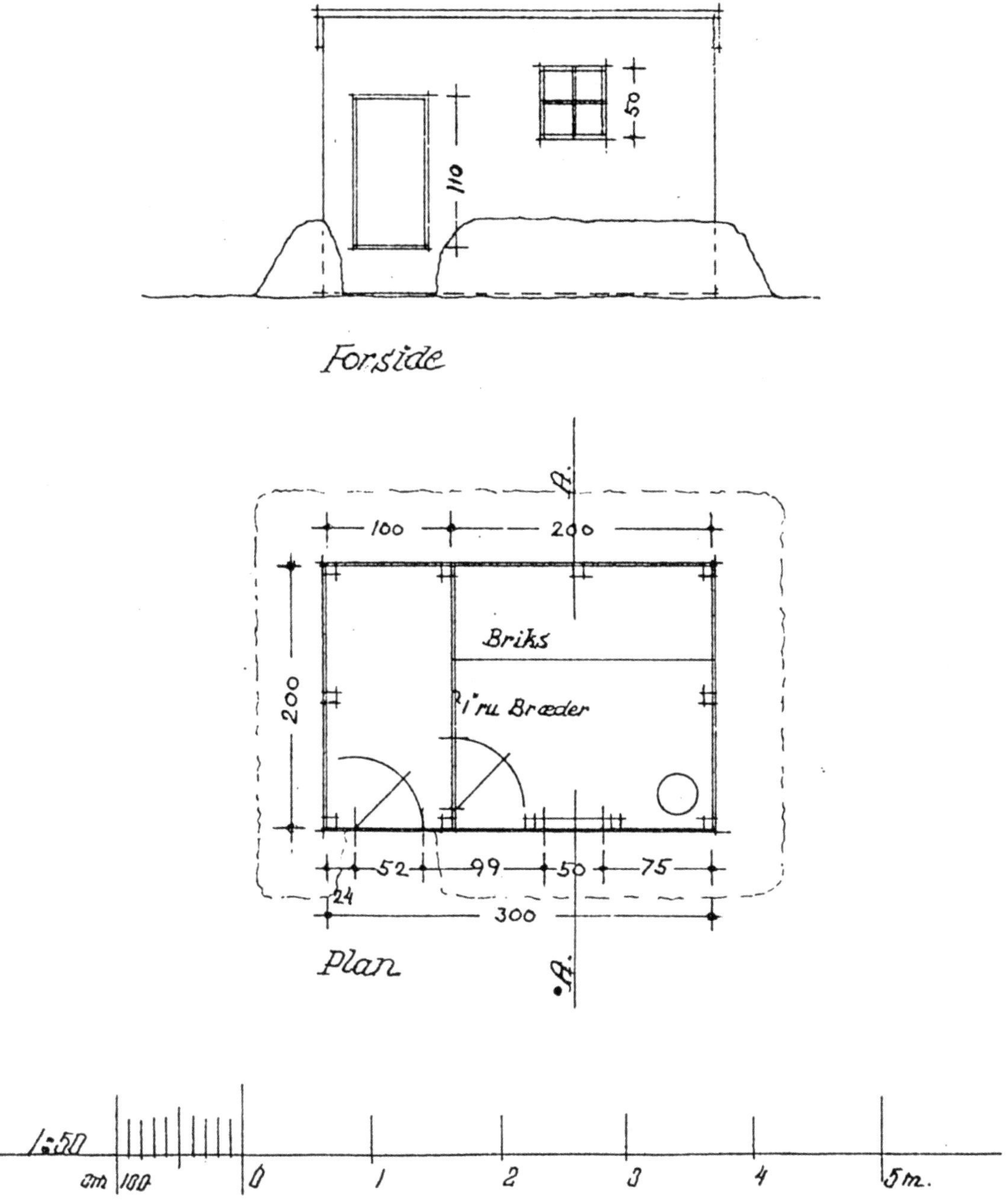

Typical trappers' hut. The Danish and Norwegian huts are almost identical as regards size and design. However, one distinct variant has a pointed roof with centre pitch, e.g. Smedal [320]. Huts of this type were only built up until the Second World War and are all of Norwegian origin – except the following three Danish huts: Henningelvhytten [416], Djævlekløfthytten [427] and Femdalhytten [524]. Forside = Front view, Briks = Bunk, Brædder = Boards.

Fleming Dal hytten [101], 12th August 2006. © NCN

101 / 71°33.05'N - 22°58.12'W / Scoresby Land[818]
FLEMING DAL HYTTEN, Pingel Dal hytten, Landhuset
■ Norwegian trappers' hut built in 1932-33 for the Helge Ingstad Expedition by Helge Ingstad and Normann Andersen, Antarctichavn.[819]
■ In Pingel Dal, on the north side of the entrance to Ærenprisdal, about 8 km south of the head of Fleming Fjord.
■ A (IIA). 210 x 130 cm plus porch 100 x 70 cm. Coal stove: Ulefos No. 158E. Floor: Wood.
■ Peder Sulebak referred to it as "Landhuset", when on the 7th February 1935 he: *"went across the area to a hut that was built by the Ingstad expedition".*[820] The hut is placed next to a large rock. It was used as late as 1955 by Otto Lapstun.[821]

102 / c. 71°34'N - 23°58'W / Scoresby Land
COLORADODAL HYTTEN
■ Danish travellers' hut built in July 1983 for the Grønlands Miljøundersøgelser (Greenland Environmental Research Institute).
■ At Qilerneq, where the rivers from Coloradodal and Major Paars Dal join in Ørsted Dal.
■ C (IIA). 450 x 220 including porch 100 x 200 cm.
■ The hut was built in connection with a muskox-marking project. The hut is made from orange fibre-glass panels that can be disassembled and moved in one load with e.g. a Bell 212 helicopter. Qilerneq is the Greenlandic word for: *"the place where something joins".*[822]

103 / 71°36.45'N - 22°36.33'W / Scoresby Land[823]
KOKKENS LYST
■ Danish travellers' hut built in the summer of 1977 for Mestersvig Airfield by Jan Juel-Brockdorff, Mestersvig.
■ On the tongue of land west of Nordenskiöld Bjerg at the head of Nathorst Fjord.
■ B (IIA). 245 x 245 cm. Coal stove: Morsø. Floor: Wood.
■ Kokkens Lyst (cook's desire) is made from an old porch taken from a caravan at Mestersvig Airfield. The hut was prefabricated at the airfield and transported to Nathorst Fjord using a GLACE helicopter. The hut was intended to be used as an emergency shelter for GLACE pilots, should there be technical problems during the helicopter flights between Mestersvig and Scoresbysund, and as an intermediate station for personnel at Mestersvig during their snowmobile trips to and from Scoresbysund. Juel-Brockdorff was cook at the Mestersvig Airfield for a number of years.[824]

Kokkens Lyst [103], 4th August 2004. © NCN

Siste-huset [104], 4th August 2004. © NCN

104 / 71°37.99'N - 22°23.73'W / Scoresby Land[825]
SISTE-HUSET, Bunn-huset
■ Norwegian trappers' hut built in August 1932 for the Helge Ingstad Expedition by Helge Ingstad and Normann Andersen, Antarctichavn.[826]
■ In Nathorst Fjord, on the west side of Canning Land, about 2 km north of Kollen.
■ C (IIA). Ruin. Originally about 200 x 200 cm.

■ On 3rd August 1932 materials were laid out with "Polarbjørn".[827] The hut was referred to by Peder Sulebak on 3rd May 1936, when during a trapping trip he came: *"to Siste-huset at the very end of the fjord"*.[828] However, trappers seldom visited Nathorst Fjord and apart from Sulebak only Nils Hanken has mentioned the hut.[829] Siste-huset (the last hut) was probably rarely used after the 1930s.
■ It is claimed that another hut, called "Fjord-eidet", was built at the location in 1931.[830] This is incorrect, as no hut was built at the location before 1932. The hut was a total ruin by the 1970s.[831]

Trapper Martin Larsen Lie at Ingstadheimen [105], August 1947. © Martin Larsen Lie

Ingstadheimen [105], 3rd August 2004. © NCN

105 / 71°37.82'N - 22°59.78'W / Scoresby Land[832]
INGSTADHEIMEN, Heimen, Bundhuset
■ Norwegian trappers' hut built in August 1932 for the Helge Ingstad Expedition by Helge Ingstad and Normann Andersen, Antarctichavn.
■ On the west side of Wegener Halvø at the south-east corner of Fleming Fjord.
■ C (IIA). 250 x 215 plus porch 175 x 165 cm. Coal stove: Ulefos No. 120. Floor: Wood/Earth.
■ Materials were laid out with "Polarbjørn" on 3rd August 1932.[833] Built as the main depot for Ingstad's and Andersen's journeys into the Scoresby Land territory. Ingstadheimen (Ingstad's home) is named after Helge Ingstad, who wrote that: *"here we were thinking of setting up our largest depot and of having a home to turn to on occasion when our bodies and souls should stand in need of overhauling after weeks of tent life in the open snow. We therefore named the place "Heimen" – "Home, Sweet Home" – and took particular pains with our work"*.[834]

Stresshytten [106], 3rd August 2004. © NCN

106 / 71°37.90'N - 22°59.54'W / Scoresby Land[835]
STRESSHYTTEN
■ Danish travellers' hut built in the summer of 1976 for Nordmine by Bjørn Thomassen and others, Mestersvig.
■ On the west side of Wegener Halvø a few hundred metres north of the south-east corner of Fleming Fjord.
■ B (IIA). 365 x 245 cm. Coal stove: L. Lange & Co, 1608M. Floor: Wood.
■ Materials were laid out with the "Ole Rømer" in the summer of 1976, when Nordmine was prospecting for copper. The hut was built of prefabricated sections delivered by "Stress Tagelementer" of Fårevejle.[836] Stresshytten is located just a few hundred metres north of "Ingstadheimen" [105].

107 / 71°43.19'N - 22°43.92'W / Scoresby Land[837]
KAP BROWN HUSET, Fleming Fjord huset, Vimmelskaftet
■ Danish travellers' house built late August 1931 for the Three-Year Expedition 1931-34 by Arne Noe-Nygaard, other members of the expedition, and the crew of "Gustav Holm".[838]
■ On the west side of Wegener Halvø, about 15 km south-west of Kap Brown.

Kap Brown huset [107] before and after the flood in 1953. Note how the house has turned anticlockwise almost 90 degrees. (Top) In the winter of 1936-37. © Arne Philbert. (Above) 3rd August 2004. © NCN. (Below) Kap Brown huset [107], 3rd August 2004. © NCN

■ C (IIA). A-type house. 570 x 575 including a living room 360 x 280 cm. No stove. Floor: Wood.

■ The smallest of the Three-Year Expedition characteristic A-type houses. In the 1930s primarily used as intermediate station for the dog sledge travels to and from Scoresbysund. In the summer of 1953 the house was lifted off the ground by a huge wave, which left it rotated by about 90°. The door originally faced south, it now faces east.[839]

108 / c. 71°44'N - 22°16'W / Scoresby Land[840]
SNEVIGEN

■ Norwegian trappers' hut built in 1932-33 for the Helge Ingstad Expedition by Helge Ingstad and Normann Andersen, Antarctichavn.

■ On the west side of Canning Land, at Snevigen at the mouth of Nathorst Fjord.

■ C (IIA). Disappeared.

■ Helge Ingstad on his map (1935) marks a hut near Snevigen.[841] There are no further references to the existence of this hut. In 2004 a Nanok team did not find any evidence for, or remains of a hut at this location.

109 / c. 71°44'N - 22°29'W / Scoresby Land[842]
KÅRES-BU, Pass-huset

■ Norwegian trappers' hut built early August 1932 for the Helge Ingstad Expedition by Helge Ingstad and Normann Andersen, Antarctichavn.[843]

■ On the east side of Wegener Halvø, at the mouth of Nathorst Fjord, about 6-7 km south of Kap Brown.

■ C (IIA). Moved. Originally about 200 x 200 cm.

■ Ingstad wrote, that: *"the first thing to meet our gaze next morning when we stuck our heads out of the tent was a raven sitting some yards away peering at us with his head cocked to one side. But when Andersen talked to it in his Nordland dialect, it uttered an ugly screech and flew off in high dudgeon in the direction of that twisted peak. To the latter we therefore gave the name Ravnefjellet – Raven Mountain. Directly in its shadow we fell to work putting up our first cabin. In the course of two days, there stood "Kaares-bu" – named after my brother, Kaare – and then we continued our way along the coast in the motor boat".*[844] Kåres-bu (Kåre's homestead) is named after Ingstad's brother, Kaare, who was a diplomat and the Norwegian ambassador in Israel 1960-71.

■ In the summer of 1955 Kåres-bu was moved to a new location [114-3] at Fleming Fjord.[845]

110 / 71°45.88'N - 22°31.76'W / Scoresby Land[846]
HOLSTAD, Kap Brown hytten, Brown-stua, Brownhuset, Raskøttet

■ Norwegian trappers' hut built 9th August 1931 for the Møre Expedition by Peder Sulebak and Odd Åmbak, Antarctichavn.[847]

■ At the west side of Wegener Halvø, about 5 km south-west of Kap Brown.

■ C (IIA). 190 x 190, plus porch 135 x 120 cm.

Trapper Peder Sulebak at Holstad [110], August 1931. © Karin Krogsæter

Holstad [110], 3rd August 2004. © NCN

Coal stove: Home-made from an old fuel drum.
Floor: Earth.

■ On 9th August 1931 Odd Åmbak wrote that: *"We found a fine location to build a hut about five km from the cape* (Kap Brown)". ... *"This hut we call "Holstad" after professor Hoel* (Adolf Hoel)".[848] Holstad was the southernmost hut built by the Møre Expedition.

111 / 71°45.38'N - 23°23.49'W / Scoresby Land[849]
ØRSTED DAL HYTTEN, Allday Dal

■ Norwegian trappers' hut built in 1932-33 for the Helge Ingstad Expedition by Helge Ingstad and Normann Andersen, Antarctichavn.[850]

■ In Ørsted Dal at the mouth of (east side) of Allday Dal, about 22 km from Fleming Fjord.

■ B (IIA). 210 x 130 cm. Coal stove: Ulefos No. 120. Floor: Wood.

■ Ottar Årsvold, who wintered at Antarctichavn 1937-38, said in 1992 that: *"Helge Ingstad had built a hut in Ørsted Dal, but we didn't know that. When the Danes Ib Poulsen and Jørgen Tvermose passed by Antarctichavn, they told us about this hut. We went there and were held up by a snowstorm for five days around the 1st February 1938"*.[851]

Ørsted Dal hytten [111], 13th August 2006. © NCN

112 / c. 71°46'N - 22°57'W / Scoresby Land[852]
SYVEREN, Midthuset, Funkis, Pasdalshuset, Mellem-huset

■ Norwegian trappers' hut built in 1932-33 for the Helge Ingstad Expedition by Helge Ingstad and Normann Andersen, Antarctichavn.[853]

■ At Fleming Fjord, at the mouth (north side) of Solfaldsdal.

■ C (IIA). Disappeared. Originally 250 x 140 cm. Coal stove: Ulefos No. 1585.

■ Peder Sulebak in 1934 referred to the hut as "Mellem-huset",[854] and Nils Hanken in 1937 called it "Midthuset"; the hut was located about halfway along Fleming Fjord.[855] Then in 1948, Martin Larsen Lie called it "Funkis".[856] Finally, in 1954 Otto Lapstun named it "Syveren" (Number seven), as all the wall panels were marked with the number 7.[857]

■ A ruin as early as the end of the 1960s. Later on it vanished. In 2006, a Nanok team could not find any trace of the hut.

113 / c. 71°48'N - 24°20'W / Scoresby Land
LOMSØHYTTEN, Lommensø hytten, Pingo Dal hytten

■ Danish travellers' hut built in the spring of 1957 for Nordmine, Mestersvig.

■ At the location where Pingo Dal joins Schuchert Dal.

■ C (IIA). Removed.

■ The hut was built in connection with the drilling for lead, and the materials were transported to the location by bulldozer. There is an old airstrip between Lomsøen and the spot where the hut was located. In 1990, the hut was removed by a Nordmine clean-up team.[858]

114-1 / c. 71°52'N - 22°45'W / Scoresby Land[859]
FLATSTRANDA, Stranda-huset

■ Norwegian trappers' hut built 10th August 1931

for the Møre Expedition by Odd Åmbak and Peder Sulebak, Antarctichavn.[860]

- At the north-west side of Fleming Fjord at Sporfjeld.
- C (IIA). Disappeared.
- Odd Åmbak called the hut "Flatstranda" as well as "Stranda-huset", because the terrain: *"from this hut and further inland is rather flat"*.[861] In 1953, the hut was taken by a big wave.[862]

Trapper Odd Åmbak at Flatstranda [114-1], August 1931. © Karin Krogsæter

Lapstun-hytten [114-2], c. 1955. © Otto Lapstun

114-2 / 71°52.18'N - 22°45.56'W / Scoresby Land[863]
LAPSTUN-HYTTEN, Surøje, Fleming Fjord hytten, Søndre Biot, Fladestrand

- Norwegian trappers' hut built in September 1954 for the Hermann Andresen Expeditions by Otto Lapstun, Antarctichavn.
- At the north-west side of Fleming Fjord at Sporfjeld, about 9 km south-west of Kap Biot.
- C (IIA). Ruin. Originally 200 x 195 cm. Coal stove: Trolla Brug No. 355 and Trolla Brug No. 80.
- After the "Flatstranda" hut had been taken by a wave in 1953, a replacement was needed. Trapper Otto Lapstun therefore dismantled "Lavøira" [208-1], and the wall and roof-panels were transported by motor boat to Fleming Fjord, where the hut was reassembled. The first year he called it "Surøje", because it had an old leaking coal stove. This stove, which Lapstun had found on the beach south of Kap Biot, probably originated from Kap Biot [116].[864]

Lapstun-hytten [114-2], 3rd August 2004. © NCN

114-3 / 71°52.14'N - 22°45.49'W / Scoresby Land[865]
FLEMING FJORD NORD

- Norwegian trappers' hut built in the summer of 1955 for the Hermann Andresen Expeditions by Otto Lapstun and others, Antarctichavn.[866]
- At the north-west side of Fleming Fjord at Sporfjeld, about 9 km south-west of Kap Biot.
- C (IIA). Ruin. Originally about 200 x 200 cm.
- In 1955 another trappers' hut was needed in Ørsted Dal. At Otto Lapstun's suggestion, Kåres-bu [109] was moved from Nathorst Fjord and placed beside Lapstun-hytten [114-2].[867] It has since remained at this location, as Lapstun never managed to transport it into Ørsted Dal. Fleming Fjord was named in 1822 by William Scoresby Junior after the Scottish zoologist, John Fleming (1785-1857).[868]

Fleming Fjord Nord [114-3], 3rd August 2004. © NCN

Øyedalshytten [115], 1950s. © Otto Lapstun

Øyedalshytten [115], 25th March 1979. © Peter Schmidt Mikkelsen

Øyedalshytten [115], 14th August 2006. © NCN

115 / 71°53.08'N - 23°00.96'W / Scoresby Land[869]
ØYEDALSHYTTEN, Minimalen, Stenrøysdalshytten

▪ Norwegian trappers' hut built in 1932-33 for the Helge Ingstad Expedition by Helge Ingstad and Normann Andersen, Antarctichavn.[870]

▪ In Henrik Møller Dal, at a small bank in the river bed about 7 km from Fleming Fjord and 3 km from the Flexurdal watershed.

▪ C (IIA). Ruin. 220 x 120 cm.

▪ "Øyedal" and "Stenrøysdal" were the Norwegian names for Henrik Møller Dal and Flexurdal. Concerning this little hut, Nils Hanken noted on 22nd January 1937: *"This hut is really something. The size is 150 x 125 cm and it is built from some few pieces of boards and turf. But the hut has one advantage; it is both tight and warm"*.[871] Trapper Otto Lapstun gave the hut the descriptive name: "Minimalen".[872]

Kap Biot [116], 3rd August 2004. © NCN

116 / 71°52.78'N - 22°39.21'W / Scoresby Land[873]
KAP BIOT

▪ Danish trappers house built between 1st and 7th September 1940 for the Igdloo company by Jørgen Tvermose, Børge Franck, Jørgen Børresen and Immanuel Starup.

▪ On the north-west side of Fleming Fjord: *"at the foot of Kap Biot"*.[874]

▪ A (IIA). Ruin. Originally 650 x 450 cm.

▪ In August 1940, a Danish trapping expedition went to North-East Greenland with the "Furenak" of Ålesund. The German Wehrmacht had financed the expedition through a stooge in order to establish a German controlled weather service in North-East Greenland. The station house at Kap Biot was: *"under cover"* on the 7th September 1940, but the very same day the Norwegian naval vessel "Fridtjof Nansen" in allied service arrived.[875] The commander, Ernst Ullring, had been informed about the expedition, and ordered the Danes evacuated and the station house burnt. Kap Biot was named in 1822 by William Scoresby Junior after the French scientist, Jean-Baptiste Biot.[876]

117 / 71°56.98'N - 22°44.11'W / Scoresby Land[877]
VILLA, Davy Sund hytten, Biot-stua, Nordre Biot

▪ Norwegian trappers' hut built 19th August 1930 for the Møre Expedition by Jonas Karlsbak and Odd Åmbak, Antarctichavn.[878]

▪ North-west of Kap Biot about 3 km west of Edderfugledal on the south side of Davy Sund.

▪ B (IIA). 210 x 210 plus porch 100 x 90 cm. Floor: Earth.

Villa [117], c. 1947. © Martin Larsen Lie

Villa [117], 5th August 2004. © NCN

■ On 10th August 1930 materials were laid out with "Veslekari".[879] Jonas Karlsbak wrote on 19th August 1930, that: *"we have now built our first trappers' hut in this direction. It only remains for us to put the roofing felt on then it is finished. We have named the hut "Villa""*.[880] The place name Davy Sund was given in 1822 by William Scoresby Junior: *"in honour of the much respected President of the Royal Society"* - Sir Humphrey Davy.[881]

118 / 71°58.50'N - 24°16.50'W / Scoresby Land

MALMBJERG

■ Danish mine built in 1958 for Nordmine, Mestersvig.

■ On the south side of Høstakken, where Arcturus Gletscher meets Schuchert Gletscher.

■ C (IIA).

■ Danish molybdenum deposit, with a trial mining adit from which drill-coring was carried out for Nordmine, Mestersvig.

■ On the south side of Høstakken, where Arcturus Gletscher meets Schuchert Gletscher.

■ C (IIA).

■ In the summer of 1958 Nordmine began investigations for molybdenum. A tunnel was excavated into the west side of Malmbjerg. From here a number of drill holes were made. The investigations were continued the following years, from 1961-62, by "Arktisk Minekompagni" (Arctic Mining Company), a consortium of Nordisk Mineselskab and the American mining company Amax. By the end of 1962, a total 20,000 metres of drill cores had been acquired, revealing an ore body about 120 Mt grading 0.25 % MoS_2. The low grade of the deposit and the location led to the evaluation that mining would not be profitable. A small mining town erected on the moraine due south of the deposit was removed by a Nordmine clear-up team. To excavate the ore, construction of an 11 km tunnel beneath three glaciers was considered in order to transport the ore to Kong Oscar Fjord.[882] In 2004, new operators entered the scene when International Molybdenum Plc (InterMoly) was established by Galahad Gold for the purpose of developing two primary molybdenum licences in Greenland. Field activities at Malmbjerg began in April 2005, and in 2007 preparations for constructing a road along Schuchert Dal to its mouth at Scoresby Sund were initiated.[883]

Malmbjerg [118]. The mineralisation is located in the lower part of the mountain between the two glaciers. March 2005. © Jesper Weiss Andersen/POLOG

The entrance to the horizontal mine shaft at Malmbjerg [118]. © Jesper Weiss Andersen/POLOG

Antarctichavn [201], 5th August 2004. © NCN

201 / 71°59.67'N - 23°06.72'W / Scoresby Land[884]
ANTARCTICHAVN, Karlsbak, Bakkehuset

- Norwegian trappers' station built in 1930 for the Møre Expedition.
- In the south-east corner of Antarctic Havn on the south side of Davy Sund.
- C (IA). Ruin. Originally 575 x 315 plus porch 180 x 180 cm.
- See chapter on stations.

Jakobsbo [202], 18th August 2006. © NCN

202 / 72°02.30'N - 24°03.65'W / Scoresby Land[885]
JAKOBSBO, Jacobsbo

- Danish travellers' huts built in 1960 for Nordmine, Mestersvig.
- At the upper end of Deltadal close to the north side of Kolossen.
- B (IIA). Cabin I: 405 x 280 cm plus porch 235 x 100 cm. Paraffin stove: Reflex Odense. Floor: Wood. Cabin II: 310 x 305 cm. Floor: Wood.
- Two cabins. The location is named after "Old Jakob", who worked as a carpenter foreman at the Mestersvig mine. Jakobsbo was established as an intermediate station during the bulldozer transports between Mestersvig via Lomsøen to Malmbjerg. Subsequently used during investigations of water availability for a possible exploitation of the molybdenum at Malmbjerg.[886]

Sorte Hjørne [203], 18th August 2006. © NCN

203 / 72°05.84'N - 24°00.79'W / Scoresby Land[887]
SORTE HJØRNE

- Danish travellers' house built in 1952 for Nordmine, Mestersvig.
- At the foot of Sortebjerg, close to Storm P. Elv, at the mouth of Nedre Funddal.
- B (IIA). 970 x 885 cm. Coal stove: Morsø.
- Built as a canteen and living quarters during drilling for lead. A former airstrip is situated close to the house.

Kap Simpson hytten [204], 27th April 1979. © Peter Schmidt Mikkelsen

204 / 72°07.99'N - 22°12.47'W / Traill Ø[888]
KAP SIMPSON HYTTEN, Simpson-stranda

- Danish travellers' hut built in 1955-56 by the Sirius Dog Sledge Patrol (and Otto Lapstun), Daneborg.[889]

Kap Simpson hytten [204], 2nd August 2004. © NCN

■ At Kap Simpson, on the east side of Føndal.
■ C (IIA). 310 x 305 including porch 310 x 100 cm. Coal stove: C.M. Hess,[890] Veile. Floor: Wood/Earth.
■ On the 12th August 1929 materials were laid out at Kap Simpson by "Veslekari".[891] However, no hut was ever built at this location using these materials. The only hut built here was the 1955-56 Sirius hut.

Jostein [205], 14th August 2006. © NCN

205 / 72°07.50'N - 23°28.56'W / Scoresby Land[892]
JOSTEIN, Pictet Bjerg hytten, Segldalen, Bjørnebu
■ Norwegian trappers' hut built on 25th August 1930 for the Møre Expedition by Odd Åmbak and Jonas Karlsbak, Antarctichavn.[893]
■ At Pictet Bjerge, about 15 km north-west of Kap Syenit on the south side of Kong Oscar Fjord.
■ B (IIA). 200 x 185 plus porch 90 x 80 cm. Coal stove: Drammen Jernstøperi No. 5. Floor: Earth.
■ On 25th August 1931 Jonas Karlsbak wrote that: *"we have been building a trappers' hut. The hut is almost finished except for the roofing felt and porch. It will be Åmbak's first trappers' hut, and therefore we call the hut "Jostein" after his first-born son"*.[894]

Ekspeditionshuset [206-1], 26th July 2003. © NCN

206-1 / 72°07.94'N - 23°51.65'W / Scoresby Land[895]
EKSPEDITIONSHUSET
■ Danish travellers house built in 1949 for the Lauge Koch Expeditions by the crew of "Gustav Holm", Mestersvig.[896]
■ In the south-western corner of Mestersvig.
■ C (IIA). Ruin. Originally 400 x 300 cm.
■ Built during the lead prospecting. The house was divided into two rooms, a living room, and a horse stable that made up 3/4 of the house. In the spring of 1973 the house was totally destroyed by an avalanche; only the foundation remains. Replaced by "Nyt ekspeditionshus" [206-2].[897]

Nyt ekspeditionshus [206-2], 26th July 2003. © NCN

206-2 / 72°07.90'N - 23°51.71'W / Scoresby Land[898]
NYT EKSPEDITIONSHUS
■ Danish travellers' hut built in 1974 or 1975 for Mestersvig Airfield, Mestersvig.
■ In the south-western corner of Mesters Vig.
■ B (IIA). 400 x 350 cm.
■ Built originally in 1954 as an office shed at Mestersvig Airfield. In 1966, it was moved to the apron and used as a terminal shed, but was damaged

during an airplane crash in 1973 and condemned. After scanty repairs it was moved to Mesters Vig by Nordmine and Statens Luftfartsvæsen in 1974 or 1975 to replace Ekspeditionshus. It is located 200 m south of the foundation of Ekspeditionshuset [206-1].

Minebyen [207], August 1979. © Peter Schmidt Mikkelsen

Minebyen [207], 16th August 2006. © NCN

207 / 72°11.09'N - 24°07.10'W / Scoresby Land[899]
MINEBYEN, Blyklippen

- Danish lead-zinc mine built in 1950 for Lauge Koch's Expeditions, Mestersvig.
- In Store Blydal on the west side of Tunnelelv at Blyklippen.
- C̲ (IB). 2 houses and 3 tanks.
- See chapter on stations.

208-1 / c. 72°13'N - 23°45'W / Scoresby Land[900]
LAVØIRA, Solstrand, Låg-Øyra, Lavøyrahuset, Lavøren

- Norwegian trappers' hut built 27th August 1930 for the Møre Expedition by Odd Åmbak and Jonas Karlsbak, Antarctichavn.[901]
- On the east side of Hovedet at Noret, about 2-3 km north-west of the Archer Øer.
- C̲ (IIA). Removed. Originally about 200 x 180 cm.
- On 27th August 1930 Jonas Karlsbak wrote that: *"here we have built a hut west of Archer Øer. It only remains for us to put on the roofing felt and build the porch. We are naming the house "Lavøren"* (low bank of gravel) *after the appearance of the place".*[902] In 1939 the Søren Richter Expeditions built the station Hamna at the same location.
- In the summer of 1954, Otto Lapstun dismantled Lavøira and moved it to Fleming Fjord. See Lapstunhytten [114-2].[903]

Hamna [208-2], 26th July 2003. © NCN

208-2 / 72°13.67'N - 23°45.31'W / Scoresby Land[904]
HAMNA, Trønderheimen, Havna

- Norwegian trappers' station built in 1939 for the Søren Richter Expeditions.
- On the east side of Hovedet at Noret, about 2 km north-west of the Archer Øer.
- B̲ (IA). 640 x 320 cm. Coal stove: Scandia. Floor: Wood. Remains of fox cages.
- See chapter on stations.

Mestersvig Airfield [209-1], 10th August 2006. © NCN

209-1 / 72°13.99'N - 23°55.30'W / Scoresby Land[905]
MESTERSVIG AIRFIELD, Mestersvig Flyveplads
■ Danish airfield built in 1952 for Statens Luftfartsvæsen.
■ West of Noret on the south side of Kong Oscar Fjord.
■ D (IB). Station area with many buildings, a control tower and an 1800 m gravel runway.
■ See chapter on stations.

Nyhavn [209-2], 10th August 2006. © NCN

209-2 / 72°15.51'N - 23°55.70'W / Scoresby Land[906]
NYHAVN
■ Danish harbour area built in 1954 for exporting ore-concentrate from the lead mine. Nordmine.
■ West side of Nyhavn on the south side of Kong Oscar Fjord.
■ D (IIA). Harbour with several buildings.
■ See chapter on stations.

Washburns hus [210], 10th August 2006. © NCN

210 / 72°13.28'N - 24°03.22'W / Scoresby Land[907]
WASHBURNS HUS, Camp Tahoe
■ American scientific station built in 1955 for A.L. Washburn, Mestersvig.
■ On the north-east side of Hesteskoen, about 5 km south-west of Mestersvig Airfield.
■ B (IIA). 845 x 660 cm. Paraffin stove: Constantin Burn. Floor: Wood.
■ Built for Dr. A.L. Washburn, who named the house Camp Tahoe after his wife, Tahoe Washburn. For almost ten years Dr. Washburn, a American geophysicist, came to North-East Greenland every summer to study the Arctic permafrost. After his project had finished the house was used by Nordmine, the staff at Mestersvig Airfield, and visiting expeditions.[908]

Skida [211], 15th August 2006. © NCN

211 / 72°16.25'N - 23°55.89'W / Scoresby Land[909]
SKIDA
■ Danish travellers' hut moved here in 1965 from Mestersvig Airfield, Mestersvig.
■ Inside a small north-facing cove at the outermost point of the peninsular west of Nyhavn.
■ B (IIA). 315 x 220 plus porch 135 x 130 cm. Paraffin stove: Refleks. Floor: Wood.
■ Originally a bathroom and toilet-shed at Mestersvig Airfield. Used for weekend trips by staff at the airfield.

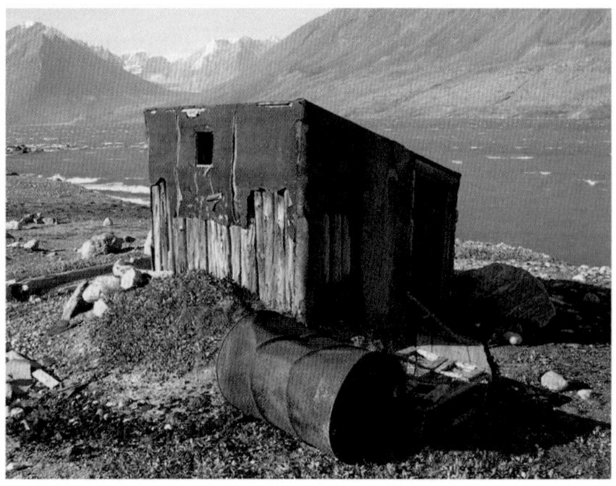

Alpehuset [212], 24th August 2006. © NCN

212 / 72°17.35'N - 25°20.48'W / Scoresby Land[910]
ALPEHUSET, Alpefjordhytten
■ Norwegian trappers' hut built in 1932-33 for the Helge Ingstad Expedition by Sverre Røstad and Arne Jacobsen, Kap Peterséns.
■ On the east side of Alpefjord, at the south side of a river delta, about 12 km south of Arwidsson Ø.
■ C (IIA). The hut walls are partly made from split wood. 200 x 170 cm. Coal stove: Dravn. Floor: Earth.
■ Probably built in August 1932. In 1934 when Peder Sulebak and Odd Åmbak took over the territory after the Helge Ingstad Expedition, they did not know the name of the hut in Alpefjord: *"we therefore called it Alpehuset"*, Sulebak wrote on 1st September 1934.[911]

Elveide [213]. In the background Nanok expedition member Niels Gyldenlund Mikkelsen, 13th July 2007. © NCN

213 / 72°17.44'N - 24°08.92'W / Scoresby Land[912]
ELVEIDE, Skeldalhytten, Skjelldalen, Havnhytta
■ Norwegian trappers' hut built 31st August 1930 for the Møre Expedition by Peder Sulebak and Knut Røbek, Kap Peterséns.[913]
■ On the east side of the Skeldal delta on the south side of Kong Oscar Fjord.
■ C (IIA). 290 x 185 cm including porch. Floor: Wood/Earth.
■ The Skeldal Elv flows into Kong Oscar Fjord about 1 km north of the hut and: *"between this river* (elv) *and the hut there is a low isthmus* (eide) *and therefore we call this place Elveide"*, Peder Sulebak wrote on 17th November 1930.[914]

214 / 72°18.45'N - 23°04.22'W / Traill Ø[915]
VÆLDDALHYTTEN
■ Danish travellers' hut built in the summer of 1970 for Mestersvig Airfield. Mestersvig.
■ At the entrance to Vælddal on the south side of Traill Ø.

Vælddalhytten [214], 27th July 2003. © NCN

■ B (IIA). 420 x 405 cm plus windbreak. Coal stove: Scandia No. 909N. Floor: Wood.
■ A so-called "Münchener Haus", which was sent to Mestersvig by Dr. Karl Herrligkoffer in the mid-1960s. Herrligkoffer, who was from München, wanted to use the hut for an expedition by tracked vehicles to the North Pole. The expedition never took place, as it was considered unrealistic and was opposed by the authorities. Herrligkoffer gave the hut to Mestersvig Airfield, where it stood until 1970, when it was transported to Vælddal on a barge.[916]

Raudberget [215], 24th July 2003. © NCN

215 / 72°24.35'N - 24°54.56'W / Scoresby Land[917]
RAUDBERGET, Raudeberg
■ Norwegian trappers' hut built 26th August 1930 for the Møre Expedition by Peder Sulebak and Knut Røbek, Kap Peterséns.
■ On the south side of Segelsällskapet Fjord, about 1 km south-west of Skipperdal.
■ C (IIA). 190 x 190 plus porch 100 x 100 cm. Coal stove: Ulefos No. 120. Floor: Wood.
■ On the 8th August 1930 materials were laid out with "Veslekari".[918] On the 27th August 1930 Peder Sulebak wrote, that: *"there is no name for*

this location on the map, so we named it Raudeberg (red mountain)".[919]

216 / 72°23.13'N - 25°15.06'W / Nathorst Land[920]
KAP MÆCHEL HYTTEN, Sentralen, Mæchel-stua

- Norwegian trappers' hut built 25th August 1930 for the Møre Expedition by Peder Sulebak and Knut Røbek, Kap Peterséns.[921]
- West of Arwidsson Ø on the south side of Kap Mæchel, Segelsällskapet Fjord.
- B (IIA). 205 x 200 plus porch 205 x 120 cm. Coal stove: L. Lange & Co. Svendborg. Floor: Wood.
- On the 8th August 1930 materials were laid out with "Veslekari".[922] Peder Sulebak called the hut Sentralen, but it is best known as Kap Mæchel hytten.[923]

Kap Mæchel hytten [216], 23rd July 2003. © NCN

217 / 72°24.47'N - 23°34.61'W / Traill Ø[924]
BÅDHYTTEN, Polypen

- Danish travellers' hut built in the summer of 1968 for Mestersvig Airfield, Mestersvig.
- On the south coast of Traill Ø south of Svinhufvud Bjerge.
- C (IIA). 530 x 235 cm. Floor: Wood.

Bådhytten [217], 9th August 2006. © NCN

- Bådhytten is made from an old boat, the "Polypen", one of Lauge Koch's boats that was stationed at Ella Ø. In 1960 it was given to Statens Luftfartsvæsen, who used it at Mestersvig. In 1968 the motor boat "Åse" was taken into use, and "Polypen" was condemned and moved to Traill Ø for use as a weekend hut. There have been two boats by the name of "Polypen"; the other is a wreck at Kap Berghaus south of Daneborg, where it has been since WWII.[925]

218 / 72°24.96'N - 24°33.75'W / Scoresby Land[926]
KAP PETERSÉNS, Sunnmørsheimen, Vardevakt

- Norwegian trappers' station built in 1930 for the Møre Expedition.
- About 2 km south-east of Kap Peterséns.
- B (IA). One building. 735 x 275 cm. Coal stove: Morsø. Floor: Wood.
- See chapter about stations.

Kap Peterséns [218], 28th July 2003. © NCN

219 / 72°24.43'N - 26°02.74'W / Lyell Land[927]
BJØRKTUN, Inderhytten

- Norwegian trappers' hut built 2nd September 1931 for the Møre Expedition by Odd Åmbak and Peder Sulebak, Kap Peterséns.[928]

Trappers Peder Sulebak (left) and Odd Åmbak at Bjørktun [219], September 1931. © Karin Krogsæter

Bjørktun [219], 24th August 2003. © NCN

■ On the north side of Forsblad Fjord about 10 km from its head.
■ C (IIA). Ruin. Originally: 190 x 160 plus porch 190 x 100 cm.
■ On 2nd September 1931 Peder Sulebak wrote, that the hut was: *"named Bjørktun because of all the birch that grows around the hut"*.[929] In the spring of 1976 the hut was completely destroyed by an avalanche.

Polheim [220], 23rd August 2003. © NCN

220 / 72°26.67'N - 25°28.94'W / Lyell Land[930]
POLHEIM, Bærtun, Polhem Dal hytten
■ Norwegian trappers' hut built 3rd September 1931 for the Møre Expedition by Odd Åmbak and Peder Sulebak, Kap Peterséns.[931]
■ On the north side of Forsblad Fjord about 2 km west of Polhem Dal.
■ A (IIA). 185 x 160 plus porch 110 x 130 cm. Coal stove: Drammen Jernstøperi No. 5. Floor: Wood.
■ On 3rd September 1931 Odd Åmbak wrote that Sulebak had named the hut "Bærtun": *"because here there is so much bilberry"*.[932] Later Sulebak changed the name of the hut to "Polheim". The roof was originally made from a sawn off, old boat.

Sporvognen [221], 8th August 2006. © NCN

221 / 72°28.64'N - 24°01.54'W / Traill Ø[933]
SPORVOGNEN
■ Danish travellers' hut built in 1976 for Mestersvig Airfield, Mestersvig.
■ On the north side of a small foreland at the mouth of Karupelv, north-east of Haslum Øer.
■ B (IIA). 600 x 220 cm divided into two rooms. Paraffin stove: Reflex. Floor: Wood.
■ Sporvognen (the tram car) is an old shed from Mestersvig Airfield. It was lent to Nordmine in 1973-76 and then moved to its present location.

Holm Bugt hytten [222], 1st August 2007. In 2001 Nanok was encouraged to restore Holm Bugt hytten, which for several years had been used by Dr. Benoît Sittler and the Karupelv Valley Project as a base and emergency shelter. © NCN

222 / 72°30.05'N - 24°00.32'W / Traill Ø[934]
HOLM BUGT HYTTEN, Karupelv hytten, Holmvika, Holmbukta, Holms Vig hytten, Holmsvik
■ Norwegian trappers' hut built 30th July 1932 for the Helge Ingstad Expedition, Kap Peterséns.
■ In Holm Bugt on the south-west coast of Traill Ø, about 2-3 km south-east of the Lunedal river delta.

■ B (IIA). 255 x 205 cm. Coal stove: Morsø. Floor: Wood.

■ On 11th August 1929 materials for a hut were laid out with "Polarbjørn" at Holm Bugt.[935] However, the hut was not built in 1929-30 by Arctic Commercial Enterprise[936] or - as claimed by John Giæver - in 1930-32 by the Møre Expedition,[937] but in fact in 1932 by the Helge Ingstad Expedition and the crew of the "Polarbjørn".[938]

■ Holm Bugt hytten was restored by Nanok in 2001.[939]

Kongeborg [224-1], 1947-48. © Martin Larsen Lie

Beinhaugen [223], 28th July 2003. © NCN

Kongeborg [224-1], 8th August 2006. © NCN

223 / 72°31.24'N - 24°39.47'W / Lyell Land[940]
BEINHAUGEN, Kap Lagerberg hytten, Beinhauen

■ Norwegian trappers' hut built 18th August 1930 for the Møre Expedition by Peder Sulebak and Knut Røbek, Kap Peterséns.[941]

■ On the south side of Kap Lagerberg, Kong Oscar Fjord.

■ C (IIA). 200 x 185 plus porch 120 x 185 cm. Coal stove: Old fuel drum. Floor: Wood.

■ On the 9th August 1930 materials were laid out with "Veslekari".[942] The name Beinhaugen (bone hill) arises from the bones associated with eskimo ruins.

224-1 / 72°35.43'N - 24°22.85'W / Traill Ø[943]
KONGEBORG, Kongsborg

■ Norwegian trappers' hut built in 1932-33 for the Helge Ingstad Expedition, probably by Sverre Røstad and Arne Jacobsen, Kap Peterséns.[944]

■ At the south-west point of Traill Ø, at the southern end of the Kongeborg mountain range.

■ A (IIA). 245 x 150 cm. The roof is made from an old boat. Coal stove: L. Lange & Co, Svendborg.

■ The oldest Kongeborg hut was most probably built in the summer of 1932. Peder Sulebak mentions it on 4th September 1934: *"We have been on Traill Ø today. First we went across the fjord to Holm Bugt and then to Kongsborg".*[945] On 27th November 1948 Per Myrvold wrote that: *"the hut is like a sieve, without a porch or wood, and with a rotten sack as door".*[946] In 1950 the hut was replaced by a new hut, "Kongeborgen" [224-2].

224-2 / 72°35.43'N - 24°22.85'W / Traill Ø[947]
KONGEBORGEN, Kongeborghytten

■ Norwegian trappers' hut built 21st August 1950 for the Hermann Andresen Expeditions by Alf Rustøen and Halvor Bjørdal, Antarctichavn.

■ At the south-west point of Traill Ø, at the south end of the Kongeborg mountain range.

Kongeborgen [224-2], 8th August 2006. © NCN

■ B (IIA). 310 x 210 including porch 100 x 210 cm. Coal stove: Morsø. Floor: Wood.
■ This hut replaced the old Kongeborg [224-1], and is located immediately adjacent to it.[948]
■ In 2001, Kongeborgen was restored by Nanok.[949]

Trapper Otto Johnsen at Vogtshytten [225], 4th May 1930. © Sverre Sørensen / Norwegian Polar Institute

Vogtshytten [225], 1st August 2004. © NCN

225 / 72°37.03'N - 22°38.39'W / Traill Ø[950]
VOGTSHYTTEN, Thorolf Vogts hytten
■ Norwegian trappers' hut built 14th September 1929 for Arctic Commercial Enterprise by Sverre Sørensen and Thor Halle, Sverresborg.[951]
■ About 4 km south-west of Kap Palander in Vega Sund.
■ C (IIA). Ruin. Originally 250 x 200 plus porch 160 x 100 cm. Coal stove: Kraakerøy Støperi No. 1.
■ On 14th September 1929 Sverre Sørensen wrote in his diary that they: *"came to the hut, which we have named Vogtshytten, at 12 o'clock. Drank a little coffee from the thermos, ate a bit and immediately started the work".*[952] The hut was named after Thorolf Vogt (1888-1958), professor of mineralogy and geology at Norges Tekniske Høgskole in Trondheim.

226 / 72°40.91'N - 22°02.14'W / Geographical Society Ø[953]
KAP MAC CLINTOCK HYTTEN, Valmuehytten
■ Danish travellers' hut built 20th August 1956 by Peter Hofman Wistisen, Jens Sonne-Harild and A. Smith-Andersen for Sirius Dog Sledge Patrol, Daneborg.
■ On the west side of a small foreland about 3 km west of Kap McClintock. It was common Danish practice to spell Scottish names beginning with "Mac" in two words.
■ B (IIA). 395 x 205 including porch 150 x 205 cm. Coal stove. Floor: Wood.
■ The inside wall has the following inscription: *"This hut – called Valmuehytten* (the poppy hut) *– belongs to the Royal Danish Sledge Patrol and was built on 20th August 1956 by Peter, Jens and Smith. May it provide refreshment for thirsty, hungry and chilled men and dogs."*

Kap Mac Clintock hytten [226], 1st May 1979. © Peter Schmidt Mikkelsen

Kap Mac Clintock hytten [226], 2nd August 2004. © NCN

227 / 72°41.98'N - 22°17.95'W / Geographical Society Ø[954]
RICHTER-HYTTEN
■ Norwegian trappers' hut built 6th September 1929 for Arctic Commercial Enterprise by Søren Richter and Sverre Sørensen, Sverresborg.[955 & 956]
■ On Geographical Society Ø, about 6 km north-east of the northernmost point of Nordenskiöld Ø.

■ C (IIA). 250 x 200 plus porch 160 x 100 cm. Coal stove: Kraakerøy Støperi No. 1. Floor: Wood/Earth.

■ On 3rd September 1929 Sverre Sørensen wrote: *"Richter and I have been outside Nordenskiöld Ø, with parts for a hut. It is not far from Kap McClintock and at a bay, which we call Thorolf Vogts Bugt".*[957] The hut, named after Søren Richter, was used only in 1929-30.

Richter-hytten [227], 1st August 2004. © NCN

228 / 72°42.39'N - 26°47.66'W / Gletscherland[958]

FESTNINGEN, Strømnæshytten, Strømhytten, Röhss Fjord hytten

■ Norwegian trappers' hut built 11th July 1934 for Arctic Commercial Enterprise by Ole Klokset and Magne Råum, Kap Humboldt.[959]

■ On the east side of Strømnæs in Röhss Fjord.

■ A (IIA). 285 x 235 cm. Coal stove. Floor: Earth.

■ On 13th September 1934 Ole Klokset wrote, that: *"the hut is named "Festningen". It is 3 x 3 metres and 2 metres high inside. On the outside earth and rocks all the way around the hut. The frame is of driftwood and then wire netting and old sacks to keep out the earth".*[960]

Festningen [228], 1st August 2003. © NCN

Jomfruen [229], 1st August 2004. © NCN

229 / 72°43.84'N - 22°37.32'W / Geographical Society Ø[961]

JOMFRUEN, Jomfru-hytten

■ Norwegian trappers' hut built 31st August 1929 for Arctic Commercial Enterprise by Sverre Sørensen and Thor Halle, Sverresborg.[962]

■ In Vega Sund, on the north side of the west-facing bay north-east of Silja Ø.

■ C (IIA). 250 x 200 plus porch 160 x 100 cm. Coal stove: Kraakerøy Støperi No. 1. Floor: Wood/Earth.

■ In 31st August 1929 Sverre Sørensen wrote: *"We have named the bay Jomfru-bukten and the house, Jomfruen".*[963] Sørensen is referring to the west-facing bay; however, the so-called "Jomfru-pollen" bay on Lacmann's (1937) map is identical with the south-facing bay known as Malia Havn.[964] Jomfruen was only used in 1929-30.

Rimhytten [230-1], winter 1934. © Ole Klokset

230-1 / c. 72°43.07'N - 26°10.53'W / Lyell Land[965]

RIMHYTTEN, Kap Hedlund

■ Norwegian trappers' hut built 11th September 1934 for Arctic Commercial Enterprise by Ole Klokset and Magne Råum, Kap Humboldt.[966]

■ On the east side of Kap Hedlund, Kempe Fjord.

■ C (IIA). Removed.

■ With respect to the oldest Kap Hedlund hut,

Ole Klokset on 26th November 1934 wrote that he went: *"to Hedlund "Rimhytten". I have named it so, because it was quite white from frost when I arrived, and it dripped for more than an hour so it was impossible to stay inside. The hut is small, just long enough for me to lie stretched out and rather narrow".*[967] In 1964 Rimhytten was removed and replaced by Kap Hedlund hytten [230-2]. See also Kap Hedlund (vestside) [903].

Kap Hedlund hytten [230-2], 1st August 2003. © NCN

230-2 / 72°43.07'N - 26°10.53'W / Lyell Land[968]
KAP HEDLUND HYTTEN

- Danish travellers' hut built in 1964 for the Sirius Dog Sledge Patrol, Daneborg.
- On the east side of Kap Hedlund, Kempe Fjord.
- B (IIA). 360 x 205 cm. Coal stove: Morsø. Floor: Wood.
- Built as a replacement of Rimhytten [230-1] and at the same location.[969]

Nordborg [231-1], 8th August 2006. © NCN

231-1 / 72°44.47'N - 24°27.50'W / Traill Ø[970]
NORDBORG, Norborg

- Norwegian trappers' hut built on 1st September 1935 for the Suløya Expedition by Peder Sulebak and Karsten Sulebak, Kap Peterséns.
- On the west side of the Kongeborgen mountain range, about 11 km south of the north-west point of Traill Ø.
- C (IIA). Ruin. Originally about 200 x 200 cm. Coal stove: Kraakerøy No. 4. Floor: Wood.
- This is the northernmost hut in the Sunnmøring trapping territory of Kong Oscar Fjord. On 29th August 1935 Peder Sulebak wrote: *"I have sawed through an old boat, which had been left by Ingstad's men. From this boat we are going to use the middle part as a roof for the hut we are going to build at northern Kongeborg on the north-western coast of Traill Ø".*[971] The newer Nordborghytten [231-2] is situated at the same location.[972]

Nordborghytten [231-2], 8th August 2006. © NCN

231-2 / 72°44.47'N - 24°27.46'W / Traill Ø[973]
NORDBORGHYTTEN, Nordborghuset

- Norwegian trappers' hut possibly built in 1937, Kap Peterséns.
- On the west side of the Kongeborgen mountain range, about 11 km south of the north-west point of Traill Ø.
- C (IIA). Ruin. Originally 245 x 190 plus porch 165 x 110 cm. Coal stove: C.M. Hess, Veile, No. 10. Floor: Wood.
- The origin of the newer Nordborg hut is unclear. With respect to the construction it resembles the Norwegian pre-war model as the roof is A-shaped, a design only used until the end of the 1930s. The trapping territory belonged to Kap Peterséns station, but neither Peder Sulebak nor Karsten Sulebak, who built the old hut, mentions the building of a new hut in their diaries from 1936-39.[974] Nevertheless, the hut is assumed built before 1939 - according to Magne Råum[975] - and therefore in this book attributed to the

Søren Richter Expedition 1937-38. Nordborghytten may on the other hand be mistaken for the marked, but never found, "Kap Dufva" hytte [902];[976] it cannot be excluded that it was built after WWII, or built before the war and later moved to its present location.[977]

Sverresborg [232], 31st August 2004. © NCN

232 / 72°50.86'N - 22°56.78'W / Geographical Society Ø[978]

SVERRESBORG, Gåsehytten

- Norwegian trappers' station built in August 1929 for Arctic Commercial Enterprise.
- On the north side of Vega Sund, about 4 km north-west of Gåseøen.
- A (IA). 510 x 310 plus porch 205 x 310 cm. Coal stove: Hess & Søn Nr. 99 Middelfart. Floor: Wood.
- See chapter on stations.

Solveigs hytte [233], 1959. © Torbjørn Torkildsen / Norwegian Polar Institute

233 / 72°51.80'N - 23°33.74'W / Geographical Society Ø[979]

SOLVEIGS HYTTE, Reveodden, Kap Rygg, Sverdrup hytte

- Norwegian trappers' hut built 19th August 1929 for Arctic Commercial Enterprise by Sverre Sørensen and Thor Halle, Sverresborg.[980]
- On the east side of a small foreland on the north side of Vega Sund, about 32 km from Kong Oscar Fjord.
- B (IIA). 245 x 200 plus porch 100 x 165 cm. Coal stove: Morsø. Floor: Wood/Earth.
- On 19th August 1929 Thor Halle wrote about the location and the hut that: *"the foreland we call Reveodden, and the hut that we have built we have named Solveigs hytte after my wife"*.[981] The Norwegians also referred to the foreland as Kap Rygg.[982]

Solveigs hytte [233], 31st July 2004. © NCN

234 / 72°52.68'N - 24°01.73'W / Traill Ø[983]

TRAILL HYTTEN, Østhytten, Snøheim, Osthytten

- Norwegian trappers' hut built 22nd August 1929 for Arctic Commercial Enterprise by Sverre Sørensen and Thor Halle, Sverresborg.[984 & 985]
- On the south side of Vega Sund, about 17 km from Kong Oscar Fjord.
- C (IIA) Ruin. Originally about 250 x 200 cm plus porch.
- On 11th August 1929 materials were laid out with "Veslekari".[986] The hut was originally named Traill

Traill hytten [234], 31st July 2004. © NCN

hytten, but Ole Klokset 1934 referred to it as Osthytten on 9th December, meaning the easternmost usable hut in Vega Sund.[987] Traill Ø was named by William Scoresby in 1822 after Sir Thomas Stewart Traill (1781-1862). Traill was born at Kirkwall in the Orkney Islands, and studied at Edinburgh University. He then practiced medicine in Liverpool. He became acquainted with Scoresby, and contributed a list of animals observed in eastern Greenland to Scoresby's "Journal of a Voyage to the Northern Whale Fishery" (1823).[988]

Ella Ø [235], 29th July 2003. © NCN

235 / 72°52.62'N - 25°06.70'W / Ella Ø[989]
ELLA Ø, Ellaøy

- Danish scientific station built in 1931 for the Three-Year Expedition.
- At Solitærbugt on the north-west side of Ella Ø.
- D (IB). Station area with about 10 buildings.
- See chapter on stations.

Maristua [236], 13th August 2003. © NCN

236 / 72°53.60'N - 24°47.35'W / Ella Ø[990]
MARISTUA, Kap Elisabeth hytten, Camp Lindquist

- Norwegian trappers' station built in 1930 for Arctic Commercial Enterprise.
- On the north-east side of Ella Ø, at Richardpynt about 2 km south of Kap Elisabeth.
- B (IA). 490 x 200 cm including porch. Coal stove: Kraakerøy Støperi No. 1. Floor: Wood.
- See chapter on stations.

Nils Hermans hytte [237], 31st July 2004. © NCN

237 / 72°53.95'N - 24°22.74'W / Geographical Society Ø[991]
NILS HERMANS HYTTE, Lindquist-hytten, Nansen-hytten

- Norwegian trappers' hut built 21st August 1929 for Arctic Commercial Enterprise by Sverre Sørensen and Thor Halle, Sverresborg.[992]
- On the north side of Vega Sund, about 5 km from Kong Oscar Fjord.
- C (IIA). Ruin. Originally 245 x 200 cm. Coal stove: Kraakerøy Støperi No. 1. Floor: Wood.
- On 7th August 1929 materials were laid out with "Veslekari".[993] Thor Halle wrote a couple of weeks later, that it was a: *"bad location, but there is nothing to do about it. Finally the hut was built and named Nils Hermans hytte"* – after Halle's son.[994]

Mineralbukta [238], 8th August 1978. © B.L. Nielsen / GEUS

238 / 72°53.81'N - 25°43.88'W / Suess Land[995]
MINERALBUKTA, Lumskebugthytten, Sunnmørsheimen

Mineralbukta [238], 2nd August 2003. © NCN

■ Norwegian trappers' hut built 7th September 1934 for Arctic Commercial Enterprise by Ole Klokset and Magne Råum, Kap Humboldt.[996]
■ About 500 metres inland on the west side of the river at Lumskebugten, Kempe Fjord.
■ B (IIA). 205 x 200 plus porch 200 x 105 cm. Coal stove: Kværner Ovnstøperi Nr. 3. Floor: Wood.
■ On the 25th November 1934 the hut was named "Sunnmørsheimen" by Ole Klokset, but as the Kap Peterséns station [218] at that time was known by the same name, Klokset later changed the name to "Mineralbukta".[997]

Eli Knudsens hytte [239-1], 10th August 2003. © NCN

239-1 / 72°57.48'N - 24°56.51'W / Ella Ø[998]
ELI KNUDSENS HYTTE
■ Danish travellers' hut built in 1941-42 for the North-East Greenland Sledge Patrol by Eli Knudsen and Hans Siewers, Ella Ø.[999]
■ In a small cove on the west side of Maria Ø.
■ C (IIA). 320 x 180 cm. Floor: Wood.
■ Inside the hut the following inscription is found: *"Bygget 1941 af Hans Siewers, Drammen og Eli Knudsen, København"* (Built in 1941 by Hans Siewers, Drammen and Eli Knudsen, Copenhagen). This is most likely correct, although Hans Siewers said in 1991: *"We did not build any huts. Eli and I repaired a hut at Maria Ø, which was in poor shape, probably built previously by people from Ella Ø".*[1000] Siewers may have confused this hut with "Maria Ø (østhavn)" [240].

Maria Ø Station [239-2], 1951. © Wagn Kromann

Maria Ø Station [239-2], 10th August 2003. © NCN

239-2 / 72°57.47'N - 24°56.65'W / Ella Ø[1001]
MARIA Ø STATION
■ Danish scientific summer station built in 1950 for Lauge Koch's Expeditions.
■ In a small cove on the west side of Maria Ø.
■ C (IIA). Removed.
■ Lauge Koch wrote: *"it has been necessary to erect a station on Maria Ø a little north of Ella Ø, where there is good holding ground for ships and motor boats, and seaplanes can run directly ashore"*[1002]
■ The Maria Ø Station no longer exists; the houses were taken down and removed about 1960. The Sirius Dog Sledge Patrol took over a so-called "Weber-barrack" and moved this to Mestersvig Airfield. The expression "Weber-barrack" originates from the construction firm "Asmussen & Weber", which in the 1950s delivered numerous buildings to North-East Greenland.[1003]
■ There are still various piles of different materials on the beach at this location, as well as a number of fuel drums of German origin labelled "Kriegsmarine".

Maria Ø (østhavn) [240], 14th August 2003. © NCN

240 / 72°57.78'N - 24°51.59'W / Ella Ø[1004]
MARIA Ø (østhavn)

■ Danish travellers' hut built 15th December 1934 for the Danish Police Service by Ib Poulsen and Allan Lind, Ella Ø.[1005]

■ Inner part of the bay on the north-east side of Maria Ø.

■ C (IIA). 215 x 205 cm. Coal stove: Middelfart Støbegods Nørrevold 10. Floor: Earth.

■ This hut has previously been confused with "Eli Knudsens hytte" [239-1]. However, in 1992 Ib Poulsen said that this hut and a similar hut, "Kap Ruth hytten" [406], were abandoned dark-room huts built by the Three-Year Expedition 1931-34 at the Ella Ø and Eskimonæs stations.[1006] *"The materials were un-insulated masonite sheets on a framework of rough timbers and boards,"* Poulsen said, and quoted his diary of the 15th December 1934: *"Drove again today to Maria Ø with materials for the porch and we finished the hut and covered it with roofing felt"*.[1007]

Svedenborg [241], 13th August 2003. © NCN

241 / 72°59.05'N - 24°33.40'W / Geographical Society Ø[1008]
SVEDENBORG, Røvballehytten, Joplassen, Valborghytten, Bakkehytta

■ Norwegian trappers' hut built in September 1930 for Arctic Commercial Enterprise by Olav Kjelbotn and Søren Richter, Kap Humboldt.

■ At the western entrance to Sofia Sund on the north-western point of Geographical Society Ø.

■ B (IIA). 245 x 195 plus porch 155 x 115 cm. Coal stove: L. Lange & Co. Floor: Wood.

■ On 11th August 1929 materials were laid out with "Veslekari" on the south side of Sofia Sund, about 8-9 km east of Kong Oscar Fjord.[1009] In 1930 the materials were moved to "Jo-nesset", at that time the Norwegian name for the north-western point of Geographical Society Ø. On 14th September 1930 Olav Kjelbotn wrote that: *we have built a trappers' hut at the outermost point of Sofia Sund on Geographical Society Ø".*[1010] By dog-sledge drivers the hut has since received the nickname "Røvballehytten" (the arse hut), as it is situated inconveniently up on a steep slope.

Laplace [301], 5th May 1979. © Peter Schmidt Mikkelsen

Laplace [301], 11th August 2003. © NCN

301 / 73°00.43'N - 22°31.89'W / Geographical Society Ø[1011]
LAPLACE, Kap Laplace

■ Norwegian trappers' station built in 1938 for the

Ole Klokset Expedition.
▪ On the north side of Geographical Society Ø, west of a small basalt cape at the foot of Laplace Bjerg.
▪ B (IA). 700 x 300 plus side shed 300 x 200 cm. Coal stove: Laxevaags Verk. Floor: Wood
▪ See chapter on stations.

302 / c. 73°01'N - 23°38'W / Geographical Society Ø [1012]
BØDTKERS HYTTE, Sejerstedt Bødtkers hytte
▪ Norwegian trappers' hut built 30th September 1929 for Arctic Commercial Enterprise by Olav Kjelbotn and Hallvard Devold, Kap Humboldt.
▪ On the south side of Sofia Sund, about 10 km west of Rudbeck Bjerg.
▪ C (IIA). Removed.
▪ On 11th August 1929 materials for Bødtkers hytte were laid out with "Veslekari".[1013] On the 30th September 1929 the hut was built by Hallvard Devold and Olav Kjelbotn. As it was located inconveniently, Kjelbotn and Søren Richter later moved it to the north side of Sofia Sund - See Stordalen [306]. Kjelbotn wrote on 20th October 1930 that: *"we agreed to move the hut in one piece. We jacked up the hut, put two sledges underneath, and there it stood with stove and everything on four runners. Harnessed our eight dogs in front of it and off we went with the entire house"*.[1014]

303 / c. 73°02'N - 22°55'W / Geographical Society Ø[1015]
STRØMHYTTEN, Strøm-hytten
▪ Norwegian trappers' hut built 25th August 1929 for Arctic Commercial Enterprise by Ingvald Strøm, Hallvard Devold and Olav Kjelbotn, Kap Humboldt.
▪ On the north side of Geographical Society Ø, south-east of Robertson Ø.
▪ C (IIA). Removed.
▪ *"One day we went across Sofia Sund to build a hut on Geographical Society Ø. It was later called Strømhytta"*,[1016] Hallvard Devold wrote. It was named after Ingvald Strøm.[1017]
▪ Strømhytten only had a short life. On 20th August 1932, it was taken down by Bernt Marø, Leif Brandal and Hans Furland, who moved it into Sofia Sund[1018] - See Stordalen [306].

304 / 73°02.80'N - 24°04.07'W / Ymer Ø[1019]
ARENTZ HYTTEN, Rødebjerghytten, Snehytten
▪ Norwegian trappers' hut built 12th October 1929 for Arctic Commercial Enterprise by Olav Kjelbotn and Hallvard Devold, Kap Humboldt.[1020]
▪ At the foot of Rødebjerg on the north side of Sofia Sund.

Arentz hytten [304], c. 1947. © Martin Larsen Lie

Arentz hytten [304], 13th August 2003. © NCN

▪ B (IIA). 240 x 195 plus porch 95 x 165 cm. Coal stove: Morsø. Floor: Wood.
▪ On the 11th October 1929, Hallvard Devold wrote that they had: *"the hut built before dark. The roofing felt will have to wait until tomorrow"*.[1021] Consul Gustav Arentz was a member of the board of Arctic Commercial Enterprise.

305 / 73°02.61'N - 24°42.43'W / Ymer Ø[1022]
NAMDALSHYTTEN, Fladedalhytten, Karl Jakobsen Bugt, Firmannsdalen
▪ Norwegian trappers' hut built 30th August 1934 for Arctic Commercial Enterprise by Ole Klokset and Magne Råum, Kap Humboldt.

Namdalshytten [305], 13th August 2003. © NCN

■ On the east side of Karl Jakobsen Bugt west of Konglomeratnæs, at the south end of Fladedal.
■ B (IIA). 200 x 200 cm. Coal stove.
■ On 11th November 1934 Magne Råum wrote that he was: *"in Firmannsdalen. Have today named the hut Namdalshytten"*.[1023] Råum originated from Namdalen, an area north of Trondheim in Norway. In the autumn of 1934, Magne Råum, Ole Klokset, Ib Poulsen and Allan Lind got together for a joint hunting trip into Fladedal, which didn't have a name at that time. In memory of their successful trip they called it "Firmannsdalen" (the four men valley).[1024]

Stordalen [306], 13th August 2003. © NCN

306 / 73°04.06'N - 23°43.31'W / Ymer Ø[1025]
STORDALEN, Barnabas, Raudalshytten, Bødker, Røvdalen, Dalhytten, Stor-dalen
■ Norwegian trappers' hut built 20th October 1930 for Arctic Commercial Enterprise by Olav Kjelbotn and Søren Richter, Kap Humboldt.[1026]
■ On the north side of Sofia Sund, east of Barnabas Dal.
■ C (IIA). 250 x 200 plus porch 160 x 100 cm. Coal stove: Dravn No. 5. Floor: Wood.
■ The original hut at this site was the former Bødtkers hytte [302], which on 20th October 1930 was moved to here by Olav Kjelbotn and Søren Richter.[1027] This hut was moved once again in August 1931, see Renbugthytten [325]. Finally, on 21st August 1932, Bernt Marø, Hans Furland and Leif Brandal moved Strømhytten [303] from the north side of Geographical Society Ø to this site.[1028]

307 / 73°05.25'N - 23°19.89'W / Ymer Ø[1029]
ORVINHYTTEN, Orvin-lia
■ Norwegian trappers' hut built 28th September 1929 for Arctic Commercial Enterprise by Olav Kjelbotn and Hallvard Devold, Kap Humboldt.
■ On the north side of Sofia Sund, about 10 km west of Kap Humboldt.

Trapper Bjarne Myrvold at Orvinhytten [307], August 1947. © Bjarne Myrvold

Orvinhytten [307], 6th August 2006. © NCN

■ C (IIA). Ruin. Originally about 250 x 200 plus porch 200 x 100 cm. Coal stove: Kraakerøy Støperi No. 4.
■ On 6th August 1929 materials for Orvinhytten were laid out with "Veslekari".[1030] Hallvard Devold wrote on 28th September 1929 that: *"we call it Orvins hytte, as engineer Orvin was the first who came ashore and climbed the hills"*.[1031] Anders Kristian Orvin (1889-1980), was a Norwegian geologist with NSIU. He took part in summer expeditions to North-East Greenland in 1929, 1930 and 1932. Awarded his doctorate in 1934. He was leader of numerous expeditions to Svalbard, and Director of the Norwegian Polar Institute 1958-61.

Kap Humboldt [308], 11th August 2003. © NCN

308 / 73°06.16'N - 23°00.03°W / Ymer Ø[1032]
KAP HUMBOLDT, Kjelbotn, Humboldt
- Norwegian trappers' station built in 1929 for Arctic Commercial Enterprise.
- On the east side of Ymer Ø, about 1 km north of Kap Humboldt and the entrance to Sofia Sund.
- B (IA). 515 x 305 plus side shed 200 x 305 cm. Coal stove: Scandia. Floor: Wood.
- See chapter on stations.

Rendalshytten [309], 2nd August 2003. © NCN

309 / 73°05.83'N - 27°18.24'W / Suess Land[1033]
RENDALSHYTTEN, Paradisdalen, Renhytten
- Norwegian trappers' hut built in the summer of 1938 for Arctic Commercial Enterprise by Bjarne and Oddvar Akre, Kap Humboldt.
- On the north side of Paradisdal in Kjerulf Fjord.
- B (IIA). 205 x 200 plus porch 105 x 200 cm. Coal stove: Kværner Ovnstøperi No. 4. Floor: Wood.
- On 8th August 1938, materials for Rendalshytten were laid out with "Polarbjørn".[1034] Bjarne Akre wrote that before: *"we left the place, we agreed to name this hut Rendalshytta"*.[1035] The Akre cousins originated from Rendalen in the eastern part of Norway.

Bjørnheimen [310], 1st August 2003. © NCN

310 / 73°07.61'N - 25°44.44'W / Suess Land[1036]
BJØRNHEIMEN, Nanortalik
- Norwegian trappers' hut built 10th September 1934 for Arctic Commercial Enterprise by Magne Råum and Ole Klokset, Kap Humboldt.[1037]
- Due south of Kap Mohn on the south side of Antarctic Sund, and east of the delta at Nanortalikdal.
- B (IIA). 205 x 200 plus porch 110 x 200 cm. Coal stove: L. Lange & Co Svendborg. Floor: Wood.
- Magne Råum recalled that he: *"learnt from the Greenlanders that Nanortalik is the Greenlandic name for the place of many bears. That's the reason why I named the hut Bjørnheimen on 1st November 1934"*.[1038]

Kikut [311], 21st May 1982. © Jørn Ladegaard

Kikut [311], 11th August 2003. © NCN

311 / 73°10.58'N - 23°08.26'W / Ymer Ø[1039]
KIKUT, Dusén Fjord hytten, Steffensens hytte
- Norwegian trappers' hut built 27th August 1929 for Arctic Commercial Enterprise by Hallvard Devold and Olav Kjelbotn, Kap Humboldt.
- At the entrance of Dusén Fjord, south of Vinterøer.
- C (IIA). Ruin. Originally 250 x 200 plus porch 160 x 110 cm. Coal stove: Kraakerøy Støperi No. 4.
- Hallvard Devold wrote on 27th August 1929 that: *"Olav and I took the rest of the materials from hut no. 2 and drove into Dusén Fjord, where we finished building the hut"*.[1040]

Snaddheimen [312], 2nd August 2003. © NCN

312 / 73°10.22'N - 26°40.03'W / Frænkel Land[1041]
SNADDHEIMEN

- Norwegian trappers' hut built in August 1938 for Arctic Commercial Enterprise by Bjarne and Oddvar Akre, Kap Humboldt.
- About 13 km south-west of Svenskenæs in the inner part of Kejser Franz Joseph Fjord.
- C (IIA). 200 x 200 plus porch 95 x 200 cm. Coal stove: Kværner Ovnstøperi No. 4. Floor: Earth.
- Bjarne Akre wrote that: *"after we had driven across Isfjord, along a several kilometres long and probably thousand metres high mountainside, we turned around Svenskenæs and into Kejser Franz Joseph Fjord. Here we found materials and immediately started to build the first hut"*.[1042] "Snadd" is the Norwegian name for the ringed seal.

Brehytten [313], 1950. © Birger Larsen

313 / 73°09.58'N - 27°33.81'W / Frænkel Land[1043]
BREHYTTEN, Gregorydalhytten, Knækelvhytten, Bræhytten

- Norwegian trappers' hut built 24th April 1950 for Arctic Commercial Enterprise by Sverre Storholt and Birger Larsen, Kap Humboldt.
- On the east side of Knækelven at the mouth of Knækdalen (Gregory Dal), innermost Kejser Franz Joseph Fjord.
- C (IIA). Originally about 215 x 150 cm. Coal stove: Dravn No. 3.
- On the 22nd March 1950, Birger Larsen wrote that he: *"had been to Gregorydalen* (Knækdalen) *today to find the hut materials, which were put ashore from "Quest" this summer. Storholt and I were supposed to build a hut here in the autumn, but that became impossible due to unceasing storms and heavy seas"*. The hut was built on the 24th April 1950: *"we came here this morning and tonight the hut is finished"*, Larsen wrote.[1044]

Brehytten [313], 1996. © Ivar Ytreland

Brehytten [313], 6th August 2007. © NCN

Trapper Bjarne Myrvold at Polarheimen [314], July 1947. © Bjarne Myrvold

Polarheimen [314], 1st August 2003. © NCN

314 / 73°11.05'N - 25°58.39'W / Suess Land[1045]
POLARHEIMEN, Røiskattlia, Gråkollen

- Norwegian trappers' hut built 29th July 1947 for Arctic Commercial Enterprise by Bjarne Myrvold and Egil Amsjø, Kap Humboldt.
- On the north coast of Suess Land, east of the river draining Sonklargletscher.
- B (IIA). 310 x 210 including porch 210 x 80 cm. Coal stove: Kværner Ovnstøperi No. 4. Floor: Wood.
- On 8th August 1938 materials for a hut were laid out with "Polarbjørn" in Kejser Franz Joseph Fjord: *"on the south side under Payertoppen".*[1046] Bjarne and Oddvar Akre were supposed to build the hut the same summer, but did not do so.[1047] Polarheimen was not built until after the war. It was from this location, that Julius Payer climbed Sonklargletscher to obtain a view of inner Kejser Franz Joseph Fjord and Petermann Bjerg in August 1870.[1048] It was assumed for many years that Payer had also reached to the summit of Payer Tinde (2320 m), but when John Haller and Wolfgang Diehl climbed it in 1952 there was no sign of a previous ascent.

315 / 73°13.88'N - 23°27.55'W / Ymer Ø[1049]
NØRVEHYTTEN

- Norwegian trappers' hut built 16th October 1929 for Arctic Commercial Enterprise by Hallvard Devold and Olav Kjelbotn, Kap Humboldt.
- On the north side of Dusén Fjord, about 6 km west of the cape south of Kap Graah.
- C (IIA). Ruin. Originally about 250 x 200 plus porch 150 x 100 cm.
- On 16th October 1929, Hallvard Devold wrote that: *"yesterday evening I made spiked shoes for my dog Trym. We loaded the materials placed at Wijkanderøya* (Vinterøer) *and drove in 4 hours to Kap Graah. It is a several hundred kilo load for two dogs but with spiked shoes they made it. We built the hut before evening".*[1050] Nørvehytten was named after Elias Nørve, a merchant in Ålesund and a member of the board of Arctic Commercial Enterprise.

Nørvehytten [315], 11th August 2003. © NCN

316 / c. 73°15'N - 22°20'W / Gauss Halvø[1051]
FUNKIS, Firkanten

- Norwegian trappers' hut built in the summer of 1937 for Arctic Commercial Enterprise by Finn Framnes-Hansen and Johan Johansen, Myggbukta.
- On the southernmost point of Gauss Halvø, about 5-6 km west of Kap Franklin.
- C (IIA). about 200 x 200 cm.

Funkis [316], 1940. © Hans K. Siewers

■ On 7th August 1937 materials for a hut were laid out with "Polarbjørn": *"about 10 kilometres west of Kap Franklin"*.[1052] On 22nd January 1940, Hans Siewers visited the hut and noted that there was: *"one foot of snow on the floor. What a pity that a construction engineer could not do better than this."* Siewers was here referring to Framnes-Hansen. The hut is said to have been completely destroyed by a landslide in 1955.[1053]

Brøggers hytte [317], 11th August 2003. © NCN

317 / 73°15.42'N - 23°59.30'W / Ymer Ø[1054]
BRØGGERS HYTTE, Brødgerhytten

■ Norwegian trappers' hut built 17th September 1929 for Arctic Commercial Enterprise by Hallvard Devold and Olav Kjelbotn, Kap Humboldt.

■ On the north side of Dusén Fjord, 10-11 km east of Zoologdalen on Gunnar Andersson Land.

■ B (IIA). 255 x 205 plus porch 160 x 95 cm.
Coal stove: CMS Veile 420T. Floor: Wood.

■ On 17th September 1929 Hallvard Devold wrote that: *"Kjelbotn and I took the material for a trappers' hut and went into Dusēns Fjord, where we put up a hut. We have named it Brøggers hytte after solicitor Brøgger"*.[1055]

318 / 73°17.66'N - 24°26.01'W / Ymer Ø[1056]
DEVOLDHYTTEN, Isboksen

■ Norwegian trappers' hut built 24th October 1929 for Arctic Commercial Enterprise by Hallvard Devold and Olav Kjelbotn, Kap Humboldt.

■ On the north side of Dusén Fjord, about 5 km west of Zoologdalen on Gunnar Andersson Land.

■ B (IIA). 250 x 200 plus porch 200 x 95 cm.
Floor: Wood.

■ On 17th August 1929 materials for a hut were laid out at Kap Graah with "Veslekari". On 24th October 1929, Hallvard Devold wrote that: *"we took with us the rest of the material for the new hut, Devoldhytten, and finished building it"*.[1057]

Devoldhytten [318], 8th May 1979. © Peter Schmidt Mikkelsen

Devoldhytten [318], 11th August 2003. © NCN

319 / 73°18.30'N - 22°05.58'W / Gauss Halvø[1058]
FRANKLIN STRAND, Franklinhytten, Kap Franklin

■ Norwegian trappers' hut built 4th September 1927 for the Foldvik Expedition by Hallvard Devold and Nils Foldvik, Myggbukta.

■ At Foster Bugt, 6-7 km north of Kap Franklin.

■ C (IIA). 280 x 280 plus porch 140 x 120 cm.
Coal stove: L. Lange & Co. Floor: Wood.

■ Built of materials from Franklin-huset [326].[1059]

Franklin Strand [319], 27th July 2004. © NCN

■ Kap Franklin was named by William Scoresby Junior in 1822 after the arctic explorer John Franklin (1786-1847): *"the persevering commander of the overland expedition for exploring the coasts of the Arctic Ocean"*.[1060] The cairn at Kap Franklin was built by the Nathorst Expedition on 30th August 1899.[1061]

Trapper Hans K. Siewers at Smedal [320], 1940. © Hans K. Siewers

Smedal [320], 10th August 2003. © NCN

320 / 73°18.72'N - 22°41.78'W / Gauss Halvø[1062]
SMEDAL, Margrethedalhytten

■ Norwegian trappers' hut built in August 1930 for Arctic Commercial Enterprise by Hallvard Devold and John Giæver, Hoelsbu.

■ On the west side of the river delta at Margrethedal, on the south side of Gauss Halvø.

■ B (IIA). 260 x 200 cm. Coal stove: Morsø. Floor: Wood.

■ On 3rd August 1930 materials for a hut were laid out with "Veslekari".[1063] Hallvard Devold wrote that: *"During the last days of August 1930 John Giæver and I built a hut in Smedalen* (Margrethedal), *that is the first valley west of Kap Franklin on the north side of Kejser Franz Joseph Fjord"*.[1064] Gustav Smedal, a Norwegian lawyer, was a driving force behind the Norwegian claim over "Eirik Raudes Land" argued at The Hague. He was the chairman of Norges Grønlandslag (Norway's Greenland Society) and of Norges Ishavsråd (Norway's Arctic Ocean Council).

Dyrstien [321], 10th August 2003. © NCN

321 / 73°19.00'N - 24°48.93'W / Ymer Ø[1065]
DYRSTIEN, Dyrfaret, Strømhytten, Trangen, Dyrstein, Strømmen

■ Norwegian trappers' hut built 19th September 1930 for Arctic Commercial Enterprise by Olav Kjelbotn and Søren Richter, Kap Humboldt.

■ South-west of Barrieren in Dusén Fjord, on the north side of the fjord.

■ C (IIA). Ruin. About 210 x 150 cm.

■ On 19th September 1930 Olav Kjelbotn wrote that: *"we continued to Dyrstien."* ... *"and before dark we had finished the hut sufficiently that we could move in"*.[1066]

Trapper Sverre Storholt at Noahytten [322], summer 1949. © Sverre Storholt

322 / 73°19.10'N - 25°02.79'W / Ymer Ø[1067]
NOAHYTTEN, Bunnhuset, Laksehytta, Holmboe-hytta

■ Norwegian trappers' hut built in August 1932 by the W. Holmboe fishing expedition, Kap Humboldt.[1068]

Noahytten [322], 10th August 2003. © NCN

- At the head of Dusén Fjord on the south side of the river draining Noa Dal.
- B (IIA). 400 x 200 including porch 125 x 200 cm. Coal stove: Ulefos 158D. Floor: Wood.
- Built for the char fishery in the river draining Noa Dal.
- On 8th February 1933 Bernt Marø wrote that: *"today I discovered a hut in the innermost part of Dusén Fjord. There is a plaque on the hut reading: 25th August 1932. The land around this stake is today annexed by Captain Alb. Bergesen m/s "Isbjørn" of Tromsø for the company F.A.W. Holmboe, Tromsø. Witness: Norse Andr. Lehne, G. Bjørnnes".*[1069]

323 / c. 73°21'N - 23°46'W / Ymer Ø[1070]
KLOKSETHYTTEN, Kap Martha hytten, Slippenhytten

- Norwegian trappers' hut built in August 1938 for Ole Klokset's expedition by Ole Klokset and the crew of "Grande", Laplace.[1071]
- At Slippen on the north side of Gunnar Andersson Land.
- C (IIA). Disappeared.[1072] A few scattered timbers were observed from the fjord in 2003.[1073]
- In 1991, Ole Klokset said that: *"we built the hut for overnight stays on the journey to Hudson Land, where I was trapping in the winter of 1938-39".*[1074] In 1991 Trygve Havold recalled that the roof of the hut was made from natural slate found near the location. It was a good roof according to Havold.[1075]

324 / 73°19.85'N - 25°16.88'W / Ymer Ø[1076]
VARGHYTTEN, Blomsterbugten, Vargbukta, Vargheim

- Norwegian trappers' hut built 25th March 1930 for Arctic Commercial Enterprise by Olav Kjelbotn and Sverre Sørensen, Kap Humboldt.[1077]

Varghytten [324] destroyed by polar bears, 9th May 1979. © Peter Schmidt Mikkelsen

Varghytten [324] being restored by Fritz Ploug Nielsen and Jannik Berntsen from Nanok in 2002. © NCN

Varghytten [324], 3rd August 2003. © NCN

- In Blomsterbugten at the west end of Noa Dal, Ymer Ø.
- B (IIA). 250 x 200 plus porch 160 x 145 cm. Coal stove: L. Lange & Co. Floor: Wood/Earth.
- On 15th August 1929 materials for a hut were laid out with "Veslekari", but the hut was not built until the following spring.[1078] The wall in the hut has this inscription: *"Varghytte, opsat 25. mars 1930 av Olaf Kjelbotn."* (Varghytte, built 25th March 1930 by Olaf

Kjelbotn).[1079] The Norwegians called Blomsterbugten (flower bay) Vargbukta (wolf bay), because a crew member of the "Veslekari" in the summer of 1929 was surrounded by a pack of five wolves while capturing a muskox calf here.[1080] The following winter Blomsterbugten was the domicile of a large wolf pack.[1081] The hut was used by Sirius until 1979.
■ In 2002 Varghytten was restored by Nanok.[1082]

Renbugthytten [325], 17th August 2003. © NCN

325 / 73°21.00'N - 26°27.99'W / Andrée Land[1083]
RENBUGTHYTTEN, Reinsbukta, Reinli, Ha-Ha-hytta
■ Norwegian trappers' hut built 17th August 1931 for Arctic Commercial Enterprise by Jonas Karlsbak and Gustav Lindquist, Kap Humboldt.
■ On the east side of Renbugten, at the mouth of Rendalen, Isfjord.
■ B (IIA). 250 x 205 cm. Coal stove: Dravn No. 3. Floor: Wood.
■ The present Renbugthytten has been placed at three different locations. In 1929-30 it was on the south side of Sofia Sund and called Bødtkers hytte [302]. In 1930-31 it was moved to the north side of Sofia Sund and named Stordalen [306]. Finally, in August 1931, it was moved to its present location in Renbugten.[1084] On 17th August 1931 Jonas Karlsbak wrote: *"Renbugten. Lindquist and I went ashore today with materials for a hut, which we have built during the day"*.[1085]

326 / 73°20.41'N - 21°57.47'W / Gauss Halvø[1086]
FRANKLIN-HUSET
■ Norwegian trappers' station built in 1922 for the Johan A. Olsen Expedition.
■ About halfway between Kap Franklin and Kap Bennet on the southern coast of Vestersletten.
■ C (IA). Removed.
■ See chapter on stations.

Franklin-huset [326], 27th July 2004. © NCN

327 / 73°22.61'N - 21°41.84'W / Gauss Halvø[1087]
FOLDVIK, Kap Bennet hytten, Giesecke, Giskehytten, Bennethytten
■ Norwegian trappers' hut built 24th August 1927 for the Foldvik Expedition by Nils Foldvik and Hallvard Devold, Myggbukta.
■ On a small point about 4 km south-west of Kap Bennet.
■ A (IIA). 215 x 210 plus porch 105 x 75 cm. Coal stove: Dravn. Floor: Wood
■ Built of materials taken from the former Franklin-huset [326]. Nils Foldvik, the leader of the Foldvik Expedition of 1926-28, wrote that: *"we rowed the materials to Giesecke* (Kap Bennet) *and built the hut there"*.[1088] Kap Bennet was named by William Scoresby Junior in 1822: *"after Captain Bennet, of the "Venerable" whaler, who furnished me with some chronometrical observations on the longitudes of two or three adjoining headlands, which very nearly correspond with my own"*.[1089]

Foldvik [327], 29th July 2004. © NCN

328 / 73°23.02'N - 23°11.60'W / Gauss Halvø[1090]
VON KROGH, Krogh-hytten, Aina Dal hytten

■ Norwegian trappers' hut built in October 1930 for Arctic Commercial Enterprise by John Giæver and Otto Johnsen, Hoelsbu.
■ East of the river draining Aina Dal on the south coast of Gauss Halvø.
■ B (IIA). 250 x 200 plus porch 165 x 100 cm. Floor: Wood.
■ On 3rd August 1930 materials for two huts were laid out with "Veslekari". Both huts were assembled here, one of which was to be moved to another site, see Giæverhytten [358-1]. Von Krogh hytten was built during a snow storm and John Giæver wrote that: *"in memory of this struggle and to add a militant aspect we named the place after commander von Krogh." ... "To cut a long story short the place and the hut are now called von Krogh".*[1091] Commander Rolf von Krogh was hydrographer on several NSIU expeditions to North-East Greenland.

Von Krogh [328], 10th August 2003. © NCN

329 / 73°26.89'N - 20°38.07'W / Hold with Hope[1092]
GNISTEN, Bjørnehytten
■ Norwegian trappers' hut built 12th September 1950 for Arctic Commercial Enterprise by Stein Sørensen, Myggbukta.

Trappers Birger Larsen and Sverre Storholt at Gnisten [329]. Winter 1952. © Birger Larsen

■ On the southernmost point of Hold with Hope.
■ C (IIA). Ruin. Originally about 200 x 200 cm. Coal stove.
■ On 10th September 1950 Stein Sørensen wrote: *"As I approach the place where the materials are located, I observe bear tracks going the same way and I have misgivings. Sure enough, the bear has made a mess, and a whole finished wall for the hut has disappeared without trace – pulled into the sea by the bear. I curse and swear, search high and low, but in vain. I have to use the materials for the floor for the wall and have therefore no boards for the floor".*[1093] Stein Sørensen was a "gnist" ("spark" = a nickname for a radio operator) at Myggbukta.

Gnisten [329], 1st August 2003. © NCN

330 / 73°27.21'N - 21°01.30'W / Hold with Hope[1094]
GEISHA
■ Norwegian trappers' hut built 24th August 1926 for the Foldvik Expedition by Hallvard Devold and Arnulf Gisvold, Myggbukta
■ 1-2 km east of the river Dyraelv on the south coast of Hold with Hope.
■ B (IIA). 315 x 225 including porch 95 x 225 cm. Coal stove. Floor: Wood/Earth.
■ Geisha has probably been replaced and moved one or more times. It was named after Geisha, one

Geisha [330], 29th July 2004. © NCN

of Hallvard Devold's sledge dogs.[1095] On 25th August 1926 Nils Foldvik wrote about the dog and the original hut: *"at 11.30 Devold and Gisvold came walking back. They had built the hut and prepared the place" ... "Geisha, who had been missing since Friday, when it ran away from Devold, came home with them".*[1096]

Kap Broer Ruys Syd [331], 28th July 2004. © NCN

331 / 73°27.53'N - 20°53.68'W / Hold with Hope[1097]
KAP BROER RUYS SYD, Sydhytten

▪ Danish trappers' hut built 7th August 1945 for Nanok by Henry V. Nielsen, Ib Bach Hansen and others, Knudshoved.
▪ At a small river south of Uglehøjene on the south coast of Hold with Hope.
▪ C (IIA). 300 x 200 cm. Coal stove. Floor: Wood.
▪ Nanok's southernmost trappers' hut. On 7th August 1945 J.G. Jennov wrote that they: *"placed a hut a little west of Kap Broer Ruys. The work was not finished, as the wind turned south-west and freshened. Half an hour of work at the hut was still needed".*[1098]

332-1 / 73°28.12'N - 21°56.85'W / Gauss Halvø[1099]
FLATA, Giesecke

▪ Norwegian trappers' hut built in the spring of 1931 for Arctic Commercial Enterprise by Eilif Herdal, Hallvard Devold, Olav Kjelbotn and Ingvald Strøm, Myggbukta.
▪ At a small lake near Fløelv at the foot of Giesecke Bjerge, north-east of Bonney Plateau on Vestersletten.
▪ C (IIA). Ruin. Originally about 200 x 200 cm.
▪ Flata was built at Myggbukta and transported by dog sledge to the site. On 29th March 1931 Ingvald Strøm wrote that: *"Hallvard and Eilif built one of the huts and prepared it to be transported westwards".*[1100] However, on 1st April 1931 Herdal wrote that they had: *"tried to drive, but the snow is too deep, so the hut must be dropped".*[1101] Strøm later, on 31st May, wrote

Flata [332-1], 1st August 2005. © NCN

that a hut, probably Flata, was transported *"southwards."* Flata was located close to Stormbu [332-2], where Oscar Bang on 21st October 1938 wrote, that: *"we saw the remnants of one of the huts that stood here before".*[1102] In 1992, Peter Melleby recalled that: *"in 1946-48 I found the remnants of a hut (blown down) on the plain not so far from Stormbu".*[1103] Judging from these accounts and the remaining materials it can be assumed that Flata was never actually assembled at the location.

Stormbu [332-2], 1st August 2005. © NCN

332-2 / 73°28.12'N - 21°56.92'W / Gauss Halvø[1104]
STORMBU

▪ Norwegian trappers' hut built 17th October 1938 for Arctic Commercial Enterprise by Oscar Bang and Eilif Herdal, Myggbukta.
▪ At Fløelv at the foot of Giesecke Bjerge north-east of Bonney Plateau on Vestersletten.
▪ C (IIA). 290 x 195 including porch 85 x 195 cm. Coal stove: Kværner Ovnstøperi. Floor: Wood.
▪ On 16th October 1938 Oscar Bang wrote that they were going to: *"drive up the materials, which are deposited on the beach at Giskehytta* (Foldvik [327]). *They have to be transported by the river, which begins here and flows out at Giske* (the Kap Bennet

mountain).[1105] On 18th October, when the hut had survived the first blizzard, Bang wrote that: *"the hut stood just as sturdy this morning as last night. We have named it "Stormbu"."* Stormbu is located just 30 metres from Flata [332-1].

Isfjordhytten [333], 17th August 2003. © NCN

333 / 73°26.81'N - 27°07.60'W / Andrée Land[1106]
ISFJORDHYTTEN, Lille Stu
- Norwegian trappers' hut built 25th March 1940 for Arctic Commercial Enterprise by Oddvar Akre, Kap Humboldt.
- On the east side of Isfjord opposite Jættegletscher.
- C (IIA). 200 x 140 cm. No stove. Floor: Earth.
- The following inscription is found inside the hut: *"Lille Stu, opsat av Oddvar Akre den 25. March 1940"*.[1107] In 1992, the former Norwegian trapper Birger Larsen recalled that in the summer of 1949 a hidden depot of American military food was discovered beneath the hut.[1108]

334 / 73°28.98'N - 20°25.34'W / Hold with Hope[1109]
KAP BROER RUYS, Kap Hold with Hope Station, Station "B"
- Danish trappers' station built in 1920 for the East Greenland Company.

Kap Broer Ruys [334] in 1924. © Gunnar Isachsen / Norwegian Polar Institute

Kap Broer Ruys [334], 28th July 2004. © NCN

- On the east coast of Hold with Hope, 5-6 km south of Kap Broer Ruys, on the south side of a small point.
- C (IA). Ruin.
- See chapter on stations.

Myggbukta [335], 29th July 2004. © NCN

335 / 73°29.44'N - 21°33.36'W / Hold with Hope[1110]
MYGGBUKTA
- Norwegian trapping and weather station built in 1922 for the Johan A. Olsen Expedition.
- The south coast of Hold with Hope at the head of Mackenzie Bugt.
- B (IA). The station consists of a large two-story house with several side sheds, and three or four other sheds and huts.
- See chapter on stations.

336 / 73°30.40'N - 23°40.15'W / Gauss Halvø[1111]
DALHEIM, Paralleldalhytten, Tromsdalen
- Norwegian trappers' hut built in October 1930 for Arctic Commercial Enterprise by John Giæver and Otto Johnsen, Hoelsbu.
- On the north side of Paralleldal on the south coast of Gauss Halvø.

■ C (IIA). 255 x 195 plus porch 165 x 100 cm. Coal stove: L. Lange & Co. Floor: Wood.
■ On 3rd August 1930 materials were laid out with "Veslekari".[1112] John Giæver wrote that: *"the hut is located at the entrance to a quite wide valley" ... "The entire terrain looks so much like the country at home around Tromsø, that we named the valley Tromsdal and the mountain peak Tromsdalstind. The hut is called Dalheim"*.[1113] Despite a tilt of 10-20 degrees the hut was used until about 1980.

Dalheim [336], 10th August 2003. © NCN

337 / 73°28.52'N - 25°02.89'W / Andrée Land[1114]
RAGNHILDS-HYTTEN, Grejsdalen, Eleonore Bukta
■ Norwegian trappers' hut built 31st March 1937 for Arctic Commercial Enterprise by Magne Råum, Kap Humboldt.
■ On the east side of Grejsdalen, at the coast of Kejser Franz Joseph Fjord.
■ B (IIA). 205 x 200 plus porch 130 x 100 cm. Coal stove: Jøtul 373. Floor: Wood.
■ On 25th August 1936 materials were laid out with "Isbjørn".[1115] One of the walls has the inscription: *"Ragnhilds-hytta. Er opsatt 31. mars 1937 av Magne Råum."* (Ragnhilds-hytten, built 31st March 1937 by Magne Råum.) In 1990 Råum recalled that: *"before I built Ragnhilds-hytten I used to turn over my dog sledge and place the sleeping bag between the runners to sleep there, when I didn't manage to return to Varghytten."* The hut was named after Råum's fiancée, Ragnhild Lien.[1116]

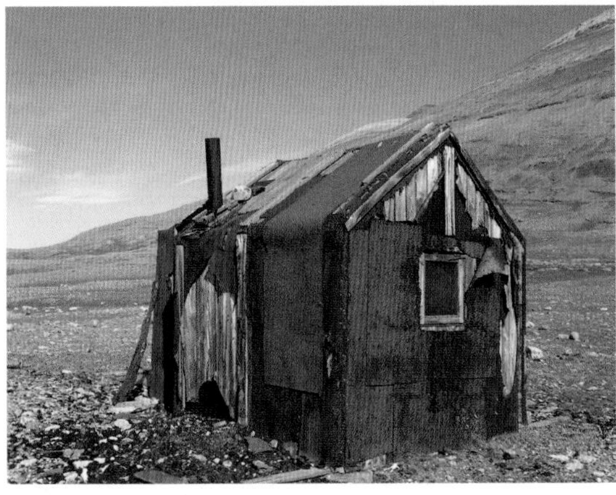

Ragnhilds-hytten [337], 6th August 2003. © NCN

Kap Broer Ruys Nord [338], 20th May 1979. © Peter Schmidt Mikkelsen

Kap Broer Ruys Nord [338], 28th July 2004. © NCN

338 / 73°32.70'N - 20°29.68'W / Hold with Hope[1117]
KAP BROER RUYS NORD, Domkirken, Kirkehytten
■ Danish trappers' hut built in September 1945 for Nanok by Carl El'Vibe and Ib Bach Hansen, Knudshoved.
■ About 100 m south of the mouth of Glommen, about 4 km north-west of Kap Broer Ruys.
■ B (IIA). 305 x 205 including porch 110 x 205 cm and a 335 cm high tower. Coal stove: L. Lange & Co. Nr. 900. Floor: Wood/Earth.
■ On 8th August 1945 materials were laid out with "Godthaab".[1118] On 7th August 1950 J.G. Jennov wrote: *"the hut is located some distance from the coast and is completely buried by snow in the winter. We put a 3½ metre high tower on the hut, so it is possible to get down into the hut through a hatch at the top of the tower"*.[1119]

This tower gave the hut a unique appearance, and gave rise to use of the name Domkirken (the cathedral).

Skandalen [339], 27th July 2004. © NCN

339 / 73°33.32'N - 20°30.47'W / Hold with Hope[1120]
SKANDALEN, Bukta, Moskusoksehytten, Tvivlsom
■ Norwegian trappers' hut built in August 1927 for the Foldvik Expedition by Hallvard Devold, Fritz Øien, Hans Olsen and Meyer Olsen, Myggbukta.[1121]
■ About 2 km north of the mouth of Glommen on the east coast of Hold with Hope.
■ A (IIA). 350 x 210 including porch 105 x 210 cm. Coal stove: Godthåb & Christianshavn. Floor: Earth.
■ Hallvard Devold wrote that the Foldvik Expedition built: *"a hut from driftwood in the bay north of Hold with Hope"*.[1122] Elmar Drastrup wrote that the hut in 1933: *"consisted of a framework of driftwood found along the beach and split into suitable sizes. The framework was covered with roofing felt and some dried, stretched muskox skins"*.[1123]

340 / 73°32.93'N - 24°25.03'W / Strindberg Land[1124]
KAP OVIBOS HYTTEN, Ovibos, Solheim
■ Norwegian trappers' hut built 18th September 1933 for Arktisk Næringsdrift by Johan Listhaug and Knut O. Brandal, Hoelsbu.
■ About 2 km west of Kap Ovibos on the south-east coast of Strindberg Land.
■ B (IIA). 255 x 200 cm. Coal stove: L. Lange & Co. Floor: Wood.
■ On 18th August 1931 materials were laid out with "Polarbjørn".[1125] On 28th October 1932 Walter Molt wrote that he planned to build the hut at the site,[1126] but this was carried out in 1933 by Listhaug and Brandal.[1127] *Ovibos moschatus* is the Latin name for the muskox. Wilhelm Solheim participated as a topographer in NSIU's expedition in 1931.

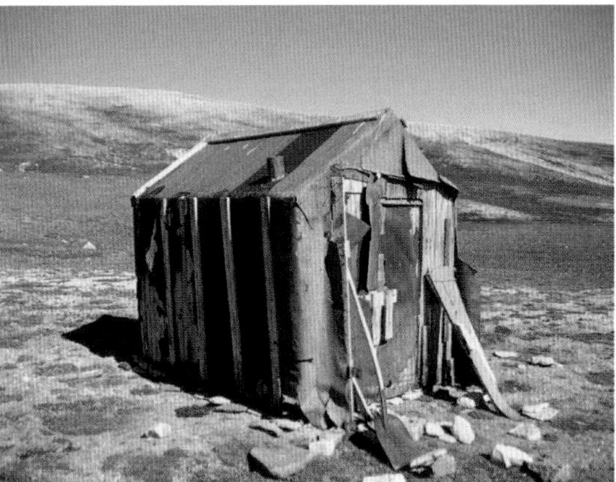

Kap Ovibos hytten [340], 8th August 2003. © NCN

■ In 2000 Kap Ovibos hytten was restored by Nanok.[1128] However, in 2003 it was necessary to move the hut several metres further inland, as it was about to be washed away by the sea.[1129]

Halle [341], 6th August 2003. © NCN

341 / 73°33.59'N - 22°44.00'W / Hudson Land[1130]
HALLE
■ Norwegian trappers' hut built 26th September 1929 for the Finn Devold Expedition by Levin Winther, Myggbukta.
■ On the north side of Moskusoksefjord, west of Prospektdal, near the southernmost point of Hudson Land.
■ B (IIA). 370 x 195 including porch 125 x 195 cm. Coal stove. Floor: Wood.
■ On 18th August 1929 materials were laid out with "Veslekari".[1131] From Bråstad hytten [345] Levin Winther went on 26th September 1929: *"three hours further out of the fjord and built another hut"*.[1132] The hut was named after Thor Halle, a trapper for Arctic Commercial Enterprise from 1929-31. The hut had a tilt of 10-15 degrees in the 1940s, but was still in regular use until about 1980.

Brandalhytten [342], August 1994. © Mike Lea & Kate Lea

342 / c. 73°34'N - 24°52'W / Andrée Land[1133]
BRANDALHYTTEN, Mørkebjerghytten, Geologhytten
▪ Norwegian trappers' hut built in September 1933 for Arctic Commercial Enterprise by Johan Listhaug and Knut O. Brandal, Hoelsbu.
▪ On the west side of Geologfjord at the point below Mørkebjerg.
▪ C (IIA). Disappeared. Originally about 200 x 220 plus porch 100 x 220 cm.
▪ In 1992 Johan Listhaug said that: *"Knut Brandal and I built the huts at Ovibos* [340] *and Geologfjord during four long days. At 2 o'clock in the morning on 18th September 1933 we were finished".*[1134] The hut was named after the trapper Knut O. Brandal, who died of an acute stomach disease less than two weeks later, on 30th September 1933.
▪ No remains of Brandalhytten could be found in 2003.

343 / 73°38.74'N - 20°28.26'W / Hold with Hope[1135]
GAMVIK
▪ Norwegian trappers' hut built in August 1927 for the Foldvik Expedition by Hallvard Devold and others, Myggbukta.
▪ On the north side of Lygnaelv on the east coast of Hold with Hope.
▪ A̲ (IIA). 220 x 150 cm. Floor: Earth.
▪ On 12th August 1927 Nils Foldvik wrote that: *"Devold was going to the outer coast to build a hut between Carlshavn* [365] *and the hut* (Skandalen [339]) *inside Holland Ø." -* And on 17th August: *"Devold came back tonight, he has built the hut up there".*[1136] Foldvik also wrote, that it was a: *"dugout, trappers' hut, built from barrel staves covered with roofing felt and earth, no stove, earth floor. Location on a seashore slope. Good anchorage, about 100-200 m from land. Sand bottom".*[1137]

Gamvik [343], 21st July 2005. © NCN

344 / 73°36.34'N - 22°02.17'W / Gauss Halvø[1138]
SCHJELDERUP-HYTTEN, Skeldruphytten, Quest-hytten, Tyvholmen, Sjelderuphytten
▪ Norwegian trappers' hut built in August-September 1936 for the Quest Expedition by Ludolf Schjelderup and others, Krogness.
▪ In Badlanddal, north-east of Ladderbjerg.
▪ C̲ (IIA). 190 x 190 cm. Coal stove: Drammen Jernstøperi . No. 3. Floor: Wood.
▪ Built as a trappers' hut for the Quest Expedition, which in 1936-37 had rented a trapping territoy at Loch Fyne from Arctic Commercial Enterprise.[1139] The hut was later used by trappers from Myggbukta.[1140]

Schjelderup-hytten [344], 1st August 2005. © NCN

345 / 73°36.49'N - 22°28.49'W / Hudson Land[1141]
BRÅSTAD, Ankerlien, Bråsted
▪ Norwegian trappers' hut built 25th September 1929 for the Finn Devold Expedition by Levin Winther, Myggbukta.
▪ On the north side of Moskusoksefjord, west of Ankerbjergselv.
▪ B (IIA). 255 x 200 plus porch 105 x 160 cm.

Coal stove: Jøtul 376. Floor: Wood.

■ On 18th August 1929 materials were laid out with "Veslekari".[1142] Levin Winther briefly observed: *"24/9. Went to Moskusoksefjord. 25/9. Built a hut".*[1143] Dr. Johan Braastad (1888-1972) was a geologist and secretary of NSIU 1924-35.

Bråstad [345], 9th August 1932. © Thor Askheim / Norwegian Polar Institute

Bråstad [345], 28th July 2007. © NCN

346 / 73°39.25'N - 20°52.69'W / Hold with Hope[1144]
ULVEDRÆBERHYTTEN

■ Danish trappers' hut built in 1939-40 for Nanok by Christian Petersen, Knudshoved.

■ C (IIA). 305 x 205 cm. Coal stove: L. Lange & Co. Floor: Wood.

■ Beside the eastern main river branch of Reinaelv on Østersletten, Hold with Hope.

■ In the summer of 1939, J.G. Jennov told Christian "Ulvedræberen" (wolf killer) Petersen to: *"build a new hut inland* (Hold with Hope) *about 17 km south-west of Knudshoved and 9 km west of point 102 on Østersletten, from materials deposited at the coast".*[1145] Due to the remote location it was uncertain until August 1951 where the "wolf killer" had built his hut.[1146] The position was then forgotten again, until Sirius located the hut in 1979; an exact position was not determined until 2005.

Ulvedræberhytten [346], 21st July 2005. © NCN

347 / 73°38.89'N - 23°10.48'W / Hudson Land[1147]
PETRAHYTTEN, Røiskattlia, 1ste hytten

■ Norwegian trappers' hut built 23rd August 1932 for Arctic Commercial Enterprise by Walter Molt and Knut Nakken, Hoelsbu.

■ On the north side of Moskusoksefjord about 11 km south-east of Hoelsbu.

■ B (IIA). 205 x 205 cm. Coal stove: Dravn No. 3. Floor: Wood.

■ Materials for a hut, Herdal [906], were laid out on 5th August 1930 at Vastidal on the south side of Moskusoksefjord.[1148] However, the Herdal hut was never built; Molt and Nakken moved the materials to the north side of the fjord and built the so-called *"1ste hytten"* her. Walter Molt on 23rd August 1932 wrote that: *"at 7.30 this morning we had finished the hut. The materials were not enough for a porch".*[1149] The hut was renamed Petrahytten in 1939 - and possibly replaced - when Levin and Petra Winther took over the Hoelsbu station.[1150] In 1992 Trygve Havold recalled

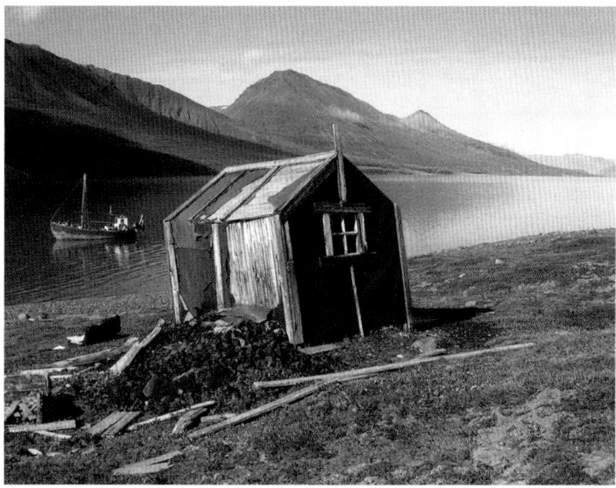

Petrahytten [347], 28th July2007. © NCN

that the hut was also called Røiskattlia, because the trapping at the location was pestered by røyskatt (ermine), that pulled down the fox traps.[1151]

Huttetu [348], 8th August 1989. © Peter Schmidt Mikkelsen

Huttetu [348], 9th August 2003. © NCN

348 / 73°38.75'N - 24°03.95'W / Gauss Halvø[1152]
HUTTETU, Sydvestpynten

▪ Norwegian trappers' hut built in October 1930 for Arctic Commercial Enterprise by John Giæver and Otto Johnsen, Hoelsbu.

▪ On the beach at the river about 5 km north of Sydvestpynten, on the south-west coast of Gauss Halvø.

▪ C (IIA). 250 x 210 plus porch 165 x 100 cm.

▪ On 4th August 1930 materials were laid out with "Veslekari".[1153] John Giæver wrote: *"Huttetu! said Otto as we woke up, and we then named the hut "Huttetu""*.[1154] The weather was namely "huttetu" (perishing cold) when Giæver and Johnsen built the hut.

349 / 73°40.56'N - 21°44.86'W / Hold with Hope[1155]
BUNNHUSET, Øiens hus, Botnhuset, Bundhuset, Bundhytten

▪ Norwegian trappers' hut built in August 1926 for the Foldvik Expedition by Fritz Øien, Hans Olsen and Meyer Olsen, Myggbukta.[1156]

▪ On the east side of Loch Fyne, 2-3 km north of Sogneelv.

▪ C (IIA). 405 x 200 including porch 85 x 200 cm plus side sheds. Coal stove: Omustad & søn Nr. 50. Floor: Wood.

▪ On 4th August 1926 Nils Foldvik wrote that: *"Øien arrived at 7 o'clock this morning. He had walked from the head of Loch Fyne, where the others were building a hut"*.[1157] Foldvik wrote elsewhere that: *"the hut was in everyday speech called "Bunnhuset", but I suggested that we named it "Øiens hus""*.[1158] As it was impossible in 1935 to reach Myggbukta, a shed was built beside Bunnhuset, in which the provisions for Myggbukta were deposited. Bunnhuset has been renewed, altered and enlarged several times, most recently in August 1955 by the trapper Hilmar Gauteplass.[1159] About 200 m south of the present hut are the remains of a former hut, possibly the original.[1160]

Bunnhuset [349], 9th August 2003. © NCN

350 / 73°40.57'N - 21°51.41'W / Hudson Land[1161]
LOCH FYNE, Loch Fyne-huset

▪ Danish trappers' station built in 1945 for Nanok.

Loch Fyne [350], 9th August 2003. © NCN

■ On the west side of Loch Fyne, 2-3 km north of the head of the fjord.
■ B (IA). Station house: 560 x 490 cm. Gas cooker. Floor: Wood.
■ See chapter on stations.

351 / c. 73°41'N - 21°51'W / Hudson Land[1162]
PROVIANTHUS (QUEST)
■ Norwegian hut built in the autumn of 1936 for the Quest Expedition, Krogness.
■ On the west side of Loch Fyne, about 2-4 km north of the head of the fjord.
■ C (IIA). Removed.
■ When the Quest Expedition wintered at the head of Loch Fyne, a provisions hut was built on the west bank of the fjord. The expedition pulled down the hut in 1937, and used the timber as fuel during the home voyage of "Quest".[1163]

GGU sommerlejr [352], 6th August 2005. © NCN

GGU sommerlejr [352], 6th August 2005. © NCN

352 / 73°40.10'N - 22°03.61'W / Hudson Land[1164]
GGU SOMMERLEJR
■ Danish depot hut built in 1973 for the Geological Survey of Greenland (GGU).
■ On the east side of Storelv, 6-7 km west of Loch Fyne at the Stordal landing strip.
■ C (IIA). 250 x 90 cm, plus a caravan.
■ From 1973-77 GGU had a base camp at this location to support geophysical surveys using fixed-wing aircraft and helicopter-supported geological and geochemical investigations. In 1977 the camp was dismantled, leaving only the depot hut. The orange-painted caravan at this location was left by others than GGU, and may have been intended for meteorological observations.

Arvehytten [353], 6th August 2003. © NCN

353 / 73°41.55'N - 22°12.66'W / Hudson Land[1165]
ARVEHYTTEN, Vuachehytten, Storelvhytten
■ Danish trappers' hut built 31st May 1947 for Nanok by Ib Bach Hansen, Loch Fyne.
■ On the north side of Storelv, about 500 m west of the junction of Storelv and the Arve river.
■ C (IIA). 200 x 200 cm. Coal stove: L. Lange & Co. Floor: Wood.
■ Trapper Ib Bach Hansen had to make five sledge trips from the Loch Fyne station to transport the materials for Arvehytten: *"I have been at Vouachebjerg with provisions and built the hut and made a bank of earth"*, Bach Hansen wrote after his final trip on the 31st May 1947.[1166]

354 / 73°41.26'N - 25°06.24'W / Andrée Land[1167]
HASTVÆRKSHYTTEN, Moränedalhytten, Villa Hastverk
■ Norwegian trappers' hut presumably built in 1938 for Arctic Commercial Enterprise by Arne Jacobsen, Hoelsbu.
■ At the north side of Moränedal in Geologfjord.
■ C (IIA). 210 x 200 cm. Coal stove: Laxevaags Værk Nr. 33. Floor: Wood.

■ It was probably the trapper Arne Jacobsen, who built the hut, from materials laid out in 1938: *"on the western side of the middle part of Geologfjorden"*.[1168]
In 1992, Fredrik Sæterdal had the following comment: *"Villa Hastverk* (hurry) *is the worst hut I've ever slept in. It was so sloping that you felt seasick as soon you came inside the door. The wind that came from the valley blew into the stovepipe, and it's a miracle that I didn't die from carbon monoxide poisoning. More than once I had to throw myself outside into the snow to save my life"*.[1169]

Hastværkshytten [354], 1st August 2003. © NCN

355 / 73°42.49'N - 20°32.21'W / Hold with Hope[1170]
KNUDSHOVED
■ Danish trappers' station built in 1930 for Nanok.
■ On the east coast of Hold with Hope, 4 km south-west of Knudshoved.
■ B (IA). 410 x 375 plus porch 330 x 200 cm.
Coal stove: Scandia. Floor: Wood.
■ See chapter on stations.

Knudshoved [355], 11th August 2003. © NCN

356 / 73°42.18'N - 23°26.25'W / Hudson Land[1171]
HOELSBU, Hoelsby
■ Norwegian trappers' station built in 1930 for Arctic Commercial Enterprise.
■ On the north side of Moskusoksefjord, about 5 km south-east of Genvejsdalen.
■ B (IA). Station house and sheds. 935 x 515 cm.
Paraffin stove: Refleks. Coal stove: OM&S No. 50.
Floor: Wood.
■ See chapter on stations.

Hoelsbu [356], 1st August 2003. © NCN

357 / c. 73°42'N - 23°48'W / Gauss Halvø[1172]
JOHNSENHYTTEN, Kolthoffhytten, Jensenhytten
■ Norwegian trappers' hut built in November-December 1930 for Arctic Commercial Enterprise by Otto Johnsen, Thor Halle, Hallvard Devold and John Giæver, Hoelsbu.
■ On the south side of Moskusoksefjord, about 7 km east of Kap Kolthoff.
■ C (IIA). Disappeared. Originally about 250 x 200 cm plus porch.
■ On 13th November 1930 Thor Halle wrote at Hoelsbu that: *"we began to build a hut down at the shore. It has since been transported to Kap Kolthoff by Otto and Hallvard"*.[1173] On the 14th November the hut was ready, but: *"the roofing felt broke constantly during mounting, so the hut never became very tight"*.[1174]
The hut, named after Otto Johnsen, was transported to the location by dog sledge in December 1930.
In 1991, Trygve Havold recalled that Johnsenhytten was so low-lying, that the door had frozen in 1949, because the floor had been flooded.[1175] In 1954 the hut was destroyed by a landslide.

358-1 / 73°42.16'N - 24°30.56'W / Strindberg Land[1176]
GIÆVERHYTTEN, Giævertun
■ Norwegian trappers' hut built in November 1930 for Arctic Commercial Enterprise by Hallvard Devold and Otto Johnsen, Hoelsbu.
■ On the south side of Lakseelv at the entrance

Giæverhytten [358-1]. Summer 1931. © Adolf Hoel / Norwegian Polar Institute

to Brogetdal, at the same location as Strindberghuset [358-3].

■ C (IIA). Removed. Originally about 200 x 200 cm.

■ As the sea had washed away the materials that had been laid out with "Veslekari" on 7th August 1930, Hallvard Devold and Otto Johnsen instead built a hut from the materials deposited at Von Krogh hytten [328] on Gauss Halvø: *"They had built the hut, put it on top of the dog sledges and it went fine on the smooth ice"*, Thor Halle wrote on 28th November 1930.[1177] On 11th June 1935, Giæverhytten was pulled down by Walter Molt, Magne Råum, Ole Klokset and Johan Listhaug, who used the materials for Strindberghuset [358-3].[1178] The foundation of the hut is still visible.[1179]

Nordfjordhuset [358-2], 7th August 2003. © NCN

358-2 / 73°42.09'N - 24°30.59'W / Strindberg Land[1180]
NORDFJORDHUSET

■ Danish travellers house built for the Three-Year Expedition from 9th to 11th August 1931 by the crew of "Gustav Holm".[1181]

■ On the south side of Lakseelv at the entrance to Brogetdal, south of Strindberghuset [358-3].

■ B (IIA). 700 x 580 cm. Coal stove: Hess & Søn Middelfart No. 30. Floor: Wood.

■ Built as a travellers' house; but for periods also used as a base for longer periods, e.g. in 1948-49 by the geologists Erdhart J. Fränkl and Rudolf Katz. The house is the same design as Kap Brown huset [107] and Kulhus [511]. Originally it was equipped with a radio station. At the beginning of the 1930s the house was also used by Norwegian trappers, who at that time just had the small hut, Giæverhytten [358-1], at the site.

Strindberghuset [358-3] after the enlargement in 1954. © Fredrik Sæterdal

Strindberghuset [358-3], 7th August 2003. © NCN

358-3 / 73°42.18'N - 24°30.58'W / Strindberg Land[1182]
STRINDBERGHUSET, Laksehytta, Strindbergdalen, Strindberg

■ Norwegian trappers' hut and summer station built in June 1935 for Arctic Commercial Enterprise by Magne Råum, Ole Klokset, Walter Molt and Johan Listhaug, Hoelsbu.

■ On the south side of Lakseelv at the entrance to Brogetdal, north of Nordfjordhuset [358-2].

■ A (IIA). 510 x 310 plus porch 205 x 310 and a sideshed 160 x 100 cm. Coal stove: Drammen Jernstøperi . Floor: Masonite on wood.

■ Strindberghuset was built as summer quarters for the local char fishery. Materials partly came from

Giæverhytten [358-1], and the materials laid out on 29th July 1932 at Junctiondal [905].[1183] From 1935, it became common practice for Norwegian trappers from Hoelsbu, Kap Humboldt and Myggbukta to meet in the summer at Strindberghuset for the char fishing. In the summer of 1938, an experiment to can char on site was made.[1184] However, the experiment was never repeated. In size Strindberghuset is much like a station house and has been improved several times. In 1954, it was renovated and enlarged by Fredrik and Solveig Sæterdal.[1185] In 1958-59, the trapper John Berg used the house as his main station for most of the season.[1186]

Tobiashytten [359], 4th August 2005. © NCN

359 / 73°43.90'N - 21°23.93'W / Hold with Hope[1187]
TOBIASHYTTEN

- Danish trappers' hut built 3rd August 1938 for Nanok by Carlos Ziebell, Marius Jensen, Alfred Hansen, Christian Petersen and J.G. Jennov, Knudshoved.[1188]
- In the inner part of Tobias Dal on the north side of the river, about 3 km east of Tobias Dal (vest) [360].
- C (IIA). 205 x 200 cm. Coal stove: L. Lange & Co. Floor: Wood.
- On 2nd August 1938 J.G. Jennov wrote: *"At 12.30 we started with three horses and three carriages with more than half of the materials for the next hut. At 5 o'clock in the afternoon we arrived at a suitable location a couple of kilometres on the other side of the watershed. At the watershed we passed a Norwegian hut* (Tobias Dal (vest) [360]) *built by Captain Schjelderup."*[1189] On the 3rd August Jennov continued: *"The hut was finished around 8 o'clock, whereupon we went back to Herjadalshytten* [361]*"*.[1190]

360 / 73°43.57'N - 21°28.84'W / Hold with Hope[1191]
TOBIAS DAL (VEST)

- Norwegian trappers' hut built in the autumn of 1936 for the Quest Expedition, Krogness.
- In the inner part of Tobias Dal on the north side of the river, about 3 km west of Tobiashytten [359].
- C (IIA). 200 x 200 cm. Coal stove: Drammen Jernstøperi No. 3. Floor: Earth.
- This unnamed hut, here called "Tobias Dal (vest)", was built and used by trappers from the Quest Expedition in 1936-37. The hut has often been mistaken for Tobiashytten [359].[1192]

Egil Halvorsen at Tobias Dal (vest) [360], 1937. © Will C. Knutsen

Tobias Dal (vest) [360], 4th August 2005. © NCN

361 / 73°44.00'N - 21°40.56'W / Hold with Hope[1193]
HERJAHYTTEN, Herjadalshytten

- Danish trappers' hut built 2nd August 1938 for Nanok by Carlos Ziebell, Marius Jensen, Alfred Hansen, Christian Petersen and J.G. Jennov, Knudshoved.[1194]
- On the south side of Herjaelv about 3 km from the coast.

Herjahytten [361], 4th August 2005. © NCN

- C (IIA). 205 x 200 plus porch 100 x 100 cm. Coal stove: L. Lange & Co. Floor: Wood.
- The materials for Herjahytten were transported from Loch Fyne to the location by horse carriages. On 31st July 1938 J.G. Jennov wrote that: *"we started at 8 o'clock with some hut materials. We were only able to use three carriages, as the red horse threw itself down with all four legs up in the air. At 10.30 we were stopped by impassable terrain at Herjaelven, only about 5 km inland".*[1195] They then fetched the rest of the materials and built the hut.

Jordly [362], 1st August 2005. © NCN

362 / 73°45.53'N - 20°59.56'W / Hold with Hope[1196]
JORDLY, Vulkanhytten
- Danish trappers' hut built in the spring of 1946 for Nanok by Ib Bach Hansen, Knudshoved.
- In the central part of Tobias Dal on the north side of the river.
- C (IIA). 205 x 205 cm. Coal stove: L. Lange & Co. Floor: Wood.
- On 28th August 1946 Ib Bach Hansen went to: *"the third hut in Tobiasdalen. The hut was wrecked and the roofing felt quite mouldy and damp. The hut should not have been built in the spring. The materials should just have been left on the site, then I could have built it now. I'll fix it temporarily and use the materials from the old Schjelderup hut* (probably Tobias Dal (øst) [363]), *which I was going to make traps from".*[1197] On the 3rd November 1946 Bach Hansen named the hut Jordly.

Trapper Hans Madsen at Arundelhytten [364], 1952. © Hans Madsen

363 / c. 73°45'N - 21°03'W / Hold with Hope[1198]
TOBIAS DAL (ØST)
- Possible Norwegian trappers' hut built in autumn 1936 for the Quest Expedition, Krogness.
- In the central part of Tobias Dal.
- C (IIA). Unknown.
- On his map[1199] John Giæver marks a Norwegian hut in the central part of Tobias Dal; and in 1992 Willie Knutsen said he believed that the Quest Expedition had had a hut here.[1200] It may be this hut that Ib Bach Hansen referred to on 28th August 1946, when he said he was going to use: *"the materials from the old Schjelderup hut"* for repairing Jordly [362].[1201] In 1993, former trapper Carl El'Vibe did not recall the hut, but said he believed that in 1945-46 there were remains of one or more small "bivouac" huts in Tobias Dal.[1202] See also Herjadal I [920] and Herjadal II [921].

364 / 73°46.01'N - 20°04.86'W / Hold with Hope[1203]
ARUNDELHYTTEN, Arundel Ø
- Danish trappers' hut built 9th August 1949 for Nanok by Iver C. Iversen, Hans Egede Jacobsen, J.G. Jennov and others, Loch Fyne.
- On the west side of Arundel Ø, east of Home Forland.
- B (IIA). 365 x 210 including porch 95 x 201 cm. Coal stove: L. Lange & Co. Floor: Wood.
- On 9th August 1949 J.G. Jennov wrote that they sailed: *"to Arundel Ø, where we arrived at 22.00.*

Arundelhytten [364], 22nd July 2005. © NCN

We began to build a hut on the west side of the island." ... *"We finished building the hut late in the afternoon"*. The hut was used by the trappers Hans Madsen and Otto Lapstun in the 1950s.[1204] Arundel Ø was named by William Scoresby Junior in 1822 as "Cape Arundel" in compliment to his brother-in-law the Reverend John Arundel.[1205]

Carlshavn [365], 22nd July 2005. © NCN

365 / 73°46.33'N - 20°29.55'W / Hold with Hope[1206]
CARLSHAVN, Station "A", Karlshavn
- Danish trappers' station built in 1920 for the East Greenland Company.
- On the south-east coast of Home Forland on the north side of Carlshavn.
- C (IA). Ruin.
- See chapter on stations.

366 / 73°48.37'N - 24°02.17'W / Hudson Land[1207]
SOLSTRAND, Rødtophytten, Brehytta, Northfjord, Stenoland
- Norwegian trappers' hut built in 1938, probably by the Ole Klokset Expedition, Laplace.

Solstrand [366], 1947-49. © Trygve Havold

Solstrand [366], 9th August 2003. © NCN

- On the east side of Nordfjord at the foot of Rødtop, about 10 km north-west of Kap Bull.
- C (IIA). Ruin. Originally about 200 x 200 cm.
- Between 2nd and 8th August 1938: *"hut material was landed between K. Bull and Waltershausenbreen"*.[1208] The hut was probably built by Ole Klokset, who used it in the winter 1938-39.[1209] In 1991, Trygve Havold recalled that the hut had been built right next to Waltershausen Gletscher; but when he used it in 1947-49, the distance to the glacier had increased to at least 2 km.[1210]

367-1 / 73°48.38'N - 21°45.80'W / Hold with Hope[1211]
MIDTSTUA
- Norwegian trappers' hut built in August 1926 for the Foldvik Expedition by Arnulf Gisvold, Fritz Øien, Hans Olsen and Meyer Olsen, Krogness.
- On the east side of Loch Fyne - about halfway between Strømmen and the head of Loch Fyne.
- C (IIA). 100 x 200 cm (the porch). Coal stove: Dravn. Floor: Wood.
- The original hut was built in August 1926 and Nils Foldvik described it as a: *"hut made from boards covered with felt and turf. Dimensions 1.80 x 1.80 m.*

No window. About 60 m from the sea and about 12 m above sea level. The hut is difficult to see from the sea".[1212] Midtstua has probably been enlarged or replaced twice; most recently in 1954, see also Mellemhuset [367-2].[1213] Only the porch remains.

Midtstua [367-1], 9th August 2003. Mellemhuset [367-2] can be seen to the right of the hut in the background. © NCN

367-2 / 73°48.36'N - 21°45.94'W / Hold with Hope[1214]
MELLEMHUSET, Midtstua, Midthuset

- Norwegian trappers' hut built in 1954 for Arctic Commercial Enterprise by Helge Nesset, Myggbukta.[1215]
- On the east side of Loch Fyne - about halfway between Strømmen and the head of Loch Fyne.
- B (IIA). 305 x 200 including porch 70 x 200 cm. Floor: Wood.
- Mellemhuset was built in 1954 by Helge Nesset to replace Midtstua [367-1]. It is situated about 100 m from Midtstua.

Mellemhuset [367-2], 9th August 2003. © NCN

368 / 73°48.89'N - 25°36.32'W / Andrée Land[1216]
WINTHERHEIMEN, Eremitdalhytten

- Norwegian trappers' hut probably built in 1936 for Arctic Commercial Enterprise by Levin Winther, Hoelsbu.[1217]
- On the north side of the mouth of Eremitdal on the west side of Geologfjord.
- B (IIA). 310 x 190 including porch 110 x 190 cm. Coal stove: Morsø. Floor: Wood.
- On 24th August 1936 Nils Hanken wrote that: *"we arrived here* (Geologfjord) *tonight. Winther is going to build a hut".*[1218] Hanken was probably here referring to Wintherheimen.

Wintherheimen [368], 8th August 2003. © NCN

369 / 73°53.23'N - 20°18.20'W / Hold with Hope[1219]
RØBEKSTUA, Kap James hytten, Røbeckstua

- Norwegian trappers' hut built 9th August 1930 for the Møre Expedition by Peder Røbek and Hermann Andresen, Kap Herschell.
- At Kap James on the north-east coast of Home Forland.
- A (IIA). 185 x 180 cm. Floor: Earth.
- On 27th July 1926 the Foldvik Expedition laid out materials at Kap James for a hut.[1220] The hut was built shortly afterwards, but in August 1927 it was pulled down and the materials used for a hut on the south

Røbekstua [369], 11th August 2003. © NCN

side of Clavering Ø, see Nes-odden [414] and Breivikhytten (ældre) [404-1]. The present Røbekstua originates from 1930 and is named after Peder Røbek or Knut Røbek, brothers who were both members of the Møre Expedition.[1221]

Knud Erik Filskov (left) and Hans Madsen at Danske Villa [370], 1952. © Laurits Storholt

Danske Villa [370], 18th August 2003. © NCN

370 / 73°53.22'N - 21°52.52'W / Hudson Land[1222]
DANSKE VILLA, Strømmenhytten, Strømshytta

- Danish trappers' hut built 16th September 1950 for Nanok by Hans Madsen and Knud Erik Filskov, Loch Fyne.
- On the west side of Loch Fyne, south of Strømmen and on the south side of the Suselv delta.
- B̲ (IIA). 300 x 200 including porch 90 x 200 cm. Floor: Wood.
- On 17th September 1950 Hans Madsen wrote that: *"during the past week we have been at Strømmen with a hut, which is now completely in order"*.[1223] This hut name is a counterpart to the Norske Villa [373] hut on the other side of Strømmen.

371 / 73°54.33'N - 20°09.58'W / Hold with Hope[1224]
JACKSON-STUA, Jacksonhytten

Jackson-stua [371], 22nd July 2005. © NCN

- Norwegian trappers' station built in 1928 for the Hird Expedition.
- On the south-west side of Jackson Ø.
- C̲ (IA). Ruin. Coal stove: LM Hess Vejle Nr. 420 T.
- See chapter on stations.

Knoph-stua [372], 11th August 2003. © NCN

372 / 73°54.97'N - 20°54.56'W / Hold with Hope[1225]
KNOPH-STUA, Rødelv

- Norwegian trappers' hut built in September 1928 for the Finn Devold Expedition by Gunnar Knoph, Krogness.
- On the north coast of Home Forland on the east side of Rødelv.
- C (IIA). 360 x 190 including porch 150 x 190 cm. Coal stove: OM&S. Floor: Wood.
- The Knoph-stua was built as a replacement for a hut the Foldvik Expedition had built at the same location in August 1926, but pulled down in 1927 and moved to Clavering Ø; see Nes-odden [414] and Breivikhytten (ældre) [404-1].[1226] Above the window in the present hut is the following inscription: *"Huset tilhører Den Norske Grønland Expedition 1928. Bygget sept. 1928. Gunnar Knoph."* (The hut belongs

to the Finn Devold Expedition 1928. Built in September 1928. Gunnar Knoph).

Trappers Helge Nesset (left) and Sverre Storholt at Norske Villa [373], 1954. © Helge Nesset

Norske Villa [373], 9th August 2003. © NCN

373 / 73°56.43'N - 21°53.19'W / Hold with Hope[1227]
NORSKE VILLA, Villaen, Tømmerhuset, Strømhytten

■ Norwegian trappers' hut built in 1927 for the Foldvik Expedition by Fritz Øien, Hans Olsen and Meyer Olsen, Krogness.

■ On the east side of Loch Fyne, about 3 km north of Strømmen.

■ A (IIA). 375 x 220 including porch 85 x 220 cm. Coal stove: Morsø. Floor: Wood.

■ In 1926 a sort of a hut already existed at this location. It was described by John Giæver: *"The most miserable of these wretched affairs and the smallest was situated in Loch Fyne, north-west of Myggbukta, and built by Fritz Øien. It was about the size of a coffin, a large coffin in all fairness; it was six feet long and just over three feet high with a trap-door in the roof for your comings and goings, that is you and your dog – and there was even room for a primus at one end! This dwelling was called "The Villa", and incredible though it may sound, Fritz used it for the entire length of a Greenland winter. It has been slightly enlarged since, but ask Fritz what it felt like when the wolves would scrape at his thin walls and eerie sounds could be heard on the roof of his hermetic cell!"*[1228]

■ In 1927 the original Villa was replaced.[1229] On 11th May 1950 Stein Sørensen described the Norske Villa as a: *"cosy trappers' hut, built from rough hewn driftwood, reminiscent of a Norwegian mountain hut"*.[1230] In 1954 the hut was enlarged again by Sverre Storholt and Helge Nesset.[1231]

Ørnereiret [374], 8th August 1931. © Wilhelm Solheim / Norwegian Polar Institute

Ørnereiret [374], 11th August 2003. © NCN

374 / 73°58.72'N - 21°17.40'W / Hold with Hope[1232]
ØRNEREIRET, Ørnereden

■ Norwegian trappers' hut built in August 1926 for the Foldvik Expedition by Arnulf Gisvold, Fritz Øien, Hans Olsen and Meyer Olsen, Krogness.

■ On the north coast of Hold with Hope, about 1 km south-east of Blåelv.

■ C (IIA). 200 x 175 plus porch 80 x 110 cm. Coal stove: Kværner Ovnstøperi. Floor: Wood.

■ Hallvard Devold wrote: *"One day Øien came back from Loch Fyne. Now we were going to build three huts along the south coast of Clavering fjord* (Gael Hamke Bugt) *and Meyer wanted more people"*.[1233] The porch was added later. In 1930 Nils Foldvik described it as a: *"trappers' hut. Made of boards with a wooden floor. Covered with turfs. Size 2.00 x 1.75 m. One window in the door. No stove. Entering from the north and west of Finsch Øer, shallow. The hut stands about 50 m from the sea. The area poor in vegetation. The house has no name".*[1234] Ørnereiret = eagles nest.

Vulkanhytten [401]. In front Nanok trapper Svend Olsen, c. 1951. © Hans Madsen

Vulkanhytten [401]. In front Nanok expedition member Kunuk Olsen Lennert, 3rd August 2005. © NCN

401 / 73°59.99'N - 22°12.09'W / Hudson Land[1235]
VULKANHYTTEN, Dyndvulkanen, Jennovs Næse

■ Danish trappers' hut built 17th August 1951 for Nanok by Hans Madsen, Svend Olsen, Knud Erik Filskov, Ernst Wind, Hans Frederiksen, Erik Larsen and J.G. Jennov, Loch Fyne.

■ On the south side of Godthåb Golf, about 5 km west of Strømtangen and about 2 km inland.

■ C (IIA). 330 x 150 including porch 130 x 150 cm. Coal stove: L. Lange & Co Nr 900. Floor: Wood.

■ On 17th August 1951 J.G. Jennov wrote that: *"at 5 o'clock we arrived somewhat west of Strømtangen. Madsen, Olsen, Filskov, Frederiksen, Wind and Larsen went ashore at 6 o'clock with dogs and carriage to build a hut in the neighbourhood of the large pingo." ... "The hut was ready at 16.00, onboard at 16.30, sailed for Loch Fyne".*[1236] A pingo (dyndvulkan) is a mound of earth-covered ice found in the Arctic, subarctic, and Antarctica that can reach up to 70 metres in height and up to 2 kilometres in diameter. The term originated as the Inuit word for a small hill. Pingos can only form in a permafrost environment.

■ In 1992, former trapper Hans Madsen said that they also called the hut "Jennovs Næse" (Jennov's Nose), as it was located at the foot of a mountain which had that name.[1237] The inside wall has the following insciptions: *"E. Wind H.E. Larsen 17/8-51 ... L. Vemø 14/8-54 J. Molver 14/8-54 ... Kochs Exp. 21/3-57 R. Stern Bagel R. Elmer Luzern Schweiz"*[1238]

Kalles hytte [402], 8th August 2003. © NCN

402 / 74°01.45'N - 22°17.84'W / Hudson Land[1239]
KALLES HYTTE, Wordie Bugt hytten

■ Norwegian trappers' hut built in the summer of 1936 for the Quest Expedition by Willie Knutsen, Karl Nicolaisen and Ludolf Schjelderup, Krogness.[1240]

■ On the south side of Wordie Bugt, about 2-3 km west of Surprise Elv.

■ C (IIA). 200 x 180 plus porch 95 x 170 cm. Coal stove: UM-Kompagni 11-02. Floor: Wood.

■ Willie Knutsen wrote: *"Schjelderup towed us twelve miles west along Gael Hamke's Bay to where Kalle had scouted for a good spot for the hut".*[1241] The hut was named after Karl "Kalle" Nicolaisen, a leading member of the Quest Expedition 1936-37 and of the Norwegian-French Polar Expedition 1938-39. Peter Melleby used Kalles hytte as a trappers' hut in 1947-48, when it was in a good condition.[1242] It was also used by trapper Hans Oddvik in 1956-57.[1243]

403 / 74°02.84'N - 21°46.76'W / Hold with Hope[1244]
KROGNESS, Kap Stosch hytten, Kap Krogness, Krognæshytten, Krogenæs

Krogness [403], 9th August 2003. © NCN

Krogness [403], 9th August 2003. © NCN

- Norwegian trappers' station built in 1926 for the Foldvik Expedition.
- On the south side of Godthåb Golf, about 2 km south-west of Kap Stosch.
- B (IA). Two huts. The main hut: 300 x 300 cm. Floor: Wood.
- See chapter about stations.

Trappers John Giæver (left) and Søren Richter visiting Breivikhytten (ældre) [404-1] c. 1930. © John Giæver / Norwegian Polar Institute

404-1 / 74°05.88'N - 21°07.01'W / Clavering Ø[1245]
BREIVIKHYTTEN (ældre), Bredevik

- Norwegian trappers' hut built in the summer of 1929 for the Finn Devold Expedition, Moskusheimen.
- On the east side of Eskimovig about 5 km east of Eskimonæs, on the south coast of Clavering Ø.
- C (IIA). 195 x 175 cm. Floor: Wood.
- The oldest of the two Breivik huts is probably identical with one of the two huts ([369] and [372]) that the Foldvik Expedition built on the north coast of Hold with Hope in 1926, and moved in 1927 to the south-west coast of Clavering Ø; see also Kap Oetker [420] and Nes-odden [414].[1246] The first of these, [420], was moved once again in 1929, to Eskimovig, probably by Henry Rudi and Finn Framnes-Hansen.[1247]

Breivikhytten (ældre) [404-1] to the left and Breivikhytten (yngre) [404-2] to the right, 25th May 1979. © Peter Schmidt Mikkelsen

Breivikhytten (ældre) [404-1], 7th August 2003. © NCN

404-2 / 74°05.88'N - 21°07.01'W / Clavering Ø[1248]
BREIVIKHYTTEN (yngre)

- Norwegian trappers' hut built in August 1938 for Arctic Commercial Enterprise, Moskusheimen.
- On the east side of Eskimovig about 5 km east of Eskimonæs, on the south coast of Clavering Ø.

Breivikhytten (yngre) [404-2], 7th August 2003. © NCN

■ C (IIA). 205 x 205 cm. Coal stove: Ulefos No. 1580. Floor: Wood.

■ The newer of the two Breivik huts was probably built in the middle of August 1938 by Gerhard Antonsen. On 14th August 1938, Sigurd Tolløfsen wrote that: *"at 8.30 Antonsen arrived from Clavering Ø, where he has built a new hut".*[1249] In 1991, Birger Larsen said that the hut may have been renewed by Normann Andersen in 1952-54.[1250]

Eskimonæs [405], about 1952. © Hans Madsen

Eskimonæs [405], 11th August 2003. © NCN

405 / 74°05.74'N - 21°16.75'W / Clavering Ø[1251]
ESKIMONÆS, Eskimohamna

■ Danish scientific station built in 1931 for the Three-Year Expedition.

■ At Østhavn on the south point of Clavering Ø.

■ B (IIA). One hut and the ruins of the original Eskimonæs station. Ground plan of the present hut: 510 x 400 cm. Gas cooker: Scandia. Floor: Wood.

■ See chapter on stations.

Niels Ove Jensen and Christian Arke at Kap Ruth hytten [406], 1938. © Niels Ove Jensen

The remains of Kap Ruth hytten [406], 21st July 2007. © NCN

406 / 74°04.91'N - 22°16.72'W / Payer Land[1252]
KAP RUTH HYTTEN

■ Danish travellers' hut built in the autumn of 1938 for the Police Service in North-East Greenland by N.O. Jensen, Ib Poulsen, Christian Arke and Jakob Senimoinaq, Eskimonæs.

■ On the south point of Jordanhill on the west side of Godthåb Golf.[1253]

■ C (IIA). Ruin. Coal stove: L. Lange & Co.

■ In 1992, Ib Poulsen said that: *"the hut was made from a dark-room hut that had been built at Eskimonæs by the Three-Year Expedition for use by the photographers from the Geodetic Institute, who were using aerial photographs for making topographical maps. The flights were carried out during 1932-33 with the Navy's open Heinkel floatplanes. The materials were uninsulated masonite sheets on a framework of rough wood and boards. Despite the simple materials the hut was sturdy and sound. In the winter of 1938-39 I spent a couple of days in the hut during a blizzard, which broke up the ice in Wordie Bugt some kilometres south of Kap Ruth".*[1254]

Elvsborg [407], 17th August 2007. © NCN

407 / 74°07.90'N - 20°39.91'W / Clavering Ø[1255]
ELVSBORG, Elfsborg, Elfborghytten
- Norwegian trappers' station built in 1927 for the Hird Expedition.
- On the south coast of Clavering Ø on the west side of Fiskeelv.
- B (IA). 360 x 350 including porch 350 x 100 cm. Floor: Wood.
- See chapter on stations.

Dødemandsbugten [408], 6th August 2003. © NCN

408 / 74°07.32'N - 20°53.17'W / Clavering Ø[1256]
DØDEMANDSBUGTEN, Daumannsvågen
- Danish station built in 1943 for the North-East Greenland Sledge Patrol.
- On the south coast of Clavering Ø at Dødemandsbugten.
- A (IB). 620 x 460 plus porch 160 x 130 cm. Coal stove: Morsø. Floor: Wood.
- See chapter on stations.

409-1 / c. 74°07'N - 22°11'W / Payer Land[1257]
JORDAN-STRANDA
- Norwegian trappers' hut built in September 1927 for the Foldvik Expedition by Hallvard Devold, Fritz Øien, Hans Olsen and Meyer Olsen, Moskusheimen.
- On the easternmost point of Jordanhill.
- C (IIA). Ruin. Originally about 200 x 200 cm.
- In 1930 Nils Foldvik wrote that it was a: *"trappers' hut made of boards with turf around it. One window. Earth floor. Size 2.40 x 2.00 m. Porch 2.00 x 1.50 m. Stove made from a zinc tub. About 20 metres from the sea, three metres above sea level. A large river on each side of the hut. No name. Usually called "Jordan".*[1258] As the hut over time fell into decay, it was replaced by Jordanhill hytten [409-2] in 1953.[1259]

Jordan-stranda [409-1], 1935. © Will C. Knutsen

409-2 / 74°06.66'N - 22°10.87'W / Payer Land[1260]
JORDANHILL HYTTEN
- Norwegian trappers' hut built late August 1953 for Arctic Commercial Enterprise by Normann Andersen and Gudrun Andersen, Moskusheimen.
- On the easternmost point of Jordanhill.
- C (IIA). Ruin. Originally about 200 x 200 cm. Coal stove: Laxevaags Verk, Bergen No. 33.
- The hut replaced the old Jordan-stranda [409-1] hut. On 26th August 1953, when Odd Bogholm and Stein Sørensen arrived at Moskusheimen, there was:

Jordanhill hytten [409-2], 21st July 2007. © NCN

"nobody home, except a bunch of howling crocodiles (dogs). *But half an hour later Normann and wife arrived from the sea just as we did. They have been building a hut at Jordan Hill, and been away for three days and hardly slept at all".*[1261] The hut was blown down in the 1950s.[1262] The place name Jordanhill was given by D.C. Clavering in 1823 after the residence of his friend James Smith, FRS (1782-1867). Jordanhill is an estate near Glasgow, Scotland.[1263]

Kap Mary huset [410-1], 6th August 2003. © NCN

410-1 / 74°09.87'N - 20°11.69'W / Clavering Ø[1264]
KAP MARY HUSET, Maryhuset

- Norwegian trappers' house built in August 1909 for the 7de juni Expedition by Vebjørn Landmark and others, Germania-hamn.[1265]
- At Kap Mary on the south-east of Clavering Ø.
- C̲ (IIA). Removed.
- The 7de juni Expedition had planned to use the house as a trappers' station, because as Martin Bjørlo wrote on 7th August 1909:[1266] *"from here we can keep a lookout for prey in both fjords, that is "Claveringfjorden"* (Gael Hamke Bugt) *and "Tyrolerfjorden"* (Young Sund). However, due to unforeseen circumstances the expedition had to spend the winter at Sabine Ø - see Germania-hamn [447-2]. Although the house was large and well built, it was never used for wintering. On the other hand it was used as a trappers' hut by both Norwegians and Danes. Due to the dangerous ice conditions at this location, which over the years led to three fatal accidents, the Norwegian trappers, Ivar Ytreland and Odd Lindhjem, decided to pull down the house in 1947 and use the materials for Dahl Skær hytten [412].

Christianshavn [410-2], 12th August 2007. © NCN

410-2 / 74°09.87'N - 20°11.69'W / Clavering Ø[1267]
CHRISTIANSHAVN, Kristianshavn

- Danish trappers' station built in 1921 for the East Greenland Company.
- At Kap Mary on the south-east coast of Clavering Ø.
- C̲ (IA). Removed. Coal stove.
- See chapter on stations.

411-1 / 74°09.28'N - 21°31.43'W / Clavering Ø[1268]
SANDVIK, Granathytten, Svampebugthytten,

Sandvik [411-1], 4th August 2007. © NCN

Granitelva, Stordal

■ Norwegian trappers' hut built in August 1926 for the Foldvik Expedition by Fritz Øien, Hallvard Devold, Hans Olsen and Meyer Olsen, Krogness.

■ At Svampebugt on the west side of Granatdal, south-west Clavering Ø.

■ C (IIA). 250 x 230 cm. Floor: Wood.

■ The hut was originally built in 1926 about 5 km east of Granatdal. The following year, in July 1927, it was moved to the present location by the Foldvik Expedition. Nils Foldvik described Sandvik as a: *"trappers' hut. Dimensions 2.50 m x 2.50 m and sloping roof. Double walls of boards with turf around on the outside"*.[1269]

Norma hytta [411-2], 4th August 2007. © NCN

411-2 / 74°09.21'N - 21°30.39'W / Clavering Ø[1270]

NORMA HYTTA

■ Norwegian trappers' hut probably built in 1953-54 for Arctic Commercial Enterprise by Normann Andersen, Moskusheimen.

■ At Svampebugt on the west side of Granatdal, south-west Clavering Ø.

■ B (IIA). 300 x 200 cm including porch. Coal stove: Kværner Ovnstøperi. Floor: Wood.

■ Norma hytta was most probably built by Normann Andersen, who named it after his daughter, Norma.[1271] In the previous Danish edition of this book Norma hytta was mistaken for Storholts hus [414-2], which was believed to have been moved from a location about 5-6 km south of Kap Oetker to the west side of Granatdal. This is incorrect, as the remains of Storholts hus are still visible at its original location close to Nes-odden [414-1]. Norma Andersen (Larsen) is married to former trapper Birger Larsen.

412 / 74°09.58'N - 20°18.49'W / Clavering Ø[1272]

DAHL SKÆR HYTTEN

Dahl Skær hytten [412], 6th August 2003. © NCN

■ Norwegian trappers' hut built in the summer of 1948 for the Hermann Andresen Expeditions by Ivar Ytreland and Odd Lindhjem, Kap Herschell.

■ On the east side of the bay north of Dahl Skær, on the south-east coast of Clavering Ø.

■ B (IIA). 350 x 250 plus porch 200 x 100 cm. Floor: Wood.

■ Materials taken from the Kap Mary huset [410-1] were used when building Dahl Skær hytten. In 1991, former trapper Ivar Ytreland said that he and Lindhjem had built the hut: *"from the remains of the old Kap Mary house, which was situated at a dangerous location and had already cost three human lives – the Norwegians Knut Røbek in 1932 and Arnljot Tolløfsen in 1933, and the Dane Aksel Nielsen in 1946; it nearly killed me too"*.[1273] It was the treacherous ice conditions in the area, which were the cause of the three fatal accidents. About 1970, Dahl Skær hytten was expanded by the Sirius Dog Sledge Patrol.[1274]

413 / c. 74°11'N - 22°13'W / Payer Land[1275]

HANSEN HAVN HYTTEN, Blåræven

■ Norwegian trappers' hut probably built in 1935 for Arctic Commercial Enterprise by Ole Sivertsen, Moskusheimen.

■ On the north side of the east-facing foreland about 3 km north-east of Kap Adam, north of Hansen Havn.

■ C (IIA). Disappeared.

■ On 2nd September 1935 Ole Sivertsen wrote that he: *"this morning was set ashore after having built a trappers' hut opposite Krogness, by the glacier"*. It was probably the Hansen Havn hytten Sivertsen was referring to.[1276]

414-1 / 74°12.12'N - 21°53.06'W / Clavering Ø[1277]

NES-ODDEN, Kap Øtker hytten

■ Norwegian trappers' hut built in July 1927 for the

Nes-odden [414-1], 8th August 2003. © NCN

Foldvik Expedition by Fritz Øien, Hallvard Devold, Hans Olsen and Meyer Olsen, Moskusheimen.
- On the south-west coast of Clavering Ø, 6-7 km south-east of Kap Oetker.
- C (IIA). 240 x 240 cm. Coal stove: Kværner Ovnstøperi. Floor: Wood.
- Probably built from the materials of one of the two huts that the Foldvik Expedition built in 1926 on the north coast of Hold with Hope. These two huts were located at Rødelv [372] and Kap James [369], but were removed in 1927. Nils Foldvik described Nes-odden as a: *"trappers' hut. Dimensions 2.50 m* x *2.50 m and sloping roof. Double walls of boards with turf around the outside"*.[1278] In 1992, Sverre Storholt said that he built a hut in the vicinity of Nes-odden in 1954, as the hut there often became snowed up. See also Storholts Hus [414-2].[1279]

414-2 / 74°12.17'N - 21°53.52'W / Clavering Ø[1280]
STORHOLTS HUS
- Norwegian trappers' hut built in August 1954 for Arctic Commercial Enterprise by Sverre Storholt, Moskusheimen.

Storholts hus [414-2], 21st July 2007. © NCN

- On the south-west coast of Clavering Ø, 6-7 km south-east of Kap Oetker and about 200 m west of Nes-odden [414-1].
- C (IIA). Ruin.
- Storholts hus was built at this location to replace Nes-odden [414-1], and was not moved to another location on the west side of Granatdal as previously assumed.[1281]

Kap Breusing hytten [415], 11th August 2003. © NCN

415 / 74°12.60'N - 20°07.03'W / Clavering Ø[1282]
KAP BREUSING HYTTEN
- Danish travellers' hut built in 1951 for Daneborg Vejrstation by S. Weber Nielsen and others, Daneborg.
- On the south side of Kap Breusing, the easternmost point of Clavering Ø.
- C (IIA). 320 x 300 including porch 80 x 300 cm. Coal stove: L. Lange & Co. Floor: Wood.
- On 14th January 1959 Knud Nielsen wrote that it is: *"not a trappers' hut, but it was built by people from Daneborg who have plenty of materials from an old American house at their disposal. Apart from a porch for coal and dog food it has a room 2½* x *3 metres inside, insulated with cardboard and plywood and equipped with a real stove, two large windows, two berths and a table with real oilcloth plus a chair"*.[1283] The American house mentioned above was that at Dødemandsbugten [408]. Materials from the Blæsedal retrætedepot [422] are also said to have been used.[1284]

416 / 74°13.43'N - 20°13.97'W / Clavering Ø[1285]
HENNINGELVHYTTEN
- Danish trappers' hut built 24th July 1930 for Nanok by J.G. Jennov, Leander E. Emskær Larsen and Evald Rasmussen, Sandodden.
- In Young Sund on the west side of Henningelv on Clavering Ø.
- B (IIA). 190 x 190 plus porch 75 x 85 cm. Coal

stove: L. Lange & Co Svendborg. Floor: Wood.

■ On 24th July 1930 Leander E. Emskær Larsen wrote that: *"Jennov, Rasmussen and I sailed to Henningelv with a small trappers' hut and built it there"*.[1286] The hut has a pitched roof, which is unusual for a Danish trappers' hut.

Henningelvhytten [416], 4th August 2003. © NCN

417 / 74°14.62'N - 19°41.05'W / Wollaston Forland[1287]

KAP HERSCHELL, Herschellhus, Herschel, Hersel

■ Norwegian trappers' station built in 1927 for the Hird Expedition.

■ On the south coast of Wollaston Forland, due south of the highest point of Herschell Bjerg.

■ B (IA). 870 x 345 cm including three rooms. Coal stove: Scandia 909-N. Floor: Wood.

■ See chapter on stations.

Kap Herschell [417], 30th July 2003. © NCN

418-1 / 74°13.78'N - 20°31.73'W / Clavering Ø[1288]

GRØNNEDALSHYTTEN

■ Danish trappers' hut built in April 1947 for Nanok by Kjeld Soelberg and Harald Mikkelsen, Sandodden.

■ About 7-8 km up Grønnedal on the south side of the valley, Clavering Ø. The ruin of Grønnedalshytten is located about 300 m west of Grønnedal [418-2].

■ C (IIA). Ruin. Coal stove: L. Lange & Co.

■ On 8th September 1946 Mogens Graae and Kjeld Soelberg deposited materials at the entrance to Grønnedal.[1289] On 20th September an attempt was made to transport the hut into the valley on a handcart; but Orla Jensen noted that they had to give up after one kilometre.[1290] On 1st May 1947 Harald Mikkelsen wrote that: *"Soelberg and I have build a hut in Grønnedal eight kilometres from the coast"*, and in 1992 Mikkelsen added that: *"due to the enormuous masses of snow it was difficult to find a spot to build the hut, so we placed it on a snow-free spot on the hill side. In the spring of 1950, when I visited the location, the hut had blown down the hill side and was completely smashed"*.[1291]

Grønnedalshytten [418-1], 27th July 2005. © NCN

418-2 / 74°13.65'N - 20°31.06'W / Clavering Ø

GRØNNEDAL

■ Danish travellers' hut built in the middle of the 1950s by the Sirius Dog Sledge Patrol, Daneborg.

■ About 7-8 km into Grønnedal on the south side of the valley, Clavering Ø.

■ C (IIA). 220 x 215 cm. Floor: Wood.

Grønnedal [418-2], 27th July 2005. © NCN

Grønlænderhuset [419], 29th July 2003. © NCN

419 / 74°15.06'N - 19°46.96'W / Wollaston Forland[1292]
GRØNLÆNDERHUSET, Grønlænderhusene

- Danish trappers' hut built 25th July 1930 for Nanok by J.G. Jennov, Leander E. Emskær Larsen and Evald Rasmussen, Sandodden.
- About 3 km east of the Blæsedalen river on the south coast of Wollaston Forland.
- C (IIA). 305 x 200 including porch 90 x 200 cm. Coal stove: L. Lange & Co Svendborg. Floor: Wood.
- On 25th July 1930 Leander E. Emskær Larsen wrote that: *"we sailed a trappers' hut to Kap Herschell and built it".*[1293] The original hut was destroyed in the autumn of 1931, and the present hut was built in May 1935 by Niels and Aage Hansen. This was mentioned by Hermann Andresen on 28th May 1935: *"They are at the old Greenlander houses to build a new hut as a replacement for the one blown into the sea by the storm".*[1294]

420 / c. 74°15'N - 22°00'N / Clavering Ø[1295]
KAP OETKER

- Norwegian trappers' hut built in August 1927 for the Foldvik Expedition by Fritz Øien, Hallvard Devold, Hans Olsen and Meyer Olsen, Moskusheimen.
- At Kap Oetker, westernmost Clavering Ø.
- C (IIA). Removed.
- The Kap Oetker hut, which should not be mistaken for Nes-odden [414], only existed for two years. In 1929 it was moved to Eskimovig by the Finn Devold Expedition. See Breivikhytten (ældre) [404-1].[1296]

421-1 / 74°15.89'N - 19°22.91'W / Wollaston Forland[1297]
BORGANES, Kap Borlase Warren, Gammen, Bjørn-heimen, Sverdrupsnes, Grønlænderhytten

- Norwegian trappers' station built in 1908 for the Floren Expedition.
- On the south side of Kap Borlase Warren on the south-east coast of Wollaston Forland.
- A (IA). "Dugout", 600 x 320 cm. Floor: Earth.
- See chapter on stations.

Borganes [421-1], 6th August 2004. © NCN

421-2 / c. 74°15.93'N - 19°22.96'W / Wollaston Forland[1298]
VALDEMARSHAAB, Kap Borlase Warren Station

- Danish trappers' station built in 1922 for the East Greenland Company.
- On the south side of Kap Borlase Warren, on the south-east coast of Wollaston Forland.
- C (IA). Removed.
- See chapter on stations.

Valdemarshaab [421-2], 6th August 2004. The square of white stones on the ground probably marks the former location of Valdemarshaab. The hut in front is the Borlase Warren hytten [421-3], with Borganes [421-1] in the right background. © NCN

421-3 / 74°15.93'N - 19°22.96'W / Wollaston Forland[1299]
BORLASE WARREN HYTTEN

- Danish travellers' hut built in the summer of 1956 for Sirius Dog Sledge Patrol by Erik Jensen, Hans

Borlase Warren hytten [421-3], 6th August 2004. © NCN

Frederiksen and Erik B. Larsen, Daneborg.

■ On the south side of Kap Borlase Warren, on the south-east coast of Wollaston Forland.

■ C (IIA). 310 x 200 plus porch 120 x 180 cm. Coal stove. Floor: Wood.

■ The hut was built as a joint project between the Sirius Dog Sledge Patrol and the Daneborg Weather Station.[1300] Knud Nielsen in a letter dated 30th April 1959 noted that: *"at Kap Borlase Warren the patrol has a nice hut, which has just one fault, namely that the window has been broken by a bear".*[1301]

Blæsedal retrætedepot [422], 25th July 2005. © NCN

422 / 74°16.90'N - 19°51.68'W / Wollaston Forland[1302]

BLÆSEDAL RETRÆTEDEPOT

■ Danish travellers' hut built about 20th December 1944 for the North-East Greenland Sledge Patrol by Niels Ove Jensen, Kurt Olsen, Alfred Hansen and others, Daneborg.

■ About 2-3 km inland on the west side of Blæsedalen.

■ C (IIA). Removed. Originally measured about 350 x 250 cm and built of plywood taken from the American Adwell huts at Daneborg. Coal stove: OVT.

■ In the autumn of 1944, the North-East Greenland Sledge Patrol began to suspect a possible German presence somewhere in Hochstetterbugten. In that case an attack on Daneborg was not unlikely and: *"in view of this we built a hut about 3 km inland in Blæsedalen – installed a transmitter and deposited weapons, fuel and provisions for four men for the rest of the winter. If OYK* (Daneborg) *was to be destroyed during an enemy attack, we would here have an excellent strong-point"*, N.O. Jensen (the head of the patrol) wrote in his annual report.[1303] Alfred Hansen, one of the patrol members said the materials were transported into Blæsedalen on dog sledges.[1304] The hut no longer exists, as the materials were used in 1951 to build the Kap Breusing hytten [415].[1305]

Kap Berghaus hytten [423], 25th August 2003. © NCN

423 / 74°16.89'N - 20°07.77'W / Wollaston Forland[1306]

KAP BERGHAUS HYTTEN

■ Danish trappers' hut built 11th September 1946 for Nanok by Jørgen Andersen and Orla Jensen, Sandodden.

■ In the cove east of Kap Berghaus on the south coast of Wollaston Forland.

■ B (IIA). 200 x 185 cm. Coal stove: L. Lange & Co. Floor: Wood.

■ On 11th September 1946 Jørgen Andersen wrote in the station journal of Sandodden that: *"Orla Jensen and I today arrived at Zackenberg after having built a hut at Berghaus".*[1307]

424 / 74°18.13'N - 19°18.86'W / Wollaston Forland[1308]

HERMANNSBU, Haredalshytten, Djevlekløft

■ Norwegian trappers' hut built 29th July 1930 for the Møre Expedition by Hermann Andresen and Peder Røbek, Kap Herschell.

■ On the east coast of Wollaston Forland, about 4 km south of Haredalen.

■ C (IIA). Ruin. Originally about 200 x 200 cm. Coal stove.

Hermannsbu [424]. Stein Sørensen standing in front of the hut, 1953. © Liv Berg

Hermannsbu [424], 6th August 2004. © NCN

■ Built as a replacement for Borganes [421-1]. On 29th July 1930 Hermann Andresen wrote that: *"we have today been north to build a hut as a replacement for Gammen* (Borganes), *as we will not use it this winter"*.[1309] Andresen, who called the new hut "Djevlekløft" in July 1935, improved it together with Nils Hanken.[1310] On the same occasion the hut was renamed Hermannsbu. In the summer of 1947, Ivar Ytreland and Odd Lindhjem installed a wooden floor in the hut and replaced the old stove, which had been made from a fuel drum.[1311] Hermannsbu burnt down sometime in the 1950s or 1960s.

425-1 / 74°18.42'N - 20°13.59'W / Wollaston Forland[1312]
SANDODDEN, Ny Valdemarshaab
■ Danish trappers' station built in 1923 for the East Greenland Company.
■ At Daneborg in Young Sund, Wollaston Forland.
■ B (IA). One station house and three sheds: Skindskuret, Sorte Skur, and Hotel Karina.
■ See chapter on stations.

Sandodden [425-1], 8th July 2007. © NCN

425-2 / 74°18.60'N - 20°13.60'W / Wollaston Forland[1313]
DANEBORG WEATHER STATION, Kystens Perle
■ Danish weather station built in 1944 for the North-East Greenland Sledge Patrol.
■ The northern part of Daneborg in Young Sund, Wollaston Forland.
■ D (IB). Station area with several buildings.
■ See chapter on stations.

Daneborg Weather Station [425-2], 8th July 2007. © NCN

Sirius Daneborg [425-3], 8th July 2007. © NCN

425-3 / 74°18.27'N - 20°13.39'W / Wollaston Forland[1314]
SIRIUS DANEBORG
- Danish patrol station built in 1951 for the Resolut Sledge Patrol (later re-named Sirius Dog Sledge Patrol).
- The southern part of Daneborg in Young Sund, Wollaston Forland.
- D (IB). Station area with several buildings.
- See chapter on stations.

Lille Vandsø [425-4], 25th August 2003. © NCN

425-4 / 74°19.38'N - 20°11.24'W / Wollaston Forland[1315]
LILLE VANDSØ
- Danish hut built for Daneborg Vejrstation, Daneborg.
- Where Lillebitte Sødal joins Lille Sødal.
- C (IIA). 200 x 190 cm. Paraffin stove. Floor: Wood.
- Until the middle of the 1970s, the hut was used to help with transport of freshwater from Lille Vandsø to the various Daneborg stations. In the winter, when the lake froze up, the hut was carried out onto the lake, where it was used as a pumping hut until 1975.

Granta-botn [426], 8th August 2003. © NCN

426 / 74°17.97'N - 22°20.40'W / Payer Land[1316]
GRANTA-BOTN, Grantafjordhytten, Grantahytten
- Norwegian trappers' hut built in September 1931 for Arctic Commercial Enterprise by Eilif Herdal and Knut O. Brandal, Moskusheimen.
- On the south point of Payer Land in Grantafjord.
- C (IIA). 280 x 200 including porch 70 x 200 cm. Floor: Earth.
- The materials for Granta-botn were taken from the porch of Krogness [403]. On 11th September 1931, Eilif Herdal wrote that: *"since my previous entry we have built the hut in Grantafjord"*.[1317] It was in this hut, that the noted trapper Gerhard Antonsen accidently stabbed himself in the eye in the autumn of 1938. The door had no handle on the inside, so Antonsen would stick his knife in the door to pull it shut - but on that occasion the knife slipped out and hit him in the eye.[1318]

Djævlekløfthytten [427], 25th August 2003. © NCN

427 / 74°20.00'N - 20°27.82'W / Clavering Ø[1319]
DJÆVLEKLØFTHYTTEN
- Danish trappers' hut built 29th July 1930 for Nanok by J.G. Jennov, Leander E. Emskær Larsen and Evald Rasmussen, Sandodden.
- On the north side of the river at Djævlekløften on the east coast of Clavering Ø.
- B (IIA). 355 x 200 including porch 90 x 200 cm. Coal stove: L. Lange & Co. Floor: Wood.
- On 29th July 1930 Leander E. Emskær Larsen wrote that: *"we have carried a trappers' hut to Clavering Ø and built it beyond the rock island* (Basaltø)*"*.[1320]
- The hut has a pitched roof, which is unusual for a Danish trappers' hut.

428 / 74°21.82'N - 19°47.66'W / Wollaston Forland[1321]
BLÆSEDALHYTTEN (Nanok)
- Danish trappers' hut built 25th May 1947 for Nanok by Mogens Graae and Kjeld Soelberg, Sandodden.
- About 12 km up into Blæsedalen, beside a large

Blæsedalhytten (Nanok) [428], May 1947.
© Mogens Graae

Blæsedalhytten (Nanok) [428], 25th July 2005. © NCN

boulder on the west side of the valley.
■ C (IIA). 370 x 205 cm. Coal stove: L. Lange & Co. Floor: Wood.
■ On 2nd June 1947 Kjeld Soelberg wrote that: *"on 25th May* (Mogens) *Graae arrived and we built the Blæsedalhytten"*. A porch was added to the hut later, probably in the 1950s.

Moskusheimen [429], 25th July 2003. © NCN

429 / 74°21.77'N - 21°51.68'W / Payer Land[1323]
MOSKUSHEIMEN, Revet, Tyrolerheimen, Ulveheimen
■ Norwegian trappers' station built in 1927 for the Foldvik Expedition.
■ At Revet between Rudi Bugt and Copeland Fjord, on the east coast of Payer Land west of Clavering Ø.
■ B (IA). A station house and a shed. Coal stove: Scandia. Floor: Wood.
■ See chapter on stations.

Blæsedalhytten (norsk/Sirius) [430], 1947. © Ivar Ytreland

Blæsedalhytten (norsk/Sirius) [430], 25th July 2005.
© NCN

430 / 74°23.59'N - 19°46.70'W / Wollaston Forland[1324]
BLÆSEDALHYTTEN (norsk/Sirius)
■ Norwegian trappers' hut built 16th May 1947 for the Hermann Andresen Expeditions by Ivar Ytreland and Odd Lindhjem, Kap Herschell.
■ At the watershed, about 15 km up into Blæsedalen.
■ B (IIA). 425 x 395 including porch 205 x 200 cm. Coal stove: L. Lange & Co 1608M. Floor: Wood.
■ About the original hut - the present porch - former trapper Ivar Ytreland recalled in 1992: *"The hut at the watershed of Blæsedalen was built by Odd Lindhjem and myself late in the spring of 1947. We drove up there by dog sledge, in all four large loads. It was firmly built with wooden floor and a cast iron*

stove – with two hot plates for cooking – from Trolla Brug A/S; the company of which 18 years later I became the managing director".[1325]

■ In 1961 the hut was enlarged by the Danish Sirius Dog Sledge Patrol, and the original Norwegian hut became the porch.

Hermann Andresen in front of Augusta Dal hytten [431], after the new porch had been built, July 1935.[1326] *© Nils-Martin Hanken*

Augusta Dal hytten [431], 21st August 2003. © NCN

431 / 74°24.22'N - 19°09.48'W / Wollaston Forland[1327]
AUGUSTA DAL HYTTEN, Stordalen, Dronning Augusta Dal hytten, Bjørnebu, Bjarnebu

■ Norwegian trappers' hut built 28th July 1928 for the Hird Expedition by Peder Sulebak, Kap Herschell.

■ On the north side of Fladebugt on the east coast of Wollaston Forland, at the entrance to Dronning Augusta Dal.

■ C (IIA). 350 x 250 including porch 110 x 250 cm. Coal stove. Floor: Wood.

■ The original hut was built by Peder Sulebak and called Stordalen.[1328] On 15th July 1935 Hermann Andresen and Nils Hanken enlarged the hut with a porch, put in a wooden floor and a stove with two hot plates for cooking. According to Andresen it was then: *"the best trappers' hut in the territory, and I don't believe there are any better huts in Greenland at all".*[1329] In 1992 Ivar Ytreland remembered it as a sturdy hut, partly made from driftwood and covered with turf.[1330]

Kuppelpashytten [432], 26th July 2005. © NCN

432 / 74°24.34'N - 20°04.91'W / Wollaston Forland[1331]
KUPPELPASHYTTEN

■ Danish trappers' hut built 17th May 1946 for Nanok by Harald Mikkelsen, Aksel Jensen, Ib Bach Hansen, Svend Søegaard and Henry V. Nielsen, Zackenberg.

■ About 3 km north-east of Kuplen (506 m) and 5-6 km inland from Isdal (Kuppelpasset).

■ C (IIA). 305 x 200 including porch 90 x 200 cm. Ovn: L. Lange & Co. Floor: Wood/Earth.

■ Harald Mikkelsen wrote, that: *"on 17th May we drove materials on five dog sledges from Sandodden to Kuppelpasset, where we built a good hut in three hours".*[1332]

Pashuset [433], 24th August 2003. © NCN

433 / 74°24.97'N - 20°19.13'W / Wollaston Forland[1333]
PASHUSET, Pashytten

■ Danish trappers' hut built 1st August 1933 for Nanok by J.G. Jennov, Walther Povelsen and others, Sandodden.

■ On Wollaston Forland between Skiferdal and Cardiocerasdal on the east side of Young Sund.

■ B (IIA). 290 x 200 including porch 85 x 200 cm. Coal stove. Floor: Wood.

■ On 1st August 1993 J.G. Jennov wrote that they: *"sailed to the location where the trappers' hut was to be built and deposited some walrus meat on the way. When we had cut up the boards, Poulsen sailed to Sandodden to fetch more materials plus window glass. Went on building and had the hut ready with a large good bank of earth around it late in the night".*[1334]

■ In 2003 Pashuset was restored by Sirius.

Leirvågen [434], 23rd August 2003. © NCN

434 / 74°26.13'N - 20°56.14'W / Clavering Ø[1335]
LEIRVÅGEN, Lerbugthytten, Eigerhytten, Ahlmanns hytte

■ Norwegian trappers' hut built in August 1939 for Arctic Commercial Enterprise by Henry Rudi, Schjølberg Nilsen and Kåre Rodahl, Moskusheimen.

■ On the west side of Lerbugt on the north coast of Clavering Ø.

■ B (IIA). 370 x 200 including porch 100 x 200 cm. Coal stove: Kværner Ovnstøperi. Floor: Earth.

■ Built to support H.W. Ahlmann's glaciological surveys on Clavering Ø. Henry Rudi wrote that: *"Ahlmann's hut was to be built at Leirvåg and we helped to do it. Rodahl was still going to help him, while Schjølberg and I left for Zackenberg with the motor boat".*[1336] It may have been at Lerbugt that the original Meyer-hus [439] was built in 1927 - see Meyer-hus [439].[1337]

435 / 74°25.77'N - 21°26.93'W / Clavering Ø[1338]
BAKKEHAUG, Bakkehuset, Louise Elv hytten

■ Norwegian trappers' hut built in August 1927 for the Foldvik Expedition by Fritz Øien, Hallvard Devold, Hans Olsen and Meyer Olsen, Moskusheimen.

■ About 1 km west of Louise Elv on the north coast of Clavering Ø.

■ A (IIA). 330 x 205 including porch 115 x 205 cm. Coal stove: Dravn. Floor: Wood.

■ The hut was built from Danish materials found at Kap Mary. In 1930 Nils Foldvik gave this description of the hut: *"Floor, but no stove. Wall of turf all around. Situated on a hill 40 m from the sea. Name "Bakkehaug". Built in 1927".*[1339]

Bakkehaug [435], 25th July 2003. © NCN

Kristian Ytreland at Gisvold [436], 1948. © Ivar Ytreland

436 / 74°25.62'N - 20°20.93'W / Wollaston Forland[1340]
GISVOLD, Norskepashytten

■ Norwegian trappers' hut built in 1927 for the Foldvik Expedition by Hallvard Devold, Fritz Øien, Hans Olsen and Meyer Olsen, Moskusheimen.

■ At a river bed on the east side of a small cove, 1-2 km north of Pashuset [433] on Wollaston Forland.

■ C (IIA). Ruin. Originally about 250 x 200 cm. Coal stove: L. Lange & Co and Laxevags Verk No. 33.

■ The hut was built from Danish materials found at Kap Mary. Named after Arnulf Gisvold, who

Gisvold [436], 23rd July 1989. © Peter Schmidt Mikkelsen

Gisvold [436], 25th July 2007. © NCN

participated in the Foldvik Expedition of 1926-28.[1341] In 1989 the hut was standing on the edge of the shore slope, and by 1991 it had almost fallen into the sea.

Bjørnnesstua [437], 1932. © Norwegian Polar Institute

437 / 74°27.07'N - 21°41.94'W / A.P. Olsen Land[1342]
BJØRNNESSTUA, Gieseckehytten, Giskehuset, Holmboehytten

- Norwegian trappers' hut built in July 1932 by the W. Holmboe fishing expedition, Moskusheimen.
- Beside the river bed 3-4 km south-east of Giesecke Bjerg (1347 m), on the south-western point of A.P. Olsen Land.
- B (IIA). 370 x 200 including porch 100 x 200 cm. Coal stove: Morsø. Floor: Wood.
- On 15th August 1932 Sigurd Tolløfsen wrote that: *"Holmboe's crew have built a hut here. Six men have been fishing char since we left. They have caught three barrels of char".*[1343] The original Bjørnnesstua was a larger hut than the present, almost the size of a station house, of which the present hut was the living room. The house then had a pitched roof and a side shed.[1344] Later the side shed and roof were removed, probably to build a trappers' hut elsewhere.

Bjørnnesstua [437], 25th July 2003. © NCN

438-1 / 74°27.88'N - 20°37.61'W / A.P. Olsen Land[1345]
ZACKENBERGHYTTEN

- Danish trappers' hut built 30th July 1930 for Nanok by Evald Rasmussen, Leander E. Emskær Larsen and J.G. Jennov, Sandodden.[1346]
- On the west side of the Zackenberg river about 100 m east of the Zackenberg trappers' station [438-2]
- C (IIA). Ruin.
- On 30th July 1930 Leander E. Emskær Larsen wrote regarding the original hut at Zackenberg that:

Zackenberghytten [438-1]. Arne Philbert sitting in front, 1932. © Arne Philbert

Zackenberghytten [438-1], 26th August 2005. © NCN

"we have today sailed a trappers' hut to the head of the fjord. It was built on the left side of the big river at Zackenberg. There was a lot of vegetation in there, everywhere – even northern willow. I shot a small char in the river – hence there are some char in the river".[1347] It was probably this hut that in May 1939 was pulled down to be used as material for Sødalhytten [446].[1348] It is, however, also possible that the hut existed until 7th July 1952, when a hut at the Zackenberg trappers' station accidently burnt down.[1349]

Zackenberg [438-2], 27th July 2003. © NCN

438-2 / 74°27.91'N - 20°37.92'W / A.P. Olsen Land[1350]
ZACKENBERG, Horsnæs trappers' station

- Danish trappers' station built in 1945 for Nanok.
- In Zackenberg Bugt on the west side of the river draining into Young Sund.
- B (IA). A station house and a shed. Station house: 705 x 550 cm. Floor: Wood.
- See chapter on stations.

438-3 / 74°27.94'N - 20°38.43'W / A.P. Olsen Land[1351]
ZACKENBERG-BASEN

- Danish scientific station built in July 1947 for the Danish Peary Land Expedition.
- On the west side of the Zackenberg river, immediately west of Zackenberg trappers' station [438-2].
- A (IIA). Provision shed 350 x 420 and 440 x 230 cm. Floor: Wood/Earth.
- Originally the Danish Peary Land Expedition had planned to establish its southern base at Loch Fyne, but chose Zackenberg because the conditions here were better: *"for start and landing with airplane than in Loch Fyne. Finally a base at Zackenberg was located about 80-100 km more northerly than a base in inner Loch Fyne" ... "Godthaab" anchored in Zackenberg Bugt on 24th July and the next day on the 25th in the afternoon the south base was already an effective reality with house, tents and radio on land".*[1352] The Danish Peary Land Expedition 1947-50, and later on the British North Greenland Expedition 1952-54, used Zackenberg-basen as the starting point for airlifts with seaplanes (Catalina and Sunderland) to Peary Land and Dronning Louise Land respectively.[1353]

Zackenberg-basen [438-3], 1956. © Jørgen Rasmussen

Zackenberg-basen [438-3], 27th July 2003. © NCN

438-4 / 74°27.88'N - 20°39.15'W / A.P. Olsen Land[1354]
FISKERHYTTEN, Laksehytten
■ Norwegian trappers' hut built in the summer of 1949 for the Hermann Andresen Expeditions by Ivar Ytreland, Odd Lindhjem and Hermann Andresen, Kap Herschell.
■ About 500 m west of Zackenberg trappers' station.
■ B (IIA). 300 x 200 cm. Floor: Wood.
■ Ivar Ytreland mentioned the hut in an article about char fishing in North-East Greenland: *"The equipment for this fishery was very spartan. For housing we had a trappers' hut, which we built in 1949 measuring 2 x 3.5 m and with a room height of about 2 m. It contained two berths and was used as a dining and living room".*[1355]

Fiskerhytten [438-4], 27th July 2003. © NCN

438-5 / 74°28.25'N - 20°33,58'W / A.P. Olsen Land[1356]
ZACKENBERG ZERO, Zackenberg Ecological Research Station, ZERO, Feltstationen Zackenberg
■ Greenlandic/Danish scientific station built in 1995 for the Greenland Home Rule authority.
■ In Zackenberg Bugt about 2 km from the shore line on the east side of the main Zackenberg river.
■ D (IIA). Nine buildings (2007).
■ The construction at Zackenberg started in 1995 and the station was officially opened in August 1997.
■ See chapter about stations.

Zackenberg ZERO [438-5], 9th July 2007. © NCN

439 / c. 74°28'N - 21°03'W / A.P. Olsen Land[1357]
MEYER-HUS, Trangfjordhuset, Zackenberghuset
■ Norwegian trappers' hut built in September 1927 for the Foldvik Expedition by Hallvard Devold, Fritz Øien, Hans Olsen and Meyer Olsen, Moskusheimen.
■ The exact location of this hut is unknown. According to a description it was situated on the *"north side of Tyrolerfjord, somewhat west* (and across from) *of the northernmost point of Clavering Ø. The hut, which is placed between large rocks, is hard to see".*[1358] It can be assumed that the hut was located about halfway between the huts Bakkehaug [435] and Gisvold [436], which were also built in 1927 by the Foldvik Expedition.[1359] Giæver's map, however, suggests the above description may be incorrect, and that Meyer-hus was actually situated in the vicinity of the present Leirvågen [434] on Clavering Ø.[1360]
■ C (IIA). 200 x 200 cm.
■ The hut was built from Danish materials found at Kap Mary. It was named after the Norwegian trapper Oskar Meyer Olsen (1880-1973) from Tennes, Balsfjord in northern Norway, who participated in the Foldvik Expedition of 1926-28.[1361]

Skrænthytten [440], 25th July 2003. © NCN

440 / 74°28.69'N - 21°53.50'W / Payer Land[1362]
SKRÆNTHYTTEN, Tyroler-heimen, Kap Ehrenberg
■ Norwegian trappers' hut built in September 1928 for the Finn Devold Expedition, Moskusheimen.
■ On the north side of the river delta 3-4 km north-west of Kap Ehrenherg.
■ C (IIA). 200 x 180 cm. Coal stove: Trolla Brug TMV 90A. Floor: Wood.
■ Probably built by Henry Rudi and Finn Framnes-Hansen. Rudi writes that: *"the territory was well equipped with trappers' hut, but we put up two new ones ..."*[1363] The hut was: *"located on the west side of the innermost branch of Tyrolerfjord".*[1364] On Orvin's map from 1930 it is mistakenly shown on the east side[1365]

of Tyrolerfjord, and on the 1:250,000 so-called "Lauge Koch maps" it is also incorrectly shown on the south side of the river bed.

Kopperneshuset [441-1], 6th August 2004. © NCN

441-1 / 74°29.58'N - 18°59.94'W / Wollaston Forland[1366]
KOPPERNESHUSET, Koppernes-tufta, Gripers Road

- Norwegian trappers' station built in 1908 for the Floren Expedition.
- About 1.5 km north-west of Kap Wynn, the easternmost point of Wollaston Forland.
- C (IA). Remains of a stone wall from the house.
- See chapter on stations.

Nothing remains of Gåsneshuset [441-2]. On this photograph it was located immediately to the left of the present Liavåg hut [441-3]. 6th August 2004. © NCN

441-2 / 74°29.36 - 18°59.61'W / Wollaston Forland[1367]
GÅSNESHUSET, Gåsenes

- Norwegian trappers' hut built 31st July 1928 for the Hird Expedition by Peder Røbek, Jørgen Furnes, Peder Sulebak and Jonas Karlsbak, Germaniahavn.
- About 1 km north-west of Kap Wynn, the easternmost point of Wollaston Forland.
- C (IIA). Originally 240 x 175 cm.[1368]
- Built from the remains of Kopperneshuset [441-1] and named after Severin Gåsnes Liavåg (1879-1909). Gåsneshuset was originally covered with turf and had a muskox skin as roof. In 1928-29 the Hird Expedition considered using it as a trappers' station. However, they chose instead to settle in the empty Danish station at Germaniahavn [447-3]. In 1929 a new hut, Liavåg [441-3], was built adjacent to Gåsneshuset. Today there are no remains of Gåsneshuset, and it may have been removed as early as the 1930s.

Liavåg [441-3], 6th August 2004. © NCN

441-3 / 74°29.36'N - 18°59.61'W / Wollaston Forland[1369]
LIAVÅG, Kap Wynn hytten

- Norwegian trappers' station built in 1929 for Arctic Commercial Enterprise.
- About 1 km north of Kap Wynn, the easternmost point of Wollaston Forland.
- C (IA). 500 x 200 including porch 160 x 200 cm. Coal stove: Damgaards Støberi No 18. Floor: Wood.
- See chapter on stations.

442 / 74°30.46'N - 18°46.51'W / Pendulum Øer[1370]
HVALROSØ DEPOTSKUR

- Danish trappers' hut built in the summer of 1921 for the East Greenland Company, Germaniahavn.
- On the western side of the southern point of Hvalrosø.
- C (IIA).
- The original hut was not built in 1920 as claimed,[1371] but in 1921 when "Teddy" was unable to call at Germaniahavn due to the ice conditions. A provision shed, 6 feet square, was built on the south-east coast of Hvalrosø, and here the supplies were unloaded.[1372] On 29th July 1928 Peder Sulebak wrote that he and Jonas Karlsbak: *"took a trip to Hvalrosø to look at the hut that stands there. The provisions that were there are*

Hvalrosø depotskur [442], 23rd July 2004. © *NCN*

completely ruined, there is a hole in the roof and no door".[1373] On 19th-22nd July 1931 J.G. Jennov and Andreas Hvidberg moved the hut to the southern point of Hvalrosø.[1374] On 23rd August 1947, Mogens Graae pointed out that the hut: *"had blown down into a small ravine by the beach, where it lay upside down".*[1375] The Swedish Nathorst Expedition of 1899 had established a depot for Otto Sverdrup on Hvalrosø.[1376]

Blæsenborghytten [443], 22nd August 2003. © *NCN*

443 / 74°30.25'N - 20°37.94'W / A.P. Olsen Land[1377]
BLÆSENBORGHYTTEN, Dalhytten

- Danish trappers' hut built 7th August 1938 for Nanok by Aage Hansen, Carlos Ziebell, J.G. Jennov, Franz Dalskov and E. Brandstrup, Sandodden.
- At the foot of the Zackenberg mountain and a few hundred metres south of the junction between Store Sødal and Lindemansdalen.
- C (IIA). 205 x 200 plus porch 90 x 85 cm. Coal stove: L. Lange & Co. Floor: Wood.
- The materials for the hut were carried here by a horse drawn cart. On 12th November 1938, Berndt Jensen found a meaningful name for the hut: *"Blizzard. It is quite heavy. I will name the hut Blæsenborg* ("windy castle"). *I never experienced a storm like this, it seemed to be raining large stones".*[1378]

Antonsens hytte [444], 29th August 2005. © *NCN*

444 / 74°30.95'N - 21°10.71'W / A.P. Olsen Land[1379]
ANTONSENS HYTTE

- Norwegian trappers' hut built in the summer of 1937 for Arctic Commercial Enterprise by Gerhard Antonsen, Moskusheimen.
- In the central part of Store Sødal, 14-15 km from Tyrolerfjord, A.P. Olsen Land.
- C (IIA). 200 x 200 cm. Coal stove: Kværner Ovnstøperi. Floor: Earth.
- On 10th March 1938 Adolf Hoel mentioned the hut in a letter to Sigurd Tøllefsen: *"Previous summer Antonsen put up a hut approximately halfway between Tyrolerfjord and Lindeman Fjord".*[1380] On 7th May 1939 Sigurd Tolløfsen arrived: *"from Svendsby* [458-1] *at 8 o'clock via Antonsen's hut in Gisikerdalen* (Store Sødal) *to Holmbohytta* [437]. *The dogs had to rest here for three hours. We then continued to Revet, where we arrived at 24.00".*[1381] On 12th February 1960, Ib Palle Madsen referred to the hut when he passed through Store Sødal on his way to Moskusheimen: *"The Danish hut* [Sødalhytten 446] *is leaky and filled with snow, the Norwegian* (Antonsens hytte) *fine with roofing felt and excellent".*[1382]

445 / 74°28.28'N - 20°22.91'W / Wollaston Forland[1383]
KUHNPASHYTTEN

- Danish trappers' hut built 28th July 1951 for Nanok by Hans Frederiksen, Ernst Wind and Erik Larsen, Zackenberg.
- About 2-3 km from Young Sund on the east side of the Kuhnpasset river, Wollaston Forland.
- C (IIA). Ruin. Originally 210 x 200 cm.
- On 18th May 1951 Hans Frederiksen wrote: *"Have this morning come back home from Daneborg,*

Kuhnpashytten [445], 21st August 2005. © NCN

have sawed up boards for the hut in Kuhnpasset". And on 20th May: *"Today starting to sledge the hut up into Kuhnpasset".* On 21st May: *"Have today come back home. We got the material for the hut up there; but we didn't get it built".* Finally on 28th July: *"Larsen and I have been up into Kuhnpasset and built the hut".*[1384] The remains of the hut have been blown 10-15 m from the original foundation.

Sødalhytten [446], 25th August 2005. © NCN

446 / 74°31.45'N - 20°59.70'W / A.P. Olsen Land[1385]
SØDALHYTTEN, Søhytten

▪ Danish trappers' hut built 4th June 1939 for Nanok by Berndt Jensen and Christian Petersen, Sandodden.

▪ On the north side of the largest lake in Store Sødal, about 1-2 km from the west end of the lake.

▪ C (IIA). 255 x 235 cm. Coal stove: L. Lange & Co. Floor: Wood/Earth.

▪ The materials for the hut were acquired by pulling down another hut [probably 438-1] at Zackenberg, where Berndt Jensen on 31st May 1939 wrote that: *"we pulled down the hut, but before we had finished it had become stormy weather".* And on 1st June: *"With two large loads we drive into Sødalen and find a very suitable location to put up the hut".* And on 4th June: *"We finish the hut and make ready to drive to Sandodden".*[1386]

Germania Havn [447-1] Western cape. Remains of a stone house from the Koldewey Expedition 1869-70 (left). Jelstrup's concrete pillar (middle foreground). Jelstrup's hut (right). Hvalrosø (background). 1932. © Norwegian Polar Institute

Germania Havn [447-1] Western cape. The concrete pillar at 74°32.06'N – 18°50.13'W built and used by Norwegian astronomer Hans Severin Jelstrup in 1932. 23rd July 2004. © NCN

447-1 / 74°32.09'N - 18°50.11'W / Pendulum Øer [1387]
GERMANIA HAVN

▪ German observatory hut built 1869 for the Koldewey Expedition.

▪ On the western cape of Germania Havn on the south coast of Sabine Ø.

▪ A (IIA). Stone ruin. 500 x 500 x 90 cm.

▪ The German Koldewey Expedition built two observatories on the western cape of Germania Havn in the autumn of 1869: *"One of these stone houses was intended for an observatory. It was built on the corner of land lying near the ship, on the edge of a steep bank; the other was for a magnetic observatory, and a north-west position seemed preferable".*[1388] The houses were used by the expedition astronomer R. Copeland (1837-1905).[1389] It was just a few hundred metres north-west of these observatories that Edward Sabine undertook his pendulum experiments in 1823 at:

Germania Havn [447-1]. Western cape. In the foreground remains of one of the German observatory houses at 74°32.09'N – 18°50.11'W. In the background on the hill top, Jelstrup's concrete base from 1932. 23rd July 2004. © NCN

Germania Havn [447-1] Eastern cape. A small solid pillar on the bare ground surrounded by stones is located on the east side of Germaniahavn at 74°32.14'N – 18°48.79'W. The pillar was most likely placed here in 1926 by the Cambridge East Greenland Expedition. 23rd July 2004. © NCN

"the site of an Esquimaux village".[1390] J.M. Wordie wanted the Cambridge East Greenland Expedition to verify Sabine's work in 1926,[1391] but noted: *"the exact place where the instruments stood was not marked in any way"*. The Cambridge Expedition therefore used a position on the: *"east side of Germania Havn"*, where they erected their pendulum stand: *"on a small firm pillar built upon the bare ground"*.[1392] In 1932 the Norwegian astronomer Hans Severin Jelstrup undertook astronomical determinations of latitude, longitude and azimuth for the Norway Svalbard- and Arctic Ocean Survey. The instrument was then mounted: *"on a firm concrete pillar, which stood in a roomy wooden hut with a partly removable roof"*.[1393] The measurements were used to confirm Alfred Wegener's theory of continental drift. Jelstrup's hut had blown down as early as 1933.[1394] Of the original two stone observatories, only the remains of one still exist; the other, situated right beside Jelstrup's pillar, was later on completely removed for unknown reasons.

Germania-hamn [447-2], 1932. © Norwegian Polar Institute

447-2 / c. 74°32.11'N - 18°50.98'W / Pendulum Øer[1395]
GERMANIA-HAMN, Gammen

- Norwegian trappers' station built in 1909 for the 7de juni Expedition.
- Probably on the west side of the western cape of Germania Havn, south coast of Sabine Ø.
- C̲ (IA). c. 600 x 300 cm.
- See chapter on stations.

The 1948 house at Germaniahavn [447-3], 21st August 2003. © NCN

447-3 / 74°32.21'N - 18°48.27'W / Pendulum Øer[1396]
GERMANIAHAVN, Sabineøen, Sabino, Villaen, Germania Havn Station

- Danish trappers' station built in 1919 for the East Greenland Company. In 1948 the original house (74°32.16'N - 18°48.36'W) was taken down and

the materials used for a new, smaller house located about 100 m to the east.
■ On the eastern cape of Germania Havn, south coast of Sabine Ø.
■ B (IA). (1948 house): 800 x 440 including porch 120 x 500 cm and two side sheds. Coal stove: Morsø. Floor: Wood.
■ See chapter on stations.

Trapper Ivar Ytreland at Falkberget [448], spring 1947. © Ivar Ytreland

Falkberget [448], 24th July 2004. © NCN

448 / 74°33.88'N - 19°18.20'W / Wollaston Forland[1397]
FALKBERGET, Falske Bugt hytten, Taymors Fjell, Falkenberg, Falkebjerghytten
■ Norwegian trappers' hut built 24th August 1928 for the Hird Expedition by Hermann Andresen and Peder Røbek, Kap Herschell.
■ On the small foreland in the north-eastern corner of Falskebugt, south-east of Falkebjerg on Brorson Halvø.[1398]
■ C (IIA). 385 x 210 cm. Coal stove: Trolla Brug TVN 90. Floor: Wood.
■ The materials were taken from Kopperneshuset [441-1]. On 22nd August 1928 Hermann Andresen wrote that: *"we left Stordalen* (Dronning Augusta Dal) *early this morning and went to Gåsenes* (Kap Wynn), *where we loaded some materials. Continued to Taymors* (Falkebjerg), *where we are going to build a hut"*. By the 24th August they had completed the hut.[1399]
■ In 1947 the Falkberget hut was renovated by Ivar Ytreland, who furnished it with a new roof and a wooden floor.[1400]

Kroneberghytten [449], 24th July 2004. © NCN

449 / 74°34.89'N - 19°13.52'W / Pendulum Øer[1401]
KRONEBERGHYTTEN
■ Danish trappers' hut built 18th August 1948 for Nanok by J.G. Jennov, Harald Mikkelsen and Erling Pedersen, Germaniahavn.
■ At the foot of Kronebjerg, westernmost Sabine Ø.
■ C (IIA). 330 x 170 including porch 120 x 170 cm. Coal stove: L. Lange & Co. Floor: Wood.
■ The materials were laid out on 7th August 1948. On 18th August J.G. Jennov wrote: *"Sailed at 12 o'clock for Kronebjergpynten, where we arrived at 14.00 and began to build the hut. We did not finish until 4 o'clock in the morning. Went to bed. Got up at 11 o'clock, made a stone bank around the hut and doors and a shutter for the window"*.[1402]

450 / 74°35.35'N - 20°02.93'W / Wollaston Forland[1403]
SLETTEHYTTEN
■ Danish trappers' hut built 17th May 1947 for Nanok by Mogens Graae, Orla Jensen and Kjeld Soelberg, Hochstetter.
■ On the west side of Albrechtsletten, about 3-4 km south of the coast of Wollaston Forland.
■ C (IIA). c. 200 x 200 cm. Floor: Earth.
■ On 17th May 1947 Mogens Graae wrote at Zackenberg: *"Prepared materials for the hut at Albrecht Bugt. Soelberg, O. Jensen and I agreed to build the huts*

at Albrecht Bugt and Svejstrup Dal. The three of us went with the materials through Kuppelpasset to Albrecht Bugt, unloaded the materials and continued to Kap Maurer, stayed for the night and drove the materials from Hochstetter to Albrecht Bugt. We built the hut at a hill on the western side of the bay".[1404] On 22nd August 1947 J.G. Jennov wrote that: *"as everything was covered with snow, we dropped the materials and built the hut four kilometres inland. An earth wall was placed around the hut".*[1405]

Slettehytten [450], May 1947. © Mogens Graae

Slettehytten [450], 8th July 2007. © NCN

451 / 74°35.27'N - 20°43.63'W / A.P. Olsen Land[1406]
LINDEMANSPASHYTTEN
▪ Danish trappers' hut built 14th May 1951 for Nanok by Ernst Wind, Hans Frederiksen and Erik Larsen, Zackenberg.
▪ A few hundred metres south of the watershed in Lindemansdalen, on the western side of the valley.
▪ C (IIA). 190 x 155 cm. No window. No stove. Floor: Earth.
▪ On 12th May 1951 Hans Frederiksen wrote in the journal of Zackenberg station: *"Have today sawed up planks meant for the hut in Lindemansdalen"*. And on 13th May: *"Today starting for Lindemansdalen with the hut"*. And on 14th May: *"Have come back home, we got the hut built"*.[1407] Lindemanspashytten was not meant to be used as a regular trappers' hut, but rather as an emergency shelter.[1408]

Lindemanspashytten [451], 24th August 2005. © NCN

452 / 74°36.37'N - 19°40.71'W / Wollaston Forland[1409]
JACKS HYTTE, Kap Berlin
▪ Danish trappers' hut built 18th August 1950 for Nanok by J.G. Jennov, Peder Vorre Thykjær and others, Hochstetter.
▪ On the west side of Brorson Halvø, about 3-4 km north-east of the head of Albrecht Bugt.
▪ C (IIA). 205 x 135 cm. Coal stove: Unknown manufacture. Floor: Wood.
▪ On 18th August 1950 J.G. Jennov wrote that they placed: *"a hut on the east side of Albrecht Bugt, where Jack Christensen got frostbite in his toes last winter. Anchored at 11 o'clock and left again when the hut was finished at 20.45"*.[1410] The designation "Kap Berlin" is geographical incorrect as a name for this hut.

Jacks hytte [452], 5th August 2004. © NCN

453-1 / 74°35.71'N - 19°51.37'W / Wollaston Forland[1411]
SLETTA, Sletten, Græstørvshytten
▪ Norwegian trappers' hut built 30th August 1928 for the Hird Expedition by Jørgen Furnes, Germaniahavn.
▪ On the west side of Albrecht Bugt, about 2 km north-west of the head of the bay.

Sletta [453-1], 5th August 2004. © NCN

■ C (IIA). 200 x 190 cm. Coal stove: Trolla Brug. Floor: Earth.

■ Built from driftwood and materials from Kopperneshuset [441-1]. On 29th August 1928 Jonas Karlsbak wrote that: *"Today we went from Sabine Ø to Gåsnes* (Kap Wynn). *Loaded materials and then headed into the fjord* (Claveringstrædet) *to begin the next hut. In order to reach the next building site we had to go around a long peninsula, so it took a long time before we arrived at Sletten* (the plain) *as we call it. We unloaded the materials, left behind Furnes and then went back to Gåsnes"*.[1412] The hut, on older maps often placed incorrectly on the east side of Albrecht Bugt, is situated adjacent to Albrechtbugthytten [453-2].[1413]

Albrechtbugthytten [453-2], with Sletta [453-1] in the background to the right. 5th August 2004. © NCN

453-2 / 74°35.72'N - 19°51.40'W / Wollaston Forland[1414]
ALBRECHTBUGTHYTTEN, Albrechtbugten

■ Danish travellers' hut built in August 1960 for the Sirius Dog Sledge Patrol by Bent Zwergius, Hans Ladefoged, Tonny Zangenberg Jakobsen and Arne Agergaard, Daneborg.

■ On the west side of Albrecht Bugt, about 2 km north-west of the head of the bay.

■ B (IIA). 305 x 210 including porch 95 x 210 cm. Coal stove: Langager & Co. Floor: Wood.

■ In 1992, former Sirius Patrol member Bent Zwergius recalled that late in 1959 he and Hans Ladefoged spent 12 days in the old Norwegian hut Sletta [453-1] due to bad weather. There was not enough food, even for the sledge dogs, two of whom starved to death. The two patrol men promised each other they would build a new hut at the location if they ever got the chance. The following summer they redeemed their promise.[1415]

Fjordbotten [454], 25th July 2003. © NCN

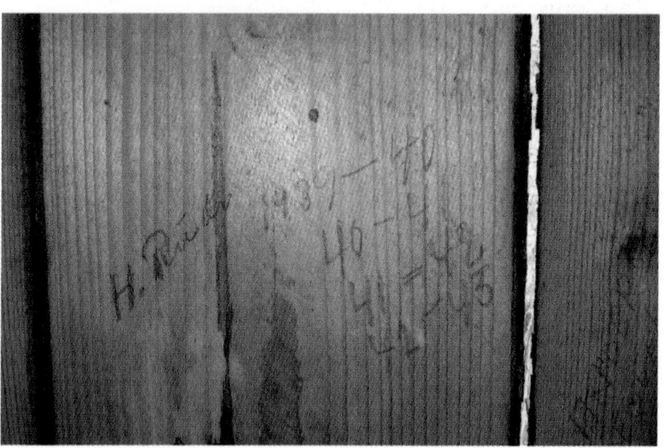

The walls inside Fjordbotten [454] are signed by several notable trappers, including Henry Rudi and Normann Andersen. 25th July 2003. © NCN

454 / 74°36.59'N - 22°05.39'W / A.P. Olsen Land[1416]
FJORDBOTTEN, Tyrolerfjord bundhytte

■ Norwegian trappers' hut built 5th September 1932 for the Sigurd Tolløfsen Expedition by Arnljot Tolløfsen and Gerhard Antonsen, Moskusheimen.

■ At the head of Tyrolerfjord, on the east side of a plateau about 500 m inland.[1417]

■ A (IIA). 240 x 200 cm. Coal stove: Ulefos 158D. Floor: Earth.

■ On 27th August 1932 Arnljot Tolløfsen wrote:

"*Rowed from home* (Moskusheimen) *to the head of Tyrolerfjord, where we are going to build a hut*". After several trips by rowing boat between Moskusheimen and the hut, Tolløfsen on 5th September 1932 wrote that they: "*rowed to Tyrolerfjord with some muskox furs for the hut, which we finished*".[1418] The noted trapper Normann Andersen considered this to be the best hut in his territory, because it was small and therefore easy to heat up.[1419]

Kap Desbrowe hytten [455], 23rd August 2004. © NCN

455 / 74°36.70'N - 18°23.95'W / Pendulum Øer[1420]
KAP DESBROWE HYTTEN, Kap Desbrowe-hus, Kap Jona, Pendelbua, Pendulumhytta

- Danish trappers' hut built in the summer of 1921 for the East Greenland Company by Gustav Thostrup and others, Germaniahavn.
- On the west side of the south point of Lille Pendulum, about 4 km south-west of Kap Desbrowe.
- C (IIA). 255 x 200 cm. Coal stove: L. Lange & Co. Floor: Earth.
- On 20th October 1921 Johan F. Petersen wrote that the crew at Germaniahavn: "*will be able to catch some foxes on Lille Pendulum, thanks to the hunters' hut that Captain Thostrup has had built at Kap Desbrowe*".[1421] The hut must therefore have been built in 1921, when Gustav Thostrup was in Greenland as master of the "Teddy", and not in 1920 as indicated by Jennov.[1422] On 7th November 1928, the hut was discovered by Jonas Karlsbak, who named it Kap Jona after one of his daughters, Jona.[1423] Later on it was claimed to be a Norwegian hut, Pendelbua.[1424] This was incorrect. On 29th July 1933, the Danish trapper Henning Nyholm-Poulsen after a conversation with John Giæver wrote: "*Giæver too was of the opinion that there had never existed a Norwegian hut at the south-west point of Lille Pendulum. The hut that his friends saw in 1927 from their ship (he himself was drunk and saw nothing), was probably the Danish hut at Kap Desbrowe*".[1425] Nevertheless, Giæver in 1939 marked it as a Norwegian hut on his map.[1426] Kap Desbrowe was named by Edward Sabine in 1823: "*so named after the late Edward Desbrowe, Esq., M.P. for Windsor, and Vice Chamberlain to her late Majesty, Queen Charlotte; to which gentleman I was indebted for my entrance into the army*".[1427]

Ingrid Havn [456-1], 12th August 1999. © NCN

456-1 / 74°37.51'N - 18°43.93'W / Pendulum Øer[1428]
INGRID HAVN, Ingrid-hamn, Hansabugthuset

- Norwegian trappers' hut built 6th September 1928 for the Hird Expedition by Peder Røbek and Jørgen Furnes, Germaniahavn.
- At a small cove on the south side of the entrance to Hansa Bugt, on the east coast of Sabine Ø.
- C (IIA). Ruin. Only few remnants remain.
- The hut was built of materials taken from Kopperneshuset [441-1].[1429] On 6th September 1928 Jonas Karlsbak wrote: "*Andresen and I today went north in the motor boat to the hut, which the others are building and to which has been given the name Ingrid* (after one of Karlsbaks twin daughters)"[1430] On 11th February 1930 Andreas Hvidberg described the hut as a: "*wooden tent, not larger than you can reach the ceiling with your legs when you're lying on your back*" ... "*It is an odd hut or tent; made from wood bars and covered with muskox skins*".[1431]
- The hut is said to have disappeared during WWII.[1432]

456-2 / 74°38.02'N - 18°44.12'W / Pendulum Øer[1433]
HANSA BUGT HYTTEN

- Danish trappers' hut built 27th August 1948 for Nanok by J.G. Jennov, Mogens Graae, Hans Thomsen, Peder Klokker and Erling Pedersen, Germaniahavn.
- On the south end of the northernmost of the three small islands or skerries at the entrance to Hansa Bugt, east side of Sabine Ø.
- C (IIA). 305 x 200 including porch 100 x 200 cm. No stove. Floor: Wood.

Hansa Bugt hytten [456-2], 23rd July 2004. © NCN

■ On 27th August 1948 J.G. Jennov wrote that they: *"were gathering materials for a hut at Hansa Bugt. Placed and built the hut at the south end of the northernmost of the three skerries at the entrance of Hansa Bugt"*.[1434]

Hansa Bugt – Alte Hütte [457], 23rd July 2004. © NCN

Hansa Bugt – Neue Hütte [457], 23rd July 2004. © NCN

457 / 74°37.10'N - 18°50.16'W / Pendulum Øer[1435]
HANSA BUGT, Alte Hütte, Neue Hütte

■ German meteorological station built in the autumn of 1942 for the German Naval Weather Service.
■ Innermost Hansa Bugt on the east side of Sabine Ø.
■ A (IB). Site of two burnt down German wintering houses and several other remains from WWII.
■ Alte Hütte: 74°37.10'N - 18°50.16'W.
■ Neue Hütte: 74°36.83'N - 18°49.70'W
■ See chapter on stations.

Svendsby [458-1], 25th July 2004. © NCN

458-1 / 74°38.47'N - 20°49.49' / A.P. Olsen Land[1436]
SVENDSBY, Stordalshytten

■ Norwegian trappers' hut built about 15th August 1932 for the Sigurd Tolløfsen Expedition by Johan Stordal, Sigurdsheim.
■ On the south side of Lindeman Fjord, west of the small peninsula where the river from Lindemansdalen flows into Lindeman Fjord.
■ C (IIA). 220 x 200 cm. Coal stove: Trolla Brug No. 91. Floor: Wood.
■ On 28th July 1932 materials for the hut were laid out. Sigurd Tolløfsen named the hut Svendsby, but it was also called Stordalshytten after the trapper Johan Stordal, who built the hut.[1437] Svendsby is located a few hundred metres from Lindeman Fjord hytten [458-2]

458-2 / 74°38.61'N - 20°49.18'W / A.P. Olsen Land[1438]
LINDEMAN FJORD HYTTEN, Fjordhytten

■ Danish trappers' hut built 10th August 1938 for Nanok by J.G. Jennov, Carlos Ziebell, Alfred Hansen, Franz Dalskov and E. Brandstrup, Hochstetter.
■ On the south side of Lindeman Fjord, west of the small peninsula where the river from Lindemansdalen flows into Lindeman Fjord.
■ C (IIA). Ruin. Coal stove: Hess No. 420T.

Lindeman Fjord hytten [458-2], 25th July 2004. © NCN

■ J.G. Jennov wrote that the hut was meant to be placed in Grandjean Fjord, but the ice blocked their way. Instead he decided to build it at: *"the location, where Zackenberg pass* (Lindemansdalen) *and Sødalen* (Slettedalen) *meet at Lindeman Fjord"*.[1439] On 31st August 1938, Sigurd Tolløfsen assumed that: *"Jennov is probably beginning to run low on territory" ... "today it turned out that he has had a new hut built 300 m from my hut Svendsby"*.[1440] The fjord was named Lindeman Bai by the Koldewey Expedition of 1869-70, after Moritz Lindeman (1823-1908), the secretary of the Bremen geographical society, the "Verein für de Deutsche Nordpolarfahrt". Lindeman was editor with G. Hartlaub of Koldewey's expedition narrative.[1441] Lindeman Fjord hytten was accidently burnt down in December 1978.

Berlin Stua [459], 24th July 2004. © NCN

459 / 74°39.96'N - 19°19.74'W / Wollaston Forland[1442]
BERLIN STUA, Kap Berlin hytten

■ Norwegian trappers' hut built 15th August 1930 for the Møre Expedition by Hermann Andresen and Peder Røbek, Kap Herschell.

■ About 3-4 km south-east of Kap Berlin on the north coast of Brorson Halvø.[1443]

■ C (IIA). 185 x 180 cm. Coal stove: Home-made from an old fuel drum. Floor: Earth.

■ On 15th August 1930 Hermann Andresen wrote: *"We have today been north to Kap Berlin and put up a hut"*.[1444] On 7th November 1931 Andresen wrote about the hut that he: *"intended to stop there, but the hut is so small, that I can't lie down, so I decided to drive on to Falkberget* [448]*"*.[1445]

460-1 / c. 74°40'N - 20°14'W / Wollaston Forland[1446]
AGNES-TUFTA, Hynes-hytten, Kap Hynes, Kap Agnes

■ Norwegian trappers' hut built 1st September 1928 for the Hird Expedition by Jørgen Furnes, Jonas Karlsbak and Hermann Andresen, Germaniahavn.

■ About 3 km west of Kap Schumacher on the north coast of Wollaston Forland.

■ C (IIA). Moved.

■ Originally the Agnes-tufta hut belonged to the Foldvik Expedition and had been standing at Krogness [403]. When the Hird Expedition took over the territory they sailed the hut by motor boat to Kap Schumacher. The hut was named for the youngest daughter of Jørgen Furnes, Agnes, who was born after Furnes had gone to Greenland in the summer of 1927.[1447] "Tufta" is the Norwegian word for a building site. On 28th August 1930 the hut was moved again by Hermann Andresen and other members of the Møre Expedition to Kap Hamburg on Kuhn Ø, where it received the new name Furnes [464].[1448]

Holmeslet [460-2], 1932-34. © Børre Holmeslet

460-2 / 74°40.07'N - 20°13.86'W / Wollaston Forland[1449]
HOLMESLET, Kap Schumacher hytten, Holmset huset

■ Norwegian trappers' hut built 11th August 1932 for the Sigurd Tolløfsen Expedition by Johan Stordal, Sigurdsheim.

■ About 3 km west of Kap Schumacher on the north coast of Wollaston Forland.

Holmeslet [460-2], 24th July 2004. © NCN

■ C (IIA). 220 x 190 cm. Coal stove: Trolla Brug. Floor: Wood.
■ On the 28th July 1932, materials for the hut were laid out with "Isbjørn" at almost the same location that Agnes-tufta [460-1] had been situated. The new hut was named after Johannes Holmeslet, who on 21st August 1932 wrote: *"Stordal had built an excellent hut"*.[1450]

Bass Rock [461], 23rd July 2004. © NCN

461 / 74°42.83'N - 18°15.52'W / Pendulum Øer[1451]
BASS ROCK, Ziegler-husa
■ American depot huts built in 1901 for the Baldwin-Ziegler Expedition, later used as a traveller's station.
■ On the east side of the island Bass Rock.
■ A (IA). Two octagonal houses, each about 400 cm in diameter. Floor: Wood.
■ See chapter on stations.

462 / 74°39.91'N - 21°03.11'W / A.P. Olsen Land[1452]
SVEJSTRUP DAL HYTTEN
■ Danish trappers' hut built in May 1947 for Nanok by Mogens Graae, Orla Jensen and Kjeld Soelberg, Zackenberg.
■ On the north-eastern side of Svejstrup Dal, about 2-3 km from Lindeman Fjord.
■ C (IIA). Ruin. No stove.
■ On 21st May 1947 Mogens Graae wrote: *"We drove materials from Fjordhytten* [458-2] *to Svejstrup Dal, and together with the materials Jørgen Andersen had sledged in, we built a hut some distance up the valley" ... "The hut lies on the north-eastern side of the valley"*.[1453]

Svejstrup Dal hytten [462], 25th July 2004. © NCN

463 / 74°43.40'N - 18°33.64'W / Pendulum Øer[1454]
KAP BUCHENAU HYTTEN
■ Danish trappers' hut built 18th September 1930 for Nanok by J.G. Jennov, Hans Bruun and Arne Schwarck, Germaniahavn.
■ At Kap Buchenau, northernmost Lille Pendulum.
■ C (IIA). 190 x 185 cm. Coal stove: L. Lange & Co. Floor: Earth.
■ On 18th September 1930 it was noted in the station log of Germaniahavn that: *"at 8.30 this morning we sailed from Germaniahavn in order to place a hut at Kap Buchenau on the north side of Pendulum. The location of the hut is not the best possible. There was*

Kap Buchenau hytten [463], 23rd July 2004. © NCN

much ice on the north side, which made it impossible for us to obtain the best location for the hut".[1455] The cape was named Cap Buchenau by the Koldewey Expedition of 1869-70, after Franz Buchenau of Bremen, who had prepared one of the botanical sections of Koldewey's narrative.[1456]

464 / c. 74°42'N - 20°08'W / Kuhn Ø[1457]
FURNES, Kap Hamburg hytten, Røsnes, Kap Norge, Kunoøya

- Norwegian trappers' hut built 28th August 1930 for the Møre Expedition by Hermann Andresen and Peder Røbek, Kap Herschell.
- On the south coast of Kuhn Ø near or just west of Kap Hamburg, also known as Kap Norge or Røsnes.[1458]
- C (IIA). Disappeared.
- Originally measuring 200 x 175 cm and located at Kap Schumacher, where it was called Agnes-tufta [460-1]. On 28th August 1930 it was moved to: *"the south point of Kuhn Ø".*[1459] It was named for Jørgen Furnes, a member of the Hird Expedition 1927-29.
- The hut no longer exists. On 31st March 1935 Hermann Andresen wrote: *"I drove from Sletten* [453-1] *this morning. At first to Kap Hamburg on Kuhn Ø, where I had planned to stop for today. When I arrived it turned out that the Devil himself has taken the house. There has been an avalanche right from the top of the mountain and it must have been the air pressure that has splintered the hut into firewood".*[1460]

Sydlige Fligely hytten [465], 25th July 2004. © NCN

465 / 74°45.23'N - 20°37.04'W / Th. Thomsen Land[1461]
SYDLIGE FLIGELY HYTTEN, Lindemanhytten

- Danish trappers' hut built in August 1931 for Nanok by Niels Hansen, Leander E. Emskær Larsen and Berndt Jensen, Hochstetter.
- On the north side of a sandy point, on the west side of the southern entrance of Fligely Fjord.
- C (IIA). 310 x 200 including porch 90 x 200 cm. Coal stove: L. Lange & Co. Floor: Wood.
- Sydlige Fligely hytten was built between 20th and 26th August 1931. Leander E. Emskær Larsen wrote that: *"we have built a hut in Fligely Fjord, at the point at Lindemanbugten* ("the Lindeman bay")*".*[1462] Trapper Henning Nyholm-Poulsen visited the hut on 29th August 1932 and wrote that it was: *"a small hut measuring 2 x 2 m without a floor and with a small porch measuring 1 x 1 m".*[1463]

Trapper Johan Stordal at Håkonshytten [466], 1932-34. © Børre Holmeslet

Håkonshytten [466], 25th July 2004. © NCN

466 / 74°47.02'N - 20°33.19'W / Kuhn Ø[1464]
HÅKONSHYTTEN, Håkonsstua

- Norwegian trappers' hut built 22nd August 1932 for the Sigurd Tolløfsen Expedition by Johan Stordal, Sigurdsheim.
- On the south-west coast of Kuhn Ø, 4-5 km south of the narrowest part of Fligely Fjord.[1465]
- C (IIA). 190 x 190 plus porch 100 x 90 cm. Coal stove: Trolla Brug No. 91. Floor: Wood.

■ On 22nd August 1932 Johannes Holmeslet wrote that: *"we then crossed the fjord to Håkonsstua. We here found Stordal. He had almost finished this hut too".*[1466] The hut was named after Haakon Karlsen, a member of the Sigurd Tolløfsen Expedition of 1932-34. Håkonshytten was only used for a few years as it always snowed down in the winter. Sigurd Tolløfsen confirmed this on 5th May 1939 when he: *"arrived at Håkonshytta at 23.00. As usual here, only a foot of the stove pipe was visible".*[1467]

Kap Maurer hytten [467], 24th July 2004. © NCN

467 / 74°47.70'N - 19°50.49'W / Kuhn Ø[1468]
KAP MAURER HYTTEN, Jennovshåb

■ Danish trappers' hut built 10th September 1930 for Nanok by Niels Hansen, Berndt Jensen and Knud Østergaard, Hochstetter.[1469]

■ About 8 km south of Kap Maurer on the east coast of Kuhn Ø.

■ C (IIA). 300 x 200 plus porch 120 x 100 cm. The floor is covered with about 30 cm of sand and gravel.

■ On 8th August 1930 Knud Østergaard wrote in the journal of the Hochstetter station that: *"we sailed over to Kap Maurer with a load of wood for the hut, and unloaded it about 6 km south of Kap Maurer".* On 10th August: *"We finished building the hut".*[1470] The hut is located about 2 km further south than estimated by Østergaard.

468 / 74°50.45'N - 19°45.27'W / Kuhn Ø[1471]
SIGURDSHEIM

■ Norwegian trappers' station built in 1932 for the Sigurd Tolløfsen Expedition.

■ About 2 km south of Kap Maurer on the east coast of Kuhn Ø.

■ B (IA). 660 x 370 including porch about 275 x 370 cm. Paraffin stove. Floor: Wood.

■ See chapter on stations.

Sigurdsheim [468], 24th July 2004. © NCN

469 / 74°50.30'N - 20°44.31'W / Th. Thomsen Land[1472]
BLÅBÆRHYTTEN, Blåbærhus

■ Danish trappers' hut built in August 1931 for Nanok by Niels Hansen, Leander E. Emskær Larsen and Berndt Jensen, Hochstetter.[1473]

■ On the south side of Blåbærdalen, on the west side of Fligely Fjord.

■ B (IIA). 415 x 220 including porch 195 x 220 cm. Coal stove: Morsø. Floor: Wood/Earth.

■ Blåbærhytten was built from 20th - 26th August 1931.[1474] On 22nd August 1951 the hut was enlarged. J.G. Jennov wrote that: *"the old hut built in 1931 and partly made of old barrel staves covered with muskox skin was repaired and used as a porch, and a new hut was added. The hut was solemnly promoted to "Blåbærhus".*[1475]

Blåbærhytten [469], 29th August 2004. © NCN

470 / 74°56.05'N - 17°39.26'W / Shannon[1476]
KAP PHILIP BROKE, Baldwin-huset

■ American depot hut built in 1901 for the Baldwin-Ziegler Expedition, later used as a travellers' station.

■ At the west side of Kap Philip Broke on the southernmost point of Shannon.

■ A (IA). An octagonal hut with a porch.

■ See chapter on stations.

Kap Philip Broke [470], 8th July 2007. © NCN

471 / 74°57.30'N - 20°02.43'W / Kuhn Ø[1477]
BOLETTESTUA

- Norwegian trappers' hut built 31st August 1932 for the Sigurd Tolløfsen Expedition by Johannes Holmeslet and Johan Stordal, Sigurdsheim.[1478]
- About 4 km south of Kap Bremen on the east coast of Kuhn Ø.
- C (IIA). Ruin. About 210 x 180 cm. Coal stove: Trolla Brug No. 91. Floor: Wood.

Bolettestua [471], 1932-34. © Børre Holmeslet

Bolettestua [471], 5th August 2004. © NCN

- Materials for Bolettestua were laid out on 28th July 1932 with "Isbjørn". Johannes Holmeslet wrote that: *"we went out of Fligely Fjord, rounded the south point of Kuhn Ø and went to Kap Bremen, where a hut was unloaded. This hut has received the name Bolettestua".*[1479] The hut was named after Sigurd Tolløfsen's wife, Bolette.

Kap David Gray hytten [472-1], Christian Rasmussen sitting in front of the hut. September 1923. © Jørgen Nielsen

Kap David Gray hytten [472-1], 1933. © Arne Philbert

472-1 / 74°58.96'N - 18°23.72'W / Shannon[1480]
KAP DAVID GRAY HYTTEN, Kap David Gray-hus, Jægerly, David Gray hytten

- Danish trappers' hut built 19th August 1923 for the East Greenland Company by Leander E. Emskær Larsen, Christian Rasmussen and Karl Richter, Kap Philip Broke.[1481]
- About 2 km north-east of Kap David Gray on the south coast of Shannon.
- C̲ (IIA). 200 x 200 plus porch 80 x 200 cm.
- Materials for a so-called "hunters' shelter" were laid out on 9th August 1923. On 19th August 1923 Christian Rasmussen wrote: *"The hut is now almost*

Kap David Gray hytten [472-1], 8th July 2007. © NCN

ready".[1482] The original hut may have been replaced or enlarged, as Andreas Hvidberg at David Gray on 11th August 1930 wrote that: *"we have built a hut".*[1483]

From left: Tåkeheimen [472-2] and Kap David Gray hytten [472-1], 8th June 1978. © Peter Schmidt Mikkelsen

The remains of Tåkeheimen [472-2] in front of Kap David Gray hytten [472-1], 8th July 2007. © NCN

472-2 / 74°58.96'N - 18°23.72'W / Shannon[1484]
TÅKEHEIMEN

■ Norwegian trappers' hut built in August 1952 for Arctic Commercial Enterprise by Stein Sørensen and Hans Hvide Bang, Ottostrand.

■ About 2 km north-east of Kap David Gray on the south coast of Shannon.

■ C (IIA). Ruin. Originally 405 x 200 cm.

■ In the summer of 1952, when the sea ice prevented "Polarbjørn" from calling at Ottostrand, the trappers Hans Hvide Bang and Stein Sørensen were set ashore at Kap David Gray, where they built a new hut beside the old "Kap David Gray hytten" [472-1]. Sørensen wrote: *"However there is a lot of fog here, so we intend to name it "Tåkeheimen"* (home of fog).[1485] The two men stayed in the hut until autumn, when they travelled on to Ottostrand. Tåkeheimen was used by Sirius until the beginning of the 1980s, when it was accidently destroyed by fire.

Kap Bremen hytten [473], 5th August 2004. © NCN

473 / 74°59.02'N - 19°58.20'W / Kuhn Ø[1486]
KAP BREMEN HYTTEN

■ Danish trappers' hut built 12th September 1931 for Nanok by Niels Hansen, Bjarne Ludvigsen, Berndt Jensen and Leander E. Emskær Larsen, Hochstetter.

■ At Kap Bremen on the east coast of Kuhn Ø.[1487]

■ C (IIA). 305 x 200 including porch 95 x 200 cm. Coal stove: L. Lange & Co. Floor: Earth.

■ On 11th September 1931 the journal of the Hochstetter station records: *"At 10 o'clock we left Hochstetter heading for Kap Bremen. We carried along a trappers' hut" ... "We came back to Kap Bremen at 9.30 in the evening – Hansen and Ludvigsen in the meantime had put up the hut".* And on 12th September: *"We finished the hut and sailed from there at 1 o'clock, and arrived at Hochstetter at 16.30".*[1488]

474 / 74°59.38'N - 20°33.99'W / Kuhn Ø[1489]
NORDLIGE FLIGELY HYTTEN, Fligelyhytten

■ Danish trappers' hut built 30th August 1930 for Nanok by Niels Hansen and Knud Østergaard, Hochstetter.[1490]

Nordlige Fligely hytten [474], 26th July 2004. © NCN

■ About 7 km south-west of Kap Mosle on the west coast of Kuhn Ø.
■ B (IIA). 300 x 220 plus porch 115 x 105 cm. Coal stove: L. Lange & Co. 1608M. Floor: Wood. On 1st September 1930 Knud Østergaard at the Hochstetter station wrote that: *"Niels and I arrived here at the station at 10 o'clock in the evening from Fligely Fjord. We have finished the hut and put an earth bank around it, so it's tight and good"*.[1491]

Mågenæshytten [501], 26th July 2004. © NCN

501 / 74°59.76'N - 21°45.00'W / C.H. Ostenfeld Land[1492]
MÅGENÆSHYTTEN
■ Danish trappers' hut built 21st August 1948 for Nanok by Hans Thomsen, Mogens Graae, J.G. Jennov and Peder Klokker, Hochstetter.[1493]
■ At the head of the small bay at Mågenæs in Grandjean Fjord.
■ C (IIA). 300 x 200 including porch 100 x 200 cm. Coal stove: L. Lange & Co. Floor: Wood.
■ On 20th August 1948 J.G. Jennov wrote that: *"when we came around Mågenæs to sail to Betulahavn, the wind was rising so much that we could not get through"*. Consequently they had to turn around and enter the small bay at Mågenæs: *"although I, of course, would have much preferred to have the hut placed at Birkedalen"*.[1494]

Citystua [502], 1932-34. © Børre Holmeslet

Citystua [502], 26th July 2004. © NCN

502 / 75°01.39'N - 20°37.86'W / Th. Thomsen Land[1495]
CITYSTUA, Kap Negri hytten
■ Norwegian trappers' hut built 6th September 1932 for the Sigurd Tolløfsen Expedition by Johan Stordal and Johannes Holmeslet, Sigurdsheim.
■ On the west side of Fligely Fjord, about 3-4 km south of Kap Negri on the south side of a river.
■ C (IIA). Ruin. About 220 x 190 cm. Coal stove: Trolla Brug.
■ Materials were laid out on 28th July 1932 with "Isbjørn". The hut was named by Sigurd Tolløfsen after the noted trapper Gerhard "City" Antonsen.[1496] The hut is also called Kap Negri hytten, and can therefore be confused with Vedethytten [505].

Grandjeanhytten [503], 26th July 2004. © NCN

503 / 75°01.55'N - 21°28.11'W / C.H. Ostenfeld Land[1497]
GRANDJEANHYTTEN, Grandjean bundhytte, Ulvebugthytten

- Danish trappers' hut built in September 1934 for Nanok by Berndt Jensen and Henry Larsen, Hochstetter.[1498]
- About 10 km north-east of Mågenæs in Grandjean Fjord.
- C (IIA). Ruin. Originally about 220 x 190 cm. Coal stove: L. Lange & Co.
- On 8th September 1934 the journal of the Hochstetter station records: *"At 4.30 in the morning B. Jensen and H. Larsen came home after having laid out a hut in the middle of Grandjean Fjord on the northern side"*.[1499] On 23rd August 1938 Sigurd Tolløfsen became aware of the hut. He wanted to build two huts in Grandjean Fjord; but then: *"it turned out that the Danes had built a hut in the territory I have occupied"*.[1500]

Birkedalhytten [504], 26th July 2004. © NCN

504 / 75°01.13'N - 22°03.53'W / Th. Thomsen Land[1501]
BIRKEDALHYTTEN, Betulahavnhytten

- Danish trappers' hut built 21st August 1951 for Nanok by J.G. Jennov and others, Hochstetter.
- On the north-west side of Betulahavn in Grandjean Fjord.
- C (IIA). 200 x 140 cm. Floor: Wood.
- On 21st August 1951 J.G. Jennov wrote that they sailed: *"into Grandjean Fjord. At Birkedal at 16.00. Good anchorage in Betula Havn" ... "While the hut was being built, I went for a walk inland about 8 km. Very beautiful country"*.[1502]

Vedethytten [505], 26th July 2004. © NCN

505 / 75°01.85'N - 20°37.50'W / Th. Thomsen Land[1503]
VEDETHYTTEN, Vedetten, Kap Negri hytten

- Danish trappers' hut built 22nd August 1951 for Nanok by J.G. Jennov and others, Hochstetter.
- On the west side of Fligely Fjord south-east of Vedetten, about 2 km south of Kap Negri. Not built beside a river, as a trappers' hut should be, but on a rocky slope.
- C (IIA). 220 x 130 cm. Floor: Wood.
- On 22nd August 1951 J.G. Jennov wrote that they sailed: *"down towards Vedetten. Went ashore at 16.00, built a hut and came onboard again at 21.00"*.[1504] The hut is also called Kap Negri hytten and can therefore be confused with Citystua [502].

506 / 75°03.93'N - 18°53.97'W / Shannon[1505]
TOMSBORG, Kap Tramnitz hytten

- Danish trappers' hut built in September 1948 for Nanok by Harald Mikkelsen and Hans Thomsen, Hochstetter.
- On the west coast of Shannon about 6-7 km north of Kap Tramnitz.
- C (IIA). 210 x 190 cm. Coal stove: L. Lange & Co. Floor: Wood.
- In 1992 Harald Mikkelsen recalled that: *"when we were approaching the location to build the weather was very foggy, but we assumed we were close to Kap Tramnitz. Despite the quite heavy seas I took*

Tomsborg [506], 2nd August 2004. © NCN

a chance and ran the boat ashore at a fair speed. It went well but wasn't without danger. After having slept a couple of hours on the foredeck of the boat, we drank coffee to go with our last bread and began building the hut. It went quite quickly as all the wood had been cut in advance. We didn't allow ourselves a break until we had finished the hut". The hut was named after Hans Thomsen.[1506]

Stormheimen [507], 8th July 2007. © NCN

507 / 75°03.00'N - 17°20.47'W / Shannon[1507]
STORMHEIMEN

▪ Norwegian trappers' hut built 18th March 1953 for Arctic Commercial Enterprise by Stein Sørensen, Odd Bogholm and Hans Hvide Bang, Ottostrand.

▪ About 12-13 km south of Kap Pansch on the east coast of Shannon.

▪ C (IIA). 335 x 210 cm including porch. Coal stove: Dravn. Floor: Wood.

▪ The three trappers had found a lot of wood at Ny Jonsbu [514-2] and decided to build a hut on the outer coast of Shannon. When they had finished the hut, they had a heavy snowstorm and the hut was therefore named Stormheimen (the stormy home). It is the easternmost trappers' hut in Greenland.[1508]

Ullahytten [508], 26th July 2004. © NCN

508 / 75°07.64'N - 21°03.31'W / C.H. Ostenfeld Land[1509]
ULLAHYTTEN, Ullestuen

▪ Danish trappers' hut built in September 1934 for Nanok by Berndt Jensen and Christian Sørensen, Hochstetter.

▪ On the south side of the large river bed north-west of Ulla Ø in Grandjean Fjord.

▪ B (IIA). 305 x 200 including porch 100 x 200 cm. Coal stove: L. Lange & Co. Floor: Earth.

▪ On 28th September 1934 the journal of the Hochstetter station records: *"It was B. Jensen and Sørensen who returned from Kap Bremen, where they have been for two days. They had gone directly to Grandjean Fjord, where they had built Ullahytten"*.[1510]

Arnljotstua [509], 1932-34. © Børre Holmeslet

509 / 75°08.25'N - 20°30.39'W / C.H. Ostenfeld Land[1511]
ARNLJOTSTUA

▪ Norwegian trappers' hut built 2nd September 1932 for the Sigurd Tolløfsen Expedition by Johannes Holmeslet and Johan Stordal, Sigurdsheim.

▪ On the south side of Kap Buch, easternmost C.H. Ostenfeld Land.

▪ C (IIA). 215 x 180 cm including porch. Coal stove: Trolla Brug No. 91 and OM&S No. 2. Floor: Wood.

▪ On 29th July 1932 the materials for the hut were

laid out with "Isbjørn". On 2nd September 1932 Johannes Holmeslet wrote: *"it must be an ideal place for wildlife. The eskimos have also been aware of this, as there are 8-10 dugouts. They are situated quite closely together over a distance of about 100 m along a ridge. It's now 24.00 and we have just finished the main parts of the hut. We have made the walls, floor and roof of the hut. It's going to be named "Arnljotstua"*.[1512] The hut was named after the trapper Arnljot Tolløfsen, who died in May 1933 during a sledge journey.[1513]

Arnljotstua [509] in the summer of 1948. Note that a porch had been added to the left side of the hut since 1932-34. © Bjarne Myrvold

Arnljotstua [509], 29th July 2004. © NCN

510 / 75°08.47'N - 19°44.86'W / Hochstetter Forland[1514]
HOCHSTETTER, Nanok, Kap Rink

- Danish trappers' station built in 1929 for Nanok.
- On the south coast of Hochstetter Forland, 4-5 km west of Kap Rink.
- B (IA). Station house and sheds. Station house: 1130 x 650 cm. Coal stove: L. Lange & Co. "Scandia". Floor: Wood.
- See chapter on stations.

Hochstetter [510], 1st August 2004. © NCN

511 / 75°11.50'N - 19°59.81'W / Hochstetter Forland[1515]
KULHUS, Jarners kulmine, Kulhuse

- Danish travellers' station built in 1932 for the Three-Year Expedition.
- At Jarners Kulmine about 6-7 km north-west of Niels Hansen Næs, west coast of Hochstetter Forland.
- A (IB). Station house: 920 x 790 cm including porch and sidesheds. Provision shed. Coal stove: L. Lange & Co and Scandia 908. Floor: Wood.
- See chapter on stations.

Kulhus [511], 1938. © Niels Ove Jensen

Kulhus [511], 30th July 2004. © NCN

Kap Buch hytten [512], 29th July 2004. © NCN

512 / 75°11.38'N - 20°34.39'W / C.H. Ostenfeld Land[1516]
KAP BUCH HYTTEN

▪ Danish trappers' hut built 8th August 1932 for Nanok by Niels Hansen and Berndt Jensen, Hochstetter.[1517]
▪ About 6 km north-west of Kap Buch on the south side of Ardencaple Fjord.
▪ C (IIA). Ruin. Coal stove: L. Lange & Co.
▪ On 7th August 1932 the journal of the Hochstetter station recorded: *"Made ready to sail to Kap Buch with a hut"*. And on 8th August: *"Sailed to Kap Buch with coal and hut"*. And on 9th August: *"Returned from Kap Buch"*.[1518] Later on trapper Henning Nyholm-Poulsen wrote: *"On Wednesday 24th August 1932 we first went to Kulhus for 20 sacks of coal and then to the huts in Ardencaple Inlet to supply these with provisions and coal for the winter. First we went to the new travellers' hut* (Kap Buch)*, where we put roofing felt on the roof and walls, put up a coal stove and berth, and stayed there for the night. I had the great opportunity to experience what a confounded ability our reindeer sleeping bags have to make one completely white from all the hairs that breaks off"*.[1519] In 2004 the ruin was only three metres from the seashore slope.

513 / 75°15.10'N - 18°49.37'W / Shannon[1520]
HARALDSBORG, Kap Copeland hytten

▪ Danish trappers' hut built in September 1948 for Nanok by Harald Mikkelsen and Hans Thomsen, Hochstetter.
▪ On the west coast of Shannon about 9-10 km south of Kap Copeland.
▪ C (IIA). 205 x 180 cm. Coal stove: L. Lange & Co. Floor: Wood.
▪ In 1992 Harald Mikkelsen said that: *"about the first of September 1948 we loaded the motor boat with materials for two huts, which we would build on Shannon. We cut up all the boards and the wood into precise lengths before we loaded the boat, so we could carry everything with us and it would ease the job once we came to Shannon. First we sailed to Kap Copeland, where we built the hut a bit south of the cape. It had become very foggy, and snowed a bit, so it was difficult to see exactly where we were. It took 8 hours to build the hut"*. The hut was named after Harald Mikkelsen.[1521] With respect to the other hut, see Tomsborg [506].

Haraldsborg [513], 2nd August 2004. © NCN

514-1 / 75°14.86'N - 20°52.76'W / C.H. Ostenfeld Land[1522]
SKYLSTAD

▪ Norwegian trappers' hut built 20th August 1932 for the John Giæver Expedition by John Giæver, Jonsbu.[1523]
▪ On the south side of the entrance to Kildedal, on the south side of Ardencaple Fjord.
▪ C (IIA). Ruin. Coal stove: OM&S No. 2.
▪ On 20th August 1932 John Giæver wrote that: *"today I have finished the house, heated and nailed on the roofing felt, put in a stove, made a berth, table and shelves, plus named the place Skylstad after my friend the editor* (Jacob Skylstad) *in Trondheim"*.[1524] In 1948 Ny Jonsbu [514-2] was built at the same location and Bjarne Myrvold recalled in 1992: *"Giæver's hut was still there, and we later on used it as a fur shed"*.[1525]

From left: Trappers Egil Amsjø, his brother Rolf Amsjø and Bjarne Myrvold at Skylstad [514-1], summer 1948. © Bjarne Myrvold

Skylstad [514-1], 28th July 2004. © NCN

514-2 / 75°14.80'N - 20°52.60'W / C.H. Ostenfeld Land[1526]

NY JONSBU

- Norwegian trappers' station built in 1948 for Arctic Commercial Enterprise.
- On the south side of the entrance to Kildedal, on the south side of Ardencaple Fjord.
- B (IA). 610 x 560 cm including porch and side shed. Coal stove: Scandia (L. Lange & Co). Floor: Wood.
- See chapter on stations.

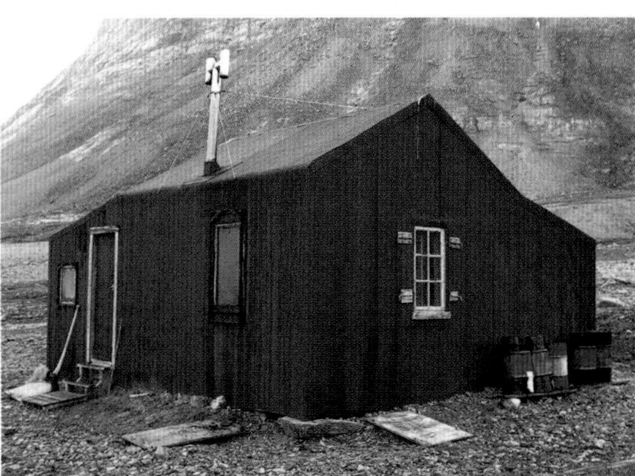

Ny Jonsbu [514-2], 28th July 2004. © NCN

515 / 75°15.93'N - 19°58.86'W / Hochstetter Forland[1527]

KOCH VIG HYTTEN, Kochsvighytten

- Danish trappers' hut built 7th September 1931 for Nanok by Leander E. Emskær Larsen, Niels Hansen and Berndt Jensen, Hochstetter.
- On the south-east side of Lauge Koch Vig on the west coast of Hochstetter Forland.
- C (IIA). 305 x 200 including porch 100 x 200 cm. Coal stove: L. Lange & Co. Floor: Earth.
- On 6th September 1931 Leander E. Emskær Larsen wrote in the Hochsettter station journal: *"Loaded the hut as well as traps and coal for Peters Bugt. We got up the hut, so we had shelter for the night"*. And on 7th September: *"Finished the hut. We took a walk around the country to look for a muskox to kill for a depot. We saw twelve in three herds, but so far from the coast that it didn't make any sense shooting any"*.[1528]

Koch Vig hytten [515], 30th July 2004. © NCN

516 / 75°15.69'N - 20°54.42'W / C.H. Ostenfeld Land[1529]

KILDEDALHYTTEN

- Danish trappers' hut built in September 1931 for Nanok by Niels Hansen, Berndt Jensen and Leander E. Emskær Larsen, Hochstetter.[1530]
- On the north side of the entrance to Kildedal, on the south side of Ardencaple Fjord.
- C (IIA). Ruin. Coal stove: L. Lange & Co.
- On 13th March 1931 the trappers Andreas Hvidberg and Berndt Jensen camped here: *"In the summer a hut is going to be built here where our tent stands"*.[1531] On 3rd September 1931 the men from Hochstetter returned: *"to the station at 18.00 with coal from the coal mine* (Jarners kulmine). *Have placed depots, built a hut and placed traps in Ardencaple Inlet"*.[1532]

Trapper Walther Povelsen at Kildedalhytten [516], 1932. © Arne Philbert

Kildedalhytten [516], 28th July 2004. © NCN

517 / 75°16.05'N - 21°25.23'W / C.H. Ostenfeld Land[1533]

AMSJØHYTTEN

■ Norwegian trappers' hut built in the spring of 1949 for Arctic Commercial Enterprise by Egil Amsjø and Bjarne Myrvold, Ny Jonsbu.

■ About 15 km up in Kildedal, c. 1-2 km west of the longest lake.[1534]

■ C (IIA). Ruin. Coal stove.

■ On 23rd October 1949 Egil Amsjø wrote, that:

The remains of Amsjøhytten [517], 4th July 1988. © A.K. Higgins/GEUS

The remains of Amsjøhytten [517] observed from a helicopter, 8th July 2007. © NCN

"I have allowed myself to name this hut after myself as is the custom when you establish a new territory".[1535] Amsjø built the hut in order to travel through Kildedal and Femdalen on his trapping trips.[1536]

Alabamahuset [518], 2nd August 2004. © NCN

518 / 75°17.19'N - 17°50.47'W / Shannon[1537]

ALABAMAHUSET

■ Danish travellers' station built in 1910 by the Alabama Expedition.

■ About 4 km south of Kap Sussi on the east coast of Shannon.

■ A (IA). 485 x 365 plus porch 105 x 90 cm. Coal stove. Floor: Wood.

■ See chapter on stations.

519 / 75°16.95'N - 19°22.46'W / Hochstetter Forland[1538]

AILSAHYTTEN

■ Danish trappers' hut built in August 1933 for Nanok by Henning Nyholm-Poulsen, Arne Philbert and Walther Povelsen, Hochstetter.

■ On the east coast of Hochstetter Forland, due east of the mountain Ailsa (197 m).

■ C (IIA). Ruin or disappeared.

■ On 6th August 1933 Henning Nyholm-Poulsen wrote that he: *"came home last night after a two day (4th-5th August) trip to the outer coast, where we placed a hut at the same latitude as Ailsa, halfway to Kap Oswald Heer".*[1539] In 1951, when "Søndmøringen" was unable to make a call at Mønstedhus due to the ice, Ailsahytten was enlarged with a depot shed on 26th August where the supplies for Mønstedhus were deposited.[1540]

■ The mountain Ailsa was named in 1823 by Captain D.C. Clavering because of its similarity to the lonely pyramidal islet Ailsa Craig in Firth of Clyde, Scotland. See also note at Haystackhytten [533].

■ In June-July 2004, Ailsahytten was taken by the sea

as a result of the considerable erosion of the sandy eastern coast of Hochstetter Forland during the summers of 2001-04.[1541]

Ailsahytten [519], c. 1932. © Arne Philbert

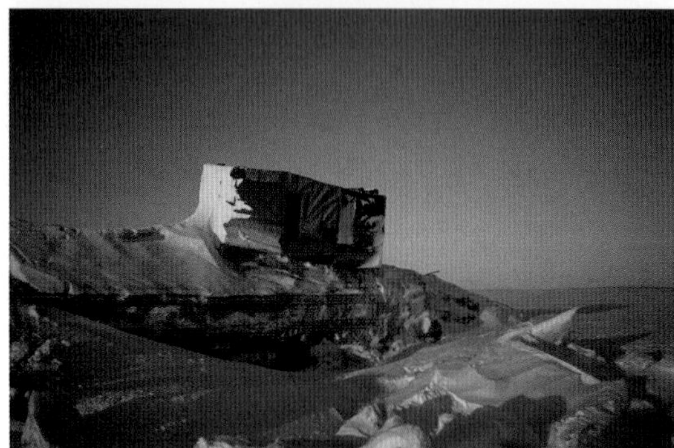

The last photograph of Ailsahytten [519]. The hut is hanging halfway over the cliff by the shore, and was taken by the sea a few months later. February 2004. © Erik Jochumsen

Ailsahytten [519], 4th August 2004. The hut has been destroyed by the sea. © NCN

520 / 75°19.18'N - 17°48.08'W / Shannon[1542]
KAP SUSSI, Funkhütte

- German meteorological station built in 1943 for the German Naval Weather Service.
- At Kap Sussi on the east coast of Shannon.
- A (IB). Ruin.
- Significant locations at Kap Sussi include: Funkhütte (75°19.18'N - 17°48.08'W), Observation post (75°19.24'N - 17°48.78'W), Zacher's grave: (75°19.15'N - 17°48.08'W).
- See chapter on stations.

Kap Sussi [520], 2nd August 2004. The Funkhütte was located between the rocks in the foreground. © NCN

521 / 75°19.15'N - 20°23.27'W / Hochstetter Forland[1543]
JONSBU, Johnsbu, Norske Petersbugt Station, Kolstad, Gamle Jonsbu

- Norwegian trappers' station built in 1932 for the John Giæver Expedition.
- On the west side of Peters Bugt, about 8 km north-east of Kap Klinkerfues.
- A (IA). Ruin. Coal stove: OM&S. No 12.
- See chapter on stations.

Jonsbu [521], 30th July 2004. © NCN

522 / 75°20.14'N - 20°11.83'W / Hochstetter Forland[1544]
PETERS BUGT HYTTEN, Bundhytten, Nummer 1-hytten

- Danish trappers' hut built 17th August 1930 for

Nanok by Niels Hansen and Knud Østergaard, Hochstetter.

■ On the east side of a delta on the north side of Peters Bugt, about 3 km east of Myrvoldhytten [523].[1545]

■ C (IIA). 380 x 195 including porch 80 x 195 cm. Coal stove: L. Lange & Co. Floor: Wood.

■ On 15th August 1930 the men from Hochstetter station according to the logbook arrived: *"at 8 o'clock in the evening and at once started building the hut. We did not go to sleep before 4 o'clock in the morning".* And the 16th August: *"We slept until 10 o'clock and then started with the hut again and worked until 10 o'clock in the evening and were almost done".* And finally on 17th August: *"We finished the hut and carried coal and everything up and got it all set, so it's all together ready for one man".*[1546]

Peters Bugt hytten [522], 1932. © Arne Philbert

Peters Bugt hytten [522], 30th July 2004. © NCN

523 / 75°19.94'N – 20°17.98'W / Hochstetter Forland[1547]

MYRVOLDHYTTEN

■ Norwegian trappers' hut built in the autumn of 1948 for Arctic Commercial Enterprise by Bjarne Myrvold and Egil Amsjø, Ny Jonsbu.[1548]

■ About 500 metres west of the small river delta on the north side of Peters Bugt and about 3 km west of Peters Bugt hytten [522].

■ B (IIA). 305 x 195 including porch 90 x 195 cm. Coal stove: Dravn. Floor: Wood.

■ Materials for Myrvoldhytten were carried by dog sledge across Ardencaple Fjord from Ny Jonsbu [514-2]. In 1992 Bjarne Myrvold recalled that: *"we built the hut in Peters Bugt in two days. The first day we put up two walls, and the next day we finished the rest of the hut".*[1549] Myrvoldhytten is named after the Norwegian trapper Bjarne Myrvold, who was in North-East Greenland from 1947-1950.

Myrvoldhytten [523], 30th July 2004. © NCN

Femdalhytten [524-1], about 1932. © Arne Philbert

Femdalhytten [524-1], 28th July 2004. © NCN

524-1 / 75°21.26'N - 21°19.41'W / C.H. Ostenfeld Land[1550]
FEMDALHYTTEN
■ Danish trappers' hut built in September 1930 for Nanok by Andreas Hvidberg, J.G. Jennov, Leander E. Emskær Larsen and James van Hauen, Hochstetter.
■ On the south side of the entrance to Femdalen, on the south side of Ardencaple Fjord.
■ C (IIA). Ruin. Coal stove: L. Lange & Co.
■ On 1st September 1930 Leander E. Emskær Larsen wrote that: *"we arrived at Femdalen in the afternoon. Here we unloaded both the hut and one barrel of paraffin plus coal. Van Hauen and Hvidberg shot four muskox immediately after we came ashore. Then we began to build the hut"*.[1551] There is a photograph of Femdalhytten opposite page 40 in Leo Hansens book: "Situationen er kritisk" (1939), although Hansen in error places the hut in Kildedalen.

524-2 / c. 75°22'N - 21°21'W / C.H. Ostenfeld Land[1552]
FEMDALEN
■ Norwegian trappers' hut built 18th November 1949 for Arctic Commercial Enterprise by Bjarne Myrvold and Egil Amsjø, Ny Jonsbu.
■ On the north side of the entrance to Femdalen, on the south side of Ardencaple Fjord.
■ C (IIA). Disappeared. A small, portable hut, possibly a ruin, or disappeared around 1951.
■ In 1992 Bjarne Myrvold said that: *"the small hut, that was placed in Ardencaple Fjord was originally meant to be placed in innermost Bredefjord, but that area was unsuitable for trapping. It was therefore put up in Femdalen, so we could drive up Kildedalen and down Femdalen"*.[1553] On 14th November 1949 Egil Amsjø wrote: *"Bjarne drove to Femdalen with the hut we made this summer"*. And four days later: *"I drove to Femdalen to put up the hut, which Bjarne drove in"*.[1554]
■ On 19th November 1952 Stein Sørensen wrote: *"I couldn't find any traps until I arrived at the Danish hut in Femdalen, where I raised seven traps all around. I drive on to stay in the hut on the other side of the river, which is Norwegian, but can't find it, so it must have been pulled down or moved away"*.[1555]

525 / c. 75°24'N - 20°20'W / Hochstetter Forland
BARTH BJERGE
■ Norwegian trappers' hut built in 1949 for Arctic Commercial Enterprise by Bjarne Myrvold and Egil Amsjø, Ny Jonsbu.
■ In the large unnamed valley, running from the head of Peters Bugt about 1 km west of Peters Bugt hytten [522] northwards and westwards into Barth Bjerge.
■ C (IIA). Ruin or disappeared in 1949-50.
■ In 1992 Bjarne Myrvold recalled that when he came back to the valley on his second or third trapping trip, he found further down the valley pieces of wood and other hut materials. The storm had been so strong that the entire hut had blown away from the place where it had been built.[1556]

Holmsnes [526], 28th July 2004. © *NCN*

526 / 75°24.77'N - 21°11.30'W / Hochstetter Forland[1557]
HOLMSNES, Halsneshytten, Berglann, Holmneshytta, Barth-hytta
■ Norwegian trappers' hut built 25th August 1932 for the John Giæver Expedition by John Giæver, Jonsbu.
■ On the north side of Ardencaple Fjord opposite Femdalen in a south-east-facing bay behind a small headland.
■ C (IIA). Ruin, the hut has been blown over. Coal stove: OM&S No. 2. Floor: Wood.
■ On 24th August 1932 John Giæver wrote that he had: *"named the hut Berglann after the editor Berglann in Bodø, and the name is quite suitable as the land here is mountainous and steep"*. Later on Giæver renamed the hut Holmsnes after the radio operator Johan Holm.[1558]

527 / 75°27.86'N - 21°38.50'W / C.H. Ostenfeld Land[1559]
TORNØESTUA, Smallefjordhytten, Thornøe-hytten
■ Norwegian trappers' hut built 8th August 1933 for the John Giæver Expedition by John Giæver and Otto Johnsen, Jonsbu.
■ On the north side of Smallefjord on the east side of the large river bed, 7-8 km west of Kap Daly.
■ C (IIA). 300 x 205 including porch 75 x 205 cm. Floor: Wood.
■ On 2nd August 1932 materials for Tornøestua were laid out with "Isbjørn". However, the hut was not built until 8th August the following year. Materials

deposited on 2nd August 1932 on the south side of Ardencaple Fjord at Niflheim [923] were also used for building the hut. Tornøestua was named after Johannes Kristoffer Tornøe, a journalist who came up with the NSIU Expedition to North-East Greenland in 1930, and later became secretary of NSIU.[1560]

Tornøestua [527], 28th July 2004. © NCN

528 / 75°30.54'N - 19°22.84'W / Hochstetter Forland[1561]
KAP OSWALD HEER HYTTEN, Oswald Heer hytten

▪ Danish trappers' hut built 12th May 1931 for Nanok by Andreas Hvidberg, J.G. Jennov, Berndt Jensen and Arne Schwarck, Hochstetter.

▪ About 9-10 km south of the Agnete Sø river on the east coast of Hochstetter Forland.

▪ C (IIA). 260 x 185 plus porch 60 x 185 cm. Coal stove: L. Lange & Co. Floor: Earth.

▪ The original hut, which consisted of just a few timbers covered with muskox skins, was brought here by dog sledge from the Hochstetter station.[1562] However, on 12th August 1932 it was improved by Evald Rasmussen, Arne Philbert, Finn Kristoffersen and Leander E. Emskær Larsen.[1563] Later, on 14th August 1933, it was again rebuilt and improved by Evald Rasmussen and Henning Nyholm-Poulsen.[1564]

▪ It was at this place that the last traces of Svend Aage Jespersen and Anders Kristian Østerlund Johannesen were found. They both disappeared without trace in February 1939.

Kap Oswald Heer hytten [528], 4th August 2004. © NCN

Bredruphytten [529], 28th July 2004. © NCN

529 / 75°32.84'N - 21°28.12'W / Hochstetter Forland[1565]
BREDRUPHYTTEN, Brædalhytten, Solstrand

▪ Norwegian trappers' hut built 10th August 1933 for the John Giæver Expedition by John Giæver and Otto Johnsen, Jonsbu.

▪ On the east side of Brædal on the north side of Bredefjord.

▪ C (IIA). Ruin.

▪ On 2nd August 1932 materials were laid out with "Isbjørn". On 10th August 1933 John Giæver wrote that they came to: *"Bredefjord. Here we put up Bredruphytten"*.[1566] On 21st August 1938 Sigurd Tolløfsen wrote that: *"the journey was continued to "Solstrand", the innermost hut in Ardencaple Fjord"*.[1567]

530 / 75°35.59'N - 20°00.07'W / Hochstetter Forland[1568]
AGNETEHYTTEN, Agnete Sø hytten

▪ Norwegian trappers' hut built in the spring of 1933 for the John Giæver Expedition by Otto Johnsen and Ove Høeg, Ottostrand.

▪ At the south end of Agnete Sø on the north side of the Agnete Sø river.

▪ C (IIA). 310 x 200 cm including porch. Coal stove. Floor: Wood.

▪ On 29th May 1933 John Giæver wrote that: *"the lads have driven materials for a hut about 15 km inland. In a valley here they have discovered a big lake* (Agnete Sø) *about 10 km long"*. In reality Agnete Sø is 18 km long. The hut was still usable in December 1977.[1569]

Ottostrand [531], 4th August 2004. © *NCN*

531 / 75°37.00'N - 19°30.12'W / Hochstetter Forland[1570]
OTTOSTRAND, Kolstad, Norske Roseneath

- Norwegian trappers' station built in 1932 for the John Giæver Expedition.
- On the east coast of Hochstetter Forland about 3 km north of the Agnete Sø river outlet.
- B (IA). One station house and three sheds. Station house: 980 x 355 cm. Stove: Dravn. Floor: Wood.
- See chapter on stations.

Ottostrand [531], 4th August 2004. © *NCN*

532-1 / c. 75°42 - 19°33'W / Hochstetter Forland[1571]
LANGSØHYTTEN

- Danish trappers' hut built 15th August 1933 for Nanok by Arne Philbert and Walther Povelsen, Hochstetter.
- On the north side of Langelv at Roseneathbugt, on the east coast of Hochstetter Forland.
- C (IIA). Disappeared.
- The hut was located where Nanok in 1938 built the Mønstedhus trappers' station.[1572] Langsøhytten, which had been used as a provision shed was in danger of being taken by the sea, and on 15th August 1948 J.G. Jennov wrote that: *"the old trappers' hut, (which was hanging over the cliff), was lifted up and put on rollers, and we pulled it more than nine metres away front the cliff"*.[1573] Langsøhytten was taken by the sea in the summer of 2001.[1574]

Trapper Walther Povelsen in front of the Langsøhytten [532-1], 15th August 1933. © *Arne Philbert*

532-2 / c. 75°42'N - 19°33'W / Hochstetter Forland[1575]
MØNSTEDHUS, Danske Roseneath

- Danish trappers' station built in 1938 for Nanok.
- On the north side of Langelv at Roseneathbugt on the east coast of Hochstetter Forland.
- C (IA). Fell into the sea due to strong coastal erosion activity in September 2002. Some remains were rescued and used to build "Ny Mønstedhus" [532-4].
- See chapter on stations.

Mønstedhus [532-2], 5th June 1978. In the background the conical mountain Haystack. © *Peter Schmidt Mikkelsen*

532-3 / 75°41.90'N - 19°34.08'W / Hochstetter Forland[1576]
LANGELV FISKERHYTTE

- Norwegian trappers' hut built in June 1949 for Arctic Commercial Enterprise by Bjarne Myrvold, Egil Amsjø, Erling Juell Ramberg and Hermod Sætre, Ottostrand.
- On the south side of Langelv at Roseneathbugt on the east coast of Hochstetter Forland.

Trappers building the Langelv Fiskerhytte [532-3], June 1949. © Bjarne Myrvold

Langelv Fiskerhytte [532-3], 4th August 2004. © NCN

■ C̲ (IIA). 305 x 205 plus side shed 190 x 205 cm. Coal stove: Dravn. Floor: Wood.[1577]

■ Langelv Fiskerhytte was built for the char fishery in Langelv.[1578] The Danish trapper, Harald Mikkelsen, was present on the occasion in 1949, and recalled in 1992 that: *"the Norwegians caught eight barrels of char, which they salted"*.[1579]

Ny Mønstedhus [532-4], 4th August 2004. © NCN

532-4 / 75°42.14'N - 19°33.75'W / Hochstetter[1580] Forland

NY MØNSTEDHUS

■ Danish travellers' hut built mid-September 2002 for the Sirius Dog Sledge Patrol, Daneborg.

■ On the north side of Langelv at Roseneathbugt, on the east coast of Hochstetter Forland.

■ B (IA). 430 x 375 cm. Coal stove: L. Lange & Co. Floor: Wood.

■ Ny Mønstedhus was built from the remains of Mønstedhus [532-2].

533 / 75°44.33'N - 19°27.59'W / Hochstetter Forland[1581]

HAYSTACKHYTTEN

■ Norwegian trappers' hut built in November 1932 for the John Giæver Expedition by Otto Johnsen and Ove Høeg, Ottostrand.[1582]

■ On the north side of the Haystack peninsula.

■ C̲ (IIA). 300 x 206 including porch 100 x 206 cm. Coal stove: OM&S No. 2. Floor: Wood.

■ On 21st May 1933 John Giæver mentioned the hut as he: *"visited Otto's hut at the peninsula and had myself a smoke"*.[1583] The Haystack mountain was observed by Captain Douglas C. Clavering from Shannon on the 12th August 1823 when he: *"ascended the heights"*.[1584] From here Clavering could see two distinctive mountains or islands, Haystack and Ailsa, that he named for their appearance.

Haystackhytten [533], 20th July 2005. © NCN

534-1 / c. 75°45'N - 20°03'W / Hochstetter Forland[1585]

LANGELV-HYTTEN

■ Norwegian trappers' hut built in May-June 1933 for the John Giæver Expedition by Otto Johnsen and Ove Høeg, Ottostrand.[1586]

■ At Langelv, about 15 km from the east coast of Hochstetter Forland.

■ C̲ (IIA). "Slatted hut".

Langelv-hytten [534-1], July 1933. © Ove Høeg / Norwegian Polar Institute

■ In 1990 former trapper Peter Nielsen recalled: *"The hut was so well hidden between the rocks, that it was a mere chance I discovered it. It was made from boards standing upright, and I believe it only had boards on one side. There was probably a foot or more between the boards, but they were covered with roofing felt. There was a stove in the hut, about a foot high, barely that wide and a bit more than a foot long. The coal stove lay on its side and had never been put up. I don't think the hut had ever been used, and placed as it was it would be impossible to find during the polar night"*. Langelv-hytten was later replaced by Fjellborg hytten [534-2].[1587] No traces of Langelv-hytten were observed during a brief helicopter-supported survey on 8th July 2007.

The remains of Fjellborg-hytten [534-2] at lower right observed from a helicopter, 8th July 2007. © NCN

534-2 / 75°45.98'N - 20°08.18'W / Hochstetter Forland[1588]

FJELLBORG-HYTTEN

■ Norwegian trappers' hut built 23rd October 1950 for Arctic Commercial Enterprise by Fredrik Sæterdal and Trygve Saga, Ottostrand.

■ On the south side of Langelv about 18 km from the east coast of Hochstetter Forland.

■ C (IIA). Ruin.

On 24th October 1950 Erik Larsen wrote at Mønstedhus: *"The Norwegians passed by on their way to Ottostrand. The last couple of days they have been at Langsø to build a hut"*.[1589] In 1992 Fredrik Sæterdal recalled that: *"the hut at Langelv* (Fjellborg-hytten) *was built as a replacement for a hut which was built before the war, but couldn't be found"*.[1590]

535-1 / 75°49.87'N - 19°39.73'W / Hochstetter Forland[1591]

SØNDERELV

■ Norwegian trappers' hut built in November 1933 for the John Giæver Expedition by Otto Johnsen and Ove Høeg, Ottostrand.

■ On the south side of Sønderelv about 12 km north of the Haystack peninsula.[1592]

■ C (IIA). Ruin.

■ On 24th November 1933 John Giæver wrote that: *"according to plan Otto has built a fourth hut between Haystack and Bessel Fjord"*.[1593] In 1949 the hut was replaced by Astralhytten [535-2].

Sønderelv [535-1], 1932-33. © Arne Philbert

Sønderelv [535-1]. The foundation of the old Sønderelv hut [535-1] in front of Astralhytten [535-2], 22nd July 2005. © NCN

535-2 / 75°49.87'N - 19°39.72'W / Hochstetter Forland[1594]
ASTRALHYTTEN

- Norwegian trappers' hut built in 1948-49 for Arctic Commercial Enterprise, probably by Hermod Sætre and Erling Juell Ramberg, Ottostrand.
- On the south side of Sønderelv about 12 km north of the Haystack peninsula.
- C (IIA). 310 x 200 including porch 85 x 200 cm. Coal stove: Dravn. Floor: Wood.
- Astralhytten was built as a replacement for the old Norwegian Sønderelv hytte [535-1].[1595]

Astralhytten [535-2], 22nd July 2005. © NCN

535-3 / 7 5°50.20'N - 19°40.16'W / Hochstetter Forland[1596]
HUNDEHUSET, Hundehushytten, Terrassehytten, Terrasso-hytten, Sønderelv-huset, Yderkysthytten

- Danish trappers' hut built 18th May 1931 for Nanok by Andreas Hvidberg, J.G. Jennov, Arne Schwarck and Berndt Jensen, Hochstetter.
- On the north side of Sønderelv about 13 km north of the Haystack isthmus.
- C (IIA). 195 x 160 cm. Coal stove: L. Lange & Co. Floor: Earth.
- Materials for the original hut were brought here by dog sledge from the Hochstetter station.[1597] On

The original Hundehuset [535-3] built in May 1931 was a "dummy" hut. August 1932. © Arne Philbert

Hundehuset [535-3] just after it was rebuilt in 1932. August 1932. © Arne Philbert

Hundehuset [535-3], 21st July 2005. © NCN

12th August 1932 the hut was renewed by Evald Rasmussen, Arne Philbert, Finn Kristoffersen and Leander E. Emskær Larsen. The last-mentioned wrote in the journal of the Hochstetter station, that: *"we built a completely new hut of wood and covered it with roofing felt".*[1598] On 5th February 1937 Poul Hennings wrote: *"When I had climbed a bit up the hill I to my surprise discovered a hut* (Hundehuset) *right north of the riverbed." ... "From the outside it looked much better than the Norwegian hut* (Sønderelv), *but the door had been broken open, so the hut was filled with snow".*[1599] See the note concerning the possibility of confusion [537-1].

536 / 75°55.17'N - 20°21.76'W / Hochstetter Forland[1600]
POLLENHYTTEN, Perka hytten

- Norwegian trappers' hut built about 12th November 1932 for the John Giæver Expedition by Otto Johnsen and Ove Høeg, Ottostrand.
- In the bay known as Pollen, south-west of Trums Ø in Eigtvedsund on the south side of Bessel Fjord.
- C (IIA). 300 x 200 including porch 100 x 200 cm. Coal stove: Dravn. Floor: Wood/earth.
- A notice in the hut has the inscription: *"Denne hytte med omkringliggende terreng tilhører John Giævers*

Pollenhytten [536], 23rd July 2005. © NCN

Grønlandsekspedisjon. Hytten lagt op her den 12/8-1932. Perka Hytten".[1601] (This hut with surrounding territory belongs to the John Giæver Greenland Expedition. The hut was put here on 12th August 1932. Perka Hytten). "Pollen" is the Norwegian word for a cove or small bay.

Mundingshytten [537-1], 22nd July 2005. © NCN

537-1 / 75°55.97'N - 19°56.48'W / Hochstetter Forland[1602]

MUNDINGSHYTTEN, Besselfjordhytten

- Danish trappers' hut built in September 1932 for Nanok by Evald Rasmussen and Arne Philbert, Bessel Fjord.
- About 1 km south-east of Kap Møbius and Kaphytten [537-2], on the south side of the entrance to Bessel Fjord.
- B (IIA). 250 x 205 cm including porch. Coal stove: L. Lange & Co.. Floor: Earth.
- In 1992 Arne Philbert said that the hut was built of surplus materials from the Bessel Fjord station.[1603] On 11th March 1937 Hans Ludvig Jensen wrote that the hut: *"is similar to "Hundehuset"* [535-3], *but more cosy as it is tight; but these huts are much too small, even for one man".*[1604] The hut has from time to time been confused with Hundehuset / Terrasso-hytten [535-3], which is located about 13 km to the south.[1605]

Kaphytten [537-2], 22nd July 2005. © NCN

537-2 / 75°56.31'N - 19°57.79'W / Hochstetter Forland[1606]

KAPHYTTEN

- Norwegian trappers' hut built in November 1932 for the John Giæver Expedition by Otto Johnsen and Ove Høeg, Ottostrand.
- At Kap Møbius, about 1 km north-west of Mundingshytten [537-1] on the south side of the entrance to Bessel Fjord.
- C (IIA). 300 x 200 cm including porch. Coal stove: OM&S. Floor: Wood/Earth.
- On 10th November 1932 Ole Sivertsen wrote: *"Arrived at the main station today after having said hello to Otto Johnsen and Ove Høeg. They were going to build two trappers' huts".*[1607] The eastern wall in the hut bears the following inscription: *"Denne hytte med omkringliggende terreng eies af John Giævers Grønlandsekspedisjon. Ilandført 12/8-1932".* (This hut with surrounding territory is owned by the John Giæver Greenland Expedition. Taken ashore 12th August 1932).

538 / 75°57.91'N - 20°48.23'W / Hochstetter Forland[1608]

FREDHAUG, Svarthammerhytten

- Norwegian trappers' hut built 3rd September 1932 for the John Giæver Expedition by Ole Sivertsen and John Johnsen, Olestua.
- On the west side of the river on the south side of Bessel Fjord, about 12 km west of Trums Ø.
- C (IIA). 295 x 195 cm including porch. Coal stove. Floor: Wood.
- On 2nd September 1932 Ole Sivertsen wrote that they started to build the hut: *"and finished*

Fredhaug [538], 8th July 2007. © NCN

the framework and made floor, walls, ceiling and doors". And on 3rd September: *"We have put roofing felt on the hut, made furniture and started to put up a wall of turf"*.[1609]

Gåseholmhytten [539], 8th July 2007. © NCN

539 / 75°58.47'N - 21°52.05'W / Hochstetter Forland[1610]
GÅSEHOLMHYTTEN Gåseholmhytten

- Danish trappers' hut built 15th August 1938 for Nanok by Christian Jensen, Franz Dalskov and Christian Petersen, Mønstedhus.
- On a small islet on the north-west side of the cove at the head of Bessel Fjord, about 2 km south of "Botten" [541].
- C (IIA). 200 x 200 cm. Coal stove. Floor: Earth.
- J.G. Jennov wrote that they arrived at: *"the head of the fjord, where we started to build a hut on a small islet, which is connected with land by a narrow bank of gravel" ... "At noon the hut was finished"*.[1611]

540 / 75°58.91'N - 21°22.03'W / Ad. S. Jensen Land[1612]
JOHNS HYTTE, John Johnsens hytte, Jonshytten

- Norwegian trappers' hut built 1st September 1932 for the John Giæver Expedition by Ole Sivertsen and John Johnsen, Olestua.
- On the west side of a small peninsula on the north side of Bessel Fjord, about 13-14 km east of the head of the fjord.
- C (IIA). 295 x 195 including porch 100 x 195 cm. Coal stove. Floor: Wood.
- Named after the trapper John Johnsen, who wintered at Olestua from 1932-34.[1613]

Johns hytte [540], 8th July 2007. © NCN

541 / 75°59.21'N - 21°53.33'W / Hochstetter Forland[1614]
BOTTEN, Bundhytten

- Norwegian trappers' hut built 28th August 1932 for the John Giæver Expedition by Ole Sivertsen and John Johnsen, Olestua.[1615]
- On the north-east side of the peninsula at the head of Bessel Fjord, about 2 km north of "Gåseholmhytten" [539].
- C (IIA). 300 x 200 cm including porch. Coal stove. Floor: Wood.
- On 26th August 1932 Ole Sivertsen wrote that: *"we started with the hut and continued working until the evening"*. And the following day: *"Today we finished the hut, and tomorrow we'll start to build a wall of turfs around it"*.[1616]

Botten [541], 8th July 2007. © NCN

601-1 / c. 76°03'N - 20°06'W / Ad. S. Jensen Land[1617]
BESSEL FJORD HYTTEN

■ Danish trappers' hut built 22nd May 1931 for Nanok by J.G. Jennov, Andreas Hvidberg, Arne Schwarck and Berndt Jensen, Hochstetter.

■ On the east side of the entrance to Trumsdalen on the south coast of Ad. S. Jensen Land.

■ C (IIA). Disappeared. In 1932 replaced by Bessel Fjord [601-2].

■ The materials for the hut were brought here by dog sledge from the Hochstetter station. On 20th May 1931 Andreas Hvidberg wrote: *"Today we camped in a valley at the entrance to Bessel Fjord. We have named the valley Trums Dal. We left Trums Ø with heavy loads, carrying with us the materials that Jennov and Jensen have brought here"*. And on 22nd May: *"We have today covered the hut with the muskox furs we had. The rest we have covered with a sleeping bag cover and with stones and gravel; now the hut is in order, and we are ready to go home tomorrow"*.[1618]

Bessel Fjord [601-2], 23rd August 2005. © NCN

601-2 / 76°03.35'N - 20°05.97'W / Ad. S. Jensen Land[1619]
BESSEL FJORD, Trumsdalen, Besselfjordstationen, Trumsødalen

■ Danish trappers' station built in 1932 for Nanok.

■ On the east side of the entrance to Trumsdalen on the south coast of Ad. S. Jensen Land.

■ A (IA). 550 x 450 cm. Coal stove: Scandia No. 909. Floor: Wood/earth.

■ See chapter on stations.

602 / c. 76°04'N - 20°03'W / Ad. S. Jensen Land[1620]
SÆTHERHYTTEN

■ Norwegian trappers' hut built 5th September 1932 for the John Giæver Expedition by Ole Sivertsen and John Johnsen, Olestua.

Sætherhytten [602], 24th August 2005. © NCN

■ About 2-4 km east of the entrance to Trumsdalen on the south coast of Ad. S. Jensen Land.

■ C (IIA). Ruin. Originally about 250 x 190 cm. Coal stove: OM&S Nr. 2.

■ On 5th September 1932 Ole Sivertsen wrote that they: *"started building the hut. While sitting and eating we had a visit from two men. It turned out to be the two* (Evald Rasmussen and Arne Philbert) *that live right next to our hut* (Sætherhytten)*"*.[1621] The hut was named after consul Carl S. Sæther in Tromsø.

Olestua [603], 25th July 2005. © NCN

603 / 76°07.30'N - 19°44.84'W / Ad. S. Jensen Land[1622]
OLESTUA, Carl Ritter hytten, Kap Carl Ritter, Beurmann, Ullestuen

■ Norwegian trappers' station built in 1932 for the John Giæver Expedition.

■ At Kap Carl Ritter on the east coast of Ad. S. Jensen Land.

■ C (IA). Ruin. Originally about 640 x 300 cm. Coal stove: C.M. Hess, Veile.

■ See chapter on stations.

Påskehytten [604], 25th July 2005. © NCN

604 / 76°08.75'N - 19°47.62'W / Ad. S. Jensen Land[1623]
PÅSKEHYTTEN, Påskenæshytten, Påskenæsset

■ Danish trappers' hut built 17th August 1938 for Nanok by Franz Dalskov, Christian Jensen, J.G. Jennov and Henning Ørnlef, Aalborghus.

■ On the north side of the Påskedalen river, about 2 km south of Påskenæsset.

■ C (IIA). 190 x 185 cm. Coal stove: L. Lange & Co. Floor: Wood.

■ On 16th August 1938 J.G. Jennov wrote that: *"at Kap Peschel we loaded some wood and then sailed to Påskedalen, where we began to build a hut at 10.30". ... "At 3 o'clock on the 17th August the hut was finished".*[1624]

Site of Trækpashytten [605] observed from a helicopter. The remains of the hut are located at the centre of the photograph. 8th July 2007. © NCN

605 / 76°10.15'N - 18°33.61'W / Koldewey Øer[1625]
TRÆKPASHYTTEN

■ Danish travellers' hut built in the summer of 1958 for Danmarkshavn Vejrstation by Gerhardt Blaase, Danmarkshavn.

■ About 200 m north of the Trækpasset river outlet on the east coast of Store Koldewey.

■ C (IIA). Ruin.

■ Trækpashytten was built from sections prepared at Danmarkshavn and sailed to the location by the boat "Petersuaq". The hut was blown down at the end of the 1970s.[1626]

Fiskerhytten [606] used for an overnight stay by the author - as a member of the Sirius Dog Sledge Patrol, 1st June 1978. © Peter Schmidt Mikkelsen

Fiskerhytten [606] visited by the author – as member of a Nanok expedition team, 8th July 2007. © NCN

606 / 76°11.14'N - 20°43.29'W / Ad. S. Jensen Land[1627]
FISKERHYTTEN

■ Danish trappers' hut built in August 1951 for Nanok by Knud Nielsen and Leo Ingwersen, Aalborghus.

■ On the north side of the moraine ridge that separates Syttendemajfjorden from Laksesø.

■ C (IIA). 300 x 200 including porch 100 x 200 cm. Coal stove. Floor: Wood.

■ Materials for the hut were laid out in the summer of 1950. On 6th August 1951 Fiskerhytten was described in detail in the journal of the Aalborghus station: *"The hut has a floor area of 3 x 2 m. The sitting room is 2 x 2 m and there is also a porch measuring 1 x 2 m for storing fishing gear, coal etc. The base has been dug about 35 cm into the ground, and a thick bank has been built around the entire hut.*

The strengthening has been made using four square beams and segments of thick trap boards have been placed at the middle of the walls and ceiling. There are berths for two persons plus a table. The heating is by means of a hut stove. The hut has a floor".[1628]

Strømsbukta [607], spring 1934. © Norwegian Polar Institute

Strømsbukta [607], 28th July 2006. © NCN

607 / 76°14.61'N - 20°01.52'W / Ad. S. Jensen Land[1629]
STRØMSBUKTA, Kap Peschel hytten

- Norwegian trappers' hut built 24th August 1933 for the John Giæver Expedition by Ole Sivertsen, Olestua.
- South of an unnamed island about 2 km west of Kap Peschel on the north coast of Ad. S. Jensen Land.
- C (IIA). 175 x 130 cm. Coal stove. Floor: Wood.
- On 24th August 1933 Ole Sivertsen wrote: *"Unfortunately I could not finish the grand building. As I was going to cover the roof and walls with roofing felt it turned out that it was impossible to open the rolls. There wasn't any sand between as there should be, but only tar".*[1630] The hut was instead covered with an old tent and turfs. On 22nd March 1937 Hans Ludvig Jensen humorously remarked that: *"the hut is 1.75 x 1.25 m, so there isn't any room for dancing between the tables".*[1631]

Hasseriishytten [608], 28th July 2005. © NCN

608 / 76°15.05'N - 20°24.47'W / Dove Bugt[1632]
HASSERIISHYTTEN, Sydlige Jægersund hytten, Jægersundhytten

- Danish trappers' hut built 6th September 1938 for Nanok by Franz Dalskov and Christian Jensen, Aalborghus.
- On the west side of the southern point of Nanok Ø (Tuxens Ø) in Dove Bugt.
- C (IIA). 210 x 200 cm. Coal stove: L. Lange & Co. Floor: Wood.
- On 6th September 1938 Franz Dalskov wrote that they had: *"placed a hut at the south end of Tuxens Ø* (Nanok Ø)*".*[1633]

Sjelnan [609], spring 1934. © Norwegian Polar Institute

609 / 76°15.83'N - 21°41.42'W / Dove Bugt[1634]
SJELNAN, Kap Ullidtz hytten

- Norwegian trappers' hut built 20th August 1933 for the John Giæver Expedition by Ole Sivertsen, Olestua.
- About 14-15 km south of Kap Niels north-west of Soranerbræen, on Rechnitzer Land, inner Dove Bugt.
- C (IIA). Ruin. Originally about 170 x 140 cm. Coal stove: Trolla Brug.
- On 19th August 1933 Ole Sivertsen wrote that

Sjelnan [609], 7th August 2005. © NCN

he sailed to a location *"across Kap Ullidtz"* to build the hut.[1635] Sivertsen probably had the impression that Kap Ullidtz was located on the east side of the fjord north of Soranerbræen, as Richard Nielsen in 1992 recalled that the hut was located on the west side of fjord.[1636] In 2005, Nielsen's recollection was confirmed by a Nanok team.

Majhytten [610], 6th August 2005. © NCN

610 / 76°17.10'N - 21°07.09'W / Ad. S. Jensen Land[1637]
MAJHYTTEN, 17. maj hytten

▪ Danish trappers' hut built 6th September 1938 for Nanok by Franz Dalskov, Christian Jensen and Marius Jensen, Aalborghus.

▪ On the north side of Syttendemajfjorden, about 1 km from the entrance, on Ad. S. Jensen Land.

▪ C (IIA). 195 x 195 cm. Coal stove: L. Lange & Co. Floor: Earth.

▪ On 6th September 1938 Christian Jensen wrote: *"This morning we made ready and sailed to Skyggefjorden* (Syttendemajfjorden) *with wood for two huts. At about 14.00 we arrived at the fjord and began building a hut at the agreed location. At 19.30 we were finished and sailed on"*.[1638]

611 / 76°18.96'N - 20°48.34'W / Dove Bugt[1639]
KROKEN, Nordlige Jægersund hytten, Tvillinghytten

▪ Norwegian trappers' hut built 23rd August 1933 for the John Giæver Expedition by Ole Sivertsen, Olestua.

▪ On the south-west side of Tvillingerne in Trangsund, at the passage in the middle part of the island. The high mountains on each side of the low-lying passage are named "The Twins".

▪ C (IIA). Ruin. Originally about 215 x 160 cm. Coal stove: Old fuel drum. Floor: Wood.

▪ Kroken, which Ole Sivertsen himself called "Kroken, Vestre Tvilling", was built on the west side of the island Tvillingerne (the twins) and not on Nanok Ø as formerly assumed, e.g. by John Giæver (1939).[1640] Hence the name Nordlige Jægersund hytten (Northern Jægersund hut) is misleading. The correct location of Kroken was indicated by Ole Sivertsen on 25th February 1934, when on a journey heading for Kap Peschel he: *"went across* (meaning through the low passage) *Vestre Tvilling and came southwards through the sound* (Jægersund) *between both* (islands, meaning Tvillingerne and Nanok Ø)*"*.[1641] In 1993 the geologist A.K. Higgins confirmed that in 1990 he had observed remains of a hut on the south-west side of Tvillingerne.[1642]

Kroken [611], spring 1934. © Norwegian Polar Institute

Kroken [611], 29th July 2005. © NCN

Rechnitzerhytten [612], 8th August 2005. © NCN

612 / 76°20.16'N - 21°39.75'W / Dove Bugt[1643]
RECHNITZERHYTTEN

- Danish trappers' hut built 24th August 1938 for Nanok by Christian Jensen and Henning Ørnlef, Aalborghus.
- At the north side of the large valley on the east coast of Rechnitzer Land.
- C (IIA). Ruin. Coal stove: L. Lange & Co.
- On 23rd August 1938 Christian Jensen wrote that Ørnlef and he sailed: *"westwards to the large valley on Rechnitzer Land"*. The following day the hut was ready. It stood: *"not quite at the spot initially thought out, but about 1 km more northerly, which we thought a more suitable location and closer to the shore, so there the hut was built. We have seen several seals over here, but have caught none. There were fresh tracks from fox in the sand by the hut today"*.[1644] Rechnitzerhytten is a ruin, and probably has been since the 1950s.

613-1 / c. 76°23'N - 20°54'W / Dove Bugt[1645]
GEFION HAVN HYTTEN

- Danish trappers' hut built 7th May 1934 for Nanok by Henry V. Nielsen, Finn Kristoffersen, Christian Jensen and Povel Povelsen, Hvalrosodden.
- At a small bay, Gefion Havn, on the south coast of Godfred Hansen Ø.
- C (IIA). Disappeared.
- On 6th May 1934 the journal of Hvalrosodden recorded: *"In the morning we arrived at Gefion Havn. Found the depot. Fine weather and the going quite good"*. And on 7th May: *"The other depot was discovered after a lot of digging. The hut now has its roof on. In the morning strong wind with snow drift. The hut is 2 x 2.5 m with a wooden floor"*. In 1938 the hut, which was named after the ship "Gefion", was replaced by Aalborghus [613-2].[1646]

Aalborghus [613-2], 4th August 2005. © NCN

613-2 / 76°23.29'N - 20°54.38'W / Dove Bugt[1647]
AALBORGHUS, Gefion Havn

- Danish trappers' station built in August 1938 for Nanok.
- At a small bay, Gefion Havn, on the south coast of Godfred Hansen Ø.
- B (IA). Station house: 705 x 565 cm, including living room, sleeping room, porch and workshop. Shed: 450 x 390 cm plus sauna/toilet 115 x 110 cm. Coal stove: Morsø - sponsored by H.M. Queen Margrethe II. Floor: Wood.
- See chapter on stations.

Kap Niels hytten [614], March 1934. © Norwegian Polar Institute

614 / 76°25.51'N - 21°37.72'W / Dove Bugt[1648]
KAP NIELS HYTTEN

- Norwegian trappers' hut built 19th August 1933 for the John Giæver Expedition by Ole Sivertsen, Olestua.
- About 4 km north of Kap Niels on the east coast of Rechnitzer Land.
- C (IIA). Ruin. Coal stove: L. Lange & Co.
- On 18th August 1933 Ole Sivertsen wrote that he: *"loaded two huts in the motor boat plus coal, stove etc., and went north to build the huts. At 11.30 in the evening I arrived here at Kap Niels, where I immediately started to unload one of the huts"*.[1649]

Kap Niels hytten [614], 8th August 2005. © NCN

615 / 76°28.51'N - 21°41.17'W / Dove Bugt[1650]

BRÆFJORDHYTTEN, Jarners hytte, Hjarnerhytten

■ Danish trappers' hut built 15th May 1934 for Nanok by Finn Kristoffersen, Henry V. Nielsen, Christian Jensen and Povel Povelsen, Hvalrosodden.

■ At a point about 4 km north of the entrance to Bræfjorden on the east coast of Lindhard Ø.

■ C (IIA). Ruin. Coal stove: L. Lange & Co.

■ On 14th May 1934 Henry V. Nielsen wrote that: *"it was the intention that Povelsen and Christoffersen should go to the northern point of Godfred Hansen Ø with a hut, Jensen and I towards Kap Stop with another. But it turned out to be impossible for us to get through, so the hut was split up on all four sledges. We reached the Norwegian hut at Kap Niels, where we camped"*. And on 15th May: *"The hut was built about 5 km from Kap Niels. Exactly 20 km from Kap Stop"*.[1651] The name "Jarners hytte" refers to the geologist Hakon Høeg Jarner (1882-1964), who participated in the Danmark Expedition 1906-08, and discovered Jarners Kulmine.

Bræfjordhytten [615], 9th August 2005. © NCN

616 / 76°30.33'N - 20°14.16'W / Dove Bugt[1652]

DEN NY HYTTE

■ Danish travellers' hut built in 1966 for Danmarkshavn Vejrstation by Carl E. Pedersen, Gert Hansen, Jens Peter Madsen and Ole Eliasen, Danmarkshavn.

■ On the north-east point of the island north-east of Licht Ø in Dove Bugt.

■ C (IIA). 490 x 260 including porch 150 x 260 cm. Coal stove: Hess & Søn. Floor: Wood.

■ This hut never received another name than "Den ny hytte" (the new hut). Unfortunately the hut has a tendency to become snowed down.[1653]

Den ny hytte [616], 2nd August 2005. © NCN

617 / 76°32.88'N - 20°45.35'W / Dove Bugt[1654]

NØRRESUNDBYHYTTEN, Nr. Sundby hytten

■ Danish trappers' hut built 25th August 1938 for Nanok by Christian Jensen, Marius Jensen, Franz Dalskov and Henning Ørnlef, Aalborghus.

■ On the south-east coast of Andreas Lundager Ø.

■ C (IIA). 205 x 200 cm. Coal stove: L. Lange & Co. Floor: Wood.

■ On 25th August 1938 Christian Jensen wrote:

Nørresundbyhytten [617], 2nd August 2005. © NCN

"We went to the north side of Godfred Hansen Ø. We couldn't find any suitable places to build a hut, so we went over to another large island, right next to Godfred Hansen Ø. Here we built the hut, so it's placed almost the same distance from Aalborghus, Port Arthur and Jarners hytte. We have made two berths in this hut, because it's placed right next to the southern main route".[1655]

Pashytten [618], 8th July 2007. © NCN

618 / 76°35.71'N - 18°44.67'W / Koldewey Øer [1656]
PASHYTTEN, Berg Fjord hytten, Yderhytten

▪ Danish trappers' hut built late August 1933 for Nanok by Finn Kristoffersen, Henry V. Nielsen and Christian Jensen, Hvalrosodden.

▪ On the east coast of Store Koldewey, on the north side of a small bay at the passage over to Berg Fjord.

▪ C (IIA). 300 x 200 including porch 100 x 200 cm. Floor: Wood.

▪ On 24th August 1933 the journal of Hvalrosodden recorded: *"We have now built huts at Snenæs and Bergs Fjord".*[1657] This hut can be confused with Bergfjordhytten [619], which is located in Berg Fjord, and with Dagmar Havn hytten [620], which is located more northerly on the east coast of Store Koldewey.[1658]

619 / 76°35.11'N - 18°49.46'W / Koldewey Øer[1659]
BERGFJORDHYTTEN, Inderhytten

▪ Norwegian trappers' hut built in September 1938 for the Norwegian-French Polar Expedition by Karl Nicolaisen and others, Micardbu.

▪ On the small peninsula in the north-eastern corner of Berg Fjord, Store Koldewey.[1660]

▪ C (IIA). 305 x 195 including porch 75 x 195 cm. Coal stove: Damgaards Støberi nr. 182. Floor: Wood.

▪ On the 11th September 1938 Christian Jensen wrote: *"Today at noon we sailed to Danmarkshavn. "En Avant" lay there; they had put people ashore at Kap Marie Valdemar, and now the ship was on the way to the north point of Store Koldewey to anchor for the winter. They had built a hut in Berg Fjord".*[1661] On 13th April 1941 Poul Hennings wrote that the hut: *"was well made of Piten-plates".*[1662]

Bergfjordhytten [619], 22nd August 2005. © NCN

620 / 76°38.89'N - 18°46.93'W / Koldewey Øer [1663]
DAGMAR HAVN HYTTEN, Øresundshytten

▪ Norwegian trappers' hut built in September 1938 for the Norwegian-French Polar Expedition by Karl Nicolaisen and others, Micardbu.

▪ On the east coast of Store Koldewey, about 3-4 km south-west of Røseløbet.

▪ C (IIA). 215 x 180 plus porch 110 x 80 cm.

▪ Standing beside the hut and looking through Røseløbet on Lille Koldewey, one can see the antenna masts at Danmarkshavn Weather station. Both names "Dagmar Havn hytten" and "Øresundshytten" are misleading as the hut is located about 2 km south of Dagmar Havn, and on the coast of "Lille Bælt". The "Øresund" is the strait between Kap Bismarck on the mainland and Lille Koldewey.[1664]

Dagmar Havn hytten [620], 8th July 2007. © NCN

621 / 76°38.80'N - 21°38.21'W / Dove Bugt[1665]
KAP STOP HYTTEN

■ Danish trappers' hut built 2nd September 1933 for Nanok by Finn Kristoffersen, Henry V. Nielsen and Christian Jensen, Hvalrosodden.

■ Inner part of a north-east facing bay about 2-3 km north of Kap Stop in Dove Bugt.

■ B (IIA). 310 x 200 including porch 90 x 200 cm. Coal stove: L. Lange & Co. Floor: Wood.

■ The original Kap Stop hytten was built in 1933.[1666] On 25th August 1939, the old hut was replaced by a new hut built by Carl Henrik Schultz and Poul Hennings. The latter wrote that: *"the following day we pulled down Kap Stop hytten and rebuilt it at a higher place where it is free of snow. With a lot of hard work we got a fine hut out of it".*[1667]

Kap Stop hytten [621], 10th August 2005. © NCN

Location of the original Kap Stop hytten [621] before it was rebuilt in 1939, 10th August 2005. © NCN

622-1 / 76°39.73'N - 19°40.72'W / Dove Bugt[1668]
WEASELHYTTEN, Weasel hut

■ Danish travellers' hut built 14th March 1953 for Danmarkshavn Vejrstation by Mike Banks, John Oakley, Hans Egede Jacobsen and Ove Hermansen, Danmarkshavn.

■ On the south side of Weaseløen, the island south of the southernmost of the Orienteringsøerne, Dove Bugt.

■ C (IIA). 320 x 300 including porch 90 x 300 cm. Coal stove: Hess & Søn nr. 1611. Floor: Wood.

■ Weaselhytten was built with the assistance of members of the British North Greenland Expedition 1952-54. *"A small staging hut with two berths had been built at Danmarkshavn, and we agreed to transport this in its prefabricated state to a site on Orienterings Ø, about seventeen miles away. We just managed to balance the unwieldy building on a trailer, and Taffy* (Oakley) *and I in two Weasels set out. Driving carefully we avoided a spill and erected the hut, thereby saving the station many tedious sledge journeys. They named the hut Weaselhytte* (Weasel hut) *in our honour".*[1669] The porch was added in the 1970s. As the hut was often attacked by polar bears, it was replaced in 1991 by Åndehullet [622-2].[1670]

Weaselhytten [622-1], 22nd August 2005. © NCN

622-2 / 76°39.70'N - 19°40.81'W / Dove Bugt[1671]
ÅNDEHULLET

■ Danish travellers' hut built 10th September 1991 for Danmarkshavn Vejrstation by Allan Nielsen, Jes Graugård, Per Rasmussen and Ejvind Larsen, Danmarkshavn.

■ On the south side of Weaseløen, the island south of the southernmost of the Orienteringsøerne, Dove Bugt.

Åndehullet [622-2], 22nd August 2005. © NCN

■ B (IIA). 445 x 300 cm. Paraffin stove: Reflex. Floor: Wood.

■ Åndehullet is a bear-proof hut built at Danmarkshavn in the summer of 1990 by Allan Nielsen and Jes Graugård. The following year the hut was sailed to Weaseløen on a raft made of empty fuel drums. It was placed about 60 m south of Weaselhytten [622-1].[1672]

Kap Bismarck hytten [623], 5th August 2006. © NCN

623 / 76°41.99'N - 18°33.04'W / Germania Land[1673]
KAP BISMARCK HYTTEN

■ Danish travellers' hut built in September 1979 for Danmarkshavn Vejrstation by Mogens Lund and Bo Mogensen, Danmarkshavn.

■ On the south point of Kap Bismarck, south-east of Danmarkshavn.

■ C (IIA). 340 x 220 including porch. Coal stove. Floor: Wood.

■ In the summer of 1979 Mogens Lund built the hut in sections at Danmarkshavn. It was originally meant to replace Trækpashytten [605], but due to heavy pack ice along the east coast of Store Koldewey they had to retreat, and instead placed the hut at Kap Bismarck.[1674]

624 / 76°43.27'N - 18°32.15'W / Germania Land[1675]
KAP QUIST HYTTEN

■ Danish travellers' hut built in 1951 for Danmarkshavn Vejrstation by Steen Malmquist, Danmarkshavn.

■ On the east side of the Kap Bismarck peninsula, about 3 km north of Kap Bismarck.

■ C (IIA). Ruin. Originally about 220 x 180 cm.

■ In 1959 some of the materials from Kap Quist hytten were used to build Syttenkilometernæsset [630-2].[1676]

Kap Quist hytten [624], 5th August 2006. © NCN

625 / 76°43.19'N - 19°06.27'W / Koldewey Øer[1677]
KAP HELGOLAND HYTTEN, Aldersro

■ Danish travellers' hut built in 1965 for Danmarkshavn Vejrstation by Carl E. Pedersen, Klaus Reindel and Ernst Simonsen, Danmarkshavn.

■ In a small cove at Kap Helgoland on the north-west point of Store Koldewey.

■ B (IIA). 480 x 255 cm. Paraffin stove: Reflex. Floor: Wood.

■ In the summer of 1965 Carl E. Pedersen built the hut in sections at Danmarkshavn. The hut is often attacked by passing polar bears.[1678] Kap Helgoland was named by the German Koldewey Expedition, that camped here on 10th April 1870.[1679]

Kap Helgoland hytten [625], 21st August 2005. © NCN

626 / 76°44.87'N - 18°26.21'W / Germania Land[1680]
HEERINGHUS, Øksebladet

■ Danish travellers' hut built in the autumn of 1949 for Danmarkshavn Vejrstation by E. Heering-Hansen, Hans Thomsen, Erik Palsby, Kaj Brandt and others, Danmarkshavn.

- On a small unnamed island between Ørnen Ø and Øksebladet.
- C (IIA). 310 x 225 plus porch 120 x 120 cm. Coal stove. Floor: Wood.
- Heeringhus was built here for bear hunting. The Danmarkshavn station manager, Hans Thomsen, wrote that: *"the outer walls we made from laths, and the inside we covered with masonite sheets. The roof was also from laths, covered with roofing felt " ... "The hut we called "Heeringhus" after Hansen's middle name".*[1681]

Heeringhus [626], 5th August 2006. © NCN

627 / 76°45.68'N - 18°48.49'W / Dove Bugt [1682]
KRADSHYTTEN
- Danish travellers' hut built in 1968 for Danmarkshavn Vejrstation by Allan Nielsen and Poul Elkjær Olsen, Danmarkshavn.
- About 500 m north-west of Bådskæret, about 4 km west of Danmarkshavn.
- B (IIA). 480 x 305 cm. Wood-burning stove. Floor: Wood.
- The name "Kradshytten" originates from an expression used at Danmarkshavn in the 1960s. To go on "krads" meant to go hunting. In September 1985 the hut was improved with a roof made from corrugated iron, and in October 1992 Allan Nielsen made a porch for the hut. [1683]

Kradshytten [627], 24th August 2005. © NCN

Villaen / Danmarks-Minde [628-1], 20th July 2006. © NCN

628-1 / 76°46.15'N - 18°41.06'W / Germania Land [1684]
VILLAEN, Danmarks-Minde, Danmark Havn Station
- Danish scientific station built in 1906 for the Danmark Expedition.
- On the south coast of Germania Land at Danmark Havn.
- A (IA). 1060 x 540 cm.
- See chapter on stations.

Danmarkshavn Weather Station [628-2], 9th August 2006. © NCN

628-2 / 76°46.15'N - 18°40.15'W / Germania Land [1685]
DANMARKSHAVN WEATHER STATION
- Danish weather station built in 1948 for Grønlands Radio- and Vejrtjeneste.
- On the south coast of Germania Land at Danmark Havn.
- D (IB). Station area with several buildings.
- See chapter on stations.

Port Arthur hytten [629], 11th August 2005. © NCN

629 / 76°45.86'N - 21°05.30'W / Dove Bugt [1686]
PORT ARTHUR HYTTEN, Spydodden

■ Danish trappers' hut built late August 1933 for Nanok by Finn Kristoffersen, Henry V. Nielsen and Christian Jensen, Hvalrosodden.

■ On the south tip of the northern cape of Port Arthur, the almost circular bay south-west of Spydodden in Dove Bugt.

■ B (IIA). 360 x 210 including porch 100 x 210 cm. Coal stove: L. Lange & Co. Floor: Wood.

■ According to the journal of Hvalrosodden, between the 28th and 31st August 1933 they: *"built a hut at Spydodden"*.[1687]

Syttenkilometernæshytten [630-1], 3rd August 2006. © NCN

630-1 / 76°49.29'N - 18°17.16'W / Germania Land [1688]
SYTTENKILOMETERNÆSHYTTEN

■ Danish trappers' hut built in 1935 for Nanok, Hvalrosodden.

■ At the bay on the east coast of Germania Land, on the north side of Syttenkilometernæsset.

■ C (IIA). Ruin. Originally about 190 x 125 cm.

■ The original Nanok hut at Syttenkilometernæsset was probably build by Ole Winstedt and Arvid Waldenstrøm Petterson.[1689] The location was named Syttenkilometernæsset by the Danmark Expedition because it was approximately 17 km sledging distance from their base at Danmark Havn.[1690]

Syttenkilometernæsset [630-2], 3rd August 2006. © NCN

630-2 / 76°49.18'N - 18°17.21'W / Germania Land[1691]
SYTTENKILOMETERNÆSSET

■ Danish travellers' hut built in March 1959 for Danmarkshavn Vejrstation by Gerhardt Blaase, Danmarkshavn.

■ At Syttenkilometernæsset on the east coast of Germania Land.

■ B (IIA). 365 x 340 plus porch 110 x 110 cm. Wood-burning stove: Bruner 472 B. Floor: Wood.

■ The hut was built partly of boards from some large wooden containers that previously housed oil pipes, and of material from the Kap Quist hytten [624]. The hut was built in sections at Danmarkshavn and transported to the location by dog sledge. It replaced the old, blown down Syttenkilometernæshytten [630-1]. In 1991 and 1992 the hut was enlarged with a side shed built by Jens Laugesen, Peter Nielsen, Jes Graugård, Ib Palle Madsen and Torben Jensen. The original part of the hut now serves as a depot.[1692]

631 / 76°48.90'N - 18°59.83'W / Germania Land[1693]
STORMBUGTHYTTEN, Stormelvshytten, Stormely-hytten

■ Danish trappers' hut built in September 1939 for Nanok by Carl Henrik Schultz, Ove Harder Jensen and Poul Hennings, Hvalrosodden.

■ On the cliff on the east side of Stormelv, on the south coast of Germania Land.

■ C (IIA). 200 x 150 cm. Floor: Wood.

■ On 12th September 1939 Poul Hennings wrote that they sailed: *"to Stormelven, where we helped*

Stormbugthytten [631], 18th August 2005. © NCN

each other with carrying the materials up to the place where the hut would be. Schultz then began to build, while Harder and I sailed out to hunt walrus".[1694]

Store Snenæs hytten [632-1], 17th August 2005. © NCN

At left Store Snenæs hytten [632-1], with behind it Ny Store Snenæs hytte [632-2], 17th August 2005 © NCN

632-1 / 76°49.20'N - 19°21.22'W / Germania Land[1695]
STORE SNENÆS HYTTEN, Snenæshytten

■ Danish trappers' hut built in August 1933 for Nanok by Finn Kristoffersen, Henry V. Nielsen and Christian Jensen, Hvalrosodden.
■ At Snenæs on the south coast of Germania Land.
■ C (IIA). 360 x 200 including porch 100 x 200 cm. Coal stove. Floor: Wood.
■ The hut was built in the period 18th to 24th August 1933.[1696] In 1939 it was improved by Poul Hennings, who wrote that he: *"laid a floor in the hut and large flat stones around the coal stove. It has now become a nice hut".*[1697]

Ny Store Snenæs hytte [632-2], 17th August 2005. © NCN

632-2 / 76°49.20'N - 19°21.28'W / Germania Land[1698]
NY STORE SNENÆS HYTTE

■ Danish travellers' hut built in 1999 for Danmarkshavn Vejrstation by Ole Lykke Larsen, Danmarkshavn.
■ At Snenæs on the south coast of Germania Land.
■ B (IIA). 440 x 335 including porch 100 x 335 cm. Paraffin stove: Refleks. Floor: Wood.
■ The hut was erected at Store Snenæs from prefabricated sections made at Danmarkshavn Vejrstation.[1699]

633 / c. 76°48'N - 20°12'W / Dove Bugt
VINDSELØHYTTEN

■ Danish trappers' hut built 2nd November 1938 for Nanok by Christian Jensen, Carlos Ziebell and Henning Ørnlef, Hvalrosodden.
■ On the east side of Vindseløen in Dove Bugt.
■ C (IIA). Disappeared.
■ On 2nd November 1938 Christian Jensen wrote: *"It was nice weather today and at 10 o'clock all three of us went to Vindseløen with a small travellers' hut and 10 traps. The going was fine, so we arrived at 1-1.30. We built the hut and put up the traps".*[1700] On 31st November 1938 Henning Ørnlef spent a night in the hut: *"it's so small, that you have to crawl in".*[1701] On 3rd September 1939 Poul Hennings raised doubts about

the existence of the hut: *"We arrived at Vindseløen, and searched more than half of the coastline looking for the hut, which should be placed there. We didn't find it and I believe it's all a bluff"*.[1702]

Syltekrukken [634], 24th July 2006. © NCN

634 / 76°50.97'N - 18°47.40'W / Germania Land[1703]
SYLTEKRUKKEN

- Danish hut built in 1966 for Danmarkshavn Vejrstation by Knud Nielsen, Danmarkshavn.
- In Germania Land on the 400 m plateau about 10 km north-west of Danmarkshavn.
- C (IIA). 750 x 400 including porch 180 x 400 cm. Paraffin stove: L. Lange & Co. Floor: Wood.
- In 1961 Knud "Sylte" Nielsen cleared a 300 m landing strip. At the same time he built a hut measuring 200 x 200 cm. In 1964, the hut was enlarged by 250 x 250 cm by Knud Nielsen, Bendt "Lille Sylte" Nielsen and Gunnar Husted Jensen. A new landing strip 1200 m long was prepared at the same time. The present Syltekrukken hut was purchased with ICAO funds and erected in 1966 by Knud Nielsen. Syltekrukken functioned as an air terminal until the middle of the 1970s, when a new airstrip closer to Danmarkshavn was taken into use. However, for special projects the 1966 hut and airstrip were occasionally used up to 1991, e.g. for fuel transports for GGU. In 1979, the original 1961/1964 hut was moved to another location - see Germania Land hytten [702].[1704]

635 / 76°51.31'N - 20°44.61'W / Dove Bugt[1705]
VÆDDERHYTTEN, Væderhytten

- Danish trappers' hut built in August 1933 for Nanok by Finn Kristoffersen, Henry V. Nielsen and Christian Jensen, Hvalrosodden.
- On the south-east coast of Vædderen, north of a small island on the north side of the entrance to Hellefjord.
- C (IIA). 195 x 195 cm. Coal stove: L. Lange & Co. Floor: Wood.
- The original Vædderhytten was built between 25th and 27th August 1933.[1706] It then measured 190 x 190 cm with a small porch. In 1938 the hut blew down, and only the coal stove and a bank of stone remained. A new hut was built on 10th September 1938 by Christian Jensen and Henning Ørnlef who: *"sailed down to Vædderen and built the hut"*.[1707]

Vædderhytten [635], 22nd August 2005. © NCN

636 / 76°52.72'N - 21°21.63'W / Dove Bugt[1708]
HELLEFJORDHYTTEN

- Danish trappers' hut built 14th September 1933 for Nanok by Finn Kristoffersen, Henry V. Nielsen and Christian Jensen, Hvalrosodden.
- On the east side of the Pusterdal river where it drains into the north side of Hellefjord.
- C (IIA). 300 x 200 including porch 85 x 200 cm. Coal stove: L. Lange & Co.
- On 12th September 1933 the journal of Hvalrosodden station records: *"Sailed to Hellefjord with materials for a hut"*. And on 14th September: *"Finished building the hut and made some traps. Went back to Hvalrosodden"*.[1709]

Hellefjordhytten [636], 12th August 2005. © NCN

Lille Snenæs hytten [637], 17th August 2005. © NCN

637 / 76°52.82'N - 19°37.93'W / Germania Land[1710]
LILLE SNENÆS HYTTEN

▪ Danish trappers' hut built in September 1939 for Nanok by Carl Henrik Schultz and Poul Hennings, Hvalrosodden.

▪ At the east side of Lille Snenæs on the south coast of Germania Land.

▪ C (IIA). 195 x 155 cm. Coal stove: L. Lange & Co. Floor: Wood.

▪ On 24th October 1939 Poul Hennings wrote that one day they sailed: *"to Lille Snenæs and built the hut there, but we became worried about the new ice growing thicker hour by hour, and not daring to wait went home and therefore didn't get the roofing felt on"*. In October 1939 Hennings had: *"a difficult and especially cold finger job getting the roofing felt on the hut, as we missed doing that when we built it"*.[1711]

Margarinecentralen [638] in August 1938. © Jess F. Tillier / Norwegian Polar Institute

638 / 76°56.49'N - 18°10.79'W / Germania Land[1712]
MARGARINECENTRALEN, Kap Steensby hytten, Resoluthytten, Centralen

▪ Norwegian trappers' hut built in August 1938 for the Norwegian-French Polar Expedition by Willie Knutsen and Leif Olsen, Micardbu.

▪ About 5-6 km north of Kap Steensby on the east coast of Germania Land.

▪ C (IIA). 320 x 180 including porch 105 x 180 cm. Coal stove: Laxevaags Verk No. 32, Bergen. Floor: Earth.

▪ Willie Knutsen wrote: *"We had lots of margarine, which the manufacturer had sold to us at a bargain price. None of us really liked margarine, but the dogs loved it and the fat was of course an important nutritional supplement for all of us. The margarine boxes, however, we didn't need. The hut got walls of materials from the margarine boxes, and the name Margarinecentralen brightened up the landscape"*.[1713]

Margarinecentralen [638], 1st August 2006. © NCN

Hvalrosodden [639-1], 17th August 2005. © NCN

639-1 / 76°55.03'N - 20°06.50'W / Germania Land[1714]
HVALROSODDEN, Odden

▪ Danish trappers' station built in 1919 for the East Greenland Company.

▪ On the north side of Hvalrosodden at the mouth of Lakseelven on Germania Land.

▪ B (IA). 495 x 480 cm plus porch and side sheds. Coal stove: Scandia. Floor: Wood.

▪ See chapter on stations.

Alwin Pedersens hus [639-2], 17th August 2005. © NCN

639-2 / 76°55.06'N - 20°06.54'W / Germania Land[1715]

ALWIN PEDERSENS HUS

- Danish scientific station built in 1938 for Alwin Pedersen.
- On the north side of Hvalrosodden at the mouth of Lakseelven on Germania Land.
- B (IB). 355 x 306 plus porch 150 x 150 cm. Coal stove: L. Lange & Co. Floor: Wood.
- See chapter on stations.

Pustervig [640], 13th August 2005. © NCN

640 / 76°55.27'N - 21°01.55'W / Dove Bugt[1716]

PUSTERVIG

- Danish scientific station built in 1907 for the Danmark Expedition.
- At the north side of the head of the bay Pustervig in Mørkefjord.
- C (IB). Ruin: About 400 x 250 cm. Coal stove: L. Lange & Co.
- See chapter on stations.

641 / 76°55.74'N - 20°19.36'W / Germania Land[1717]

MØRKEFJORD

- Danish scientific station built in 1938 for the Mørkefjord Expedition.
- On the north side of the mouth of Mørkefjord, about 5-6 km west of Hvalrosodden.
- A (IB). Station house and provision shed. Station house: about 1500 x 800 cm. Coal stove: S. Hess & Søn Comfort No. 81. Floor: Wood. Provision shed: 410 x 310 cm. Coal stove: L. Lange Co. Floor: Wood.
- See chapter on stations.

Mørkefjord [641], 13th August 2005. © NCN

The provision shed at Mørkefjord [641], 13th August 2005. © NCN

642 / 76°56.41'N - 20°48.47'W / Dove Bugt[1718]

MØRKEFJORDHYTTEN

- Danish trappers' hut built 17th August 1933 for Nanok by Finn Kristoffersen, Henry V. Nielsen and Christian Jensen, Hvalrosodden.
- On the north side of Mørkefjord, about 3-4 km east of the mountain Danmarks Monumentet.
- C (IIA). Ruin. Coal stove: L. Lange Co.
- H: On 17th August 1933 the trappers at Hvalrosodden sailed: *"the finished hut to* (a place across from) *Danmarks-Monumentet, and made it ready"*.[1719]

Mørkefjordhytten [642], 13th August 2005. © NCN

701 / c. 77°01'N - 20°01'W / Germania Land[1720]
TREKRONERHYTTEN, Pashytten, Schultzhytten, Hvalsletten, Slettehytten

■ Danish trappers' hut built in the spring of 1938 for Nanok by Carl Henrik Schultz, Hvalrosodden.

■ East of the Trekroner mountain north of Hvalrosodden, south-west Germania Land.

■ C (IIA).

■ Built in the spring of 1938 at Hvalrosodden by Carl Henrik Schultz, who then transported the hut inland by dog sledge. On 18th August 1938 J.G. Jennov wrote that: *"Schultz said that due to the late time he began to lay out the huts he had just managed to lay out one hut in the pass leading to Flade-Bugt"*.[1721] In 1959 the hut was rebuilt by Gerhardt Blaase and Knud Ernø, Danmarkshavn.[1722]

■ No traces of "Trekronerhytten" were observed during a helicopter-supported survey on 8th July 2007.

702 / 77°01.05'N - 19°05.75'W / Germania Land[1723]
GERMANIA LAND HYTTEN

■ Danish travellers' hut built in late May 1979 for Danmarkshavn Vejrstation by Mogens Lund and Bo Mogensen, Danmarkshavn.

Germania Land hytten [702], 31st July 2006. © NCN

■ About 220 m above sea level in the central part of Germania Land.

■ B (IIA). 460 x 250 cm. Coal stove. Floor: Wood.

■ Originally the hut was built in 1961 by Knud Nielsen and used as an air terminal; see Syltekrukken [634]. Between 25th May and 3rd June 1979 Mogens Lund and Bo Mogensen used snow scooters to transport the hut to its present location.[1724]

Tvillingnæshytten [703], 17th August 2005. © NCN

703 / 77°02.51'N - 20°16.41'W / Germania Land[1725]
TVILLINGNÆSHYTTEN, Sælsøhytten

■ Danish trappers' hut built 16th October 1933 for Nanok by Finn Kristoffersen, Henry V. Nielsen, Christian Jensen and Povel Povelsen, Hvalrosodden.

■ About 4 km east of Tvillingnæs in Sælsøen.

■ C (IIA). Ruin. Coal stove: L. Lange & Co. Floor: Wood.

■ The materials were carried to Sælsøen from Hvalrosodden by dog sledges.[1726] Eigil Knuth mentioned the hut: *"After four hours of walking in a headwind we reached the first hut about 20 km from the station. When we succeeded in opening the door, we found the entire room filled with snow, and lacking a shovel we had to empty it using our hands and an empty can. Finally we came down to the upper edge of the coal stove, to the berth and to the floor, where we found small lumps of frozen coal to use in the stove"*.[1727]

704 / 77°04.25'N - 18°11.41'W / Germania Land[1728]
MICARDBU

■ Norwegian scientific and trappers' station, originally built in 1938 for the Norwegian-French Polar Expedition. It was replaced in 1960 by a smaller hut.

■ On the east coast of Germania Land, about 17-18 km south of Thomas Thomsen Næs.

■ C (IA). The Micardbu hut from 1960: 455 x 300 including porch 110 x 300 cm. Coal stove. Floor: Wood.
■ See chapter on stations.

Micardbu [704] (the hut from 1960), 28th July 2006. © *NCN*

705 / c. 77°05'N - 20°47'W / Germania Land[1729]
MIDTERNÆSHYTTEN, Inderhytten, Bundhytten
■ Danish trappers' hut built 16th November 1938 for Nanok by Christian Jensen and Henning Ørnlef, Hvalrosodden.
■ At Midternæs on the north side of Sælsøen.
■ C (IIA). 200 x 150 cm.
■ Christian Jensen wrote that at first they tried to carry the materials all the way to Anneksøen on dog sledges, but had to give up as the river bed between Anneksøen and Sælsøen was impassable due to lack of snow. Instead they went about 20 km further into Sælsøen, where they built the hut at Midternæs.[1730] Eigil Knuth wrote that he: *"came to the innermost small hut at the northernmost bend of the lake. It was very small, just about 1 1/2 x 2 metres and 1.35 metres high, without any berths or floor".*[1731] Midternæshytten is without any doubt identical to the so-called Inderhytten [918], or Bundhytten, a hut which was wrongly considered to have been built at the western end of Sælsøen.
■ No traces of "Midternæshytten" were observed during a helicopter-supported survey on 8th July 2007.

706 / c. 77°09'N - 23°36'W / Dronning Louise Land
BRITANNIA SØ, Britannia Lake
British scientific station built in 1952 for the British North Greenland Expedition.
■ On the north side of Britannia Sø, originally about 2 km east of the front of Britannia Gletcher.
■ C (IB). Crushed by an advance of Britannia Gletscher in the 1980s. It was a wintering station for about 20 persons.
■ See chapter on stations.

707 / 77°10.45'N - 18°11.26'W / Germania Land[1732]
THOMAS THOMSEN NÆS HYTTEN
■ Norwegian trappers' hut built in the autumn of 1938 for the Norwegian-French Polar Expedition by Willie Knutsen and Leif Olsen, Micardbu.
■ At Thomas Thomsen Næs on the east coast of Germania Land. Note that Thomas Thomsen Næs is misplaced northwards on some maps, and is actually about 11 km south-east of Kap Marie Valdemar.
■ C (IIA). 330 x 245 including porch 100 x 245 cm. Coal stove: Laxevaags Værk Nr. 32. Floor: Earth.
■ Willie Knutsen wrote that: *"Kalle* (Nicolaisen) *put Leif Olsen and me ashore, so we could finish the new hut at Thomas Thomsen Næs".*[1733] On 15th April 1939 trapper Christian Jensen mentioned the hut when he: *"arrived at the Micard depot at Th. Thomsen Næs, where I made coffee and turned in".*[1734] Thomas Thomsen (1870-1941), was a Danish ethnographer and archaeologist.

Thomas Thomsen Næs hytten [707], 29th July 2006. © *NCN*

708 / 77°15.45'N - 19°25.43'W / Germania Land[1735]
KNUTHSMINDE, Kap Li hytten, Kløfthytten
■ Danish travellers' hut built in 1940 for the Mørkefjord Expedition by Andreas Hvidberg and Carlos Ziebell, Mørkefjord.
■ On the south side of the low-lying east-facing point on the west side of Flade Bugt, about 13-14 km south-east of Kap Li.
■ C (IIA). 200 x 190 cm. Floor: Earth.
■ Named after Eigil Knuth (1903-1996), who wrote that: *"materials were transported to Fladebugt, where the hut* (according to a letter from Hvidberg) *was placed "on the first north-western cape after the descent to the bay from Passet, about 18-20 km out", that*

is to say, in all probability on Kap Li. The hut contains two berths and is free of snow and surrounded by a low wall of stones".[1736] It later turned out that the hut was located further south on the east-facing point about 13-14 km to the south-east of Kap Li in Flade Bugt.[1737]

Knuthsminde [708], 8th July 2007. © NCN

709-1 / 77°32.07'N - 19°08.02'W / Skærfjorden[1738]
KAP AMÉLIE HYTTEN

- Danish travellers' hut built 15th March 1941 for the Mørkefjord Expedition by Ib Poulsen, Carlos Ziebell and Kristian Madsen, Mørkefjord.
- On the east side of the Chatham Elv river, about 3 km north-east of Kap Amélie on the south side of Stormlandet.
- C (IIA). 200 x 200 cm. Floor: Earth.
- In 1942 Eigil Knuth wrote: *"In order to earn part of the increased expenses due to the unintentional doubling of the personnel caused by the war an attempt was made to establish a hunting territory in Skærfjorden in connection with the building of a hut at Kap Amélie, the erection of which had been planned during the first wintering of the expedition. This hut was i.e. to serve as a base for climatological observations in Skærfjorden during a continuous period, so that it might be found out whether or not the cold minima ascertained up there*

From left: Kap Amélie hytten [709-1] and Thors Café [709-2], 12th May 1978. © Peter Schmidt Mikkelsen

From left: Kap Amélie hytten [709-1] and Thors Café [709-2], 13th May 2005. © Thomas Hansen

in 1939 were phenomena recurring every year. In the first days of February 1941, Poulsen and Ziebell, travelling via Danmarks Havn (Villaen), *sledged the main part of the materials for the hut to Kap Amélie, where the hut was built by Poulsen, Ziebell, and Madsen on March 15th".*[1739] In 1991 Ib Poulsen explained that: *"the hut was built in 1941, when communication with Knuth was impossible, and the hut was just used for meteorology and as a depot for travels".*[1740]

709-2 / 77°32.07'N - 19°08.02'W / Skærfjorden[1741]
THORS CAFÉ, Kap Amélie hytten

- Danish travellers' hut built in the spring of 1966 for the Sirius Dog Sledge Patrol by Kjeld Sørensen, Jørgen Andersen, Mogens Guldbrandsen and Hans Henrik Larsen, Daneborg.
- On the east side of the Chatham Elv river. about 3 km north-east of Kap Amélie on the south side of Stormlandet.
- C (IIA). 400 x 300 including porch 100 x 100 cm. Coal stove: Hess & Søn. Floor: Wood.
- The hut was built in the period 25th April - 4th May 1966 by Sirius, who needed another and larger depot hut at Kap Amélie. It is situated adjacent to the Mørkefjord Expedition's old Kap Amélie hut [709-1], and was named after Thors Café in Reykjavik.[1742]

Thor's Café [709-2], 10th March 2004. © Thomas Hansen

901 / c. 72°24'N - 25°49'W / Nathorst Land
CALEDONIAHYTTEN, Sulebak

- On the south side of Forsblad Fjord, about 2 km south of Caledoniaø.
- C (IIC). Non-existent.
- The "Description des Stations de chasse Norvégiennes dans l'Eirik-Raudes-Land"[1743] claims a Norwegian trappers' hut, "Sulebak", was built in the autumn of 1931 in Forsblad Fjord, but this was not the case. The diary of the trapper Peder Sulebak confirms that huts were built only on the north side of Forsblad Fjord. "Caledoniahytten" is another name for this non-existent hut.[1744]

902 / c. 72°39'N - 24°44'W / Lyell Land
KAP DUFVA

- About 3 km south of Kap Dufva on the west side of Kong Oscar Fjord.
- C (IIC). Non-existent.
- John Giæver marked a hut at this location on his 1939 map.[1745] On 23rd August 1931 Peder Sulebak recorded that he gave up building a hut at Kap Dufva: *"as it is snowy terrain up there"*,[1746] and while he used the territory for a number of years there is no other mention of the Kap Dufva hut in his diaries. Giæver may have confused the hut with one of the so-called Nordborg huts [231], which are located on the opposite side of Kong Oscar Fjord and not marked on Giæver's map. After WWII, Norwegian trappers were not aware of the supposed hut at Kap Dufva and do not mention it in their diaries. A search in the summer of 1989 did not reveal any traces of a hut at the location.[1747]

Kap Hedlund (vestside) [903], 21st July 2007. © NCN

903 / 72°42.84'N - 26°13.70'W / Lyell Land[1748]
KAP HEDLUND (vestside)

- Norwegian material site built 12th July 1934 for Arctic Commercial Enterprise by Ole Klokset and Magne Råum, Kap Humboldt.
- In Rhedin Fjord about 2 km south-west of Kap Hedlund.
- C (IIB). 240 x 200 cm. Floor: Earth.
- On 12th July 1934 Magne Råum wrote: *"Today westarted to build a hut of driftwood at the cape here. Went on building until the afternoon, but then the mosquitoes became too annoying and we stopped"*.[1749] On 11th September 1934, when Råum and Klokset returned to finish their driftwood hut, they were prevented by strong winds blowing out of Rhedin Fjord. So instead they built another hut, Rimhytten [230-1], on the east side of Kap Hedlund.[1750]

904 / c. 72°44'N - 23°00'W / Traill Ø[1751]
TRAILL Ø

- Norwegian material site laid out in September 1929 for Arctic Commercial Enterprise by Søren Richter, Sverre Sørensen and Thor Halle.
- On Traill Ø on the south side of Vega Sund, due south of Sverresborg.
- C (IIB). Disappeared or removed.
- On 20th September 1929 Thor Halle wrote: *"Richter and I took a trip with the boat to Traillhytta* [234] *with some materials, which we put ashore due south of Sverresborg"*.[1752] And on 22nd September 1929 Sverre Sørensen wrote: *"Have carried the rest of the materials for the hut on the other side of the sound"*.[1753] Since then the materials are not mentioned; the hut was never built. A search in the summer of 2004 did not reveal any traces of materials at the location.[1754]

905 / c. 73°15'N - 25°55'W / Andrée Land
JUNCTIONDAL

- Norwegian material site laid out on 29th July 1932 by "Polarbjørn" for Arctic Commercial Enterprise.
- At Junctiondal on Andrée Land, north-west of Kap Mohn.
- C (IIB). Removed.
- A hut was never built at Junctiondal. On 25th April 1935 the materials were taken by dog sledge to Nordfjord by the trapper Magne Råum, and later on were used for building Strindberghuset [358-3].[1755]

906 / c. 73°34'N - 22°57'W / Hudson Land[1756]
HERDAL

- Norwegian material site set out on 5th August 1930 by "Veslekari" for Arctic Commercial Enterprise, Hoelsbu.
- At the entrance of Vastidal on the south side of Moskusoksefjord.
- C (IIB). Removed.
- A projected hut "Herdal" was never built. On 22nd August 1932 Walter Molt and Knut Nakken instead used the materials for building Petrahytten [347].[1757]

A view over a likely location of Brogetdal [907], 29th July 2007. © NCN

907 / c. 73°46'N - 24°49'W / Strindberg Land[1758]
BROGETDAL

- Norwegian material site laid out in 1946 for Arctic Commercial Enterprise by Bjarne Akre, Hoelsbu.
- In Brogetdal on Strindberg Land.
- C (IIB).
- In 1939 John Giæver marked a hut in Brogetdal on his map.[1759] This hut was never built. After WWII another attempt was made, and Trygve Havold later on related: *"In 1946 materials were laid out at Strindberg. These materials were taken into Giæverdalen* (Brogetdal) *by Bjarne Akre. In August 1947 I walked in to build the hut by the middle lake, but the materials had been blown away by a storm. I only found a roll of roofing felt and two boxes of nails"*. Neither Havold nor Fredrik Sæterdal knew of any other hut in Brogetdal.[1760] In 2007, a Nanok-team tried to find the material site, but was unable to cross the river a short distance before reaching the estimated location of the site.[1761]

908 / 73°47.34'N - 20°19.06'W / Hold with Hope[1762]
KAP KRAUS

- Danish material site laid out in August 1951 for Nanok.
- About 1 km west of Kap Kraus.
- C (IIB). Material site.
- On 18th August 1950 the journal of Loch Fyne records: *"We have now returned to the station after a trip with "Søndmøringen" along the coast and laying ashore materials for huts at Broer-Ruys-syd and Kap Kraus"*.[1763] However, the projected hut at Kap Kraus was never built.

Kap Kraus [908], 22nd July 2005. © NCN

909 / 73°46.38'N - 22°26.99'W / Hudson Land[1764]
DYBENDAL

- Danish material site laid out in 1952 for Nanok by Svend Olsen, Loch Fyne.
- In Stordal at Granitelv, at the entrance to Dybendal on Hudson Land.
- C (IIB). Material site.
- On 15th March 1952 Svend Olsen wrote: *"Tonight I have arrived at Arvehytten. This morning I left home with a load of materials for the hut at Dybendal. I went all the way into Dybendal with the load"*.[1765] Due to the closing down of Nanok activities in the summer of 1952, the materials were never used to build a hut.

Dybendal [909], 7th August 2005. © NCN

910 / 74°37.51'N - 20°02.62'W / Wollaston Forland[1766]
ALBRECHT BUGT

- Danish material site laid out in August 1950 for Nanok.

Albrecht Bugt [910]. The hut materials are located beside the large boulder, 7th July 2007. © NCN

- Beside a large boulder on the west side of Albrecht Bugt.
- C (IIB). Material site.
- On 18th August 1950 J.G. Jennov wrote: *"We sailed across Albrecht Bugt and laid out hut materials by the large boulder on the western shore of the bay" ... "but we didn't manage to build it"*.[1767]

Svejstrup Dal (norsk) [911], 25th July 2004. © NCN

911 / 74°39.30'N - 20°58.66'W / Th. Thomsen Land[1768]
SVEJSTRUP DAL (norsk)

- Norwegian material site laid out in August 1938 for the Sigurd Tolløfsen Expedition.
- At the entrance to Svejstrup Dal on the northern side of the head of Lindeman Fjord.
- C̲ (IIB). Material site. Stove: OM&S No. 2.
- In the spring of 1938 Arctic Commercial Enterprise had plans to build two huts in the valleys between Tyrolerfjord, Svejstrup Dal and Lindeman Fjord. However, these plans were never carried through. On 31st August 1938 Sigurd Tolløfsen wrote that he unloaded at the head of Lindeman Fjord: *"a hut including stove, pipes, roofing felt, fuel etc., and 10 traps. The rest of the hut must be brought here later on"*.[1769] However, neither Tolløfsen nor anyone else built this hut.

912 / c. 75°19'N - 20°04'W / Hochstetter Forland[1770]
PETERS BUGT (Norwegian)

- Norwegian material site laid out 2nd August 1932 for the John Giæver Expedition by "Isbjørn".
- On the north side of Peters Bugt.
- C̲ (IIB). Non-existent.
- On 2nd August 1932 materials for five trappers' huts in Ardencaple Fjord were laid out with "Isbjørn" for the John Giæver Expedition. Giæver wrote that "Isbjørn" on the way out called at Jonsbu: *"to put ashore paraffin and the sixth hut"* on the north side of Peters Bugt.[1771] The sixth hut was never built and it is not known where it was planned to be located. Giæver may have planned a trappers' hut on the north-eastern side of Peters Bugt as an intermediate stop when travelling north to Ottostrand station.

913 / c. 75°38'N - 20°15'W / Hochstetter Forland[1772]
AGNETE SØ

- On the south side of Agnete Sø about 10 km west of the Agnete Sø outlet.
- C (IIC). Non-existent.
- It has been claimed that a Norwegian trappers' hut was built at this location in 1948 for Arctic Commercial Enterprise; if so it would have been by Hermod Sætre and Erling Juell Ramberg. However, this information must be incorrect, as Fredrik Sæterdal stated in 1992 that there had never existed any hut at the location. As early as 1933, the John Giæver Expedition had plans to place a hut inland on Hochstetter Forland between Agnete Sø and Peters Bugt. This third hut, in addition to Agnetehytten [530] and Langelv-hytten [534-1], was not built at the time.[1773] No traces of "Agnete Sø" were observed during a brief helicopter-supported survey on 8th July 2007.

914 / c. 75°46'N - 20°14'W / Hochstetter Forland[1774]
LANGELV

- Danish material site laid out in March 1952 for Nanok by Hans Frederiksen and Erik Larsen.
- On the south side of Langelv, about 22 km inland.
- C̲ (IIB). Disappeared or removed.
- On 4th March 1952 Erik Larsen wrote: *"Frederiksen and I today drove materials inland for the first hut in Langelv. The hut is going to be 2 x 2 m and will be located 22 km up the river on the south side of the river"*.[1775] However, the hut was never built. No traces of the "Langelv" hut or the materials were observed during a brief helicopter-supported survey on 8th July 2007.

Langsø [915] observed from a helicopter. The hut materials are located in the barren area in the centre of the photograph, 8th July 2007. © NCN

915 / 75°48.68'N - 20°47.58'W / Hochstetter Forland[1776]

LANGSØ

▪ Danish material site laid out in April 1952 for Nanok by Hans Frederiksen and Erik Larsen.

▪ On the south side of Langsø about 35 km inland, 4-5 km east of Smøgen.

▪ C (IIB). Material site.

▪ On 29th April 1952 Erik Larsen wrote: *"Today Frederiksen and I carried materials for a large hut about 40 km inland along Langelv. The hut will be located at the entrance to Smøgen"*. The hut was never built.[1777]

916 / c. 76°07'N - 20°29'W / Ad. S. Jensen Land

LAKSEHYTTEN

▪ On: *"the north side of the westernmost lake in Påskedalen"* in Ad. S. Jensen Land.

▪ C (IIC). Non-existent.

▪ According to J.G. Jennov "Laksehytten" was: *"laid out by Nanok in 1939"*.[1778] The hut was never built, a fact confirmed in 1992 by Richard Nielsen and by notes from the trappers Knud Nielsen and Leo Ingwersen.[1779]

917 / 76°40.60'N - 18°43.80'W / Koldewey Øer[1780]

TYSKERDEPOTET

▪ German material site laid out on 1st October 1944 for the German Naval Weather Service by Dr. Karl Schmid and others.

▪ On the north side of Røseløbet, the narrow sound between the two islands making up Lille Koldewey.

▪ C (IIB). Material site.

▪ At the beginning of October 1944, a German expedition, "Edelweiss II" (formerly "Goldschmied"), made an attempt to establish a manned weather station on Lille Koldewey. The eleven members of the expedition sailed to Greenland on the weather observation ship "Externsteine" (WBS 11). However, the landing was discovered by the US Coast Guard, and on 4th October the Germans were taken as prisoners of war by a military task force from the USCG "Eastwind". At the location there still remain a number of 200 liter drums of German "Kraftstoff" labelled: "Kriegsmarine".[1781]

Tyskerdepotet [917], 20th August 2005. © NCN

918 / c. 77°05'N - 21°33'W / Germania Land

BUNDHYTTEN, Inderhytten

▪ *"I den indre del af Sælsøen"*. (In the inner part of Sælsøen).

▪ C (IIC). Non-existent.

▪ It has been claimed that a Danish trappers' hut was built for Nanok in the innermost part of Sælsøen. This is not correct. In reality the so-called "Bundhytten" is identical with Midternæshytten [705].[1782]

919 / c. 76°40'N - 22°30'W / Dove Bugt

BORG

▪ Danish scientific station built in October 1912 for the Danish Expedition to Dronning Louise Land and across the Greenland Ice Cap 1912-13 by Johan Peter Koch, Alfred Wegener, Vigfus Sigurdsson and Lars Larsen.

▪ Disappeared. Originally located about 5 km inland on Brede Bræ, north-west of Kap Jarner on Lindhard Ø, the hut was carried eastwards by the glacier into Borgfjord and Dove Bugt.

▪ C (IB). J.P. Koch wrote: *"The house was 6.6 metres long and 5 metres wide, not including the snow shed. The walls consisted of two triple layers of plywood, placed on each side of a slender wooden frame, thus making an air gap of a couple of centimetres inside the wall. The north and south sides of the living room had double walls with three decimetres spacing (that is in all 12 layers of plywood with three air gaps). The roof was double; there was no attic. All the individual pieces of the house slotted together in an airtight manner and were joined together by fasteners and staples. Only the floor for the living room was brought along from home. The chest benches with cushions served in the daytime as seating, and at night as sleeping benches. The house, that was built by the Army armoury workshops, is the best that has ever been used in an Arctic expedition to uninhabited places".*[1783] It was Marie Kristine, Koch's wife, who had named the winter house Borg, after the home of the Icelandic saga hero Egil Skallegrimsson. The house parts were carried up onto Brede Bræ using horse-drawn sledges. The expedition members lived in the house from October 1912 until the 20th April 1913.[1784]

Borg [919], Autumn 1912. © Arctic Institute

920 / 73°43.02'N - 21°44.47'W / Hold with Hope[1785]
HERJAELV I

- Danish material site laid out in July-August 1939 for Nanok by Knud Bavngaard, Niels Haarløv, Ove Harder Jensen, Christian Petersen and others, Knudshoved.
- On the south side of Herjaelv, 100 m from the east shore of Loch Fyne on Hold with Hope.
- C (IIB). Material site.
- In the period 28th July - 7th August 1939 Nanok made several attempts to transport hut materials into the Herjaelv and Tobias Dal area of central Hold with Hope, using horse-drawn carriages. Unfortunately it was an unusually rainy and wet season. In his report J.G. Jennov wrote: *"The attempt to transport huts into Tobias Dal by means of horses from Loch Fyne failed, due to the fact that the ground was so wet that the horses sank in up to the middle of their legs and from time to time right up to the middle of the chest, even in places where the terrain is usual easily passable. The hut materials, which had been brought ashore at Loch Fyne, were cut up partly for huts and partly for traps, and placed at a location that should stay free of snow, so they can later be carried on by dog sledge".*[1786] It is likely that some of the material has been transported over the years to various other locations on Hold with Hope. Two material sites, here named Herjaelv I [920] and Herjaelv II [921], were discovered by a Nanok team in the summer of 2005.

Herjaelv I [920], August 1939. © Knud Bavngaard

Herjaelv I [920], August 1939. © Knud Bavngaard

Herjaelv I [920], 4th August 2005. © NCN

Herjaelv II [921], 4th August 2005. © NCN

921 / 73°43.72'N - 21°39.55'W / Hold with Hope[1787]
HERJAELV II

- Danish material site laid out in July-August 1939 for Nanok by Knud Bavngaard, Niels Haarløv, Ove Harder Jensen, Christian Petersen and others, Knudshoved.
- On the south side of the Herjaelv, about 3 km from the east shore of Loch Fyne on Hold with Hope.
- C (IIB). Material site.
- See further description under Herjaelv I [920].

Entrance of Guldminen [922] (the gold mine) in 1933.[1788] *Koch 1955 p. 129*

922 / 74°06.10'N - 21°04.57'W / Clavering Ø[1789]
GULDMINEN, Mining camp, Klondyke

- Danish excavation carried out in 1933 for the Three-Year Expedition by Olaf Eklund and others, Eskimonæs.
- About 1-2 km east of Breivikdalen at 134 m above sea level, on the south coast of Clavering Ø.
- C (IIB). Excavation.
- In the summer of 1933 the Three-Year Expedition had a mining party, led by the geologist Olaf Eklund, working in the southern part of Clavering Ø. Lauge Koch wrote: *"A pit was made by means of dynamite down to a mineral-bearing dyke. Eklund stayed in East Greenland during the winter and continued the work next spring, among other things making a number of mineral analyses"*.[1790]

Entrance of Guldminen [922], 9th August 2005. © NCN

923 / 75°23.70'N - 21°21.73'W / C.H. Ostenfeld Land[1791]
NIFLHEIM

- Norwegian material site laid out on 2nd August 1932 by "Isbjørn" for the John Giæver Expedition.
- At the foot of the mountain Niflheim, 3-4 km north of Femdalen on the south side of Ardencaple Fjord.
- C (IIB). Material site.
- On 2nd August 1932 materials for five trappers' huts were laid out with "Isbjørn" in Ardencaple Fjord for the John Giæver Expedition. The fourth location was at Niflheim north of Femdalen. In 1933, John Giæver decided not to build a hut at the location and instead he and Otto Johnsen on 8th August 1932 picked up: *"a boat load of the materials and went in to Tornøestua [527] in Smallefjord"*.[1792] The wood remaining at the material site, here named Niflheim [923], was discovered by a Nanok team in the summer of 2004.

Niflheim [923], 28th July 2004. © NCN

LIST OF ABBREVIATIONS

ABP Allan Broholm Pedersen
AUI Anders Ibsen
BID Bill Davis
CAMP Changes in Arctic Marine Production
CHA Christian Holm Andersen
CZJ Christina Zinck-Jørgensen
DMU National Environmental Research Institute
DPC Danish Polar Center
ERJ Erik Jochumsen
GEUS De Nationale Geologiske Undersøgelse for Danmark og Grønland / Geological Survey of Denmark and Greenland
GGU Grønlands Geologiske Undersøgelse / Geological Survey of Greenland
GNA Greenland National Museum & Archives
GTO Grønlands Tekniske Organisation / Greenland Technical Organisation
HEN Henrik Nevers
HHC Hans Henrik Carlsen
JES Jens Erik Schultz
JMS Jesper Mølbæk Stentoft
JUS Justin Mark Smallbone
JWB Jannik William Berntsen
KGH Den Kongelige Grønlandske Handel / Royal Greenland Trading Company
KMJ Klaus Mynzberg Jensen
KOL Kunuk Olsen Lennert
KRN Kristian Nevers
LAB Lars Bønding
LAK Line Anker Kyhn
MES Mette Stentoft
MOH Morten Hauerbach
MOL Morten Lindhard
NCN North-East Greenland Company Nanok
NFS Niels Fæster Sørensen
NGM Niels Gyldenlund Mikkelsen
NPI Norwegian Polar Institute
NSIU Norwegian Svalbard- and Arctic Ocean Survey
OLS Ole Sten
OSN Ole Schirmer Nielsen
PSM Peter Schmidt Mikkelsen
RAG Rasmus Gregersen
SØA Søren Andersen
SØK Søren Kristensen
STH Steffen Holberg
TEJ Torben E. Jeppesen
THH Thomas Hansen
USAAF United States Army Air Force
USCG United States Coast Guard

DANISH / NORWEGIAN – ENGLISH DICTIONARY

bakke / bakke	hill
bjerg / berg	mountain
bjergtop	mountain peak
bred	beach / bank
bræ / bre	glacier
bo / bu	home
bugt	bay
bund / bunn, botn	head (e.g. of a fjord)
bæk / bekk	creek
dal / dal	valley
delta	delta
landtange / eid	isthmus
elv / elv	river
elvleje	river bed
fjeld	mountain
flod / elv	river
fos / foss	waterfall
gletscher	glacier
halvø	peninsula
hav	sea
havn	harbour
hjem / heim	home
holm	holm, islet
hus	house
hytte / hytta	hut
høj / haug	hill
højderyg	range of hills
kap / kapp	cape
klippe	rock
klippeblok	boulder
kløft	canyon/ravine
kyst	coast
land	land area
lavland	lowland
mark	field
mose	moor/bog
munding	mouth (e.g. of a fjord)
nord	north
næs / nes	point
odde	elongate peninsula
pas	pass
pynt	point
sandbanke / øyr	bank of sand or gravel
skrænt	cliff
skråning	slope
slette	plain
sten	rock
strand / stranda	beach
stræde	strait
strøm	current
stua	hut
sund	sound
syd	south
sø	lake
tinde	peak
tufta	site
tun	yard
vandskel	watershed
vest	west
vig / vik	cove
vold / voll	rampart, embankment
våg	small inlet
ø / øy	island
øst	east
å	creek

LITERATURE

125 *Jahre deutsche Polarforschung*. Alfred-Wegener-Institut für Polar- und Meeresforschung, Bremerhafen, 1993.

Akre, Bjarne: *Fri manns liv*. Oslo, 1957.

Akre, Bjarne: *"Heltene" i kald krig*. Oslo, 1983.

Aktstykker vedrørende Grønland og de med den norske regering indtil 1. september 1923 førte forhandlinger. Trykt på Udenrigsministeriets foranstaltning. København, 1923.

Amdrup, G.C. et al.: *Danmark-Ekspeditionen til Grønlands Nordøstkyst 1906-1908 under ledelse af L. Mylius-Erichsen*. Meddelelser om Grønland. bd. 41. København, 1913.

Andreasen C. & H. Elling: *Biologisk-arkæologisk kortlægning af Grønlands østkyst mellem 75°N og 79°30'N: Del 5: Arkæologisk kortlægning mellem Shannon og Île de France, sommeren 1989*. Teknisk rapport, nr. 18. Nuuk, Grønlands Hjemmestyre, Miljø- og naturforvaltning, 1990.

Andreassen, Janni: *Eigil. Biografi om polarforskeren og kunstneren Eigil Knuth*. København, 2003.

Andrée, S.A., Nils Strindberg og Knut Frænkel: *Andrées Polarfærd 1897*. København, 1930.

Arnesen, Odd: *Vi flyver over Eirik Raudes land*. Oslo, 1932.

Asher, G.M.: *Henry Hudson the Navigator*. New York, 1860.

Astlund, Bertil et al.: *Greenland Lead-Zinc Mine Beats Elements With Underground Mill*. In: Mining World, November 1957, pp. 46-50. 1957.

Aune, Tormod: *Magne Råum – fangstmand og soldat*. Namsos, 1991.

Balchen, Bernt, Corey Ford and Oliver La Farge: *War below zero. The Battle for Greenland*. Boston, 1944.

Balchen, Bernt, Corey Ford and Oliver La Farge: *Kampen om Grønland*. København, 1947.

Balchen, Bernt: *Kom Nord med meg*. Oslo, 1958.

Bang, Oscar: *Blant fangstfolk og bikkjer i Eirik Raudes land*. Fangstmann stud. jur. Oscar Bang's dagbok fra en overvintring 1938-39 på Nordøst-Grønland. Oslo, 1944.

Banks, Mike: *High Arctic. The story of the British North Greenland Expedition*. London, 1957.

Barr, Susan: *Jan Mayen. Norges utpost i vest. Øyas historie gjennom 1500 år*. Oslo, 1991.

Bartlett, Robert A.: *Sails over Ice*. New York, 1934.

Bartlett, Robert A & Junius Bird: *The Bartlett East Greenland Expedition*. In: Geographical Review, vol. 21, 1931, pp. 398-414. 1931.

Beskrivelse av de norske fangststasjoner i Eirik Raudes Land. In: Den Norske Regjerings motinnlegg angående den rettslige status for visse deler af Østgrønland. Fremlagt for Den Faste Domstol for Mellemfolkelig Rettspleie 15 Mars 1932. Norges Svalbard- og Ishavs-undersøkelser. Oslo, 1932.

Bistrup, Henning: *"Teddy"s sidste togt. Uddrag af mine dagbogsoptegnelser*. København, 1924.

Bjerre, Jørgen: *Sirius. Danmarks slædepatrulje i Nordøstgrønland i 50 år*: København, 1999.

Blom, Ida: *Kampen om Eirik Raudes Land. Pressgruppepolitikk i grønlandsspørgsmålet 1921-31*. Oslo, 1973.

Blyklippen lead-zinc mine at Mesters Vig, East Greenland. In: Geology and ore. Exploration and Mining in Greenland. No. 5 - December 2005. GEUS. Copenhagen 2005.

Boyd, Louise A.: *The Fiord Region of East Greenland*. Special publication no. 18. American Geographical Society. New York, 1935.

Boyd, Louise A.: *The Coast of Northeast Greenland with hydrographic studies in the Greenland Sea. The Louise A. Boyd Arctic Expeditions of 1937 and 1938*. American Geographical Society. Special publication no. 30. New York, 1948.

Brandal, Adolf: *Dagbok ført av Adolf Brandal under en overvintring på Østgrønland 1908-09*. Meddelelse nr. 10. Norges Svalbard- og Ishavs-undersøkelser. Oslo, 1930.

Brandt, Kai M.: *Nordlys og slædespor*. Nuuk, 1995.

Brinch, Viggo: *Er der økonomisk grundlag for minedrift i Østgrønland?* In: Grønland, pp. 171-179. Charlottenlund, 1969.

Brun, Eske: *Mit grønlandsliv. Erindringer af Eske Brun*. København, 1985.

Brøgger, A.W.: *Dommen i Haag*. Oslo, 1933.

Böcher, Tyge W.: *Det grønne Grønland*. 2000.

Castberg, Frede: *Østgrønlandsavtalen*. Kristiania, 1924.

Dahl, Kai R.: *På en isflage langs Østgrønland. Motorskonnerten Teddy's forlis i Ishavet og besætningens vidunderlige frelse*. København, 1924.

Dahl, Kai R.: *The "Teddy" Expedition. Among the ice floes of Greenland*. London, 1925.

Dahl, Kai R.: *Et frygteligt forlis i Ishavet. Motorskonnerten Teddy's undergang*. København, 1926.

Danmarkshavn 1948-1988. Særnummer af "Teleposten". NunaTek Tele. København, 1988.

Dansk Pearyland Ekspedition. Forekspeditionen 1947.

Ekspeditionens videreførelse. København, 1947a.

Dansk Pearyland Ekspedition. Sommeren 1947. Haandbog. Seehusen, Svend (editor). København, juli 1947b.

Dansk Pearyland Ekspedition 1948-49-50. Haandbog. Seehusen, Svenn (editor). København, juni 1948.

Description des Stations chasse Norvégiennes dans L'Eirik-Raudes-Land. Norges Svalbard- og Ishavs-undersøkelser. Oslo, 1932

Devold, Hallvard: *Polarliv*. Oslo, 1940.

Statusrapport for Nationalparken/ Biosfærereservatet i Nord- og Østgrønland. Direktoratet for Miljø og Natur. Nuuk, 2001.

Drastrup, Elmar: *Blandt danske og norske fangstmænd i Nordøstgrønland*. København, 1932.

Drastrup, Elmar: *Contributions to the Geography of Ingolfs Fjord and the Interior of Kronprins Christians Land.* Meddelelser om Grønland, bd. 142, nr. 1. København, 1945.

Drastrup, Elmar: *Polarnattens farer*. København, 1956.

Elander, Magnus: *Stilla dagar i Arktis*. Stockholm, 1992.

Ellefsen, Einer and Odd Berset: *Veslekari*. En *fortelling om is og menn*. Bergen, 1957.

Erngaard, Erik: *Grønland gennem tusinde år*. København, 1973.

Erskine, Angus B. og Kjell-G. Kjaer: *The Polar ship Quest*. In: Polar Record 34 (189): 129-142 (1998).

Feltrapport fra rejsen til Nordøstgrønland. Field report from the journey to Northeast Greenland. North-East Greenland Company Nanok, 1991-.

Fiala, Anthony: *Fighting the Polar Ice*. New York, 1907.

The first blow. In: Life, 24. august 1942 p. 63. Chicago, 1942.

Fischer, B. E. et al.: *Der Blei-Zink-Bergbau Mesters Vig in Ostgrönland.* In: Berg- und Hüttenmännische Monatshefte, Jahrgang 103, Heft 8. Wien, 1958.

Fischer, Knud: *Polarsommer*. København, (1983).

Fischer, Knud: *Polardage*. København, 1993.

Fredning af dyrebestanden i Nordøstgrønland. Publikationer om Østgrønland, nr. 6. København, 1938.

Freuchen, Peter: *Min grønlandske ungdom*. København, 1936.

Friis, Achton: *Danmark Ekspeditionen til Grønlands Nordostkyst*. København, 1909.

Génsbøl, Benny & Carl Christian Tofte: *Grønlands dyr og planter*. København, 1998.

Giæver, John: *Fangsthyttene. Jegerliv på Øst-grønland*. Oslo, 1930.

Giæver, John: *To mann i Moskusfjorden. Da vi bebygget og okkuperte Eirik Raudes Land*. Oslo, 1931.

Giæver, John: *Norges Svalbard- og Ishavsundersøkelsers ekspedisjoner til Øst-Grønland sommeren 1937*. Meddelelse nr. 41. Oslo, 1937a.

Giæver, John: *Kaptein Ragnvald Knudsens ishavsferder. Norges Svalbard- og Ishavs- undersøkelser*. Meddelelse nr. 38. Oslo, 1937b.

Giæver, John: *Den norske fangstvirksomheten på Østgrønland*. Publikationer om Østgrønland, nr. 8B. København, 1939.

Giæver, John: *Maudheim. To år i Antarktis. Den norsk-britisk-svenske vitenskapelige ekspedisjon til Antarktis 1949-1952*. Oslo, 1952.

Giæver, John: *Dyretråkk og fugletrekk på 74°Nord*. Oslo, 1955.

Giæver, John: *Hardbalne polarkarer*. Oslo, 1957.

Giæver, John: *Ishavets glade borgere*. København, 1959.

Giæver, Magnus K.: *Turister og jegere i Ishavet*. Oslo, 1944.

En grav i Arktis. In: Gardehusaren nr. 11, november 1989.

Grønland under den kolde krig – Dansk og amerikansk sikkerhedspolitik 1945-68. Dansk Udenrigspolitisk Institut (DUPI). København, 1997.

Grønlands forhistorie. Edited by Hans Christian Gulløv. København, 2004

Grønlandserindringer. Grønlandske Selskabs Skrifter XXVI. Charlottenlund, 1983.

Gulløv, Hans Christian: *Syv skinnende hvide rener. Dagbog ført på Den Danske Ekspedition til Østgrønland 1891-92 af Premierlieutenant Helge Vedel*. København, 1991.

Haag-dommen af 5. April 1933 om Østgrønlands retsstilling. København, 1933.

Hamilton, R.A (editor): *Venture to the Arctic*. Middlesex, 1958.

Hansen, Leo: *Situationen er kritisk. Dagbogsoptegnelser fra min filmekspedition til Østgrønland og Hvidehavet 1934-35 og 1937*. København, 1939.

Hartz, Nicolay: *Skibsexpeditionen til Grønlands Østkyst. For tidsrummet fra d. 18. Juli til d. 12. September 1900*. Meddelelser om Grønland XXVVII. København, 1902.

Henriksen, Niels: *Grønlands geologiske udvikling fra urtid til nutid*. København, 2005.

Higgins, A.K.: *Place names of East Greenland, 72°- 75°N*. Unpublished volume. Copenhagen, 1997.

Higgins, A.K.: *The place names of East Greenland, 69°- 82°N*. (In preparation).

Hoff, Erik: *Ekspeditioner. Grønland og Island*. København, 1992.

Holzapfel, Rupert: *Die Tätigheit des Deutschen Wetterdienstes der Luftwaffe in der Arktis wärend des Krieges*. In: Berichte des Deutschen Wetterdienstes in der U.S. Zone Nr. 12, 1950, p. 129-134, map. (Account of meteorological work

of Luftwaffe in arctic regions, 1940-45.: Bad Kissigen, 1950.
Holzapfel, Rupert: *Deutsche Polarforschung* 1940/45. In: Polarforschung 21 (1951) pp. 85 - 97. 1951.
Howarth, David: *The Sledge Patrol*. London, 1957.
Hvidberg, Andreas: *Pelsjægerliv i Nordøstgrønland*. København, 1932.
Hydle, Halvdan: *I Erik Raudes kjølvann. Små epistler fra den norske grønlandsekspedisjon 1931*. Oslo, 1931.
Høy, Thorkild: *Fra Himmerland til Pearyland. Fra Danmarks søer til Stillehavets øer*. 2003.
Høygaard, Arne og Martin Mehren: *"Ajungilak" eller Grønland på tvers*. Oslo, 1931.
Håndbog for Slædepatruljen Sirius. Søværnskommandoen. 1956.
Haarløv, Niels: *En Foraarstur langs Grønlands Østkyst*. In: Naturens Verden pp. 78-90. København, 1941.
Ingstad, Helge: *Øst for den store bre*. Oslo, 1935.
Ingstad, Helge: *East of the Great Glacier*. New York, 1937.
Ingstad, Helge: *Oppdagelsen av det nye land*. Oslo, 1996.
Isachsen, Gunnar: *Norske fangstmænds færder til Grønland*. In: Det Norske Geografiske Selskaps Aarbok 1919-1921 pp. 201-261. Kristiania, 1922.
Isachsen, Gunnar: *Grønland og Grønlandsisen*. Oslo, 1925.
Isachsen, Gunnar & Fridtjof: *Norske fangstmenns og fiskeres ferder til Grønland 1922-31*. In: Meddelelse nr. 18. Norges Svalbard- og Ishavs-undersøkelser. Oslo, 1932.
Jackson, C. Ian: *The Arctic Whaling Journals of William Scoresby the younger*. Volume I. The Voyages of 1811, 1812 and 1813. London, 2003.
Jennov, J.G.: *Østgrønlandsk Fangstkompagni "Nanok"s "Gefion"-Ekspedition til Danmarks Havn og Hvalrosodden juli-september 1932 og nogle iagttagelser vedrørende isforhold ved den Grønlandske nordøstkyst*. Publikationer om Østgrønland. Bd. 2. København, 1935.
Jennov, J.G.: *Redegørelse vedrørende de danske og norske fangstvirksomheder i Nordøstgrønland*. Østgrønlandsk fangstkompagni NANOK. København, 1937.
Jennov, J.G.: *Østgrønlandsk Fangstkompagni Nanok A/S*. Publikationer om Østgrønland Nr. 8C. København, 1939.
Jennov, J.G.: *Moskusoksebestanden i Nordøstgrønland og nogle spredte iagttagelser og betragtninger vedrørende dyrelivet i Nordøstgrønland*. København, 1945.
Johnsen, Palle: *Zoolog i Nord og Syd*. København, 1967.
Journal of a Voyage to Spitzbergen and the east coast of Greenland in His Majesty's Ship Griper. The Edinburgh New Philosofical Journal, vol. 9, April-June 1830. Edinburgh, 1830.
Kampmann, P.: *Bly- og zinkforekomster i Nordøstgrønland*. In: Ingeniörvetenskaps-akademien, meddelande nr. 24, 1953, pp. 294-303. Stockholm, 1953.
Keulen, Gerhard Van: *De groote nieuwe Zee-Atlas*. Amsterdam, 1710.
Kjær, Kjell-G.: *Belgica in the Arctic*. In: Polar Record 41: 205-214 (2005).
Kjær, Kjell-G.: *The polar ship Frithjof*. In: Polar Record 42: 281-289 (2006).
Kjær, Kjell-G. and Hillary Foxworthy: *The Arctic ship Danmark*. In: Polar Record 40: 31-38 (2004).
Kjær, Kjell-G. and Magnus Sefland: *The Arctic ship Veslekari*. In: Polar Record 41 (216): 57-65 (2005).
Kjær, Kjell-G. and Magnus Sefland: *The Arctic ship Polarbjørn*. In: Polar Record 42 (220): 51-57 (2006).
Kmunke, Rudolf: *Auf Eisbären und Moschusochsen. Tagebuchblätter der Jagderlebnisse in Ostgrönland*. Wien, 1910.
Knuth, Eigil: *Under det nordligste Dannebrog. Beretning om Dansk Nordøstgrønlands Ekspedition 1938-39*. København, 1940.
Knuth, Eigil: *Report on the expedition and on subsequent work at Mørkefjord station. Dansk Nordøstgrønlands Ekspedition 1938-39*. Meddelelser om Grønland, bd. 126, nr. 1. København, 1942.
Knuth, Eigil: *The Danish Expedition to Peary Land, 1947-49*. In: The Geographical Journal, vol. CXVIII, Part 1, March 1952: København, 1952.
Knuth, Eigil: *Kap Moltke 1972*. Rapport. København, 1973.
Knuth, Eigil: *Independence. The philosophy of a dog sledge journey*. Nuuk, 1995.
Knutsen, Willie: *Mitt arktis*. Oslo, 1992.
Knutsen, Willie and Will C. Knutsen: *Arctic sun on my path*. Connecticut, 2005.
Koch, J.P.: *Bemærkninger vedrørende de paa Skibsexpeditionen til Grønlands Østkyst 1900 opmaalte Kyststrækninger mellem 69°20 N.Br. og 72°20 N.Br.* Meddelelser om Grønland XXVII. København, 1902.
Koch, J.P.: *Gennem den hvide ørken. Den danske forskningsrejse tværsover Nordgrønland 1912-13*. København, 1913.
Koch, Lauge: *Treaarsekspeditionen til Chr. X's Land 1931-34*. København, 1934.
Koch, Lauge: *Vi flyver over isbjørnens land*. København, 1938.
Koch, Lauge: *Fra Lissabon til Pearyland*. København, 1939.
Koch, Lauge: *Survey of North Greenland. Index*

to Survey of North Greenland. The East Greenland Ice. Meddelelser om Grønland, bd. 130, nr. 1-3. København, 1940.
Koch, Lauge: *Report on the expeditions to Central East Greenland 1926-39*. Meddelelser om Grønland, bd. 143, nr. 2. København, 1955.
Koldewey, Karl: *Die zweite Deutsche Nordpolarfahrt in den Jahren 1869 und 1870 unter des Führung des Kapitän Karl Koldewey herausgeben dem Verein für die Deutsche Nordpolarfahrt*. Leipzig, 1873.
Koldewey, Karl: *The German Arctic Expedition of 1869-70*. London, 1874.
Kolthoff, Gustaf: *Till Spetsbergen och nordöstra Grönland år 1900*. Stockholm, 1901.
Kristoffersen, Finn: *Jæger og fangstmand*. København, 1969.
Lachmann, Otto: *Karte von Nordöstgrönland*. Gotha, 1937.
Lassen, Fin Kløve: *Blyminen i Mesters Vig*. 2005.
Lauritsen, Birthe: *Fangstmandsliv og de danske fangstkompagnier i Nordøstgrønland 1919-1952*. København, 1984.
Laursen, Dan: *The Place Names of North Greenland*. Meddelelser om Grønland, bd. 180, nr. 2. København, 1972.
Leverkus, Alfred: *Im Banne des Eismeers. Grönländische Jagd- und Reise-erlebnisse*. Leverkusen, 1909.
Lister, Hal: *Ice – High and Low*. Cumbria, 2005
Luncke, Bernhard: *Norges Svalbard- og Ishavs-undersøkelsers luftkartlegning i Eirik Raudes land 1932*. Meddelelse nr. 23. Norges Svalbard- og Ishavs-undersøkelser. Oslo, 1933.
Lund, Thoralv: *Kalde krigsår. Svalbard 1940-1945*. Bergen, 1990.
Lund, Viggo S.: *Jægerliv og nordlysnætter*. København, 1926.
Lundbye, Vagn: *Omkom 79' fjorden. Tragedien på Danmark-ekspeditionen 1906-08*. København, 1984.
Madsen, Marius: *Shipwreck and struggle. True life adventures of a Danish-born Canadian shipwrecked and stranded on the world's last land of the Ice Age*. Toronto, 1963.
Madsen, Marius: *Strandet i Østgrønland. To års kamp for livet efter Dagny's forlis 1920*. København, 1989.
Manniche, A.L.V.: *Midnatssol og mørketid. Stemninger og hændelser på "Danmark-Ekspeditionen"*. København, 1909.
Mikkelsen, Astrid Duus: *Fangstmændene i Nordøstgrønland 1908-60*. In: Tidsskriftet Grønland, nr. 7 - November 2001. København, 2001.
Mikkelsen, Ejnar: *Tre år på Grønlands Østkyst*. København, 1914.
Mikkelsen, Ejnar: *Alabama-expeditionen til Grønlands Nordøstkyst 1909-1912 under ledelse af Ejnar Mikkelsen*. Meddelelser om Grønland, bd. 52. København, 1922.
Mikkelsen, Ejnar: *Fra hundevagt til hundeslæde*. København, 1953.
Mikkelsen, Ejnar: *Farlig tomandsfærd*. København, 1955.
Mikkelsen, Peter Schmidt: *Tusind dage med Sirius*. København, 1986.
Mikkelsen, Peter Schmidt: *I kajak mellem moskusokse og hvalros*. In: "Levende Natur", nr. 1, marts. København, 1990.
Mikkelsen, Peter Schmidt (editor): *SIRIUS gennem 50 år*. København, 2000.
Mikkelsen, Peter Schmidt: *Nordøstgrønland 1908-60, fangstmandsperioden*. København, 1994 / 2001.
Mikkelsen, Peter Schmidt: *Twin Otter – Flyvning og rejser i Grønland*. København, 2006.
Mindeblade om Danmark-Ekspeditionen 1906-08. Grønlandske Selskabs Skrifter XXV. Publikationer om Østgrønland, nr 10. København, 1983.
Mulvad, Søren (editor): *Katastrofen i Ishavet 1777. Beretninger fra hval- og sælfangsten ved Grønland*. Esbjerg, 2002.
Munck, Ebbe: *Strejftog i nord*. København, 1959.
Muus, Bent, Finn Salomonsen and Christian Vibe: *Grønlands fauna. Fisk-fugle-pattedyr*. København, 1990.
Münsterhjelm, Ludvig: *Bland isbjörnar och myskoxar på Nordost-Grönland*. Stockholm, 1937.
Münzing, Joachim: *Die Jagd auf den Wal. Schleswig-Holsteins und Hamburgs Grönlandfahrt*. Heide in Holstein, 1978.
Møller, N.C.Th.: *Historiske meddelelser om A/S Østgrønlandsk Kompagni*. Publikationer om Østgrønland, nr. 8A. København, 1939.
Nathorst, A.G.: *Två somrar i Norra Ishafvet*. I-II. Stockholm, 1900.
Nielsen, Kay Søren: *Sirius 1950 – 1990*. København, 1990.
Novak, Thaddeus D., P.J. Capelotti (editor): *Life and Death on the Greenland Patrol, 1942*. Florida, 2005.
Nusser, Franz: *Die Arktisunternehmen des deutschen Marinewetterdienstes in den Jahren 1940-45*. Einzelveröffentlichungen nr. 96. Deutscher Wetterdienst Seewetteramt. Hamburg, 1979.
Nyholm-Poulsen, Henning: *Fangstmand på Østgrønland 1932-33*. København, 1985.
Nyquist, R.B.: *En håndfull nordmenn. Forpostene i Ishavet*. Oslo, 1945.
Odsbjerg, Anders: *Nordøstgrønlands Slædepatrulje*

1941-45; besættelsestidens militære forsvarspatrulje. København, 1990.
Odsbjerg, Anders: *Lauge Koch – Grønlandsforskeren.* København, 1992.
Olsen, Kurt: *Et hundeliv. Oplevelser med slædepatruljen i Nordøstgrønland under 2. Verdenskrig.* København, 1965.
d'Orléans, Louis Philippe Robert Duc: *A travers la banquise de Spitzberg au Cap Philippe mai-aout 1905.* Paris, 1905.
Orleans, The Duke of: *Hunters and hunting in the Arctic.* London, 1911.
Orvin, A.K.: *Ekspedisjonen til Østgrønland med "Veslekari" sommeren 1929.* Meddelelse nr. 11. Norges Svalbard- og Ishavs-undersøkelser. Oslo, 1930.
Orvin, A.K.: *Ekspedisjonen til Jan Mayen og Øst-Grønland sommeren 1930.* Meddelelse nr. 13. Norges Svalbard- og Ishavs-undersøkelser. Oslo, 1931.
Orvin, A.K.: *Norges Svalbard- og Ishavs-undersøkelsers ekspedisjoner til Nordøst-Grønland i årene 1931-1933.* Isfjord fyr og radiostasjon, Svalbard. Meddelelse nr. 25. Norges Svalbard- og Ishavs-undersøkelser. Oslo, 1934.
Orvin, A.K.: *Norges Svalbard- og Ishavs-undersøkelsers ekspedisjoner i årene 1934 og 1935.* Meddelelse nr. 32. Norges Svalbard- og Ishavs-undersøkelser. Oslo, 1935.
Orvin, A.K.: *Norges Svalbard- og Ishavs-undersøkelsers ekspedisjoner til Øst-Grønland og Svalbard i året 1936.* Meddelelse nr. 37. Norges Svalbard- og Ishavs- undersøkelser. Oslo, 1937.
Pantenburg, Vitalis: *Langt inne i isen.* Oslo, 1944.
Payer, Julius: *Den østerrigsk-ungarske Nordpol-Expedition i Aarene 1872-1874. tilligemed en skitse af Den anden tydske Nordpol-Expedition 1869-70 og af Polar-Expeditionen i 1871.* København, 1877.
Pedersen, Alwin: *Polardyr.* København, 1934.
Pedersen, Alwin: *Et naturens reservat.* København, 1940.
Pedersen, Alwin: *Rosmarus. En beretning om hvalrossens liv og historie.* København, 1951.
Pedersen, Alwin: *Polar Animals.* London, 1962.
Pedersen, Carl Emil: *Farvel Rundø.* Oslo, 1979.
Pedersen, Einar Sverre: *Polarbasillen. Tredve år rundt Arktis.* Oslo, 1969.
Polarboken. Norsk Polarklubb. Oslo, 1954-.
Polarprofiler: J.P. Koch og A. Wegener. Temanummer af Forskning i Grønland/tusaat, nr. 2-3/93. København, 1994.
Polarprofiler: Lauge Koch. Temanummer af Forskning i Grønland/tusaat, nr. 3/92. København, 1992.
Polarårboken. Norsk Polarklubb. Oslo 1933-1953.
Poulsen, Charles: *Yngstemandens dagbøger. Fra Danmark-Ekspeditionen 1906-1908.* København, 1991.
Price, Scott: *Master of the Ice. The Capture of the Externsteine.* In: Sea Classics July 1995, pp. 45-61. 1995
Report on the Activities of Norges Svalbard- og Ishavs-undersøkelser 1927-1936. Skrifter om Svalbard og Ishavet, nr. 73. Norges Svalbard- og Ishavs-undersøkelser. Oslo, 1937.
Report on the Activities of Norges Svalbard- og Ishavs-undersøkelser 1936-1944. Skrifter om Svalbard og Ishavet, nr. 88. Norges Svalbard- og Ishavs-undersøkelser. Oslo, 1945.
Richter, Søren: *A Contribution to the archaeology of North-East Greenland.* Skrifter om Svalbard og Ishavet, nr. 63. Norges Svalbard- og Ishavs-undersøkelser. Oslo, 1934.
Ries, Christopher Jacob: *Retten, magten og æren. Lauge Koch Sagen – en strid om Grønlands geologiske udforskning.* København, 2003.
Rodahl, Kåre: *Et år under breen.* Oslo, 1946. (1)
Rodahl, Kåre: *The Ice-capped Island:* Greenland. London, 1946. (2)
Rodahl, Kåre: *Nytt land under vingerne.* Oslo, 1948.
Rodahl, Kåre: *Den lange veien hjem.* Oslo, 1992.
Rogne, Frode: *Ishavsliv. Norske fangstfolk på Grønland.* Oslo, 1981.
Rohan, Philippe, Gérard Loucel, Jacques Godin: *Apsuma. Dans les traces de Jørn Riel. Larbey, 2003.*
Rostock-Jensen, Louis: *M/S Teddy. Dagbog fra en grønlandsekspedition 1923-24.* København, 2004.
Roy, Iain Brownlie: *Beyond the imaginary gates. Journeys in the fjord region of north east Greenland.* Stockport, 2004.
Rud, Mogens: *Grønlandsforskeren Alfred Wegener og de drivende kontinenter.* København, 2007.
Ruge, Friedrich: *Der Seekrieg 1939-1945.* Stuttgart, 1954.
Ryder, Carl: *Beretning om Den østgrønlandske Expedition 1891-92.* Meddelelser om Grønland, bd. 17, nr. 1. København, 1895.
Sabine, Edward: *An account of experiments to determine the figure of the earth by means of pendulum vibrating seconds in different latitudes as well as on various other subjects of philosophical inquiry.* London, 1825.
Sandell, Hanne & Birger: *Rapport over Grønlands Landsmuseum/KNK's arkæologiske rekognoscering på Jameson Land Nordøstgrønland 1988.* Grønlands Landsmuseum. Nuuk, 1988.
Schatz, Heinrich: *Die katastrophe der Coburg im Eis vor Shannon am 18.-19. November, 1943.* In: Polarforschung, bd. 2, Jahrgang 20,Heft 1/2, 1950

(pub. 1951), p. 336-38. (The fate of Coburg during operation Bassgeiger in East Greenland). 1951.

Scheina, Robert L.: *U.S. Coast Guard Cutters and Craft of World War II*. Annapolis, 1982.

Schwarzenbach, Fritz Hans (editor): *Towards New Horizons. John Haller 1927 – 1984*. Zürich, 1993.

Schwerdtfeger, Werner & Franz Selinger: *Wetterflieger in der Arktis 1940-44. Erlebnisse und Erfahrungen der Wettererkundungs-Staffeln im Hohen Norden*. Stuttgart, 1982.

Scoresby, William, Junior: *Journal of a voyage to the northern whale-fishery including researches and discoveries on the eastern coast of West Greenland made in the Summer of 1822, in the ship Baffin of Liverpool*. Edinburgh, 1823.

Scoresby, William, Senior: *Seven log-books concerning the Arctic voyages of Capt. William Scoresby, Senior of Whitby, England*. The Explorers Club. New York, 1917.

Seidenfaden, Gunnar: *Eventyret om Østgrønland*. København, 1936.

Seidenfaden, Gunnar: *Moderne arktisk forskning*. København, 1938.

Selinger, Franz: *Abriss der Unternehmungen des Marinewetterdienstes in der Arktis 1940-45 nach dem Erkenntnisstand von 1990*. Einzelveröffentlichung Nr. 96a. Deutscher Wetterdienst Seewetteramt. Hamburg, 1991.

Selinger, Franz: *Von NANOK bis Eismitte – Meteorologische Unternehmungen in der Arktis 1940-1945*. Hamburg, 2001.

Siewers, Hans: *Grønland 1939-1945*. In: Drammen Trekkhundklubb 50 års jubilæumbog 1933-1983, pp. 37-51. Oslo, 1983.

Silis, Ivar: *Hvide horisonter*. København, 1995.

Simpson, C.J.W.: *North Ice. The British North Greenland Expedition*. London, 1957.

Slædepatruljen Sirius. Nord- og Nordøstgrønland. Inspektøren for Søværnet. Vedbæk, 1990.

Slædeposten. Foreningsblad for "Foreningen af tidligere medlemmer af den nordøstgrønlandske slædepatrulje". København, 1963-.

Smedal, Gustav: *Opgjør og forståelse med Danmark. Grønlandssaken, historisk og politisk*. Oslo, 1928.

Smedal, Gustav: *Erhvervelse av statshøihet over polarområder*. Oslo, 1930.

Smedal, Gustav: *Acquisition of sovereignity over Polar areas*. Skrifter om Svalbard og Ishavet, nr. 36. Norges Svalbard- og Ishavs-undersøkelser. Oslo, 1931.

Smedal, Gustav: *Nationalt forfall. Tilbakeblikk og fremtidsmål i Grønlandssaken*. Oslo, 1934.

Stamp, Tom & Cordelia: *William Scoresby – Arctic scientist*. Whitby, 1975.

Steen, E.A.: *Norges Sjøkrig 1940-1945. Bind VII. Marinens operasjoner i arktiske farvann og i Island, på Grønland, Jan Mayen og Svalbard*. Oslo, 1960.

Stuhr, Werner: *Abenteuer vor Grönland. Unbekannte Episode von der Abholung des Marine-Wettertrupps Bassgeiger*. In: Koehlers Flottekalender 1974, pp. 183 - 187. 1974.

Sørensen, Lars Normann: *Henry Rudi, Isbjørnkongen*. Oslo, 1958.

Sørensen, Ove (editor): *Et andet Sirius*. København, 2002.

Talcott, Dudley Vaill: *A/S Norkap II av Tromsø*. Oslo, 1937.

Thomas, Charles W.: *Ice is where you find it*. New York, 1951.

Thomsen, Elsebeth, Svend Erik Bendix-Almgreen og Peter Schmidt Mikkelsen: *Om Tromsø Museums forsvunnede flyveøgle eller 15 geologiske prøver og en mann, Oskar Meyer Olsen, in memoriam*. In: Årbok 1998 for Malangen og Balsfjord, pp. 4-12. Balsfjord, 1998.

Thomsen, Hans: *Danmarkshavn kalder*. København, 1966.

Thormann, Tomas: *Slædepatruljen Sirius, 4000 km med verdens bedste hunde*. 1997.

Thorson, Gunnar (editor): *Med Treaarsekspeditionen til Christian X's Land. Af Deltagere i Ekspeditionen*. København, 1937.

Tilley, John A.: *The Coast Guard & the Greenland Patrol*. Publication of the Coast Guard Historian's Office / Commandant's Bulletin insert for August 1992. Washington, 1992.

Topografisk Atlas Grønland. In: Atlas over Danmark, serie II, bind 6. Det Kongelige Danske Geografiske Selskab og Kort & Matrikelstyrelsen. København, 2000.

Torkildsen, Torbjørn (editor): *Svalbard. Vårt nordligste Norge*. Oslo, 1991.

Traces – 4400 Years of Man in Greenland. (editor Claus Andreasen et. al.). Greenland National Museum and Archives. Nuuk, 2004.

Tutein, Peter: *Dramaet i Storisen. "Teddy"s forlis*. København, 1945.

Tutein, Peter: *Grøn ungdom hele livet*. København, 1951.

Ventegodt, Ole: *Den sidste brik. Mylius-Erichsens Danmark-ekspedition til Nordøstgrønland 1906-08*. København, 1997.

Vervarslinga for Nord-Norge 25 år. Festskrift utgitt i anledning av 25-års jubileet 1. februar 1945. Tromsø, 1945.

Vervarslinga for Nord-Norge 50 år. Festskrift utgitt i anledning av 50-års jubileet 1. februar 1970. Tromsø, 1970.

Vibe, Christian: *Ene ligger Grønland. Livet i Grønland under de 6 lange adskillelsens aar 1939-46.* København, 1946.

Vollan, Odd: *Ishavsfart. Selfangsten fra Sunnmøre gjennem femti år.* Oslo, 1951.

Walthew, Kenneth: *From rock to tempest. The life of Captain George William Manby.* London, 1971

Washburn, A.L.: *Geomorphic and vegetational studies in the Mesters Vig district, North-East Greenland.* Meddelelser om Grønland, bd. 166, nr. 1. København, 1965.

Weiss, Gottfried: *Das arktische Jahr. Eine Überwinterung in Nordostgrönland.* Braunschweig, 1949.

Willoughby, Malcolm F.: *The U.S. Coast Guard in World War II.* Annapolis, 1989.

Wordie, J.M.: *The Cambridge Expedition to East Greenland in 1926.* In: Geographical Journal, vol. 70, 1927, pp. 225-265. London, 1927.

Wordie, J.M.: *The Cambridge East Greenland Expedition 1929.* In: Geographical Journal, vol 75, no. 6, June 1930, pp. 481-504. London, 1930.

World's Greatest National Park in North and East Greenland. The Greenland Home Rule Authorities. Nuuk, 1989.

Zackenberg – a research station in North East Greenland. Dansk Polarcenter. København, 1993.

Zorgdrager, Cornelis Gijsbertsz: *Alte und neue Grönlandische Fischerei und Wallfischfang/mit einer kurzen historischen beschreibung von Grønland/Island/Spitzbergen/Nova Zembla/Jan Mayen Eiland/der Strasse Davis u.a. ausgefertiget durch Abraham Moubach.* Leipzig, 1723.

Årsskrift. Hareid Historielag 1974. Hefte nr. 1. Brandal, 1974.

Årsskrift. Hareid Historielag 1984. Hefte nr. 10. Brandal, 1984.

OTHER SOURCES

Archives:

A: Arkivfond A 265, Arctic Institute. Copenhagen
G: Mogens Graaes collection, Arctic Institute. Copenhagen
N: Norwegian Polar Institutte. Tromsø
P: Private ownership
R: Hyllenummer 2A078.24 - 2A078.33, Riksarkivet. Oslo
U: Naval Historical Center. Washington DC
Ø: Arkivfond A 267, Arctic Institute. Copenhagen

Dagbog, Dagbok, Journal (Diary, journal, logbook)
Rapport, Rapporter (Report or diary)

A127 Jennov, J.G.: Jennovs rapport fra Germaniahavn 24/8-1929
A128 Jennov, J.G.: Jennovs rapporter fra Østgrønland 12/12-1929 - 11/7-1930
A129 Jennov, J.G.: Jennovs rapporter fra Østgrønland 1930 - 31
A130 Jennov, J.G.: Jennovs rapport fra sommerturen 1933
A131 Jennov, J.G.: Jennovs rapport fra sommerturen 1934
A132 Jennov, J.G.: Jennovs rapport fra sommerturen 1935
A133 Jennov, J.G.: Jennovs rapport fra sommerturen 1938
A134 Jennov, J.G.: Jennovs rapport fra sommerturen 1939
A135 Jennov, J.G.: Jennovs rapport fra sommerturen 1945
A136 Jennov, J.G.: Jennovs rapport fra sommerturen 1946
A137 Jennov, J.G.: Jennovs rapport fra sommerturen 1947
A138 Jennov, J.G.: Jennovs rapport fra sommerturen 1948
A139 Jennov, J.G.: Jennovs rapport fra sommerturen 1949
A140 Jennov, J.G.: Jennovs rapport fra sommerturen 1950
A141 Jennov, J.G.: Jennovs rapport fra sommerturen 1951
A142 Jennov, J.G.: Jennovs rapport fra sommerturen 1952
A143 Jennov, J.G.: Jennovs rapport fra sommerturen 1954
A144 Dagbog for Germaniahavn 25/8 1929 - 31/7 1931 og Hvalrosodden 11/8-1933 - 24/10-1934 og 9/5-1935 - 10/3-1936
A145 Rasmussen, Jensen: Dagbog for Knudshoved, 27/1 1931 - 9/8 1931
A146 Journal for Hochstetter, 28/8-1934 - 17/8-1935
A147 Journal for Hochstetter, 20/8-1936 - 7/8-1938
A148 Journal for Sandodden 1938-39
A149 Journal for Aalborghus, 25/8 1938 - 12/8-1939 og Zackenberg, 15/9-1945 - 26/7-1946
A150 Larsen, L.E.: Dagbog (Hochstetter og Germaniahavn), 18/10-1931 - 18/8-1932
A151 Dagbog for Arne Philbert og Walther Povelsen, 12/8-1933 - 20/9-1934
A152 Dagbog for Frantz Dalskov, Aalborghus, 23/8-1938 - 16/8-1939
A153 Jensen, Berndt: Dagbog Sandodden, 10/10-1938 - 9/8-1939
A154 Dagbog for Chr. Jensen, Hvalrosodden, 24/8-1938 - 1/3-1939
A155 Dagbog for H. Ørnlef, Hvalrosodden, 15/10-1938 - 15/3-1939
A156 Dagbog for Chr. Jensen, 4/3-1939 - 19/4-1939
A157 Dagbog for Poul Hennings, 23/8-1939 - 28/3-1940
A158 Dagbog, Loch Fyne, 21/11-1949 - 27/11-1949, 13/3-1950 - 22/3-1950, 19/7-1950
A159 Journal for Loch Fyne, 15/8-1950 - 18/8-1951
A160 Journal for Loch Fyne, 27/8-1951 - 28/7-1952
A161 Journal for Mønstedhus, 11/10-1951 - 19/5-1952
A162 Journal for Zackenberg, 3/8-1950 - 31/7-1951
A163 Journal for Zackenberg, 6/11-1951 - 1/8-1952
A164 Journal for Hochstetter, 22/8 1950 - 16/5 1951
A165 Stationsdagbog for Hochstetter, 28/8-1951 - 3/4-1952
A166 Larsen, H.E.: Dagbog, Hochstetter, 1/11-1950 - 30/3-1951
A167 Dagbog for Hans Frederiksen, Hochstetter, 9/10 1951 - 14/3-1952
A168 Frederiksen, Hans: Dagbog fra Zackenberg, 27/9-1952 - 24/8-1953
A169 Larsen, H.E.: Hyttedagbog 11/10-1950 - 5/4-1951, 1/10-1951 - 2/12-1951, 19/1-1952 - 30/7-1952
A170 Hyttedagbog for fangstmand Hans E. Madsen, Loch Fyne, 5/11-1950 - 18/4-1951
A171 Madsen, Hans E.: Dagbog, Loch Fyne, 1/11 1951 - 1/4 1952
A172 Dagbog for Svend Olsen, Loch Fyne, 9/12-1951 - 20/4-1952

A173 Hyttedagbog for K.E.P. Wind, Sandodden, 1/11-1950 - 18/4-1951

A174 Erik B. Larsens dagbogsoptegnelser, Hochstetter og Mønstedhus, 24/8-1954 - 14/9-1955

A175 Radiotelegrafist Ib Palle Madsens dagbog, Zackenberg, 31/6-1959 - 18/4-1960

A178 Beskrivelse af hytterne ved Sandodden, Germaniahavn, Hochstetter, Danmarkshavn, Hvalrosodden

A181 Kort over Nordøstgrønland med danske og norske hytter indtegnede

A190 Bemandingsplaner. Besselsfjord 1932-33, Loch Fyne, Hochstetter og Aalborghus 1951-52

A241 Jensen, Hans Ludvig: Dagbog fra Hochstetter, 2/8-1929 - 1/5-1930, 1/5-1930 - 27/7-1930, 30/7-1930 - 25/8-1930

A244 Jensen, Hans Ludvig: Dagbog fra Hochstetter, 23/8-1936 - 10/9-1938

A270 Jennov, J.G.: Besejlingen 1929, heri Jennovs rapport til styrelsen om den første besejlings forløb

A278 Fangststationer og fangstresultater 1929-34

A279 Konstruktionstegning til jagthytte, including fortegnelse over materialer

A280 Jennov, J.G.: Anlæg af nye fangststationer og varetransport med hundeslæde

A282 Fangststationerne 1944

A283 Fangststationerne 1945

A296 Fangstmand Poul Hennings breve og dagbogsoptegnelser 1936-41

G101 Mogens Graaes dagbog fra Hochstetter og Mønstedhus, 18/10-1946 - 23/5-1947

G102 Mogens Graaes dagbog fra Hochstetter og Mønstedhus, 20/8-1947 - 21/5-1948

G103 L.E. Larsens dagbog fra Sandodden, 25/8-1929 - 29/3-1931

G104 Chr. Petersens dagbog fra Sandodden/Knudshoved, 2/9-1938 - 26/7-1939

G105 Journal for Loch Fyne, 12/8-1946 - 10/8-1947

G106 Journal for Loch Fyne, 12/8-1947 - 14/5-1947

G107 Journal for Loch Fyne, 1/8-1948 - 4/4-1949

G108 Iversen, Iver C.: Dagbog fra Loch Fyne, 16/8-1949 - 30/8-1950

G109 Journal for Hochstetter, 16/8-1938 - 2/8-1941

G110 Hyttedagbog ført af Leo Ingwersen på Aalborghus, 28/10-1950 - 18/3-1952

G111 Hyttedagbog for Jack Engelbrecht Christensen, 20/11-1949 - 14/3-1950

G112 Dagbog for Erling Pedersen, 4/2-1948 - 9/6-1948

G113 Hyttedagbog for K.B. Soelberg, Sandodden, 23/10-1946 - 10/8-1947

G115 Marius Jensens dagbog, Aalborghus, 8/2-1939 - 5/5-1939

G116 Hyttedagbog for Jørgen Andersen, 20/2-1947 - 13/5-1947

G117 Dagbog for Station I, Hochstetter Forland, 22/8-1929 - 15/8-1931, 8/8-1933 - 31/8-1934

G118 Dagbog for Station I, Hochstetter Forland, 16/8-1931 - 18/8- 1932

G119 Journal for Zackenberg, 8/8-1946 - 14/7-1947

G121 Journal for Aalborghus, 31/8-1959 - 3/8-1952

G123 Journal for Mønstedhus, 23/9-1938 - 31/8-1940, 5/11-1947 - 9/11-1947

G124 Journal for Mønstedhus, 1/9-1940 - 25/7-1941, 3/2-1947 22/4-1947

G125 Hyttedagbog for Orla Jensen, 25/10-1946 - 11/5-1947

G126 Hyttedagbog for Orla Jensen, 14/8-1947 - 28/5-1948

G127 Forhandlingsprotokol for Østgrønlandsk Fangstkompagni Nanok A/S, 20/5-1929 - 18/11-1930

G128 Forhandlingsprotokol for Østgrønlandsk Fangstkompagni Nanok A/S, 16/12-1930 - 26/9-1935

G129 Forhandlingsprotokol for Østgrønlandsk Fangstkompagni Nanok A/S, 27/11-1935 - 27/11-1940

G130 Forhandlingsprotokol for Østgrønlandsk Fangstkompagni Nanok A/S, 27/11-1940 - 17/11-1948

G131 Forhandlingsprotokol for Østgrønlandsk Fangstkompagni Nanok A/S, 17/11-1948 - 3/1-1989

G132 Beskrivelse af Nanoks stationer og hytter (ca. 1940)

G133 Graae, Mogens: Mønstedhus, February 1947

N018 Dagbog ført paa overvintringen med Floren af Adolf Brandal, Liavågs ekspedisjon 1908-1909

N026 Dagbok for Sigurd Tolløfsen, Kap Herschell 1933-34

N027 Dagbok for Sigurd Tolløfsen, Kap Herschell 1932-33

N028 Dagbogsavskrift for Arnljot Tolløfsen, Revet 1932-1933

N029 Avskrift av dagbok for Haakon Karlsen og Gerhard Antonsen, Revet

N030 Klokset, Ole: Dagbok ført under overvintring på Grønland 1933-1935

N031 Andresen, Hermann: Hermann Andresens dagbok, 15/8-1931 - 16/8-1932

N032 Andresen, Hermann: Dagbok fra Hird-ekspedisjonen, Østgrønland 1927-28-29

N033 Andresen, Hermann: Møre Grønlandsexpedisjon overvintring, 9/7-1930 - 14/8-1931

N034 Åmbak, Odd: Dagbok ført av Oddmund Åmbak, 10/7-1930 - 1/8-1932
N035 Andresen, Hermann: Dagbok for Suløya Grønlandsekspedisjon 1934-36
N048 Råum, Magne: Dagbok ført under overvintring på Grønland 1933-1934
N050 Lindquist, Gustav: Dagbok for overvintringen på Østgrønland 1930-31
N051 Dagbog ført av Bernt Marø 1932-33
N052 Holmeslet, Johannes: Dagbok. Sigurd Tolløfsens Grønlandsekspedisjon 1932-34
N053 Dagbok ført av Sverre Sørensen under overvintringen på Østgrønland, 1932-33
N054 Sørensen, Sverre J.: Dagbok 14/7-1929 - 27/5-1930, 28/5-1930 - 6/2-1931, 7/2-1931 - 22/8-1931
N055 Råum, Magne: Dagbok ført under overvintring på Grønland 1934-1935
N056 Halle, Thor: Dagbok Østgrønland 1929-31
N057 Devold, Hallvard: Dagbok, 14/7-1929 - 5/11-1929, 6/11-1929 - 20/5-1930, 21/5-1930 - 20/7-1931
N059 Peder Sulebaks dagbok fra Østgrønland, 1930-32
N060 Kjelbotn, Olaf: Dagbok fra overvintringen på Østgrønland 1929-31
N061 Herdal, Eilif: Dagbok fra overvintringen på Østgrønland 1930-32
N062 Stordal, Johan: Dagbok for Johan Stordal, Jacksonøen 1933-34
N063 Hanken, Nils: Dagbok fra Østgrønland 1935-1936
N064 Dagbok for Ingvald Strøm, Kap Humboldt, 1929-30
N065 Dagbok for Ingvald Strøm, Myggbukta 1930-31
N069 Dagbok for Sigurd Tolløfsen, Østgrønland 1937-39
N070 Dagbok av Dagfinn Egeberg, Hoelsbu, Østgrønland 1949-50
N072 Larsen, Birger: Kap Humboldt. Enkelte betraktninger omkring høstens motorbåtturer
N075 Molt, Walter: Dagbok fra overvintringen på Grønland 1934-35
N076 Johnsen, John: Dagbok fra Østgrønland 1933-1934
N077 Molt, Walter: Dagbok fra overvintringen på Østgrønland 1932-33
N080 Dagbog fra Carl Ritter nedtegnet av Ole Sivertsen, 1932-1934
N082 Dagbok ført på Østgrønland 1932-34 av John Giæver
N084 Dagbok for Ole Sivertsen, 1935-37
N085 Foldvik, Nils: Dagbok fra Den Norske Grønlandsekspedisjonen 1926-28
N086 Dagbog for 7de Junis overvintringsekspedisjon 1909-1910. Skrevet av Martin Bjørnlo
N087 Liavåg, Severin: Dagbok 1908-09
N088 Furland, Hans: Dagbok 1932-33
N090 Johansen, Johan: Dagbok 1/8-1939 - 10/9-1942
N091 Journal og Fremmedbok for Myggbukta fangst- radio- og meteorologiske, stasjon. Begyndt 1933
N142 Karlsbak, Jonas: Dagbok for Hird-ekspedisjonen 1927-1928
N143 Karlsbak, Jonas: Bak Østgrønlands ismur høsten og vinteren 1928-1929.
N144 Karlsbak, Jonas: Dagbok fra overvintringen på Østgrønland, 13/4-1931 - 19/8-1931
N145 Karlsbak, Jonas: Dagbok fra overvintringen på Østgrønland, 9/7-1930 - 12/4-1931
N189 Johnsen, Øivind Holm: Dagbok 1935-36

P101 Dagbok for Nils Hanken 1934-37, Kap Herschell og Antarctichavn
P102 Jensen, Niels Ove: Årsberetning for 1944-1945, Daneborg 26. July 1945.
P105 Egil Amsjøs dagbog 1947-48, Kap Humboldt
P106 Amsjø, Egil: Dagbok 1949 - 1950, Ny Jonsbu
P107 Trygve Havolds dagbok 1947-49, Hoelsbu
P108 Per Myrvolds dagbog 1948-50, Hamna
P109 Martin Larsen Lie's dagbog 29/7-1947 - 9/8-1948, Hamna
P111 Birger Larsens dagbog 1949-50, Kap Humboldt
P112 Birger Larsens dagbog 1953-54, Myggbukta og Loch Fyne
P128 Levin Winthers dagbøger 1928-30, Krogness
P130 Karsten Sulebaks dagbog 29/7-1934 - 8/7-1936, Kap Peterséns
P131 Karsten Sulebaks dagbog 9/7-1936 - 31/8-1937, Kap Peterséns
P132 Peder Sulebaks dagbog 28/7-1934 - 24/8-1935, Antarctichavn
P133 Peder Sulebaks dagbog 21/7-1937 - 18/6-1939, Kap Peterséns
P134 Peder Sulebaks dagbok 1928-29, Jackson Stua
P135 Peder Sulebaks dagbok 1927-28, Elvsborg
P142 Peder Sulebaks dagbog 25/8-1935 - 5/8-1936, Antarctichavn
P143 Hans Madsens dagbog 10/8-1950 - 31/7-1952, Loch Fyne
P144 Stein Sørensens dagbog 7/8-1948 - 2/8-1949, Myggbukta
P145 Stein Sørensens dagbog 13/8-1949 - 10/8-1950, Myggbukta
P146 Stein Sørensens dagbog 10/8-1950 - 20/8-1951, Myggbukta
P147 Stein Sørensen dagbog 22/8-1952 - 18/8-1953, David Gray/Ottostrand

P148 Stein Sørensens dagbog 19/8-1953 - 25/8-1954, Kap Herschell
P149 Stein Sørensens dagbog 22/8-1955 - 20/8-1956, Myggbukta
P150 Dagbog ført af Iver Iversen, Alabamaekspeditionen 1909-12
P152 Christian Rasmussens dagbog 17/6 1923 - 27/4-1924
P153 Dagbog for August F. Nielsen. Ført af stationens sekretær, hofjægermester C. Larsen. Hvalrosoddens St. Grønland 1919-1921.
P154 Ove Simonsens dagbøger fra Treårsekspeditionen til Østgrønland 1931-33
P155 Sig. Tolløfsens Grønlandsekspedisjon 1932-34. Hovedstasjonen på Kunøya (Kapp Maurer), Sigurdsheimen. Fangstleder Johan Stordal. Dagbøkene er ført av Johs. Holmeslet.
P156 Arne Philbert. Dagbøger fra Nordøstgrønland 1932-37
P157 Bror Sandbergs dagbog. Grønland 1920-21

R103 Andresen, Hermann: Korrespondance
R108 Devold, Finn: Finn Devolds eksp. 1928-30
R109 Fangst- og fiskeekspedisjonen til Grønland 1933
R110 Foldvik, Niels, m.fl.: Foldvikekspedisjonen. Grønland
R111 Framnes Hansen, Finn: Grønland
R114 Gisvold, Arnulf: Grønland
R114 Giæver, John: Grønland
R114 Halle, Thor: Grønland
R114 Hansen, August: Grønland
R118 Herdal, Eiliv: Grønland
R118 Hird-ekspedisjonen, Grønland
R119 Ingstad, Helge: Grønland
R123 Karlsbak, Jonas: Grønland
R126 Landmarks overvintringseksp., Grønland
R128 Meyer Olsen: Grønland
R130 Møre-ekspedisjonen til Grønland. Nr. 1 1930
R135 Radiostasjoner og met. stasj. Østgrønland
R136 Rudi, Henry: Grønland
R137 Sivertsen, Ole: Grønland
R137 Smedal, Gustav: Grønland
R141 Tolløfsen, Sigurd: Ekspedisjonen til Grønland 1937-38. (1932-39)

U001 War Diary, USS Northland, CG

Ø001 Love for A/S Østgrønlandsk Kompagni, 1919
Ø002 Generalforhandlingsprotokol 1919-27
Ø030 Brev til udenrigsministeriet vedr. oversigt over kompagniets virksomhed
Ø035 Inventarlister fra stationerne A, B, C, E, F
Ø038 Jensen, Hans Ludvig: Beretning og Redegørelse for Danmarkshavns Station, 5/8-1919 - 13/8-1920
Ø039 Hans Ludvig Jensens beretning om en sejlads mellem Snenæs og Hvalrosodden
Ø040 Hans Ludvig Jensens rapporter (København 12/10-1921) og (Germaniahavn 21/8-1922)
Ø043 Jensen, Hans Ludvig: Journal 1922-23 samt breve til fangstlederne
Ø044 Kristen Larsens dagbogsuddrag fra Hvalrosodden 1919-21 og Bass Rock 1923-24
Ø045 Stjernebo, Hugo: Rapport fra Station A (Carlshavn)
Ø046 Nielsen, Hans: Stationsdagbog fra Germaniahavn 1919-20 og Shannon 1920-21
Ø047 Jæger Carl Meyers rapport om rævefangst på Kap Hold with Hope, (station B)
Ø048 Johan Petersens iagttagelser i Nordøstgrønland 1919-21 (Germaniahavn og Shannon)
Ø050 Oversigt over mandskab på stationer og skibe 1919-21
Ø054 Richter, Karl m.fl.: To erklæringer vedr. jæger Axel Christensens død

REFERENCES

Key to specific references and sources of quotations are indicated throughout the text with raised numbers. p.m.: personlig meddelelser / personal communication.

1 The World's greatest national park 1990 p. 1
2 http://www.statgreen.gl/
3 Traces - 4400 Years of Man in Greenland. Nuuk 2004 pp. 16-17
4 Asher 1860
5 Walthew 1971 p. 51
6 Jackson 2003 pp.xxvi-xxxii
7 ibid.
8 Edinburgh NPJ 1830 pp. 20-21
9 125 Jahre ... 1993 p. 9
10 Nathorst 1900 p. 357
11 Kjær 2006
12 Orléans 1911 pp. 27-49
13 A.K. Higgins e-mail 15th February 2008
14 www.zackenberg.dk
15 Gulløv 1991 p. 18
16 Giæver 1937 p. 23
17 ibid. p. 24
18 Blom 1973 p. 67
19 Giæver 1944 p. 39
20 A.K. Higgins e-mail 15th February 2008
21 Hareid Historielag 1974 p. 72
22 ibid. p. 7
23 ibid. p. 71
24 Love for A/S Østgrønlandsk Kompagni 1. § 2.
25 Devold 140 p. 110
26 Jennov 1939 p. 9
27 Jennov 1935
28 ibid. p. 61
29 ibid. p. 62
30 G129
31 Blom 1973, p.168
32 Kjær and Sefland 2005
33 Ministeriet for Videnskab, Teknologi og Udvikling. Udkast til Finansudvalget. September 2002.
34 "Hvid safari". Article in Danish newspaper BT, 7th November 1966
35 Aktstykker 1923
36 ibid. p. 24
37 Balchen 1944 p. 4; 1947 p. 15
38 Steen 1960 pp. 21-34
39 Brun 1985 p. 96
40 Balchen 1944 pp. 24-28
41 P 102
42 The Greenland Home Rule Authorities 1990
43 http://www.dpc.dk/sw444.asp
44 Ø048
45 Polarfronten nr. 3/oktober 2003 p. 16
46 Nathorst 1900 p. 302
47 N145
48 ibid.
49 ibid.
50 Rogne 1981, p.96
51 N145
52 ibid.
53 Ingstad letter to the author, 5th January 1993
54 Ingstad 1937 p. 23
55 ibid. 24
56 ibid. 92
57 ibid. 123
58 ibid. 268
59 Ingstad letter to the author, 4th September 1990
60 P142
61 ibid.
62 P101
63 ibid.
64 ibid.
65 ibid.
66 ibid.
67 ibid.
68 Polarboken 1949 p. 65
69 ibid. p. 67
70 Årsvold letter to the author, 6th March 1992
71 A136
72 Lie interview with author, 13th June 1992
73 P109
74 Lie interview with author, 13th June 1992
75 P108
76 P145
77 P108
78 ibid.
79 ibid.
80 Aasen interview with author, 7th August 1993
81 Polarboken 1963-64, p.104
82 Storholt interview with author, 13th June 1993
83 Lapstun interview with author, 15th September 1991
84 A168
85 Sæterdal interview with author, 7th July 1992 / Polarboken 1963-1964, p.105
86 Polarboken 1963-1964, p.105
87 ibid.
88 Sørlie interview with author, 4th April 1992
89 Feltrapport ... 2001; Feltrapport ... 2002.
90 Mikkelsen 1953 p. 145
91 Kjær 2005; http://journals.cambridge.org/action/dis playAbstract?fromPage=online&aid=3 24099
92 Mikkelsen 1953 pp. 145-178
93 P150
94 Ø046
95 Lund 1926 p. 52
96 Ø044
97 ibid.
98 ibid.
99 Orvin 1931 p. 387
100 Hvidberg 1932, p.134
101 Koch 1955 p. 85
102 Philbert interview with author, 1993
103 ibid.
104 Nyholm-Poulsen 1985 pp. 235-241
105 Edinburgh NPJ 1830 p. 17
106 Hareid Historielag 1974 p. 18
107 ibid. p. 51
108 Ø045
109 Tutein 1951 p. 59
110 ibid. p. 63
111 ibid. p. 63
112 ibid. p. 63
113 ibid. p. 62
114 ibid. p. 77
115 Jennov 1939 p. 18
116 R110
117 Tutein 1951 p. 69
118 Ø040
119 ibid.
120 Dahl 1925 pp. 45-46
121 N142
122 Polarboken 1965-1966 p. 30
123 N142
124 ibid.
125 NCN report 2007
126 Isachsen 1925 p. 146
127 Devold 1940 p. 107
128 NCN field report 2004
129 Payer 1877 p. 542
130 Sabine 1825 p. 161; Wordie 1927 p. 227
131 Giæver 1939 p. 15; Hareid Historielag 1984 pp. 7-30
132 N086
133 ibid.
134 Giæver 1944 p. 133
135 N086
136 Ø046
137 Madsen 1963 p. 60
138 Madsen 1989 p. 119
139 Ø043
140 Lund 1926 p. 14
141 ibid. p. 65
142 ibid. pp. 134-135
143 N143
144 A127
145 Hvidberg 1932 p. 11
146 A127
147 Hvidberg 1932 p. 43
148 Bartlett 1934 p. 202
149 A129
150 "Kyst, menneske og miljø i Nordøstgrønland". I: "Geografi 2005", published by The Royal Danish Geographical Society. pp. 12-14
151 Aune 1991 pp. 124-134

152 Steen 1960 p. 31
153 Aune 1991 pp. 135-167
154 A241
155 ibid.
156 ibid.
157 ibid.
158 ibid.
159 Hvidberg 1932 pp. 124-126
160 G118
161 Olsen 1965 pp. 78-79
162 Jens Berendt p.m. 16th September 1997
163 Nyholm-Poulsen 1985 p. 14
164 ibid. p. 11
165 Kristoffersen 1969 p. 9
166 ibid. p. 10
167 A151
168 ibid.
169 Hansen 1939 p. 39
170 ibid. p. 154
171 A244
172 ibid.
173 A147
174 ibid.
175 A244
176 A147
177 G109
178 "Slædeposten" nr. 77, 1988
179 Jennov, J.G.: "Faldt brikkerne på plads". In: "Jagt og Fiskeri". 20. December 1965 pp. 385-387.
180 G109
181 ibid.
182 ibid.
183 ibid.
184 ibid.
185 G101
186 ibid.
187 G125
188 G126
189 G102
190 ibid.
191 ibid.
192 Mikkelsen interview with author, 1992
193 ibid.
194 ibid.
195 A169
196 ibid.
197 A165
198 Frederiksen interview with author, 1992
199 A174
200 ibid.
201 ibid.
202 ibid.
203 Frederiksen interview with author, 1992
204 Nathorst 1900 p. 352
205 Orvin 1931 p. 381
206 Giæver 1931 p. 22
207 Polarboken 1963-1964 p. 125
208 N050
209 N077
210 ibid.
211 ibid.
212 Listhaug interview with author, 1992
213 ibid.
214 N075
215 ibid.
216 ibid.
217 ibid.
218 Giæver 1957 pp. 188-194
219 Bang 1944 p. 56
220 Ellen Danielsdottir interview with author 1993.
221 Petra Winther interview with author 1992.
222 Polarboken 1969-1970 p. 10
223 ibid. p. 11
224 ibid. p. 12
225 Polarboken 1979-1980 p. 110
226 Akre 1983 p. 109
227 P107
228 Free translation by the author
229 Trygve Havold interview with author, 1991
230 P107
231 Free translation by the author
232 N070
233 P145
234 N070
235 Knud Erik Filskov interview with author, 1992
236 P146
237 "Slædeposten" nr. 86/1991
238 Fredrik Sæterdal interview with author, 1992
239 ibid.
240 Birger Larsen interview with author, 1991
241 Helge Nesset interview with author, 1993
242 Odd Uthi interview with author, 1993
243 ibid.
244 P148
245 P149
246 Fredrik Sæterdal interview with author, 1992
247 P149
248 ibid.
249 ibid.
250 John Berg interview with author, 1991
251 NCN field reports 1999, 2000
252 Ø039
253 Ø044
254 Lauritsen 1984 p. 88
255 N082
256 Jennov 1939 p. 69
257 Newspaper "Fyns Amts Avis", 23rd July 1973 p. 11
258 "1000 km med Hundeslæde - Nordøstgrønland 1940" ved Niels Haarløv. Redigeret af Lars Christian Ingerslev (In preparation, June 2004)
259 A296
260 ibid.
261 Reindel interview with author, 1993
262 ibid.
263 Scoresby 1822 p. 104; Higgins 1997 p. 77
264 P135
265 N143
266 P135
267 Thorson 1937 pp. 211-212
268 Giæver 1939 p. 49
269 N082
270 ibid.
271 ibid.
272 ibid.
273 ibid.
274 R141
275 ibid.
276 ibid.
277 ibid.
278 ibid.
279 ibid.
280 ibid.
281 ibid.
282 ibid.
283 Life Magazine, October 24, 1942
284 U101
285 Ø047
286 Madsen 1963 p. 14
287 Ø047
288 Iver Ytreland interview with author, 1991
289 Polarboken 1965-1966 pp. 29-30
290 N032
291 ibid.
292 Ivar Ytreland interview with author, 1991
293 N032
294 Giæver 1930 p. 18
295 N057
296 ibid.
297 N033
298 ibid.
299 ibid.
300 N031
301 N061
302 N031
303 N027
304 ibid.
305 N026
306 N035
307 P101
308 N035
309 Polarboken 1963-1964 pp. 82-83
310 Ytreland interview with author, 1992
311 ibid.
312 Letter to author, 14th December 1990
313 ibid.
314 ibid.
315 Polarboken 1965-1966, pr. 39
316 ibid.
317 ibid. pp. 40-41
318 ibid.
319 A138
320 P145
321 P106
322 P145
323 Arvid Svoren interview with author, 1993
324 ibid.
325 Otto Lapstun interview with author, 1992

[326] P148
[327] ibid.
[328] ibid.
[329] P149
[330] Herman Ingebrigtsen interview with author, 1993
[331] ibid.
[332] ibid.
[333] Polarboken 1963-1964 pp. 104-105
[334] Scoresby 1823 p. 116
[335] Orvin 1930 p. 112
[336] N060
[337] N057
[338] Devold 1940 p. 128
[339] N060
[340] N057
[341] N060
[342] N051
[343] N048
[344] N055
[345] N075
[346] N055
[347] ibid.
[348] N084
[349] ibid.
[350] ibid.
[351] ibid.
[352] Ellen Danielsdottir interview with author, 1993
[353] ibid.
[354] Akre 1957 p. 11
[355] ibid. p. 31
[356] ibid. p. 93
[357] ibid. p. 94
[358] ibid. p. 96
[359] ibid. p. 98
[360] ibid. pp.102-103
[361] N090
[362] P105
[363] ibid.
[364] ibid.
[365] ibid.
[366] Birger Larsen interview with author, 1993
[367] P111
[368] ibid.
[369] ibid.
[370] Egil Grindflek interview with author, 1992
[371] ibid.
[372] N059
[373] ibid.
[374] ibid.
[375] ibid.
[376] ibid.
[377] ibid.
[378] Orvin 1934 p. 9
[379] Ingstad 1937 p. 98
[380] N030
[381] N049
[382] ibid.
[383] N030
[384] Orvin 1935 p. 2
[385] P132
[386] P130
[387] ibid.
[388] P131
[389] P101
[390] P133
[391] ibid.
[392] ibid.
[393] ibid.
[394] Karin Krogsæter interview with author, 1992
[395] NKN report 1997
[396] Edinburgh New Philosophical Journal, April-June 1830 p. 18
[397] Ø046
[398] P152
[399] Lund 1926 p. 144
[400] Orvin 1931 p. 387
[401] A241
[402] A129
[403] P101
[404] Hansen 1939 p. 101-105
[405] A286
[406] ibid.
[407] G104
[408] Carl El'Vibe interview with author, 1991
[409] Giæver 1957 pp. 156-157
[410] Hareid Historielag 1974 p. 10
[411] Orléans 1911 p. 40
[412] Devold 1940 p. 75
[413] Thomsen et al. 1998 pp. 4-12
[414] ibid. p. 73
[415] ibid. p. 108
[416] N142
[417] Sørensen 1958 p. 133
[418] Giæver 1957, p.189
[419] Orvin 1931, p.377-378
[420] N084
[421] ibid.
[422] ibid.
[423] Erskine and Kjaer 1998
[424] Knutsen 1992 p. 22; Knutsen 2005 p. 25
[425] ibid p. 26-27
[426] Halvorsen interview with author, 1992
[427] Knutsen 1992 p. 23
[428] ibid p. 51
[429] Pedersen 1969 p. 45
[430] ibid pp. 48-49
[431] ibid p. 50
[432] Ole Klokset interview with author, 1992
[433] ibid.
[434] Polarboken 1963-1964, p.118
[435] Giæver 1939 p. 24
[436] Hvidberg 1932 p. 35
[437] Edinburgh New Philosophical Journal, 1830 p. 23
[438] A135
[439] ibid.
[440] ibid.
[441] G130
[442] G105
[443] A137
[444] Ivar Ytreland interview with author, 1991
[445] G106
[446] G107
[447] ibid.
[448] A140
[449] G108
[450] A140
[451] Hans Madsen interview with author, 1992
[452] ibid.
[453] Knud Erik Filskov interview with author, 1993
[454] P143
[455] ibid.
[456] P143
[457] ibid.
[458] ibid.
[459] ibid.
[460] NCN report 1993
[461] Sirius team 2000-02
[462] NCN report 2007
[463] N054
[464] ibid.
[465] Sørensen 1958 p. 114
[466] N050
[467] ibid.
[468] Knutsen 1992 p. 102; Knutsen 2005 p. 126
[469] Polarboken 1963-1964 p. 118
[470] Knutsen 1992 p. 138; Knutsen 2005 p. 164
[471] Willie Knutsen interview with author, 1991
[472] R110
[473] N085
[474] Sørensen 1958 p. 83
[475] ibid. pp. 126-129
[476] ibid. p. 129
[477] ibid. pp. 129-130
[478] ibid. p. 144
[479] ibid, 144
[480] Devold 1940, p.144
[481] N061
[482] ibid.
[483] ibid.
[484] ibid.
[485] N027
[486] N028
[487] N026
[488] Bang 1944, p.138
[489] ibid. p. 137
[490] ibid. p. 144
[491] ibid. p. 140
[492] Fredrik Sæterdal interview with author, 1992
[493] Pantenburg 1944 p. 180
[494] Rodahl 1946 (1) p. 22
[495] Rodahl 1992 p. 9
[496] ibid. p. 10
[497] Rodahl 1946 (2) pp. 40-42
[498] Sørensen 1958 p. 194
[499] ibid. pp. 196-197
[500] Rodahl 1992 pp. 59-60
[501] Sørensen 1958 p. 201
[502] Giæver 1952 p. 371
[503] ibid. p. 204
[504] ibid. p. 209
[505] ibid. p. 211
[506] ibid. p. 213
[507] ibid. p. 220
[508] Norma Larsen interview with author, 1993
[509] ibid.
[510] ibid.

511 ibid.
512 Polarboken 1961-62 p. 88-101
513 P143
514 ibid.
515 Sverre Storholt interview with author, 1992
156 ibid.
517 ibid.
518 P111
519 P148
520 Viggo Block interview with author, 1993
521 ibid.
522 ibid.
523 NCN report 1994
524 Erik Jochumsen, Klaus Mynzberg Jensen, Kunuk Olsen Lennert, Martin Ove Jacobsen
525 R135
526 Devold 1940 p. 24
527 Polarårboken 133 p. 136
528 R110
529 Devold 1940 p. 93
530 ibid. p. 107
531 N085
532 Sørensen 1958 p. 127
533 ibid. p. 126
534 Devold 1940 p. 111
535 Orvin 1931 p. 387
536 N056
537 ibid.
538 Smedal 1934 pp. 123-124
539 Norsk Polarinstitutt
540 N056
541 N065
542 Devold 1940 pp. 143-144
543 ibid. pp. 146-147
544 Orvin 1934 p. 8
545 N053
546 ibid.
547 ibid.
548 Orvin 1934 p. 21
549 Giæver 1957 p. 203-204
550 Henry Haug interview with author 1993
551 ibid.
552 Polarboken 1965-66 p. 33
553 ibid. p. 36
554 Polarboken 1959-60 p. 78
555 Pantenburg 1944 p. 134
556 Giæver 1939 p. 36
557 Bang 1944 p. 60
558 Giæver 1957 p. 207
559 Bang 1944 p. 38
560 ibid.
561 Siewers 1983 p. 37
562 N90
563 Siewers 1983 p. 38
564 N090
565 Siewers interview with author, 1993
566 ibid.
567 Siewers 1983 p. 40
568 The Life Support Newsletter, May 98 edition, USAF
569 N090
570 ibid.
571 ibid.
572 ibid.
573 Polarboken 1949, p.53
574 Giæver 1952 p. 370
575 Ytreland interview with author, 1992
576 P144
577 ibid.
578 ibid.
579 ibid.
580 P145
581 ibid.
582 ibid.
583 P145
584 P146
585 ibid.
586 ibid.
587 ibid.
588 ibid.
589 P143
590 Storholt interview with author, 1992
591 ibid.
592 P112
593 ibid.
594 Helge Nesset interview with author, 1992
595 ibid.
596 P149
597 ibid.
598 ibid.
599 ibid.
600 Hans Oddvik interview with author, 1993
601 ibid.
602 ibid.
603 Polarboken 1959-60 pp. 69-71
604 Elander 1992
605 Dennis Carter, unpublished expedition report, November 1992
606 NCN reports 1999 and 2002
607 A133
608 A244
609 Slædeposten nr. 77, 1988
610 Olsen 1965 p. 105
611 G123
612 Slædeposten nr. 77, 1988
613 G123
614 A134
615 Slædeposten nr. 77, 1988
616 G123
617 G124
618 Ivar Ytreland interview with author, 1992
619 Mogens Graae interview with author, 1992
620 ibid.
621 ibid.
622 ibid.
623 ibid.
624 Mogens Graae's obituary
625 A169
626 ibid.
627 NCN report 2003 pp. 16-17
628 Bjarne Myrvold interview with author, 1991
629 ibid.
630 ibid.
631 P106
632 ibid.
633 Bjarne Myrvold interview with author, 1991
634 Anne Marit Myrvold comm. 2007
635 NCN report 1995
636 N080
637 ibid.
638 ibid.
639 ibid.
640 ibid.
641 ibid.
642 ibid.
643 N082
644 ibid.
645 ibid.
646 ibid.
647 Munck 1959 pp. 130-131
648 N069
649 P106
650 ibid.
651 ibid.
652 ibid.
653 Fredrik Sæterdal interview with author, 1992
654 ibid.
655 ibid.
656 P147
657 Ivar Ytreland interview with author, 1992
658 P147
659 ibid.
660 ibid.
661 Higgins 1997 p. 143; Scoresby 1823 p. 104
662 Ø043
663 ibid.
664 Dahl 1925 p. 68
665 Hvidberg 1932 p. 81
666 Lund 1926 p. 135
667 A127
668 Jennov 1939 p. 10
669 A129
670 Lauritsen 1984 p. 108
671 ibid., 117
672 A129
673 A129
674 ibid.
675 N033
676 Drastrup 1932 pp. 11-12
677 P101
678 N035
679 Jennov 1939 p. 69
680 A286
681 Jennov 1939 pp. 81-82
682 Giæver 1937a p. 5
683 A286
684 G104
685 ibid.
686 ibid.
687 Foreningsbladet "Garderhusaren" 11/1989
688 A134
689 Sørensen 1958 p. 207
690 Peter Nielsen interview with author, 1993
691 A149
692 ibid.
693 G113

694 A137
695 ibid.
696 G102
697 ibid.
698 G111
699 ibid.
700 ibid.
701 ibid.
702 ibid.
703 ibid.
704 Giæver 1957 pp. 215-221
705 Devold 1940 p. 12
706 R141
707 ibid.
708 N027
709 N052
710 Nyholm-Poulsen 1985 pp. 117-118
711 ibid.
712 ibid.
713 ibid.
714 Nyholm-Poulsen 1985 pp. 185-186
715 ibid., pp.199-200
716 N027 p. 9
717 Iver Ytreland interview with author, 1991
718 P155
719 Tommy Pedersen e-mail 1st January 2004
720 Nathorst 1900 p. 293
721 N050
722 N030
723 Jens Mathiesen e-mail 9th May 2007
724 E-mail from Erik Borup Larsen, 13th 2002 & 27th May 2007
725 Tutein 1951, p. 90
726 Bistrup 1924 p. 19
727 R110
728 ibid.
729 R110
730 Unpublished report "Tilstandsrapport for "Villaen" i Danmarkshavn. Sommeren 2006"
731 Unpublished report "Tilstandsrapport for "Villaen" i Danmarkshavn. Sommeren 2006"
732 G103
733 G130
734 A135
735 Harald Mikkelsen interview with author in 1992
736 ibid.
737 G119
738 Harald Mikkelsen interview with author in 1992
739 ibid.
740 ibid.
741 ibid.
742 ibid.
743 ibid.
744 ibid.
745 Obituary, Berlingske Tidende, 5th May 2002
746 Berlingske Tidende, 5th May 2002
747 G111
748 Harald Mikkelsen interview with author, 1992
749 Hans Frederiksen interview with author, 1992
750 A140
751 ibid.
752 Hans Frederiksen interview with author, 1992
753 ibid.
754 A168
755 Ib Palle Madsen interview with author, 1993
756 A175
757 ibid.
758 ibid.
759 ibid.
760 ibid.
761 Magazine "Naturens Verden" 1992 No. 8
762 NCN report 1991
763 A133
764 A244
765 A133
766 Olsen 1965 p. 19
767 P156
768 Richard Nielsen interview with author, 1993
769 ibid.
770 ibid.
771 ibid.
772 A140
773 ibid.
774 G121
775 A142
776 Sirius team 1997-99
777 Thomas Hansen, e-mail 5th January 2008
778 Knuth 1940 p. 43
779 Knuth 1942 p. 51
780 Pedersen 1940 p. 10
781 Simpson 1957 pp. 155, 352-354
782 P102
783 ibid.
784 ibid.
785 G102
786 Rysgaard et al. 2007, p 9
787 Slædeposten nr. 6/1964
788 Nuna-Tek, August 1988
789 ibid.
790 ibid.
791 Olsen 1965, pp.65-66
792 Thorson 1937 p. 58
793 Koch 1955 p. 295
794 Thorson 1937 p. 47
795 Koch 1955 p. 284
796 Thorson 1937 p. 47
797 Thorson 1937, pp.48-53
798 Howarth 1957 p. 131
799 Weiss 1949 p. 113
800 Nusser 1979 p. 55
801 Franz Selinger p.m. 1993
802 Balchen 1944 pp. 27-28
803 NCN report 1998
804 Selinger 2001 p. 202
805 P102
806 Koch 1955 pp. 290-91
807 Andreasen & Elling 1990 pp. 46-47
808 Kristoffersen 1969 p. 58
809 Knuth 1940 p. 9
810 ibid. p. 11
811 Knuth 1942 p. 48
812 ibid. p. 155
813 Friis 1909 p. 489
814 Freuchen 1936 pp. 13-14
815 Ø044
816 Knuth 1940 p. 196
817 Peter Schmidt Mikkelsen, e-mail December 2006
818 Nanok (JMS, OSN, TEJ) 12th August 2006
819 Ingstad 1935 p. 147. Ingstad 1937 p. 215
820 P132
821 Otto Lapstun p.m. 1992
822 Henning Thing p.m. 1993; Otto Lapstun p.m. 1992.
823 Nanok (JMS, LAB, OSN) 4th August 2004
824 Jan Juel-Brockdorff p.m. 1993
825 Nanok (JMS, LAB, OSN) 4th August 2004
826 Ingstad 1935 pp. 16-20. Ingstad 1937 pp. 24-30
827 Orvin 1934, p.10
828 P101
829 P142
830 Beskrivelse ... 1932 p. 19. Description ... 1932 p. 30
831 Bjørn Thomassen p.m. 1993
832 Nanok (JMS, LAB, OSN) 3rd August 2004
833 Orvin 1934, p.10
834 Ingstad 1935 p. 23. Ingstad 1937 pp. 35-36
835 Nanok (JMS, LAB, OSN) 3rd August 2004
836 Bjørn Thomassen p.m. 1993
837 Nanok (JMS, LAB, OSN) 3rd August 2004
838 Koch 1955 pp. 285-299
839 Otto Lapstun p.m. 1992
840 Nanok (JMS, LAB, OSN) 4th August 2004
841 Ingstad 1935, map
842 Nanok (JMS, LAB, OSN) 4th August 2004
843 Orvin 1934 p. 11
844 Ingstad 1935 p. 16. Ingstad 1937 p. 24
845 Otto Lapstun p.m. 1991
846 Nanok (JMS, LAB, OSN) 3rd August 2004
847 N059
848 N034
849 Nanok (JMS, OSN, TEJ) 13th August 2006
850 Ingstad 1935, map
851 Ottar Årsvold p.m. 1992
852 Nanok (JMS, OSN, TEJ) 13th August 2006
853 Ingstad 1935, map
854 P132
855 P101
856 P109
857 Otto Lapstun p.m. 1991
858 Otto Lapstun p.m. 1992; Bjørn Thomassen p.m. 1993
859 Nanok (JMS, OSN, TEJ) 13th August 2006

860 N059 p. 85
861 N034 p. 99
862 Otto Lapstun p.m. 1991
863 Nanok (JMS, LAB, OSN) 3rd August 2004
864 Otto Lapstun p.m. 1991
865 Nanok (JMS, LAB, OSN) 3rd August 2004
866 Otto Lapstun p.m. 1991
867 Norsk Polarklubb 1964 p. 99
868 Scoresby 1823 p. 272
869 Nanok (TEJ) 14th August 2006
870 Ingstad 1935, map
871 P101
872 Otto Lapstun p.m. 1991
873 Nanok (JMS, LAB, OSN) 3rd August 2004
874 Ib Poulsen p.m. 1992
875 Jørgen Tvermose p.m. 1992
876 Scoresby 1823 p. 272
877 Nanok (JMS, LAB, OSN) 5th August 2004
878 N034
879 Orvin 1930 p. 383
880 N145
881 Scoresby 1823 p. 248
882 V. Brinch p. 171-179; Bjørn Thomassen p.m. 1993.
883 Greenland Mineral Resources, Fact Sheet No. 11. GEUS 2005.
884 Nanok (JMS, LAB, OSN) 5th August 2004
885 Nanok (JMS, MES) 18th August 2006
886 Bjørn Thomassen p.m. 1993
887 Nanok (JMS, MES) 18th August 2006
888 Nanok (JMS, LAB, OSN) 2nd August 2004
889 Otto Lapstun p.m. 1991
890 Nanok 2nd August 2004
891 891 Orvin 1931 p. 383
892 Nanok (JES, MOL) 26th July 2003
893 N034
894 N145
895 Nanok (JES, MOL) 26th July 2003 / (JMS, MES) 17th August 2006
896 Tusaat 1992 p. 61
897 Bjørn Thomassen p.m. 1993
898 Nanok (JES, MOL) 26th July 2003 / (JMS, MES) 17th August 2006
899 Nanok (JMS, OSN, TEJ) 16th August 2006.
900 Nanok (JES, MOL) 26th July 2003 / (OSN, CZJ) 17th August 2006
901 N034
902 N145
903 Otto Lapstun p.m. 1991
904 Nanok (JES, MOL) 26th July 2003
905 Nanok (JMS, OSN, TEJ) 10th August 2006
906 Nanok (JMS, OSN, TEJ) 10th August 2006
907 Nanok (JMS, OSN, TEJ) 16th August 2006
908 A.K. Higgins p.m. 1993
909 Nanok (JMS, OSN) 15th August 2006
910 Nanok (JMS) 24th August 2003
911 P132
912 Nanok (JES, MOL) 27th July 2003
913 N145
914 N059
915 Nanok (OSN, TEJ) 9th August 2004
916 Norwegian Polarklubb 1966 p. 147
917 Nanok (JMS, OSN) 24th July 2003
918 Orvin 1931 p. 383
919 N059
920 Nanok (JMS) 23rd July 2003
921 N034
922 Orvin 1931 p. 382
923 N059
924 Nanok (JMS, OSN, TEJ) 9th August 2006
925 Olsen 1965
926 Nanok (JES, MOL) 28th July 2003
927 Nanok (JMB, NFS) 24th August 2004
928 N034
929 N059
930 Nanok (JMS, NFS, OSN) 23rd August 2003
931 N059
932 Rogne 1981 p. 97. N034
933 Nanok (JMS, OSN, TEJ) 8th August 2006
934 Nanok (JMS, OSN, TEJ) 8th August 2006
935 Orvin 1930 p. 120
936 N057
937 Giæver 1939 p. 38
938 Orvin 1934 p. 9
939 NCN field report 2001
940 Nanok (ML) 28th July 2003
941 N059
942 Orvin 1931 p. 383
943 Nanok (JMS, OSN, TEJ) 8th August 2006
944 Ingstad 1935
945 P132
946 P108
947 Nanok (JMS, OSN, TEJ) 8th August 2006
948 Halvor Bjørdal p.m. 1993
949 NCN field report 2001
950 Nanok (JMS, LAB, OSN) 1st August 2004
951 N056
952 N054
953 Nanok (JMS, LAB, OSN) 1st August 2004
954 Nanok (JMS, LAB, OSN) 1st August 2004
955 Description ... 1932 p. 21
956 Koch 1955 p. 507
957 N054
958 Nanok (JMS, NFS, OSN) 1st August 2003
959 N055; N048
960 N030
961 Nanok (JMS, LAB, OSN) 1st August 2004
962 N056
963 N054
964 Lacmann 1937
965 Nanok (JMS, NFS, OSN) 1st August 2003
966 N055
967 N030
968 Nanok (JMS, NFS, OSN) 1st August 2003
969 Sirius p.m.
970 Nanok (JMS, OSN, TEJ) 8th August 2006
971 P142
972 P108
973 Nanok (JMS, OSN, TEJ) 8th August 2006
974 P131; P133
975 Magne Råum p.m. 1993
976 Giæver 1939 p. 48
977 P108
978 Nanok (JMS, LAB, OSN) 31st July 2004
979 Nanok (JMS, LAB, OSN) 31st July 2004
980 N054
981 N056
982 Orvin 1930 p. 119
983 Nanok (JMS, LAB, OSN) 31st July 2004
984 N054
985 N056
986 Orvin 1930 p. 119
987 N030
988 Scoresby 1823 p. 247
989 Nanok (JES, MOL) July 2003 & (KRN, HEN, STH) July 2007
990 Nanok (JES, MOL) 13th August 2003
991 Nanok (JMS, LAB, OSN) 31st July 2004
992 N054
993 Orvin 1930 p. 117
994 N056
995 Nanok (JMS, NFS, OSN) 2nd August 2003
996 N055
997 N030
998 Nanok (JMS, NFS, OSN) 10th August 2003
999 Ib Poulsen interview with author, 1992
1000 Hans Siewers letter to author, 25 October 1991
1001 Nanok (JMS, NFS, OSN) 10th August 2003
1002 Koch 1955 p. 288
1003 Ove Hermansen p.m. 1993
1004 Nanok (JMS, OSN) 14th August 2003
1005 Ib Poulsen letter to author, 31st March 1992
1006 Koch 1955 p. 289
1007 Ib Poulsen letter to author, 31st March 1992

1008 Nanok (JMS, NFS, OSN) 13th August 2003
1009 Orvin 1930 p. 116; N057; N054
1010 N060
1011 Nanok (JES, MOL) 11th August 2003; (JMS, OSN, TEJ) 7th August 2006
1012 Nanok (JMS, OSN, TEJ) 8th August 2006
1013 Orvin 1930 p. 116; N057; N054
1014 N060
1015 Nanok (JMS, OSN, TEJ) 8th August 2006
1016 Devold 1940 p. 126
1017 N050; N057; N064
1018 N088
1019 Nanok (JES, MOL) 13th August 2003; (JMS, OSN, TEJ) 6th August 2006
1020 Orvin 1930 p. 116
1021 N057
1022 Nanok (MOL) 13th August 2003
1023 N055
1024 N030
1025 Nanok (JES, MOL) 13th August 2003; (JMS, OSN, TEJ) 6th August 2006
1026 N057
1027 N060
1028 N051
1029 Nanok (JES, MOL) 13th August 2003; (JMS, OSN, TEJ) 6th August 2006
1030 Orvin 1930 p. 116
1031 N057
1032 Nanok (JES, MOL) 11th August 2003; (JMS, OSN, TEJ) 7th August 2006
1033 Nanok (JES, MOL) 2nd August 2003
1034 NSIU 1945 p. 16
1035 Akre 1957 p. 21
1036 Nanok (JES, MOL) 1st August 2003
1037 N055; N030
1038 Magne Råum p.m. 1990
1039 Nanok (JMS, OSN) 11th August 2003
1040 N057; N064
1041 Nanok (JES, MOL) 2nd August 2003
1042 Akre 1957 p. 17
1043 Nanok (KRN, HEN, STH) 6th August 2007
1044 P111
1045 Nanok (JES, MOL) 1st August 2003
1046 NSIU 1945 p. 16
1047 Akre 1957 p. 21
1048 Payer 1877 p. 612-621
1049 Nanok (JMS, OSN) 11th August 2003
1050 N057
1051 Nanok (JMS, LAB, OSN) 27th July 2004
1052 NSIU 1945 p. 11
1053 Hans Siewers p.m. 1992
1054 Nanok (JMS, OSN) 11th August 2003
1055 N057
1056 Nanok (JMS, OSN) 11th August 2003
1057 N057
1058 Nanok (JMS, LAB, OSN) 27th July 2004
1059 N085; R110
1060 Higgins 1997 p. 81; Scoresby 1823 p. 116
1061 Nathorst 1900 p. 363
1062 Nanok (JMS, NFS) 10th August 2003
1063 Orvin 1931 p. 380
1064 Devold 1940 p. 125
1065 Nanok (JMS, OSN) 10th August 2003
1066 N060
1067 Nanok (JMS, OSN) 10th August 2003
1068 Orvin 1934 p. 18
1069 N051
1070 Nanok (JES, MOL) 10th August 2003
1071 Pedersen 1969 p. 50
1072 Nanok (KRN, HEN, STH) 8th August 2007
1073 Nanok (MOL, JES)
1074 Ole Klokset p.m. 1991
1075 Trygve Havold p.m. 1991
1076 Nanok (JES, MOL) 3rd August & BID 2007
1077 N054
1078 Orvin 1930 p. 128
1079 N060
1080 Devold 1940 p. 122
1081 Devold 1940 p. 122
1082 NCN field report 2002
1083 Nanok (JES, MOL) 17th August 2003
1084 Orvin 1934 p. 3
1085 N144
1086 Nanok (JMS, LAB, OSN) 27th July 2004
1087 Nanok (JMS, LAB, OSN) 29th July 2004
1088 N085
1089 Higgins 1997 p. 80; Scoresby 1823 p. 117
1090 Nanok (JMS, NFS) 10th August 2003
1091 Giæver 1931 p. 84
1092 Nanok (JMS, LAB, OSN) 29th July 2004
1093 P146
1094 Nanok (JMS, LAB, OSN) 29th July 2004
1095 Devold 1940 p. 87
1096 N085
1097 Nanok (JMS, LAB, OSN) 28th July 2004
1098 A135
1099 Nanok (RG) 1st August 2005
1100 N065
1101 N061
1102 Bang 1944 p. 96
1103 Peter Melleby p.m. 1992
1104 Nanok (RG) 1st August 2005
1105 Bang 1944 p. 92-97
1106 Nanok (JES, MOL) 17th August 2003
1107 J.D. Friderichsen p.m. 1993
1108 Birger Larsen p.m. 1991
1109 Nanok (JMS, LAB, OSN) 28th July 2004
1110 Nanok (JMS, LAB, OSN) 29th July 2004
1111 Nanok (JMS, NFS) 10th August 2003
1112 Orvin 1931 p. 380
1113 Giæver 1931 p. 82
1114 Nanok (JES, MOL) 6th August 2003 & BID 2007
1115 Orvin 1937 p. 3
1116 Magne Råum p.m. 1990
1117 Nanok (JMS, LAB, OSN) 28th July 2004
1118 A135
1119 A140
1120 Nanok (JMS, LAB, OSN) 28th July 2004
1121 N085
1122 Devold 1940 p. 108
1123 Drastrup 1956 p. 35
1124 Nanok (JMS, NFS, OSN) 7th August 2003 & BID 2007
1125 Orvin 1934 p. 4
1126 N075
1127 Johan Listhaug p.m. 1991
1128 NCN field report 2000
1129 NCN field report 2000 p. 12
1130 Nanok (JMS, NFS, OSN) 6th August 2003 & Nanok (KRN, HEN, STH) 28th July 2007 & BID 2007
1131 Orvin 1930 p. 132
1132 P128
1133 Nanok (JMS, MOL) 8th August 2003
1134 Johan Listhaug p.m. 1992
1135 Nanok (CHA, KOL, RAG) 21st July 2005
1136 N085
1137 R110
1138 Nanok (RG) 1st August 2005
1139 Willie Knutsen p.m. 1992
1140 Trygve Havold p.m. 1991
1141 Nanok (JMS, NFS, OSN) 6th August 2003 & Nanok (KRN, HEN, STH) 28th July 2007
1142 Orvin 1930 p. 132
1143 P128
1144 Nanok (CHA, KOL, RAG) 21st July 2005
1145 A134
1146 A151
1147 Nanok (JMS, NFS, OSN) 6th August 2003 & Nanok (KRN, HEN, STH) 28th July 2007 & BID 2007
1148 Orvin 1931 p. 381
1149 N077
1150 Petra Winther p.m. 1991
1151 Trygve Havold p.m. 1991
1152 Nanok (JMS, NFS)

9th August 2003
1153 Orvin 1931 p. 381
1154 Giæver 1931 p. 80
1155 Nanok (KMJ, ERJ, SØA) 9th August 2003
1156 Description ... 1932 pp. 8, 39
1157 N085
1158 R110
1159 P149
1160 Robert Burton & Dennis Carter p.m. 1992.
1161 Nanok (KMJ, ERJ, SØA) 9th August 2003 & BID 2007
1162 Nanok (KMJ, ERJ, SØA) 9th August 2003
1163 Willie Knutsen p.m. 1991.
1164 Nanok (CHA, KOL, RAG) 6th August 2005
1165 Nanok (CHA, KOL, RAG) 6th August 2005
1166 G105
1167 Nanok (ML, NFS) 8th August 2003
1168 NSIU 1945 p. 16
1169 Fredrik Sæterdal p.m. 1992.
1170 Nanok (KMJ, ERJ, SØA) 10th August 2003
1171 Nanok (JMS, NFS, OSN) 6th August 2003 & BID 2007
1172 Nanok (JMS, NFS, OSN) 6th August 2003
1173 N056
1174 ibid.
1175 Trygve Havold p.m. 1991.
1176 Nanok (JES) 7th August 2003
1177 N056
1178 N030; N055; N075
1179 Nanok (JES) 7th August 2003
1180 Nanok (JES) 7th August 2003 & BID 2007
1181 Koch 1955 p. 284-299; Thorson 1937 p. 55.
1182 Nanok (JES) 7th August 2003 & BID 2007
1183 Orvin 1934 p. 9;N030; N055; N075
1184 Bang 1944 p. 51
1185 Fredrik Sæterdal p.m. 1992
1186 John Berg p.m. 1992
1187 Nanok (CHA, KOL, RAG) 4th August 2005
1188 Jennov 1939 p. 89; Giæver 1939 p. 37
1189 A133
1190 ibid.
1191 Nanok (CHA, KOL, RAG) 4th August 2005
1192 Willie Knutsen p.m. 1992
1193 Nanok (CHA, KOL, RAG) 4th August 2005
1194 Jennov 1939 p. 89; Giæver 1939 p. 37
1195 A133
1196 Nanok (CHA, KOL, RAG) 1st August 2005
1197 G105; Carl El'Vibe p.m. 1991
1198 Nanok (CHA, KOL, RAG) 1st August 2005
1199 Giæver 1939 pp. 48
1200 Willie Knutsen p.m. 1992
1201 G105
1202 Carl El'Vibe p.m. 1993
1203 Nanok (CHA, KOL, RAG) 22nd July 2005
1204 Hans Madsen p.m. 1992
1205 Scoresby 1823 p. 104
1206 Nanok (CHA, KOL, RAG) 22nd July 2005
1207 Nanok (NFS, JMS) 9th August 2003
1208 NSIU 1945 p. 16
1209 Ole Klokset p.m. 1992
1210 Trygve Havold p.m. 1991
1211 Nanok (KMJ, ERJ, SØA) 9th August 2003 & Nanok (ABP, HHC, JUS) 4th August 2007 & BID 2007
1212 R110; Beskrivelse av de norske fangststasjoner 1932 ... p. 7
1213 Devold 1940 p. 83; Helge Nesset p.m. 1992.
1214 Nanok (KMJ, ERJ, SØA) 9th August 2003 & Nanok (ABP, HHC, JUS) 4th August 2007 & BID 2007
1215 Helge Nesset p.m. 1992.
1216 Nanok (NFS, MOL) 8th August 2003
1217 Orvin 1937 p. 3
1218 P101
1219 Nanok (KMJ, ERJ, SØA) 11th August 2003
1220 Devold 1940 p. 75; N085
1221 N033
1222 Nanok (KMJ, ERJ, SØA) 8th August 2003 & BID 2007
1223 A159
1224 Nanok (CHA, KOL, RAG) 22nd July 2005
1225 Nanok (KMJ, ERJ, SØA) 11th August 2003
1226 Description ... 1932 p. 17
1227 Nanok (KMJ, ERJ, SØA) 9th August 2003
1228 Giæver 1955 pp. 41-42; Giæver 1958 p. 38
1229 Devold 1940 p. 83
1230 P145
1231 Sverre Storholt p.m. 1991; Helge Nesset p.m. 1992.
1232 Nanok (KMJ, ERJ, SØA) 11th August 2003
1233 Devold 1940 p. 83
1234 Description ... 1932 p. 9; R110
1235 Nanok (CHA, KOL, RAG) 3rd August 2005
1236 A141; 159
1237 Hans Madsen p.m. 1992
1238 Nanok (CHA, KOL, RAG) 3rd August 2005
1239 Nanok (KMJ, ERJ, SØA) 8th August 2003 & BID 2007
1240 Willie Knutsen p.m. 1992
1241 Knutsen 1992 p. 37; Knutsen 2005 p. 46
1242 Peter Melleby p.m. 1992
1243 Hans Oddvik p.m. 1992
1244 Nanok (KMJ, ERJ, SØA) 9th August 2003
1245 Nanok (KMJ, ERJ, SØA) 7th August 2003
1246 Devold 1940 p. 108
1247 Description ... 1932 p. 12; R110.
1248 Nanok (KMJ, ERJ, SØA) 7th August 2003
1249 N069
1250 Birger Larsen p.m. 1991
1251 Nanok (KMJ, ERJ, SØA) 10h August 2003
1252 Nanok (ABP, HHC, JUS) 21st July 2007 & BID 2007
1253 Bang 1944 p. 145
1254 Koch 1955 p. 76; Ib Poulsen p.m. 1992
1255 Nanok (KMJ, ERJ, SØA) 6th August 2003
1256 Nanok (KMJ, ERJ, SØA) 6th August 2003
1257 Nanok (KMJ, ERJ, SØA) 8th August 2003 & Nanok (ABP, HHC, JUS) 21st July 2007
1258 R110; Description ... 1932 p. 11; Bang 1944 p. 145
1259 Lauritz Storholt p.m. 1991
1260 Nanok (KMJ, ERJ, SØA) 8th August 2003 & Nanok (ABP, HHC, JUS) 21st July 2007 & BID 2007
1261 P148
1262 Sverre Storholt p.m. 1992
1263 Higgins 1997 p. 78
1264 Nanok (KMJ, ERJ, SØA) 6th August 2003& Nanok (ABP, HHC, JUS) 12th August 2007
1265 Giæver 1939 p. 15; Description ... 1932 p. 6.
1266 N086
1267 Nanok (KMJ, ERJ, SØA) 6th August 2003 & Nanok (ABP, HHC, JUS) 12th August 2007
1268 Nanok (KMJ, ERJ, SØA) 8th August 2003 & Nanok (ABP, HHC, JUS) 4h August 2007
1269 Description ... 1932 p. 11; R111
1270 Nanok (KMJ, ERJ, SØA) 8th August 2003 & Nanok (ABP, HHC, JUS) 4th August 2007
1271 Norma Larsen p.m. 2007
1272 Nanok (KMJ, ERJ, SØA) 6th August 2003
1273 Ivar Ytreland p.m. 1991
1274 Claus Birkbøll p.m. 1993
1275 Nanok (ABP, HHC, JUS) 21st July 2007
1276 N084
1277 Nanok (KMJ, ERJ, SØA) 8th August 2003 & Nanok (ABP, HHC, JUS) 21st July 2007
1278 Description ... 1932 p. 12; R111
1279 Bang 1944 p. 185; Sverre Storholt

p.m. 1992
1280 Nanok (ABP, HHC, JUS) 21st July 2007
1281 Sverre Storholt p.m. 1992
1282 Nanok (KMJ, ERJ, SØA) 11th August 2003
1283 Bendt Nielsen p.m. 1992
1284 Carl El'Vibe p.m. 1991
1285 Nanok (KMJ, ERJ, SØA) 3rd August 2003
1286 Jennov 1939 p. 26; A241; G103
1287 Nanok (KMJ, ERJ, SØA) 30th July 2003
1288 Nanok (CHA, KOL, RAG) 27th July 2005
1289 G101; G113
1290 G119
1291 Harald Mikkelsen p.m. 1992
1292 Nanok (KMJ, ERJ, SØA) 29th July 2003
1293 A129; G103
1294 N031; N035
1295 Nanok (ABP, HHC, JUS) 21st July 2007
1296 Devold 1940 p. 108; R110; Orvin 1930 p. 142; Description ... 1932 p. 12.
1297 Nanok (ERJ, PSM, SØK) 6th August 2004
1298 Nanok (ERJ, PSM, SØK) 6th August 2004
1299 Nanok (ERJ, PSM, SØK) 6th August 2004
1300 Erik Jensen p.m. 1992
1301 Bendt Nielsen p.m. 1992
1302 Nanok (CHA, KOL, RAG) 25th July 2005
1303 P102
1304 Alfred Hansen p.m. 1991
1305 Carl El'Vibe p.m. 1991
1306 Nanok (ABP, HHC, JUS) 25th July 2007
1307 G119
1308 Nanok (ERJ, PSM, SØK) 6th August 2004
1309 N033
1310 N035
1311 Ivar Ytreland p.m. 1992
1312 Nanok (PSM) 8th July 2007
1313 Nanok (PSM) 8th July 2007
1314 Nanok (PSM) 8th July 2007
1315 Nanok (KMJ, SØA) 14th August 2004
1316 Nanok (KMJ, ERJ, SØA) 8th August 2003
1317 N061
1318 Bang 1944 p. 138
1319 Nanok (KMJ, ERJ, SØA) 25th August 2003
1320 A129; G103; Jennov 1939 p. 26
1321 Nanok (CHA, KOL, RAG) 25th July 2005
1322 G113
1323 Nanok (KMJ, ERJ, SØA) 25th July 2003 & BID 2007
1324 Nanok (CHA, KOL, RAG) 25th July 2005
1325 Ivar Ytreland p.m. 1990
1326 Nils-Martin Hankens archive
1327 Nanok (SA) 21st August 2003
1328 N143; P134
1329 N035; P101
1330 Ivar Ytreland p.m. 1992
1331 Nanok (CHA, KOL, RAG) 26th July 2005
1332 A149; Harald Mikkelsen p.m. 1992.
1333 Nanok (KMJ, ERJ, SØA) 24th August 2003
1334 A130; Jennov 1939 p. 57
1335 Nanok (KMJ, ERJ) 23rd August 2003
1336 NSIU 1945 p. 16; Sørensen 1958 p. 192
1337 Description ... 1932 p. 13
1338 Nanok (KMJ, ERJ, SØA) 25th July 2003 & BID 2007
1339 Devold 1940 p. 108; Description ... 1932 p. 13; R110
1340 Nanok (ABP, HHC, JUS) 25th July 2007
1341 Orvin 1930 p. 142; Description ... 1932 p. 13; R110
1342 Nanok (KMJ, ERJ, SØA) 25th July 2003
1343 N027
1344 Orvin 1934 pp. 15, 18; Giæver 1939 p. 48
1345 Nanok (RG) 26th August 2005
1346 Drastrup 1932 p. 110-117; Jennov 1939 p. 26
1347 G103
1348 A148; G104
1349 A163
1350 Nanok (KMJ, ERJ, SØA) 27th July 2003
1351 Nanok (KMJ, ERJ, SØA) 27th July 2003
1352 Dansk Pearyland Ekspedition 1947 p. 4-5; Dansk Pearyland Ekspedition 1947b; Dansk Pearyland Ekspedition 1948
1353 Simpson 1957
1354 Nanok (KMJ, ERJ, SØA) 27th July 2003
1355 Norwegian Polarklubb 1966 p. 51; Ivar Ytreland p.m. 1992
1356 Nanok (MOH, NGM, OLS, PSM) 9th July 2007
1357 Nanok (CHA, KOL, RAG) 2005
1358 Description ... 1932 p. 13; R110; Orvin 1930 p. 142
1359 Devold 1940 p. 108
1360 Giæver 1939 p. 48
1361 Thomsen et al. 1998 pp. 4-12
1362 Nanok (KMJ, ERJ, SØA) 25th July 2003
1363 Sørensen 1958 p. 129
1364 Description ... 1932 p. 17
1365 Orvin 1930 p. 143
1366 Nanok (ERJ, PSM, SØK) 6th August 2004
1367 Nanok (ERJ, PSM, SØK) 6th August 2004
1368 Description ... 1932 p. 5
1369 Nanok (ERJ, PSM, SØK) 6th August 2004
1370 Nanok (ERJ, PSM, SØK) 23rd August 2004
1371 Jennov 1939 p. 116, 123;
1372 Hvidberg 1932 p. 23; Ø061
1373 P135
1374 Hvidberg 1932 p. 143; Jennov 1939 p. 123; A144
1375 G102; A138 (6/8-1948)
1376 Nathorst 1900 p. 97; Giæver 1944 pp. 23, 90
1377 Nanok (KMJ, ERJ) 22nd August 2003 / Nanok (LAK, RAG) 23rd August 2005
1378 Jennov 1939 p. 89; A133; A148 Nanok (CHA, KOL, RAG) 29th July 2005
1380 R141
1381 R141
1382 A175
1383 Nanok (RG) 21st August 2005
1384 A162; A181
1385 Nanok (RG) 25th August 2005
1386 A133; A148; A181; G104
1387 Nanok (ERJ, PSM, SØK) 23rd July 2004
1388 Koldewey 1874 p. 335; 1873 p. 372; Payer 1877 p. 542
1389 Die Zweite ... p. XXII; Wordie 1927 p. 245
1390 Sabine 1825 p. 161
1391 Wordie 1927 p. 227
1392 Wordie 1927 p. 260
1393 Orvin 1934 p. 16
1394 Nyholm-Poulsen 1985 p. 201
1395 Nanok (ERJ, PSM, SØK) 23rd July 2004
1396 Nanok (ERJ, PSM, SØK) 23rd July 2004
1397 Nanok (ERJ, PSM, SØK) 24th July 2004
1398 Orvin 1930 p. 142
1399 N032; N143
1400 Ivar Ytreland p.m. 1992
1401 Nanok (ERJ, PSM, SØK) 24th July 2004
1402 A138; A181
1403 Nanok (MOH, NGM, OLS, PSM) 8th July 2007
1404 G101; G113; G119
1405 A137
1406 Nanok (LAK, RAG) 24th August 2005
1407 A162; A181
1408 Hans Frederiksen p.m. 1992
1409 Nanok (ERJ, PSM, SØK) 5th August 2004
1410 A140; A181
1411 Nanok (ERJ, PSM, SØK) 5th August 2004
1412 N143
1413 Description ... 1932 p. 16
1414 Nanok (ERJ, PSM, SØK) 5th August 2004
1415 Bent Zwergius p.m. 1992
1416 Nanok (KMJ, ERJ, SØA) 25th July 2003
1417 Bang 1944 p. 80

1418 N027; N028
1419 Birger Larsen p.m. 1991
1420 Nanok (ERJ, PSM, SØK) 23rd July 2004
1421 Ø048; A241
1422 Jennov 1939 p. 123
1423 N143; Letter from Jona Karlsbakk Torske, 16th November 1994
1424 Description ... 1932 p. 16
1425 Nyholm-Poulsen 1985 pp. 206, 249-250
1426 Giæver 1939 p. 48
1427 Sabine 1825 p. 420
1428 Nanok (PSM) 12th July 1999
1429 Description ... 1932 p. 16
1430 N032; N143; Letter from Jona Karlsbakk Torske, 16th November 1994
1431 Hvidberg 1932 p. 49
1432 Norwegian Polarklubb 1964 p. 103
1433 Nanok (ERJ, PSM, SØK) 23rd July 2004
1434 A138; A181
1435 Nanok (ERJ, PSM, SØK) 23rd July 2004
1436 Nanok (ERJ, PSM, SØK) 25th July 2004
1437 N027; N052; R141
1438 Nanok (ERJ, PSM, SØK) 25th July 2004
1439 A133; Jennov 1939 p. 90
1440 N069
1441 Higgins 1997 p. 96
1442 Nanok (ERJ, PSM, SØK) 24th July 2004
1443 Hansen 1939 p. 114; Nyholm-Poulsen 1985 p. 200
1444 N033
1445 N031
1446 Nanok (ERJ, PSM, SØK) 24th July 2004
1447 N143
1448 N033; Description ... 1932 p. 16; Giæver 1939 p. 20
1449 Nanok (ERJ, PSM, SØK) 24th July 2004
1450 N027; N052; R141; Koch 1955 p. 564
1451 Nanok (ERJ, PSM, SØK) 23rd July 2004
1452 Nanok (ERJ, PSM, SØK) 25th July 2004
1453 G101; G116; G113; G119
1464 Nanok (ERJ, PSM, SØK) 23rd July 2004
1455 A129; A144; Jennov 1939 p. 30
1456 Higgins 1997 p. 80
1457 Nanok (ERJ, PSM, SØK) 24th July 2004
1458 Nyholm-Poulsen 1985 p. 74
1459 Description ... 1932 pp. 16, 30; N033
1460 N035
1461 Nanok (ERJ, PSM, SØK) 25th July 2004
1462 G117; Jennov 1939 p. 41
1463 Nyholm-Poulsen 1985 p. 74
1464 Nanok (ERJ, PSM, SØK) 25th July 2004
1465 N027; Nyholm-Poulsen 1985 pp. 116-118
1466 N052
1467 R141
1468 Nanok (ERJ, PSM, SØK) 24th July 2004
1469 A129; A135; A137; Jennov 1939 p. 29; Nyholm-Poulsen 1985 p. 74, 108
1470 G117
1471 Nanok (ERJ, PSM, SØK) 24th July 2004
1472 Nanok (ERJ, PSM, SØK) 29th July 2004
1473 Nyholm-Poulsen 1985 p. 72
1474 G118; Jennov 1939 p. 41
1475 A141
1476 Nanok (MOH, NGM, OLS, PSM) 8th July 2007
1477 Nanok (ERJ, PSM, SØK) 5th August 2004
1478 N026; N027; R141; Nyholm-Poulsen 1985 p. 185
1479 N052
1480 Nanok (MOH, NGM, OLS, PSM) 8th July 2007
1481 Ø044; Dahl 1924 pp. 60, 72; Dahl 1925 pp. 77-78
1482 P152
1483 Hvidberg 1932 pp. 77, 86
1484 Nanok (MOH, NGM, OLS, PSM) 8th July 2007
1485 P147; Hans Hvide Bang p.m. 1992
1486 Nanok (ERJ, PSM, SØK) 5th August 2004
1487 Nyholm-Poulsen 1985 pp. 61, 107
1488 G118; Jennov 1939 p. 41
1489 Nanok (ERJ, PSM, SØK) 26th July 2004
1490 A129; A135; G103; Nyholm-Poulsen 1985 pp. 71, 123
1491 G117; Jennov 1939 p. 29
1492 Nanok (ERJ, PSM, SØK) 26th July 2004
1493 A181; Mogens Graae p.m. 1992
1494 A138
1495 Nanok (ERJ, PSM, SØK) 26th July 2004
1496 N027; N052
1497 Nanok (ERJ, PSM, SØK) 26th July 2004
1498 A138
1499 A146; Jennov 1939 p. 65
1500 N069
1501 Nanok (ERJ, PSM, SØK) 26th July 2004
1502 A141; A181
1503 Nanok (ERJ, PSM, SØK) 26th July 2004
1504 A147; A181
1505 Nanok (ERJ, PSM, SØK) 2nd August 2004
1506 A181; Harald Mikkelsen p.m. 1992.
1507 Nanok (MOH, NGM, OLS, PSM) 8th July 2007
1508 P147; Hans Hvide Bang p.m. 1992
1509 Nanok (ERJ, PSM, SØK) 26th July 2004
1510 A146; A181; Jennov 1939 p. 65
1511 Nanok (ERJ, PSM, SØK) 29th July 2004
1512 P155
1513 N027; N052; Nyholm-Poulsen 1985 p. 110.
1514 Nanok (ERJ, PSM, SØK) 1st August 2004
1515 Nanok (ERJ, PSM, SØK) 30th July 2004
1516 Nanok (ERJ, PSM, SØK) 29th July 2004
1517 Hansen 1939 p. 69
1518 G118
1519 Nyholm-Poulsen 1985 p. 70
1520 Nanok (ERJ, PSM, SØK) 2nd August 2004
1521 A181; Harald Mikkelsen p.m. 1992
1522 Nanok (ERJ, PSM, SØK) 28th July 2004
1523 Nyholm-Poulsen 1985 p. 70
1524 N082
1525 Bjarne Myrvold p.m. 1992
1526 Nanok (ERJ, PSM, SØK) 27th July 2004
1527 Nanok (ERJ, PSM, SØK) 30th July 2004
1528 G118; A150; Jennov 1939 p. 41
1529 Nanok (ERJ, PSM, SØK) 28th July 2004
1530 Hansen 1939 p. 70
1531 Hvidberg 1932 p. 118
1532 G118; Jennov 1939 p. 41
1533 Nanok (MOH, NGM, OLS, PSM) 8th July 2007
1534 A.K. Higgins p.m. 1993
1535 P106
1536 Bjarne Myrvold p.m. 1992
1537 Nanok (ERJ, PSM, SØK) 2nd August 2004
1538 Nanok (ERJ, PSM, SØK) 4th August 2004
1539 Nyholm-Poulsen 1985 p. 251; Jennov 1939 p. 46
1540 A141
1541 Erik Jochumsen p.m. 2004
1542 Nanok (ERJ, PSM, SØK) 2nd August 2004
1543 Nanok (ERJ, PSM, SØK) 30th July 2004
1544 Nanok (ERJ, PSM, SØK) 30th July 2004
1545 P147; Andreasen & Elling 1990 p. 48
1546 G117; Jennov 1939 p. 29
1547 Nanok (ERJ, PSM, SØK) 30th July 2004
1548 P147; Andreasen & Elling 1990 p. 47.
1549 Bjarne Myrvold p.m. 1992
1550 Nanok (ERJ, PSM, SØK) 28th July 2004
1551 G103; G117; Jennov 1939 p. 29; Hvidberg 1932 p. 81

1552 Nanok (ERJ, PSM, SØK) 28th July 2004
1553 Bjarne Myrvold p.m. 1992
1554 P106
1555 P147
1556 Bjarne Myrvold p.m. 1992
1557 Nanok (ERJ, PSM, SØK) 28th July 2004
1558 N082
1559 Nanok (ERJ, PSM, SØK) 28th July 2004
1560 NSIU 1937 p. 99; N082
1561 Nanok (ERJ, PSM, SØK) 4th August 2004
1562 Hvidberg 1932 p. 132; Jennov 1939 p. 34; A129
1563 G118
1564 G117; Nyholm-Poulsen 1985 p. 259
1565 Nanok (ERJ, PSM, SØK) 28th July 2004
1566 N082
1567 N069
1568 Nanok (MOH, NGM, OLS, PSM) 8th July 2007
1569 N082; Giæver 1939 p. 49
1570 Nanok (ERJ, PSM, SØK) 4th August 2004
1571 Nanok (ERJ, PSM, SØK) 4th August 2004
1572 G117; Jennov 1939 p. 46
1573 A138
1574 e-mail from Sirius to author 14th November 2001
1575 Nanok (ERJ, PSM, SØK) 4th August 2004
1576 Nanok (ERJ, PSM, SØK) 4th August 2004
1577 Andreasen & Elling 1990 p. 44
1578 Bjarne Myrvold p.m. 1992
1579 Harald Mikkelsen p.m. 1992
1580 Nanok (ERJ, PSM, SØK) 4th August 2004
1581 Nanok (AUI, ERJ, HHC) 20th July 2005
1582 Andreasen & Elling 1990 p. 41
1583 N082
1584 Journal of ... 1830 p. 18
1585 Nanok (MOH, NGM, OLS, PSM) 8th July 2007
1586 N082; Giæver 1955 p. 40, 1958 p. 36
1587 P. Nielsen p.m. 1990; Nyholm-Poulsen 1985 p. 236
1588 Nanok (MOH, NGM, OLS, PSM) 8th July 2007
1589 A164
1590 Fredrik Sæterdal p.m. 1992
1591 Nanok (AUI, ERJ, HHC) 22nd July 2005
1592 G101
1593 N082
1594 Nanok (AUI, ERJ, HHC) 22nd July 2005
1595 Harald Mikkelsen p.m. 1992
1596 Nanok (AUI, ERJ, HHC) 21st July 2005
1597 Hvidberg 1932 p. 134; Jennov 1939 p. 34
1598 G117; G118
1599 A296
1600 Nanok (AUI, ERJ, HHC) 23rd July 2005
1601 N080
1602 Nanok (AUI, ERJ, HHC) 22nd July 2005
1603 Arne Philbert p.m. 1992
1604 A296; Jennov 1939 p. 46
1605 Nyholm-Poulsen 1985 p. 220
1606 Nanok (AUI, ERJ, HHC) 22nd July 2005
1607 N080
1608 Nanok (MOH, NGM, OLS, PSM) 8th July 2007
1609 N080; N076
1610 Nanok (MOH, NGM, OLS, PSM) 8th July 2007
1611 A133; Jennov 1939 p. 90
1612 Nanok (MOH, NGM, OLS, PSM) 8th July 2007
1613 N080; N076
1614 Nanok (MOH, NGM, OLS, PSM) 8th July 2007
1615 Boyd 1948 p. 74
1616 N080; N076
1617 Nanok (AUI, ERJ, HHC) 23rd July 2005
1618 Hvidberg 1932 p. 134
1619 Nanok (AUI, ERJ, HHC) 23rd July 2005
1620 Nanok (AUI, ERJ, HHC) 24th July 2005
1621 N080
1622 Nanok (AUI, ERJ, HHC) 25th July 2005
1623 Nanok (AUI, ERJ, HHC) 25th July 2005
1624 A133; Jennov 1939 p. 93
1625 Nanok (MOH, NGM, OLS, PSM) 8th July 2007
1626 Bjerre 1980 p. 127; Gerhardt Blaase p.m. 1990; Allan Nielsen p.m. 1990
1627 Nanok (MOH, NGM, OLS, PSM) 8th July 2007
1628 G121
1629 Nanok (AUI, ERJ, HHC) 28th July 2005
1630 N080
1631 A244
1632 Nanok (AUI, ERJ, HHC) 28th July 2005
1633 A149; A152; Jennov 1939 p. 93
1634 Nanok (AUI, ERJ, HHC) 7th August 2005
1635 N080
1636 Richard Nielsen p.m. 1992
1637 Nanok (AUI, ERJ, HHC) 6th August 2005
1638 A140; A154; Jennov 1939 p. 93.
1639 Nanok (AUI, ERJ, HHC) 29th July 2005
1640 Giæver 1939 p.48
1641 N080
1642 A.K. Higgins p.m. 1993.
1643 Nanok (AUI, ERJ, HHC) 8th August 2005
1644 A154; A244; Jennov 1939 p. 93
1645 Nanok (AUI, ERJ, HHC) 4th August 2005
1646 A144; Jennov 1935 p. 17, 1939 pp. 57, 90
1647 Nanok (AUI, ERJ, HHC) 4th August 2005
1648 Nanok (AUI, ERJ, HHC) 8th August 2005
1649 N080
1650 Nanok (AUI, ERJ, HHC) 9th August 2005
1651 A144; A154; Jennov 1939 p 57
1652 Nanok (AUI, ERJ, HHC) 2nd August 2005
1653 Allan Nielsen p.m. 1990; Bendt Nielsen p.m. 1990
1654 Nanok (AUI, ERJ, HHC) 2nd August 2005
1655 A154; A152; Jennov 1939 p. 93
1656 Nanok (MOH, NGM, OLS, PSM) 8th July 2007
1657 A144
1658 Finn Kristoffersen p.m. 1989; Allan Nielsen p.m. 1993
1659 Nanok (ERJ, HHC) 22nd August 2005
1660 H. Thomsen 1966 p. 125
1661 A154
1662 A296
1663 Nanok (MOH, NGM, OLS, PSM) 8th July 2007
1664 Allan Nielsen p.m. 1993; Bendt Nielsen p.m. 1990
1665 Nanok (AUI, ERJ, HHC) 10th August 2005
1666 A144; Jennov 1939 p. 57
1667 A296
1668 Nanok (ERJ, HHC) 22nd August 2005
1669 Banks 1957 p. 151; Ove Hermansen p.m. 1993
1670 Allan Nielsen p.m. 1991
1671 Nanok (ERJ, HHC) 22nd August 2005
1672 Allan Nielsen p.m. 1993
1673 Nanok (ERJ, HHC) 5th August 2006
1674 Allan Nielsen p.m. 1993
1675 Nanok (ERJ, HHC) 5th August 2006
1676 Allan Nielsen p.m. 1991; Bendt Nielsen p.m. 1991; Ove Hermansen p.m.
1677 Nanok (ERJ, HHC) 21st August 2005
1678 Allan Nielsen p.m. 1993
1679 Payer 1877 p. 581; Koldewey 1874 490
1680 Nanok (ERJ, HHC) 5th August 2006
1681 Thomsen 1966 p. 62
1682 Nanok (ERJ, HHC) 24th August 2005
1683 Allan Nielsen p.m. 1993
1684 Nanok (ERJ, HHC, JES, JWB) August 2005

1685 Nanok (ERJ, HHC, JES, JWB) August 2005
1686 Nanok (AUI, ERJ, HHC) 11th August 2005
1687 A144; Jennov 1939 pp. 57, 98
1688 Nanok (ERJ, HHC) 3rd August 2005
1689 Jennov 1939 p. 65
1690 email from A.K. Higgins 26th December 2007
1691 Nanok (ERJ, HHC) 3rd August 2005
1692 Gerhardt Blaase p.m. 1991; Allan Nielsen p.m. 1993
1693 Nanok (AUI, ERJ, HHC) 18th August 2005
1694 A296
1695 Nanok (AUI, ERJ, HHC) 17th August 2005
1696 A144;; Jennov 1939 p. 57
1697 A296
1698 Nanok (AUI, ERJ, HHC) 17th August 2005
1699 email from Danmarkshavn/ Ulrik Capito 15th August 2007
1700 A154; Jennov 1939 p. 93
1701 A155
1702 A296
1703 Nanok (ERJ, HHC) 24th July 2006
1704 Bendt Nielsen p.m. 1990
1705 Nanok (ERJ, HHC) 22nd August 2006
1706 A144; Jennov 1939 pp. 57, 93
1707 A154
1708 Nanok (ERJ, HHC) 12th August 2006
1709 A144
1710 Nanok (AUI, ERJ, HHC) 17th August 2005
1711 A296
1712 Nanok (ERJ, HHC) 1st August 2006
1713 Knutsen 1992 p. 97, Knutsen 2005 pp. 121-122. Knuth 1942 p. 64
1714 Nanok (AUI, ERJ, HHC) 17th August 2005
1715 Nanok (AUI, ERJ, HHC) 17th August 2005
1716 Nanok (AUI, ERJ, HHC) 13th August 2005
1717 Nanok (AUI, ERJ, HHC) 13th August 2005
1718 Nanok (AUI, ERJ, HHC) 13th August 2005
1719 A130; A144; Jennov 1939 pp. 57, 91
1720 Nanok (MOH, NGM, OLS, PSM) 8th July 2007
1721 Nanok (ERJ, HHC) 1st August 2006
1722 Allan Nielsen p.m. 1993
1723 Nanok (ERJ, HHC) 31st July 2006
1724 Bendt Nielsen p.m. 1990; Allan Nielsen p.m. 1993
1725 Nanok (AUI, ERJ, HHC) 17th August 2005
1726 A144; Jennov 1939 p. 57
1727 Knuth 1940 p. 72; Knuth 1942 p. 159
1728 Nanok (ERJ, HHC) 28th July 2006
1729 Nanok (MOH, NGM, OLS, PSM) 8th July 2007
1730 A154; A155
1731 Knuth 1940 p. 73
1732 Nanok (ERJ, HHC) 29th July 2006
1733 Knutsen 1992 p. 102; Knutsen 2005 p.125
1734 A156
1735 Nanok (MOH, NGM, OLS, PSM) 8th July 2007
1736 Knuth 1942 p. 154
1737 Allan Nielsen p.m. 1993
1738 Thomas Hansen email 20th July 2007
1739 Knuth 1942 p. 156
1740 Ib Poulsen p.m. 1991
1741 Thomas Hansen email 20th July 2007
1742 Claus Birkbøll p.m. 1992
1743 Description ... 1932 p. 30
1744 N059; R130; A.K. Higgins p.m. 1992; Otto Lapstun p.m. 1992
1745 Giæver 1939 p. 48
1746 N059; P133
1747 PSM 18th August 1989
1748 Nanok (HEN, KRN, STH) 21st July 2007
1749 N048
1750 N030; N055; A.K. Higgins p.m. 1992
1751 Nanok (JMS, LAB, OSN) 2004
1752 N056
1753 N054
1754 Nanok (JMS, LAB, OSN) 1st August 2004
1755 Orvin 1934 p. 9; N053; N055
1756 Nanok (KRN, HEN, STH) 2007
1757 Description ... 1932 p. 23; Orvin 1931 p. 381; N077
1758 Nanok (HEN, KRN, STH) 29th July 2007
1759 Giæver 1939 p. 48;
1760 Trygve Havold p.m. 1991; Fredrik Sæterdal p.m. 1992
1761 NKN field report 2007 p. 13
1762 Nanok (CHA, KOL, RAG) 22nd July 2005
1763 A159; A138
1764 Nanok (CHA, KOL, RAG) 7th August 2005
1765 A172
1766 Nanok (MOH, NGM, OLS, PSM) 8th July 2007
1767 A140
1768 Nanok (ERJ, PSM, SØK) 25th July 2004
1769 R141; N069
1770 Nanok (PSM, ERJ, SØK) 30th July 2004
1771 N082
1772 Nanok (MOH, NGM, OLS, PSM) 8th July 2007
1773 Fredrik Sæterdal p.m. 1992
1774 Nanok (MOH, NGM, OLS, PSM) 8th July 2007
1775 A161
1776 Nanok (MOH, NGM, OLS, PSM) 8th July 2007
1777 A161
1778 Jennov 1939 p. 120
1779 Richard Nielsen p.m. 1992; G121
1780 Nanok (ERJ,) 20th August 2005
1781 Nusser 1979 p. 104; Price 1995; Selinger 1991 p. 45; Thomas 1951 p. 196
1782 Lauritsen 1984 p. 164; Bendt Nielsen p.m. 1992
1783 Koch 1913 p. 124
1784 Mindeblade ... 1983 p. 70-71
1785 Nanok (CHA, KOL, RAG) 4th August 2005
1786 A134
1787 Nanok (CHA, KOL, RAG) 4th August 2005
1788 Koch 1955 p. 129
1789 Nanok (CHA, KOL, RAG) 9th August 2005
1790 Koch 1955 p. 156; Seidenfaden 1936 pp. 88-93
1791 Nanok (ERJ, PSM, SØK) 28th July 2004
1792 N082

INDEX

Normal font — text
Italic font — photo & text

STATIONS, HOUSES & HUTS

VESSELS, AEROPLANES, ETC.

PERSONS, EXPEDITIONS, ETC.

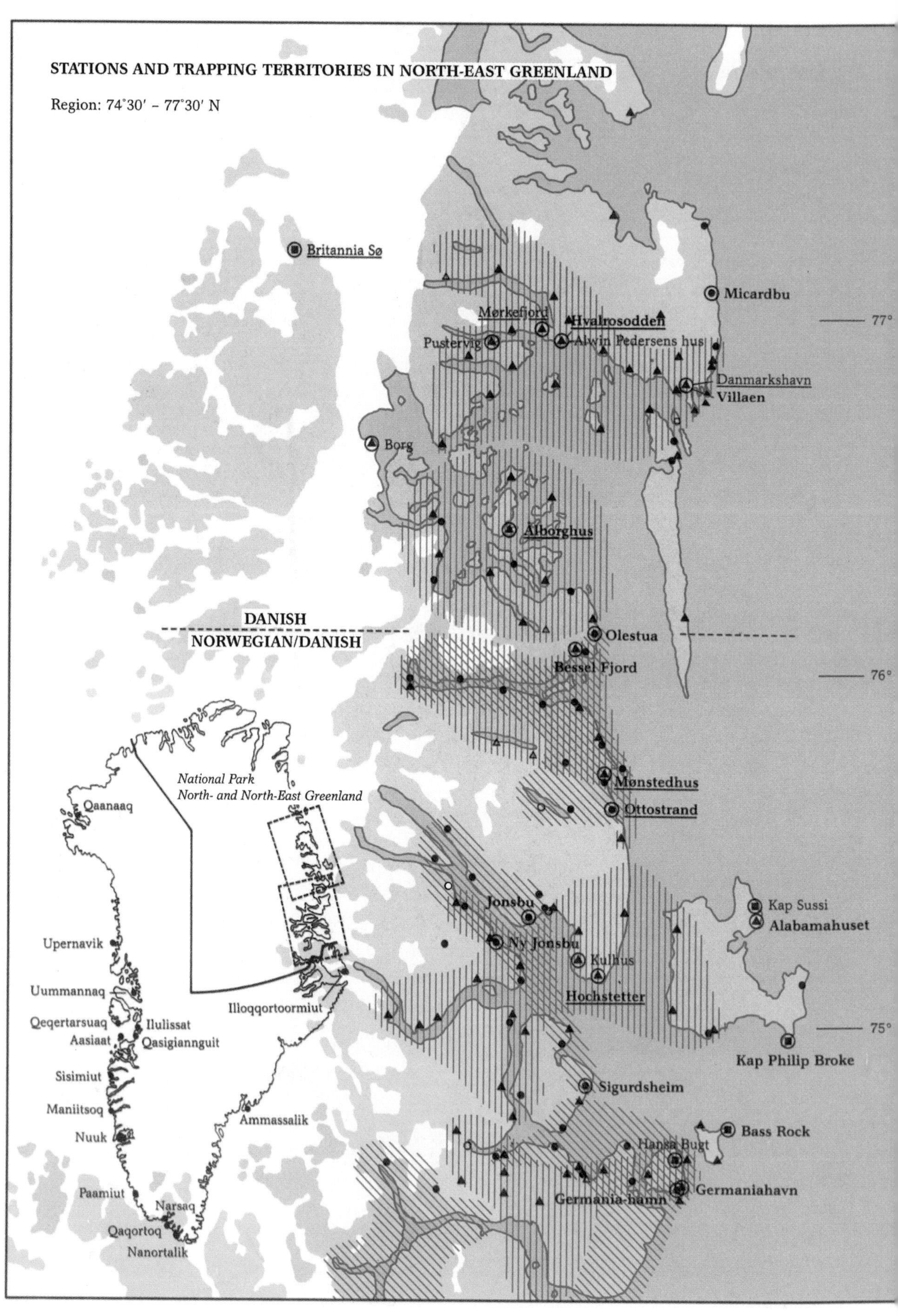

STATIONS AND TRAPPING TERRITORIES IN NORTH-EAST GREENLAND
Region: 74°30′ – 77°30′ N
Britannia Sø
Micardbu
77°
Mørkefjord
Hvalrosodden
Pustervig
Alwin Pedersens hus
Danmarkshavn
Villaen
Borg
Ålborghus
DANISH
NORWEGIAN/DANISH
Olestua
Bessel Fjord
76°
Mønstedhus
Ottostrand
National Park
North- and North-East Greenland
Qaanaaq
Jonsbu
Ny Jonsbu
Kulhus
Hochstetter
Kap Sussi
Alabamahuset
Upernavik
Uummannaq
Illoqqortoormiut
Qeqertarsuaq
Ilulissat
Aasiaat
Qasigiannguit
75°
Kap Philip Broke
Sisimiut
Sigurdsheim
Maniitsoq
Ammassalik
Bass Rock
Nuuk
Hansa Bugt
Germaniahavn
Germania-hamn
Paamiut
Narsaq
Qaqortoq
Nanortalik